*Goodhue County, Minnesota*

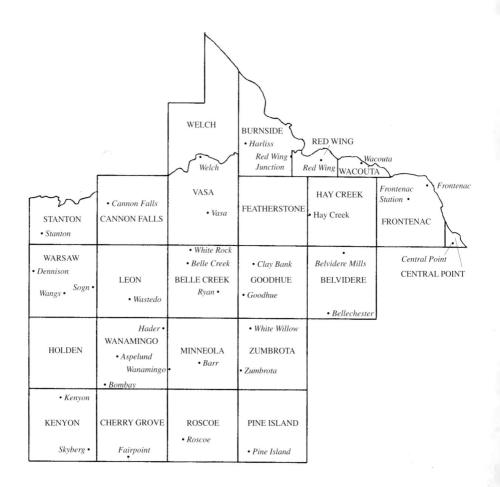

Goodhue County Townships

# Goodhue County, Minnesota

## A Narrative History

*Frederick L. Johnson*

Goodhue County Historical Society Press • Red Wing, Minnesota • 2000

*On the Jacket*
Contour farming in Goodhue County, *Paul Chesley photo*

*Endsheets and Page 8*
Artist John Koepke's conception of communal living in the villages of the
Red Wing Locality, A.D. 1100–1250. See "Introduction."

*Photo Credit Abbreviations*
CFHS for Cannon Falls Historical Society
GCHS for Goodhue County Historical Society
MHS for Minnesota Historical Society

*Editing, Design, Production*
E. B. Green Editorial, St. Paul

*Indexing*
Patricia Harpole, Stina Enterprises, St. Paul

*Printing*
Sexton Printing, Inc., St. Paul

*Binding*
Midwest Editions, Minneapolis

© 2000 by Goodhue County Historical Society Press
1166 Oak Street
Red Wing, MN 55066

All rights reserved.

Library of Congress Card Number: 00-106133

ISBN: 0-9617197-3-7

Manufactured in the United States of America

10 9 8 7 6 5 4 3 2 1

# *Contents*

# *Preface*

This is not the first history of Goodhue County. Publishers and authors produced three 19th-century histories within 40 years of the county's inception and added others in 1909 and 1935. In the early 1990s the time seemed right to the leadership of the Goodhue County Historical Society to resume the story of the county and its people. The society worked to put in place the financial and human resources required to do so. The result is this volume.

Throughout the narrative, I have applied the principles of historiography to provide information and interpretation that illustrate some of the major themes in Goodhue County history. I used primary materials including letters, diaries, journals, memoirs, oral histories, and personal interviews, as well newspapers and periodicals. I relied on several published histories for background information, making careful use of the earlier ones, which have been rightly criticized for their lack of documentation. I have also used contemporary county newspapers in the knowledge that they too are not perfect sources. When questions arose in interpretation of specific events, I corroborated accounts with other references. I assume full responsibility for any errors that have reached print in this volume.

Space limitations did not permit the publication of annotations to the book's footnotes, but the Goodhue County Historical Society in Red Wing has copies available of that complete 37,000-word source. The annotated footnotes contain pertinent information and the names and deeds of many county residents. These should be helpful to researchers and casual readers as well.

Many people have been supportive to me during the writing of this book. First among them are Jean Anderson Chesley and Elizabeth Anderson Hedin. These two sisters have been instrumental in the development of this project and a host of others over their many years of involvement with the historical society. Their fingerprints figuratively, and in many case literally, are on much of what the society has produced. They came up with the idea of getting a new county history published, and their many talents got the project off the ground. They volunteered to work on the committee to develop the book and served as its first readers. If two more gracious people exist, I've not met them.

The other members of the history book committee—Dan Dietrich, John Schwartau, Robert Hedin, and Charles O. Richardson—also provided their considerable abilities to the project. The staff at the Goodhue County Historical Society gave valued assistance as well. Interim director and curator Char Henn painstakingly reviewed first drafts and made valuable suggestions. Archivist Heather Craig put the society's collection at my fingertips. In Cannon Falls, I received expert assistance and cordial cooperation from Heidi Holmes-Helgren, curator for the collections of the Cannon Falls Historical Society. My thanks to the Anderson Center for Disciplinary Studies, Red Wing, for allowing me the use of its outstanding facility for my preliminary research.

The Minnesota State Historical Society and its vast repository provided a remarkable collection of resources and the skilled and friendly staff to make it accessible. They certainly made my job easier. Also helpful were the State Legislative Library and its archivists. I am grateful to other friends of history, too numerous to name here, who shared their time and talents.

I am indebted to my father, Frederick K. Johnson, for his expertise and advice in the preparation of this manuscript. He was born in Claybank, Goodhue township and over the years passed on to me his interest in local history. He taught me much about the county and of his adopted Red Wing, the town he came to love.

Ellen Green has served as my editor before yet was willing to work with me on this project. Ellen got the book into print—editing and designing the text, then shepherding it through the publication process. We work well together, and I hope we have the opportunity to team up again.

My wife, Diane, has been a partner in this enterprise. As with all of my writing, she serves as the first reader and editor. She is precise and perceptive and makes insightful suggestions. As always, I am deeply indebted to her for her patience, skill, and loving support.

Note: Towns and cities mentioned in the text are in Minnesota unless otherwise noted or generally known.

# *Goodhue County, Minnesota*

Archaeologist Clark A. Dobbs led this 1984 excavation of the Bryan site, the largest of the eight ancient village locations found in the Red Wing Locality. The fortified community overlooked the Cannon River. *GCHS*

# Introduction

## The Prehistoric People
## of the Upper Mississippi River Valley

At the dawn of the second millennium A.D., what would become one of the Western Hemisphere's most advanced cultures developed around a growing city-state near the confluence of the Missouri and Mississippi Rivers. This new cultural force, the Mississippian tradition, centered on Cahokia, a budding metropolis near present-day St. Louis. Within 200 years the Mississippians spread their influence along the great river. This powerful society made inroads into the upper Mississippi River valley, bringing remarkable changes to the indigenous people of the area, including those of the future Goodhue County.[1]

Mississippian tradition produced the most sophisticated pre-Columbian civilization north of the Valley of Mexico. At its peak, between A.D. 1000 and 1400, its influence was felt from the Gulf of Mexico to the upper Mississippi. Cahokia, its cultural capital, was larger, then, than London. In A.D. 1150, Cahokia's population of more than 20,000 made it one of the largest urban centers in the world. Not until 1800 did another American city surpass the population of Cahokia at its height.[2]

Mississippian society, based on agriculture with corn the staple, grew stronger and spread to other cultures. Empowered by Cahokia's central location, its people interacted with forest dwellers of the northeast woodlands, nomadic people of the plains, and other Mississippians in the southeast. Water and land routes brought the Cahokians copper from the upper Great Lakes, mica from the southern Appalachians, and seashells from the Gulf of Mexico. Historian Claudia Mink wrote: "For 500 years, Cahokia was the major center of a culture that, at its peak, stretched from Red Wing, Minnesota, to Key Marco, Florida, and across the Southeast."[3]

The organizers of Cahokia and other river cities used thoughtful urban-planning techniques and mobilized large workforces. These crews constructed a variety of earthen mounds, including massive flat-topped temple structures. Cahokia's still-standing Monks Mound covers more than 14 acres and rises to 100 feet. It was the Western Hemisphere's largest prehistoric earthen structure.

Around 1200, the influence of the Mississippians became evident some 500 miles north of Cahokia, at the junction of the Cannon, Trimbelle, and Mississippi Rivers. The Cannon flowed through what would become Goodhue County. The Trimbelle cut through the future Pierce County in Wisconsin. The surrounding lands contain evidence of prehistoric people—several thousand mounds and earthworks as well as major villages and dozens of secondary sites. The area became the northernmost center of Mississippian interaction in eastern North America. Archaeologists examining the area in the 20th century named 58 square miles of this territory the Red Wing Locality.[4]

Humans have lived in the Goodhue County area for about 12,000 years. Mississippian visitors of the 12th century were relative newcomers. Archaeologists classify prehistoric North American people by their cultural traits and adaptations to their surroundings. These divisions apply to the Minnesota region:

- Paleo-Indian stage (also known as the Big Game Hunter stage)—12,000 to 10,000 years ago. Humans lived in small family groups and hunted mastodon, bison, and caribou.
- Archaic tradition—10,000 to 3,000 years ago. Humans became more adept at tool making. Social organization probably became more complex.
- Woodland stage—2,500 years ago (500 B.C. to A.D. 1000). Humans began to make pottery, build earthen mounds, and near the end of this era, raise crops.
- Mississippian stage—A.D. 1000 to A.D. 1700. Mississippians relied on agriculture in the floodplain including, in the Red Wing Locality, that of the Cannon River. They produced fine pottery tempered by crushed freshwater clamshell. Inventions related to cultivation, preparation, and storage of agricultural products also occurred. The bow and arrow, which may have appeared in the late Woodland stage, was perfected at this time.[5]

Proof of Paleo-Indian and Archaic cultures in the Goodhue County area is sketchy. Clovis and Folsom spearpoints have been found not locally but elsewhere in the region, suggesting Big Game Hunters were in the Red Wing Locality. Artifacts related to Archaic peoples have been found along the Cannon River, Hay Creek, and Spring Creek.

Two distinct cultures occupied the Red Wing Locality during the Mississippian period—the Oneota (a later Woodland group) and the Mississippian. The locality likely was the most densely populated area in the upper Mississippi valley during the 12th and 13th centuries. It was also the site of one of the earliest centers of corn cultivation in the upper Midwest. A debate over the evolution of the Oneota in relation to Middle Mississippian expansion has gone on for decades. Some believe the Oneota culture resulted from the expansion of Mississippians into the Woodland regions. Others suggest the Oneota developed from an existing Woodland base and only later were affected by the Mississippians.[6]

The Red Wing Locality consists of eight large village or town sites with related locations including mounds, petroglyphs, rock cairns, and processing sites. Archaeologist Clark Dobbs believes this series of sites was the northernmost extension of the Middle Mississippian culture. He says the locality was a center for trade between the northern frontier and the Middle Mississippian groups to the south. "Complex social relationships based on Cahokian religious, belief, and kinship systems," drove interactions between the groups.[7]

Silvernale and other villages in the locality have differing features. This implies that the communities were occupied in sequence for a century or more. In its first configuration, Silvernale contained a living area of more than ten acres, surrounded by 225-plus earthen mounds. It appears to be one of the earliest sites in the Mississippian sequence. Construction during the 1970s largely destroyed the site, but it may still contain evidence of the transformation of local Late Woodland hunters and gatherers to Mississippian corn farmers.

Bryan, the largest of the Red Wing Locality villages, overlooked the Cannon River from a high terrace. Farmers and traders occupied the site about A.D. 1200. Archaeological studies show that its citizens fortified the site with a palisade of logs. A mound group on the south and east may have been the site of village burials and ceremonies. Spring floods washed rich topsoil onto the river plains and gardens of Bryan, providing fertile fields for corn, beans, and squash. The villagers also ate fruits and berries and caught fish, clams, and turtles. The immediate area offered plentiful hunting sites, with game including deer, bear, rabbit, squirrel, fox, raccoon, ducks, and geese. Bryan contains evidence of Oneota and Mississippian culture and is likely a mixture of the two. This fortified village also had links to the prairie people to the west.[8]

Some Bryan villagers lived in dwellings dug partially into the ground, with the upper portions covered by grasses. One house unearthed for study was about six by seven feet, had a smooth black floor, perhaps of tar, and a center fireplace. Another home, about 8.5 feet in diameter, was nearly round, with a hard-packed dirt floor.

People living at the Bryan site made pottery and did stonework. They used crushed shell to temper their pottery and produced functional containers. The pottery featured designs usually on the upper portions only. Archaeologists have uncovered stone artifacts–projectile points, chert knives, scrapers, and other tools—at the site. Flat stones with slight depressions, apparently used as paint palettes, were an unusual find at Bryan. One recovered palette still contained red ocher.

Bryan and other sites in the Red Wing Locality clearly show Middle Mississippian influence as well a connection with other regional groups during the Silvernale phase (A.D. 1050–1300). Archaeologists found Middle Mississippian ceramic forms and artifacts, including a flat-topped pyramidal mound, copper ornaments, a long-nosed God mask, and Cahokian tri-notched projectile points.[9]

Archaeologists believe that the location of the Red Wing sites led to relationships with other groups. The eastern edge of the North American prairie is just west of the locality, and the Cannon River provided easy access to bison-hunting areas. The Mississippi and St. Croix served as river roads north to wild-rice regions and deposits of copper.

Continued exploration by the Institute for Minnesota Archaeology (IMA) in the 1980s and 1990s has deepened the understanding of Red Wing Locality sites and provided a basis for their protection. In May 1989, the Minnesota legislature furnished funds to purchase land containing a well-preserved village site recently discovered by IMA researchers. This ancient community, between the Bryan and Silvernale villages, is now the Red Wing Archaeological Preserve.[10]

So where do the prehistoric people of Goodhue County fit in the complicated mix of cultural evolution? Decades of investigation and analysis by teams of experts have produced a growing body of information and theory. Research shows occupation of the Red Wing Locality for 250 years—from about A.D. 1050 to 1300. Eight major village locations, including two on the Wisconsin side of the Mississippi, have been discovered.[11]

The region was home to a Late Woodland people whose lifestyle followed hunting and gathering patterns similar to the way Archaic people lived for millennia. The Late Woodland groups in the Red Wing Locality, however, underwent great cultural changes in a short time. Late Woodland society transformed from a hunting and gathering culture to one developing a reliance upon corn cultivation to augment its traditional food supply.

New developments occurred in ceramics, food preparation, and storage. Also unfolding was a feature new to Woodland communal living—semipermanent villages. After thousands of years of slow, almost imperceptible lifeways evolution, more rapid change came to the people living at the river junction. These innovations presumably occurred during the 11th century. They provided a basis for the Oneota culture that still existed at the time of mid-17th-century contact with Europeans.[12]

These changes in the area can be attributed to the influence of the Mississippian culture. During the 12th and 13th centuries, the reach of the Mississippians lengthened to include the upper Mississippi River valley and Woodland people living there. Evidence of contact between the Woodland culture and Mississippians has been found throughout this region. Most interactions, though, seem centered on two specific areas—the Mill Creek sites of northwestern Iowa and the Red Wing Locality. Experts on the Red Wing Locality believe that Oneota culture evolved from a Woodland base, later affected by Mississippians. The Oneota occupation began around A.D. 1000. The Bartron site of Prairie Island is one example. Later sites (such as Bryan) were more of a mixture of Oneota and Mississippian cultures, with other regional influences also involved.[13]

The mounds that so fascinated early researchers continue to provide some of the most tangible evidence of prehistoric people. Dobbs's 1985 archaeological survey of Red Wing lists five "distinct" mound subtypes within the sites containing mounds. Examples remain, though hundreds have been destroyed. The establishment of the Red Wing Archaeological Preserve protected the only rectangular flat-topped mound in the region. This mound is similar to Mississippian temple mounds found in sites in the southeastern United States.[14]

The power and influence of the Mississippian tradition had lasting significance for the people it touched, even though Cahokia weakened and disappeared. The city began a decline about A.D. 1250 and eventually was abandoned. Theorists believe a combination of factors brought on the Mississippian sunset. These include excessive use of the land and forests, poor diet, and a climate change towards cooler, drier summers and shorter growing seasons. Analysis of Cahokian human skeletal remains shows that even during the city's most dominant days, people were malnourished because of a high-carbohydrate diet and seasonal food scarcity.[15]

Changes also occurred in the upper Mississippi valley. Villages like those in the Red Wing Locality withered, perhaps affected by the same problems plaguing the Cahokians. The disintegration of the wide-reaching Mississippian trade network may have speeded the decline. By A.D. 1300, cultural changes caused the extinction of some communities and modifications in those surviving. Large villages such as Bryan, Silvernale, Bartron, Mero, and Adams disappeared.[16]

Well-trained and -equipped archaeological teams continue to study the Red Wing Locality and its prehistoric people. They acknowledge the work of the antiquarians who proceeded them, even if earlier research standards were not so exacting as today's. Teams of researchers working in the area in the future can only envy the rich prehistoric panoramas beheld by earlier archaeologists.

From Goodhue County's amateur archaeologists of the mid-19th century to the painstaking researchers of the 21st runs a common thread of respect for the people who first lived in this area. For thousands of years these ancients per-

severed in an often-harsh climate. They developed stone tools for every kind of need, designed pottery for storage, cooking and ceremonial purposes, and developed tools for gardening. They exhibited respect for their dead in the carefully built and uniformly shaped burial mounds next to every village.

These intelligent, adaptable, resourceful prehistoric people prepared the way for those who later lived in Goodhue County.

# *1*

# *The Mdewakanton and the Challenge of Euroamericans*

Mid-17th-century Europe was in turmoil. The Thirty Years War, a bitter and bloody conflict between Protestants and Catholics, had come to an inconclusive end in 1648. Three decades of carnage had ravaged north central Europe, particularly the German states. Exhausted by war, the French, Dutch, Germans, Swedes, and Swiss signed the Treaty of Westphalia.[1]

But the treaty hardly meant peace for Europe. The French and Spanish continued fighting until 1659. England was in the throes of a civil war that had cost its people their peace and their king his head. War continued to divide the English even after Puritan leader Oliver Cromwell supplanted the English monarchy following the execution of Charles I in 1649. Compromise finally led to the restoration of Charles II in 1660.[2]

While monarchs and their minions struggled for supremacy in Europe, nearly half a world away other Europeans built small outposts on the North and South American continents. After a hundred years of their probing along its coast, the New World lured the adventurous farther inland.

New France, an eastern Canadian colony on the St. Lawrence River, was one important base of European operations. French explorers Cartier and Champlain helped establish the outpost, well sited to facilitate examination of the North American interior. New France, with its access to the Great Lakes, became a natural starting point.

In 1654, two French fur-trading brothers-in-law began a journey that would take them to the upper Mississippi and possibly to Goodhue County. Médard Chouart des Groseilliers and Pierre Radisson came to New France as young men, probably teenagers. They survived adventures that, in Radisson's case, included captivity among the Iroquois. The Frenchmen made two major exploratory expeditions westward between the years 1654 and 1660.³

Groseilliers and Radisson proved hardy adventurers and traders if not effective cartographers. In the course of their two expeditions the young men traversed the Great Lakes and eventually reached Minnesota. Some argue that they stayed more than a year at Prairie Island in what is now Goodhue County, but the tangle of lakes, rivers, and forests, combined with the inconsistencies of Radisson's records, obscured their path.

The first Europeans known to have reached the Goodhue County region arrived as captives. On April 11, 1680, a 33-canoe flotilla of warriors from the tribe known to the French as *Naduesiu* (rooted in the Algonquian *Nadouess-iw,* roughly *snake*) overwhelmed Louis Hennepin, a Franciscan of the Recollect Order, and his two companions. The missionary's party, treated in kindly manner by its captors, advanced up the Mississippi through a broad river passage that Father Hennepin named *Lac des Pleurs* (Lake of Tears), today's Lake Pepin. They finally arrived at Izatys, a village near Lake Mille Lacs. Daniel Greysolon, Sieur du Luth, later helped to free them.⁴

The Ojibway applied the name *Nadewisou* to the people living in the upper Mississippi and western Great Lakes region, equating the term with *enemy.* The French later shortened this name to *Scioux* and finally *Sioux*. The Europeans met mostly with the eastern Sioux, a people who called themselves *Dakota* (Friends, or Alliance of Friends).⁵ Most government documents, newspapers, magazines, and personal letters of the day referred to the Dakota people as *Sioux*, bringing the term to common usage and perpetuating the error.⁶

The subdivision of people within the Dakota nation also confused the Europeans. The Dakota divided into separate but allied tribal groups, with four— the Mdewakanton, Wahpekute, Wahpeton, and Sisseton—becoming known to the French as the Sioux of the East. They called the others—Yankton, Yanktonais, and Teton—the Sioux of the West. The French applied the term *Santee,* a corruption of *Issati* (Knife Lake, where one of the bands once lived) to the four eastern groups. Since the term referred to only one band of 17th-century Mdewakanton, this too was in error.

So, as the French moved more aggressively into the Mississippi River valley, they dealt mostly with the Dakota. The Yankton and Yanktonais moved westward, while the Teton (Dwellers on the Plains) migrated to the northern prairie, later dividing into seven subtribes.

On paper the claim of France to the upper Mississippi territory, compared with that of its European rivals, appeared strong indeed. French forts, trading posts, and wide-ranging *coureurs de bois*—free-lance fur traders—were the most visible sign of European presence. England also had designs on the area, and the two enemies began positioning to renew their old conflict in the "new" world.

The Europeans contrived to ally themselves with the Indian nations of the region. Sometimes they exploited existing differences between tribes or created new conflicts. They did not view the land rights of indigenous people as a major impediment to their designs on North America. Nicolas Perrot formalized France's attempts to establish itself along the Mississippi when he proclaimed in May 1689 that the "Country of the Nadouesioux" was a part of New France.[7]

In the 1720s French emissaries tried to drive a wedge between the Fox nation and its eastern Sioux allies. The French had temporarily withdrawn from the region and now wanted to return. The Fox maintained control over the fur trade in the upper Mississippi valley while the eastern Sioux were driving the Ottawa and Huron from their position of influence. The attempt to split the Indian allies failed, however, and the Fox and French established an uneasy peace in 1726. The arrangement allowed Frenchmen to return to the Mississippi River eastern Sioux country and resume their lucrative trade for furs.[8]

The French did not give up their attempts to dissolve the Fox-eastern Sioux alliance. In 1727 the French set up trading posts with the Sioux, including Fort Beauharnois, an outpost on Lake Pepin. The mission of the fort and its small garrison was to maintain ties with the eastern Sioux and facilitate the fur trade. Soon about 150 Sioux, ready to trade, encamped near the fort. The French saw this more direct relationship with the Sioux as strengthening ties between them.

But a blundered French campaign against the Fox in 1728 succeeded only in inspiring the Indians to greater resistance. Fort Beauharnois, now dangerously exposed, had to be abandoned. The French would not easily give up the idea of a Lake Pepin base. They twice again established forts on Pepin. The first outpost was built sometime between 1731 and 1736, the second in 1749.

French claims along the upper Mississippi formally ended with defeat at the hands of the English and their American allies in the French and Indian War (1754–1763). That failure, coupled with losses in Europe's Seven Years War, forced France to assign its North American possessions east of the Mississippi River to England. Through an earlier treaty with Spain, France managed to keep her territory west of the Mississippi out of English hands.[9]

The effects of the English and American victory over the French were far-reaching for the native people living along the northern reaches of the Mississippi. The European rivals differed fundamentally in their methods of interaction in the region. The French mainly wished to exploit the vast resources of New France. They came to trade—not to settle. The English and their American allies took a different tack, as shown by their methods in establishing New England and the middle colonies. Through a series of treaties and wars, these colonists obtained and occupied former Indian lands. The colonists took root, eventually prospered, and widened their holdings until they encountered other Indian-owned territory. Then they repeated the process.

———

The Mdewakanton considered Red Wing among the greatest of their military leaders. His people, a formidable tribe of eastern Sioux, lived along the upper Mississippi near Lake Mille Lacs. In his prime, roughly between the late 1770s and early 1800s, Red Wing was the tribe's preeminent war chief—valued by his people as one of the bravest warriors in the nation. Many said he never lost a battle—no small feat for a man who fought many times with enemy tribes. One of his village sites later became Red Wing, the seat of government for Goodhue County as well as its largest city.[10]

The times in which he lived obscure the early part of the Red Wing legend. He had little contact with Europeans during his formative years in a village near the confluence of the St. Peter's (later Minnesota) River and the Mississippi. European and American explorers, traders, adventurers, and government officials encountered the chief during his middle and later years. Their recorded meetings, however, were infrequent and occurred over many years.

His people called the Mdewakanton chief *Tatankamani* (Walking Buffalo) though he is known to history as *L'Aile Rouge* (French for Red Wing). Later in life he took the name *Shakea* (The Man Who Paints Himself Red). Recent interpretations suggest that this tribal leader, once thought descended from a series of Red Wings, was not. Instead, he was born around the year 1750 into the Mantanton tribe and was related to the Mdewakanton chief Wabasha I, possibly as his nephew.[11]

Red Wing grew to adulthood under the customs of the eastern Sioux, which for males stressed the duties of protection, hunting, and warfare. He first fought the Ojibway during their incursions into his tribe's territory. Later he battled the Fox and Sac as he moved his band south along the Mississippi. The Fox war chief Morgan said his people knew Red Wing as a brave enemy who would long be remembered for "the injury he had done to them."[12]

Many believed Red Wing possessed mystical powers and connections with the spirit world. As a war shaman, he led others who believed in his powers. He credited his remarkable success in battle to prophetic dreams.[13]

During the War for Independence, the British convinced the eastern Sioux to join in their fight against the Americans. Red Wing and his men were probably with Wabasha in the 1780 campaign against American forces at St. Louis. Red Wing appeared at a 1787 Indian conference at Michilimackinac, on the Straits of Mackinac, following the British and American peace. Acknowledged there as "first war chief" of his tribe, Red Wing served as spokesman for the Mdewakanton.[14]

In the late 18th century the Mdewakanton tribe divided into smaller bands, each following a particular leader. Wabasha, the most influential Mdewakanton patriarch, moved about 500 people south and east, where they migrated between Lake Pepin and the mouth of the Upper Iowa River. A group under Red Wing joined Wabasha but reportedly fell away when the two chiefs quarreled.

Red Wing took his followers, more than a hundred, to the mouth of the Cannon River, north of where Red Wing is today.[15]

Still a fighting war chief, Red Wing saw frequent combat with the Ojibway. His warriors repelled an Ojibway attack in about 1795, killing enemy leader Big Chippewa during the battle. In 1807 they repulsed an Ojibway assault with the help of a dream warning Red Wing of the enemy's approach. Many of the attackers, after being trapped on an island, suffered a grisly fate at the hands of Red Wing's men.[16]

Lt. Zebulon Pike, on an American exploratory mission into the upper Mississippi valley, met Red Wing in September 1805 and again in the spring of 1806. Red Wing was present when Pike and the Mdewakanton signed the treaty ceding land at the confluence of the Mississippi and St. Peter's (Minnesota) Rivers for what would become the American base of Fort Snelling. Pike ranked Red Wing as a "very celebrated war chief" and a "man of sense." Red Wing was upset to hear that other Sioux had fired upon the Pike party. The combative chief, by that time at least 50, said he could arrange to put Pike in command of 1,000 warriors to take revenge.[17]

Red Wing had experience dealing with whites; both English and French had become more common among the Mdewakanton in the final two decades of the 18th century. The traders, seeking to expand their relationships with the eastern Sioux, pursued approved unions with female members of important family groups. Kinship bonds were of great importance to the eastern Sioux and most helpful to the Europeans trying to expand and protect trade privileges.[18]

Joseph Renville purchased a woman from Red Wing's village in 1779. Eighteen years later their son married a Mdewakanton woman from Little Crow's band. Renville thus tied himself to both groups. The wife of Joseph Ainsé, an Englishman, also came from Red Wing's band. Ainsé's connection to Red Wing served him well. When Ainsé sought the chief's help in getting a hunter to turn over animal skins owed him, for instance, Red Wing forcefully settled the matter in the English trader's favor. The daughter of Ainsé and his Mdewakanton wife later married Jean Baptiste Faribault, further extending the trader's influence.

The military base and trading facilities that Pike claimed would be coming did not soon materialize. Meanwhile, rumors of a new war between England and America reached the eastern Sioux, and both prospective combatants wished to make allies of the Indians. In May 1812 the Americans convinced the Sioux to send a delegation of leaders, including Red Wing's eldest son, to Washington for a meeting with President James Madison.[19]

The Mdewakanton war leader kept his options open. With his son headed to Washington, Red Wing, along with Little Crow and Wabasha II, met with British representatives on June 10. The British tried to incite the Indian leaders with claims that the Americans would soon war on the eastern Sioux. An an-

gry Red Wing sided with the British, asserting that his people had been de-
ceived by American lies. "We abandon forever any connection with the Liars
. . . and we throw ourselves for protection and advice . . . on the brave and generous English nation."[20]

The Sioux warriors, apparently including Red Wing, joined the British in
their move against Fort Mackinac, the American base near the junction of Lake
Michigan and Lake Huron. On July 17 the fort fell to the attackers without a
fight. The British moved on to Detroit. There on August 16 they and their Indian allies scored another bloodless victory over the Americans.[21] The eastern
Sioux returned home, awaiting rewards for their service from the English.

Red Wing had second thoughts about his British allies after discussions
with his son, recently returned from Washington. The son had taken part in a
conference with President Madison and bore a document signed by Secretary
of War William Eustis, praising "Tar-ton-ga-ma-nee" (Tatankamani). After pon-
dering several dreams about the future, Red Wing switched his allegiance to the
Americans.[22]

To make matters worse for the British, Red Wing's second son was agitat-
ing the Ojibway, threatening to disrupt their tenuous partnership with the eastern Sioux. According to exasperated English trader Robert Dickson, Red
Wing's son killed some Ojibway in January 1814 "on purpose, to prevent any
Sioux coming this way [to Green Bay]."[23]

Red Wing persisted in his attempts to disrupt the British-Sioux alliance,
trying to convince the Sisseton and Yanktonais to make peace with the Americans. He also aided the American force that captured the British fort at Prairie
du Chien in June 1814. The war chief later avoided an apparent assassination
attempt by some pro-British warriors among Wabasha's men.[24]

Capt. Thomas Anderson, an American curious about the reasons behind
Red Wing's decision to abandon the English, asked the chief to explain. Red
Wing replied with a metaphor, likening the war to a struggle between a lion (the
English) and an eagle (the Americans):

> He (the eagle) will light on a tree over the lion, and they will scold at each
> other for a while; but they will finally make up and be friends, and smoke
> the pipe of peace. The lion will then go home, and leave us Indians with
> our foes. That is the reason for not taking up my war-club.[25]

Red Wing's prediction was correct. England and the United States made peace,
leaving the Americans a free hand in the upper Mississippi valley. The eastern
Sioux now had to work out their own deals with the Americans, and Red Wing
acted quickly. He led a delegation of Mdewakanton and Wahpeton to Portage
des Sioux near St. Louis. There, on July 19, 1815, he signed a treaty of friendship with the Americans. The Americans considered Red Wing the spokesman

for the "Sioux of the Lakes." Other leading Mdewakanton chiefs, including Wabasha, Little Crow, and Shakopee, displeased with their departing British allies, journeyed to Lake Huron to confront the English command in late spring 1816.[26]

American representatives also sought to confirm with leaders of the eastern Sioux all previous agreements and pledges of peace. More than 40 Sioux, including Red Wing plus Iron Cloud and Marching Wind of his band, "touched a pen" to the agreement signed near St. Louis in the summer of 1816.[27]

During the War of 1812 Red Wing moved his village east from the Cannon River to the foot of a river bluff rising 334 feet above the Mississippi. The Mdewakanton called the site *Khemnichan* (Hill, Wood, Water). More than half-a-mile long and 300 feet high, the bluff reminded the French of a barn. Hence their name for it—La Grange. Red Wing's village, one of the smaller Mdewakanton communities, contained about ten bark lodges set 20 feet above the waterline on the river's south bank. The villagers planted and raised corn, fished

Red Wing (Tatankamani), leading a delegation of Mdewakanton and Wahpeton called the "Sioux of the Lakes," signed this treaty with the United States near St. Louis on July 19, 1815. "Ta-tan-gamanie The walking Buffalo" appears just below the names of the American delegation, led by William Clark, who with Meriwether Lewis received credit for opening the American West. *GCHS*

in the river, and traveled west on buffalo hunts. At this location Euroamerican visitors encountered Red Wing and his people. In less than 40 years it became the Goodhue County seat.[28]

Mdewakanton villages along the Mississippi—Wabasha, Red Wing, and Kaposia, at what is now St. Paul—became stops for the growing number of Americans traveling up the river. Those coming face-to-face with Red Wing noticed a decline in the aging leader. Benjamin O'Fallon wrote, after meeting the chief on May 20, 1818, that Red Wing had "no more than about 20 men both young and old" and that "this old chief has seen better days."[29]

The American government became more of a presence in the region with the appointment of "Indian agents" following the War of 1812. The War Department employed the agents, technically civilians, to safeguard tribal rights. They concentrated on carrying out a U.S. government policy that centered on the purchase of Indian lands in settled territories and the voluntary removal of involved tribes to lands elsewhere.

Stephen Kearny, leader of an army unit trying to establish a land route to the one-year-old Fort Snelling, stopped at Red Wing's village during the summer of 1820. Kearny noted the chief's reputation as a warrior and friend of Americans. Later that summer, Michigan territorial governor Lewis Cass and Henry Schoolcraft found Red Wing unhappy over an attack on his tribe by the Sac and Fox. About 70 years old, the chief nevertheless threatened action: "I can command many men. I may do something for which I shall afterward be sorry, and by which they will long remember me."[30]

Around this time Red Wing bestowed his name on his surviving son. (His oldest son, who had traveled to Washington in 1812, had died.) The aging leader then took the name *Shakea*. Also stepping up in the band's hierarchy was the chief's nephew Wakute (Shooter).[31]

The old warrior Red Wing, now Shakea, still held the reins, but rivals questioned his leadership. The chief continued to deal with resentment from other Mdewakanton leaders because of his advocacy of the American cause in the War of 1812. And, of course, the British were unhappy with him. Indian agent Lawrence Taliaferro told him, in 1821, that the British trader Robert Dickson was bad-mouthing the chief. Shakea relished the Englishman's comments:

> I am glad to hear you say that when Dickson speaks bad of a chief, you then begin to think that the chief is a good man. You are right. Dickson thinks me the Devil, perhaps something worse, for what?—because I would not spill my blood for the British.[32]

The old warrior continued to impress his visitors. The adventurous counterfeit Italian count Giacomo Beltrami, searching in the region for the source of the Mississippi River, met the chief in 1823. Beltrami was aboard the *Vir-*

*ginia,* the first steamboat to reach the area, when Red Wing came aboard to meet with Major Taliaferro.[33]

In the summer of 1825 Shakea attended the great Prairie du Chien tribal council, which among other things established a boundary line between the eastern Sioux and Ojibway. He reminded American officials there that he adhered to their advice and had no "bad thoughts" about them. In late spring 1827 he displayed continued allegiance to the Americans by refusing to join in a Winnebago warrior's proposed uprising.[34]

Shakea died on a hunting trip during the winter of 1828–29. Renowned throughout the upper Mississippi River valley, he was then about 80 years old. Major Taliaferro wrote in his journal of Shakea's (Red Wing's) death, observing that his "war club preserved his band for many years and he used it decisively but with discretion, and was greatly respected not only by the whites and his own people, but by all the surrounding nations—even his enemies."[35]

Stephen Kearny's view of Red Wing, written after the meeting in 1820, provided a fitting epitaph for the Mdewakanton warrior: "Red Wing was an early example of the self-made American. Not born in a chief's family, he rose from warrior ranks by sheer force of character to be second only to Wabasha."[36]

For more than 30 years, from settlement during the War of 1812 to the appearance of Swiss missionaries in 1837, life in the Mdewakanton village of Red Wing continued in the tradition of the eastern Sioux. The people adjusted to their new location on the banks of Mississippi after leaving their homes around Lake Mille Lac. From this site, trade with the whites also increased.[37]

By 1823 tribal diffusion had created seven Mdewakanton villages along the Mississippi and Minnesota Rivers. The Mississippi River communities included the Red Wing band, estimated at 100 people, sited between Wabasha's village to the south and Little Crow's (Kaposia) to the north. Wabasha's village contained 400 people, and Little Crow's had 300. Including the villages on the Minnesota, the Mdewakanton population was estimated at 1,500. [38]

Growing trade with the whites changed the daily lives of the eastern Sioux. By the 1830s they made their clothing mostly from cloth obtained from traders. For everyday use women wore blue broadcloth skirts gathered at the waist, coats of printed cotton, leggings of red or blue broadcloth, moccasins, and blankets. They often had finer clothes, including colorful skirts with hems embroidered in ribbons and beads. Men wore cotton shirts, leather or cloth leggings, foot-wide blue wool breechcloths, moccasins, and wool blankets—usually white. For hunting in cold weather the men might wear buffalo robes. Some winter coats were made from blankets, while mittens came from animal skin with fur left on. [39]

The physical appearance of the Indian impressed many of the white visitors. The eastern Sioux were taller on average than their Euroamerican counterparts, and their range of height was more uniform. Women combed their hair back into two braids worn behind the ears. Men trimmed their hair across the forehead, above the eyes. Younger men often braided their hair, wearing two braids behind and smaller ones on each side of the face. They fastened the braids with small metal ornaments. Both genders wore bead and ribbon ornaments, especially for social occasions, and women often wore earrings.[40]

A New England visitor to Cannon Falls gave his impression of the Sioux he met at their hunting camp in July 1855: "The men were all young & most of them really fine looking fellows & the girls rather handsome; a very different looking set from those of La Crosse."[41]

Kinship ties were of great importance to the Dakota. Village members viewed all individuals in their community as close relatives. For example, the term *father* might apply not only to the biological parent but also to the father's brothers and male cousins. The word *mother* had similar connotations when applied to females of the birthmother's generation. Generally, the Mdewakanton used kinship identification in addressing one another. [42]

Dakota courtship and marriage involved families as well. One chose a mate from another band, a practice that maintained strong relationships among Mdewakanton villages. Before a marriage could take place, the family had to accept the suitor's gift (horses, guns, cloth, kettles, for example). Villages celebrated marriages with feasting and gift-giving. Parents valued and treated their children well and taught them to develop a self-reliant spirit.[43]

Summer homes were of bark supported by a framework of poles lashed together with basswood bark. Live elm trees supplied the covering layers—a single bark from each tree. These bark pieces sometimes were five or six feet square and quite heavy when green. Overlapping bark served as shingles for the roof, which had a hole to allow smoke from the fire to escape. Larger houses had doors at each end; smaller houses had just one. Women provided most of the labor for building homes, though men always attached the roof. The residents sat, ate, and slept on benches built about two feet high and five to six feet wide on each side of the interior and covered with bark or buffalo robes and mats. A single family or two or more families might occupy these homes.[44]

The typical tipi had a framework containing three long poles tied together at the top, against which nine more poles, arranged in a circle, leaned. The women sewed buffalo skins with sinew, lifted them by pole to wrap around the standing poles, and fastened them with pins. They reserved a space three to four feet square in the center of the tent for the fire. The tipi ran about 12 feet high and 10 to 12 feet in diameter.

The Mdewakanton men provided for their people as hunters and protected them as warriors. A man's rank depended largely on his skills at both endeavors. During wide-ranging hunts the men encountered members of rival tribes—Ojibway, Sac, and Fox—which often resulted in conflict over the hunting territory. All sides conducted deadly, recurrent raids in continuing struggles of retribution.

Red Wing's band did most of its hunting and fighting in Wisconsin. Along with other Mdewakanton, the band conducted raids deep into enemy territory. From 1835 to 1845 the eastern Dakota suffered 80 killed in battle and accounted for about 150 enemy dead. The warfare was almost exclusively between Indians. Government Indian agent Taliaferro noted that the eastern Sioux killed no white people during his term in office from 1819 to 1840.[45]

Women of the band planted, tended, and harvested corn, their chief cultivated crop. They gathered wild vegetables, berries, plums and nuts, hauled water and wood, prepared food, dressed animal skins, and made clothing. Women were the main builders of summer lodges, and they took down and put up tipis as the hunting parties moved—a daunting task during the cold winters. They wielded heavy, short-handled hoes in cornfields and axes for cutting wood.[46]

Women's labors freed men for the hunt. There were no guarantees that a hunter, even after walking all day, would return with food. When game was scarce, a hunter could work for weeks with little or no success. The women's self-reliance facilitated the hunt, which they well understood was difficult and often dangerous.

White Americans, accustomed to different social conventions, questioned the heavy labor assigned to women. Criticism became more prevalent as more settlers arrived and Dakota lifestyles changed. The depletion of game, noted as early as 1820, made more difficult the hunting tasks of the men. And the annuity system, developed to pay the Indians for their land, reduced to a degree their dependence on hunting and gathering. Settlers arriving later had firsthand knowledge of the work the Dakota women performed but little understanding of the traditional male roles of hunter and protector.

Mdewakanton women worked terribly hard but were far from slaves to their husbands. Men treated them as equals in most respects, and though women had no formal voice in tribal politics, they did have considerable influence. The woman owned the home and all that was inside it. After living and working in Dakota villages, Samuel Pond wrote that " but a slight acquaintance" with the Santee would show that "the women were not afraid of their husbands [and] are not the right material to be made slaves."[47]

This 1829 government document recognizes Wakute (Wahcoota) as the new chief "of the Sioux at the head of Lake Pepin." Indian agent Lawrence Taliaferro believed Wakute to be Tatankamani's son and gave the date of the former chief's death as March 4, 1829. *GCHS*

# 2

## 'A Thoroughly Sordid Affair'
## —The Land Transfers of 1851

Red Wing's death on March 4, 1829, led to disagreement among his followers. Who would assume leadership of the band? Red Wing's first son had died. His second son suffered from a bone disease affecting his leg and died about a year after his father. The majority supported Wakute—variously referred to as son, stepson, or nephew of Red Wing. Agent Lawrence Taliaferro also recognized Wakute as Red Wing's heir.

Intelligent, well-proportioned, and six feet tall, Wakute faced a challenge to his leadership that would trouble him and the band for years. Two months after the old chief's death, Wakute told Taliaferro that the "young men" of his village were determined to war against the Ojibway and that "he thought it useless to attempt to stop them."[1]

Wakute's main challenger was Iron Cloud (Marpiyamaza), who, like Red Wing, was a war shaman who believed he could foresee events. Iron Cloud attracted the support of the warriors and young men. He was the nephew of Red Wing's surviving son. Whites viewed Iron Cloud with suspicion. For instance, village physician William W. Sweney called him a "crafty, intriguing politician . . . a base, bad man." But that caused no damage among his followers. On August 22, 1830, Iron Cloud told Major Taliaferro he wished to replace Wakute, a suggestion the Indian agent firmly rejected.[2]

The Red Wing band temporarily split in 1832, when Wakute led his followers south to live near Wabasha's village. They stayed about eight years. Geologist George Featherstonhaugh, who stopped at the Red Wing village in September 1835, noted that "Mahpayah Maza" (Iron Cloud) was principal chief. Government officials recognized both Wakute and Iron Cloud when they conferred with the two Mdewakanton and other eastern Sioux leaders. Iron Cloud signed an 1836 treaty surrendering land in southwestern Iowa. The next year he joined Wakute and 20 other Dakota leaders on a trip to Washington, where they negotiated further land cessions. Wakute, using the name *Tautunga-munne* (Walking Buffalo), signed the treaty of 1837, as did Iron Cloud.[3]

Iron Cloud seemed well aware of the significance of signing away land in 1837, and he openly admitted losing sleep over it. "I hope it [the treaty] will satisfy our people," he said to government negotiators. "I feel very uneasy about giving up these lands as you would not give us our price."[4]

The treaty of 1837 had far-reaching effects for those who signed. The eastern Sioux received annuities for relinquishing rights to lands east of the Mississippi as well as funds dedicated to the "education and civilization" of the Sioux. That referred to the encouragement of missionary activity and the hiring of government farmers to teach agricultural techniques in each village. Missionaries already worked in some Mdewakanton communities, and Red Wing's village had just received its own.

Samuel Denton and his wife, Persis, arrived early in 1837. Daniel Gavin and his new wife—16-year-old Lucy Stevens—followed. The men were Swiss Presbyterians sent by a missionary society in Lausanne. They both married upon reaching America. From two log cabins they built themselves, the missionaries taught the tenets of Christianity to those of the Red Wing band willing to listen. In October 1838, Denton was appointed government farmer in the village for $600 a year.[5]

Political issues beyond the control of the missionaries frustrated their efforts. The Mdewakanton believed the government was not living up to agreements in the 1837 treaty. Unhappiness over the disbursement of "education funds" caused friction. The treaty made provision for funds to the eastern Sioux, but the money did not reach them. The Indians came to believe that the missionaries intercepted their money. These feelings led to an effort to sabotage the mission schools.

The Dentons and Lucy Gavin opened a school at the Red Wing village in 1842 and reported just 15 students enrolled that year. They hoped more pupils would appear upon completion of the proposed schoolhouse. Average enrollment crept to 16 the next year. Eleven girls and six boys attended regularly, and others came sporadically. Wakute, who had returned to Red Wing's village with his followers in the 1840s, supported the school, but his enthusiasm waned. In 1844 Gavin wrote that Wakute seemed determined to eliminate the program. Wakute was by this time chief of the village; Iron Cloud served as head soldier.[6]

The future of the Red Wing mission was in doubt. Complaints from village leaders resulted in Denton's dismissal as government farmer on March 31, 1845. Meanwhile, Lucy Gavin's health problems made it necessary for the Gavins to leave their posts. A discouraged Denton wrote to fellow missionary

Rev. John F. Aiton with his second wife,
Mary Briggs Aiton, in April 1855. *MHS*

Samuel Pond, complaining that his superiors wanted to keep the Red Wing mission going even "after a full understanding of our utter failure here, and the probability that we never shall do anything." Denton soon left Red Wing.

On June 13, 1849, the side-wheel steamer *Dr. Franklin* edged towards shore at Red Wing's village, attracting a crowd of Mdewakanton men, women, and children. The villagers were by this time familiar with steamboat arrivals, but the New England couple about to disembark was unprepared for the "fantastically dressed" Indians awaiting them. The couple, Joseph Hancock, his wife, Maria Houghton Hancock, and their 18-month-old daughter, Marilla, had to adjust rapidly to their new life at the missionary station.[7]

John Aiton and John Bush also greeted the Hancocks. Aiton had known Hancock during their days at Lane Seminary in Cincinnati and was expecting their arrival. Hancock told Aiton in early 1848 that he was willing to "go to the Sioux" if Aiton was. The birth of Marilla delayed his departure. Meanwhile, with the help of his first wife, Nancy, Aiton reestablished the Red Wing mission. The 60-year-old Bush was the new government farmer hired to replace Samuel Denton. He lived in the village with his "mixed-blood" wife, Charlotte.[8]

Bossy, the Hancock's cow, was an unwilling immigrant to Red Wing. She broke from the riverside assemblage and swam across the river. Maria Hancock identified with Bossy's feelings, writing in her diary, "I really don't blame her for being frightened. I am frightened myself at the thought of living in a village of 300 Indians. I shall be the only white woman here for some time." Aiton's wife had given birth to a daughter while at Dr. Thomas Williamson's mission at Little Crow's village Kaposia. The Aitons spent the winter there, and Nancy had not yet returned to Red Wing.[9]

The Aiton-Hancock partnership proved short-lived. The families shared a former Swiss mission home. The Aitons lived downstairs and the Hancocks above. They apparently got along well, but John Aiton objected to the disparity of pay between a missionary (himself) and the newly created government teacher (Hancock). Aiton and his wife, as missionaries, received $300 a year plus $30 for their child. The teaching position paid $500. The arrangement upset Aiton, even though Hancock returned the difference between teacher and missionary pay to the missionary board.[10]

Aiton and Hancock argued about the management of the school. Both were concerned about inconsistent attendance. Aiton averaged 27 students per day for several weeks in the fall of 1848, but then the Mdewakanton left the area to collect annuities and hunt. April 1849 attendance, while Aiton ran the school, averaged 13, though about 50 pupils attended sometime during the session. He reported in September 1849, "I teach in Dakota only as yet, as it is much easier learned than English." Aiton decided to leave the mission.[11]

Problems with school attendance continued under Hancock. The concept of formal schooling was foreign to the Mdewakanton. But Hancock also reported: "In intellectual capacity, I do not consider the North American Indian inferior to the Anglo-Saxon race." The children, he wrote, "were generally unwilling to stay long in the schoolroom. The work seemed like trying to tame a lot of young foxes."[12]

Teaching and proselytizing produced mixed results for Hancock and the Mdewakanton, but the 34-year-old missionary made better progress on a personal level. He began learning the Dakota language on his first day in the village and soon became fluent. Hancock developed a positive personal relationship with Wakute and other members of the band, noting they were "a kind people to those who were friendly and kind to them." He came to understand and respect Dakota culture but worked vigorously to convert the people to the ways of Christianity. Often frustrated, he wrote in June 1852: "I can think of nothing that has transpired during this year which may be considered favorable to our success."[13]

The whiskey trade was of particular worry to Hancock. He believed liquor destructive to the people of Red Wing's village. John Aiton shared that concern and opened an antiwhiskey campaign during his short stay, convincing Wakute and 60 others to sign a temperance pledge.[14] Hancock traveled to St. Paul in the summer of 1850 to enlist territorial governor Alexander Ramsey in a war against Wisconsin whiskey-sellers. Wisconsin provided a sanctuary for the liquor traders barred from Indian lands across the Mississippi.[15]

Joseph Hancock and Maria Houghton Hancock arrived by
steamboat at the Red Wing village on June 13, 1849. *GCHS*

Hancock started his own war against whiskey as a self-appointed prohibition agent. Once he intercepted six young men as they returned from Wisconsin with a pail of whiskey. Hancock surprised the men, snatched the pail, and
dumped its contents. One of the young men vowed to return with more whiskey and dare the missionary to dump it. A few days later the six men were back,
their leader carrying a two-gallon jug secured to a strong cord around his neck.
Hancock understood the challenge and confronted him. During a violent wres-
tling match the missionary managed to pull the jug's cork and spill the liquor.
Hancock claimed, "If any more whiskey was brought over to Red Wing . . . it
was carefully concealed from me."

Good health came with no guarantees on the Minnesota frontier, as the
Mdewakanton and Hancocks well understood. Maria had not been well since
giving birth to son Joseph on August 25, 1850, and her health failed as win-
ter came. Jane Williamson, sister of Kaposia missionary Thomas Williamson, came to nurse her. But 30-year-old Maria weakened, and on March 20
she died. Six months later the Hancock's year–old son died. The lonely mis-
sionary left three-year-old Marilla with the Williamsons and sat out the Minnesota winter as a boarder with John Day's family in nearby Diamond Bluff,
Wisconsin.[16]

Disease took a great toll among the eastern Sioux throughout the settlement
period. A "scourge," most likely cholera, which was a danger for all those living along the Mississippi, struck the Red Wing band during the summer of
1852, killing 11 in three weeks. Indian agent Amos Bruce reported epidemics in 1846 and 1847 "carrying [the Indians] off at a fearful rate." Iron Cloud,
longtime rival of Wakute, was among the victims of the 1852 contagion.

Hancock recorded that "the voice of wailing for the dead—the conjurers rattle—[were] very common affairs at the village of Red Wing."[17]

Mary Sampson contracted cholera during the 1852 summer outbreak while on a river steamer. Sampson, along with her husband, Francis, and their five children, were moving from Maine to Minnesota Territory when she became ill. The steamer's captain, for the safety of his passengers, required the Sampsons to disembark at Red Wing. Mary died two hours after they landed. Francis fashioned a rough coffin and, with his grieving children, buried his wife at midnight. John Bush and his wife, Charlotte, provided shelter to the Sampsons. They were asked to assume temporary care of the family's seven-month-old while Francis took the other children to St. Anthony. The child who stayed in Red Wing died later that fall.[18]

At midcentury the ever-advancing American frontier threatened to breach the upper Mississippi River valley. In 1830 President Andrew Jackson's Indian removal bill had forced the remaining tribes of the Old Northwest (north of the Ohio River and east of the Mississippi) to emigrate across the Mississippi. Now settlers neared the northern reaches of the great river. During the 1830s and 1840s the Sioux people experienced growing pressure to cede their land to the government. The March 1849 decision by Congress to establish Minnesota Territory guaranteed more white presence and more desire for Indian land.[19]

Stephen A. Douglas, senator from Illinois and proponent of territorial status, claimed "somewhere between eight and ten thousand" living in Minnesota in 1849—generous beyond the territorial census listing 4,852 citizens. Neither figure included Indian people. The vast Minnesota Territory, as first constituted, stretched to the Missouri River and was divided into three "organized counties"—Washington, Ramsey, and Benton. Six more sprawling and sparsely white-settled areas linked to the trio of organized counties to create a semblance of government. Red Wing's village fell into the northern section of Wabashaw (1849 spelling) County, one of the six yet to be officially organized.[20]

The American government had sought the purchase of Mdewakanton lands since Zebulon Pike's explorations in 1805. Tatankamani, head of the Red Wing band, witnessed the sale of two small tracts of land to the Americans in September that year. In 1819 one of those land parcels became the site of the U.S. military base later known as Fort Snelling. Iron Cloud and Wakute, of the Red Wing band, signed treaties in 1836 and 1837. With these, the Mdewakanton relinquished claims to land at the periphery of the nation. In 1841 the Red Wing and Wabasha bands firmly opposed a new government land purchase, which prompted the frustrated Indian agent Amos Bruce to suggest the government forcibly remove them.[21]

The new territorial governor, Alexander Ramsey, understood from the time of his arrival in St. Paul the importance of acquiring the eastern Sioux territories known as "Suland" in the newspapers. His first message to the territorial legislature in September 1849 called for pressure on Congress to make a land agreement with the Dakota. By summer 1851 the government negotiators, led by Ramsey and the new Commissioner of Indian Affairs, Luke Lea, dispatched from Washington, were positioned to deal. The eastern Sioux heard rumors of a land sale, and the Mdewakanton, in particular, were skeptical. The Red Wing band talked openly of its opposition.

In July the treaty commissioners proceeded to Traverse des Sioux, near present-day St. Peter, to meet with the Sisseton and Wahpeton living farther to the west. Ramsey and Lea believed those groups less sophisticated, thus easier to persuade, than the Mdewakanton and Wahpekute. Tribal leaders signed the Treaty of Traverse des Sioux, reluctantly ceding most of the land in southern and western Minnesota Territory. A notable exception was a reservation on either side of the upper Minnesota River. The Dakota were to receive for their land a total of $1,665,000, less a $275,000 payment to satisfy debts to traders and $30,000 for costs including the opening of reservation farms. Interest on the principal would produce a $40,000 yearly cash payment.

The Indian leaders, after signing the treaty, initialed another instrument prepared by traders. The document amounted to a blank check with which the Indians agreed to pay unspecified debts supposedly owed to the traders. The traders' claims exceeded the cash available from the land sale. These were later reduced, but the issue of "traders' papers" greatly embittered the Indians.[22]

Ramsey and Lea knew that procuring the signatures of the Mdewakanton and Wahpekute would be more difficult. Those bands would have to leave their homes and villages if they agreed to the new treaty. The negotiations opened at Mendota beginning July 29; the first meeting indicated that hard bargaining lay ahead. The Mdewakanton, led by Wabasha III, Little Crow, and Wakute, talked of earlier unfulfilled government promises and demanded immediate payment of money owed them. Wabasha wanted to know what had become of the money from the Treaty of 1837 education fund, discomfiting Ramsey. Little Crow also complained about the administration of the 1837 agreement. Ramsey tried to deflect the complaints, but Little Crow replied, "We will talk of nothing else but that money if it is until next spring."[23]

Wakute also spoke of broken promises. He recalled the trip to Washington in 1837 when the Mdewakanton leaders "were told many things which . . . we found out could not be done. At the end of three or four years, the Indians found out very differently from what they had been told—and all were ashamed." The leader of the Red Wing band feared more treachery from Washington.[24]

As negotiations wore on, Little Crow came to view the sale of the Mdewakanton land as inevitable. Wabasha continued to resist compromise with Ramsey and Lea. Little Crow changed tactics, attempting to secure a reservation in the east, as close to the woodlands as possible. Wakute, who had deferred to Wabasha earlier in the talks, by this time was following Little Crow's more conciliatory line.[25]

Wakute also hoped to obtain an eastern woodland reservation for the Red Wing band. He made a specific request: "I was not brought up in a prairie country, but among woods; and I would like to go to a tract of land called Pine Island, which is a good place for Indians. I want you to write this in the treaty." He added that if his wishes could not be accommodated he would "say no more about it."[26]

Little Crow agreed to the treaty of Mendota after government concessions on reservation locations, defying the rumor that the first to sign it would be killed by other warriors. A resigned Wabasha signed next, then 63 others including Wakute, Iron Cloud, Good Iron Voice, Stands on the Ground, Stands Above, Sacred Fire, the Ghost Killer, Red Stones, Sacred Blaze, and Iron Cave—all from Red Wing's band. The Mdewakanton and Wahpekute received $1,410,000 for their land, with interest on the principal yielding annual payments for the bands. The Mdewakanton, aware of the "traders' paper" controversy at Traverse des Sioux, refused to initial other documents. Yet through their signing of the treaty at Mendota, the Mdewakanton grudgingly agreed to leave their Mississippi River valley homes and move farther west.[27]

The treaties of Traverse des Sioux and Mendota still needed U.S. Senate ratification, a process that, as Wakute recalled, involved risk for the eastern Sioux. His concerns were valid. The Senate agreed to the treaties on June 23, 1852, but did not like the idea of Minnesota reservations for the Dakota people and removed that clause. The Indians felt betrayed by a proposal that left them without a home. When asked about the Senate action, Wabasha, who had not wanted to sell, answered, "There is one thing more which our great father can do, that is gather us all together on the prairie and surround us with soldiers and shoot us down."[28]

The eastern Sioux were in a precarious position. They would have to move, but because of government indecision they did not know when and where they were expected to go. They had missed their summer hunt and lost much of their corn to flood. Meanwhile, in the spring of 1852, new settlers learning of the impending sale of Suland began moving into lands west of the Mississippi. The government was powerless to halt the flood of illegal immigration as the newcomers set up town sites and farms and hunted on tribal lands.[29]

Governor Ramsey scrambled to save the treaties. He asked Washington to allow the Mdewakanton use of the reservations for 20 to 25 years. He hired St. Paulite and future U.S. senator Henry Rice to cement the deal. The governor then traveled to Washington to secure funding for the treaties. Ramsey, upon his return in November, proposed to settle with treaty money the Indian debts claimed by the traders. He suggested the Indians sign "receipts" for the cash and trust him personally to handle payment to the traders. Wabasha and

Wakute insisted *they* would make such distributions. The Mdewakanton leaders later signed the receipts, each after receiving nearly $3,000 in cash. In July 1853 the U.S. Senate held hearings on Ramsey's dealings with the eastern Sioux. He was exonerated. [30]

Henry Hastings Sibley had grave reservations about government policies towards the eastern Sioux. He had acquired firsthand knowledge of the Sioux from his start in Minnesota as a 23-year-old fur trader and through his early political career. He warned of the dire consequences of continued ill-treatment:

> Your pioneers are encircling the last home of the red man, as with a wall of fire . . . You must approach these [Indians] with terms of conciliation and friendship, or you must suffer the consequences of a bloody and remorseless Indian war . . . The time is not far distant when, pent in on all sides, and suffering from want, a Philip, or a Tecumseh, will arise to band themselves together for a last and desperate onset upon their white foes.[31]

Sibley's warning was remarkable for its prescience. In August 1862 his "bloody and remorseless war" swept across the Minnesota prairie.

Minnesota historian Newton H. Winchell labeled the treaties of 1851 a "monstrous conspiracy," a comment echoed by Roy W. Meyer in his history of the eastern Sioux. Meyer's indictment was uncompromising:

> From beginning to end—the tactics used to get the Indians to accept the treaties in the first place, the bad faith of the Senate in amending them, the devices employed to force the Indians to accept the amendments, the whole nefarious business of the traders' paper—it was a thoroughly sordid affair, equal in infamy to anything else in the long history of injustice perpetrated upon the Indians.[32]

Strafford Western Emigration Company's search for a place "suitable for a colony of New England families" in Minnesota ended with the the selection of Zumbrota in August 1856. This early photograph shows the young community. *GCHS*

The Vasa cabin of Eric Anderson illustrates construction typical of the log structures built in Goodhue County during the Euroamerican settlement period. *GCHS*

# 3

# Settling Suland—
# The New Minnesotans Arrive

From his home on the Wisconsin side of the Mississippi, John Day cast covetous eyes on land in Red Wing's village. Day was one of those unable to wait for Senate ratification of the 1851 land treaties at Traverse des Sioux and Mendota. In April 1852 he crossed the river, occupied one of the mission houses, then built a cabin and established a claim. The Mdewakanton showed their displeasure with Day's illegal action by tearing down his cabin. When Day rebuilt the structure, the Indians again razed it. Day retreated across the river but soon returned to continue building. Day built and the Indians tore down the cabin half a dozen times.[1]

Benjamin Young also wanted Red Wing land. Young, part Indian, part French, laid claim to land so near Day's that an argument ensued. The two settled the dispute, and Young later sold his claim to William W. Sweney, a St. Paul physician. Sweney and his brother-in-law William Freeborn, a past St. Paul city councilman, liked Red Wing's prospects, and both planned to move there. Sweney settled in May 1852, before the treaty ratification, but the Mdewakanton did not harass him.[2]

The white population grew with the addition of Calvin Potter and James McGinnis. In spring 1852 the widower missionary Joseph Hancock traveled to the mission station at Lac qui Parle to marry 19-year-old Sarah Rankin. She had helped out at the Red Wing mission following Maria Hancock's death. Their marriage took place on May 2, and the couple returned to Red Wing.[3]

Sickness and disease took a fearsome toll of Mdewakanton in 1852. Seven adults and 11 children died during the summer and fall of that year, a heavy loss to the small group. By September the Red Wing band was scattered throughout the area, with only a small encampment near the old village.[4] Meanwhile, the trickle of illicit immigrants became a flood. By late summer 1852, government agent Nathaniel McLean estimated about 5,000 whites lived on the Indians' lands in Minnesota Territory. He had no power to stop the settlers. Their growing number also emboldened the immigrants to challenge the Native Americans more directly.[5]

The Red Wing band, returning from a winter hunt in April 1853, discovered its homes burned to the ground. Hancock later wrote that the Mdewakanton made no attempt to retaliate after discovering the destruction. They surveyed the ashes of their homes yet "made no signs of ill temper." Wakute and his people "rebuilt in other places where the whites would not use the land."[6]

Presidential politics caused further delays in settling eastern Sioux reservation issues unresolved since the signing of the 1851 treaties. The election of Democrat Franklin Pierce in November 1852 overshadowed the establishment of the new Indian reservation in Minnesota Territory. Pierce's election meant that the territory received a new Democratic governor, Willis A. Gorman, and a new superintendent of Indian Affairs, Robert G. Murphy. On February 24, 1853, the government, after a delay of nearly two years, proclaimed the sale of Suland. Discussion regarding the resettlement of the eastern Sioux continued. Superintendent Murphy overruled earlier plans and declared his intent to locate the Sioux Indian agency on the Minnesota River about 15 miles above the new base at Fort Ridgely.[7]

During the summer of 1853 most members of the Red Wing (Wakute as leader) and Wabasha bands left their homes on the Mississippi. By September 10 they had encamped at Little Crow's village near St. Paul. Hancock reported that some in the Wakute group invited him to join them when they moved west —an idea he would consider. The missionary also observed that the Indians were "not all satisfied with going up the St. Peters [Minnesota River]."[8]

Hancock felt frustrated, after four years with the Red Wing band, by his inability to interest the Mdewakanton in the Christian religion. In March 1853 he reported that the few present at one of his services "left the house while I was reading the word of God in their language." The Mdewakanton, he added, expected some "favor" if they stayed until he finished. Yet the missionary was not without hope. Earlier he had written of the positive changes that treaty ratification would bring to the "circumstances of this people." Without this hope, he observed, "Their future prospects [are] dark indeed, both for this world and the next."[9]

The federal government certified the land sale in 1853, officially claiming the Indian lands. The removal of the Mdewakanton and Wahpekute began, stopped temporarily, then continued over several years. The people of Red Wing left their village, but their exodus was far from final. Tribal members returned to their old hunting grounds around the Cannon River and Red Wing for several years. Yet fewer than 20 families lived outside the new reservation by the time of the 1862 Dakota uprising in the Minnesota River valley.[10]

Joseph Hancock decided against joining the Mdewakanton on their Minnesota River reservation, opting to stay at the old village site and minister to its increasing white population. As for the prospects of Wakute's Red Wing band, Hancock's missionary society could only express grave concern. Rev. S. B. Treat, secretary of the American Board of Commissioners for Foreign Missions, wrote to Hancock from his Boston office: "My heart is pained when I think of the Dakotas. Is there no bright future for them? I am not willing to give up yet. Let us pray & hope on."[11]

The acquisition of the vast Suland did not legitimize the status of the estimated 20,000 settlers now living in southern Minnesota. The newcomers moving in were trespassers, despite the area's being largely empty of permanent Indian residents. By law, a survey of the land had to precede settlement. In spring 1853 that process was just beginning.[12]

Settlers ignored legal niceties. Throughout the settlement period in the Northwest, land surveys lagged behind the arrival of immigrants, so "squatters"—those who claimed land still owned by the United States—frequently lived on their claims. In Minnesota the territorial government overtly encouraged the illegals by repeatedly petitioning Congress to allow the purchase of the land. In 1851, Gov. Alexander Ramsey appealed to Washington, observing of the immigrants: "They cost the Government neither monthly pay, nor rations—they solicit no bounty—but they make the country, its history, and its glory."[13] Still, Congress would delay until August 4, 1854, the allowance of the claims of those living on unsurveyed land.

In the meantime, settlers pinned their hopes on a provision of the Preemption Act of 1841 that allowed an individual to claim government-owned land *before* it was put on sale. This meant "preemptors" could put off paying for the land they settled until the government declared it on the market.[14]

Daunted but undeterred by lack of a proper survey, the territorial legislature began, on March 5, 1853, to divide the massive Wabashaw County into smaller units—Goodhue County and eight others. The next February the legislature modified the first vague boundaries along lines laid down by the U.S. survey. To be considered "organized," the new counties had to hold a general election in which at least 50 voted. Citizens in Wacoota (later spelled *Wacouta*) and Red Wing, the only two villages of size within the new county's borders, schemed to make their communities the county seat.[15]

Goodhue County is the namesake of James Madison Goodhue, the colorful founder of the territory's first newspaper, St. Paul's *Minnesota Pioneer*. He was a master of insult, something of a necessity for newspapermen of the day, and his ability to skewer his opponents was well known. In January 1851, Goodhue unleashed a slashing written attack on a political enemy that nearly cost the editor his life.[16]

The feisty Goodhue, incensed by the political intrigues of his enemies, fired a broadside at a Minnesota Supreme Court judge, David Cooper. Among other things, Goodhue wrote that Cooper was a "miserable drunk" who had to "feel upward for the ground." He added, "Off the Bench he is a beast and on the Bench he is an ass, stuffed with arrogance."[17] Cooper's brother Joseph took exception to Goodhue's remarks and attempted to make his point with a bowie knife. The fight began when Joseph Cooper accosted Goodhue on a St. Paul street. After an exchange of words, both men pulled pistols. Sheriff Cornelius Lull intervened, temporarily disarming the two men, but Cooper produced the knife and charged the editor. Goodhue then pulled a second pistol. In the melee Goodhue was stabbed twice and Cooper shot once. Their wounds were serious, but both men recovered.[18]

Goodhue's tempestuous career ended quietly with his death on August 27, 1852. The 42-year-old newsman had been a Minnesotan for just over three years. Goodhue received high praise for his contributions to Minnesota via a generous send-off, even by rival newspapers. The state commemorated his name by attaching it to one of the territory's new counties.[19]

Promoters in Wacouta and Red Wing developed strategies for procuring the new county seat. The small Lake Pepin settlement at Wacouta, home of the George W. Bullard trading post, and the equally tiny Red Wing scrambled to find voters in time for Goodhue County's election. Bullard traded with the Indians but also attracted business from lumbermen, potential pro-Wacouta voters living across the river in Wisconsin. Red Wing boosters feared the voting power of the woodsmen and countered by hiring 20 young, unmarried St. Paul men to work and then vote in the village. Meanwhile, Benjamin Young of Red Wing, duly certified as an election judge, proved painstakingly careful in checking the address of "every woodchopper" to make sure each was qualified to vote. Red Wing became the Goodhue County seat.[20]

The voters also decided on their representative in the territorial legislature. Elected was James "Bully" Wells, who ran unopposed. Bully Wells deserved his nickname. The rough, rugged New Jersey-born frontiersman had come to Minnesota as a teenage member of the 1819 Leavenworth Expedition. He began a career as an Indian trader after a dozen years in the army, finally settling on the shores of Lake Pepin in 1831. For more than ten years Wells was the only white man other than Red Wing missionaries living within what is now Goodhue County. Wells shared the Lake Pepin trading post (at what would become Old Frontenac) with his mixed-blood wife, Jane (a daughter of pioneer trader Duncan Graham), and their seven children.[21]

Wells enhanced his reputation by his election to the first territorial legislature in 1849, though his opponent, Harley White, accused him of vote-rigging. Wells had outpolled White 33–29, but White claimed six of Wells's voters were not legal residents. A resolution to unseat Wells resulted in a tie vote, a weak show of support for the Lake Pepin trader but enough to leave him in office. Wells the politician, described as "somewhat illiterate" in Holcombe's analysis of territorial legislators, still managed a profitable trade relationship with the eastern Sioux. Jane Wells's family connections facilitated his trading deals. The skin lodges of Jane's "relatives and friends" surrounded their Lake Pepin trading post.[22]

Many Americans knew little of this land on their northwest frontier, though Minnesota Territory and its counties bordering the Mississippi received growing interest from prospective settlers in the eastern United States. Knowledge of Minnesota and its increasing accessibility soon would greatly expand. Former President Millard Fillmore, accompanied by a large party of guests, agreed to make a rail and river journey to St. Paul. The "Grand Excursion" was set for the summer of 1854.[23]

The completion of the Chicago and Rock Island Railroad line triggered the promotional trip, which proved to be Minnesota's coming-out party. The journey celebrated the extension of tracks to Rock Island, Illinois, located safely on the Mississippi's east bank. In early June, 1,200 travelers, including Fillmore, reached Rock Island, then boarded five large steamers for travel upriver to Minnesota Territory. The convoy of steamers passed by Red Wing before reaching St. Paul on June 8.

Journalists from the major Eastern newspapers joined the excursion, also called the "Fashionable Tour," and provided trip coverage for their readers. Fillmore declared the Grand Excursion one for which "history has no parallel, and such as no prince could possibly undertake." A later historian labeled the trip "by far the most brilliant event of its kind that the West had ever witnessed." Chicago, during the warm season, was now within 30 hours of Minnesota, and Washington, D.C., just four days and nights away.

Nine days after the Grand Excursion swept past Red Wing, county officers, all appointed by the governor, met in that city and opened the first meeting of the Goodhue County Board of Commissioners. The organization of the county was official.[24]

"Old-stock" Americans made up most of the first wave in the growing flood of Minnesota's newcomers. The old stock were members of white European families whose ancestors migrated to North America. Many of those moving west left homes in New England and the mid-Atlantic states. The pattern was the same for Goodhue County, beginning with its first permanent white settlers— New Englanders Joseph and Maria Hancock.[25]

During the 1830s, Midlanders traveled the National Road out of western Maryland and Pennsylvania into the lands of the Northwest Territory where upland southerners from Kentucky joined them. A deluge of New England Yankees followed the mix of southern Midlanders, who described themselves as "Western." By 1860, demographer John Rice noted, "Nearly half of the Yankees then living had left New England." Most headed for Ohio, Indiana, Illinois, or Michigan, and eventually toward Wisconsin, Iowa, or Minnesota. By 1860, 79 percent of non-Indian Minnesotans had origins in the Northeast, with another 16 percent from Pennsylvania and New Jersey.[26]

So culturally uniform were the New Englanders that demographers later argued for their inclusion in the state's immigration history as a distinct group. Many settlers from back east would have agreed. At the conclusion of a December 1857 Minneapolis gathering of the New England Society of the Northwest, the evening's final toast was to "New England and each of the New England states, and Minnesota. May she [Minnesota] imitate the heroic virtues of her foster mother, till New England industry, New England enterprise, and New England thrift shall build here a glorious superstructure of education and Gospel truth and make the land we live in like the land we left."[27]

As spring 1855 approached, New Englanders and others looked forward to the opening of navigation on the Mississippi. The Grand Excursion of 1854 helped publicize Minnesota Territory, and newcomers jockeyed to be among the first arrivals of the year. The steamer *War Eagle* arrived on April 17 carrying 814 passengers. The packet-boat company delivered 30,000 by season's end.[28]

A young Connecticut man, David W. Humphrey, arrived in Red Wing in mid-June 1855 and began the long walk to the Cannon Falls area. Settlers moved slowly into rural Goodhue County in 1853 and 1854, but a land rush was now under way. Humphrey, writing to friends back home, clearly enjoyed his experiences in a region that reminded him of New England. After a two-day walk, the traveler got his first look at Cannon Falls: "This renowned place we found to consist of two log hotels & two cabins for private residences." After that lighthearted slap at the city, he continued, "It doubtless will soon be quite a town."[29]

The speed of settlement in and around Cannon Falls amazed Humphrey. He wrote of his interest in Prairie Creek, "a gem of a prarie [*sic*]," settled mostly by Vermonters. He told of the explosion of immigration there:

> To give you a little idea of the rapidity with which the country is filling up, this prarie of prarie creek was all unclaimed last Monday morning, & in three days 3,000 acres were taken. One man can have only 160 acres . . . All the settlers there are N. Englanders.

The Prairie Creek lands later became part of Stanton township, named for William Stanton Sr., one of that area's early settlers. Stanton and a party of New Englanders left their previous settlement in Dodge County, Wisconsin, and arrived around the time of Humphrey's visit.

"Only let the New England enterprise & industry be transplanted to this country," Humphrey wrote, "& we shall soon see these magnificent prairies blossom like the rose." Like others, he quickly spotted weaknesses in the regulations regarding the establishment of claims:

> This claiming business is rather rich. The law requires that any man to hold 160 acres must build a house on it, live on it, make it his home, but does not require any particular length of time. The way the merchants, lawyers & speculators take up claims and reside on them is amusing.

Humphrey's concise, first-person study of such a land fraud near Cannon Falls sums up the situation. That others employed similar practices throughout the county and elsewhere in the territory, serves to make Humphrey's account even more relevant:

> The law requires a house. A log cabin that had already been one *home* was bought for $2. The logs drawed on to the claim & put up in the form of a pen 12 ft square and 6½ high. A board roof & floor is required & they were borrowed of the next neighbor for a couple of days. One glass window must be had & it was lent by the landlord of the hotel. A door was necessary & it was brought two miles on our backs one evening to be returned early the next morning. The cabin must be *chinked* & *mudded*. Fifteen minutes sufficed for that operation. The *preemptor* must make it his home there & the landlady furnished a pail of provisions for two days support. A witness to all this must needs be had & of course I accompanied him. Two nights we slept in our cabin, on our prarie [*sic*] home & two very comfortable nights they were . . . The third morning we took up our borrowed blankets, window & all fixins & came in.[30]

A woman could not preempt under law unless she was a widow or "head of a family." But clever pioneer females found ways to circumvent the restrictions. If they couldn't borrow a movable house in the manner of David Humphrey's friend, they *could* borrow babies. A young woman, to prove she headed a household, might temporarily adopt a child, swear to family status, and preempt a piece of land. Later she had the adoption annulled and returned the child to its natural parents.[31]

Morris P. Dennison and his wife, Rebecca, left the stony foothills of Vermont's Green Mountains in spring 1856 and headed toward the rich prairie of Minnesota. He knew the western Goodhue County area, having made an exploratory trip there in 1849. On his second trip, the Vermonter, weighed down by gold sewn into his vest, nearly drowned when he fell off a raft crossing the Mississippi at Wabasha. The Dennisons walked wagon roads and old Indian trails to reach land near the Goodhue County-Rice County borders, where they staked their claim. The Dennison land stretched across the county borders, a problem later addressed in platting the village bearing the Dennison name.[32]

Massachusetts native Levi Hillman arrived in Cannon Falls on May 17, 1856, and saw the "Promised Land—New England of the West." The adventuresome Hillman, a veteran of the California gold rush, now took part in the Minnesota land rush.

"You behold a thousand acres of smooth, level land lying before you richer than the best of our lands in the east," he wrote to his wife, Mary. It was a "beautiful sight," especially to a New Englander "reared upon one of those cramped Hill Farms." He also reported that "very fine families" from Massachusetts, Maine, New York, and Connecticut lived in the area.[33]

Vermont native Helen Rudd came to Goodhue County as a newlywed in April 1856. When Helen was a child, her family joined the New Englander western movement and settled in Michigan. At age 25, Helen married Quinton Bunch. The couple then set out for Minnesota, arriving in Red Wing just 17 days after their wedding. There they would first live in a boardinghouse.

"We are going to have chairs soon," she wrote. They did have a bench and lounge: "These are what we sit on at table in this new country!" Helen was thankful for a present of soap, not readily available in the city, and for a cup and plate: "We can drink in the cup and warm gruel in it and bake turnovers on the plate."[34]

Zumbrota's Strafford Western Emigration Company provides a Goodhue County example of a well-organized group determined to settle an area "suitable for a colony of New England families." Samuel Shaffee, D. B. Godard, and Joseph Bailey scouted Minnesota Territory for colonists in Lowell, Massachusetts. The trio ascended a hill at sunset on August 8, 1856, and discovered, spreading out before them, the kind of land they'd been looking for—the Zumbro River valley near today's Zumbrota.[35]

The scouting party met with others of the group upon their return to Red Wing and made arrangements to buy the land from C. W. Smith and Aaron Doty, owners of the proposed town site. Smith was a land speculator who, along with partner Doty, held title to the choice land.

The wily Smith had increased the value of the land in the future Zumbrota by single-handedly changing the route of the Red Wing-Mantorville road. He intercepted wagons passing on the old road near present-day Roscoe and convinced drivers to take a new route, over his land, to Red Wing. Smith, his wife, and Doty, who lived in a rough and roofless shanty on the town site, were willing to sell a hundred acres.

The Strafford company spelled out its goals in the preamble to the group's constitution signed on August 13, 1856: "The undersigned with the purpose and hope of being more widely useful as citizens and Christians, agree to form ourselves into an agricultural community for the purpose of making a town site and settlement here in the west."[36]

Former citizens of America's Northeast provided the bulk of early white settlements in Goodhue County, with heaviest concentrations in Zumbrota and Red Wing. Rice concluded, "It was settlers from the East . . . who laid the groundwork for the future state of Minnesota. They built and managed towns, founded industries, and established institutions." They fully expected that "Minnesota would become the New England of the West."[37]

"In 1852 . . . Ole Swenson Sumbren and his brother Erik got the 'America Fever,'" wrote Ole's son Swen O. Swenson in 1939. The two young men decided to leave their home in Norway, the first of six brothers to cross the ocean to America. The Sumbrens, after three years of summer farmwork and winter logging, began a search for their own land in the summer of 1855. The brothers walked across Goodhue County to Minneola township where they encountered the sod house of another native of Norway, 21-year-old Christian Peterson Lunde. He had not seen a white person for more than a month and was happy to receive visitors.[38]

Lunde and the Sumbrens were in the vanguard of thousands of Norwegians who chose Goodhue County as their home, making it "the most prominent of Norwegian settlements in Minnesota." Goodhue County's own Norse immigration is particularly significant considering that Minnesota attracted more Norwegians than any other state. The United States saw the influx of about 850,000 Norwegian immigrants between 1825 and 1928.[39]

By the mid-19th century, expanding population and a lack of decent farmland distressed Norway and its people. The population doubled from 1815 to 1865, making jobs in the nation's traditional labor markets—agriculture, fishing, and lumbering—scarce. The American Midwest, with its tracts of rich, unsettled farmland, provided an outlet for Norwegians dreaming of a fresh start.[40]

Thousands of Norwegians came to America and Minnesota, in many cases leaving family and friends behind and accepting the risks of a long ocean crossing. "I stood ready to say to my fatherland, my kindred, my parish and my parents, farewell," wrote Lewis Larson of his April 1855 departure from Stavanger, Norway. Larson and his wife, Anna, moved to Goodhue County. Fifty years later he could still see the image of his crying parents bidding him good-bye, perhaps forever. Four passengers who died during Larson's crossing were buried at sea.[41]

The journey of the Johann Kildahl family to America and Goodhue County in 1866 proved a terrible trial. With all preparations for the voyage complete, tragedy struck just two days before their scheduled departure. Their three-year-old daughter, Johanna, contracted scarlet fever and died. The family could not cancel its trip so had to leave the burial to their child's uncle. The journey from Trondheim on the *Nicanor*, a converted salt freighter, was challenging. The 300 passengers slept in several rows of bunkbeds, and passengers furnished their own bedding except for a straw tick. People sat on their beds, trunks, or chests during the five-week trip. In mid-June the family's 16-year-old son, Nils, became ill; he died five days later. The family buried Nils at sea, then continued on to Goodhue County, settling in Leon township.[42]

And so the Norwegians came. Near the Sumbren and Lunde claims in Minneola, their countrymen began to settle in what would become Wanamingo township. Henrik (Henry) Nelson Talla and Toge Nelson Talla, a pair of adventurous brothers who earned their capital searching for gold—Henrik in California and Toge in Australia—were in the vanguard of the group. Henrik was known as "Rich" Talla because of his alleged success in the goldfields. The brothers' two married sisters—Ollegaard Ottun, whose husband Jens was still in Norway, and Kirstina Fenne, whose husband Nils was in California—joined the Talla party. Then, on June 12, 1854, the immigrants crossed the north fork of the Zumbro River in what is now Wanamingo township. The rich land with water and woods to the north and a treeless, grassy plain as far as they could see to the south were just what they were looking for.[43]

The immigrant overflow moved west to Holden township when settlers had taken the best available land in Wanamingo township. By the end of 1856, Norwegians and some New Englanders had also settled Warsaw.

In spring 1858 Mathias and Ingeborg Ringdahl, traveling in an ox-drawn covered wagon behind which trailed a cow, reached the northwest part of Pine Island township. It was Mathias Pederson Ringdahl's second trip to the area. He emigrated to Wisconsin with his mother in 1851 and two years later traveled through the county en route to St. Paul. In 1853 Ringdahl, who lived and worked in Red Wing at the time, explored the southern sections of the county and staked his claim. Apparently, he was the first Norwegian to enter Goodhue County. Christian Peterson and the Sumbren brothers, established Norwegians of nearby Minneola, welcomed the 1858 return of Mathias and immediately looked to Ingeborg for cooking and baking advice.[44]

Ingeborg's knowledge of baking interested the bachelor Sumbren brothers, who soon sought to learn how to bake bread and cookies. Their first attempt at bread failed when they didn't let the dough rise before baking. Later, while entertaining the Ringdahls, Ingeborg complimented the brothers on the biscuits they served. A disappointed Erik recalled, "We thought we had made some pretty good cookies."[45]

Holden and Wanamingo townships would become the center of Goodhue County's Norwegian colony, but many of their countrymen settled in Roscoe,

Matthias Ringdahl, pictured later in life with his wife, Ingeborg, and their daughter Olive, arrived in Goodhue County in 1853 and temporarily worked in Red Wing. Early histories thus named him the first Norwegian to enter the county. *GCHS*

Kenyon, Cherry Grove, Warsaw, and Minneola. In 1874, a visitor to the area noted that southwest Goodhue County had indeed become "a compact mass of Norwegians."[46]

About the time Norwegians filled the county's southwest townships, immigrant Swedes began claiming land along the Cannon River and Belle Creek in the north and east. Swede Prairie, an area roughly based around and between present-day Vasa and White Rock, became the center of concentration for the growing numbers of Swedish immigrants.

In late September 1853, seven Swedes journeyed from St. Paul to Red Wing to search for land suitable for a settlement. Their late autumn start, not the best time to set up a farm community in Minnesota, did not deter the group. The scouting party, with assistance from James McGinnis of Red Wing, followed Indian trails westward and found acceptable land in what would become Vasa. They then returned to St. Paul to gather their belongings. [47]

On October 5, four men returned to Vasa. According to one member, "None of us were skilled in any trade, and besides we had only a few poor tools."[48] The group included 52-year-old Carl Roos from Varmland, Gustaf Kempe, 42, a gardener and preacher's son from Vestergotland, and a man named Jon, who left within four days. The "foreman" of the settlers was the young and ambitious Hans Mattson from Onnestad. Mattson's leadership derived from his ownership of oxen and his ability to control them. Just 20, Mattson would be a leader in the county and state for decades to come.[49]

The ill-prepared Swedes struggled through their first months in Goodhue County. A prairie fire started, as Roos noted, "through our own carelessness" and destroyed their early construction work and the hay they had gathered. The men managed to save their tents and belongings by throwing them through the raging fire to land already burned. The prairie fire produced a spectacular evening view as it "wrote different figures over the hills," and pillars of flame shot up through the woods.[50]

The men finished a rough cabin in late November, finally giving them shelter as well as protection from the wolves that troubled them "quite often." The cold bothered the men. Roos had no mittens or gloves, and none could be bought in Red Wing. In December, Roos and Kempe nearly died from exposure when they became lost during a trip to town. Then in January, Roos attempted a trip to Red Wing to deliver mail. He arrived safely but could not return because of blizzard conditions. The persistent Swede started walking on three consecutive mornings, making eight to ten miles before being forced to return to the city due to lack of visibility.

Mattson also experienced the dangers of frontier life. Mattson's brother-in-law Swante J. Willard arrived at the onset of winter, and the two men headed to Red Wing, where Willard's wife, Anna, and infant daughter, Zelma, awaited them. The men found work as woodcutters for William Freeborn and in their spare time tried to haul logs for their own home. The men nearly died during one frigid night when their fire went out while they slept. John Day had joined them on this trip, and he saved the party after his hand fell into the snow, awakening him.[51]

The "Swede Prairie" settlement grew during the next year. Twelve more families from St. Paul arrived, along with other Swedes from Red Wing. The group included the families of Carl Carlson, Erick Erickson, Peter Nelson, Nels Peterson, and Samuel Johnson. The settlers named the village Vasa in honor of

Swedish King Gustavus Vasa, the man credited with building the foundation for a national Swedish state following his rise to power in 1523.[52]

Many of the Swedes arrived in *skrikervogn,* ox-drawn carts whose poorly lubricated wooden wheels and axles emitted a penetrating wail never to be forgotten by those who heard it. These screech-wagons, called *kuberulla* by Norwegians, who also used them, provided reliable transportation and prairie background music for what one settler called "the ox age."[53]

The Swedish immigrants were, on the whole, a religious group. The majority were Lutherans, but Methodists and Baptists were also among them. Hans Mattson conducted Lutheran services at Vasa until the arrival of Rev. Eric Norelius in 1855. The 23-year-old Norelius married Inga Peterson in 1856 and moved into a 16-foot-square structure that served as church, school, and home. His salary that first year was just a hundred dollars. In the depression year of 1858 he received one barrel of beans and a few bushels of corn in partial payment.[54]

Encouraging letters mailed home to families in Sweden helped to speed the early immigration. Swen Olson sent a missive from Vasa in late 1855 describing the new land: "Here are very good plains which have neither stones nor trees, but here is a shortage of woodland because it is taken." He added, "If you want to and have the desire, it's certainly better here than in Sweden, because this is the land of freedom, but one has to work."[55]

The Swedish-American colony of Vasa, started in 1853 by three Swedish immigrants including young Hans Mattson, showed signs of growth 19 years later. Vasa Lutheran Church, constructed in 1869, dominated the prairie village. The home of Rev. Eric Norelius and his wife, Inga, was across the road. *CFHS*

A letter by Ola Anderson of Vasa in January 1857 echoed Olson's. He wrote to his family in Sweden, "I thank you kindly for helping me to get to this land of freedom." Anderson, too young to make a land claim, planned to do so when eligible. He reported that travel was easy, with no questions about passports: "They were meaningless."[56]

Successful Swedish immigrants sent money home to enable more of their family and friends to come to America—a powerful factor in attracting new Swedish migrants. This was also true for other nations sending large numbers to the United States. An estimated $100 million in postal money orders returned to Sweden alone from 1885 to 1937.[57]

The Swedish movement into Goodhue County eventually produced settlements that grew until they took in parts of nine north-central townships. Of the 339 township farms owned by Swedes in 1870 Goodhue County, 147 were in Vasa, 71 in Cannon Falls, 53 in Leon, and 21 in Belle Creek. Other Swedes concentrated in Red Wing, Featherstone, and Burnside.[58]

While generally pleased with their land of choice, the Swedes joined other immigrants in their hatred of the pesky Minnesota mosquito. Carl Roos's colorful description of his war with the pests in the spring of 1854 described settlers' frustrations. The mosquitoes "came like foam-bubbles out of the stream" and were "just as bold as they were plenty." Roos noted the difficulty of eating, since the insects might creep into the mouth or nose and ears. The men tried to drive their antagonists away by puffing on tobacco until they "could hardly see each other across the table," but they could still hear the humming of the mosquitoes inside the cloud of smoke. Roos remembered, in terms possibly exaggerated but definitely respectful, that mosquitoes bit Hans Mattson so badly, "his eyes were swollen shut . . . for fourteen days."[59]

The men escaped the insects by sleeping in the cellar—a refuge in which they encountered more acceptable "crawling creatures." Roos gratefully observed that the mosquito plague eased in later years.

New Englanders, Norwegians, and Swedes dominated pre-Civil War settlement in Goodhue County, but immigrants from other European countries also arrived. Germans began settling Hay Creek, and a group of Irish families chose land in eastern Belle Creek. More of their countrymen followed, with the number of Germans, in particular, growing in the south-central and eastern sections of the county. Also, small and scattered pockets of other northern Europeans, namely former citizens of Great Britain, Denmark, Switzerland, and the Low Countries (Belgium, the Netherlands, and Luxembourg), reached the county.[60]

The study of German immigration patterns has provided a particular challenge to ethnologists. Prussians under the leadership of Otto von Bismarck united the nation that became known as Germany in 1870. Until then, the shifting boundaries of the smaller German-speaking states meant that lands on the periphery of those areas—Luxembourg, the Alsace, along with parts of Switzerland, Poland, Austria, Bohemia, and the Slavic regions—were considered German. The results of World War I and World War II in the 20th century continued the pattern of boundary change.[61]

Most of Goodhue County's earliest German settlers came from northern rural districts of that country—mainly Pomerania, Mecklenberg, Hanover, Westphalia, and Saxony. The majority were experienced farmers who journeyed to America hoping to be "better rewarded for their labor." As with other immigrant groups, successful newcomers often saved as much money as they could to send for family members waiting in Europe.[62]

John Tubbesing, his wife, Maria, and their children left Westphalia in September 1852 to journey eventually to Goodhue County. They boarded a ship at Bremerhaven and began a voyage that tested their endurance and patience, one similar to that faced by countless other European immigrants unused to the sea. The mostly poor passengers traveled in steerage—the lower decks of these cramped and crowded vessels. Tubbesing later recalled that steerage compartments were "dark like a cellar with no windows" with the only air coming from a passageway full of steam. Passengers could not see well enough during the evenings even to be able to eat.[63]

Maria Tubbesing, seven months pregnant as the trip began, had to battle illness during the voyage. She endured the journey and later gave birth to a daughter in America. The child did not survive, however; she died at six months of age. John and Maria persevered and later farmed near Red Wing, from 1860 to 1876.

Seven counties along the Minnesota River became the center of the German immigrant community in Minnesota, but Hay Creek was the heart of new Germany in Goodhue County. In 1854 three brothers from Prussia—William, George, and Henry Meyer—took claims along Hay Creek and began farming. George Meyer and his new bride, Mary Tebbe, worked 160 acres. Eleven years later Meyer and partner John Hack built a waterpowered flour mill. Other Germans arriving in 1854 included Charles Ahlers, Henry Isensee, Ernst Schubert, and Charles Dahling. By 1860, people of German stock comprised 80 percent of the population in Hay Creek township.[64]

Emigration became a matter of survival for many people living in the Ireland of the mid-19th century. Famine and disease, stemming from the failures of the potato crops between 1845 and 1851, resulted in the deaths of as many as one million of Ireland's 8.5 million people. This disaster, combined with poverty, overpopulation, lack of opportunity, and domination by Great Britain, spurred a massive exodus. More than two million people left Ireland between 1841 and 1854, with over 75 percent of them moving to the United States.[65]

Irish immigrants in America tended to congregate in large East Coast cities, where wages were far superior to what they had known. In the words of one scholar, they lived together as "pioneers of the American urban ghetto." Farming was not often their first choice of occupation. In general, the Irish were unfamiliar with large-scale American farming methods, and many well remembered the years of crop failure and famine on the small farms they abandoned. The new Irish-American settlers needed encouragement to move west to the agricultural heartland.

The Irish also confronted the challenge embodied in the anti-Catholic, anti-immigrant "Know-Nothing" political party of the 1850s. Catholics from Germany and other European countries faced the hostility of the Know-Nothings and their followers. The power of this nativist group peaked during the election of 1856. By 1860 the Know-Nothings had all but disappeared, but the feeling against immigrants in general and Catholics in particular persisted among some nativists. During this period a small group of Irish families reached Goodhue County.[66]

Irish immigrants Walter Doyle and James O'Neill developed a friendship while helping build a railroad line near La Salle, Illinois. They agreed to work together to lay claim to available public land and begin farming. Doyle and O'Neill moved their families to Minnesota Territory, reaching Red Wing in July 1854. They walked south and west across the Featherstone prairie into Belle Creek township, where they established claims.[67]

Doyle and his wife, Johanna, received help from their six children in working the 160-acre farm. Wheat yields the following year immediately encouraged Doyle and other Irish farmers. The Doyles' log cabin also became a stop on the St. Paul-to-Dubuque stagecoach line, enabling the family to entertain territorial celebrities including governors Alexander Ramsey and Henry Sibley and the prominent Ojibway leader Hole in the Day.[68]

O'Neill, a County Wexford native, and his Irish-born wife, Margaret, began farming near the Doyles in the north central section of Belle Creek. The O'Neills brought four sons with them, and Margaret gave birth to daughter Anna while at Belle Creek. The following year John and Mary McNamara, originally from County Clare, arrived in Belle Creek with their two children. They purchased 160 acres, the beginning of a farm that grew to 480 acres by the turn of the century.

The greatest growth in the Belle Creek Irish community occurred after the Civil War. In 1865 Patrick Walsh and his sister Mary, from County Mayo, established a farm in the northwest section of Zumbrota township near the Belle Creek Irish. Later that year Robert Heaney, brother-in-law of the Walshes, purchased land nearby. As the Irish community grew, Felix Tissot, a priest who ministered to 25 Catholic missions in Wabasha and Goodhue Counties, encouraged the construction of a church dedicated to St. Columbkill.[69]

Irish Catholics, as well as Catholics from Germany, Luxembourg, and other European nations, settled near the original Belle Creek Irish community. The colony continued to grow, occupying most of the township's eastern sections and extending into portions of Featherstone, Goodhue, and Zumbrota townships. Luxembourg Catholics claimed an area on the border of Belvidere township in Goodhue County and Chester township in Wabasha County. In 1865, Catholics established St. Mary's parish in Belvidere. Thirteen years later, the leaders of the growing church incorporated their congregation as the Belle Chester Church Society. Later, the name Bellechester was given to the village itself.[70]

The Mdewakanton presence lessened as the tide of Euroamerican immigrants continued to roll into Goodhue County. Indian hunting parties often returned to the area even after ratification of the land treaties of 1851, but these forays diminished as members of the Red Wing band spent more time in the Minnesota River valley. Wakantape, brother-in-law to the prominent former village chieftain Tatankamani, decided, however, to live among the whites and adopt their lifestyle.[71]

Pioneer Red Wing physician William W. Sweney greatly admired Wakantape as a man "whose word and character were above reproach." Sweney had camped with the "old fellow" and had listened to stories of Mdewakanton history and culture for hours. The doctor wrote several letters to the territorial Indian agent at Wakantape's behest, explaining the Indian's desire to exchange his claim to government annuities for 80 acres of the band's old winter hunting grounds in the southeast section of Goodhue County. No one answered.

White attitudes towards Indians hardened in March 1857, when the Wahpekute leader Inkpaduta orchestrated a series of attacks against settlers along the Minnesota Territory-Iowa border. More than 30 whites died in the "Spirit Lake Massacre." Members of a settlement group that originated in Red Wing were among the victims. Four Red Wing men made the trip to the border to help with burials and settle the affairs of the dead.

Wakantape stayed in the Goodhue County area after the Spirit Lake affair, but threats of violence finally drove him to rejoin his band. Sweney kept in contact with the old warrior even after the arrest and confinement of the Mdewakanton people following the month-long Dakota uprising in 1862. Wakantape died while still under guard at Davenport, Iowa. Sweney lamented his passing and wrote, "If previous good character in any man is to be relied on, then was Wakontoppi an innocent victim."[72]

Life in America wasn't for everyone. Some who left Europe had planned from the beginning to return to their homelands. Others, disillusioned or discouraged with their new lives, later opted to go back home. During the 156-year period from 1820 to 1975, at least 47 million immigrants reached America from countries around the world. About 13 million migrants between the years 1820 and 1950 returned to their native countries or moved to other nations. The percentage of returnees varied, with higher rates, for example, from Mediterranean Europe and lower ones for Scandinavia.[73]

That few of Goodhue County's Norwegian and Swedish immigrants re-migrated might be attributed to the rural nature of their colonies. To claim land, one had to be at least 21 years of age and a citizen, or one who declared intent of citizenship. Such requirements encouraged putting down roots. By 1900, nearly 93 percent of Swedish-born males in Vasa's largely agricultural community had become citizens or were in the process of formally changing their allegiance. Generally, Scandinavian immigrants living in cities were more likely to leave America for home.

Others who settled in Goodhue County left in search of better locations. Among the more mobile Norwegian immigrants were those who abandoned claims and colonies in Wisconsin and Iowa to come to the southwestern sections of the county. When no land remained there, some moved farther west and, joined by latecomers, established colonies in western Minnesota. Carleton Qualey, an expert in the study of Norwegian immigration, labeled Goodhue County "the mother area" of many Norwegian settlements in western Minnesota and other colonies in the Dakotas.[74]

Life on the remote Minnesota frontier could be lonely for the many who stuck it out. Some early immigrants to Goodhue County felt a sense of isolation in their new home. David Humphrey wrote from Cannon Falls of his despair of "ever receiving one word from N. England." He added, "Perhaps none of you were ever 2,000 miles away in the wilderness, away from friends (& foes too) for months & anxiously looking, waiting, longing, & wondering & all about a sheet of inked paper you hoped to receive." One woman wrote of her loneliness: "Back of the cabin is the forest, and in front of it stretches the wearisome prairie; half a mile off is the nearest neighbor." James Page, after a trip from Red Wing to Mantorville, wrote in his diary, "The sun no longer looks bright to me. I am lonesome, forsaken & I fear forgotten."[75]

Levi Hillman discovered that his wife, Mary, at home in Connecticut, was none too eager to join him on the Minnesota frontier. A New England friend of Mary, returned from the Mankato area of Minnesota, provided "the awfulest description of the place." Mary heard that the log homes were bad, that the roads were enough to "kill anyone," and that there was nothing to eat "but pork, and ham and potatoes." She understood there were "lots of Indians and I cannot go out where their [sic] is such kind of people." Levi eventually convinced his wife to come to Minnesota.[76]

Although letters from America to the "Old World" were generally positive and instrumental in encouraging immigration, some immigrants wrote negatively of the new land. John Tubbesing, a strict German Methodist, wrote from his Red Wing farm of his concern about American morality: "For those easily tempted . . . it would be better if he did not come to this country." He included a more direct warning: "From what I have learned, misfortune falls upon many who come to this country. It would be much better for many lads to stay in Germany because they would not go astray." Swen Olson made it clear to his family in Sweden that life in America was challenging: "You have to ponder it hard—all of you who have it good in Sweden" before coming to Minnesota.[77]

The pre-Civil War pioneer period is just one chapter in the story of immigration to Goodhue County. From the movements of prehistoric groups to the area to the present day, people have chosen the county as a place in which they might build successful lives.

Throughout the first 150 years of its history, the county felt the effect of this wave of pioneer immigration with its large numbers of New Englanders, Norwegians, Swedes, and Germans. Yankees and Yorkers helped build the villages and towns of Goodhue County and founded many of their industries and institutions. This northeastern influence was of particular note in the towns of Zumbrota, Cannon Falls, Pine Island, and Red Wing. The majority of European immigrants, meanwhile, came intending to claim land and become farmers. Ethnic agricultural colonies such as "Swede Prairie" in the Vasa-White Rock area and the cluster of Norwegian communities in the south and west attracted thousands. Descendants of these early arrivals continue to live and work in the county, in some cases on land originally claimed by their ancestors.[78]

Settlers could hire sod-breaking rigs such as this one to cut through the tough, densely rooted prairie grass. A Cannon Falls farmer wrote in 1856: "We plant here with an axe instead of a hoe . . . the sod is so tough that we can do nothing with a hoe the first year." *GCHS*

# 4

## Staking a Claim for a New Life—
## The Struggle for Goodhue County Land

For early American settlers, claiming and taming land was a daunting task, but safeguarding that claim proved, at times, an even more difficult proposition. In Goodhue County and other open settlement areas in Minnesota Territory, those struggling to establish ownership of land dealt with swindlers, speculators, and claim jumpers. Some settlers also made illegal claims, encroached on a neighbor's land, or resorted to violence to settle arguments. Ironically, many of those involved in these first disputes had illegally settled Indian land not yet sold to the government.

Those establishing claims received some protection from the Preemption Act of 1841, which allowed individuals to assert their claims to government land before it was offered for sale. This system worked fairly well in Goodhue County from the summer of 1852 to the establishment, in August 1855, of a U.S. Land Office in Red Wing. With government supervision virtually nonexistent in rural Goodhue County, however, the claiming of land often proved an every-man-for-himself deal.[1]

Wanamingo's "Battle of the Clubs" was one instance of settler violence. The Talla brothers, Henry and Toge, had led a small group of Norwegian settlers into the county in summer 1854. A group of their countrymen soon followed. These early arrivals selected land and established claim boundaries. The claims often stretched farther than the allotted 160 acres. To protect their land, the settlers agreed to fend off others interested in establishing holdings in the area. Brandishing stout oak clubs and ax handles, they intimidated newcomers. This plan worked for about a year until the arrival of an emigrant group from Iowa led by Sven Nordgaarden, another Norwegian immigrant. He made it clear his group would not move on, and a battle ensued. Nordgaarden's Norwegians, armed with clubs, prevailed. A court decision in Red Wing later went against the Tallas, and they had to surrender all but 160 acres each.[2]

Land speculators, opportunists looking to buy and sell land for profit, plagued settlers. One newspaperman reported: "Speculators were hovering like buzzards over the county."[3] A large group of "land sharks" watched with anticipation the opening of the land office in Red Wing. They hoped to acquire choice tracts of land by outbidding original settlers when government auctioneer William Le Duc offered the claims for sale. Settlers readied for the challenge by forming the protective Claim Association headed by David Hancock. Association members appointed Royal Lovel to bid on land claimed by members. The determination of the settlers intimidated the speculators, who elected not to bid.[4]

The following March settlers again organized, this time to deal with land ownership issues related to the "Half-Breed Tract." This reserve, established in the treaty signing at Prairie du Chien in 1830, was set aside for mixed-blood relatives of the eastern Sioux. The treaty noted that the tract began "at a place called the Barn, below and near the village of the Red Wing chief, and running back fifteen miles. Thence in a parallel line with Lake Pepin and the Mississippi about 32 miles." Although the government had reserved the land, surveyors ignored the tract while laying out Goodhue County townships and sections. Upon opening, the U.S. Land Office staff forwarded to Washington a list of those qualified to share in the reserve, provoking a volatile ownership controversy.[5]

Children descended from early white traders and settlers and their Indian spouses accounted for the majority of people listed as qualified to receive "Half-Breed Tract" land. In spring 1857, those on the list received government scrip along with a designation of the amount of land to which each person was entitled. Persons receiving the government paper, including legal guardians in some cases, used this scrip to secure title. Land speculators also attempted to acquire scrip from those holding it. Complicating the issue were 200 families already living on the tract *without* the required scrip. By law they were squatters, although many had improved the land and begun farming there. The speculators moved in with the legal scrip and began procuring title to some tract farms. Their actions prompted outrage among the settlers.

The aggrieved settlers met at Red Wing's Kelly House on March 17, 1856, and organized a committee charged with preventing more land purchases with the scrip. The 21-member group also demanded the return of land already acquired with scrip. The committee worked with determination. Two armed guards stood watch at the land office, on the alert for the scrip speculators, while other members arrested those who had already bought land.[6]

Land register William W. Phelps, a lawyer and former Michigan legislator, and receiver Chris Graham, a former Indiana legislator, ran the land office. Both

were friendly to the interests of settlers, dimming the prospects of the speculators. With no local court of law in existence, the vigilance committee took
control of the land dispute.[7]

Bully Wells, the 52-year-old, rough-and-tumble former territorial legislator, was among the speculators. He had also operated as a Lake Pepin Indian
trader, and his mixed-blood wife, Jane, had seven children who qualified for
scrip. Wells had already made one land purchase when the vigilance committee's armed guards apprehended him as he tried to make another. Wells refused when the guards ordered him to renounce his previous claim, and he
dared them to make him sign.[8]

The committee convicted Wells of refusing to obey its authority and presented the recalcitrant land buyer with a choice. The members escorted him to
the bank of the still-frozen Mississippi and pointed out a hole in the ice. They
then told Wells he could go to the land office and "raise the entry of scrip" or
face a dip in the icy river. He agreed to go to the office. Other speculators facing this ice-water option also backed down. In May 1858 the federal government granted settlers within the tract rights to the land. Parcels unclaimed were
soon occupied.

While speculators suffered in Red Wing, a Zumbrota opportunist endured
censure. Several members of Zumbrota's Strafford Western Emigration Company illegally reserved claims, allegedly for friends who would occupy the land
later. This caused little trouble until one of them sold a reserved claim for $350.
Other Zumbrotans bitterly denounced the claim seller as a speculator. C. W.
Smith, the original owner of the land, protested the sale. He had surrendered his
chance for excess profit in land sales when he sold to the Strafford group. He
now threatened to place a new settler on every claim not occupied. The Zumbrotans resolved the argument, but hard feelings lingered. Meanwhile, outsiders
learned of unsettled claims in the colony and moved in.[9]

Claim jumpers concerned but did not intimidate several early Minneola
settlers. Erik Sumbren heard someone chopping timber on the parcel of land he
claimed near the Zumbro River. When confronted, the intruder lifted his ax and
threatened to "split" the head of Sumbren. But Sumbren also held an ax and
wouldn't back down. The two men parleyed. Sumbren prevailed when he
showed his rival his rough sod shanty. Erik's brother Ole fended off a challenge
to his claim in unusual fashion. He found a stranger cutting trees on his claim
and told the unwelcome visitor to stop. The man said the wood was his: "I
chopped here first." A woodcutting contest ensued, with Ole felling four trees
to his challenger's none. The stranger gave in and left when shown Ole's nearby
sod house. In another incident the Sumbrens' neighbor, Christian Lunde, who
owned a firearm, used that weapon to chase away a claim jumper.[10]

Cherry Grove settlers battled, often unsuccessfully, with marauding bands
of claim jumpers. Some of the area's first settlers, tired of persistent harassment,

left the township. Community members formed a committee of vigilance in the winter of 1855, with Thomas Haggard, a newly arrived settler, as captain. Haggard's force put an end to claim jumping in the township.[11]

U.S. government land surveys officially ended disputes between neighbors. The government recognized and protected officially registered claims. A Gunter's chain became the standard measure used by surveyors to divide land. One chain was 66 feet long, with 80 chains equaling one mile. Ten square chains equaled one acre. Goodhue County was divided into townships, most of which were six miles square. A square mile contained 640 acres, called a section.[12]

After establishing their claims, the settlers secured title by visiting the land office in Red Wing. Money was hard to get, and frequently the settlers had to borrow the $200 required to cover the costs of registering their 160-acre farms. Annual interest rates ranged from the more standard 25 percent upward to 40 percent.[13]

Most of Goodhue County's pioneer farmers faced the challenges of clearing and breaking land. Farmers could hire "breaking rigs," which consisted of three to five teams of oxen hitched in pairs to pull a large plow. One man drove the oxen while another handled the plow. This effort would "throw a furrow" about 18 to 24 inches wide. One settler told of making a breaking rig strong

William Freeborn's 1855 log home, above in 1872, with some of the town's earliest settlers, was the first structure in Cannon Falls. L to r: Rev. J. R. Barnes, William Stranahan, Swante Anderson, Capt. David L. Davis, Charles A. Scofield (seated), James H. Wright, George McKenzie, Rev. Elizah W. Merrill, James L. Scofield, Rev. and Mrs. James Peckham, Mr. and Mrs. Giles Slocum, Mrs. James Wright, Sherman and Mrs. Hale, William P. Tanner, and Archibald M. Knox. *GCHS*

Sod homes, about the size of their log counterparts, typically measured 10 by 12 feet and featured a wood frame with sodded walls to the eaves. This soddie likely was in the Cannon Falls area. *CFHS*

enough to turn over brushland. It required six yoke of oxen. Breaking teams usually worked from mid-May to mid-July and typically charged five dollars per acre. The farmers used felling axes or crosscut saws to clear trees. They also needed a chain and oxen to clear stumps from their timbered land, a task that often took several years to complete.[14]

When no breaking rig was available, the early farmers had to be creative. A Cannon Falls farmer wrote in 1856: "We plant here with an axe instead of a hoe . . . the sod is so tough that we can do nothing with a hoe the first year." He added that first-year plantings gave smaller yields than subsequent seasons.[15]

The log house was the most popular home style, but some lived in sod huts and dugouts cut into the sides of hills. Settlers could erect log homes quickly. They arranged logs horizontally, notching the corners to produce a good fit. Some made sturdier homes by hewing the timber into square shapes by use of broad axes and adzes. They typically added sod roofs to the log structures, satisfactory except in rainy weather. The small frontier cabins often measured just 10 by 12 feet, with one all-purpose room, a cellar for food storage, and an attic sometimes used for sleeping. Sod homes, about the same size as their log counterparts, had a wood frame with walls sodded to the eaves. Open fireplaces provided a cooking station and heat when needed.[16]

Goodhue County's first rural settlers labored to establish themselves and their farms. As subsistence farmers, they grew vegetables, particularly potatoes, for their own use while beginning to establish fields for wheat. The farmers first sowed their grain by hand, tossing seed to the ground while walking toward an aligning pole placed at the end of a field. Skillful sowing prevented overlapping and uneven crops. Oats constituted the most common small grain until about 1860. Wheat then became dominant.

Farmers wielding grain sickles or cradles harvested wheat in the 1850s. They laid the falling grain on the ground, raked it into piles, and tied it into bundles, which they gathered into shocks and stacked to await threshing. An effective worker could harvest about five acres a day. At first, workers threshed with hand flails or by walking oxen over the grain on the barn floor or some smooth place. Later, when horses became common, one county farmer used a machine powered by four teams of horses to thresh 400 bushels in a day.[17]

Goodhue County became home to 21 waterpowered mills providing flour and feed, but in the early years of settlement getting grain to a mill was a challenge. Burnside resident Rev. J. G. Johnson raised two acres of wheat in the summer of 1856. He took a wagonload of grain 30 miles to Northfield, only to find the water too low to power the mill. He later carried wheat on a four-day trip to a mill eight miles past Prescott, Wisconsin.[18]

The very character of these new Goodhue County farms and the lonely prairies nearby isolated the settlers within the rigid rectangles set forth by survey. Typical farms in the county covered 160 acres, or a quarter section, with 80-acre parcels also common. The homesteader was thus separated from neighbors, often by a half-mile or more. For the more sociable farmers the sense of isolation, particularly during the long winter months, was profound. E. V. Smalley wrote of the northwest prairie as a land where:

> There is a short hot summer followed by a long cold winter, and where there is little in the aspect in nature to furnish food for thought . . . [In winter] the silence of death rests on the vast landscape, save when it is swept by cruel winds that search out every chink and cranny of the buildings, and drive through each unguarded aperture the dry, powdery snow . . . Neighborly calls are infrequent because of the long distances which separate farmhouses . . . An alarming amount of insanity occurs in the new prairie States among farmers and their wives.[19]

The isolation and monotony of their new lives troubled some of the women as they first arrived. One wrote:

> The store may be three, or it may be ten miles away. Church there is none. Silence is all around . . . The musquitoes come early in the evening and

stay all night . . . When the excitement is over and the family begins to look the fact in the face, that they have really come West to *live*; and, if the wife and daughters don't have some "good crying-spells" then they are made of superior stuff.[20]

*Giants in the Earth*, Ole E. Rolvaag's classic novel of the Norwegian immigrant experience on the Minnesota frontier, relates the terrible cost to the human spirit. In one scene Beret Hansa becomes disconsolate with the realities of her life on the prairie, tormented because she can find no tree behind which to hide.[21]

Farmwomen faced a host of expected duties along with the sense of isolation they shared with their husbands. Chores included cooking, baking, canning fruits and vegetables, skimming milk, making cheese, and churning butter, washing clothes, making soap, carding wool, spinning yarn, weaving cloth, and knitting, along with making, mending, and ironing clothes. They also assisted in planting and harvesting crops and tended the chickens, cattle, and oxen. Hand-milking of the cows often fell to women and children.[22]

David Humphrey, in the summer of 1855, told of a woman he met living on the prairie 12 miles from Cannon Falls. Humphrey sought shelter in her family's 12-by-16-foot cabin: "The wife was a lady who would grace any circle either in an eastrn [*sic*] parlor or a western log house." The home had one table, four chairs, and three homemade pine stools. Living in the cabin with her family of five were "two hired men, & also two single men & one man & wife & one child." The woman honored Humphrey's request for lodging. The "equanimity of our lady was not in the least disturbed, but cheerfully & without apology we were provided for."[23]

Childbirth on the Minnesota frontier presented danger, particularly in cases of difficult delivery. Ellen Season and her husband, George, faced such a challenge. The Seasons settled in Stanton on the Little Cannon River in 1854. The next year she experienced problems during the birth of a child and required medical help. Alonzo Dibble, the Seasons' neighbor, walked 30 miles to Red Wing, the location of the nearest doctor, to get assistance. Both the young mother and her infant were beyond help by the time the doctor arrived in Stanton.[24]

When Dibble's wife, Louisa, was due to deliver a child in the spring of 1856, the concerned Stanton farmer transported his wife by oxcart to her parents' home in Hay Creek. There she received her family's support. The move also meant she was much closer to a doctor in Red Wing. The pregnancy came to a happy conclusion for the Dibbles when daughter Sarah was born.[25]

Holden Lutheran Church records detail a terrible death toll among the congregation's children. An 1860 account tells of a family with three children, all ill with whooping cough. The eldest child, a four-year-old, died, prompting the father to head to Red Wing on foot to get medicine for the two survivors. He found another child dead upon his return. A remaining infant recovered. From December 1861 to December 1862, there were 56 deaths in the congregation; 40 were children under five, and four were mothers 35 or younger.[26]

Women of the prairie—stoic helpmates and mothers of legend—were more than stereotypical saints in sunbonnets. Thousands of female settlers spent at least a segment of their adult lives alone through choice, divorce, desertion, or death of a spouse. A number of unmarried women claimed and settled land. In a sample of Minnesota Homestead Final Certificates for 1863, one in five homesteaders was an unmarried woman. Some "girl homesteaders" later married and combined their farms with those of their husbands.[27]

Despite the hardships, determined immigrants continued to acquire public land and seek their fortunes in the boom years of the mid-1850s. Settlers and speculators alike sought the land west of the Mississippi River, from Minnesota in the north to Texas in the south. Improved transportation, easier credit, and comparatively high prices for grains and cotton lured those interested in the purchase of vast government-owned territory. Neighboring Wisconsin, where the population had more than doubled from 305,000 in 1850 to an estimated 730,000 in 1857, provided those heading toward Minnesota with a lesson. Land values in the Northwest rose quickly, and acquiring a piece of the new Minnesota Territory was an investment almost guaranteed to pay off.[28]

Business boomed in America. Textile mills expanded in New England, while the iron works of western Pennsylvania prospered. Improved agricultural practices increased the productivity of western farmers and southern planters. The explosive expansion of railroads in the East gave rise to a mood of enthusiasm for entrepreneurs and investors alike. Since the gold rush of 1849, the flow of California bullion increased specie (money in coin) reserves, enlarging the basis for bank loans. Banks doubled in number between 1850 and 1857.

The demise of the second Bank of the United States in 1836 and the subsequent withdrawal of the federal government from banking no longer appeared to discourage investors. Regulation of American banks devolved to the individual states, whose inconsistent supervisory practices were occasionally lax. Banks issued their own notes backed by supposedly adequate reserves, a system vulnerable to failure.

In Minnesota the most popular form of land speculation involved the platting of township sites. Between 1855 and 1857 developers surveyed and platted at least 700 towns in the territory, providing lots for as many as 1.5 million newcomers. Prospective Minnesotans began arriving to occupy the sites. Among those encouraging settlement was New York *Tribune* editor Horace Greeley, a prominent booster of the westward movement. Wrote Greeley on July 4, 1857: "Minnesota *is* a good State—one of the most fertile, best timbered, best watered, of all the New States."[29]

Speculation fever swept Minnesota Territory during 1856 and 1857. Aggressive investors borrowed freely to buy land, knowing they could sell quickly for a profit. Personal debt grew. Minnesota lawyer and politician George A. Nourse wrote in April 1857 that people in the territory were "so engrossed in speculating" that they no longer had time for politics. Farmers, mechanics, and laborers gave up their jobs to become real-estate operators.[30]

In Goodhue County, Vasa settler Hans Mattson became enmeshed in "this mad fury of speculation." The 23-year-old Swedish immigrant purchased several parcels of land and sold them for a profit. He also took mortgages on other pieces, confident of quick sales and more profit. Mattson then bought land in two "paper cities" farther south and west, in Dodge and Freeborn Counties. Paper cities sprang up like prairie grass, laid out by promoters and speculators. These cities had plats but no people. Mattson moved his family to Geneva in Freeborn County, intending to start a city in what appeared to be a can't-miss proposition.[31]

America's financial house of cards collapsed on August 24, 1857. Ohio Life Insurance and Trust Company of New York suspended payment, forcing its creditors to default. This in turn caused other institutions to suspend operations. Before the day was out, financial entities throughout the country failed. Banks and creditors called their loans, soaking up available money, and the Panic of 1857 was on. Minnesota sustained a particularly harsh blow.[32]

Mattson's days as a speculator were over. He could barely raise enough money to return to Vasa. Analyzing his debt upon his return, Mattson found he owed $2,000 plus interest at a boomtime rate of 5 percent a *month*. To raise money, Mattson and his wife, Chersti, sold everything they had, including their furniture and Chersti's gold watch. They could not return to their old farm because it was mortgaged for about twice its value. The young couple managed to rent a 16-foot-square room in Red Wing, and Hans began studying law. During that dark winter Chersti made a lamp for Hans by lighting cotton wicks placed in saucers full of melted lard received from her parents.[33]

The village of Cannon Falls had incorporated on March 10, 1857. Charles Parks, its first elected president, later recalled the enthusiasm of its people:

> Town property was advancing rapidly; corner lots were worth a fortune and we all believed our wildest dreams were about to be realized . . . To become rich all you needed was a pocket full of deeds and a hazy idea of where there was some land to sell. There was no end to the money in the real estate business.[34]

With the economic collapse, property values eroded, disputes over land ownership arose, and confusion reigned. There seemed to be no way to make a living in Cannon Falls, and people left the area as quickly as they had appeared. Before the panic, the population of Cannon Falls was about 1,200. A year later the number had dwindled to 300, and the remaining settlers abandoned the village charter.[35]

Thomas Kellett, one of Strafford Western Emigration Company's leaders in Zumbrota, noted that the Panic of 1857 hit his village hardest the following year. He termed 1858 "that year of Ruta Bagas [*sic*] And Corn Cake." The crisis slowed growth in Zumbrota in a stagnation that continued until 1865.[36]

Hard times also prevailed in the Goodhue County seat of Red Wing. Steamboats coming upriver carried flour and meat, but too often there was not enough local money to buy. Those few people holding banknotes carefully monitored the "daily depreciation" of their currency. Some merchants issued their own scrip. The territorial government paid its bills with warrants of doubtful value. Confidence in land as a basic unit of value quickly evaporated. Land was no longer worth the inflated dollars many had paid for it. In some cases the land had virtually no value at all.[37]

Citizens of Dennison observed deflation. A farmer there reported that $12 would buy as much as $25 did two years previous—if one had the cash: "They [*sic*] is no money. I have not seen a dollar for a great while. They [*sic*] is no money around. Everything is closing up. Poor folks must die."[38]

A letter written to President James Buchanan by a group of farmers described the economic box in which they found themselves. They moved west expecting that "years of labor, economy, prudence and deprivation" would enable them to live successfully. The farmers raised enough produce and stock but had no local market and no way to transport:

> We are not presenting to you the cause of the indolent or the profligate—
> we have worked late, and we have worked early, and have used as much
> frugality and prudence as any class of people in the Union. Still, we are
> not able to pay for our lands.[39]

Minnesotans were drowning in debt. By decade's end more than 20,000 Minnesota settlers could not pay for their claims without selling all of their possessions. Another 10,000 could not pay under any conditions.[40]

The financial crisis began to ease in 1859. Citizens began to exchange some hoarded coin, often French five-franc pieces and Mexican silver. A good harvest produced a wheat crop that could command 50 cents a bushel in gold. Minnesota began for the first time to export grain, a positive development for the many wheat-producing farmers of Goodhue County.[41]

Yet as the settlers battled back from the punishing blows of the economic depression, an even more serious crisis awaited Minnesota and the nation.

# 5

# *Minnesota's Two Civil Wars—*
# *A Nation and a State Divided*

The divisive issue of slavery plagued the delegates to the Philadelphia constitutional convention of 1787. Perplexed nation-builders faced a sectional contrast between the South, where African slavery had emerged as a significant factor in the economy, and the North, where forced labor, never crucial to economic success, was on its way out. The constitution's framers agreed, through careful preparation, skillful negotiation, secret debate, and compromise, on a philosophy and framework for the new republic. But they did not resolve the slavery question.

The nation's political leadership, after years of equivocation and compromise and decades of debate on the slavery issue, managed only grudging agreement on a series of temporary solutions. By 1850 increasing numbers of Americans felt compelled to confront the national dilemma they had preferred to ignore.

Argument about the expansion of slavery into the vast trans-Mississippi River territories provided a new and dangerous wedge between the factions. The growth of the country threatened the balance of voting power between proslavery and antislavery groups in Congress. Slavery's expansion into the new territories put the future of America at stake.

Far from the eye of the storm, the citizens of remote and sparsely settled Minnesota Territory dealt with the slavery issue, too. The case of Dred Scott, a slave brought to Minnesota by his owner, became a national controversy. When Scott's owner died, the slave, supported by friends, sued for his freedom. He lost but in 1857 carried his case to the Supreme Court. There his fate became secondary to a larger issue—the course of slavery's expansion. The court's

March 6 ruling went decisively against Scott, eliminating all restrictions on slavery in the territories. A storm of criticism swept the northern states, further widening the chasm. Meanwhile, a member of the family that had owned the nearly forgotten Scott, acquired title and freed him and his family. Dred Scott, whose request for freedom ignited a national debate, died after living free for little more than a year.[1]

The slavery question also complicated Minnesota's efforts towards admission to the Union. Territorial representatives and their allies in Washington pressed the case for statehood during the first three months of 1858. They found the pursuit of their goal frustrating. Henry M. Rice, who would become a U.S. senator upon the state's admission to the Union, noted the tension. Rice wrote, in a January 15 letter to Judge William H. Welch in Red Wing, of the "intense feeling" in the capital. It "produced ill will between prominent Democrats, that nothing but death can wipe out. The sectional hate is very strong."[2] Southern forces in the Senate hoped to balance Minnesota's request for admission to the Union by adding Kansas and recognizing that territory's proslavery Lecompton faction. Senator Albert Brown of Mississippi warned his Republican opponents: "If you admit Minnesota and exclude Kansas . . . the spirit of our revolutionary fathers is utterly extinct."[3]

In the House, southern representatives waged a bellicose campaign against Minnesota statehood. A Missouri representative talked of antislavery foreigners filling northern territories such as Minnesota: "I warn the gentlemen from the South of the consequences . . . The great body of [foreigners] are opposed to slavery . . . They are enemies of the South and her institutions."[4]

William W. Phelps of Red Wing was one of three Minnesotans elected to the House of Representatives during the statehood debates, but the House wished to give Minnesota just one representative. A compromise resulted in the acceptance of two. Phelps and James Cavanaugh won a coin toss for the seats. In May, after five months of maneuvering and acrimony, Congress allowed the delegation to be seated. Minnesota became the 32nd state in the Union.[5]

The election of 1860 highlighted the division of the nation over slavery issues. Abraham Lincoln's victory in the presidential contest came without benefit of a single southern electoral vote. This, in turn, led disaffected states in the South to leave the union and subsequently form the Confederate States of America. Conflict broke out when Lincoln refused a demand to remove federal troops from Fort Sumter in Charleston, South Carolina. Confederate artillery units opened fire on April 12, 1861, then battered into submission the fort's garrison. Lincoln called for volunteers to defend the Union, and civil war commenced.

Local pro-Union organizers in Goodhue County, upon hearing of Lincoln's request for assistance, beckoned the public to an April 19 meeting at the courthouse in Red Wing. Stirring speeches from a number of men inspired the

Col. William Colvill in later years
*GCHS*

crowd, and in answer to a call for volunteers, many rushed to enroll. The formidable William Colvill, a Red Wing newspaper editor, and A. E. (Ed) Welch, a 22-year-old Hamline student, competed to be the first to sign. Colvill seized the pen, relegating Welch to second position.[6]

Men from throughout the county joined the Goodhue County Volunteers, with more than 100 recruits quickly oversubscribing the unit. The men elected Colvill captain and Welch first lieutenant of the force designated Company F and assigned to the Minnesota First Volunteer Infantry Regiment. Students from Hamline made up 20 percent of Company F, including Welch, 2nd Lt. Mark Hoyt, and Sgts. Martin Maginnis and Henry Bevans. Patriotic Pine Island matched the Hamline total.[7]

Company F's elected leaders, Colvill and Welch, were destined to be war heroes. Colvill, a native New Yorker, attended Fredonia Academy, then moved to Buffalo, where he studied law in the office of Millard Fillmore. At age 24 he emigrated to Goodhue County, where he established the *Sentinel*, a Red Wing newspaper supporting the Democratic Party. Thirty-one years old and still a bachelor, Colvill readied for war. Welch came from the prominent family of Judge William H. Welch, the man elected to preside over the April 19 Goodhue County recruiting meeting. His son, known as Edward or Ed, was about to enter his junior year at Red Wing's Hamline University. Colvill, at six-feet-five-inches, towered by nearly a foot over the slender, shorter Welch.[8]

Other Goodhue County men sought to form additional volunteer companies as the first unit filled. Pine Island, which had sent 20 soldiers into Company F, now organized the Pine Island Rifles under Capt. N. D. Marble and 1st Lt.

William Haskins. The new unit enlisted 47 men by May 10. In early May, a new Red Wing company enlisted 49 officers and men.[9]

Military life was new for the officers and men of Company F. "From the captain down we had it all to learn," the company historian later wrote. The unit drilled in Red Wing for a week, preparing for its April 27 riverboat departure to Fort Snelling. The men had no formal uniforms and few weapons as they marched on Broadway in front of the Parker Hotel.[10]

Turning untrained citizens into proper soldiers required time far greater than the allotted two months. The ten companies of the First Minnesota, eager and full of fight, soon became restless under the restrictions of army life. The average enlisted man felt himself the equal of his superiors and occasionally found accepting orders difficult. Complaints about the food served at Fort Snelling resulted in "bad-beef riots," during which soldiers rained plates and food on the cooks and their cookhouse. Still, such disturbances from the regiment were rare.[11]

Rumors that the First Minnesota might relieve regular army garrisons on the Minnesota and Dakota frontier concerned the men. The volunteers reacted angrily to the idea, insisting that they enlisted in response to an insult of the American flag and the bombardment by the Confederates of Fort Sumter. The Goodhue County *Republican* fumed that exile to the frontier would, "hardly please the boys, as they expected more active duty than the stupid business of watching Indians."[12]

On June 22 the First Minnesota, more than 900 strong, gathered on the Fort Snelling parade ground in what passed for uniforms—black pants, red flannel shirts, and black felt hats. The men marched to the river to board two boats–the *Northern Belle* and *War Eagle*—to begin their trip east. The steamers stopped at river cities including Hastings, Red Wing, Wabasha, and Winona. The companies organized in those places were able to spend a brief time ashore, but the boats and their cargoes of men soon continued the trip. Whistles in Red Wing sounded as the *Northern Belle,* which carried Company F, left the city and moved down the river. As the ship passed Barn Bluff it sounded its whistle— then slowly steamed out of sight.[13]

The regiment left the riverboats at La Crosse, Wisconsin, and boarded trains for Baltimore via Chicago and Pittsburgh. The unit reached Baltimore on June 26, four days later. Many Confederate sympathizers lived in Baltimore; a week earlier some of them had fired on a passing federal unit. An unfriendly crowd now awaited the arrival of the Minnesotans at a city train station. The unit commander, Col. Willis Gorman, pointedly ordered his men to load their muskets in the presence of the spectators. The First Minnesota marched through the city unmolested and reached Washington, D.C., at midnight.[14]

The Minnesotans joined the Union army in its advance into northern Virginia less than three weeks after arriving in Washington. Still wearing their red flannel shirts and black pants, the men marched on July 16 toward Manassas and combat, along a stream called Bull Run.

The Union army, consisting of 50 regiments under command of Gen. Irvin McDowell, hoped to deal the rebel army a crippling blow. The day started well for McDowell and his Federals. As the battle wore on, the Minnesotans, led by Company F, moved to the center of the Union line and advanced. The regiment soon came under heavy fire, causing the men to bob repeatedly under the volleys. Lt. Welch angrily called on his company to "stand up like men." Second Lt. Martin Maginnis, another of the Hamline men, didn't like the "bows" the men made as they ducked enemy fire. "Shame!" Maginnis thundered, calling the unit the "damnedest politest regiment I ever saw." The Minnesota soldiers held fast, but the battle turned against the northern army. A disorderly retreat toward Washington followed. The Minnesotans continued to perform well, however, and their division commander noted that First Minnesota retired in good order, among the last to leave the field.[15]

Company F had suffered badly. Hiram Rush, called by Colvill one of the unit's best men, took a bullet through the neck and died. Deeply religious and patriotic Joseph Garrison and Elijah Thomas from Stanton took hits and later died in captivity. A musketball tore through the neck and out of the mouth of Cpl. Amos Scofield, 24, from Roscoe, knocking out four teeth. He walked to a hospital in Alexandria only to die there several days later. Company F suffered eight dead in the engagement.[16]

First Lieutenant Ed Welch emerged from the battle a hero. He helped repulse an enemy assault, shooting down four attackers with his pistol. A second attack overwhelmed Welch and the men with him. Last seen surrounded by Confederate soldiers and reported dead, Welch was in Richmond's Libby Prison with seven men from Company F and 16 others from the First Minnesota. In a letter to his father in Red Wing, Welch, slightly wounded, maintained, "If all, or even a majority, had followed where Company F led, the field would have been ours."[17]

Confederates nearly captured Colvill late in the day. The captain noticed enemy soldiers closing in as his company slowly fell back. He ran for a nearby ravine, chased by the Southerners. Colvill heard the "chuck" of the pursuers' muskets being raised to fire and dove to the ground just as a volley of shots buzzed over his head. The lanky captain sprang to his feet, glanced back at the astonished Confederates, and made his escape.[18]

More Goodhue County men enlisted for service in 1861. The Red Wing unit, first organized under A. D. Whitney, became Company I of the Second Minnesota, with John Foot as captain. Hans Mattson resigned as county auditor and called on Scandinavians to "rise with sword in hand" to defend their adopted country. Mattson organized Company D of the Third Minnesota and was captain. Red Wing men formed Company E of the Third, captained by Clinton Gurnee. The city's mayor, Edward L. Baker, resigned his office and joined Company E as its first lieutenant. The Roscoe Union Guards enrolled in the southern sections of the county under the command of Capt. C. C. Sent.[19]

Goodhue County soldiers of the Third Regiment unwillingly became involved in an inglorious surrender at Murfreesboro, Tennessee. On July 12, 1862, the able Confederate cavalry leader Nathan Bedford Forrest attacked the Ninth Michigan and Third Minnesota. The Northerners, though surprised, fought well, keeping Forrest's horse soldiers at bay. The Confederate leader managed to capture the Third's 20-man-camp guard but only after three separate charges.[20]

Brigade commander Col. W. W. Duffield of the Michigan regiment suffered a serious wound during the fighting and asked Forrest for a truce to consider his options. Duffield wished to meet Col. Henry Lester, the Third's commander. Lester, a Winona man, had come to the regiment following a transfer and promotion from the First Minnesota. The Confederate Forrest allowed the meeting, carefully gathering his men along the path Lester would take. Forrest hoped to convince the Minnesota officer that the Southerners outnumbered them. The ploy worked. After a council of war, the shaken Lester polled his officers regarding surrender. Capt. Hans Mattson, leader of Goodhue County's nearly all-Swede Company D, was on leave, and his second in command, John Vanstrum, stayed with his men and didn't vote. Capt. Gurnee of Company E, the Red Wing unit, voted to give in. The Minnesota leadership argued among themselves before finally deciding to surrender. They notified Forrest.[21]

The surrender came as a shock to the Minnesota men who had fought well and maintained strong defensive positions through the day. They laid down their weapons with sorrow and indignation. The Third Regiment's noncommissioned officers and men received paroles, agreeing not to bear arms until the completion of prisoner exchange. They then marched back to Union army control. The unit's officers headed to a Georgia prison camp from which they were paroled three months later. The "disgraceful" affair tarnished the reputation of the Minnesota and Michigan regiments. The men of the Third Minnesota considered themselves betrayed by the timid Lester and could only hope for a chance to erase the stain on their honor. On December 1, President Lincoln issued Lester, Gurnee, and all the officers who voted for surrender a dishonorable dismissal.[22]

The Third's Capt. Hans Mattson returned to his unit shortly after the surrender and received the duty of escorting the regiment's enlisted men to St. Louis for formal parole. The Red Wing officer wrote to his wife:

> It is a horrible affair that this proud and splendid Rgt. was surrendered to the enemy—the men feel awful bad about it, and some of our highest of-

ficers will have to look out for themselves if they ever get out of the Southern prison, the men swear vengeance.[23]

The fate of the displaced Dakota people, following the purchase of "Suland," was no longer on the minds of other Minnesotans. The 1851 land sale transferred nearly all the Indian lands of southern Minnesota to government control. Settlers soon claimed the former Indian territory and worked to establish themselves there. The Mdewakanton and Wahpekute, exiled to a narrow reservation along the upper Minnesota River valley, still returned on occasion to their former homes, but they did so sporadically and in small numbers.

David Humphrey, while spending the summer of 1855 in Goodhue County, encountered small groups of eastern Sioux and visited them "several times." Humphrey apparently enjoyed conversing with the Indians and studying their culture, but he entertained few doubts about their fate. In uncompromising terms no doubt reflecting the views of other settlers, he wrote:

> It was & is interesting to see them [the Sioux] but sad too. They are fast fading away & soon will be gone. But another reflection, perhaps no less sad, but a compensating one for the last, if I may so say, is that they are apparently *good for nothing* [his emphasis], no blessing or good to themselves or to anybody else & in a practical view their decrease is not to be regretted however much romantic sympathy may weep. One thing is certain, the question what we shall do with them is fast being settled, whether right or wrong, & with a rapidity that will apparently put an end very soon to its discussion. That they have been most unrighteously used is true & one cannot blame them for the resistance they are now making against the whites in the west. Their list of grievances is long but the *might* of the white man is greater than the *right* of the Indian.[24]

The flood of white immigration that had washed over Goodhue County in the early 1850s now flowed into the upper Minnesota River valley, reaching the eastern Sioux reservation in the early 1860s. By the summer of 1862, the settlers encroached on Indian land, creating tension on the prairie.

Some Indians, under pressure from the government and Christian missionaries, tried to take up farming and adopt other "white" ways. Individuals, as a part of that process, discarded Indian dress, and some men even cut their scalp locks. Several prominent Mdewakanton men, including Mankato, Wabasha III, and the leader of the Red Wing band, Wakute II, became "cut hairs."[25]

Other Sioux lived true to tribal tradition, preferring the chase to farming. Some, particularly younger men, still warred on the Ojibway. Their warrior societies or soldiers' lodges opposed government programs and conversion to Christianity. Wamditanka (Big Eagle), a Mdewakanton warrior, recalled the deep resentment of traditionalists about the pressures: "Then the whites were

always trying to make the Indians give up their life and live like white men—
go to farming, work hard, and do as they did—and the Indians did not know
how to do that, and did not want to anyway."[26]

Minnesota's own civil war began on August 17, 1862. A four-to-six-man
hunting party from Red Middle Voice's band quarreled with settlers living near
Acton in Meeker County, and the hunters killed five settlers. The hunting party
then headed to the cluster of eastern Sioux villages along the Minnesota River
with the news. Later that night tribal leaders gathered at Little Crow's home to
consider all-out war. The Sioux still saw Little Crow as the man to take his nation to war, though his accommodation of the settlers had tarnished his reputation among the young warriors. The Mdewakanton leader well understood the
power of the federal government, having traveled cross-country to Washington,
D.C., in 1854. He had no illusions about what war might mean.[27]

In a prophetic speech, Little Crow warned the hotheaded young warriors
that the U.S. soldiers greatly outnumbered them and that they had little chance
to prevail. The chief responded chillingly when others questioned his courage:
"You will die like rabbits when the hungry wolves hunt them in the hard moon
[January]. Taoyateduta [Little Crow] is not a coward: he will die with you."[28]

At seven o'clock Monday morning, Sioux soldiers, mostly from Mdewakanton bands, struck the Lower Sioux (Redwood) Agency near present-day
Morton. In a brief but bloody affair they killed 20 whites, captured ten, and sent
the remainder fleeing toward Fort Ridgely. Capt. John Marsh and a relief column of 43 men rushed to the agency, only to be ambushed. Marsh and more
than half of his men died. Warriors swept the prairie clean of settlers, then
moved to attack the fort and the nearby German settlement at New Ulm. In all,
the Dakota soldiers scoured an area 200 miles long and about 50 miles wide as
refugees fled eastward.[29]

Members of the Red Wing (under Wakute) and Wabasha bands took part
in the combat, though their leaders opposed the war. On the first day of conflict
Wakute and Wabasha assisted in keeping white women and children from
harm's way. Wabasha, wielding two pistols, single-handedly dispersed warriors
seeking to capture a small group of refugees including Jannette DeCamp, who
later related the story. Wakute eventually rescued this same group. Telling them
they were in danger, the Mdewakanton chief picked up the four-year-old son
of Mrs. DeCamp and said, "Come with me."[30]

Wakute hid the fugitives in an empty cabin. Shortly thereafter three more
women—Mattie Williams, Mary Schwandt, and Mary Anderson—arrived and
received sanctuary from Wakute. Two Indians had helped Anderson to the
cabin. The young woman, shot in the back, needed medical help.

After the day's battles a group of warriors arrived at the cabin flushed with
victory and boasting of the ambush of Captain Marsh. The noise of the warriors
brought Wakute back to the cabin. Jannette DeCamp believed nearly all in the

crowd of men were from Wakute's band. The chief noticed two of his teenage sons in the group of warriors and evicted them from the cabin. He then dispersed the rest of the men. To DeCamp, Wakute "seemed distressed beyond measure" to learn his sons were involved in the fighting. As the room cleared, Mary Anderson asked the chief whether he could remove the bullet still lodged in her flesh. Wakute probed the wound with a knife until he found and extracted the bullet. He guarded the refugees through the night.

The next morning Wakute advised the women to remain in the cabin. The Dakota were preparing for an attack on Fort Ridgely, and Wakute planned to join them. His decision to take part in the fighting surprised the women whose safety he guarded so carefully. Wakute explained that his band would kill him if he did not engage in the attack. Whether Wakute believed his men would kill him is open to conjecture, but according to DeCamp, that is what he told the women. His actions the next day proved again that he advocated peace.[31]

Hachinwakanda (Lightning Blanket), a Mdewakanton warrior, attended a council of war on the second day of battle. There Wakute and Wabasha spoke against attacks on New Ulm and Fort Ridgely. Hachinwakanda asserted that Wabasha's jealousy of Little Crow was behind that decision. Regardless of motive, Wabasha and Wakute demonstrated the traditionally close relationship of their Mdewakanton bands at this meeting. But the majority of young men wanted to fight and disregarded their advice.[32]

For two weeks the Sioux warriors dominated the western prairie, causing a panic that reached to settlements on the Mississippi. Settlers and soldiers fought off repeated attacks on New Ulm and Fort Ridgely. Citizens of New Ulm evacuated their town on August 25. Their community, before the outbreak, held nearly 1,000 people.[33]

After receiving reports of imminent Indian attack, nervous settlers in Goodhue County took flight. Near Holden, Cleng Dale and his wife abandoned their farm and fled toward Osmund Wing's home near Aspelund in Wanamingo township. The Dale and Wing families headed east toward Torger Rygh's house, previously used as a meeting place. The men, armed with axes and pitchforks, stood guard below as the women and children went upstairs. Also in Wanamingo, 15-year-old Ellen Wilson joined her father and mother, Ole and Hannah, on the 30-mile walk to Red Wing. They started in the dark, and the road was full of people. But the rumors of Indian attack proved false, and they returned to their homes. Nevertheless, Hannah Wilson had had enough of the prairie. The Wilson family moved to Red Wing.[34]

Minnesota desperately needed trained soldiers to put down the Sioux rebellion, but it had few on hand. Governor Ramsey turned to Henry Sibley for assistance. Sibley's wide knowledge of Dakota culture and acquaintance with Indian leaders, including Little Crow, made him a logical choice. Sibley had four companies of undertrained recruits from the Sixth Minnesota infantry immediately available; he took them up the Minnesota River. A motley mix of volunteers also joined the relief column. Upon reaching Fort Ridgely, Sibley, under pressure to put his untried army into the field, allowed a 170-man burial party to leave the fort. The Sioux promptly ambushed the group at Birch Coulee on September 2, and the detail sustained heavy losses.[35]

The federal government now swung into action, creating the Department of the Northwest on September 7 and sending Gen. John Pope to Minnesota to take command. The bombastic Pope, fresh from a stinging defeat at Second Bull Run, was eager to restore his reputation. His first letter to Sibley called upon the Minnesota field commander to put a final stop to the Indian troubles by "exterminating or ruining all the Indians engaged in the late outbreak."[36]

On September 13, about 270 members of the Third Minnesota Infantry, the unit earlier surrendered to the Confederates at Murfreesboro, reached the front, enhancing greatly the prospects of Pope and Sibley. The Third was spoiling for a fight. The unit was now under the command of recently promoted Maj. Ed Welch, First Regiment hero from Red Wing. Welch, freed from a Confederate prison and recovered from the wounds sustained at Bull Run, was ready for combat.[37]

Sibley and his men began a pursuit of the Dakota, who retreated westward with more than 250 white and mixed-blood prisoners in tow. Little Crow's warning to his warriors about the power of the government proved true as Sibley and 1,619 well-armed men moved against the Dakota. In response, Little Crow and other leaders called for an ambush of Sibley's contingent.

Early on September 23, more than 700 Sioux attempted to encircle Sibley's camp on the east shore of a small lake, mistakenly identified as Wood Lake, near present-day Echo. Welch and his Third infantry advanced aggressively, and Sibley twice ordered the unit back. The Sixth Minnesota, led by two Red Wing officers—Maj. Robert N. McLaren, a regimental staff officer, and former Hamline professor Capt. Horace Wilson of Company F—also attacked.[38]

The battle soon subsided and the Indians withdrew to their camps, allowing both sides time to count their casualties. The Dakota lost 16 men, including Chief Mankato; about 50 were wounded. Sibley suffered seven dead and 34 wounded. All but seven of the casualties were from Welch's Third Regiment. Sibley's army had just two officers wounded; both of them, Welch and Wilson, were from Red Wing.

The defeat at Wood Lake dispirited some Sioux, who, tired from the length and growing cost of the conflict, decided to approach Sibley. Men like Wabasha and Wakute, opposed to the war from the beginning, hoped for decent treatment. Their cases strengthened when the Indians surrendered 269 prisoners, mostly women, at Sibley's Camp Release near Montevideo.[39]

Little Crow understood there could be no surrender for soldiers like himself who had assumed leadership roles in the uprising. Those who refused to

Wacouta (Wakute) in captivity at Fort Snelling, in 1863. *Upton photo, MHS*

give in took their families and scattered over the western plains. Theirs was a wise decision. In a dispatch to Colonel Sibley on September 28, General Pope made clear his intentions. He wanted no treaty with the people who committed "horrible massacres of women and children . . . It is my purpose utterly to exterminate the Sioux . . . They are to be treated as maniacs or wild beasts."[40]

Those surrendering found little mercy. A five-man military commission held trials for Dakota accused of taking part in the fighting. The commission concluded some cases in three weeks but was under pressure to move faster. The court responded, holding as many as 40 hearings in a day, with some completed in as little as five minutes. In all, the court tried 392 Indians during the five weeks after fighting ended and sentenced 307 to death.[41]

President Lincoln resisted the nearly unanimous pressure from Minnesota to execute the convicted prisoners. He reduced to 39 the number of Indians to be killed. One of the condemned Dakota was later removed from the death list. On December 26, 1862, the remaining 38 men were taken to a large scaffold in Mankato and executed simultaneously by hanging.

As the prairie conflict with the Dakota wound down, members of Minnesota's military concentrated on the struggle with the Confederacy. The state's ten in-

fantry regiments as well as its cavalry and artillery units, all of which included
Goodhue County men, soon were fighting in the South.

The First Minnesota continued serving in Virginia as part of the Army of
the Potomac. The regiment took part in heavy fighting, suffering more attrition.
Goodhue County soldiers Ferris Johnson (Cherry Grove), Edward Davis (Zumbrota), Bob Leeson (Burnside), Edwin Cox (Leon), and Goodhue's "Dixie"
Milliken died in fighting at Savage Station and Antietam.[42]

By early summer 1863, the First Minnesota was among the Army of the
Potomac's most experienced and reliable regiments and about to face its most
serious test of the war. Southern forces led by Gen. Robert E. Lee slipped
around the Union army and made a drive into Pennsylvania. The Federals regained their balance and began a pursuit. In a grueling march, they caught up
to Lee at Gettysburg.[43]

The three-day Battle of Gettysburg was underway by the time the Minnesotans, now under Col. William Colvill of Red Wing, reached the battlefield.
Preliminary fighting commenced on July 1, precipitating orders from the federal command to hurry reinforcements into position. At 3:00 A.M. on July 2, division commander Gen. John Gibbon ordered his units, including the First Minnesota, awakened and prepared to move.[44]

The First Minnesota joined the rest of the Second Corps on Cemetery
Ridge, where the regiment moved into reserve. Colvill's Minnesotans, with two
companies detached, was at reduced strength. Goodhue County's Company F
rooted out suspected Confederate sharpshooters on the left, and Company C
served as provost guard. Colvill had just 262 men.[45]

Late in the afternoon Lee launched a full-scale attack on the Union line, a
blow that sent the exposed Third Corps reeling back. A dangerous gap opened
in the Union defenses as the Federals retreated. If Lee's army could exploit the
opening, the entire Army of the Potomac would be in peril. At this juncture Gen.
Winfield Scott Hancock, northern corps commander on the scene, recognized
the danger and looked for men to stop the charging Confederates. Hancock
noticed the First Minnesota and rode to Colvill with a plaintive question, "My
God! Are these all the men we have here?"[46]

Hancock had no choice but to order the Minnesota regiment forward in an
attack he considered a "sacrifice." Coming at Colvill and his men were the
nearly 1,600 men of Cadmus Wilcox's brigade of Alabamians. The men of the
First Minnesota, in position on the high ground in the center of the northern
line, had a panoramic view of the Southern army's sunset attack. Hancock ordered Colvill to advance, and Colvill asked the men whether they were ready.
They answered "yes," and he immediately ordered, "Forward, double-quick."[47]

With bayonets fixed, the Minnesotans started down the hill at a slow trot,
forming a line almost a hundred yards across. Southern fire cut into their ranks,
but Colvill and his well-disciplined veterans kept coming, partially obscured by

smoke. As they neared Wilcox's men, the regiment charged at the Confederates with leveled bayonets. The southern line, staggered by the First's assault, fell back. Only then did Colvill order his men to fire; their volley struck the Confederates' second line a devastating blow. Colvill pressed the attack, but soon he and his men had to take cover.[48]

The surviving Minnesota men crouched under a hail of fire. Many of the unit's officers were down—dead or wounded. Colvill took a plunging shot through the "top of the right arm." The ball passed under the shoulder blade and struck his backbone, causing him "to see stars." Colvill ordered Capt. Henry Coates to assume command and "take care of the men." Almost immediately Colvill felt another "pang" and fell to the ground. This shot hit his right foot, "smashing up the joint." Badly wounded, he rolled into a small gully.[49]

Darkness descended upon the battlefield. Wilcox's call for support had not been answered, and the southern brigade commander felt his unit exposed. He ordered a withdrawal. The battleground belonged to the Minnesotans, but they also abandoned the field, moving back to the relative safety of the ridge. Command of the First Minnesota devolved to Capt. Nathan Messick, who counted just 47 officers and men present.[50]

Colvill's old command, Goodhue County's Company F, missed the charge. Busy dealing with the Confederate snipers to the left of the Union line, they suffered three wounded in the process. Company F's Capt. John Ball, upon returning his unit to the federal position, asked permission to rejoin the Minnesota First. He received orders to wait until the following morning. Desperately concerned about the fate of their comrades, the men tried to get some sleep. Ball nervously paced through the evening.[51]

Early on the morning of July 3 the men of Company F found the First Minnesota's survivors gathered around Captain Messick and the regimental flag. They enjoyed a happy yet melancholy reunion. The First Regiment had been reduced to less than the size of a company, with only about 70 men fit for action. Those returning from special duty swelled the number to 150 as renewal of the battle neared. Every one of the men knew that at least another long day of fighting lay ahead.[52]

At 3:00, Lee's lieutenants sent 15,000 men on a terrible mile-long journey to a meeting with the Army of the Potomac. The Confederates emerged from a stand of timber into the bright sunlight. They headed toward the Union lines, focusing the assault on a clump of trees about 400 feet to the right of First Minnesota.[53]

The men of the First Minnesota waited for orders to fire. They received instructions to aim their shots at the feet of the attackers to correct a tendency to overshoot. As the Confederates came into range obscured by clouds of smoke, the Minnesotans poured a volley into the enemy lines, then began firing individually as fast as they could. The First and other units in the brigade then received orders to assault the exposed flank of the attackers.[54]

Company F's James Wright and Joe Richardson charged down the slope towards the Confederates. Shouting "we'll show 'em there is a God in Israel," Richardson ran forward. The northern brigade advanced, shooting, then stabbing and clubbing as there was no time to reload. Sgt. Wright heard an explosion and discovered his face, neck, and chest covered by splinters, probably from a shattered gunstock. The wounds did not stop Wright as he ran to catch Richardson. "We're getting some satisfaction now, ain't we, Sergeant?" he yelled.[55]

The Confederate attack collapsed, and its survivors withdrew. Both sides, exhausted by the fighting and in desperate need of food and rest, returned to their lines. Lee expected a counterattack the following day. When none came, the general decided to begin a movement back to Virginia.

The First Minnesota and the men of Company F once again assessed their losses. Captain Messick was dead after having commanded the First for less than 24 hours. Also dead were Sgt. Philip Hamlin and Len Squires, two of Company F's most popular members. Squires was far from a saint in the view of his comrades. The husky, broad-shouldered 26-year-old used profanity and "did not always refuse a drink." Hamlin, 23, was a religious, "old fashioned Methodist" from Pine Island, known for honesty, courage, and absolute faith.[56]

As Company F's survivors sat and drank coffee on the evening of July 3, they resolved to find Hamlin's body and bury it. They located the sergeant's corpse, disfigured by four bullet holes, near a walnut tree. His comrades dug a shallow trench next to the tree and placed a blanket and tent cloth in the depression. They laid Hamlin in the grave, covered the corpse with dirt and stone, and marked the place with a simple identifying board.[57]

The Civil War dragged on for nearly two more years, but Lee's once powerful army weakened, forcing the astute southern leader into a more defensive stance. The war was nearly over for the First Minnesota and the surviving members of Company F. After duty in New York and some action in Virginia, they learned they'd be going home. The men had earned the praise that federal officials showered upon them as they prepared to leave. Gen. Winfield Scott Hancock, the officer who ordered the desperate charge on the second day at Gettysburg, wrote of his appreciation, including a powerful declaration about the actions of the First Minnesota: "There is no more gallant deed recorded in history."[58]

The unit reached St. Paul on February 15, 1864, and the men received a 30-day furlough allowing them time to consider reenlistment. Their three-year tour of duty was expiring. Some of the veterans—15 from Company F alone—decided on another tour. Others had had enough of war, among them Sgt. James Wright, one of the enlisted Hamline students. Wright returned to his mother's

Abraham Edwards Welch, Company F,
First Minnesota Volunteer Regiment.
*Whitney photo, MHS*

new home on Seventh Street in Red Wing, writing with relief in his diary, "I am at home, at last, once more, and as gratefully glad as a mortal can be."[59]

The Civil War produced heroes from both the North and the South. Goodhue County certainly provided its share, none more renowned than William Colvill. Despite lingering disabilities from his Gettysburg wounds, Colvill agreed to take command of Minnesota's First Regiment of Heavy Artillery during the final months of the war. The army later brevetted Colvill a brigadier general of volunteers in recognition of his service.[60]

Lucius Hubbard, like Colvill, was a Red Wing newspaper editor who decided to go to war. He enlisted as a private in the Fifth Minnesota on December 19, 1861, but by September 1, 1862, was a full colonel in command of the regiment. His heroic performances at the battles of Corinth and Nashville—he was wounded in both—earned him the rank of brevet brigadier general.[61]

The brave and reckless A. Edwards Welch recovered from his wound at the Battle of Wood Lake and served with the Fourth Minnesota during the critical Vicksburg, Mississippi, campaign. There on May 21, 1863, he was wounded again. His sister Felicity later joked about his susceptibility to injury, writing that she had heard of the wounding of a different Major Welch. Felicity knew it wasn't Ed, but she "could not help thinking that 'Major Welch wounded' sounded very familiar." This time the young officer did not recover so quickly, and he returned to Red Wing to recuperate. F. F. Hoyt, M.D., wrote that Welch was "wholly unfit for duty," but he tried to return to combat nonetheless. His health deteriorated until he was taken to Memphis Officers' Hospital #17, where he died on February 1, 1864.[62]

A hero's death in combat brought the faint solace of acclaim to his survivors. A soldier's slow and quiet death from disease was just as final and keenly felt. The Third Minnesota suffered terribly from malaria while stationed near Pine Bluff, Arkansas, in the spring and summer of 1864. New recruits were particularly susceptible. Eighty-nine died in May. Another 30 replacements died in June.[63] Forty-one Goodhue County men in the Third Regiment succumbed to disease in Arkansas. The dead came from 17 townships, with the heaviest losses in Red Wing (nine), Vasa (five), Florence (four), and Wanamingo, Holden, and Warsaw each with three.[64]

The Sixth Minnesota, including Company F, a unit filled with Goodhue County soldiers, languished in Arkansas in the summer of 1864. In July the regiment reported 815 men fit for action and a month later had only 185. At one time just 26 soldiers were healthy enough to report for duty. The Sixth sent 600 men to hospitals in Memphis, Milwaukee, Chicago, and Prairie du Chien. Six Company F men died during the scourge.[65]

Goodhue County, with a population of less than 9,000 before the war, sent 1,508 men into service. One hundred twenty-two died in battle or of wounds or disease. County soldiers were most heavily represented in the First and Third Regiments, which coincidentally suffered the highest losses. The Third Regiment contained 184 Goodhue County soldiers and the First Regiment 104.[66]

Memories of the Civil War had faded 63 years later, when President Calvin Coolidge traveled later to Cannon Falls to dedicate a statue placed over the grave of Col. Colvill. The president spoke of the reasons for his July 27, 1928, trip to Goodhue County and of the heroism of the First Minnesota and its colonel. His praise was characteristically succinct. Said President Coolidge, "Colonel Colvill and those eight companies of the First Minnesota are entitled to rank among the saviors of their country."[67]

# 6

## *Postwar Prosperity—*
## *Agricultural Boom and Industrial Growth*

The Civil War produced years of pain for those left awaiting the return of Goodhue County's citizen soldiers. Early defeats dashed hopes for a quick, decisive victory by the North, and the toll of local men—dead from disease, killed or wounded, missing or captured—shocked the people back home. Some of the county's most promising young men fell even in the first days of combat. More died with each successive battle. The nearly simultaneous return to the county of the shattered First Minnesota's Company F and the body of Maj. A. Edwards Welch in February 1864 vividly demonstrated the cost of the war. The funeral of Welch, the thrice-wounded hero of three major battles, produced a massive outpour of grief and reduced Red Wing to a city in mourning. And still the war continued.[1]

The Civil War also changed life on the home front. The demand for soldiers created manpower shortages particularly challenging for labor-intensive farms. With sons and some fathers gone to war, mothers and daughters found their workloads increased. Before the war a field hand got from 50 to 65 cents per day. That rate soared to between three and four dollars as the fighting wore on. Yet crops were plentiful and wheat prices jumped from prewar lows of 35 cents per bushel to $2.75 later in the war.[2]

The loss of three sons forced Wacouta settler and Ireland native John Jordan out of farming. "We were prosperous until the breaking out of the war, when all the help I had went to fight for the Union," he wrote. "Three sons went away; one returned broken down in health, and the other two lie in some southern ditch for the sake of their country." Jordan, nearly 60 at the time his sons left to fight, was forced to rent his land to others. "The war was a sorrowful thing on me and mine," Jordan lamented, "but it had to be, or freedom was no more, and if I had been young I would have been there too."[3]

Soon there was a new price to pay for the continuing war. On March 3, 1863, Congress declared men between 20 and 45 eligible for conscription. Those drafted received the same bounty given earlier volunteers and also served three years. A controversial provision in the conscription law allowed a man to avoid the draft by paying $300 for a substitute. Peace Democrats, unhappy with the course of the conflict, claimed it a rich man's war and a poor man's fight.[4]

Goodhue County citizens felt the pressure to fill assigned manpower quotas. Township residents taxed themselves heavily to offer bonuses to those who would enlist, thus attempting to send only the men willing to go. A September 6, 1864, town meeting in Welch resulted in a special bounty tax of $600 and another $700 five months later. Prosperous Holden raised $14,000 to hire volunteers for the war and needed no draft. Zumbrota took in $5,300 to provide enlistment bounties. Some drafted men provided their own substitutes, paying as much as $500 for a replacement.[5]

The armies of the North and South stubbornly fought to near total exhaustion. Finally, in April 1865, the depleted southern forces capitulated. In July 1865, Minnesota's Second, Fourth, and Eighth Regiments came home, followed in August by the Sixth, Seventh, and Tenth. The Third Regiment, stationed in Arkansas, and the Fifth in Alabama did not return until September.[6]

The veterans returning to Goodhue County immediately began to reestablish themselves. Among them were war heroes Lucius Hubbard, William Colvill, and Hans Mattson, who built futures based at least partially on their outstanding war service. Dozens of little-known returning soldiers resumed civilian life and, in their turn, assumed leadership positions in the county and state.

Marriage was on the mind of many former soldiers. Weddings of veterans and their brides flourished in the county's towns and townships in 1865 and 1866. The Third Regiment's Frank Carlson went back to Vasa, where he married Signild Turner. Hezekiah Bruce, a First Minnesota hero at Fredericksburg, returned to Goodhue township to farm and marry Emma Saunderson. Jacob Christ, a member of the Seventh Regiment, wedded Catherine Koerner. Joseph Dickey, who fought with the 2nd Minnesota Sharpshooters and was wounded at Antietam, married Sarah Steele. James Scofield, from the Eighth Regiment, returned to Cannon Falls and married Mary Hillman.[7]

These men and women were among many to achieve success in Goodhue County. The Carlsons opened a general store in Red Wing. The Bruces became successful farmers in Hay Creek. Christ founded the Red Wing Brewery. The Dickeys specialized in raising sheep on their 160-acre Pine Island farm. James Scofield, along with his brother Wilbur, founded Scofield Brothers Drug Store, a Cannon Falls institution.

James L. Scofield, third from left, and his brother Wilbur, in doorway, made a success of their Cannon Falls drug store and post office in the years after the Civil War. The family-owned business still operates as of this writing. *CFHS*

One postwar match was doomed. Ole Nelson and Julia Bullard, two former classmates at Hamline University in Red Wing, married on September 25, 1866, and moved to his land in Belvidere to farm. The couple celebrated the birth of a son in the fall of 1868, but the child died before his first birthday. Five months later Ole died, at age 27. His unit, the Sixth Minnesota, had been ravaged by malarial fever while on duty in Arkansas. Ole became ill while stationed there and never regained his health.[8]

Julia Bullard Nelson was the niece of one of the county's first white settlers, George W. Bullard. He settled in what became Wacouta, a tiny township of about four sections at the head of Lake Pepin. Bullard had a license to trade with the Indians. Seven years later Edward Bullard arrived to join his brother George. He had two daughters in tow, including 15-year-old Julia.[9]

Julia, as a young woman, had studied for a teaching certificate. As the widowed Julia B. Nelson, she decided to return to teaching and "consecrate her life to work among the lowly and down-trodden." At 26 she embarked upon a career that put her in the forefront of both the state and national woman's suffrage and temperance movements. Her first step was to heed a call from the American Missionary Association (AMA), which needed a force of northern teachers willing to teach freed slaves. The Freedmen's Bureau, established by Congress in 1865, developed schools in the South devoted to educating former slaves, and the AMA planned to help staff them. The missionary association accepted Nelson and assigned her to a school in Houston, Texas.

Julia B., as she was called for most of her life, headed south in September of 1869. The white citizens of the South had little time for the new teachers and

Julia Bullard Nelson and student
in Texas in 1869. *MHS*

so ostracized, persecuted, and even physically assaulted them. Still, the number of teachers grew. By 1869 hardly a southern city or town was without what some Southerners derisively called the "Nig schools." [10]

The AMA sent Nelson to Columbus, Texas, after a bout with illness temporarily halted her work in Houston. She shrugged off the hostility of the white population in Texas and told of her protection from the "Ku Klux" by her students and their families. Nelson wrote to the Goodhue County *Republican* asking for more teachers to come south. She frankly stated the situation: "Those who come should understand that they will be ostracized by white society, and that they will be loved and trusted by the colored people." [11]

Goodhue County's most famous veteran, Col. William Colvill, married native New Yorker Jane Elizabeth Morgan two years after the war's end. Colvill was 37 and his new wife 33 at the time of their April 1867 marriage. Jane Morgan came to Minnesota as a woman of some wealth, with a family line that could be traced back to the *Mayflower*.

Upon her arrival in Goodhue County, the new Mrs. Colvill took pains to protect her financial assets. She filed a "Schedule of Married Women's Property, Book 1st" with the county recorder, listing holdings that included $4,000 in U.S. securities, an interest in her deceased mother's unsettled estate, an Illinois farm worth $2,000, and $1,700 in cash and household furniture. Jane made her reasons for developing the statement of assets clear: "The above document is filed as notice to the creditors of William Colvill of Goodhue County . . . of the separate property claimed and owned by his said wife at the time of their marriage." [12]

Colvill had suffered a disappointing defeat at the polls the year before he married. The colonel began a political career immediately after the war, getting off to a promising start in 1865 when elected state attorney general. The next year Colvill ran unsuccessfully for Congress from the Second District.[13]

Within three weeks of her marriage to the colonel, Jane Colvill bought 18 acres of land for $1,000 in what is now east Red Wing and 160 acres near Zumbrota for $800. In November 1867 she paid $5,000 for 158 acres of land that became the Colvill farm. Part of this property eventually became Red Wing's Colvill Park. Later that month she bought for $1,250 another 320 acres in Zumbrota Township.[14]

Colvill received a small political plum in 1887 when President Grover Cleveland appointed him register of the Duluth land office. William and Jane moved to that city, where seven years later she died at age 60. Jane's grip on the purse strings held even in death. She willed some property to her husband, but her estate still was not settled when he died in 1905. The total of William's assets, $1,237, went to funeral costs, taxes, creditors, and taxes.

The people of Minnesota and Goodhue County tried to put the war behind them with a return to the more comfortable rhythms of life. The state's population continued to grow—even during the years of fighting it increased by 250,000 —and government officials hoped for even more newcomers. The legislature, at the conclusion of the war, established a state board of emigration to encourage more settlement. Former Third Regiment colonel Hans Mattson, a founder of Vasa, was appointed secretary of the new board. Mattson ordered an advertising campaign with circulars encouraging immigration to Minnesota printed in Swedish, Norwegian, and German.[15]

A life in agriculture and related businesses lay ahead for the great majority of immigrants, likewise for war veterans returning to Minnesota and other parts of the trans-Mississippi region. In the 30 years following the Civil War, more of the nation's land came under cultivation than in the previous two-and-a-half centuries. The emerging Midwest became home to a new agricultural empire where the population (Minnesota, Nebraska, Kansas, and the Dakotas) grew from 300,000 in 1860 to well over two million in 1880. These years of growth also marked the last heyday of the family farmer—an era in which families owned their own land and were independent of world markets, the vagaries of transportation expenses, and the cost of fertilizer and machinery.[16]

From the beginning of cultivation in territorial Minnesota, spring wheat was the cash crop of promise. Goodhue County farmers were among the first to refine and improve their wheat-raising methods. In 1856 John Lawson managed a yield of 56 bushels of wheat to the acre on his Belle Creek farm. In 1860, the year before the war began, the Minnesota wheat crop reportedly reached five million bushels. Ten years later that number had more than tripled.[17]

Wheat became the basis for much of Goodhue County's rural economy, yet in the early postwar years a lack of local mills meant that most county farmers carried their grain to Red Wing or Hastings. The river markets offered good prices, luring farmers into long hauls over treacherous trails. Grain haulers faced snowdrifts blocking the roads and flooding that left streams unfordable. A farmer living within three days of a market by ox team was fortunate.[18]

The river towns of Winona, Hastings, and Red Wing competed for honors as the state's primary wheat market before the Civil War and in the decade following. Winona led as early as 1860, when it shipped a million bushels of wheat downriver to outstrip Hastings, with 600,000 bushels, and Red Wing, with 350,000. Yet the river would turn against the farmers and shippers. Low water curtailed the shipping season in Red Wing in both 1860 and 1861, and 1863 was another poor year for river trade. Between 1850 and 1867 the river was closed to shipping due to low water or winter ice an average of 142 days a year.[19]

During the late 1860s a technological breakthrough in the milling of spring wheat revolutionized the grain business. Spring wheat was best suited to the state's land and climate, yet it was considered inferior to winter wheat because of its darker flour that more readily gathered moisture. The milling of spring wheat separated meal into flour, bran, and residual "middlings." The middlings contained wheat's nutritional qualities but were inferior in appearance. [20]

Spring wheat's value soared with the development of a process to purify middlings, becoming the first choice of markets in the eastern United States and later in foreign countries. Spring-wheat flour soon commanded a premium of a dollar per barrel over winter-wheat flour. Perfectly positioned to capitalize on this development, the state entered into the era of "King Wheat."

Many viewed Minnesota after the war as one vast "wheat-field," and Goodhue County boasted some of the state's prime land. By 1872, wheat grew on more than 61 percent of the state's cultivated acres—the largest proportion devoted to one grain in any northern state. That year the county ranked first in the state in wheat acreage (116,977), bushels produced (2,311,674), and bushels per acre (19.76). The county claimed 13 percent of the state's total wheat acreage, and its farmers produced 14 percent of the entire wheat harvest.[21]

But King Wheat did not guarantee financial success to those raising the grain. Wheat growers harbored suspicions of unfair treatment at market, even though farmers in Goodhue County and other wheat-producing areas profited from the new spring wheat-processing system. The farmers complained that their loads were "short weighed" and improperly graded. Weighing-in, with its imperfect technology and lack of standardization, was irregular at best. There were no public scales or inspections of weights and measures.[22]

The Chicago Board of Trade in 1858 initiated an analysis of wheat quality, establishing three grades for the grain. The price difference between grades one and two was about 10 cents per bushel. The difference between grades two and three fell in the 10-to-20-cent range. A load of number-one wheat downgraded at sale to number-two quality lost 5 to 10 percent of its value.

Farmers suspected price-fixing among buyers. They claimed there was only an appearance of competition and that prices were artificially low. Buyers at the Red Wing market in the late 1860s were aggressive, often meeting farmers and their ox-drawn wagons two or three miles from town. Sometimes wagons backed up as farmers waited for sales to proceed. Buyers climbed onto the wagons, opened bags, examined the contents, and began bidding.[23]

In the late 1860s, Red Wing grain merchant James Marshall developed a concept by which a farmer could sell wheat in the late fall for May delivery. Before the futures market, business suffered during winter months as the frozen Mississippi prohibited grain shipment. Farmers getting $1.80 a bushel for grain destined for immediate shipment saw that price fall to 40 cents in winter. Marshall made the first futures transaction with a Chicago firm agreeing to buy fall wheat at a fixed price and take delivery of the grain the next spring.[24]

In 1873 Red Wing overcame other regional competition to claim the title of the world's largest primary wheat market. The city exported 1,800,385 bushels, all received directly from the producers and valued at more than two million dollars. On December 15 alone, city buyers took in a record 33,462 bushels. Red Wing's warehouse capacity of a million bushels remained under strain four months later with 950,641 bushels stored, not counting grain held in mills for flour manufacture. With Red Wing its main market town, Goodhue County became in 1874 "the banner wheat county in America."[25]

Complaints from wheat farmers continued, focusing even more on grain-buying middlemen, able dealers who knew markets well and negotiated the best possible deals. Farmers felt grain buyers' grading methods were too strict and that weighing practices favored those handling the scales. Buyers at the region's primary markets kept abreast of the competition's price levels, information not typically available to farmers. If a buyer's bid for a farmer's grain seemed low the farmer could try another market, but this was a time-consuming gamble that could result in failure and frustration. In an effort to reassure farmers about pricing systems, some cities instituted local boards of trade to regulate grain sales. Still, many growers remained uncomfortable with the selling process.[26]

Farmers saw money being made in wheat growing and processing but believed they did not get enough. Frank Sterrett, a grain dealer and later wheat superintendent for Red Wing Mills, organized a free dinner and dance for the local citizenry on August 1, 1870. He was celebrating a "killing" he had made in the grain market. While they no doubt appreciated Sterrett's generosity, success like his raised issues of fairness with the wheat farmers.[27]

Many of those growing wheat resisted a change to other crops despite the unpredictability of wheat production and equitable pricing. Farmers generally were poor, and wheat was the crop with a guaranteed market. Few could afford to construct buildings for livestock or experiment with other crops. They lacked the knowledge and experience to change their ways. Some forward-thinking agriculturalists touted crop diversification as early as the late 1860s, but farmers did not readily practice the concept. Committed to growing wheat, they began instead to see the need to band together to combat the inequities in the market.[28]

In February 1869, Minnesota became home to the first national farmer's organization, the National Grange of the Patrons of Husbandry. Minnesotan Oliver H. Kelley, Elk River farmer and founder of the grange, also worked as a Department of Agriculture clerk in Washington, D.C. Grangers tried to organize farmers and convince them to use their economic and political strength.[29]

The Grangers were not the first Minnesota farmers to form groups dedicated to promoting the common good. In 1868, a group of Vasa and Belle Creek farmers in Goodhue County organized to "assist each other." Some 60 farmers established the "Vasa Farmer's Union" to obtain goods at reasonable rates. They built and stocked a general merchandise store that reportedly did "a fine business" by 1869. John Paulson, postmaster of Vasa, served as salesman and secretary for the company. Nearby, on the Vasa-Belle Creek township boundary at White Rock, 15 farmers also organized the "Farmer's Commercial Union," a general store run by Mons Munson.[30]

Two other leading citizens of the area, John W. Peterson and T. G. Pearson, helped develop another cooperative venture, "The Scandinavian Transportation Company." The cooperative bought a Red Wing warehouse to provide the farmers of Vasa a place to store and from which to ship their grain. The warehouse process kept transportation costs low.[31]

Vasa farmers weren't the only ones seeing a need to control transportation costs. The pace of railroad construction quickened. Trains could shorten the haul to market for many farmers, yet transport costs remained high. In 1868 the average shipping rate per mile on the Chicago and Northwestern was 31 percent higher in Minnesota than that charged by the three largest eastern railroads. In 1871 rail lines linked Red Wing to St. Paul and Winona, bringing hope for competition among railroads and a reduction in freight rates. By 1873, Red Wing's boom wheat year, nearly 2,400 miles of track crossed Minnesota land.[32]

But Minnesota, in its eagerness to encourage railroad development, had no system to regulate the new industry. Railroads claimed the right to determine the conditions under which freight could be carried. Their rates were high and irregular. Where there was no competition, the carriers set rates at what the traffic would bear.[33]

The evolution of railroads introduced new classes of grain middlemen, who placed storage elevators along rural stretches of rail line. Farmers could market their grain more readily and avoid the long haul to river ports. But they soon discovered that "line" elevator operators controlled the pricing. Trade centered around these large buyers, and the monopolistic features of their operations angered farmers. The web of elevators built by two famous line operators, Will Cargill and Frank Peavey, laid the foundations for 20th-century agribusiness giants Cargill, Inc., and Peavey (later Conagra, Inc.). On a smaller scale, Goodhue County grain dealer Theodore. B. Sheldon established a line, adding to his assets and making him one of the wealthiest men in the region.[34]

Sheldon, born in Massachusetts in 1820, came to Red Wing in 1856 with his wife, Mary. He joined Jesse McIntire, another Massachusetts native, in the mercantile business. Sheldon sold out to McIntire in 1860, built a warehouse, and went into the grain business. He helped McIntire establish Red Wing's First National Bank in 1865 and had interests in Goodhue County Bank, Minnesota Stoneware Company, Red Wing Furniture Company, and several other enterprises. The construction of the Duluth, Red Wing and Southern Railroad, of which he was a principal, prompted Sheldon to build grain elevators in Goodhue, a village he helped establish and name, and at Rice (White Willow).[35]

Sheldon also helped establish Red Wing Mills, a combination of the Bluff and Diamond flour mills and the pride of the city. The older Bluff mill, built in 1873, used a combination of traditional millstones and the newer roller technology. It featured 11 sets of flat millstones or burrs, three sets of iron rollers, and six porcelain rollers. A series of rollers crushed the wheat in the newer process, supplanting a system of passing the grain between flat millstones. Diamond, which cost $140,000 to construct, was a "new process" mill, commonly called a roller mill. It used porcelain and metallic rollers for grinding.[36]

Construction of the Diamond was big news in the milling industry. "Hurrah for Rollers! Genuine Roller Mill to be Built in Minnesota" read a July 1877 headline of the *Northwestern Miller*. The story told of how Oscar Oexle, a well-known civil engineer and millwright from Bavaria, came to Red Wing to design Diamond Mill. Diamond adopted a Hungarian system that featured four or more grindings of the same grain and careful purification of the product. A 150,000-barrel capacity warehouse connected the Diamond and Bluff mills, featuring a 136-foot octagonal boiler house chimney. Upon completion, the chimney became a city landmark. The milling complex stretched between the river and the railroad tracks from Potter Street toward Barn Bluff.[37]

By 1878, the Bluff and Diamond plants, then unified as Red Wing Mills, operated under the control of 58-year-old Theodore Sheldon, the firm's president. Red Wing Mills was perfectly sited for the shipment of flour. The basement floors were on a level with freight cars standing on the tracks. The Mississippi River dock stood just a hundred feet from the mills. River steamers from the Diamond Jo line provided biweekly service between St. Paul and St. Louis. The Bluff Mill could produce 400 barrels of flour per day, and the Diamond 600. Together they employed a hundred men and had a daily payroll exceeding $250.

Post-Civil War milling enterprises also developed along the waterways of rural Goodhue County. Entrepreneurs constructed 21 mills to meet farmers' demands for new and more accessible markets. Small businesses such as general stores, blacksmith shops, hotels, and cooperages, often sprang up around local gristmills. Churches and schools also appeared.[38]

The Little Cannon and Cannon Rivers in the Cannon Falls and Stanton area were home to early Goodhue County mills. Cannon Falls' first mill, the Little Cannon Mill, later known as "Old Stone Mill," was completed in 1857. But with the economic panic limiting its prospects, it did not open until 1861—with machinery for manufacturing woolen goods. The Little Cannon Mill, refitted in 1875, became a flour mill with a grinding capacity of 600 bushels of wheat per day. The junction of the two Cannons became the site of the city's second mill, known over the years as Cannon Falls City, Knox, Sorghum, and Phoenix Roller Mill. A flood in 1867 destroyed the original structure, but (Mrs.) Cornelia Grosvenor immediately rebuilt it and prospered from her effort. The four-story mill contained eight "run of stone." A run consisted of two grooved millstones, the lower stationary stone, called the bedder, and the upper known as the runner. The heavy stones crushed the grain between them. Grosvenor's millstones handled a thousand bushels per day and employed 40 workers. This building burned on April 8, 1894. Flooding ruined another reconstruction, and the site was abandoned.[39]

The most successful milling enterprise in Cannon Falls was Goodhue Mill. Its original 1873 site was about a half-mile west of the confluence of the two Cannons. The Goodhue operation employed 43 men and featured a warehouse, barrel and bran houses, and a cooperage. Later conversion to a roller mill increased capacity to 800 barrels of flour per day.

Red Wing port facilities in the 1870s: The 136-foot smokestack of the Diamond and Bluff Mills is at center left. The St. Paul and Chicago railroad traces the riverfront, and a log rafter is visible on the Mississippi. *Chas. A. Tenney photo, MHS*

Martin Gunderson (inset) helped establish this mill, his first in Kenyon. *GCHS*

The Little Cannon River in Stanton township provided a natural location for a mill. The first Oxford Mill, a $16,000 wooden structure with a limestone foundation, went up in 1867 near a shallow Little Cannon crossing or "ox ford." C. N. Wilcox, a Rice County miller, and two partners built the 30-by-70-foot, four-story mill. It soon handled 70,000 bushels of wheat each year and received a first-place medal for its flour in the Philadelphia Centennial Exposition of 1876. In 1878 Wilcox, by this time sole proprietor, built a second and larger mill at Oxford. The 44-by-56-foot mill had a daily capacity of 400 bushels of wheat. Wilcox hauled the flour to Hastings for shipment.[40]

Martin Gunderson learned milling in Cannon Falls and later founded in Kenyon one of the county's most prosperous mills. Gunderson's Norwegian immigrant parents brought him to Holden in 1857. He began his career with wheat by helping his family grow and transport the grain. In his early twenties, he began milling work for John Mattson in Cannon Falls. Later he was head miller at $75 at month. In 1881 Gunderson married his boss's daughter Ella.[41]

The Gundersons, along with James McReynolds, purchased half-interest in a Kenyon gristmill. A year later Gunderson's brother G. B. bought out McReynolds, and the mill became known as Gunderson Brothers. Martin became sole owner in 1887 and seven years later constructed a mill and elevator along the Chicago Great Western tracks in eastern Kenyon. Gunderson's Mill, a steam-powered operation, had a capacity of 200 barrels of flour a day and storage for 30,000 bushels of wheat. It operated around the clock for 15 years.

Minnesota's continued economic expansion in the last decades of the 19th century depended upon the development of railroads. The state's growing grain production needed railroad links to reach eastern markets. But by 1866 five

Hay Creek's Hawkeye, or Meyer, Mills also served county farmers. *GCHS*

different railroad companies had built just 105 miles of track. A traveler leaving the state undertook long, tiring, costly trips by steamboat or stagecoach.[42]

Stagecoach routes evolved early in Goodhue County's history, the first stageline developing in 1855 out of a need to deliver mail. David Hancock operated the route connecting Red Wing, the only steamboat stop in the area, with the Mississippi River settlements of Wacouta, Westervelt (later Frontenac), and Central Point. This route later expanded to Wabasha County's Lake City and Read's Landing. Hancock used a horse to make deliveries to Winona during the winter of 1855–56. He earned $16 for the round trip, using the old military road between Fort Snelling and Prairie du Chien.[43]

The St. Paul-to-Dubuque stage route, established in 1854, cut diagonally across the county. Originally it featured three county stops—Cannon Falls, Burr Oak Springs in Belle Creek township, and Poplar Grove in Pine Island township. In 1857 a more direct route sent the coaches through Wastedo, Hader, Minneola, and Zumbrota. U.S. Highway 52 later traced the path of this road.[44]

A trip from St. Paul to Dubuque began at 4:00 A.M., when a four-horse stagecoach left the Minnesota capital. The coach passed through Goodhue County during midday before reaching Rochester at 5:00 P.M. That 90-mile, 13-hour leg of the journey required frequent changing of teams. Hader had a station with 16 horses ready for work and another 16 recovering from travel.[45]

The typical Concord-style stagecoach carried six people riding on narrow, padded leather cushions, three facing forward and three back. Its rocky ride buffeted the passengers despite a carefully designed suspension system. The coach's body rested on two long slings of thick, layered bullhide extending from front to back and attached to a metal standard bolted to the axle.[46]

Three other early stagecoach routes radiated from Red Wing. One headed west to Faribault through Vasa, Spring Creek, and Cannon Falls. The first regular mail route to Cannon Falls, it ran three times a week. A southwesterly coach road along the old wheat trail linked Red Wing to Kenyon as well as Featherstone, Belle Creek, and Wanamingo. A southerly trail joined Red Wing with the Dodge County seat, Mantorville. This coach road crossed Hay Creek, Goodhue, Zumbrota, and Roscoe as well as Ayr and Fairpoint in Cherry Grove township.[47]

While stagecoaches linked many communities of the area, the people of Minnesota impatiently awaited the arrival of the railroads. Local and state governmental bodies, in their eagerness to secure rail links, provided land and financial aid to railroading entrepreneurs. Railroad companies began to expand into a welcoming Minnesota as the Civil War concluded.[48]

One proposed rail route along the Mississippi River valley joined the capital of St. Paul with the well-established river towns of Hastings, Red Wing, Winona, and points south. A pontoon bridge at McGregor, Iowa, already linked that town to the east bank of the Mississippi and Prairie du Chien, Wisconsin. A Minnesota traveler could reach Chicago in less than two days once railroads connected with McGregor. The St. Paul and Chicago Railroad began construction from the north end of this new river line, joining St. Paul and Hastings in July 1869. On October 8, 1870, the tracks reached Red Wing. A 40-mile stretch between Red Wing and Weaver was all that remained unfinished.[49]

A formidable roadblock in the person of Civil War hero William Colvill temporarily halted construction the next summer. The money offered by the railroad for right-of-way over the land owned by his wife, Jane, left Colvill feeling cheated and angry. In response, Red Wing's most famous resident thwarted the railroad men by rapidly constructing a house on the rail grade. When the crew returned, Colvill, sporting a pistol in his belt, ordered the men off the land. If Robert E. Lee and the Army of Northern Virginia could not intimidate William Colvill, a mere railroad-construction gang could not shake his resolve.[50]

Representatives of the rail company explained to Colvill that their charter allowed them to proceed. The colonel returned to his house, defying continued construction. After the railroaders' attempts to remove the veteran failed, they neatly stacked his belongings outside the house and tore it down around him. That afternoon Colvill had 11 of the railroad men arrested. Colvill, a lawyer, argued that the construction violated his constitutional rights, contending that when private property is condemned for public purposes, "just compensation" is required. He called the railroad's offer unfair because its charter allowed payment only for appropriated land. He wanted consideration of the resulting devaluation of remaining land. Colvill's arguments failed to halt construction, but he received several hundred dollars more than the original offer.

Finally, on October 7, 1871, the St. Paul and Chicago Road announced regular train service between St. Paul and Minnesota City, just north of Winona. Trains left St. Paul at 8:45 A.M., making stops in Newport, Cottage Grove, Hastings, and Etter before reaching Red Wing at noon. The trains also stopped at Frontenac and six more stations before reaching Minnesota City at 4:05. Later completion of a railroad bridge at Winona extended service to Chicago with two daily passenger trains each way. The Winona bridge also carried freight traffic. Trains from Chicago could reach St. Paul in 18 to 20 hours.[51]

Travel by train took some getting used to. Initially the arrival of trains, signaled by their whistles and bells, drew people to the depot to observe the activity. In January 1871, the third month of rail service, a train reached the Red Wing depot to the usual excitement. "Great was the disappointment of our citizens, and great was the astonishment of the conductor . . . when it was discovered that there was not a single passenger," wrote Justice of the Peace Chris Graham. The passenger car had somehow broken free of the engine. The engineer reversed and later found the car and its passengers near Hastings. The passengers, assuming there was reason for their predicament, waited quietly. Upon discovering the "facts in the case, they were one and all very indignant."[52]

In the mid-1870s the Minnesota Midland Railway Company commenced operations in an attempt to answer the demand for rail service to the southeastern sections of Goodhue County. Midland's organizers proposed a narrow-gauge line (with tracks closer together than the standard 4 feet, 8.5 inches) between Wabasha and Zumbrota, with a continuation to the Dakota Territory border. Midland grading crews went to work in April 1877. Workers completed 25 miles by mid-September when funds for the project ran out. Crews halted with 61 miles of developed grade and just 30 miles of track down, all in Wabasha County. The towns providing Midland with cash had little more than a raised path of earth to show for their investment.[53]

Lucius F. Hubbard of Red Wing soon eyed the incomplete Midland route. By 1878 Hubbard, 42, had amassed a small fortune in the grain and milling industry. The Civil War hero also took interest in politics and within three years was elected governor of Minnesota. Hubbard knew the area to be serviced by Midland. Since the late 1860s he had held a major interest in a mill at Forest Mills on the Zumbro River, two miles east of Zumbrota. The mill, run under the name Hubbard, Wells and Company, was among the largest in the county.[54]

Forest Mills was a thriving community of about a hundred people. It grew around the mill, which according to the 1870 census produced 24,500 barrels of flour worth $85,000 and $12,000 in feed. The cooper's shop made $13,000 worth of barrels. The village had a blacksmith shop, two livery barns, a sash-and-door factory, harness shop, and other businesses established around the economic base provided by the mill. Every Thursday about 30 teams pulling wagons hauled flour from the village to Red Wing. Clearly, Forest Mills would benefit from completion of the Minnesota Midland Railroad and its access to Wabasha.[55]

Hubbard, his Forest Mills partner William "Billy" Wells, and James G. Lawrence bought five-ninths control of Midland, and rail construction recommenced in spring 1878. Billy Wells, key to the partnership's hopes, had suffered severe war wounds in the Civil War. After his discharge in March 1864, he returned to Goodhue County, married Emma Dickey, and three years later helped establish the Forest Mills flour mill. The energetic Wells, now in charge of the Midland railroad construction, made quick progress. His crews built 45 miles of track in 50 days, a remarkable achievement considering the twisting terrain of the lower Zumbro valley. On May 12 they reached Mazeppa. Less than ten miles away lay Forest Mills and Zumbrota.[56]

At that same moment, another line's tracks stretched towards Zumbrota. The Rochester and Northern Minnesota Railroad (later part of the Northwestern system) received a bonus to run a connection between Rochester and Zumbrota and ultimately to forge a link to St. Paul. Pine Islanders favored this route over Midland's since it would pass through their town. Those in Forest Mills and Mazeppa opposed the Rochester-to-Zumbrota track since it bypassed their villages. A rumor spread that Pine Islanders burned effigies of Billy Wells and Thomas Kellett, one of Zumbrota's founding fathers. The Pine Island correspondent of the Red Wing *Argus* later denied the account in print.[57]

Rumors aside, one thing was certain—two competing railroads were racing for Zumbrota. Citizens in Zumbrota township gave the Rochester and Northern a boost when they voted it $10,000 for construction. Newspaper reports noted that the crew worked by lamplight on a Saturday night to gain an edge on the Midland men. The Rochester and Northern reached the outskirts of Zumbrota first but still faced considerable grading and track-laying.[58]

More than pride was at stake. Railroad tradition dictated that when two competing railroad grades met, the company that *crossed* the competitor's line must build and maintain the crossing. All day Sunday May 19 and again on Monday, workers for both companies struggled to finish their tracks. The lines were parallel, and the crews graded side by side with little evident friction.[59]

What happened next became county legend. Around 2:00 P.M. Tuesday, a train drawing a party of Midland officials, their backers, and a brass band reached the work parties. The Midlanders demanded that Rochester and Northern contractor George W. Flower give way. He would not. Zumbrota officials then called a town meeting and decided to ask Flower to allow Midland the right of way since "blood would be shed" if he didn't. Flower didn't budge.[60]

While negotiations continued in Zumbrota, a Minnesota Midland officer, in quest of an injunction against the enemy line, took a locomotive back to Wabasha, then north to Red Wing. The next morning he returned with Goodhue County Sheriff Martin Chandler and the injunction. Nonetheless, as the

This crew prepared grade for tracks in the 1878 "race for Zumbrota." *GCHS*

legal wrangling continued, the Midland men made a preemptive strike. During the opposing crew's dinner break, Midland workers, observed by a reporter, "formed two lines and quietly took up the Northwestern [Rochester and Northern] track and lowered their grade about two feet, put in a switch, and established themselves squarely on the grading of the Northwestern company, in fact they are there now."[61] Thus the Midland men took possession of the "battlefield." The Rochester crew returned to find a Midland engine and train on the tracks. The fact that the land the train stood on was the property of Midland's co-owner and construction chief, Billy Wells, settled the issue.

On June 2, 1878, Minnesota Midland began its 61-mile passenger service with three trains daily between Wabasha and Zumbrota. The completed Midland line became a takeover target. In August the Chicago, Milwaukee and St. Paul (CM&STP) took control of Midland, although official transfer was still a few years off. The Minnesota Midland's twisting route through the Zumbro valley caused it to be known locally as the "crookedest railroad in the world." Midland maintained its narrow-gauge trackage until 1903 when the line was adjusted to the standard and the route extended to Faribault.[62]

Citizens of Belle Creek and Leon showed interest in a railroad through the center of the county. In the mid-1870s Minnesota Midland was the logical line to extend such service. Its narrow-gauge track and the need to raise bonus money to entice rail companies raised serious concerns, however. One Hader resident wrote to the Goodhue County *Republican* welcoming railroads but criticizing the narrow-gauge concept. He added, "Neither Belle Creek, Wana-mingo, nor Leon will take advice of Minneolians [or] the Zumbrotians on the subject of bonuses."[63]

Wanamingo received rail service, but Belle Creek and Leon never were connected to the railroad net. The CM&STP route to Faribault cut through Wanamingo, a move finalizing a change in the village's location. The original site of "Old Wanamingo" was a mile northeast of the present town. The community's gradual shift to the west commenced in 1858 with construction of a flour mill on the Zumbro. The extension of CM&STP railroad through Wana-mingo triggered the platting of the newer town site by the Milwaukee Land Company in 1904, relegating the original site to secondary status.[64]

Cannon Falls was the object of another railroad competition. In 1882 the Minnesota Central and Milwaukee railroads each tried to be the first to link Northfield with Cannon Falls. The Milwaukee took the lead as the lines neared the city. On October 27, 1882, the first train, an excursion from Northfield, entered the town on Milwaukee tracks. The train included four coaches, four boxcars with seats, one caboose, and a flat car. Some of the train's crowd of passengers rode on top of the cars. The excursion train reached Cannon Falls around 3:00 P.M., greeted by an excited crowd estimated at 1,500.[65]

The Minnesota Central later reached Mankato with its Cannon Valley di-vision in May 1887. The Cannon Valley line did not make money, however, and the financial panic of 1893 caused its foreclosure. The canny A. B. Stickney, president of the more powerful Chicago Great Western (CGW), bought it af-ter another railroad could not make a success of the old Cannon Valley route. Stickney figured that carrying carloads of stone, lime, and cement from Man-kato and clay products from Red Wing would be profitable. The CGW retained its strong presence in Goodhue County until the mid-1960s.[66]

Railroads were crucial to the development and growth of several Goodhue County villages and significant in the death and abandonment of others. The Chicago Great Western (CGW), for example, ran through villages in western Goodhue County. The arrival of the CGW in 1884 resulted in the platting of the village of Dennison. Straddling the Goodhue and Rice County border, the vil-lage claimed the distinction of incorporation in two counties. The same line stretched through the village of Kenyon. The growth of Kenyon after the Civil War was slow until 1885, when the coming of the railroad produced a boom as-suring the town's future. The first CGW train chugged into Kenyon over the high wooden trestle spanning the Zumbro River on September 24, 1885.[67]

The railroads bypassed Leon, Belle Creek, and Roscoe townships while barely touching Cherry Grove and Warsaw. Several small villages in those ar-eas soon experienced the isolation caused by an absence of rail service. The first of three villages known as Belle Creek, for instance, grew up around Samuel

Grain elevators, such as this one in Stanton township, popped up along newly established rail lines of the region. The Chicago Great Western built this track. *CFHS*

P. Chandler's way station on an early wheat road to Red Wing. A post office, blacksmith shop, general store, and an Episcopal church Chandler helped found were part of the hamlet located in section 20 of the township. The village lost much of its importance with the construction of the Minnesota Central Railroad in 1882.[68]

Roscoe in southwestern Roscoe township and Wastedo in south-central Leon township also suffered from a lack of rail service. Hopeful developers platted both villages in the summer of 1857, yet neither fulfilled the expectations of their proprietors. The absence of waterpower also limited the prospects of Roscoe and Wastedo.[69]

The ambitions of railroad developers could not always be fulfilled. Underfinanced, overreaching attempts to cash in on the railroad boom carried no guarantees. In the late 1880s, for example, leading Red Wing and Duluth businessmen developed the Duluth, Red Wing and Southern (DRW&S) in an attempt to establish a connection between Great Lakes shipping and Iowa agriculture through Red Wing. Silas Foot, founder of Foot Tanning Company, was the driving force behind the DRW&S. He dreamed of making Red Wing the principal city of the Northwest.[70]

In a promotional pamphlet, the DRW&S proprietors envisioned a more industrialized Goodhue County with stoneware factories using local clay, fields of flax for Cannon River linen-producing factories, "flocks of sheep . . . bleating their consent to part with their fleeces" for the new woolen mills of the Cannon, and the Red Wing wharves piled with bales of southern cotton. Meanwhile, trains would ship Lake Superior iron and copper deposits to "the future smelting works, foundries, machine shops and rolling mills of Red Wing."[71]

The project could not meet such great expectations, but it did result in the creation of Goodhue village, a new community in the county. The new rail route south cut through Hay Creek and on to Zumbrota despite the spirited efforts of Belle Creek citizens to route the proposed railroad through their township. In the summer of 1888, about 600 men and 500 teams of horses worked to prepare the track roadbed between Red Wing and Zumbrota. A year later, in June 1889, Theodore Sheldon, another major force in the DRW&S organization, saw need for a train station between Red Wing and Zumbrota and purchased 30 acres for a village site he named Goodhue. Soon a Sheldon grain elevator went up, along with interest in the new town. Lots along Broadway were going for $100, and a building boom was underway. [72]

The DRW&S was soon under fire, with the billing by its organizers as the "Most Important Projected Line in the Northwest" seriously undermined. The Stillwater *Democrat* commented in the winter of 1891 that the DRW&S was the "worst managed, worst equipped and unreliable bob-tail, one-horse, Jim Crow railroad on the face of the North American continent." The Chicago Great Western system eventually assumed its control.[73]

A like attempt to link Red Wing with the Lake Superior region also failed. Owners of a new railroad, the Superior, Red Wing & Southern, also known as the Red Wing Route, had hired crews to grade the road's first segment when the Panic of 1893 halted construction.[74]

Several factors combined to usher the era of King Wheat into post-Civil War Minnesota and its premier wheat-growing county, Goodhue. Yet even as Red Wing celebrated its achievement as the world's largest primary wheat market in 1873, an omen of problems with wheat cultivation loomed. That year Rocky Mountain locusts, commonly called grasshoppers, began cutting a swath through northern Colorado and southern Wyoming. The crop-devouring grasshoppers reached Nebraska and Dakota Territory, then northern Iowa and Minnesota. The plague ranged as far south as Texas and New Mexico and north into Canada. Farmers struggled to survive crop destruction through one growing season, only to find the grasshoppers returning in succeeding years. People said that "the hoppers would eat everything but the mortgage."[75]

To their great good fortune, the farmers of Goodhue County were largely spared the grasshopper plague ravaging the south-central and western sections of the state. But days of reckoning lay ahead for prosperous Goodhue County and its neighbors in the southeast. The nation's economy was about to dip into another damaging financial slump, and farmers spared the scourge of the hopper would see destruction wrought by stem rust and chinch bugs reaching into their wheat fields. King Wheat was about to be dethroned.

Warehouse.                    Mill.                    Cooper Shop.

**GARDNER & MOORE,**

*Merchant Millers,*

**GOODHUE MILLS,**

**CANNON FALLS,**

**Goodhue County, Minnesota.**

STEPHEN GARDNER,          CHAS. A. MOORE,
     Hastings.                         Cannon Falls.

# 7

## *Growth of Business and Industry—*
## *The Stirrings of Labor*

As the wheat harvest strained the storage capacity of Red Wing and other nearby grain ports in the autumn of 1873, Goodhue County's economic prospects had never looked better. The nation's premier wheat-growing county was also broadening its economic base. From 1870 to 1873, Red Wing saw the opening of a stone quarry, a cooperage, a furniture factory, and a tannery, as well as the expansion of industries including wagonworks, lumber mills, breweries, printing plants, and harness factories.[1]

While the farmers of Goodhue County gathered the 1873 harvest, another event rocked America's financial establishment. One of the country's most powerful banking concerns, Jay Cooke and Company, failed in September, precipitating a crisis that overwhelmed the nation's credit system. What would become the "Panic of 1873" caused bank failures, factory layoffs, and the temporary closing of the New York Stock Exchange. The effects of the panic continued until the end of the century, shattering the confidence of those who believed in the inevitability of continuing economic progress. For Americans familiar with the words "as rich as Jay Cooke," the collapse was staggering.[2]

Cooke's financial empire floundered when he overextended his resources in an attempt to establish the Northern Pacific Railroad, which he hoped would become the nation's second transcontinental line. His proposed rail link was to join Lake Superior and Minnesota with the Pacific Northwest. Cooke marketed $100 million in bonds to underwrite the project and quickly built support, but the money-devouring railroad required more cash. Shortly before noon on September 18, with reserves dwindling and no help from political allies in sight, Cooke closed his firm. By the end of the day, 37 New York banks and brokerage houses did the same. On September 21, to save Wall Street from collapse, the stock exchange announced suspension of operations for ten days.[3]

The post-Civil War railroad boom, under full steam across the nation as well as in Goodhue County, suffocated in the Cooke-inspired meltdown. Over-expansion, poor management, and speculative credit combined to send more than half of America's railroads into receivership by 1876. The Minnesota Midland's 1877 attempt to link southern Goodhue County to Wabasha ran out of money with just 30 miles of track laid. Rail construction in the county and state slowed or stopped until the early 1880s.[4]

Residents of the state did better than other Americans during the downturn. This was especially true in comparison to the economic depression of 1857, when Goodhue County and Minnesota suffered terribly from the nation's financial plight. The farm economy of the 1870s did not depend on the forces that combined to cripple heavy industry. Minnesota farmers, however, experienced a combination of low prices for farm products and high costs of handling and transport.[5]

---

Gloomy reports are coming in from all quarters [of Goodhue County] today, of the condition of the crops. Many samples of wheat, said to be a fair average, have been brought in, which show a heavy blight—from 50 to 75 percent. The stalks from the head down several inches are dead and covered with black rust and the heads also are turning black.

The ominous newspaper report from July 21, 1878, also noted that while wheat on higher ground seemed in better condition, few fields would yield ten bushels per acre, and a great many might not reach five.[6]

The Goodhue County crop report echoed others received from considerable areas of Minnesota, Wisconsin, and Iowa; stem rust was destroying significant portions of the wheat crop. In 1878 Minnesota, where wheat occupied 69 percent of the cultivated land, the plant disease was potentially ruinous. The rust, also called "mildew," degraded the grain to little more than fodder for stock.[7]

Ironically, the 1878 growing season had begun with great promise. On June 1, the agriculture bureau reported spring wheat at 106 percent of normal growth, even better in Iowa and Wisconsin. On July 10, predictions called for a Minnesota wheat yield of 19 to 20 bushels per acre. But a change in the weather dimmed early hopes. A period of hot, muggy weather combined with frequent rain and storms punished the region, probably promoting the blight. By July 22, Minnesota and Iowa farmers expected 27 percent of their wheat crop to be affected. Neighbors in Wisconsin figured the blight would damage 17 percent of their crop. The plague also infected oats and barley.[8]

On July 29, the St. Paul *Pioneer Press* wrote an epitaph for the fields affected by the rust: "To those unfortunate enough to own wheat fields in southeastern Minnesota and northern Iowa it will not be necessary to speak of blight and rust and general failure . . . it has for some days been too apparent." Actual wheat yields in Minnesota that autumn averaged 12 bushels per acre. The fields of the southeast produced less. Mower County farms, hardest hit in the state, saw yields of 6.7 bushels per acre. In the years before 1878, the average yield was 15 to 17 bushels.

Goodhue County's leadership in wheat production was now under threat, and stem rust wasn't the only factor. The railroad network and line elevators reached north and westward to Minnesota's newest fields, inspiring a fundamental shift in the location of state wheat production. The change was startling. In 1875, eight Minnesota counties raised more than a million bushels of wheat. All were in the southeast, bounded by the Mississippi and Minnesota Rivers and the Iowa border. Ten years later, only one of the state's leading wheat-producing counties, Goodhue, was in southeastern Minnesota. The northwestern area boasted three of the top five wheat-producing counties.[9]

With the new land dedicated to wheat production, the American farmer, despite blight in some areas, began to produce more grain than the domestic market could handle. This resulted in sales of wheat on the international market. Likewise, increased world production of the grain, particularly in Canada, Argentina, Australia, and Russia, brought competition to American wheat-growers. In 1866, U.S. farmers received $1.45 per bushel of wheat. By 1889 the price had fallen to 69 cents and then to 49 cents in 1894.[10]

Farmers in Minnesota's southeast began losing confidence in wheat. They would have to make fundamental changes.[11] James J. Hill, the St. Paul railroad baron, told of new approaches to farming practice in an address to the Minnesota Historical Society in January 1897:

> Minnesota has been called a wheat-field and our farmers have been told that they can only raise wheat successfully. In . . . southern Minnesota, that is an exploded idea; they know better . . . Red Wing . . . for a few years was considered the champion wheat market, the largest primary wheat market in the world . . . but the wheat market of Red Wing has passed away, and the farmers there are doing other and better things.[12]

Hill spoke with knowledge. His success in advancing his Great Northern Railway empire into the fields of the Red River Valley and beyond played a part in the decline of wheat farming in Goodhue County and the southeast.

In 1861 a German immigrant named John Paul arrived in Goodhue Township. The 42-year-old newcomer, a potter by trade, had discovered that the north central sections of the township contained the kind of clay needed for his work. For $7.50 he bought an old schoolhouse and converted it into a small pottery. From this humble beginning sprang a Goodhue County industry that flourished for more than a hundred years.[13]

Paul produced earthenware jars, jugs, and crocks in his small pottery, selling most of them to neighbors. In September 1868, the potter married Margaret Liebe, a 27-year-old German-American. When the couple needed money for a mortgage five months later, Paul secured the cash by agreeing to repay the loan with earthenware totaling 800 gallons' capacity at 12 cents per gallon. Several years later the father of the county's pottery industry moved his family to Shakopee. In September 1881, Red Wing Stoneware Company bought the tax-delinquent Paul property for $4.22.[14]

William M. Philleo also saw promise in making earthenware and, in the late 1860s, built a manufacturing plant in his hometown of Red Wing. He used coarse clay, likely from the Trout Brook area not far from his West Main pottery, to turn out unglazed terra-cotta products. After losing the first building to fire, Philleo tried to rekindle his pottery idea by starting a new terra-cotta company in St. Paul. He attempted to enlist prominent banker Ferdinand Willius, among others, in bankrolling his idea, but all rebuffed him.[15]

David Hallum, another associate of Philleo, opened his own pottery on Red Wing's Third Street, operating a backyard kiln. Using better-quality clay from Goodhue township, Hallum had some success. He soon felt the pressure of others interested in establishing a much larger stoneware operation in the city.[16]

In February 1877 a group of Red Wing business leaders created Red Wing Stoneware Company, capitalizing the firm at $10,000. E. T. Howard was superintendent of the facility. Proceeding cautiously, the owners bought the kiln of David Hallum and conducted stoneware manufacturing experiments through August. By January 1878, the owners were ready to order production to begin in a new 40-by-70-foot West End building. Red Wing Iron Works manufactured the 24-horsepower engine and boiler that provided power and steam for grinding, turning, and drying clay. By midsummer the plant turned out 6,000 gallons of high-quality stoneware per week, and demand for its products grew.[17]

That Red Wing Stoneware was an immediate hit was not lost upon Theodore Sheldon, the city's leading businessman. In 1883 Sheldon helped spearhead a successful drive to erect a new pottery, Minnesota Stoneware Company, across West Main Street from Red Wing Stoneware. Ed Mallory, who learned the trade from his uncle E. T. Howard, the competition's factory boss, was key man and plant superintendent in the new business. Upon opening, Minnesota Stoneware boasted 18 pottery wheels to its rival's 12.[18]

The stoneware business in west Red Wing became even more competitive in 1892 with the founding of North Star Stoneware. E. T. Howard, returning to the industry after a temporary absence, took over supervision of the North Star operation. By this time John Rich joined Edward Baker in management at Red Wing Stoneware. At Minnesota Stoneware, meanwhile, ambitious E. S. Hoyt advanced from a sales position to manager. All three companies made nearly identical products, including butter crocks, large pickle jars, and jugs.[19]

Shortly after 1900, executives of Minnesota Stoneware and Red Wing Stoneware linked their sales forces so as to expand their markets and improve efficiency. They called their new concern Red Wing Union Stoneware Company. North Star Stoneware, now at a disadvantage, weakened and was soon absorbed by its powerful neighbor. The three former rivals, united under the title Red Wing Potteries, became a mainstay of the city and county clay industry.

While the natural clay deposits of Goodhue County provided the basis for one thriving industry, its deposits of limestone, remnants of the ancient oceans that once covered the region, provided another. The county's quarries produced stone ranging from rough, durable building material to the finest sawed and dressed stone. The quarries also provided stone for curbing, paving, and riprapping (erosion protection) as well as lime for building and agricultural uses.[20]

The inhabitants of the area had long used limestone. Prehistoric limestone cairns found on hills overlooking the Cannon River demonstrate ancient stone construction. Euroamerican settlers used the stone first for foundations and later for larger buildings. By the last quarter of the 19th century, Goodhue County quarries furnished stone and lime throughout the nation. Prairie du Chien or Oneota dolomite formations, which cap the bluffs of the Mississippi River valley, produced "Frontenac stone," the county's best-known building material. In 1874, one expert called the straw-colored dolomite, quarried from the river bluffs in Old Frontenac, the best stone for architectural purposes he had seen "either in Europe or America." [21]

Quarries in other parts of the county produced limestone for smaller projects such as foundations for farm homes and buildings. G. P. "Stone" Johnson of Cannon Falls owned a quarry on a bluff a half-mile from the Great Western rail tracks, providing limestone for local buildings including the First Congregational Church. Stone for the 1893 construction of the Cannon Falls school also came from Johnson's quarry. The school cost $16,000, but the practical citizens of Cannon Falls estimated that they saved at least $4,000 by using local material. The smaller, Bert Johnson quarry south of Cannon Falls also provided stone for local projects. In the Zumbrota area, five small farms, including John P. Operun's, operated quarries.[22]

Kilns reduced lime from the stone of the dolomite formations. Sufficiently burned, the stone produced lime, which stonemasons needed for mortar. Red Wing's Barn and Sorin's bluffs were major sources of stone for lime production. Quarries on the south end of town later provided tons of stone for use in the lime manufacturing process.[23]

Around 1853 Phineas Fish, Red Wing's first limestone burner, reduced large fragments of stone that had fallen from the face of Barn Bluff. The industry expanded and began to mature by the mid-1870s. The city's kilns produced nearly 400 barrels of lime per day, sold for 75 cents a barrel. Red Wing lime was rated as the best in the state, and the city became known as Minnesota's "lime center."

The lime and stone industry in Red Wing began to wane as the century ended, but over the years the city provided a home to 16 quarrying companies. Among the prominent: Gustaf Adolf Carlson's large quarry on the east end riverside of Barn Bluff provided stone for his three lime kilns. The F. J. Linne quarry in the middle of the bluff faced the city's east end with two kilns and a supply of building stone. The Charles Betcher quarry on Sorin's Bluff overlooked "Swede Hill" on Red Wing's East Seventh Street. Andrew Danielson's building stone quarry on Zumbrota Road, now Highway 58, was just inside the city. Robert Berglund's (later Gust Lillyblad's) lime-and-building-stone operation was across the road from Danielson's. The Lille-John quarry adjacent to the Lillyblad site took its name from operator John Johnson. The Andrew Haglund quarry was next to Johnson's, a former partner. G. A. Carlson's second quarry, the "Little Carlson" lime manufactory, was on Sorin's Bluff.[24]

Although best known for lime production, the Red Wing quarries provided stone for several well-known structures. The Berglund-Lillyblad quarry fur-

Workers dump limestone from a Barn Bluff quarry into rail cars in 1904. *GCHS*

nished much of the material for James J. Hill's famous stone-arch bridge near St. Anthony Falls in Minneapolis as well as for the Hastings spiral bridge. Danielson and Lille-John provided stone for Red Wing's first span across the Mississippi—the 1895 Wagon Bridge. Carlson's quarry on Sorin's Bluff produced stone for city construction projects, including the Sheldon Auditorium. At its busiest, the Berglund quarry, with the masts of its many stone-lifting derricks and guy cables, appeared to be a "veritable little shipyard or harbor."[25]

Some owners prospered in the stone and lime industry. G. A. Carlson, an alderman and chairman of the city council in 1890, did well with his Pioneer Lime and Stone Company. His Barn Bluff quarry featured a 90-foot perpendicular shaft leading to a 150-foot tunnel with a railroad track to move stone. Robert Berglund worked for Carlson for five years before opening his own business. By 1874 Berglund employed seven to ten men in summer and quarried stone valued at $12,000 to $15,000 annually. Andrew Danielson, an early lime dealer, expanded into quarrying of building stone and contracting.[26]

Carlson proved the most innovative of the quarry owners. His large, productive "tunnel" kiln on Barn Bluff threw off intense heat, punishing the lime burners who operated it. He employed a practical delivery method to move stone from his "Little Carlson" quarry on Sorin's Bluff to the kiln below. Carlson had his workers dump the stone over the edge of the quarry, letting it thunder downhill to the kiln. He also originated a small cable rail system that allowed the weight of a loaded dump car lowered down the bluff to pull an emptied car back up to the quarry.[27]

Carlson's Pioneer Lime and Stone Company's six kilns and three stone quarries produced four carloads of lime daily when running at capacity. The kilns each burned 20 cords of wood to provide the required heat. He employed 65 men, and all but one, a German named Bren, were Swedes like himself. Carlson paid his workers in "Kempe-pengar" (Kempe-money) or scrip, which could be exchanged at Charles Kempe's store for food, clothing, and other necessities.[28]

Sandblasting with explosives proved the most efficient method of quarrying stone. The process required quarrymen to drill through the layers of desired stone. Dynamiters then cleared and filled the hole with a powder charge and attached a fuse. They added fine dry sand on top of the charge; its weight allowed the sand to "pack itself," making unnecessary any dangerous ramming. The initial sandblast usually started a slight crack in the limestone. Then the blasters packed more powder into the hole and repeated the process until they freed the stone mass.[29]

Blasting on Barn Bluff in 1907 incited a civic debate over the future of the bluff and, indirectly, the prospects of quarrying in the city. The CM&STP railroad secured a contract for the removal of 200,000 cubic feet of stone from the famous landmark. Jens K. Grondahl, editor of the Red Wing *Daily Republican*, declared that the bluff was in danger and challenged citizens to save it. The newspaper secured a pledge from the Milwaukee Road president to cease attempts to open a quarry on the bluff. The promise proved of no value. Investigators discovered that a Minneapolis contractor planning to use stone for riprapping along rail tracks controlled the rights to rock on the face of the bluff.[30]

The quarriers' assault on Barn Bluff persisted as the leading citizens worked to halt operations. They also moved to purchase the bluff. Meanwhile, on January 24, 1907, a dynamite explosion injured six workers, and on February 18 falling rock killed a laborer. On March 9 the *Daily Republican* reported more problems, including explosions "felt over the entire city." Two days later the newspaper claimed the shock of bluff explosions laid bare of plaster many east Red Wing homes. In April a "monster charge" produced enough rock to keep a crew of 100 men working several days.[31]

The *Daily Republican* renewed its attack against quarrying the following year. The March 17 edition reported that the storage of explosives in a poorly secured tunnel on the eastern end of the bluff endangered the entire city. The newspaper claimed witnesses spotted boys using the door to the tunnel as a rifle target. The paper added that a falling stone, a clumsy workman, or "some maniac might break in and set off the charge."[32]

The war of words continued from March through May. Some believed the quarrying on the bluff was a proper business that should be left alone. One bluff property owner supporting the quarrymen wrote that he would "like to cut a hole right through the bluff out of sheer spite." Commenting on reports that people in Ellsworth, Wisconsin, felt tremors from the Red Wing blasting, the *Daily Republican* observed, "When the vibrations can be discerned a distance of twenty miles or more, it is not strange that the people in East Red Wing are annoyed." The campaign against the quarrying wore down the contractors, who announced operations would cease within a month. They finally halted blasting on May 9, 1908.[33]

City leaders immediately solicited money to buy Barn Bluff and make it a public park. James Lawther, a wealthy ex-Red Wing businessman retired and living in his native Ireland, offered to buy and donate a major part of the bluff. Charles A. Betcher, the Red Wing Manufacturing Company, and the Pierce-Simmons Bank offered their portions of bluff land without charge. On December 2, 1910, city leaders accepted transfer of Barn Bluff to the City of Red Wing.[34]

After the Barn Bluff controversy, Goodhue County's once flourishing lime-and-stone industry quickly faded. A 1921 survey of state limestone quarries contained just one mention of Goodhue County—a reference to a small quarry three miles from Kenyon "where farmers help themselves to blocks for foundations and footings for their farm buildings." The county industry became little more than a footnote in a state report.[35]

An 1843 accident near Stillwater provided an idea for the start of another Goodhue County industry. A boom on the St. Croix River broke, freeing logs awaiting processing at local sawmills and scattering timber as far downriver as St. Louis. This demonstration of the river's ability to move logs led to the development of sawmills along the Mississippi, including Red Wing and Central Point in Goodhue County.[36]

Central Point boasted the only steamboat landing in its portion of Lake Pepin, and by 1857 it became the site of two sawmills. Charles Moe erected a steampowered mill there in 1856. A second plant, later purchased by Red Wing mill owners Sidney and George Grannis, opened the next year. The Grannis brothers, Vermont natives, and two partners had established a new lumber mill competing with the Cogel and Blakely sawmill in Red Wing.[37]

By the mid-1870s, the county's sawmill industry was largely in the hands of the Grannis brothers at Central Point; Charles Betcher, a Red Wing hardware dealer in control of the former Cogel and Blakely mill; and Orrin Densmore, owner of the Red Wing Sawmill. The Grannis brothers moved from Red Wing after selling their mill property near the Mississippi to the Chicago, Milwaukee and St. Paul Railroad, which was beginning construction of the first line to the city. The Grannises then concentrated on their Central Point sawmill.[38]

The Betcher mill grew to a major concern employing nearly a hundred men. Its two steam driven circular saws, one 54 inches in diameter and the other 36, could cut 40,000 feet of lumber in 11 hours. The plant's annual production by the late 1870s was 5.5 million feet of lumber, 2 million shingles, and 1.25 million lath. Betcher kept 3.5 million feet of lumber on hand to meet retail demand. Also in the complex along the river was a planing mill that produced sash, door, window blinds, moldings, and related items.[39]

Orrin Densmore and his son Benjamin scouted possible locations for a sawmill in Minnesota Territory for two years before settling on Red Wing. Orrin wrote on December 27, 1856, that, "Red Wing seems quite a place but the growth of Cannon Falls may change the condition of things materially." Two weeks later he was considering Pine Bend, Red Wing, and Hastings. The Freeborn Mill in Red Wing was for sale in a deal that included other buildings and four acres of land running 300 by 208 feet from Main Street to the river. The Densmores decided to buy that operation.[40]

The increase in lumber mills directly affected the quality of life in Goodhue County and the state. The mills featured all the materials a prospective homebuilder needed to construct a comfortable farmhouse or city dwelling. Construction of a typical home involved the nailing together of a balloon frame of light timber upon a prepared foundation. The roof boards and shingles followed, then the sheathing of walls that might be insulated by tarred paper. The builder attached siding planed at the factory, placed window and door frames, then laid the floors and adjusted the windows and doors, making the house

This family farm, thought to have been near Cannon Falls, featured a frame house typical of the post-Civil War era. The home had a small addition. Besides owning horses and cattle, the family apparently had a pet fox. *CFHS*

fairly complete. Plastering the walls and ceiling or lining the interior with building paper finished the project. Wood- or coal-burning stoves supplied heat.[41]

The lumber, stoneware, and stone industries provided exceptions to the economic dominance of agriculture in Goodhue County in the last quarter of the 19th century. Most people of the county worked in farming, provided goods and services to farmers and their families, or processed and shipped farm produce. But entrepreneurs began to see other opportunities and moved to capitalize.

The growth of county business and industry produced a fundamental change in how people worked. The majority of farmers labored for themselves, raising food for their families and selling the surplus. Most of the small merchants and service providers who catered to the needs of the farmers were also self-employed. Industrialization began to change that picture. Those working in Goodhue County's flour-milling, stoneware, lumber, stone, and lime industries worked for manufacturers. The wage earners served at the pleasure of management, following the orders of supervisors. As the century moved to its close, a growing number of workers elected to labor for others.

Increased industrialization produced startling changes. The gross value of manufactured products in the state rose from $58,300 in 1850 to more than $76 million in 1880 and $192 million ten years later. National farm production was at an all-time high in 1890, but the value of manufactured goods had surpassed the agricultural total. The United States had become an industrial nation.[42]

Groups of workers began organizing in Minnesota before the Civil War, most actively in the St. Paul and Minneapolis area. The labor movement gained momentum in the 1870s, with at least seven strikes recorded in the state. Fifty people met in Lake City to organize, stating their object was "to protect the interests of the laboring man." Railroad workers, telegraphers, cigar makers, bricklayers, coopers, mill workers, and others formed unions, although total membership statewide remained small. The Panic of 1873 damaged the postwar climate of prosperity and unions as well.[43]

Labor activism in Goodhue County started in the county seat of Red Wing. The city featured an ample business and industrial base that provided jobs for expanding numbers of wage earners—the base from which labor organizers would build. Goodhue County, according to the 1870 census, took claim to being the state's fourth largest in population. Of its 22,618 citizens, 19 percent (4,260) lived in the growing riverport. A labor union founded there in 1869 left few traces after a short life. By 1878 a cooper's union had formed among workers in the Red Wing barrel-making industry. Shippers used the wooden barrel "almost universally as a container," and it became known as the "king of packages." Goodhue County cooperages of the 1870s concentrated on supplying oak barrels for the booming flour industry.[44]

By the late 1870s, however, reduced wheat yields in the rust-ravaged fields of southeast Minnesota combined with the development of linen flour sacks to reduce the need for barrels and the coopers who made them. The sack did not have the solid reputation of the barrel, but by then the crop diseases had degraded flour quality. The impression in Red Wing was that milling companies would "use the cheaper sacks so long as they are unable, on account of poor wheat, to turn out superior brands of flour." Red Wing's union coopers threatened a strike over job issues and were fired.[45]

La Grange Mill used sacks on European shipments only, while Diamond and Red Wing Mills shipped almost entirely by sack, with "140 pounds being the size used most." Early in 1879 La Grange sent 28 freightcar loads of sacked flour (about 630,000 pounds) to Great Britain. The mill also received 40 carloads of wheat for processing from the west. By mid-February 1879, Obediah Eames Cooperage, the city's largest, had laid off 30 men due to a decrease in barrel demand.[46]

The flour mills of Cannon Falls continued to ship their products in barrels. Mills there had their own cooperages. In 1882 Goodhue Mill, with a capacity of 200 barrels per day, employed 23 coopers, and the Cannon Falls Mill, also rated at 200 barrels, used 13. The Little Cannon Mill had a large stone cooperage to supply its 300-barrel-per-day need, and the nearby Oxford Mill also featured a cooperage.[47]

The coopers of Goodhue County survived the hard times of the 1880s, but in depleted numbers. Improved machinery reduced the need for men as well as

Workers at the Goodhue Roller Mill gathered for this photograph. This mill and others in the city made Cannon Falls a leader in flour milling. *CFHS*

the cost of barrel manufacture. Improvements in steel hoops and the use of kiln drying rather than air drying for barrel staves provided uniformity. Although the flour industry no longer relied on coopers, other manufacturers did ship their products in barrels. Still, the days of the cooper throughout the country were numbered.[48]

The rumble of labor unrest and the ensuing growth of unions became evident in the early 1880s. At least 73 unions organized around the state by 1884; St. Paul and Minneapolis accounted for 44 of them. Many of the early unions were short-lived, but their increasing number indicated interest in the movement among workers. The emergence of the Knights of Labor at mid-decade helped bring cohesion to labor organization.[49] In the meantime, occasional work stoppages or job actions drew the attention of the public. Roustabouts on the steamer *Red Wing* made news during a stop downriver in June 1876. They went on strike, demanding a dollar per day plus pay for three days off. The strikers, 20 "colored" and eight white men, left the boat, then later asked to return to work. Eight white and two black roustabouts were reemployed, but a mate brandishing a revolver ordered the others off the boat. Elsewhere, St. Cloud's stonecutters' union called nine strikes from 1881 to 1883. Duluth longshoremen reportedly won a wage strike in 1882. And Moorhead printers lost an 1882 job action in which they demanded more money.[50]

Minnesota's first labor groups were generally craft organizations—bricklayers, plasterers, carpenters, and boilermakers among the earliest—but the Knights of Labor attracted a broader membership in the eastern United States. Organizers built the Knights by developing local assemblies of men and women working in the trades. Banned from the labor society were lawyers, bankers, stockbrokers, and those involved in the liquor business. The Knights operated under rules of secrecy for fear of employer retribution; thus few knew of its early efforts. A series of successful job actions, especially the massive railroad strike of 1877, helped to publicize the group and draw new members. By 1886, Minnesota claimed 10,000 Knights. Both skilled and unskilled workers flocked to the organization, raising the prospect of craft and trade unions merging under the Knights' banner.[51]

In 1888 local interest resulted in formation of a Goodhue County Knights of Labor chapter under John J. Ferrin, president, and Byron Wilmot, secretary. The county Knights soon dissolved. Nationwide, the membership also evaporated, slumping to 100,000 actives by 1890. Another labor organization, the American Federation of Labor (AFL), was on the rise, however, building its strength by appealing to skilled workers. Local assemblies shifted their allegiance to the AFL, and the Knights of Labor declined irreversibly.[52]

Similarly, the National Grange of the Patrons of Husbandry, which prospered in the 1870s, lost strength nationally and in Goodhue County during the late 19th century. Minnesotan Oliver Kelley originated the grange concept, organizing farmers frustrated by tight money, questionable shipping rates, and opportunistic middlemen. Goodhue County's *Grange Advance*, a strong news-

This winter scene at the Kenyon Farmers Mercantile and Elevator company shows farm wagons loaded with sacks of grain to sell or grind. *John L. Cole collection*

paper voice for the Minnesota organization, articulated some farmer concerns in a representative January 1877 attack on two favorite targets. The *Advance* charged warehouse men with being "proverbial for short weights and noted for their dishonest stealings." The editorialist claimed the faults of "our politicians" defied characterization, writing, "a description of these pests would exhaust all the enunciatory adjectives in the English language." Still, improving conditions in the Midwest heartland of Grange power lessened the need for a farmer organization. The Red Wing *Republican* absorbed the *Grange Advance* in 1880.[53]

Goodhue County granges at Goodhue and Burnside typified the organizational malaise. Goodhue's grange began with 20 members in 1873, and six years later, when recordkeeping stopped, its membership had increased by just three. W. H. Bruce and his wife, Sarah, along with T. M. Lowater led the Goodhue group, whose business meetings were largely social in nature. The Burnside grange, organized in 1874 with the help of Featherstone's Master of the Grange Thomas Featherstone, had 28 charter members, 13 of them women. The membership charge was three dollars for men and 50 cents for women. Four years later the Burnside group had 24 members, eight female.[54]

The Goodhue and Burnside organizations formed during the height of grange expansion in Minnesota. Between August 1873 and September 1874, granges in the state mushroomed from 327 to 538. Two years later, as interest waned, that peak number had been nearly halved.[55]

The Grange left an impressive legacy. It chiefly was responsible in raising the Department of Agriculture to cabinet status, actively sought rural mail services, fought against the dangers of food adulteration, supported conservation measures, and began to bring ordinary citizens of the North and the South together, helping to dispel the lingering bitterness of the Civil War. The Grange also had female members and supported a woman's right to vote.[56]

A grange in decline did not mean the end of farmers' attempts to organize. Another group, the Farmers' Alliance, drew increased support, particularly in the South and Southwest. The National Farmers' Alliance, better known as the Northern Alliance, had a dual base of power in the Midwest and New York and became a part of the movement. Its growing strength pushed the alliance to the forefront of the agrarian reform movement. Minnesota felt the expansion of the Farmers' Alliance in the 1880s as the local alliances grew to 438 by 1886.

Echoing the principles of the Knights of Labor, the alliance excluded groups considered "obnoxious" to them. Included among the banned were "bankers, brokers, real-estate dealers, railroad officials, cotton buyers, and 'any person who keeps a store, who buys or sells grain.'"[57]

The Alliance and the Knights of Labor, still in their ascendancy, held a joint convention in St. Paul on September 1, 1886—a portent of a new and powerful farmer and labor coalition that would influence both local and national politics.[58]

# 8

## *Becoming 'American'—*
## *The Challenge of Assimilation*

The turbulent age of the settlement in Goodhue County gradually gave way to an era of increased social and economic stability. Beginning new lives on the Minnesota frontier developed in the people a sense of independence and pride. Impressive transportation and communication systems linked the county with the rest of the nation and the world. The populace could look with growing confidence to a brighter future for themselves and their children.

America now entered the Gilded Age, a period of industrial expansion and economic growth producing unheard-of wealth and a new class of self-made tycoons. The names and success stories of Andrew Carnegie, John D. Rockefeller, and J. P. Morgan, among others, became well known to Americans. In Minnesota, James J. Hill, the "Empire Builder," built a prodigious fortune from a powerful railroad base. Largely unchecked by government regulation, the barons of industry strained to consolidate their power. The wealth they created also enriched their associates and thousands of other minor moguls while providing jobs for American workers. Goodhue County produced its own set of industrialists, mainly in the economic seat of power in Red Wing. Theodore Sheldon, Charles A. Betcher, and John Rich were among those who started with small business bases from which they developed financial success.

The expansion of wealth depended largely on an industrial base. Most of Goodhue County's citizens, still involved in agriculture, received comparatively fewer benefits from the economic expansion. But fluctuations in the American economy also affected them less than they did industrial workers. Although the typical worker, the farmer, and the factory wage-earner kept watch for hard times, they could hardly resist spending when the economy hummed.

As early as 1880 Osee Matson (O. M.) Hall warned the people of the county about their "wild, foolish, prodigal waste of money." The Red Wing lawyer, politician, and future congressman lectured a Zumbrota audience about the increasing desire for luxury:

> We require more things to live with than did our fathers—and therefore we live better. We must have finer houses, richer furniture, more delicate and a greater variety of food—a hired girl in the kitchen and a hired man in the stable; our farms must be more extensive, our stock . . . fancier, our machinery of the latest pattern . . . Weddings are so expensive that few men can afford to marry . . . Funerals are so extravagant that it seems to cost more to put a man under ground than to keep him above."[1]

In small but noticeable increments, life became easier for the American people. They found they had more time and energy for other interests. Many chose to become active in social organizations, which were undergoing remarkable growth. In Goodhue County, national fraternal organizations such as the Free and Accepted Masons, Knights of Pythias, Independent Order of Odd Fellows, Ancient Order of United Workmen, Improved Order of Red Men, and the Benevolent and Protective Order of Elk took root. Women's affiliates soon formed, countering complaints about the cost and secrecy of the male-only orders and time spent away from home. Groups such as Order of the Eastern Star (Masons), Daughters of Rebekah (Odd Fellows), and Pythian Sisters (Knights of Pythias) sprang up in villages around the county.

Many other social organizations attracted new members. Zumbrota alone, between 1870 and 1900, formed active chapters of all the associations listed above as well as Royal Arch Masons, Modern Woodmen of America, Modern Brotherhood of America, Modern Samaritans, Brotherhood of American Yeoman, Independent Order of Good Templars, Grand Army of the Republic, Women's Relief Corps, Luren Singing Society, Mitchell Literary Society, Zumbrota Cycle Club, Tennis Club, Toboggan Club, Rifle Club, Driving Club, King's Daughters, Anti-Saloon League, Good Fellows Club, Women's Christian Temperance Union, YMCA, the Prohibition Society, and the Independent Order of Foresters.[2]

Social clubs helped to erase the ethnic distinctions of Goodhue County's population, still very much in evidence in the late 19th century. The earliest arrivals in rural Goodhue County divided according to their European origins. A simple geographic delineation showed Norwegians dominant in the southwest townships, Swedes in the north and northwest, Germans in the east, with pockets of Irish, Luxembourgers, New Englanders, and others scattered throughout.

Some, particularly in positions of religious leadership, resisted the "Americanization" of their people. Bernt J. Muus, the Norwegian-born Lutheran min-

Norwegian-born minister Bernt J. Muus, an
influential churchman of the region. *GCHS*

ister who settled in Goodhue County with his wife, Oline, in 1859, was a prominent opponent of cultural assimilation. Upon arrival, Muus began fulfilling his
task of forming Lutheran congregations in an eight-county area. He worked
industriously to complete this assignment from his base at Holden Lutheran
Church in Holden township.

The minister became known for his marathon travels to Norwegian congre-
gations by foot, ox team, or horse. In one year he led 84 religious services in
Holden and still traveled to the counties of Dakota, Carver, Meeker, Kandiyohi,
Watonwan, Nicollet, and Ramsey, and other sites to conduct 60 more meetings.
While most did not consider Muus a good preacher, his training and knowledge
nevertheless commanded the respect of his audiences.[3]

By 1870 the minister started, in Goodhue County alone, churches including Dale in Cherry Grove, Urland in Leon, Vang in Holden, and Gol and Hegre
in Kenyon. Muus, who later had two assistants, also created 20 parochial
schools.[4] His support of these Norwegian Lutheran schools resulted in a well-
publicized controversy in the spring of 1870. County Superintendent of Schools
Horace B. Wilson made a pointed attack on Muus and his schools. A former
Hamline professor and combat-tested captain of the Sixth Minnesota during
the Civil War, Wilson had standing enough to challenge the powerful minister.
He wrote of clerical mistrust of public schools and attitudes that hindered
school attendance. And he observed some instances in which children were sent
to foreign-language private schools while public schools were in session.[5]

Muus replied to the criticism, declaring common (public) schools "heathen" and ineffective because of their "essential principle" in "opposition to the kingdom of God." The minister charged the public schools with being a dangerous influence from which Lutheran children should be guarded. He also confessed that "these young republicans" (American educated youth) terrified him; he compared such students to "wild animals."

An indignant Wilson replied in the Goodhue County *Republican,* saying many Norwegian-American residents opposed the ideas of Muus. He charged Muus with being a "foreign priest and aristocrat" who stood for perpetuating "a foreign language, a foreign sentiment, and foreign institutions." The superintendent said a wave of enlightenment would "roll over our prairie, and bring all bigotry, intolerance, and superstition, ten thousand fathoms deep." He asked Muus, "If you do not like our institutions, why do you come among us?"[6]

Muus countered in the *Republican,* again criticizing the county's common schools. He began his direct, if undiplomatic, reply: "In this country, where the majority of the people don't understand so well what is good for them . . ." He claimed public schools would "mix up their [Norwegian Lutheran] Christianity," and that "There can, of course, be no common school teaching the doctrines of God set forth to men for the sake of their salvation." The minister then fired a parting shot at America in general: "[That] children here are generally behaving much worse than the children of my fatherland, is a very general impression among my countrymen."[7]

The Lutheran clergyman dedicated himself to the preservation of Norwegian culture and Lutheranism and was unyielding in his defense of the Norwegian schools. (A well-educated honors graduate from the University of Christiania, Muus also had served in Norway as editor of the *Norsk Kirketidende,* or *Norwegian Church News*).[8]

Muus's unbending ministerial style caused problems within his congregation—none larger, however, than a dispute within his home. Oline Pind Muus came from a wealthy Norwegian family, and like her husband, Bernt, was well educated and well read. They began their courtship in Norway at the height of a religious revival. The young couple married, then moved to Goodhue County in 1859. Bernt's dedication to his job and its travel demands meant often leaving his wife alone to manage the homestead.[9] Fundamental disagreements about money tore at their marriage. Bernt was generous with charitable causes but stingy with his wife. The interior of their home was spartan, and Bernt allowed only one room besides the kitchen to be used in winter so as to conserve wood. When Oline broke her leg in 1877, their neighbor, physician Just Christian Gronvold, was away, and Bernt refused to seek another doctor. Bernt told his wife to "let patience be your liniment." He refused her request for a visit home though he himself had taken a trip to Norway. As her spiritual leader, he refused her Communion after lapses in her household duties.

Their marital differences might have remained unknown were it not for a legal issue that soon became public. Oline's father died in Norway, leaving her an inheritance, which Bernt took for himself under Norwegian law; neither he nor Oline had applied for American citizenship after moving to the United States. Unwilling to accept his decision, the frustrated wife brought suit in Goodhue County District Court. Norway still operated under the principle of civil death for married women. Once married, a woman no longer had legal identity, and her rights, including that of property ownership and guardianship of children, were under the control of her husband. That law had become effective in early American courts but was in the process of change, state by state.[10]

The court ruled that since the couple had lived in Minnesota for 20 years, they were subject to Minnesota law. Oline's inheritance had reached Bernt in two installments, and since the statute of limitations had run out on the first portion, he was able to keep it. The judge ordered Bernt to pay Oline the second share of $1,118.

Such a public dispute between husband and wife was rare. That one of the parties involved was a spiritual leader of the state's Norwegian community made it extraordinary. A crowd estimated at 1,000 gathered in Holden at a February 1880 meeting to discuss Bernt's future as pastor. Oline expressed concern about the controversy, explaining that she had acted only as a last resort. The congregation voted to allow Bernt to stay until resolution of the matter.

The controversy damaged Bernt Muus's position in the community and in his home congregation, where "many chafed under the restrictions imposed by him." Giving general approval of his powerful character and leadership ability, parishioners nevertheless considered him "unyielding and sometimes harsh in dealing with human frailties." He seemed unable to tolerate those who would not or could not accept his views.[11] Furthermore, Muus and like-minded supporters of parochial education were still under fire for their part in leading the parochial school movement. The 1870 dispute with Horace Wilson was behind him, but the debate between supporters of common and parochial schools continued into the 1880s. The Goodhue County *Republican* assailed Muus and the Norwegian Lutheran Synod for its opposition to public schools, portraying their congregations as having "no principle, no will, excepting those of their master. The majority of them are empty bottles . . . filled by Muus."

Muus was more than a martinet. He went to great lengths to assist immigrant countrymen, finding them lodging, providing transportation, lending wagons and oxen. A sense of humor could shine through his austere visage. Muus once demanded to know whether a 15-year-old in confirmation class had chewing tobacco. When the boy nervously answered yes, the minister said, "Give me a chew."[12]

The longer he stayed in Goodhue County, the more Muus felt the effect of American culture on his congregations. A differing set of customs loosened his steadfast grip on his flock as he fought for what he believed to be their salvation. In Norway the Lutheran Church was the state-sponsored religion under which a pastor had civic authority. America's constitutional separation of church and state left religion an open field, where Lutherans had no more or less power than others. The more comfortable certainties of the Old World were disappearing. Muus was losing his struggle against "Americanization."

In January 1883 the courts granted Oline a limited divorce. She received $2,500 of the money her husband had taken from her father's estate and $150 a year for ten years. Bernt kept custody of their minor children. A stroke in 1894 partially paralyzed him, and in 1899 he returned to Norway for good.

The entire Holden congregation turned out to say good-bye. With tears running down his cheeks, Muus, moved beyond words, pointed towards heaven, appearing to indicate, "Meet me there." Upon reaching Kenyon, Muus rode through the streets in his carriage, taking a final look. Hundreds gathered at the train depot for his departure. He died the following year in Norway at age 68.[13]

Oline Muus taught music late into her life and, in 1896, moved to Fruithurst, Alabama, where she owned and operated a hotel. She left women in Goodhue County and Minnesota an unintended yet significant legacy, having taken a stand in court on principle under risk of public ridicule. Those who knew Oline in her declining years described her as "happy and interested in people." She died in her adopted country on September 4, 1922.[14]

Concerns about ethnic differences and cultural assimilation in Goodhue County continued well into the 20th century. As with Bernt Muus, individuals in some ethnic groups resisted "Americanization," preferring to preserve the long-held cultural traditions they brought to Minnesota. The clannish nature of groups, along with the all-consuming effort to establish themselves in a new world, slowed the mixing of the European immigrants.[15]

Among the earliest cultural interchanges in rural Goodhue County were those with Indians. Rural farmers, unlike their city-dwelling brethren, were more isolated, and their meetings with Indians were typically one-to-one encounters. Operating on little knowledge of the decreasing local Indian population, farmers generally resisted contact. Despite such concern, settler accounts of their meetings with Indians on the prairie reported virtually no violence. Complaints usually centered on the way in which the Indians traded.[16]

A woman from the Swedish enclave in Leon township's Spring Garden area reported a wordless transaction with an Indian hunter. She told of an Indian coming to her farmhouse as she was baking. He left but then returned with a piece of venison, placing it on a table. He then picked up a loaf of bread and went on his way. The same family said Indians never bothered them.[17]

An Irish immigrant woman, afraid when she saw an Indian with bloody hands approaching her Belle Creek cabin, hid her two children and met the man

Eric Jonasson, Jens Zackrison, and Olaf Hanson owned these three farms (l to r, respectively) in the Swedish colony of Vasa. *GCHS*

at the door. He pointed to the fresh bread on her table, and she gave him some. The Indian returned with venison, probably from a fresh kill. This may have explained the blood on his hands.[18]

Rev. J. C. Johnson of Burnside reported frequent pre-Civil War visits from Indians who hunted in the Cannon River valley: "Our women, although alone generally through the day, were not disturbed in those early days by the visits of the redmen."[19]

A Norwegian farmwoman recalled an Indian who asked for shelter during a fierce storm. She gave him some food and fixed him a place in the corner to sleep. After breakfast the following morning he told her that he had no money and nothing to give her for the lodging but that he would return with payment. Two weeks later he brought her a "magnificent pair of moccasins."[20]

Historian Bruce White has warned that the accuracy of many accounts of white-Indian interaction during the settlement era "is hard to gauge." He noted that many such stories passed from one person to another through the filter of the white point of view. The anecdotes of such meetings included here, with the exception of Rev. Johnson's first-person account, qualify for caution. But the unembellished, straightforward stories support each other and concur with Johnson's contemporaneous assertion that the farmwomen in Goodhue County "were not disturbed" by Indians.[21]

The "melting pot" concept of cultural assimilation simmered in Goodhue County but did not always produce blending. Pride in various European heritages and a desire to preserve them combined with uncertainty about the customs and cultures of neighboring national groups to slow the mix. The settlers frowned upon intermarriage, for example. Most believed "old country" bloodlines should not be mixed. In an era when a Norwegian-Swedish union was to some a "mixed marriage," the joining of a Belle Creek Catholic man and Swedish Lutheran woman caused some to reject the couple. "We would walk to church and people would even pass us by," recalled the couple's daughter years later. She added with laughter, "If you were all Irish, you were better than if you had half-Swede in you."[22]

Schools within the irregular confines of European immigrant communities reflected their surrounding culture. Teachers used the native tongue of their students' parents for instruction, and youngsters often did not learn English until later in life. A man born in Hay Creek, one of the most heavily German townships in the state, went to school there in the 1890s and learned in that language. When his children attended the same school, they received one hour of English a day, with the rest of their schooling in German.[23]

A Belvidere man with a German heritage remembered the importance of the family's native language: "People who could talk German, talked German." But since his family lived "between Norwegians and everything," he had to learn English as well. One confused Goodhue boy of German background grew up speaking German, then moved with his family to Featherstone township, where English was the rule. After six years of school in English at Featherstone, he returned to Goodhue, where he boarded with another family. He struggled with his studies because "when I got to the school [in Goodhue] all the kids could talk German . . . but I had lost most of my German.[24]

Rev. Christian Bender of Red Wing's St. John's (German) Lutheran began a parochial school in 1881. Well known to German Lutherans in the area, he had helped establish congregations in Frontenac and West Florence. His school provided religious instruction and basic skills in German. Returning home from school, students often heard the question, *"Was hast du heute von dem Schullehrer gelernt?"* ("What have you learned from the schoolteacher today?")[25]

The predominance of Norwegian parochial schools in the Wanamingo, Holden, and Kenyon areas lessened towards the end of the 19th century. Children continued to receive religious instruction in their parents' native language, but the Norwegian school met only in the summer months. A Wanamingo girl who attended School District 148 recalled five months of English (public) school and three months of Norwegian school. The English school began on the first Monday in November and ended in the last week of March. Likewise, a Spring Garden Swedish woman remembered going to "Swedish school" in summertime and public school during the rest of the normal school year.[26]

The neatly manicured grounds and large barn of the Jacob Behrens farm near Zumbrota fit with the stereotypical image of German organizational skill. Some longtime county residents claimed they could identify the nationality of a farm's owner by looking at the barn. *GCHS*

Being bilingual could be an advantage in getting work or running for office. Hans Johnson of Zumbrota, campaigning for clerk of court in 1874, claimed to be "a young American citizen of Scandinavian birth." He was "well-educated, intelligent and speaking English well, popular among his neighbors . . . American as well as foreign-born." The editor of a book about "successful Scandinavians" commented on the language capability of a Vasa immigrant and later Minnesota governor, John Lind. He wrote that Lind "speaks English without a foreign accent."[27]

Belle Creek, in the geographic center of the county, proved a mix of ethnicities. That township had Swedes to the north and west, Norwegians to the south and southwest, Germans to the east, and Irish in the middle. Schools located in border districts, like Number 49 in Leon township on the Belle Creek border, had Norwegian, Swedes, English, and Irish students. Everyone in that small district spoke English at school. Where the mix was more one-sided, there were occasional problems. In a Goodhue school on Belle Creek's eastern border, the Irish and German minority teased the Swedish majority with, "The Irish and Dutch didn't amount to much, but to heck with Scandinavians!"[28]

Occasional ethnically charged skirmishes broke out in the county's midsection. The White Rock dance hall in northern Belle Creek was a problem spot. Fights there between Swedes and Irish were common, particularly after the combatants drank alcohol. One Swede who grew up in White Rock recalled "battle royals" between Irish and Swedes. A man whose Irish parents emigrated to Goodhue recalled some "pretty good old tangles!" at the dance hall. Another observer noted, "Everything used to go along pretty good . . . at White Rock . . . with the Irish and the Swedes until the Irish boys started dancing with the Swede girls." One family's Swedish hired man went to White Rock whenever there was a dance. The Swede didn't dance, "but he had to go help the Swedes lick the Irish!"[29]

Germans also participated in fights. One German-American resident remembered, "They got along fine until they went to a dance and got drunk . . . In Goodhue it was the Irish and the Germans; in White Rock it was the Swedes and the Irish."

In some ways the fighting seemed a form of recreation. Few reported lasting problems or more than minor injuries. Scrapes between ethnic railroad construction crews were common. A family history tells of Munka Mons Person, whose all-Swedish crew sometimes fought with rival Irish work gangs. Sometimes the Swedes won and sometimes the Irish, but Munka Mons never took a licking. If the Swedes were losing, he ran away despite the risk of revenge from his own countrymen. The younger men said he couldn't fight well anyway.[30]

The battles were "all in fun," said one German, and an Irish account noted that typical fights produced only a "few hard feelings at the time." An Irish auctioneer once had to stop a Belle Creek sale in which a vigorous snowball fight broke out between Irish and Swedes. The disgusted auctioneer told them to stop the snowballing or he would halt the bidding: "So they quit the fight and then he continued on with the auction."[31]

The very concentration of Norwegians in some areas isolated them from the rest of the county. A Swedish boy brought up in Spring Garden's Swedish colony "never heard anything" about the Norwegians to the south and west. Once Norwegians had claimed most of the land in the county's southwest sections, newcomers who wished to settle tried to buy property near their countrymen. Immigrants from Norway bought out the New Englanders who first staked claims around Hader in northeast Wanamingo township, for example. A woman whose grandparents bought land from the Easterners contended "the Yankees and Norwegians had nothing in common," and the Yankees "should be put out of the county."[32]

Zumbrota hardware merchant Edward Sohn echoed the concerns some had about "Yankees." Sohn operated his store at the turn of the century and observed that, "The Norwegians and Germans got along first rate, but it couldn't be said they loved the 'Yankee' storekeepers." Immigrants uncomfortable with the English language shied away from some of the Easterners. A man "with a German or Norwegian name . . . was sure of getting plenty of patronage from his own people."[33]

Prominent Norwegian-born physician Just Christian Gronvold of Holden stereotyped his Goodhue County countrymen with this assessment: "The Norwegians prefer to build each at a distance from the other. Everybody likes to have his own for himself, and a distance to the next neighbor." In comparison, Gronvold asserted that, "The Americans, like most other nationalities, are gregarious and like to live many together. They move together in villages." [34]

Goodhue County's ethnically divided Lutheran Church congregations, in their role as religious and cultural centers, were often slow to change. Many of these churches retained into the 20th century the language of the Old World as well as some of the doctrines originating there. The Lutheran church was the largest and most fractious in the county, organized under the "old country" divisions of Norwegian, Swedish, and German. English Lutheran churches later added to the mix.

When St. John's (German) Lutheran Church of Red Wing called pastor John Baumann in September 1901, it understood he would preach in English as well as German. Services conducted in English that November aroused strong opposition. A parishioner recalled:

> What some of these people were trying to do . . . was to transport a portion of Germany here and make it all German, the language and everything else; and of course when others started talking about having English services, why man alive! God was German! He couldn't understand English! You know, it was sacrilegious to them . . . and the Swedes and Norwegians were no different.[35]

Norwegian Lutherans, at the turn of the century, remained divided, with 19 Goodhue County congregations split among three organizations. The United Church of the Norwegian Evangelical faith had 12 Lutheran congregations in the southwest townships of the county. Three churches of the Norwegian Synod met in Red Wing, Holden, and Zumbrota, and the Hauge Synod had congregations in Roscoe Center, Kenyon, Aspelund, and Red Wing.[36]

Eight Swedish Lutheran congregations grew up in ethnic strongholds such as Vasa, Welch, and Spring Garden. Others took root in Goodhue, Red Wing, Prairie Island, Cannon Falls (St. Ansgar's) and Cannon River (Cannon Falls township). German Lutheran congregations built churches in Red Wing, Frontenac, Belvidere, Minneola, Zumbrota, Hay Creek and two in Goodhue. English Lutheran churches, taking their name from the language they adopted, organized later and drew members from the Swedish, German, and Norwegian Lutheran community. They built houses of worship in Zumbrota, Cannon Falls, Red Wing, and Goodhue.

In 1909, Red Wing alone featured congregations from nearly all the ethnic Lutheran church groups—Norwegian Synod, Hauge (Norwegian) Synod,

Swedish, German, and English Lutheran. It lacked only a Norwegian Evangelical Lutheran church.

Other Christian denominations identified less with northern European nations. "Old Stock" Americans, who left the states of New England, the Mid-Atlantic, and the old Northwest Territory to settle in Minnesota, typically made up their membership. English was the dominant language of these groups, their members well assimilated into American culture. Presbyterian missionaries Joseph and Maria Hancock became the county's first permanent white residents in 1849, but a congregation of their denomination did not formally organize until January 1855. The Methodist Episcopal (M.E.) Church in Red Wing, under the leadership of Rev. S. L. Leonard and Rev. Matthew Sorin, held services as early as 1852. The Methodists started congregations in Cannon Falls and Pine Island before statehood and in 1869 began another in Zumbrota. In 1856 and 1857 Congregationalists organized among the early New Englanders in Cannon Falls and in Zumbrota's colony of Yankees.[37]

The Protestant Episcopal church in southeastern Minnesota grew under the watchful eye of Bishop Henry B. Whipple, known for his interest in and defense of the area's Indian population. Whipple supported the Church of the Messiah at Prairie Island, a small congregation mainly of Christian Indians who returned to the area in the 1870s. Red Wing's Christ Episcopal, in keeping with its early interest in reaching the Mdewakanton people, also linked to the Prairie Island church. Episcopalians also organized churches in Pine Island, Belle Creek, Florence, Cannon Falls, Holden, and Kenyon.[38]

Old World influences were evident in Roman Catholic churches in the county, particularly in the ethnically uniform rural parishes. Irish Catholics in Belle Creek built the first St. Columbkill church in 1860. In 1865 members of the Luxembourg colony established St. Mary's parish, straddling Belvidere township's southern border with Chester township of Wabasha County. Catholics founded other parishes in the county's towns and villages, including Pine Island, Zumbrota, Cherry Grove, Cannon Falls, and Red Wing.[39]

The cacophony of foreign languages and clashes of culture gradually subsided. New generations educated in the language and traditions of their New World homeland grew up in Goodhue County. They did not require the protection afforded by the tightly knit ethnic communities that had evolved in some areas of the county. The younger generation found it easier to find a place in the more homogenous American society with one exception—that of the Mdewakanton community on Prairie Island.

Some Mdewakanton left the Santee Reservations in South Dakota and Nebraska in the 1870s and headed to Minnesota. A few returned to Goodhue County to live on sparsely settled Prairie Island in Burnside township. Sandy soil covered the low-lying Prairie Island, adjacent to the Mississippi and its flood plain. The island contained lakes and sloughs, making the area less attractive to white farmers. Because of these negatives and its comparative inaccessibility, Prairie Island was the last settled area of Goodhue County. Thus, it contained room for a small number of Indians.[40]

Recognizing this Dakota exodus, Congress in 1884 dedicated $10,000 to provide Indians returning to Minnesota with supplies, including stock and tools. Two years later legislators appropriated $20,000 for lands, seed, provisions, and lumber for homes. The government first purchased land for the Indians in Goodhue, Scott, Dakota, and Redwood counties in the summer of 1887. It acquired more acreage in 1889, 1890, and 1891. Robert B. Henton, an agent appointed to make land purchases at Prairie Island, opposed the acquisition but wrote in 1889, "These Indians are of the Red Wing or Wacoute band and this is their old home, therefore though the soil is poor they are loth [*sic*] to leave it, and we have no means of compelling their removal." [41]

Thomas H. Rouillard brought his family to Prairie Island in September 1887 and later bought seven acres there. Rouillard and his wife, Julia, had been born in 1860 and were just two years old at the time of the Dakota conflict along the Minnesota River. Julia's mother was born in the Red Wing Indian village in 1846. The Rouillards survived the postwar exile of their people and returned to Minnesota, hoping to settle at Prairie Island. The number of Indians moving to Prairie Island was small, with 46 listed by the Goodhue County auditor in 1890.[42]

Not all of the Indians coming to Prairie Island were members of the Red Wing band. Those returning were mostly Mdewakanton, but members of other eastern Sioux bands, including Wahpekute and Sisseton, married into the community or moved there.[43]

Their location on Prairie Island to a large extent isolated the Indians both geographically and culturally from the rest of Goodhue County. They farmed, raising potatoes and corn and also some wheat, oats, and beans. They supplemented their incomes through activities such as dance presentations at Red Wing Fourth of July programs, picking and selling wild grapes, and collecting bounties.[44]

Poverty plagued the community. On the occasion of two funerals in the spring of 1888, the Episcopal rector requested that clothing be donated to relatives attending the funeral. In February 1895, a newspaper reported that a Prairie Island Indian woman died of starvation, leaving three children. The writer observed that nearly all of the Indians "are in want of the necessities of life." In an appeal for charity, he added that the Indians are unable to "make their wants known, and they don't know how to work and could not obtain employment if they did." [45]

Life was difficult, with little prospect for improvement for the Indian community of Prairie Island in the 1890s. Yet because of the Native Americans' poverty and geographic isolation, other Americans largely left them alone. Perhaps because of this relative seclusion, the community persisted.

Goodhue County's medical community grew substantially in the decades following the Civil War—a welcome development for those living in rural areas. With physicians sometimes days away, early settlers on the prairie lived in dread of medical emergencies. A handful of doctors began to practice in Red Wing before 1861, but only Charles Hill worked in the other townships. Dr. Hill arrived in Roscoe in 1857 and moved to Pine Island two years later.[46]

Medical quackery proved a serious problem in the county and throughout the state. Traveling "doctors" and natural healers endangered those who sought their help. Patent medicines, claiming by far the largest portion of newspaper advertisements, promised cures to afflictions from catarrh to "indiscretions of youth." One traveling cure-all, claiming to be a doctor, tried to stir interest in his impending arrival in Red Wing:

> Dr. Purinton, the renowned Lung Physician, will visit Red Wing, Saturday, October 17, and will remain four days. Dr. Purinton has devoted his attention for the last 20 years to the treatment of Chronic Diseases of the Throat and Lungs; also those of the Heart, Liver, Kidney, etc., Scrofula, Chronic and Inflammatory Rheumatism, together with Female Diseases in all their forms. Dr. Purinton defies the whole medical Faculty to beat him in curing Dyspepsia . . . The affected are invited to call . . . He claims he can tell their complaint without asking any questions free of charge.[47]

Medical science was improving, but dreaded epidemics vexed even the most skilled practitioners. Before the Civil War, deadly outbreaks of cholera and typhoid struck the county. In October 1861 a limited smallpox outbreak affected Vasa. Soon, immigrants living in a crowded tenement house in east Red Wing contracted smallpox, forcing closure of a nearby school. The city paid for vaccinating hundreds of people. Then, in the winter of 1862, a diphtheria epidemic caused alarm in Red Wing and on the adjacent Wisconsin side of the Mississippi. Mortality rates associated with the disease were high, particularly among children.[48]

In August 1864 cholera struck Red Wing. Once again disease hit the young in particular, though the illness struck adults as well. A newspaper bluntly reported the problem: "Almost every family in this city can attest the truth of what we say. One physician . . . made the remark that he had twenty patients, all children, and that he did not expect any of them to recover."[49]

In 1867 Red Wing officials, with an eye towards another summer cholera outbreak, tried to adopt some of the sanitary measures—eliminating sources of filth, disinfecting buildings and vessels, establishing quarantines— recommended by the International Sanitary Conference. Nevertheless, cases of the disease, many fatal, occurred among immigrants. The last report of cholera victims reaching Red Wing by boat (docking prohibited) occurred in 1868. One of the city's new physicians, Charles Hewitt, offered to treat the afflicted. The city also provided a house on an "isolated" island for ailing passengers.[50]

Charles Hewitt, later described as Minnesota's "Apostle of Public Health," moved to Red Wing in 1867 after serving as a regimental surgeon in the Civil War. He soon became a leading figure in the local and state medical communities, providing the impetus for creation of the Minnesota State Board of Health in 1872, of which he became permanent secretary. From that position Dr. Hewitt pushed for a public health code for the state. Gov. Lucius Hubbard, the former Red Wing newspaperman and business leader, backed him, and the legislature supported the concept. Public health laws mandated the establishment of a board of health for every town, village, and city in the state.[51]

The law also required a health officer to inspect sanitary conditions in the district and submit a written report on the findings. Officers examined public buildings, schools, and sanitation systems throughout the state. The law empowered health officers to take action against those creating unsanitary conditions and harboring filth. Violators were subject to fines and imprisonment.

Hewitt pursued his activism beyond the establishment of his public health ideas as law. Through his research and writings, the Red Wing physician worked to improve the general health knowledge of the medical community. In 1873 he became a nonresident professor for the University of Minnesota, delivering lectures on sanitary science and public health. Hewitt, along with William Folwell, lobbied for a state medical examining board to ensure standards for the licensing of physicians. With the board's establishment at the university's College of Medicine in 1882, Hewitt became its chair. He founded in 1855 and edited for nine years the monthly magazine *Public Health in Minnesota*. He later became the president of the American Society of Public Health.[52]

Hewitt possessed remarkable talent as a creative and effective researcher. In the late 19th century, medical science concentrated on fighting the contagious diseases of typhoid, cholera, smallpox, tuberculosis (TB), and diphtheria. Hewitt joined this struggle in 1889, taking leave of his Red Wing practice to examine European developments in bacteriological research. He studied in Paris for about a year under the renowned Louis Pasteur, learning of Pasteur's treatment for rabies and tuberculosis among other techniques.[53]

In Paris Hewitt learned to prepare smallpox vaccine from infected calf lymph rather than from human pox sacs. Applying what he had learned abroad, Hewitt established his own laboratory in Red Wing. He began producing vaccine at his own expense and distributed supplies around the region.[54]

A colleague of Hewitt, another county physician with an interest in research, Norwegian-born Just Christian Gronvold, settled in Holden township.

Charles Hewitt, above with his youngest son,
Nathaniel Hewitt, was later described as Minnesota's "Apostle of Public Health." *GCHS*

Even while maintaining his practice, Dr. Gronvold became a foremost authority
on leprosy in the United States. Gronvold knew this disease was common in
Norway, and his interest in measures to prevent its spread drew him to study
leprosy in Minnesota. The *Bulletin of the History of Medicine* in 1950 credited
Gronvold "for contributing more to the study and understanding of leprosy in
the Northwest than any other single person."[55]

County doctors fought outbreaks of contagious diseases throughout the last
three decades of the 19th century. Typhoid fever and scarlet fever struck
Zumbrota in 1870, and scarlet fever plagued Red Wing in 1872 and Goodhue
six years later. Pine Island and Zumbrota had many cases of "fever," likely dys-
entery, in 1873.

Progress in public health continued. In 1884 civic leaders established a
county hospital in Red Wing. Physicians Bruno Jaehnig, Charles Hewitt, and
George Leininger donated their services free of charge for one year. German-
born Jaehnig was the first superintendent. As a cost-saving measure, the hospital accepted patients who otherwise would have gone to the county poorhouse. The charge for those who could pay was five dollars per week for food
and nursing, with medical attention and medicine extra. A total of 44 patients
received care the first year; 18 of them paid for the service.[56]

Diseases familiar to the first settlers in the county continued to reappear periodically despite advances in technology and facilities. In 1880 diphtheria closed several county schools and hit hard in Cannon Falls. That same year typhoid returned to the tenements of Red Wing, and in 1881 it struck Goodhue. Reports of measles, mumps, and scarlet fever outbreaks continued into the 1880s. Dr. Hewitt reminded citizens to get vaccinated even though smallpox was coming under control. In June 1881, Hewitt warned newspaper readers of a smallpox problem in Dakota and Todd counties: "Smallpox is being introduced into our state by immigrants." He asked that adults see that "all children are vaccinated, and that persons over 16 years of age be re-vaccinated."[57] Diphtheria plagued Goodhue County throughout the 1890s and in some years took a devastating toll. The development of a grayish membrane on the throat and tonsils, which impeded breathing, proved the most dangerous symptom of the disease. Some believed the killer was gradually being contained. Diphtheria claimed 1,607 Minnesotans in 1882, reduced to 788 five years later.

Yet the dying continued. Cannon Falls suffered a serious outbreak in 1891, during which physician Hiram Conley and his wife, Sarah, saw their daughters Mira, six years old, and Emma, 19 months, die within two days of each other.[58]

A particularly deadly outbreak of diphtheria hit the Red Wing area in the early fall of 1893. Eight-year-old Nannie Peterson was the first victim, dying on August 23 in her West Main Street home and buried that afternoon. Five days later, the *Daily Republican* reported four more cases in Red Wing and several in Featherstone and Burnside. The next week two children died in Burnside and one in Featherstone. The cases began to mount.[59]

Diphtheria claimed 13-year-old Nellie Anderson on September 9. In three days' time, health officials quarantined 13 homes and a hotel in Red Wing. The press declared an epidemic. Officials added four homes to the isolation list on September 13 and, as in the other cases, published the address and family name of the afflicted. Administrators closed city schools on September 15. The next day Clara Pirius, 13, died, followed two days later by nine-year-old Arthur Ellingson. City officers appointed special police to enforce the quarantine, and by mid-October they had ordered the isolation of 33 families.

Twenty-one Red Wing children died during the siege—a severe shock to the city. Diphtheria antitoxin became available toward the end of the decade, but control was still some years away, as illustrated by Hay Creek's report of 48 cases in 1895.[60]

Measles and typhoid also materialized in the 1890s. Cannon Falls had three deaths from typhoid in 1891, with cases reported in Vasa in 1898 and Kenyon the following year. The Minnesota State Training School in Red Wing had 40 cases of measles in the winter of 1897.

The quality of care for the sick did improve. A group of Red Wing women led by Lydia Foot, Isabelle Sterling, and Elizabeth Smith, wives of prominent

Dentist C. E. Conley (seated) and his doctor
brothers, Hiram (left) and Alva T. (right), at
a lighthearted moment. *GCHS*

community leaders, assumed business control of the county hospital in 1891
and managed it for five years. That association reorganized in 1896 under the
leadership of president Elijah Blodgett. Lydia Foot became first vice president.
In 1898 the hospital association purchased Samuel P. Jennison's home on College Hill and remodeled "City Hospital" to accommodate 15 patients.[61]

Construction began the following year on the county's second hospital, this
in more centrally located Zumbrota, under the leadership of physician K. E.
Gryttenholm. Lutheran Hospital could handle as many as 24 patients, but persistent financial problems forced the hospital to close in 1903.[62]

Tuberculosis continued to plague the nation at the century's turn, and the
1913 Minnesota legislature dedicated funds to control it. The infectious disease,
commonly known as consumption in the 19th century, attacked the respiratory
tract, causing chronic health problems and, in acute cases, debilitation and
death. Early Minnesotans did not understand the nature of the disease and
bragged that the area's cold, dry, air made the region free of such afflictions.
They advanced the healthy, invigorating climate as a reason for settling in
Minnesota. The disease's spread soon proved Minnesota had no special immu-
nity. TB was the leading cause of death in the state between 1910 and 1914. An
average of 2,373 people succumbed to it annually during that period.[63]

Goodhue County acted quickly, building the Mineral Springs Sanatorium five miles east of Cannon Falls on the Big Cannon River. Commissioners dedicated the original poured-concrete structure on October 20, 1915. It cost $27,882 and contained 30 beds. The building featured a T-shaped design, with patients occupying space at the top of the T and the service areas at the base. Physicians first used a fresh-air treatment popular in Europe. Prescribed bed-rest superseded the fresh-air program. Five nearby counties joined in ownership of the facility in the 1920s, and expansion followed. The county erected a residence for nurses in 1921 and added a three-story, 100-bed building in 1929.[64]

The "San," as its employees called the Mineral Springs facility, added a physician-superintendent in 1919. Many women, mostly from Cannon Falls, worked at the sanatorium, riding to their jobs in a special van. Mineral Springs sought employees with previous exposure to tuberculosis, determined by watching for a reaction after injecting a protein extract of the disease with a needle (Mantoux test).[65]

Deaths from tuberculosis in Goodhue County between 1902 and 1911 stood at 389. Red Wing experienced 139 deaths in that period, and Kenyon and Zumbrota (townships and villages combined) each saw 27 die. Efforts at Mineral Springs and other state sanatoriums made progress but did not eradicate the disease. In the mid-1940s a Mineral Springs patient was the first person in the world cured of tuberculosis by treatment with streptomycin, a new antibiotic.

In 1915, Goodhue County officials opened the Mineral Springs Sanatorium in Cannon Falls. Five other counties eventually joined in its sponsorship. *GCHS*

Physicians visited from around the world to study the new treatment. Drugs later added to the fight against tuberculosis brought the disease under control.[66]

A serious fire at Goodhue County's poorhouse in October 1889 brought the welfare of the county's indigent back to the attention of the public. The fire caused no fatalities but demolished the building originally purchased in 1864.

The people of Goodhue County took pride in being the first in the state to respond to the state legislature's 1864 law requiring counties to assume responsibility for the destitute. The legislators believed the solution to poverty issue lay in the establishment of poor farms and poorhouses for the indigent. County officials had a committee working on the idea even before it became law. The lawmakers felt a poor farm could provide food and work for inmates, helping contribute to their support. Commissioners also authorized the farm's overseer to confine recalcitrant inmates "in a strong room, on bread and water."[67]

One Red Wing newspaper endorsed the legislature's reasoning: "It will be but a short time before our poor will be able to pay their own way, a thing they will greatly prefer to being indebted to the county." Another paper even saw profit in a poor farm. "Such an institution can in a few years be made to pay its own way and put money into the county treasury," claimed the *Daily Republican*. From the start, however, the Burnside township farm did not produce profits. Its first residents were "mostly old persons or children, and immigrants," not the kind of work force necessary for a moneymaking farm.[68]

Perhaps persuaded by the county's early demonstration of responsibility to the poor, Red Wing businessman Orrin Densmore encouraged action in another area of social concern—treatment of the insane. In 1866 Gov. William Marshall appointed Densmore to a six-man board of trustees assigned to select a site for a proposed hospital for the insane. Densmore suggested land in Red Wing for the permanent site and a hotel in Wacouta as a temporary location. The Densmore plan gained early favor, but St. Peter's bid eventually prevailed.[69]

During the winter of 1890–91, the county erected in Burnside an impressive two-story brick facility for the indigent. The first floor contained the overseer's office  area, women's apartments, bathroom, sick room, day room, dining room, and kitchen. Male paupers lived in the second-floor dormitory, while the basement featured the furnace, the janitor's room, and smoking, bath, and sitting rooms. The county's poorest citizens once again had a home.[70]

# 9

## *Progressivism on the Prairie— The Politics of Reform*

A political thunderstorm brewed on the plains and prairies of the American heartland in the 1880s, waiting to break with surprising ferocity on a new decade. Expanding industrialization had changed the face of America, and its altered image adversely affected some of its population. Many farmers, vexed by a downward trend in crop prices and a gut-level suspicion of railroads and banks, looked for political outlets through which to vent their frustration. That outlet came in the form of the People's (Populist) Party, a new organization rooted in Farmers' Alliance philosophy. The group dedicated itself to fighting the growing power of corporate capitalism and the politicians under its influence. This third-party movement quickly coalesced, immediately affecting state and national elections.

Seeds of the new political movement found fertile ground at an 1890 Topeka meeting that helped launch the People's Party. With an almost religious fervor, speakers promised their enthusiastic audiences a war on those who exploited them. Mary Lease of Kansas, a charismatic orator, drew the battle lines: "What you farmers need to do is to raise less corn and more Hell! We want money, land, and transportation. We want the abolition of the National Banks . . . We want the accursed foreclosure system wiped out . . . We will stand by our homes and stay by our firesides by force if necessary."[1]

Goodhue County resident Omar Morse was one of the seldom-discussed failed farmers. Morse and his wife, Delia, battled high interest rates unsuccessfully and lost three prairie farms. Whether their failures were due to bad luck, unscrupulous lenders, their own shortcomings, or other factors, the Morses lived a hard life. Such settlers, in the words of historian James Marshall, "starved while freezing to death on a government claim." After Delia died in 1882, Omar tried to live off his remaining 20 acres on a Roscoe farm he called the "old home in the woods." He died in 1901 in Pine Island.[2]

Midwestern farmers, the voting base of the new party, got the reformers' message. Activists organized the People's Party in the summer of 1892 when the Populists convened in Omaha. The protest movement, however, had already made an auspicious debut during the 1890 elections. In Minnesota, dissatisfaction among the voters was evident. Its five-man Republican congressional delegation was reduced by four, with only ex-Goodhue County resident John Lind surviving in his Second District seat. The voters, looking for opposition candidates, elected two Democrats, a Democrat-Farmer Alliance candidate, and a Farmer Alliance-Prohibition man. Meanwhile, the People's Party took control in five states. Washington, D.C., also felt the shift. The Republican Party lost almost half its seats and its majority in the House of Representatives.[3]

The 1890 election dealt a body blow to the Republican Party and its representatives in the Minnesota legislature. It now held just 40 of 114 seats in the house and 27 of 54 senate seats.[4]

Even in traditionally Republican Goodhue County, the most heavily populated of the Third Congressional District's counties, voters showed their unhappiness. Beginning in 1857, Goodhue County had voted Republican in every congressional election held in the state. The streak continued unbroken in 1890, but just barely. Republican incumbent Darwin Hall's slim (2,451–2,332) Goodhue County majority would not allow him to hold office. The remainder of the Third District voted heavily for Osee Matson Hall of Red Wing, providing the Democrat with a 4,533-vote victory.[5]

O. M. Hall was a Democrat, but on the stump he sounded like a People's Party candidate. That party's issues were his issues. He railed against trusts (monopolies) and tariffs, the taxes imposed on foreign goods to protect American manufacturers. The hated tariff, in the eyes of the rebels, allowed American business to keep consumer prices artificially high. Hall, nominated by his party in 1890, spoke out against the nation's rich and powerful:

> So selfish and so extortionate have been these monopolists, so remorselessly have they plundered the people, that there has sprung up in this protected hot-bed of America an unwholesome crop of millionaires poisoning the social, the business, and the political life of our people.[6]

Hall's pre-election remarks echoed other voices of protest. Grangers, Greenbackers, Alliance members, Prohibitionists, Women's Alliance, Anti-Monopolists, the American Federation of Labor, and other populist groups represented new constituencies focusing on a growing resentment of corporate power and greedy monopolists.

The People's Party faded and disappeared by the late 1890s, a victim of the decision to fuse with the Democratic Party in backing William Jennings Bryan for president in 1896. Yet the mood of protest engendered by the Populists lived on to overlap with a more significant period of reform—the era of progressivism. Through the 1890s and until America's entry into World War I, other reformers—intellectuals, social scientists, journalists, and theologians who also believed the machinery of government should be a force for the common good—joined with the Populists. The progressives struggled to move the country in a direction they believed better for ordinary Americans. This "progressive" era had profound effects upon the nation as it entered the 20th century.[7]

Among the progressives were women enlistees in a small but rapidly growing army dedicated to national social and political reform. The largest women's group was the Woman's Christian Temperance Union (WCTU), organized to fight the manufacture and sale of intoxicating liquor. The WCTU organizers brandished a large umbrella under which its members worked on a variety of social issues important to women, including child welfare, women's working conditions, health, pay equity, and international peace.[8]

Women's rights groups concentrated largely on obtaining the right to vote but also labored to pass "woman laws" securing rights of property and income. Other women's service clubs enrolled members who focused on bettering the community, as well as themselves. Women once involved in a reform-minded group were likely to take interest in related issues. In Minnesota, for example, the WCTU became identified with women's suffrage when, in 1881, the membership added gaining the vote for women to its platform.

Women who became active in such groups risked ridicule. Former president Grover Cleveland saw women's clubs as a threat to "the integrity of our homes." The male editor of the *Ladies' Home Journal* advised women to join "merely one club" and to take care not to put such activity "before the higher duties of the home."[9]

Goodhue County's Julia B. Nelson, a prominent lobbyist for women's suffrage, was also at the forefront of the state's WCTU leadership. She began working for women's rights during interludes from her teaching in the postwar Freedman Schools of the South. By the turn of the century, Nelson had been an advocate for women for more than 20 years.

A well-known orator, Nelson spoke in the grandiloquent style of the day. She often alluded to the Bible and its lessons and pulled few punches in her talks. Her October 1881 speech at the state WCTU convention provides a sample of her style: "What issue is now of such vital importance as temperance? What enemy is so deserving of good men's best blows as the rum oligarchy, which fattens on the tears of widows and the woes of orphans; which grows rich and strong by filling the land with paupers, criminals, and lunatics."[10]

Goodhue County women formed chapters of the Woman's Christian Temperance Union. Pine Island's chapter is shown here. *GCHS*

Nelson's debating style proved formidable, and her reputation usually assured a good crowd. A December 9, 1882, newspaper report of a Red Wing meeting notes with more than a hint of condescension that Nelson's talk was "racy and full of saucy feminine repartee . . . whatever may be said of its logic." Two months later she debated temperance issues with J. R. Barry before a packed Frontenac house of 487. The chairman of the meeting ruled that Nelson won the debate, but the audience gave the nod to Barry. Later in her career, Nelson became a paid lecturer for the National Woman Suffrage Association.[11]

Nelson's sense of obligation to Freedman Schools caused her to leave her Belvidere farm in August 1883 to return to Tennessee for another stint of teaching. She rented her farm to George Patterson, a black hired man who had worked there for two years. Frederick Douglass, perhaps the most prominent black leader of 19th century, wrote to Nelson: "I am almost sorry to have you leave . . . for a life of conflict at the South—but somebody must go there and suffer there as you have before."[12]

Harriet Hobart, a former New York teacher, joined Nelson in leading the temperance struggle in the county and state. Hobart had moved to Red Wing in 1868 after marrying Rev. Chauncey Hobart, a widowed Methodist minister. She served the Minnesota WCTU in several major roles. Her 13-year tenure as state president (1881–1894) was the longest in the organization's history.[13]

In 1883 Pine Island and Kenyon became the first communities in Goodhue County to form WCTU chapters. Other county groups organized in the years following: Zumbrota in 1885, Cannon Falls in 1886, Oxford, Stanton and Red Wing in 1887, Dennison in 1894, West Oxford in 1896, Goodhue in 1898, Red Wing (Sterling Chapter) in 1922, Burnside in 1925, and Wanamingo in 1928. The WCTU also encouraged the organization of Young Woman's Christian Temperance Union (YWCTU) chapters. Goodhue County had five.[14]

Antiliquor activists pursued their campaign against alcohol on many fronts. Isabelle Sterling, temperance leader from the Methodist Church in Red Wing, organized Saturday antiliquor classes for children. She lectured them on the dangers of alcohol and, at the end of class, provided the students with glasses of juice or water. When they finished, the children sang a song that concluded, "When we are offered a drink of booze, or alcohol, or whiskey, we turn our glasses upside down." The children punctuated the tune's end by turning their emptied glasses bottoms up.[15]

The Irish communities of Belle Creek and west Goodhue township enrolled in the temperance movement in 1875, forming a 48-man chapter of the Catholic Church's Total Abstinence Union of America. Women of the community created their own branch in 1888, with 35 members. Mary Igoe, Mary Ryan, and Celia Hutcheson of Belle Creek joined the first women to attend a WCTU annual convention. Within three years, women's membership in the Belle Creek branch of the Total Abstinence Union surpassed that of the men.[16]

Nellie Igoe, speaking as chairperson at the WCTU's 1891 convention, challenged women to keep at the struggle. "Rise in your majestic might . . . veritable Amazons, in defense of domestic virtue and temperance without which happiness is impossible and the social eminence of women a myth."

Famed temperance orator John G. Woolley launched a major initiative against alcohol at Goodhue County's Central Point with his decision to construct a "home for inebriates and drunkards." Woolley, a recovering alcoholic, was a leading Minneapolis lawyer who became Hennepin County Attorney before "drink became his master." He left Minneapolis in 1887 a broken man, then recovered and dedicated himself to helping others addicted to drink.[17]

Woolley's solution was to establish a "Christian home . . . strict in tone, but flexible in rules; with reasonable liberty . . . and absolute outlawry of terms 'inmate,' 'patient,' 'ward,' 'keeper' . . . etc." He had come upon the Central Point site while driving along Lake Pepin and decided the beautiful lakeside was perfect for his purposes. He planned a complete farm, intending to have residents unable to pay for room and board work the land and help provide their own food. He also planned a series of cottages to house 20 to 40 men each. His major backers were Mrs. E. A. Russell, who operated a temperance restaurant in Minneapolis, and Etta Thompson, prominent in the Methodist church.

Woolley's home, known as Rest Island, opened in July 1891 with a week-long series of well-attended activities including the orations of speakers from "all parts of the country." The financial panic of 1893 slowed progress on the project, however, and Woolley's dream faded. He turned over the operation of Rest Island to Etta Thompson in November of that year. The facility was used as a site for religious conventions for several years.[18]

As formidable as the late-19th-century temperance organizations may have been, conquering "demon rum" required more than their efforts and those of like-minded lawmakers. Temperance advocates wanted to alert a wider audience to the dangers they believed inherent in the consumption of alcohol. Liquor was easily available in many towns, and patrons of local saloons weren't much interested in joining the "dry" movement. According to the Goodhue County *Republican*, Red Wing in 1876 had more than 49 places "in which to buy . . . liquid poison."[19]

Also standing in the way of abstinence was the aptly named porcine provider of alcohol—the "blind pig." In reality, blind pigs were off-the-record liquor-supply stops where transactions could be conducted secretly. The pig could be as simple as a drawer that extended from the wall of a home or business to the outside. A buyer knocked on the wall, and the drawer opened. The buyer placed money in the drawer. The seller replaced the money with a bottle of liquor. Buyers sometimes knew the owners of blind pigs, but neither party saw the other. Pigs tended to flourish where liquor sales were illegal and where dealers were in short supply.

Wanamingo fought a decade-long battle with blind pigs in the 1870s. Before their 1871 vote to legalize liquor sales, the cautious citizens agreed to raise $50 to build a jail. They expected trouble should the proposal become law, but the voters elected to stay dry. Nevertheless, a year later the citizenry made efforts to halt the operation of three blind pigs reported in the area.[20]

Citizens of Zumbrota, a temperance town from its inception, kept a wary eye out for blind pigs. In 1858 Zumbrota boosters claimed that "intoxicating liquors are not sold . . . nor is any person in the community known to use them as a beverage." Thomas Kellett, one of the town's founders, reported that his career as a justice of the peace was relatively uneventful since he had "little to do in a temperance town." The Zumbrota *News* reported elimination of a pig at nearby Rice Station on November 3, 1893. The newspaper suggested that its proprietor, Fred Persic, would not be missed and that "the blind pigger" had left town, "taking everything that belonged to him and some things that didn't."[21]

One sensational blind-pig case turned into a two-year melodrama. In January 1891, county commissioners granted a liquor license to James Ahern of Goodhue village. There were rumors of a thriving blind pig in Goodhue, and the commissioners approved Ahern, believing perhaps that the required $500 fee and licensing would bring control to the situation. Instead, their actions created an uproar.[22]

Angry township residents, hearing of the commissioners' actions, petitioned the board to rescind its ruling and stop Ahern. Harriet Hobart, wielding the power of her WCTU state presidency, believed the township had voted to be dry and never revoked that status. She asked for a ruling from the Minnesota attorney general, who decided that a liquor license was indeed illegal if the township had voted to ban the sale of intoxicating beverages. Ahern wasn't intimidated by the maneuvers. He had a license, and he kept selling.

County Attorney S. J. Nelson took Ahern and his bartender, Harry Tisdale, to court in February, charging them with selling liquor illegally. The defendants received a change of venue from Goodhue to Featherstone, but Ahern was found guilty and fined $50 plus costs. Tisdale was ruled not guilty.

A town election in March 1891 provided Goodhue voters with another chance to consider licensing liquor. Citizen speculation about the election's outcome dominated talk in Goodhue, and people in other parts of the county also took an interest. A Red Wing news reporter and election handicapper believed the drys would prevail, observing that the "Swedes and Americans will vote almost solidly against . . . the Irish and the Germans are divided against it." The antiliquor forces did prevail but by just 23 votes, 117–94.[23]

Ahern admitted defeat and pledged to close his saloon. He requested the withdrawal of charges and the return of his $500 license fee. The county commissioners agreed to revoke the license they erroneously granted and return the deposit. The *Daily Republican*, fed up with an issue that created ill will, pondered in print about "the cost to the county of this little cotillion."[24]

County Attorney Nelson met with Ahern and was assured by the would-be liquor dealer that he was ceasing operations. Nelson decided against pursuing the issue further, only to discover later that Ahern double-crossed him. On the same day Ahern talked with Nelson about closing down, he ordered several kegs of beer to sell in Goodhue. The irate attorney then pledged in a public letter that if Ahern or anyone else in his building sold "another drop of liquor," he would take immediate action.[25]

In August 1892, the controversial Ahern engaged in a fight with James McHugh on a Red Wing street. The *Advance Sun* reported that Ahern, upset with McHugh because of an alleged insult, hit McHugh with a billy club. The newspaper report said McHugh responded with weapons "nature had given him," and "the 'pig' squealed lustily for help."

In November 1892, Ahern and Tisdale sustained convictions in Judge William Williston's First District Court for illegal sale of alcohol. They planned to appeal that decision and clear themselves of all charges.[26]

Goodhue village voters, in the meantime, decided to go "wet" at their annual town meeting in March 1893. Temperance advocates claimed a snowstorm that blanketed the area blocked roads and kept the dry forces home. The 77 voting favored the pro-license cause, 41–36. With his appeal still pending, Ahern wasn't able to apply for a now-legal license, but his wife, Margaret, obtained one.

Before the courts could rule on the appeal of their earlier conviction, authorities arrested Ahern and Tisdale and charged them with trying to intimidate a witness. In September 1892 a group of hooded men had cornered Ben Pehrson near Goodhue. Shots fired during the incident aroused citizens who rushed to the scene and chased the intruders away. Ahern and Tisdale allegedly were members of the gang of intimidators. While awaiting grand jury action on the Pehrson case, the two men learned that the state supreme court had upheld their earlier, district-court conviction. Judge Williston sentenced Ahern to 150 days in jail and a $250 fine. Tisdale got 180 days and a fine of $300.

Ahern and Tisdale finally were locked up. Nevertheless, in the spring of 1893 the village of Goodhue had three legal saloons on Broadway.

Those toiling in the movement to secure a woman's right to vote continued to mobilize even as the temperance struggle continued. The 14th Amendment to the Constitution, enfranchising African-American men without doing the same for women, gave the suffrage movement impetus in 1869. Angry at the exclu-

Nowhere was the battle over Prohibition more hard-fought than in the village of Goodhue. Above, c. 1904, two saloons and a liquor store on Broadway. *GCHS*

sion of their gender from the amendment, Susan B. Anthony and Elizabeth Cady Stanton decided to promote the cause by forming the National Woman's Suffrage Association. Meanwhile Lucy Stone and her husband, Henry Blackwell, worked toward a similar end by organizing the American Woman Suffrage Association.[27]

The issue of a woman's right to vote became a popular topic for debates, lectures, editorial comment, and general public discussion. Opponents to suffrage voiced concern that the movement would alter the traditional notion that a woman's place was in the home. Some feared suffrage would allow women more independence and damage family structure. One minister, quoted in the *Daily Republican*, warned of calling woman "down from her white throne to a lower throne" to her "degradation and enslavement."[28]

Suffrage and other women's rights issues also became objects of ridicule. The most conspicuous function of the suffrage and prohibition movement, wrote Mark Sullivan in his widely read history of the era, "was to provide material for newspaper jokes."[29]

Chris Graham, the prominent, longtime Red Wing justice of the peace, used his well-known wit to tease his wife, Louise, about the rights issue. He wrote his good-natured jab at Louise's concerns in a letter to their daughters. The Grahams were going to the Red Wing Music Hall in January 1871 to hear a lecture on women's rights:

> Your mother is determined to go, as she is anxious to find out what her rights are; and once knowing them she is determined to maintain them, even if it destroys the harmony of the family. From this day henceforward she is going to live up to and enjoy her rights, when found out.[30]

Males who supported suffrage grew in number by the last quarter of the 19th century. Some gave grudging support. In February 1876, a Goodhue County *Republican* editorialist wrote a tepid endorsement of suffrage. He didn't believe "politics or women would be much changed for the better, nor yet for the worse, by the extension of suffrage to adult females." Three months later the *Republican* took note of a Red Wing speech by national suffrage leader Elizabeth Cady Stanton and offered her some advice. She should focus her appeals to the ladies because when women express the "general sentiment" that they want to vote, men will not oppose them.[31]

Few men were as vociferous in their support of suffrage as Red Wing Baptist preacher Claude Raboteau. In an October 29, 1887, speech, he maintained a woman had the right to "carry out her plans and aims of life after her marriage to the same extent as men." He condemned the idea that women should look "to marriage as the only object, and then settling down to a listless life with no mental activity above making chair tidies, [as] weakening if not degrading." He maintained a woman could enter business or professional life with the "same prospects" as a man and considered it "barbarous" that some women did the same work as men for lesser salaries.[32]

In 1881 Julia B. Nelson formally signed onto the continuing struggle for the vote by joining 14 other women to form the Minnesota Woman Suffrage Association (MWSA). She continued her interest in the WCTU but became the driving force behind the state suffragists during her 1890–1896 presidency.[33]

A trip to the Washington, D.C., national convention of the Woman Suffrage Association in 1886 again proved Nelson's skill in advocating for the cause. The 44-year-old crusader testified before the House Judiciary Committee:

> As a law-abiding citizen and taxpayer and one who has given all she could give to the support of this government, I have a right to be heard. I began teaching freedmen when it was so unpopular that men could not have done it. A woman gets for this work $15 per month; if capable of being a principal she has $20. A man in this position receives $75 a month. I ask you to remove the barriers which restrain women from equal opportunities and privileges with men.[34]

Her oratorical skills earned Nelson a job as a paid lecturer for the National Woman Suffrage Association, and speaking tours took her around the region. Nelson addressed audiences in western Minnesota and the Dakotas, and during an 1894 spring journey to Kansas and Missouri, she stopped to talk in different communities nearly every day. When one heckler claimed women shouldn't vote because "they don't bear arms," Nelson riposted, "Women don't bear arms, but they bear armies."[35]

Nelson also convinced state officials to declare one of the days scheduled for the annual state fair in 1894 to be "Woman's Day." The MWSA encouraged suffrage supporters to visit its fair booth and pledge support for the movement. Among the first to sign on were Vice President Theodore Roosevelt and Minnesota's Gov. Samuel Van Sant.[36]

The MWSA president wasn't so successful in securing passage of suffrage legislation. Nelson worked assiduously but without success for the passage of a series of bills backed by the association. An attempt to get Minnesota women the vote in 1892 failed. An 1892 bill requesting suffrage in municipal elections failed. An 1895 bill allowing women to vote on questions relating to liquor traffic failed. An 1897 attempt to franchise taxpaying women failed. During Nelson's presidency the persistent women's group also presented suffrage petitions to each gathering of the state legislature.

In 1911 Nelson broke with the MWSA, the organization she helped found, and started another suffrage group. Perhaps impatient with the lack of progress, she tried to find another route to success. She came to regret that move and rejoined the MWSA in 1914, still working at age 72. Weakened by a two-week fall suffrage campaign through North Dakota, she died on December 24, 1914.[37]

Other changes in the societal position of women occurred as people of the Victorian age gradually opened to new ideas. One of the most notable and controversial was the beginning of a new way of dress, inspired in the 1890s by the popular bicycle. As women became interested in the new fad, manufacturers tried to adapt bicycles to prevent skirts from becoming entangled in the spokes. A few daring women began wearing shorter skirts. For modesty's sake, the hems carried small lead weights.[38]

Other sports also created clothing problems. A woman could hardly play lawn tennis in stays and corset. Playing basketball in a long skirt was as difficult. Amelia Bloomer popularized the use of full-cut, loose-fitting trousers gathered at the ankles or knees to allow freedom of movement. Many social critics believed women should not take part in unrefined games in the first place. For them the unladylike "bloomers" made matters worse. Many years passed before such specialized clothing effected change in ordinary women's wear.

Women's fashion in 1900 focused on "smallness," resulting in dress that included tight-laced corsets, kid gloves, and the smallest shoes possible. Women strove to reach the standard of a waist "easily clasped with two hands." One account summarized the attire of the conventionally dressed woman of the day prepared to meet the public:

> She wore a wide-brimmed hat that caught the breezes, a high choking collar of satin or linen, and a flaring gored skirt that swept the street on all sides. Her full-sleeved shirt-waist blouse had cuffs that were eternally getting dirty . . . and her skirt was a bitter trial. Its heavy "brush binding" had to be replaced every few weeks, for constant contact with the pavement reduced it to dirty fringe in no time at all. In wet weather the full skirt got soaked and icy. Even in fair weather its wearer had to bunch it in great folds and devote one hand to nothing else but the carrying of it.[39]

More ready-to-wear women's clothing appeared in stores. In the 1870s and 1880s, most women made their own clothes or sought out seamstresses to create finer wear. One Zumbrota account recorded requisites for a fine dress of the period—15 yards wide silk, five yards skirt lining, three yards horsehair cloth to stiffen the skirt, 12 inches buckram for the collar, four dozen fancy buttons, one card of hooks-and-eyes, five spools silk thread, three spools cotton thread, one bolt of seam binding, and two-and-a-half yards of feather bone.[40]

The job of seamstress, among the vocations considered proper for a woman, often attracted young, unmarried females. Mothers taught daughters sewing skills. In the mid-1890s, sewing schools, such as the one in Alma Larson's

Cannon Falls home, sprang up. The Northfield College of Dressmaking recruited in the county in 1904. A dressmaker might go from home to home, sometimes staying several weeks while outfitting members of the family. The seamstress could make house calls or, if she had the space, see customers at her home or shop.[41]

Throughout the nation, Victorian rules of behavior ruled women's lives. Family members or chaperones regulated dating. Love, as it had through the centuries, still found a way, but parents of young women definitely policed the route.

One 15–year–old found that the authorities backed her parents in their desire to regulate dating. The family committed her to the State Training School at Red Wing for being incorrigible. According to a newspaper report, "She insisted on keeping company with a vile fellow and was bent on marrying him against the wishes of her parents who made the complaint."[42]

The rules of society cautioned young women to protect their reputations jealously. In a letter labeled "secret," Chris Graham, the Red Wing justice of the peace, warned his daughter, Mattie, to avoid a Mrs. Foster who had left her husband. "Prudence would dictate that you give her the cold shoulder. I am

The Women's Relief Corps, an affiliate of the Grand Army of the Republic, remained active well into the 20th century. Broom-wielding women of Zumbrota's chapter gathered with the national guard for a community celebration. *GCHS*

Members of the Floradora Club enjoyed an outing on the steamer *J.S.*—in their "casual" clothes  Back row, l to r: Carl Hemberson, Jessie Glardon, unidentified, Miss Hempfling, Lizzie Becker, and Kate Rice; front row: unidentified. *GCHS*

truly sorry for her as I respect her, but you must guard your reputation and have nothing to do with persons who are talked about." Mattie's father also admonished her not to, "under any circumstances visit a place she may want you to go. There is no telling into what company she might take you."[43]

Close supervision of its female students was a hallmark of the Lutheran Ladies' Seminary in Red Wing. Young women found it almost impossible to get away on their own. While they could go downtown once a week for shopping, they had to walk with partners, with chaperones front and back. Each Sunday they walked as a group to Trinity Lutheran Church. A student plotted to get out one night by borrowing clothes from a kitchen maid to avoid recognition. The teacher in charge apprehended the young woman before she escaped.[44]

Even in death a woman's reputation was of concern. Holden school teacher Eliza Crawford died in the 1890 Lake Pepin capsizing of the steamer *Sea Wing*. Her uncle, H. W. Keller of Hay Creek, wrote Eliza's parents in Ohio that the propriety of her taking the Sunday steamer excursion was not in question. He said there were "many good people on the boat," and that Eliza's companion, Katie Burkhard, who also died, was of "unquestionable character."[45]

Self-appointed social arbiters felt comfortable offering judgment on the behavior of women. One writer to the *Daily Republican* wondered whether mothers of Red Wing girls knew where their daughters were at night. The writer saw a group of about 22 teenage girls at the train depot to "see and be seen." He presumed the mothers of most of the girls "thought they were at church." The writer did not explain why he believed mothers alone were responsible for teenager behavior. He did report that most of the girls were "chewing gum."[46]

The newspaper page reporting the girls at the depot also included an editor's observation that the paper often had mentioned "the same matter." He did not limit criticism to girls but noted the "common saying among outsiders that Red Wing has the worst boys and girls of any town in the state."[47]

Bearing children was a danger as well as a trial for Goodhue County women, from the days of the Mdewakanton into the 20th century. Midwives assisted with the earliest births in the county, but a lack of knowledge and medical instruments hampered their work. Difficult births increased the likelihood of death for mother and child. Physicians, present by the late 19th century in the towns and villages of the county, assumed more responsibility for assisting with births. Professional medical care reduced the number of midwives, but some families, especially in rural areas, still called upon them to assist in delivery.

Victorian attitudes about women also figured in the decline of midwifery. A "proper" woman exhibited four "virtues"—piety, purity, domesticity, and submissiveness. Such a woman likely would find a problem during childbirth too much to handle. Midwifery by middle- and upper-class women thus was improper at best.[48] Prairie Island nevertheless had two midwives, Margaret Kuhns and Thelena Larson. Kuhns practiced for 35 years around the turn of the century. In Kenyon, Christine Severson delivered hundreds of babies, and Gunhild Nesseth occasionally turned her home into a maternity hospital. Caroline Scherf was a midwife in Frontenac, and Maria Schenach helped expectant mothers in Old Frontenac.[49]

In the larger city of Red Wing, midwives apparently developed their own territories. Marie Timmerberg, best known as "Old Lady Timmerberg," worked in the south end of town. Wilhelmia Anderson lived at Fourth and Bluff. Grandma Bielfeldt covered the College Hill and fairgrounds area. One of Marie Timmerberg's patients recalled the midwife's requirements for a new mother: "We had to stay in bed at least two weeks after the baby came, and she would come in each morning to bathe the baby and see that I was doing well."[50]

A neighbor called upon Amanda Johnson of Claybank to assist an expectant mother while the prospective father raced off to find a doctor. The physician made it in time, and Johnson assisted with the delivery. The baby boy was a few weeks premature, and the doctor asked Johnson to assume temporary care of the infant. He recommended keeping the child warm and giving him a few drops of warm water. Later that day, despite her best efforts, the child died in Amanda's arms. Mrs. Johnson went home to get the "prettiest dress and little shirt" she could find, then dressed the baby for burial. She remembered later, "He was such a cute baby. Then I asked the mother if she wanted to see him, but [she] said she would rather not."[51]

The presence of doctors did not insure successful childbirth. Minnie Newman, wife of school superintendent A. W. Newman, experienced difficulty for a week in the final stages of pregnancy. Mary Scofield wrote of the woman's ordeal in a February 1908 letter. Dr. A. T. (Alva) Conley, later assisted by other physicians, attended her. The medical men had to "crush the skull of the baby" to deliver it and save the mother's life. The doctors anesthetized the mother for the operation and later told her what happened. Mrs. Scofield reported that the baby boy was "full time" and weighed about 12 pounds. During the birth, wrote Scofield, nurse Emma Kowitz and Dr. A. T. agreed that, "It just seemed as if the mother and child could not be seperated [*sic*]."[52]

Dr. Conley felt the mother was doing well after the traumatic birth, but Nurse Kowitz soon called him back to his patient. Minnie Newman experienced complications from birth and was weakening. The doctor's struggles to save her were unsuccessful. Scofield recounted that the surviving husband said he "hasn't anything to live for."

Mary Scofield, herself the mother of a six-month-old, described the funeral of the mother and child. Mrs. Newman was "laid out in the parlor" dressed in her white wedding gown, "her baby lying on her left arm." The infant's body, "buried two or three days," was exhumed for reburial with the mother. To Scofield, the casket bearing the mother and child was "the most touching sight I ever saw."[53]

Women's issues gained scant political traction as the century turned. The reform movement was in disarray. The People's Party agrarian crusade had been co-opted and destroyed, largely by its ill-fated 1896 alliance with the Democratic Party. "Fusionists," dedicated to linking the party with the Democrats and their presidential candidate William Jennings Bryan, prevailed over hard-line party veterans at the People's Party raucous St. Louis convention. Fusionists, most of whom, according to one historian, "held office, had once held office, or sought to hold office," believed their "future was now." They thought their best hope for the coming election lay in allying with the Democrats to defeat the Republicans.[54]

The nation, throughout the election process, continued its struggle to recover from the lingering effects of another economic panic. That devastating blow struck the country in the spring of 1893 following the collapse of the Philadelphia and Reading Railroad and several other major rail systems. More than 600 banks closed, financial institutions foreclosed thousands of farm mortgages, and 20 percent of the nation's industrial workers eventu ally lost their jobs. Populists blamed the downturn on the "tight money" resulting from the nation's policy of backing its currency with gold. Bryan and his followers advocated coining silver to get more money in circulation. In at least one Red Wing factory, a cash-starved employer paid his employees in scrip, which for a time was virtually the city's "only circulating currency."[55]

The candidacy of Bryan, the "boy orator of the Platte," did give Republicans pause, but they soon developed a broad-themed, well-organized, and well-financed campaign of "peace, progress, patriotism, and prosperity." The Republicans chose William McKinley of Ohio as their standard-bearer. Bryan carried the solidly Democratic South, but the industrial North and three midwestern agricultural states, including Minnesota, voted for the Republican McKinley. Overall, the election was a bloodbath for the Democrats. They lost 113 seats in the House of Representatives and five in the Senate.[56]

Minnesota gave McKinley a plurality of 53,767 votes and 64 counties to Bryan's 17. Traditionally Republican, Goodhue County put itself solidly behind McKinley, providing him the largest winning margin in the state—80 percent of the votes cast. Republicans David Clough, winner of the governor's contest, and Joel Heatwole, elected to Congress from the Third District, scored similar victories in the county.[57]

The success of McKinley and the Republicans in 1896 hardly dispelled the disquiet. Many felt continuing resentment at inequities in an economy they perceived as rewarding a few to excess while others toiled without advance. Countering such sentiment were those labeling America a land of opportunity, allowing those with talent and willingness to work the freedom to advance. To supporters of America's capitalistic economy, hard work was the remedy for people struggling within the system. Others applied the lessons of Charles Darwin's *Origin of the Species*, broadly implying that the nation's most successful individuals were examples of the survival of the fittest.[58] Still, America's leaders at the turn of the century had to deal with the concerns of the men and women who believed themselves the underdogs of the current political and economic system.

Goodhue County in the 1890s was no longer a backwater. Improved rail and communications allowed citizens better access to the rest of the nation and the world. Changes altering the face of America were visible in Goodhue County. The infrastructure improved as railroad construction continued, townships worked to improve roads, and the interstate bridge at Red Wing, a major engineering accomplishment, opened. The county economy still centered on agriculture, but its growing industrial base attracted workers, some of whom left the farm for better jobs in town. The county's small towns and villages provided an array of businesses and cultural activities not readily available to those on distant prairie farms.

Goodhue County's population, according to the 1890 census, decreased from 29,651 in 1880 to 28,806 ten years later. Nineteen of the county's 23 townships showed a drop. Townships in the south and west, where Cherry Grove, Holden, Minneola, Warsaw, and Wanamingo averaged declines of more than 14 percent, sustained the largest losses. Pine Island township had a 22 percent loss, and Pine Island village dropped to 548 citizens, a loss of 108. Other villages and towns increased in population: Red Wing was the county's largest city with 6,294 citizens in 1890, up nearly 7 percent. Cannon Falls was next largest with 1,078, a 12 percent gain, and Zumbrota third with 867 residents, an increase of nearly 9 percent.[59]

A fundamental change in American immigration patterns occurred in the decades immediately before and after 1900. In 1882, 87 percent of immigrants had come from northwestern Europe. By 1907, 81 percent of the new Americans were natives of south, central, and eastern Europe. The more recent immigrants could not rely on the availability of cheap land. Whereas the northern European immigrants often lived in rural ethnic enclaves, the newcomers tended to concentrate around urban and industrial centers that needed large numbers of workers.[60]

Immigration to Goodhue County slowed. The largely Scandinavian and German base provided a more stable population than found in other sections of the state and country. The county's foreign-born population decreased from 12,502 in 1880 to 10,401 in 1890, while the number of native-born residents increased from 17,149 to 18, 405. By 1900 the number of foreign-born county residents fell to 8,988 as a new generation counted among the native-born.[61]

Goodhue County's people were rooted to established farms and communities. Their economic base subsequently was sound. Some newer Americans weren't so fortunate. The nation's remarkable economic growth, largely unrestrained by government, created dreadful social ills, particularly in its sprawling urban centers. Progressives labored to address the problems.

Pioneers of social work Jane Addams and Ellen Gates Starr founded Chicago's Hull House in 1889. John Dewey's pragmatism was at the root of the country's new "progressive education" concepts. Social scientists like Richard Ely and politicians including Wisconsin's Robert La Follette became part of the reform movement. Novelists wrote about political corruption and other evils. Upton Sinclair's *The Jungle*, a stunning 1906 account of the meatpacking industry, exposed the filth of the Chicago stockyards and gave Americans a collective stomachache. It also helped reformers muscle a pure-food law through Congress.[62]

Investigative journalists reached out to the public with compelling stories that captured readers' interest and sympathy. These "muckrakers" repeatedly shocked the American public with their tales of greedy and immoral business and government practices. Jacob Riis's haunting accounts of New York tenements horrified readers. Ida Tarbell's exposé of Standard Oil Company and its excesses hit *McClure's Magazine* in 1902. Lincoln Steffens's series on municipal corruption and Ray Stannard Baker's "The Railroad on Trial" soon followed.

America, while still the land of opportunity, clearly could be improved. Progressives would continue their attempts to remedy the nation's ills through the first two decades of the new century.

# *10*

## *The Growing Economic Base—*
## *A Better Life for Working People*

The approach of the year 1900 was more than just an arbitrary demarcation in time for the citizens of Goodhue County. The existing business leadership, along with new entrepreneurs, modified and expanded the county's industrial base. The county was in the midst of an economic evolution that would change the agricultural system that had produced much of the county's early wealth. King Wheat had given way to increased crop diversification, and farmers exploited the potential of dairying as a major moneymaker.

Farmers in Goodhue County, described in 1874 as America's banner wheat county, had understandably resisted diversification. Overspecialization in wheat, however, had resulted in depleted soil that, when combined with infestations of chinch bugs and other insects, produced near crop failure in 1880. Forced by necessity, farmers switched to barley for malting as their leading cash crop. Meanwhile, the dairy industry evolved into a sophisticated and profitable venture. Dairying adapted well to the county's rolling farmland with its ample reserves of pasture.[1]

The factory system of making butter and cheese had been introduced into Minnesota around 1870. Martin Anderson's history of the state's dairy industry notes that in 1869 Eli Ellsworth operated a Cannon Falls cheese factory. But most dairy farmers concentrated on butter production. Relatively few Swiss immigrants in the state had proven expertise in cheesemaking, but their countrymen had already made neighboring Wisconsin famous for the product. Only later did Minnesotans become adept at making quality cheese.[2]

To make dairying viable, county and state farmers would have to obtain milk-processing machinery, just for starters. They had to deal with other issues, too. During the early years of county dairying, overstocked farms resulted in the improper care of cows. Farm buildings were often substandard and unsanitary, and purebred dairy stock was rare. Time-consuming chores associated with the upkeep of property kept farmers busy; they had few laborsaving devices.

Even as it was, Goodhue County farmers managed well. In 1879 they produced 723,368 pounds of butter from their own farm dairies, the largest amount of any county in Minnesota. They also sold 20,277 gallons of milk to dairy factories. The county's dairy herd increased from 1,851 cows in 1860 to 9,461 just 20 years later. By 1890 the number reached 21,607.[3]

The state's dairy farmers in the early 1880s based their industry on butter and cheese production. Butter could be made from whole milk or from cream separated from milk, while cheese required whole milk. Dairy farmers could deliver their milk to factories under the whole-milk system or have their cream collected by factory pickup. The formation of the Minnesota Butter and Cheese Association in 1882 fostered the development of milk-processing factories.[4]

Factory owners complained that too many of their clients delivered "poor cream." Some farmers foiled the testing for quality with infractions including the stirring of air into their cream. In the early days creameries had no simple way to determine the butterfat content of milk, so they used the "stick method." Factory owners dumped cream into a standard container, then lowered a marked stick into it. Each inch of depth supposedly produced one pound of butter. Operators of Kenyon's North Star Creamery set prices by the inch until the development of more reliable measures.

Considering their early successes with butter production, the dairy farmers of Goodhue County might have been surprised to learn that their county would dominate the state's cheesemaking industry by 1904. The county's cheese industry had its roots near Pine Island, in a small Swiss enclave on the Goodhue-Dodge County border. In the late 1860s Rudolph Schmidt, Chris Martig, Jacob Figy, and Chris Closner, all natives of Switzerland, made Swiss and brick cheese at home, using wash boilers and cheese kettles. They kept some for themselves and sold the surplus "cheese weighing . . . 12 to 40 pounds." Figy was the first to peddle cheese to nearby stores.[5]

Settlers wanting their milk processed began to deliver it to local cheesemakers who took a portion of the finished product as payment. The cheese was satisfactory but did not match the quality of what the Swiss-Americans had made in their native land. They would have to improve their product to fend off the challenge of a new-style American (or Yankee) cheese.

American cheese was easy to produce, cured faster, and allowed farmers to sell the product sooner. This helped American cheese to dominate locally. Historians credit Swiss immigrants Susan and Jacob Bringgold as the first to make cheese in Pine Island, which soon became the center of the Minnesota industry. Susan learned how to make cheese from her father.[6]

Other Pine Islanders became involved in making cheese. Vern Parker worked for the Crescent Cream and Cheese Factory before developing his successful general store. Baumgartner brothers Walter, Jake, and John had long careers in the industry—Walter with 50 years and Jake with 44. John received more state fair first-premiums for his cheese than any other competitor. He also became the state's third dairy and food inspector. Hub Irish and George Lee also count among Pine Island's earliest cheesemakers. Arthur Parkin became the state's most prominent advocate for the cheese industry during the first three decades of the 20th century.[7]

Cheesemaking caught on in a major way, especially in the southern sections of the county. One or two people, often just a cheesemaker and his wife, operated the small plants, by necessity located within a two-to-three-mile radius of a farm. To prevent spoilage, farmers required brief travel time for their daily trips. Groups of farmers organized dairy cooperatives, member-owned associations that marketed products, to save money by eliminating middlemen.[8]

An early cooperative, formed in Sogn south of Cannon Falls, began a half-century of cheese production in the 1890s, starting with a cream-separating station a mile south of the Sogn store. It moved the skimming station across the road from the store as the area's dairy herds increased. Farmers brought milk to be separated and returned home with the remaining skim milk. The cream traveled on to Kenyon's North Star Creamery.[9]

After severing their agreement with North Star in January 1899, farmers in the area developed the Sogn Cooperative Dairy Association, one of the county's more successful cooperatives. Co-op members donated most of the plant's construction work. The group incorporated, issuing a hundred shares of

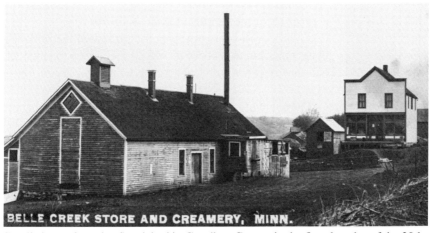

Small cheese factories flourished in Goodhue County in the first decades of the 20th century. This Belle Creek creamery faced the general store at right. *GCHS*

stock for $100 each. Cheese manufacturing began in April, with A. T. Jones of nearby West Concord serving as cheesemaker.[10]

Roscoe Butter and Cheese factory, another cooperative venture, had staying power. Township farmers built the factory in 1898. The facility and its successor, Roscoe Dairy Association, operated until 1949. The utilitarian brick structure was later placed on the National Register of Historic Places.[11]

Amund Steberg was president of the Steberg cheese factory, a cooperative venture begun in Minneola in 1889. Local farmers established the factory with a capital stock of $600. R. O. Lund soon purchased the operation. He later sold it to Gutzler Brothers of Kenyon, who remodeled it into a creamery. This firm failed, and its patrons, because of money owed them by the creamery owner, claimed the facility. They created the Minneola Creamery in December 1893.[12]

The invention of the centrifugal separator, which separated cream from milk, greatly increased the efficiency of dairy operations. This machine, perfected in the 1890s, enabled dairy farmers to get all the cream from the milk and produce a consistently high-quality cream. It also helped to move the farmwife out of the dairy barn. One female reporter for the Bureau of Dairy Information tried to imagine a man involved in premechanized dairy work, "straining the milk, skimming the shallow pans, ripening the cream, churning and working the butter, cleaning everything and everywhere." She conceded that farmer's wives and daughters "have been relieved of their work," but it might have been "even better for the dairying business itself that it remain in [their] hands." [13]

Another industry breakthrough was the 1890 development of the Babcock test for butterfat, which provided a more scientific basis for the manufacture of dairy products. The test allowed dairy farmers to determine the production value of each cow, an aid to improving their herds through culling and selective breeding. "Nothing in the history of dairying," wrote Martin Anderson in 1913, "has done so much for its development as the Babcock test."[14]

Minnesota's dairy industry underwent dynamic growth in the final two decades of the 19th century. Butterfat production increased 102 percent in the 1880s and 154 percent in the 1890s. Farm-made butter outpaced factory-made in quantity by nearly 250% in 1895. Cheese factories, however, produced five times the product of farm manufacturers. Goodhue County ranked third in the state in cheese production with 51,850 pounds, and fourth in butter with just over a million pounds.[15]

Goodhue County cheesemakers, almost by default, dominated in Minnesota by the early 1900s. Cheese production elsewhere in the state fell off, and butter production soared when the University of Minnesota's dairy school emphasized it. Meanwhile, dairy farmers in southern Goodhue County readily challenged the presence of New York and Wisconsin in the cheese industry. By 1906 county dairies produced 1,095,464 pounds of cheese, more than double the amount of their second-place neighbor, Dodge County.[16]

Cheese cooperatives underwent a period of growth especially between 1908 and 1916. Cooperative societies brought producers together to market jointly their goods and share in the profits. The Pine Island-Roscoe area near the Dodge County border was a center of this activity. Fair Point, Stanton, Cannon Falls, Kenyon and White Willow also had cheese co-ops.[17]

Much of the credit for Goodhue County's strength in dairying, and in the cheese industry in particular, goes to Pine Island's Arthur W. Parkin. As a young man Parkin studied at the University of Wisconsin under Stephen Babcock, inventor of the butterfat test. Parkin brought his expertise in cheesemaking to Goodhue County. Along with his brother and partner, Edgar, he owned or bought the cheese production of 11 different factories. Arthur Parkin won many awards for his cheeses and was a respected dairy-show judge. His skills were such that state agriculture officials asked him to become Minnesota's first dairy and food inspector. With no existing civil-service examination for the post, the officials asked Parkin to make his own list of questions and answer them. He passed the test.[18]

In a 1911 demonstration of his cheesemaking ability and as a publicity stunt, Arthur Parkin engineered the making of the world's largest cheese. Eighteen cheese factories within a 12-mile radius of Pine Island brought more than 7,000 pounds of curd to a Parkin-engineered form located on a railroad flatcar. The cheese was ready for curing after careful packing and pressing of the curd for 24 hours. Measuring six feet in diameter, four-feet-six-inches in height, and

Arthur Parkin (second from right), Pine Island, and his brother Edgar (far right) organized the making of the world's largest cheese, 1911. *George A. Fenton photo, MHS*

19 feet in circumference, it contained 70,000 pounds of milk, the production for one day of 3,300 cows from 250 farms. Parkin trucked the cured cheddar to the state fair for exhibition, but not before he displayed it in a drive through downtown St. Paul and Minneapolis. The truck carried the mammoth cheese, with Parkin and a bugler perched on top. An Atlantic City firm later purchased the cheese for 40 cents a pound—ten cents over the standard price.

Throughout his adult life Parkin was a booster of Pine Island, and he served as mayor of the town for 26 years. He chose Pine Island for the production of the giant cheese because he considered it the center of the Minnesota cheese region and the only point where such a monumental project was possible. Parkin claimed for Pine Island the leadership of the Minnesota cheese industry, an assertion unchallenged in his lifetime.[19]

The strong back of Red Wing potteries carried the clay industry of Goodhue County in 1890. Mining and transport of clay, along with the fabrication and sale of pottery products, resulted in hundreds of jobs. It also produced tons of surplus, lower-grade clay substandard for making stoneware.

Some believed the excess clay could serve a useful and profitable purpose—most likely as sewer pipe.[20] George Cook was among those experimenting to create durable pipe. He produced a sample piece for exhibition in the window of the Pierce, Simmons Bank in Red Wing. Its label read, "Red Wing Sewer Pipe, Why Not?" In October 1891, Red Wing Sewer Pipe incorporated, with Elijah Blodgett president. A year later John Rich formed a sewer-pipe company bearing his name. The two companies later completed a friendly merger and moved into the "spacious and substantial" factory erected by Rich.

The quality of Goodhue County clay proved almost perfect for the sewer-pipe industry, but its factories produced equally well-made chimney tops, flue linings, gutters, and cistern tops. An advertising booklet claimed that authorities the country over listed Red Wing pipe the best available and that pipe buyers submitted specifications "insisting upon Red Wing quality." It also quoted Heinrich Reis's assessment of Minnesota clay: "The cretaceous beds [clay] are probably the most valuable clay resource of the state, but unfortunately, the only important occurrence occupies only a very limited area near Red Wing." [21]

Zumbrota Clay Manufacturing also took advantage of the county's clay resources. In operation by 1906, it constructed buildings, kilns, and a steam plant for power built on 16 acres of Minneola township land. The clay in the immediate area proved inferior, necessitating horse-drawn wagons and later a small rail line to import a better-quality material. The company floundered and was reorganized two years later.[22]

Ed Barr jumped into the county clay industry in July 1911, when he bought the Minneola farm of Andrew and Bertine Olson for the then-substantial price of $10,000. Barr had prospected for clay a year earlier, finding it on the Olson farm. He later hired a Twin Cities contractor to drive 50 teams of mules and horses to the site and begin construction of his Barr Clay Products factory. He imported brick and tile and completed 12 kilns, 32 feet in diameter, with eight more planned.[23]

Mule teams dragged wheeled scrapers to strip the clay, but later a steam shovel operating on rails did that job. The shovel required a three-man crew— engineer, fireman, and boom operator. Workers hauled the clay into the plant for crushing and combining with water. From this mixture they produced brick and hollow tile. Barr Clay made silo tile, a popular building material in the area. A farmer writing to the Zumbrota *News* in March 1912 testified to the superiority of the clay block silo over those made of wood stave.[24]

Ed Barr was not in the business for the long haul. He sold out before the end of the year, leaving the stock company in the hands of Charles Roe, who managed Farmers' Elevator in Kenyon, and Harry Swan, manager of Wanamingo Lumber Company. Roe and Swan tried to sell stock in the firm and occasionally took prospects to the factory site on railroad handcars. The company reorganized in 1914 and operated sporadically over the next 25 years.[25]

Brick was also manufactured in Red Wing, as it had been since 1855. Charles Brink and William Williams ran their factory in the last quarter of the 19th century. A new business, Red Wing Brick Company, opened in 1905 near the sewer-pipe complex, its annual capacity ten million bricks. It employed as many as 18 men before closing in 1914.[26] Smaller clay manufacturers operated around the county. Loomis Irish, the Pine Island banker and entrepreneur, used his own modest brickyard west of town to supply construction material for his bank building. Builders used Irish brick in several other Main Street buildings.[27]

Claybank was a turn-of-the-century collection of about a dozen homes and two boardinghouses built literally on one of the county's best sources of clay, three miles north of Goodhue. Workers used the small houses mainly as sleeping quarters. The company later moved the buildings for access to the clay deposits.[28]

Most Claybank workers, immigrants from Sweden and Norway with an admixture of Germans, were single men. A few families lived on site. The work was physically demanding, and few stayed long. Laborers paid for board and room at company-owned-and-managed boardinghouses. Peter Olson, company superintendent at Claybank, and his wife, Jenny, ran one such home. The clay pit's owners paid workers 12 cents an hour until 1906, when a raise boosted the rate to 17.5 cents.

Surveyors usually found clay about four feet beneath the surface. After removing the topsoil with horse-drawn scrapers, workmen dug out and loaded the clay into horse-powered dump cars. In later years a steam-powered dragline attached to a large boom crane removed the topsoil. The crane operator lowered a capacious steel bucket, attached by cables to the boom, into the earth, then

These clay miners worked in the Claybank pits. Foreman Albin Johnson (grand-father of the author) leans on the clay car holding his son Vernold. *GCHS*

dragged it back toward the crane. Workers scraped the clay into the bucket, which was empted into a railroad car.

Men working nine- to ten-hour days required large, nutritious meals. Pit operators employed two or three young women for washing, cooking, baking, bedmaking, and waiting on tables. Mary and Olga Nelson worked at Clay-bank's upper and lower boardinghouses and, along with their other duties, served meals for crews of 26 to 32 men. Their workdays stretched from 4:30 in the morning to 7:00 in the evening, with a "breather" in between.[29]

Bellechester's "New Town," also a product of the clay industry, began to take shape around the railroad tracks just north of the village. In 1908, clay was discovered on land owned by Nick and Matt Strauss. Red Wing Sewer Pipe purchased 160 acres from the Strausses for $150 an acre—three times the typi-cal cost of land there. Mining operations began in 1912 with the completion of an imposing aerial tramway to carry loads of clay.[30] The tramway featured two towers, one 80 feet high, the other 70, placed almost two city blocks apart. Heavy steel cables linked the towers, which could be moved along three pairs of rails as required by the opening of new pits. Steam power, applied through large sets of gears, turned drums upon which cables wound and unwound, car-rying loaded buckets to railroad cars for dumping. Crews of 12 filled buckets.[31]

The Duluth, Red Wing & Southern Railroad and its Red Wing manage-ment, having established the Red Wing–Zumbrota route in 1889, turned its cor-porate eyes to the clay pits. With land-condemnation suits, the DRW&S had previously steamrolled farmer opposition to their plans. The most visible victim of DRW&S threats was a bachelor Irishman, Patrick Walsh, from the White Willow area. He sued the railroad over its land condemnation award and won $400 in damages. Walsh tore down railroad fencing and threw it on the track; he was arrested and convicted, but later he appealed and won. He again cut the wire fencing but lost two cows when a southbound train ran into them on the track. The stubborn bachelor was still battling when he died in January 1899.[32]

The railroad then looked to the clay pits of Claybank and Bellechester as targets for a new "Clay" line. The DRW&S completed a branch to the pits by 1893, and the three Red Wing potteries operated spur lines at Claybank. The DRW&S purchased two clay cars in 1889 and added ten more two years later. That growth pushed the railroad to run 32 cars. The first clay carriers, in reality, were flat cars with two-foot-high sides.

Operations at Claybank ceased unexpectedly in the last week of December 1925, and the little community never recovered. In the mid-1930s Red Wing Sewer Pipe started a digging operation in the old pit area, looking for previously missed clay. Bellechester meanwhile returned to the pre-clay-mining days with comparative ease. With restoration of some of the clay-mined farmland, the scars of its mining era partially healed.[33]

The leather and shoe industry, a part of Red Wing's manufacturing base before statehood, began a major expansion early in the 20th century. Silas B. Foot, an enterprising Pennsylvanian, had arrived in the city in 1857, trying his hand in several ventures before settling on the shoe business. The following year competition arrived in the person of George Sterling, another Pennsylvanian who manufactured boots and shoes. The production of footwear, Goodhue County's longest-lived industry, evolved from this base.[34]

Foot and Sterling soon formed a partnership, with Foot commuting by train to the St. Paul branch and Sterling running the Red Wing operations. The firms made shoes and boots as well as the popular shoepacs, rough moccasins tanned with the fur remaining. Growing demand for leather products, coupled with a lack of reliable sources of hides, created an opportunity for a local tannery. Trout Brook Tannery, later known as S. B. Foot Tannery, filled that need.

Foot built a three-story wooden tannery in 1872, in Featherstone township just southwest of Red Wing. Ample fresh water from the brook facilitated the treatment and preparation of hides. The crew of 15, working with 30 vats, could produce just 25 to 50 tanned sides per day. The unpleasant odors created by the processing proved a considerable drawback to the job.[35] As the century turned, Foot's son Edwin (E. H.), who professed a "fever to go into this tanning," became the driving force at the Trout Brook plant. E. H. Foot directed a major expansion of the old tannery in 1907, convincing his family to plow $250,000 into the venture and raising another quarter-million by selling stock in the re-

vamped company. Upon his father's death in May 1908, E. H. took the lead of
the family business.

Foot addressed the need to attract and maintain an able work force by forming Trout Brook Realty in October 1908 and building 14 houses near the plant.
A factory boardinghouse, a railroad platform, two stores, and a chapel completed his immediate vision of the small community.[36] Seventeen-year-old
German immigrant Charles Beckman began working at Trout Brook in 1873
and became something of a Silas Foot protégé. Ten years after his arrival at the
tannery, Beckman moved to retail boot and shoe sales on Red Wing's Main
Street, with Foot as a partner. But Beckman had bigger ideas.[37]

Beckman carefully secured local financial backing for a shoe-production
company and in January 1905 announced the opening of the plant. The idea received favorable front-page Red Wing newspaper coverage. Beckman declared
the full amount of proposed capital for the project already raised and announced
that construction of the new factory would start, weather permitting. The business would employ 100 to begin with, but "several times that number" might
be added. Beckman's new concern became Red Wing Shoe Company.

The county's smaller industries provided needed manufactured goods as well
as employment for those who made them. Wagonworks, breweries, ice houses,
and fur factories, among others, flourished in Goodhue County.

Red Wing had five wagon-making companies and Zumbrota two by the
late 1870s. Wagonworks in Red Wing included N. Lovegren's, which began
production during the Civil War, about 50 per year. Henry Helmeke's small factory employed ten workers. Charles Erickson's company made wagons, sleighs,
and other conveyances. Andrew Newstrom later joined with Erickson. Their
firm, which had nine workers, manufactured a hundred wagons a year. The
Kappel brothers, Michael and John, used 15 workers in their factory. Goodhue
County's largest wagonmaker was Red Wing Wagon Works Company, with a
workforce fabricating 15 wagons each day. A major fire ended that business in
1902.[38] In Zumbrota, Herman Koehler's Wagon Shop started operations on
Main near Fourth and later moved to larger quarters. H. J. Klein's wagon business was a half block east of Main and Second.

With the decline of wheat production, farmers turned to other crops and
discovered a moneymaker in malting barley—malt being the chief ingredient
for beer. They increased acreage for the new cash crop, with some raising as
much as 5,000 bushels annually. Red Wing's entrepreneurs, seeing an opportunity, built two malting companies in 1900 and 1901. In less than ten years the
malt business surpassed that of the city's powerful flour-milling industry.[39]

Minnesota Malting organized first, taking over and remodeling the old
North Star Stoneware facility in Red Wing's West End. The factory soon employed ten men, with an annual capacity of a half-million bushels. The larger

Red Wing Malting rose in 1901 and expanded the next year. With 11 tanks, the new factory by the Mississippi River levee doubled the capacity of its rival. William Krise served as plant manager. Lines of farmers with wagonloads of barley stretched along the streets of Red Wing, reminding many of the days when the wagon trains of wheat sellers jammed city thoroughfares. Farmers received between 37 and 45 cents per bushel in the early days of malting operations. Some barley purchased in the city was shipped directly to breweries. Anheuser-Busch of St. Louis stationed a buyer in Red Wing.

Goodhue and Cannon Falls became directly involved in malting. A branch of Red Wing's Minnesota Malting opened in Goodhue in 1900, and American Malting Company, managed by John Davis, a leading Goodhue businessman, started the next year. In 1912 A. R. "Tony" Mensing left his position as vice president with Minnesota Malting in Red Wing to start Commercial Grain and Malting in Cannon Falls. Mensing learned the maltster's trade in Chicago.[40]

Red Wing's breweries did not fare as well as the malting concerns. Small breweries existed in the 1860s, but by the end of the century only two viable companies—Remmler's and Jacob Christ's Red Wing Brewery—remained. Christ's, located on West Main Street, employed four men and produced 1,400 barrels of beer a year. William Heising began what would evolve into Remmler's brewery. After Heising died in 1873, his widow, Christiana, ran the business at Bush and Fifth Streets. Three years later she married Adolph Remmler, who took over management of the brewery.[41]

Flax joined malting barley as another cash-producing crop for county farmers. The J. K. Brady Tow Mill in Kenyon was one flax buyer. The mill removed the coarse and broken fibers of the flax to produce "flax moss" used in the manufacture of rope and twine. The plant and its stock covered ten acres six blocks east of the CGW depot. A 45-horsepower engine powered the flax processing machinery and produced 700 tons of moss in 1896.[42]

In 1901 city businessmen founded Red Wing Linseed Mills, a riverfront flax-crushing factory. Workers made linseed oil, an important ingredient of paints and varnishes, by crushing flaxseed. Six years after opening, the plant's annual production was 15,000 barrels of oil and 6,000 tons of oil meal.[43]

The need for ice resulted in an important wintertime business. Although refrigerating machinery was being perfected in the large cities, small-town Minnesota relied upon its frigid winters to produce tons of ice. Cutters harvested huge slabs of ice from rivers and lakes, stacking the chunks in icehouses made of four bare walls hooked to studding. Placing the ice a foot or two from the walls allowed the packing of insulating sawdust around it.[44] To obtain the ice, harvesters first removed any snow covering so that the cleared area could freeze to a greater depth. Horse-drawn plows scored the surface with three groove-cutting chisels. Chunks of ice called head blocks were then removed so the remaining ice could be split into large rafts. Workers pulled the ice rafts to a platform where they could cut individual pieces with splitting bars. The ice broke along the score lines, producing pieces about 18 by 36 inches, ranging in weight from 200 to 300 pounds.[45]

J. A. Mogren's ice operation in Kenyon provided double service. In early winter, skaters kept the rink near the Mogren Zumbro River dam clear. The clearing process allowed the ice to freeze deeper, enhancing the February ice harvest and the stocking of the large Mogren icehouse.[46]

Clamming, the hunt for freshwater mollusks, was another job-creating river activity. The shells, used in the area since prehistoric times, were in particular demand in the 1890s, when the pearl-button industry flourished. The shells with the more salable "mother of pearl" on their smooth inner surfaces provided decoration for buttons and jewelry items. Clamming became popular around Goodhue County. Searchers found clam beds along the Cannon and Vermillion Rivers as well as the Mississippi and Lake Pepin.[47]

Clammers operated from flat-bottomed boats made with enclosed square ends providing a platform for gear. They built racks to hold the clam bars on each side of the boat. The bars were of heavy fish cord or chain, about a yard long, attached to heavy pipe. Clammers attached blunt hooks with four prongs to the cords. When they lowered the bars into underwater clam bars, the bivalve mussels opened and clamped onto the prongs. The clammers raised the bars, collected the clams, and repeated the whole process.

The work of steaming the mollusks to remove the meat from the shell followed. Clammers sorted shells by variety, with their contents searched individually for pearls. Most pearls were of modest value, but fortunate clam gatherers made excellent finds. A Sunday picnicker started a "pearl rush" in Cannon Falls by finding a medium-sized pearl. A 35-grain wine-colored ball pearl, found later, sold for $500, and a 30-grain pink pearl of lesser value also was found. The hunt for valuable pearls continued, most often frustrating the hopes of searchers. Too much clamming and pollution combined to reduce the profitability of the industry, largely abandoned after three decades.

The daily lives of Goodhue County residents slowly improved during the years of industrial expansion. Increased mechanization in the factories and farms of the county reduced heavy labor for workers. Laborsaving devices helped to make chores at home easier. The advent of these timesaving inventions added leisure time somtimes filled by organized athletic competition. Arguments about who possessed the faster horse produced occasional races, later scheduled attractions. Managers of the Cannon Valley Fair in Cannon Falls found saddle- and harness-racing popular. Likewise, discussions about the relative skills of a local boxer or wrestler produced competition. Settling debates about the fastest runner, skater, rower, or bicyclist prompted challenges as well.

A few in the county played baseball as early as 1859, but not until 1866 was a Red Wing team ready to compete statewide. St. Paul's tough North Stars challenged the Crescents of Red Wing and traveled downriver for a game. Their hosts treated the North Stars to a tour of the city, entertaining them "in a very handsome style." But hospitality did not help the home team. After playing evenly early in the game, the St. Paul team pounded out a 52–34 win. The following year the Red Wing Crescents went on the road, playing two games with Lake City's Union club and meeting Rochester's Gopher State team before an estimated crowd of 1,000. As a paying-fan following increased, baseball teams pursued cash prizes instead of trophies. Citizens in Red Wing offered a purse of $20 to attract visiting clubs from outside the county.[48]

Cannon Falls began its tradition as a "baseball town" in 1867, when local players organized a team. Little is known of that first club, but by the 1880s, Cannon Falls had put together a winning team. Some of the town's early standouts went on to professional ball, including Ed Wilson and his son, George. Orville Kilroy pitched for both Minneapolis and St. Paul. Ab Hollister

The Cannon Falls 1887 baseball team: (standing, l to r) Ed Wilson, Sid Swanson, Justus Swanson, Dick Dibble, Fred Hillman; (seated) Will Platt, manager, Fred Alpstag, Frank Barlow, Clarence Stevenson, and Jim Wheat. *CFHS*

and Wallace Van Guilder, city players in the 1870s, signed contracts with the New York Knickerbockers.[49]

Baseball was a hit around the county. In Pine Island, locals gathered at the Loomis Irish pasture to enjoy games. Goodhue held early competitions between two teams of village men known as the Fats and the Leans. Kenyon's team had some fan favorites, including Frank Held, a catcher who disdained the standard protective equipment of his position, and "Wily Joe" Corrigan, who earned free passes to first by placing his padded legs in the way of pitches.[50]

Enthusiasts organized teams around the county for informal fun or serious competition, the players bearing their club's name on uniformed chests. They occasionally played games on Sundays, a practice questioned by Christians who considered Sundays a day reserved for religious observance and rest. An 1892 Sunday baseball game at the Zumbrota fairgrounds, for example, started talk in the village about banning the sport "on the Sabbath."[51]

Bicycling became a sensation in America in the 1880s and particularly caught on in Zumbrota and Red Wing. Throughout the summer of 1895, cycle enthusiasts organized competitions between teams from those cities. Red Wing cyclists built a racecourse—the West End Driving Park—and Zumbrota riders created a track west of their town. Some of the bicyclists took part in the

Quite a crowd turned out to watch this 1896 race in Red Wing, probably part of a Fourth of July celebration. *MHS*

Zumbrota Fair that September as well as the bicycle parade and competitions at the Minnesota State Fair.[52]

Local riders began to build reputations for their skills. Zumbrota's "Stub" Warren received first prize—a $100 diamond stud—in the 1895 Fourth of July race in Faribault. He covered the 18.5-mile course in 58 minutes, 20 seconds. Will Newton of Red Wing showed skill on high-wheeled bicycles, and distance-rider Mabel Miller biked 50-mile routes.[53]

The new sport attracted women as well as men, and they worked together to develop new venues for bicycling. Members of the Red Wing Bicycle Club took part in club runs, cycle picnics, lantern parades, and long- and short-distance rides. The Red Wing group proposed a bicycle path connecting the town with Lake City and raised $900 for the effort by contributing $450 for the path, a total later matched by the Goodhue County Board of Commissioners.

This route seemed perfect to everyone except farmers and property owners whose land it might affect. Landowners claimed the path, so near the wagon road to town, would cause them delays. Farmers believed that "city folks propelling themselves by on their bikes" unsettled horses. Taking matters into their own hands, some farmers plowed parts of the path into oblivion. The cyclists unsuccessfully sued Wacouta township over the issue. They abandoned the path project, but the sport of bicycling maintained its popularity in the county.

Rowing competition in racing shells proved another popular activity—one that frequently attracted wagering. As with other sports, the level of competition ranged from informal meetings, held mainly for fun, to hotly contested prize battles held among top athletes. River communities such as Red Wing prided themselves on producing fine racing teams.

An 1875 boat race between Stillwater and Red Wing shell crews became more of a "shell game." Stillwater boasted state-champion oarsman Norman Wright, who led his favored team to Red Wing for a racing meet. Unknown to the confident Stillwater visitors, conspirators in Red Wing had added a "ringer" to their lineup. World-class rower Ellis Ward had joined the host crew several weeks before the event. Ward, using the name John Fox, was more than a match for Wright. Stillwater backers bet heavily on their champion, but the powerful "John Fox" left Wright in his wake. The Red Wing four-man crew, with the added strength of Fox in its lineup, defeated Stillwater handily.[54]

Jeptha Garrard of Old Frontenac drew considerable attention for his 1890s efforts to develop the world's first airplane. Jeptha was one of the prominent Garrard brothers, whose combined resources established the village on Lake Pepin. Ed Hunecke constructed several Garrard designs under the supervision of the inventor, but they met with scant success. Garrard imported a parachute jumper to test-fly his experimental aircraft. The pilot, who boarded at the Lake Side Hotel, lounged around the scenic rest spot, relaxing and recovering from jumps.[55]

One especially unsuccessful model had double sets of wings in front and back, with the front pair pointed down and the rear up. To Hunecke, the design guaranteed a nosedive on takeoff, but he built the aircraft as directed. For the takeoff of his machines, Garrard had designed a ski-jump-styled, tracked ramp, steep at the start, then leveling over the lake. A wheeled undercarriage allowed the Garrard airships to gain speed as they reached takeoff. The test of the double-wing design didn't go well. The pilot steered the ship down the ramp and into the air. As Hunecke had predicted, the machine immediately nosed over. The pilot continued flying onward without his craft. Eyewitness Hunecke recalled, "He hit the water flat, and you could hear the crack half a mile. We always had a boat handy, but generally he'd swim in by himself. He didn't that morning. He just grabbed ahold of the boat, and he didn't say anything."[56]

Motorboating also reached the Goodhue County area early in the evolution of that sport. John Trautner moved his boat- and engine-building business to Red Wing in 1903. There he built fishing craft powered by single-cylinder, two-cycle engines. Trautner's company became known as Red Wing Motor Company, and by 1906 it produced a boat that exceeded the existing Mississippi River speed record.[57]

Fishing was a popular activity in the county in the 1890s, practiced more for food than fun. Hunting served a similar function. Decades would pass before some sportsmen and women viewed fishing and hunting as recreational sports rather than practical sources of food.

Winter sledding, tobogganing, and skating provided entertainment, but skiing became a more serious winter sport. Cross-country skiing and ski jumping, in particular, allowed Red Wing's never-shy boosters to claim the city, with some justification, the "birthplace of skiing on the North American continent." Minnesota historian Bertha L. Heilbron supported the Red Wing claim in a 1958 article in *Minnesota History*.[58]

Four leading Norwegian skiers who immigrated to Goodhue County in 1883 provided the impetus for competitive skiing in the area. The Hemmesvedt brothers, Mikkel and Torjus, along with Paul Henningstad and Bengdt Hjermstad, formed the nucleus of the Aurora Ski Club. The newcomers were "riders"—ski jumpers—with considerable experience in their homeland. The Aurora club membership mushroomed from 28 members in 1886 to 64 in 1887.[59]

The Aurora riders built a modest 20-foot jump overlooking "Tumble Valley" on the south end of Red Wing's Wilkinson Street. The ski jump helped in developing talented competitors who represented the club in tournaments. Francis Kempe was a national champion in 1911. The Red Wing team later hosted ski-jumping meets, including two national championships.[60]

County residents found a host of other entertainments—among them, dances, masquerades, school plays, traveling theatrical companies, and lectures. Public holidays, especially the Fourth of July, became major events. Commu-

Riders performed the "Leap the Death Gap" on Zumbrota's Main Street during the fairs of 1905–1910. A rider died during one such attempt. *GCHS*

nities commonly formed musical groups, including singing and instrumental societies. Local musicians organized bands, with Zumbrota alone featuring a brass band, a cornet band, a banjo-and-mandolin band, and Slosson's String Orchestra. Zumbrota's reputation for musical performance stretched back to 1872, when singers from that village and elsewhere in the county attended the state musical convention in Minneapolis.[61]

In 1893 local Zumbrota talent produced a cantata under the direction of a Chicago professor, and later the Goodhue County Singers attended the Second Annual Norwegian Sangerfest in Eau Claire, Wisconsin. In 1894 the Sangerfest moved to Urland Church in Holden and gathered a crowd of 4,000, supposedly the largest gathering of Norwegians in the history of the county.[62]

Special events included the arrival of showboats at ports along the upper Mississippi.[63] Excursion boats also attracted crowds to the Red Wing levee. Popular excursions from Red Wing went to Stillwater, with a visit inside the state prison included, and to St. Paul, where a passenger could "spend the afternoon . . . and visit the capitol." Also popular were moonlight excursions.[64] In 1890 a summer excursion provided an unlikely scenario for one of America's most appalling river disasters—the loss of the steamer *Sea Wing* and 98 of its passengers on Lake Pepin just off Goodhue County's Central Point.

National guardsmen used the barge *Jim Grant* as a base from which to remove bodies of the drowned from the steamer *Sea Wing*. The *Ethel Howard* (background) hauled many of the disaster victims back to Red Wing. *GCHS*

*11*

*Surviving Adversity—*
*Overcoming Challenges at Home and Abroad*

Citizens of Goodhue County could not escape the 19th century without confronting the sorrows that have confounded humankind through history. Fire, a terrible peril for the county's farmers and city dwellers, was particularly dangerous in towns and villages where a lack of firefighting resources could lead to an uncontrolled blaze. Violent crime provided its share of misery, and the region's unpredictable and severe weather claimed a material and human toll.

The capsizing of the steamer *Sea Wing* during a powerful summer storm on July 13, 1890, became a part of the collective memory of Goodhue County citizens. Capt. David N. Wethern, co-owner of the 135-foot *Sea Wing*, which typically hauled log rafts downriver, led a river excursion on that hot, muggy day. Wethern was a merchant and part-time steamer pilot from Diamond Bluff, a village on the Wisconsin shore of the Mississippi. He announced a Sunday trip, cost 50 cents, to Lake City, where the Minnesota National Guard held summer exercises. For the trip, Wethern tied the covered barge *Jim Grant* alongside the port bow of his sternwheeler to accommodate the expected crowd. His wife, Nellie, and their two young sons joined the captain on the journey.[1]

Wethern picked up more than 200 passengers at Red Wing and steamed on. The festive scene at Lake City featured guard demonstrations at the camp. A late-afternoon storm scattered the audience, forcing most to seek shelter. After the wind and rain subsided, Wethern decided to make the run home. The *Sea Wing's* whistle recalled the passengers, and at 8:00 P.M. Wethern began the return trip. He couldn't know it, but a storm already was headed his way. The tempest had blown into the Red Wing area, tearing off roofs, knocking down trees, and flattening crops. The storm raced toward Lake Pepin and the *Sea Wing*.[2]

Captain Wethern saw the effects of powerful winds off the Minnesota shore as he neared Maiden Rock point. He turned the ship into the gale. Suddenly, winds buffeted the *Sea Wing* and wrenched its barge free. Those on the barge watched as the *Sea Wing* rocked, tipped to a 45-degree angle, and rolled over.[3]

The ship's cabin plunged upside down beneath the raging waters. Passengers packed inside had no chance of escape. The storm pitched those on the outside decks into the water; each began a lonely struggle to survive. Some managed to scramble onto the overturned steamer's slippery, flat bottom. People on the barge *Jim Grant* watched helplessly as lightning illuminated the lake and the calamitous scene.

The barge ran aground on Central Point, and many passengers jumped into the water to wade ashore. They alerted Lake City and the National Guard camp of the accident. Rescuers, disregarding the danger of the still-perilous waters, rowed to the accident site. Too late to be of much help, they soon began to search for the dead. The waters calmed by midnight, and the workers started moving bodies from the boat's cabin to the Lake City ship *Ethel Howard*. By 3:00 A.M., the *Howard* left with 52 of the dead for Red Wing.[4]

The recovery of bodies continued through the next day, and a thorough search of the wreckage produced 18 more. Among them were Nellie and Perley Wethern, the wife and youngest son of the steamer's captain. Not until Thursday were all 98 victims recovered. Red Wing, meanwhile, was a city in shock. Families and friends buried 56 on Monday and Tuesday in what seemed an endless stream of funerals.[5]

Five weeks later, following a hearing in St. Paul, steamboat inspectors found Wethern guilty of "unskillfulness" in starting out in the face of the storm, overloading his vessel, and failing to run close to the Minnesota shore, where there were good harbors "every mile or so." They suspended Wethern's pilot's license, referring his case to the U.S. District Attorney for prosecution.[6]

The accident temporarily paralyzed Red Wing. The small river town suffered 77 dead, a staggering loss. The death toll among female passengers was particularly grim. Fifty-seven women and girls boarded for the return trip from Lake City; only seven survived.[7]

H. W. Keller, uncle of Holden teacher Eliza Crawford, had the melancholy duty of notifying her parents in Ohio of their daughter's death. His letter undoubtedly expressed the feelings of many: "There are whole families lost. There is mourning in Red Wing as nearly all were from there. God only knows the sorrow it has and will cause . . . Such a disaster has never befallen this country."[8]

Damaging fires twice threatened the business district of Cannon Falls in the 1880s. The first blaze struck at 11:30 on the night of May 21, 1884, when A. O. Sather's store caught fire. Fire bells roused the citizens to fight the flames that quickly endangered nearby buildings. Sather's general merchandise store and nearby warehouse soon were beyond saving. Van Campen Brothers store to the southeast also was lost. Bucket brigades used Scofield's Drug Store, a stone building, as a defense against the westward progress of the fire. " A *Beacon* reporter wrote: "A ceaseless stream of water was kept pouring upon it [Scofield's], and men and women never wearied in carrying water from the mill pond and wells."[9]

A more terrible May conflagration three years later leveled large parts of Cannon Falls. Local observers believed the disastrous blaze proportional in its devastation to that of the great Chicago fire of 1871. The fire began in the rear of Ben Rodger's saloon around 10:30 P.M. Rodger's building was in the midst of seven wood-frame structures between Scofield's Drug Store and the Estergreen block. Within a half-hour the blaze engulfed all of them. The fire then swept across the street, involving six more wooden buildings. Firefighters hoped the stone Clifford and brick Yale buildings could withstand the flames, but they too succumbed. The Ellsworth House, Thoorsell's furniture store, and the Citizen's Bank on the north side of Mill Street began to burn. Eli Ellsworth's home soon followed.[10]

Now nothing could stop the flames. They destroyed Ellsworth's barn and the Yale warehouse on the west side of Fourth Street, then Thoorsell's warehouse, Johnson's photograph gallery, and Wold's house and store on the east side of that same street. The fire approached Hoffman Street where firefighters organized another attempt to halt it.

Citizens unsuccessfully assaulted the stubborn conflagration on several fronts. The people of Cannon Falls battled the inferno for nearly two hours,

The Cannon Falls fire of May 1887 destroyed 27 businesses as well as homes and other buildings. Above, citizens gathered to view the aftermath. *CFHS*

staying with the buildings until flames and heat forced them to retreat. The fire reached the Estergreen block's large warehouse. Alfred Johnson's blacksmith shop and attached buildings were the next to go, and soon the nearby barns went too. Finally, the firefighters checked the fire's progress by drenching with water the exposed east side of the Thompson and Smith cooper shop.[11]

Flames destroyed 27 businesses along with other buildings and homes. City leaders immediately took steps to make Cannon Falls less vulnerable to fire in the future. They tightened building codes and monitored the materials used in reconstruction. The city installed a water system, purchased fire equipment, organized a hook-and-ladder company, and completed a fireman's hall. Cannon Falls was ready for the next fire.[12]

Goodhue suffered a devastating fire on September 28, 1895. The barn at the rear of James Ahern's Headquarters Hotel caught fire late in the evening. A brisk northwest wind carried it to nearby buildings. The unincorporated village had no fire department, so volunteer bucket brigades fought the flames threatening structures at the corner of Broadway and Second Avenue. The Anderson building burned, and across Broadway the Sheldon grain elevator and six nearby freight cars caught fire. The C. E. Rucker building, the Doxey Flats, and the P. D. Kelly machinery depot also fell under the flames.[13]

The fire caused about $35,000 in damage. Authorities suspected arson but could not prove their theory. Not much remained on Broadway, though among the buildings still standing were James Ahern's hotel and saloon, which had earlier survived the blind-pig temperance battles.

The alarm for Kenyon's April Fool's Day fire of 1908 first came in at about 3:00 A.M., when Ole Lee awakened and spotted flames coming from the roof of the Hilland and Knutson General Store. Firefighters believed they were responding to a prank until they reached Main Street and found several businesses ablaze. Flames destroyed half of Main Street's north side, ruining eight businesses and causing an estimated $50,000 in damage. No one was injured.[14]

The most costly Goodhue County 19th-century fire consumed Red Wing Milling's Diamond and Bluff flour mills. Shortly after midnight on March 4, 1883, railroad workers noticed an unusual light through windows on Diamond Mill's fourth floor. Realizing the mill was on fire, the men gave the alarm but, despite water pumps and a hose on every floor, could do little to save the mills. Evidence at the scene convinced investigators the blaze was purposely set, but no charges were filed. The damage was $240,000, and no one rebuilt the facility.[15]

A sudden storm early in the winter of 1855–56 beset Dennis Cavanaugh of Belle Creek as he walked to his brother's house. He died in the blizzard, his body not found until spring. Civil War veteran George Lantz of Roscoe encountered a blizzard while riding home on horseback during the winter of 1865–66. He died a short distance from his home, but his horse reached the safety of a neighbor's barn. Joseph Thatcher, future state legislator from Zumbrota, nearly died during one of his first winters in Minnesota. He got lost while trying to reach his home and, near total exhaustion, stumbled upon a settler's cabin. Minnesota winters, throughout the county's history, claimed others as well.[16]

The sheer volume of seasonal snow caused problems, too. The winter of 1856–57, for example, became known as the season of "The Big Snow." Snow lay four feet deep on level ground, with drifts much higher. Winter held hostage 22 boats and delayed 1,500 passengers at Read's Landing on Lake Pepin. In January 1873, a storm heaped snow so high around Frederick Richter's barn in Goodhue that he had to chop a hole in the roof so as to feed his horses. A New Year's Day storm in 1886 piled snow on the Gladstone Building construction site in Red Wing, collapsing the unfinished structure. A storm of snow, rain, and hail all in one day assaulted Cannon Falls in March 1888, giving the area the appearance of "an immense ice-field."[17]

Damaging and deadly tornadoes struck the county in 1865 and 1879, following nearly identical paths through Vasa and Burnside and finally into Wisconsin. The tornado of June 17, 1865, forced county sheriff Martin Chandler to leave his carriage and take cover. The gale carried his horse and buggy nearly a half-mile, leaving both in relatively good condition. As the tornado passed along Spring Creek, it struck a house, killing a man inside.[18]

A tornado on the evening of July 2, 1879, was part of an immense weather system that caused destruction in northwestern Iowa and southern Minnesota. The storm's first Goodhue County victims lived in Wanamingo township near Aspelund. Ole Moeslet and his wife, Birit, their five children, and Moeslet's father and mother were swept into a pasture and nearby trees. Three of the children, John 21, Berthea 5, and Marie 1, died; their parents were severely injured. Moeslet's parents escaped injury. The midnight tempest swept on to Thorstein Vegum's farm, where it carried the house more than 30 feet, "scarcely racking it." Then it demolished Vegum's barn, killing two horses. The swirling storm sent a scythe whistling through a pasture, where it cut the throat of a calf.[19]

The winds roaring north and east toward Belle Creek and Vasa destroyed John F. Pehrsson's home, injuring three. They severely damaged Joe Reginald's house without injuring anyone inside, leveled Walter Doyle's Belle Creek home, and damaged three others nearby.

Hardest hit was Vasa. The tornado plowed into the village, killing nine-year-old Emil Lundstedt and injuring four others in his family. Winds carried Gustaf Holm's residence past the nearby Vasa Orphans Home, killing Holm, his wife, Hedda, and son Otto. The tornado then came upon the orphans home and its 24 residents. Three children—Ella Brandt 7, Ellen Ekland 9, and Minnie

Ekland 7—died outright, and two-year-old George Hamberg later died from injuries. The storm injured 15 other children and the two adults in charge.[20]

The tornado roared on, destroying the Erick Swenson home and killing him and his daughter. Frank Hallberg's son was also among the dead. The storm then charged to the northeast, leveling more houses, barns and property, flooding creeks and fields, damaging crops, and destroying bridges and fences. The massive front also caused damage in Wacouta, Hay Creek, Red Wing, Frontenac, and Florence, before muscling across the Mississippi.[21]

Crime was not unknown in Goodhue County, even though the first term of the District Court in 1854 concluded without trying a single case or issuing any indictments. From the days of settlement through 1900, 125 cases of assault and 14 murders occurred.[22]

Authorities quickly solved the county's early murder cases. The Congdon-Churchill incident of April 6, 1875, involved more detective work. William Churchill succumbed to a gunshot while sitting in his Cherry Grove home. The sheriff arrested neighbor Thomas Congdon, who had quarreled with Churchill earlier that day, on suspicion of murder. Congdon denied guilt, but paper gunwadding found next to the victim's body linked him to the crime. This led to a guilty verdict and a life sentence.[23]

Temperance advocates cited alcohol as a cause in the 1905 murder of Goodhue saloon-owner Charles Zemke. Zemke threw Henry Prolow, an itinerant harvest worker, out of his bar after Prolow became involved in a drunken brawl. Prolow returned later in the day, and Zemke physically threw him from the saloon. Prolow, kneeling in the street, pulled a revolver and fired at Zemke. The first bullet went through the victim's arm and also wounded Jim Lally, standing at the bar. Pralow fired three more times, hitting the 31-year-old Zemke in the back and killing him. Authorities took Prolow to the county jail in Red Wing for trial.[24]

A sensational and tragic shooting case shocked Red Wing on January 14, 1907, when a deranged man shot chief of police James Daily and officer John Peterson. The deed occurred in the Sibley Hotel when Daily confronted August Bloom, a former Red Wing barber recently confined as a mental patient at the Rochester asylum. As Daily questioned him, Bloom stepped back and warned the chief to get away. Daily advanced and began to pull his nightstick. Bloom drew a pistol. They wrestled, with Bloom getting free long enough to fire. His first shot missed, but the second hit the chief's shoulder. Another shot hit Daily in the abdomen as he fell.[25]

Officer Peterson responded to the gunfire, and Bloom shot him as well. Peterson walked to a doctor's office for treatment. Word of the shooting spread as citizens took the two police officers to Red Wing's St. John's Hospital and summoned J. T. Rogers, a St. Paul surgeon, who soon arrived on a special train.

Bloom, meanwhile, walked around town on that cold January evening, looking for shelter. He stopped at the home of Peter Martenson and offered a dollar for a night's lodging. Martenson, unaware of the incident downtown, allowed Bloom inside. The next morning Martenson's daughter saw a newspaper account of the shooting and summoned the police. Sheriff P. J. Lundquist arrived with 25 to 30 men, but he didn't need their help. Lundquist went to Bloom's room and arrested him. The suspect's revolver was still in his pocket.

Both wounded police officers died the evening of January 15, despite the efforts of physicians. A wife and one child survived Chief Daily; Peterson was married with five children. As the city mourned, Bloom was recommitted to the Rochester asylum.

World affairs were not a high priority for most Minnesotans in the 1890s, though most enjoyed the advances made during the state's 30-plus years of statehood. They strove to take advantage of technologies that made everyday life easier and more enjoyable. For many in Goodhue County, the concept of local men fighting and dying in a war half a world away was beyond consideration. Yet in 1898 Americans watched with interest a lingering and potentially dangerous international problem.

Cuba seethed with revolution as its citizens fought for independence from their Spanish colonial masters. The Cuban insurrectionists had met with a brutal, if ineffective, reaction from Spain, producing sympathy for their movement from the American public. Concern about the Cuban unrest had grown among U.S. government officials by the mid-1890s, though the administration of President Grover Cleveland assumed a neutral stance. Aggressive American expansionists castigated Cleveland and other neutralists for their reluctance to confront Spain.[26]

On January 23, 1898, President William McKinley ordered the battleship *Maine* to Cuba, ostensibly on a neighborly visit. *Maine's* "show the flag" mission ended disastrously three weeks later, when it mysteriously exploded while at anchor in Havana harbor, killing more than 250 Americans.

A March 21 report to the president assigned blame for the blast to an underwater mine detonated by unknown parties. McKinley, reluctant to plunge the nation into war, still had to act quickly. On April 11 he referred the issue to the Senate, with war the result. McKinley ordered Cuban ports blockaded and called for volunteers. America, woefully unprepared, had to produce an army in a hurry.[27]

Zumbrota's Company D, which later claimed the honor of being the first in the state to volunteer, prepared to join a stream of national guard units en route to St. Paul. Every man in the company advanced when Capt. William Kinne asked those willing to volunteer for active duty to step forward. Maj. John Friedrich and Capt. Oscar Seebach led Company G of Red Wing, mustered into state service as a national guard unit. They had just a few days to prepare for movement.[28]

Zumbrota's Company D arrived in Red Wing the evening of April 28 to join Company G in the journey to St. Paul. The next morning, a crowd estimated at 4,000 gathered for a formal send-off at the Milwaukee depot. Former congressman O. M. Hall told the men that they were "cast in the same mold as the Goodhue County boys of '61." Deafening cheers washed over the soldiers.

Minnesota's guard units, all mustered into service by May 8, divided into three regiments—the 12th, 13th, and 14th Volunteers. Zumbrota's Company D was assigned to the 14th and Red Wing's Company G to the 13th. After a scant week for equipping and drilling the troops, the regiments left the state for assignments. The 12th and 14th headed to Camp Thomas in Chickamauga, Georgia, the 13th to San Francisco to prepare for service in the Pacific.[29]

The American military command shipped the Minnesota 13th to the Philippine Islands, the distant, Spanish-controlled archipelago off the coast of southeast Asia. The conflict with Spain had immediately outgrown the island of Cuba, reaching Spain's other colonial possessions. Six days after the declaration of war, the U.S. Navy's Asiatic Squadron steamed into Manila Bay and destroyed the Spanish ships deployed there. The American naval force then blocked Manila and awaited the arrival of infantry. The Minnesotans and Red Wing's Company G were among units assigned to take the city.[30]

Minnesota soldiers settled in for a prolonged guerrilla war in the Philippines after the successful battle for Manila during the Spanish-American War. Some of the men above are believed to have been members of Red Wing's Company G. *GCHS*

But the 13th Minnesota needed six weeks of training and outfitting in San Francisco before it was ready for combat. The unit left for the Philippines on June 26.[31]

While the 13th Regiment underwent preparations for combat, the men of the 14th, including Zumbrota's Company D, drilled at Camp Thomas in Georgia. The 14th Regiment included the state's newest infantry units and, unlike Zumbrota's men, most enlistees were raw recruits. The condition of the camp and its equipment was crude. The entire brigade had the use of just one water pump. It also suffered from a shortage of everything from clothing to rifles. Fever (286 probable cases of typhoid and malaria) ravaged the camp.[32]

Soldiers of the 14th were painfully aware that while they languished in Georgia, the war raged on in the Philippines and Cuba without them. In July, American forces had forced the surrender of the Spanish in Cuba, and a month later Manila had fallen. Still the desire of the 14th's men to fight went unfulfilled. On August 27 the men of the Minnesota regiment were ordered to Knoxville, Tennessee, and 23 days later they returned home for a 30-day furlough. On November 18 the soldiers were mustered out of the service.[33]

While men of the 14th fumed, Minnesota's 13th Regiment endured a 40-day voyage across the Pacific. Seasickness plagued the men as did a monotonous diet and a shortage of good water. A three-day stay in Hawaii helped refresh the unit for the final leg of the journey. On July 31, the Americans arrived in Manila Bay to the enthusiastic salutes of U.S. Navy vessels anchored there.

The 13,000 Spanish troops awaiting the Americans in Manila were already in grave danger. The Spanish army, weakened by the three-month American naval blockade and beset by 12,000 Filipino nationalists led by Emilio Aguinaldo, prepared to resist the fresh Americans. Aguinaldo had returned to Manila in May with the knowledge and consent of the Americans. He proclaimed a Philippine Republic and hoped for American recognition. The Filipino desire to eliminate Spanish control of the country was identical to that of the United States. But Aguinaldo later disagreed with Americans about who would run the islands once they were free of the Spanish.[34]

The American force of 8,500 moved toward Manila on August 13, with the 13th Minnesota in the lead. The Spanish contested the advance, and the Minnesotans, including Company G, became engaged. Captain Seebach, walking among his men, urging them to keep down, took a bullet in his left side. Pvts. Frank Crowel, William Jones and Cpl. Charles Ahlers were wounded too.[35]

Sgt. Charles Burnsen suffered a serious head wound and was dying. The sergeant, a Red Wing potter in civilian life, was leading a squad of men when shot. In a letter home, Burnsen had tried to calm his aunt's fears for his safety, requesting that his uncle reassure her. "You must tell Aunt not to worry about me for I will come back some day all right." Sergeant Burnsen died at the brigade hospital in Manila on August 16.[36]

Two days after Burnsen's death, friends from Company G, resentful that the sergeant had been buried without proper honors, requested a reburial service and a proper coffin for the body. Officers refused the request. Defying authority, the men raised money for a coffin. On August 18, an advance group of 20 soldiers went to the Camp Cavite cemetery, exhumed Burnsen's body, and provided him a formal military funeral.[37]

Minnesotans represented a disproportionate share of the American casualties—23 members of the 13th Regiment killed or wounded during the fighting around Manila and three disabled from noncombat causes, a total greater than that of all other regiments combined. Captain Seebach wrote home that the bullet that had hit him passed through both lungs and "generally disturbed my insides." He was lucky to be alive. All five Company G casualties were from Red Wing.[38]

The Goodhue *Enterprise* hailed the accomplishments of the 13th Minnesota and its leadership in the attack. The story claimed that the names of the local men who fought would "be placed upon the county roll of honor for all time."[39]

News of a peace protocol made between the United States and Spain the day before battle had not reached Manila until August 16, the day after the fighting. With the Spanish vanquished, Filipino leader Aguinaldo insisted on joining the American army in its occupation of the city. But the American representatives requested the insurgent Filipino forces to withdraw entirely. Aguinaldo moved his men 20 miles north of Manila to ponder his options.

The warring nations reached formal agreement, ending the war on December 10, 1898. Included among the treaty's 16 articles was Spanish cession to the United States of Puerto Rico and Guam. The United States paid $20 million to Spain to assume control of the Philippines. The American public supported ratification of the treaty, apparently accepting the concept of territorial expansion. Sen. William E. Mason of Illinois spoke for many opponents to the proposed agreement, maintaining that the United States must not attempt to govern another people "without the consent of the people themselves."[40]

While the Senate debated, word arrived that Filipino insurgents had entered American-held territory in Manila on February 4, 1899, drawing fire from an American sentry. The fighting continued. Americans, including the 13th Regiment, patrolled the streets of Manila. Company G was involved in putting down a general insurrection on February 22, but the men chafed at garrison duty and hoped to get into the field. They were about to have that opportunity.[41]

The Red Wing unit and six other companies of the Minnesota 13th went on a 33-day mission to suppress Aguinaldo's forces. From April 22 to May 26 they covered 120 miles, captured 28 towns, and destroyed enemy supplies. The rainy season began, and in the monotony and boredom of midsummer, the men of the Minnesota regiment started thinking of home.

Sgt. Edmund Neill expressed the growing impatience of Company G's men: "We are ready to go home now; we don't care who has the Philippines or how soon they get them; all that longing for glory and honor and the glorious desire to distinguish ourselves on the field of battle has passed." Neill wrote that the men would continue to do their duty, "but every letter that goes back to the old town will contain a protest against the injustice of keeping us [here]."[42]

News of relief finally reached the 13th in late July, and on August 12 the Minnesotans headed back to the United States on the transport *Sheridan* via Japan. As the ship began to move, the band, for the first time since leaving America, played "Home Sweet Home."

Not all Goodhue County men left the Philippines. Bruce Dickey, son of Pine Island settlers Joseph and Sarah Dickey, was a government worker assigned as an assistant cashier in Manila's customhouse. His newsy letters home provided a firsthand view of America's position in the Philippines.

Dickey, during in the early years of his Manila assignment, watched with growing disillusionment the roller-coaster ride of American success and failure in putting down Aguinaldo's rebellion. On December 19, 1899, he wrote to his parents that "The insurrection is practically broken up; Aguinaldo's cabinet is captured and he is in the mts." The next day he sent another letter to Pine Island with news of the combat death of American commander Gen. Henry Lawton in a battle at San Mateo.[43]

In June 1900, Dickey speculated on China's Boxer Rebellion and his hope to be a part of the America relief expedition. Dickey believed the brief but violent outbreak in China might distract America and encourage Filipino resistance. In case of trouble, wrote Dickey, "Nearly every Filipino would get his gun and commence fighting again." The talk about Filipinos being friendly to the United States was, according to the Minnesotan, "pure nonsense . . . 99 out of every 100 Filipinos are insurrectors at heart."[44]

The enthusiasm of newly arrived September replacements didn't impress the Pine Island man, now a one-year veteran in Manila. Exasperated by the long guerrilla war, Dickey wrote that replacements were "anxious to meet the gugus [derogative for rebels]; they will soon be just as anxious to get back to the states, and there are a great many who will go back in a long pine box."[45] By January 1901, Dickey believed the end to the war was in sight. American prospects brightened even more with the capture of Aguinaldo on March 23. Other important members of the resistance were arrested and exiled to Guam. William Howard Taft, later president, went to the islands as head of the 1901 Philippine Commission and became governor general there the next year.[46]

Soldiers of the 13th Minnesota received a joyous welcome on their return to St. Paul the morning of October 12, 1899. That afternoon the veterans paraded past cheering crowds on Minneapolis's Nicollet Avenue, reviewed by President William McKinley, Gov. John Lind, and other dignitaries.[47]

The appearance of John Lind on the reviewing stand signaled that the progressive movement had come of age in the state. Lind, who came to Minnesota and Vasa with his Swedish immigrant parents in 1867, received training in law, then advanced in state politics and in the ranks of the Republican Party. He stood in front of the parading veterans as a governor carried into office by the coordinated efforts of three groups—Silver Republicans, Populists, and Democrats—breaking a Republican hold on the office stretching back to 1860.[48]

Lind's political career began in New Ulm, and he ascended to the governor's office after experience as a teacher, lawyer, and congressman. Beginning in 1886, voters elected him to Congress for three consecutive terms as a Republican. He was the only Republican in the Minnesota delegation to the House of Representatives to survive the 1890 election purge of fellow party members.[49]

In the mid-1890s Lind joined other politicians looking to the coinage of silver to help reinvigorate an American economy still affected by the Panic of 1893. Those supporting "free silver," such as the charismatic Democrat William Jennings Bryan, believed that continued reliance on the gold standard placed an unfair burden on farmers and laborers. Bryan thundered his famous challenge to those supporting gold in an electrifying speech at the Democratic National Convention in Chicago on July 7, 1896: "You shall not press down upon the brow of labor this crown of thorns; you shall not crucify mankind upon a cross of gold!"[50]

Lind, a "Silver Republican," accepted an 1896 draft to run for governor as a fusion candidate representing a coalition of Democrats and Populists, with Silver Republicans thrown in. With a decent showing in his old home county, Lind might well have won that election. But Goodhue County voters chose David Clough over Lind—5,073 to 1,991. Clough defeated Lind by just 3,452 votes statewide, greatly boosted by his Goodhue County plurality of 3,082. Lind's fusion candidacy proved successful two years later, when he ran for governor again. He received 37 percent of the Goodhue County vote, an improvement of 10 percent but still a poor showing.[51]

The county's citizens kept a watchful eye on the political and social movements of the day. They followed the ups and downs of their favorite parties and politicians with an enthusiasm that, in some cases, rivaled baseball fans' support of their home team. Political loyalties ran to a pre-Civil War depth in the families of many of the longtime residents. Often a man's political affiliation was carefully noted and attached to published biographies or obituaries.[52]

At the turn of the century, Goodhue County voter loyalty to the Republican Party remained unquestioned, much as the party's strength was evident in pre-statehood days. Democrat William Phelps, given the job of Land Register at Red Wing, in 1857 had joined the race for Congress with two other Democrats and three Republicans, all running at large. County voters turned their backs on all the Democrats, giving Republicans nearly 65 percent of the vote. This made Phelps the first of a long line of county Democratic congressional candidates to be outpolled at home. Phelps did go to Congress, however, as he gathered the most total votes among the six who ran.[53]

Lucius Hubbard, editor of the Goodhue County *Republican*, celebrated the next Republican triumph in the 1859 governor's contest. Hubbard, who would later become a two-term Republican governor, proudly revealed in his paper the Norwegian vote in southern county townships where Alexander Ramsey crushed Democrat George Becker. Holden voted 99–5, Zumbrota 100–10, Warsaw 29–13, and Leon 42–21 for Ramsey. Wanamingo, with its dominant Yankee population, went Democratic, 54–51. Red Wing's Democrat Chris Graham lost his congressional bid and could not prevail in Goodhue County.[54]

Joseph Thatcher, one of the founders of Zumbrota and an early Republican leader in the state legislature, earned election to the House twice and the Senate three times during the 1860s. During the Civil War he served with the legislature's enrollment committee, involved in drafting soldiers. He returned to the Senate in 1879, replacing Holden's Andrew Finseth and chairing the committee on education. The 1902 election started Zumbrotan Anton Julius Rockne, a power in the Minnesota legislature for nearly 50 years, on a career that eclipsed that of Thatcher, the "farmer statesman."[55]

Political leaders struggled to earn and maintain the support of Minnesota's immigrant population. They also cultivated ethnic leaders in various communities in their attempt to secure votes. St. Paul banker Ferdinand Willius wrote Red Wing businessman Charles Betcher in August 1879, asking for support for the renomination of Republican and German-American William Pfaender as state treasurer. German-born Willius asked Betcher, a native of Prussia, for his help "and that of the German-American population in your city and county at large." Willius had heard that Red Wing newspaperman and politician Samuel P. Jennison was backing Pfaender's opponent Charles Kittelson.[56]

Betcher replied that he could not be of much help. Republicans in Red Wing and Goodhue County wished to advance their man, Lucius Hubbard, to the governorship: "None of them would do the least thing to offend the Skandinavians [*sic*] and would . . . sacrifice anything to gain their objective."[57]

Four days later Betcher again wrote Willius about prospects for the ethnic vote in Red Wing. Some Scandinavians would support Pfaender, but the majority "favor their own countrymen." Betcher also reported on his attempt to meet with Michael Kappel, who he said was the only prominent German American in the local Republican Party. Kappel was out of town.

Betcher, in another letter to Willius, admitted surprise at Jennison's tactics. "Jennison has aspirations and wants to make himself solid with the Skan-

Leonard A. Rosing
*CFHS*

dinavians [*sic*] who I judge make up half of your party. I can see Col. [Hans] Mattson's hand in it too—a man who is in bad oder [*sic*] down here." In the end, the Hubbard and Pfaender forces met only frustration in advancing their candidates in 1879.[58]

Republican loyalty, particularly among Norwegian Americans, ran deeper in Goodhue County than elsewhere in the state. When John Lind, a convert to the Democrat-People's Party, broke the Republicans' 39-year hold on the governorship in 1898, most credited his win to success with the Scandinavians. That phenomenon did not occur in the heavily Norwegian-American southwest townships of Goodhue County. Voters there chose Republican William H. Eustis over Lind by startling margins: Minneola 147–20, Holden 115–20, Wanamingo 147–34, Warsaw 100–19, Kenyon township 86–17, and Zumbrota 100–21. The vote was better than five-to-one against Lind. Overall, Eustis carried Goodhue County 3,107–1,878.[59]

Goodhue County did not shut the Democrats totally out of office. O. M. Hall's two terms in Congress from 1891 to 1895 gave local Democrats some solace. Peter Nelson, as a state senator from 1887 to 1889, helped secure Red Wing as the site of the new state training school. Charles E. Friedrich started, in the 1880s, a multigenerational family affiliation with the Democratic Party.[60]

Cannon Falls Democrat Leonard A. Rosing advanced quickly within party ranks and became chairman of its State Central Committee in 1886, the same year he married May Season. A native of Sweden, Rosing arrived in the Cannon Falls area when he was eight. In 1888, while staying involved in politics, he started a shoe-retailing business that evolved into Rosing and Kraft. Rosing received credit for managing well the fusion forces of the Democrats, People's Party, and Silver Republicans during the 1898 John Lind campaign. Rosing became private secretary to Lind, the man he helped elect.[61]

When Lind failed to win reelection, Rosing sought his party's backing for the governorship in 1902. Party convention delegates nominated him in June after recovering from the "Lind fever" that, according to one newspaper, had dominated Democratic thinking for six years. The Republican incumbent Samuel Van Sant convincingly defeated Rosing. Unlike Lind, Rosing ran with Democratic Party backing only. Yet, even with the combined votes of Democratic, Prohibition, People's Socialist, and Socialist Labor Parties, the Cannon Falls Democrat could not have won.[62]

Progressive thinkers in the state and county established three new educational institutions in Goodhue County in the 1890s—the Minnesota State Training School for Boys and Girls, the Lutheran Ladies' Seminary, and Villa Maria Academy.

Formerly the Minnesota State Reform School, the training school underwent its name change after relocating from St. Paul to Red Wing. Believing *reform school* an unhappy word choice, the legislature renamed the facility. The school newspaper, *Riverside*, endorsed the decision, saying, "the name 'Training School' more clearly expresses the character of the school."[63]

Several Minnesota cities had maneuvered to secure the school and its jobs, but Red Wing finally took the prize. For $17,377.25, the state purchased a 450-acre site overlooking the Mississippi River, two miles east of the city.[64]

In the spring of 1890 Gov. William Merriam addressed an audience of 3,000 as workers laid the cornerstone for the administration building. He saw the institution as a place where residents would be "lifted up by education, hand-in-hand with the public and charitable institutions [and where] the old idea of brutal treatment [was] past, and in its place had come kindly forbearance and patience."[65]

In October 1891, the St. Paul reform facility transferred 50 boys to the new Red Wing campus. During its early years in Red Wing, the training school's administration operated under a semi-military system. Uniformed students followed a strict schedule beginning with reveille at 6:00 A.M. and ended with taps at 10:00 P.M. In between was time for school, eating, and drilling. The model changed periodically.[66]

Downriver from the construction site of the training school, Ursuline nuns opened, in 1890, the Villa Maria, an educational institution for young women. They located the Catholic school's campus in Old Frontenac near Lake Pepin, on 120 acres of land donated by Israel Garrard.[67]

Israel Garrard, after distinguished Civil War cavalry service for which he earned the rank of brevet brigadier general, returned to Frontenac to supervise expansion of the town he loved. He converted a grain-storage building into the Lake Side Hotel, soon a popular summer resort. Garrard and his brothers Kenner and Lewis, along with Everett Westervelt, purchased in 1857 the town site for what would become Frontenac. The Garrards built handsome homes overlooking Lake Pepin, while other businesses, including a stone quarry, lime kiln, sawmill, and brewery, grew up in the town. Many of its residents were former Cincinnati employees of the general.[68]

In the early 1870s, Israel Garrard blocked the Chicago, Milwaukee, and St. Paul Railroad from running its tracks along the peaceful lakeshore and through Frontenac. Eventually he agreed to the railroad laying rails two miles from the shore. The decision left Frontenac in peace but resulted in a newer village along the tracks. The Lake Pepin town site became known as Old Frontenac.

In 1890 the legislature approved funds to relocate the Minnesota State Reform School to Red Wing as the Minnesota State Training School for Boys and Girls. Above, the boys stood in formation in front of the Industrial Building. *GCHS*

Israel Garrard noted the success of the Ursline nuns' rapidly growing school in Lake City, and he offered them Frontenac land in 1885. Mother Kostka Bowman accepted the donation, and construction of the Villa Maria began in 1888. When completed two years later, its main building, shaped in the form of a cross, stood four stories high, 301 feet long, and 90 feet wide. The school drew students from around the state.[69]

Another institution for young women, the Lutheran Ladies' Seminary, opened in Red Wing in 1894. The Gothic-style main building housed classrooms, offices, and some dormitory rooms. The south wing contained more dorm rooms, along with kitchens and a dining room. Lavatories were on each floor, and bathrooms in the basement. The river-bluff site of the seminary campus overlooked the valley of the Mississippi.[70]

Seminary founders gave its first president, the Rev. Hans Allen, total control of the academic operation of the new facility. Its organizers modeled the Lutheran Ladies' Seminary on the successful Rockford (Illinois) Seminary, which evolved into a fully accredited college. Dedication ceremonies for the facility, held on June 6, 1895, considered the ethnic backgrounds of the students and their families. Prayers were in Norwegian, with the speeches in both English and German.[71]

The seminary became known for its school of music, led by Bernard Laukandt. The German-born Laukandt possessed perfect credentials for the job. He was an ordained minister who also held a doctorate in music. In 1908 the seminary added a music hall featuring an auditorium with 332 opera seats and a 150-seat gallery. The building also boasted 36 practice rooms, each equipped with a piano. Its basement provided room for gymnastics, bowling, and billiards and could be converted for roller-skating.[72]

Nickie Johnson's garage, Red Wing's first, opened in 1909 on Plum Street between Third and Fourth. It featured the city's first curbside gas pump. Johnson, far left, later became better known in the county for his popular dance band. With Johnson are (l to r) Abel Thygeson, unidentified, and Olaf Benson. *GCHS*

This nine-man threshing crew worked on a farm near Zumbrota. *GCHS*

# 12

# *The March of Progress—*
# *Technology Improves Daily Life*

Americans advanced into the new century in a self-congratulatory mood. The United States now assumed a prominent place among the leading nations of the world. Newspapers and magazines reported on material gains made in the country during the 19th century—coast-to-coast growth from 15 to 45 states and technological marvels such as the railroad, telegraph, steamboat, streetcar, electricity, and reaper. More Americans joined the march to prosperity, thanks to an economy based on the nation's inventiveness and industry. What lay ahead was unclear, but the citizenry was confident and optimistic.[1]

American society underwent fundamental change as the 20th century dawned. The nation was increasingly an urban, industrial society as its people migrated from the rural areas to live and work in the cities. Minnesota followed the trend. Historian Theodore C. Blegen later observed, "The factory was becoming nearly as familiar a landmark of [Minnesota's] economic life as the barn." In 1880, 81 percent of the state's population lived in rural areas—places with fewer than 2,500 inhabitants. By 1900 the rural population had dropped to 66 percent and ten years later to 59 percent of the total.[2]

Improved communication made possible by telephones, reliable automobiles, and dependable roads linked people, both rural and urban. Railroads neared their peak in miles of track in service. In 1900 there was about one telephone for every 66 people. By 1925 there was nearly universal access, with one phone for every seven people. In 1900 Americans owned fewer than 8,000 automobiles, and the contraptions were still considered a novelty. Fifteen years later the number of cars had mushroomed to 17 million. In 1900 just ten miles of concrete road existed in the nation; by 1925 there were 20,000.[3]

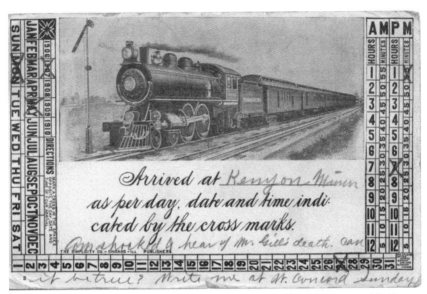

Train travelers could use postcards to confirm arrival. This Kenyon card indicates the passenger arrived on May 27, 1907, at 1:55 P.M. *John L. Cole Collection*

Rapid improvements in mechanization changed the America in which people worked and lived. In 1890 the nation employed 1,216,000 servants, a number in precipitous decline in the decades following. With the proliferation of laborsaving devices, the country nearly halved the army of domestics employed between 1880 (8.4 percent of total population) and 1920 (4.5 percent).[4]

Modernization of the American home made life easier for those who could afford new conveniences. Electric lights became more common. Improved plumbing and sewage systems allowed for the indoor water closet, a predecessor to the 20th-century toilet, as well as sinks and bathtubs.

Richard Sears, a Minnesota farmer's son, perfected a new way of marketing goods—the mail-order system. Montgomery Ward of Chicago introduced the concept in 1872 of supplying goods to rural customers by mail. By 1894 Sears's company, by then Sears, Roebuck, was building a mail-order empire. He filled his merchandise catalogs with an eye-popping variety of items for what Sears stated was a "sensationally low price." With his high volume of purchasing power, Sears pressured manufacturers to lower the prices he had to pay. He then passed part of the reduced cost to his growing legion of buyers.[5]

The people of Goodhue County continued to work towards better lives for themselves and their children. They reacted to changes in the greater culture and advanced in step with the rest of American society by exploiting the natural and human resources of the county. Goodhue County's dual agricultural and industrial economic base left most citizens well situated as the new century began.

Few changes in the chores and duties of farmwomen had appeared since early settlement. May L. Spencer addressed that problem in a magazine article in which she claimed that the mother was the most overworked person on the farm. She cooked, washed, sewed, raised the children, and also fed chickens and calves, milked cows, and tended vegetable gardens. Spencer suggested that the husband give his wife an afternoon off each week and attempt to lighten her workload with home improvements.[6]

The beginnings of rural free delivery (RFD) of mail proved an important step in reducing the isolation of farmers. The U.S. postmaster general claimed in 1900 that RFD would bring the farm "within the daily range of the intellectual and commercial activities of the world" and mitigate the "isolation and monotony, which have been the bane of agricultural life." Receiving mail, newspapers, magazines, and the popular mail-order catalogs allowed families to stay in touch with the world without leaving the farm. Sears, Roebuck and its competitor, Montgomery Ward, increased their volume of mail-order business to American farms. The inauguration of parcel post in 1913 allowed all but the largest items to be delivered within a few days.[7]

Village merchants, especially those who doubled as postmasters, saw rural free delivery as a threat. Besides losing the small salary they received as postmasters, they worried about a reduction in trade from farmers who came in to pick up mail. Their concern was legitimate. In Goodhue County, 20 of the 34 post offices in existence in 1900 had closed by 1905.[8]

Besides mail delivery itself, RFD provided other benefits. The value of individual farms increased, according to Cannon Falls postmaster Peter A. Peterson. In a 1908 speech, he claimed that a "good part of these increased valuations may be directly attributed to the introduction of the rural delivery." Also,

A threshing crew in Goodhue County takes a break. Farmwomen were called upon to feed the large crews of hungry workers. *GCHS*

he told the Postmasters' Association of Minnesota, well-maintained roads were necessary to ensure continued service.[9]

The first RFD routes in Minnesota, beyond the experimental, began in 1899 from Red Wing's post office. The carriers received $400 per year for their services. By 1901, nine routes ran from Red Wing. In Zumbrota, where the first post office was established in June 1857, RFD service began late in 1900. The postal service established five routes, covering all of Minneola and Zumbrota townships and parts of Roscoe and Pine Island. The mail routes varied from 24 to 30 miles each, with deliveries every day but Sunday.[10]

Between 1900 and 1915, postal authorities greatly expanded rural mail routes in Goodhue County. Two RFD routes began in Goodhue township on March 1, 1901. Otto Boxrud handled the east route and Oliver Olson the west. By 1903 that number had grown to six. Mary Heaney soon joined in as one of the first regular female mail carriers in the state. The mail activity prompted the Goodhue *Enterprise* to run a weekly news column about the carriers, the road conditions they faced, and other general news regarding delivery.[11]

Minnesota weather played havoc with the state's county roads, providing headaches for anyone wishing to travel. Pressure built for road improvements to facilitate transportation in the region. As a result, the state participated in the nation's "Good Roads" movement. St. Paul hosted a Good Roads convention in 1893, and the Minnesota State Fair held its first Good Roads Day the following year. In 1896 Goodhue County staged a well-attended convention in Zumbrota. Osmund J. Wing reported that Holden township roads were sound, while James Scofield of Cannon Falls noted poor roads in his region. The meeting produced agreement about the need for improved roads but no details on how to reach that goal. The Red Wing Commercial Club sponsored the Zumbrota meeting, creating a suspicion in rural districts that the meeting was "simply a move to make access to Red Wing easier."[12]

On June 22, 1897, F. I. Johnson, the former state senator from Leon, led a second county Good Roads convention in Cannon Falls. Those gathered compromised on county road width, agreeing to a standard of 27 feet. The convention also declared in favor of wide-tired wagons. County surveyor William Danforth asked for the use of wide-track, long-runner sleds in winter. The discussion kept to practical road-building concepts, with no consideration of financing and construction.[13]

The two conventions represented the beginning of a road-improvement discussion that continued through World War I. The costs of road construction and maintenance worried farmers who felt that they would have to carry too much of the financial load. Farmers had formerly built their own roads, and they were nervous about change. After the Cannon Falls meeting, editor Silas S. Lewis suggested in the *Beacon* that constructive engagement between farmers and city folk would eventually solve this problem: "It seems that a lively inter-

Workers perched on the 1895 Red Wing Wagon Bridge. The tollbridge linked Goodhue County to west central Wisconsin. *GCHS*

est in this [good roads] matter will certainly be productive of great good to town and country alike."[14]

Red Wing had experienced one vast improvement to its rural-to-city road network with the completion in May 1895 of a wagon bridge over the Mississippi River. The extensively debated project went forward after more than 20 years of often rancorous discussion. Practical plans for bridging the river began with the formation of the Red Wing & Trenton (Wisconsin) Transit Company in 1875. The 1880s saw plans for a railroad-and-wagon bridge, but demands by railroaders that the city provide $100,000 for its construction stopped the project.[15]

Red Wing voters authorized construction of an interstate tollbridge in February 1894 and issued $75,000 in bonds to fund the project. Toledo Bridge Company completed construction in 11 months for a total cost of $66,728. This gave the people of west central Wisconsin a direct link to Goodhue County and eliminated the 30-year-old ferry system joining Trenton Island and Red Wing.

The dirt roads in the county's towns and villages were particularly susceptible to spring thawing and rain. To keep village roads passable, the workers often had to haul in sand as filler and regrade the streets. An apocryphal tale of a man who rode his horse into Pine Island on a muddy day has an element of truth. Because of its depth, the story goes, only the horse's head and the man sitting in the saddle showed above the mud.[16]

Road improvements would not wait for community consensus. Spurred by RFD routes and the appearance of motorized vehicles, Minnesota created the State Highway Commission in 1898 and passed laws to regulate motor vehicle traffic in 1903. It added a state-aid road tax in 1905, adopted the New Road and Bridge amendment in 1910, and the next year passed the Elwell Act for "state rural highways." The Elwell bill provided state money for half the cost of road improvement, getting the remainder, a fourth each, from affected counties and property owners.[17]

The Dunn Amendment for new roads and bridges stirred citizens in Goodhue County. Farmers, alarmed at prospective tax increases, staged a protest in Zumbrota on March 27, 1914. Vocal opponents of the amendment shouted down speakers from the State Highway Commission. An April meeting at the Kenyon Opera House produced protests about the high tax rate in Goodhue County and a resolution to repeal Dunn.[18]

Samuel Lockin, cashier of Red Wing's First National Bank who also served as president of the city's automobile association, assured farmers that supporters of the Dunn proposal did not wish to force the amendment upon them. Farmers tended to be suspicious of city leaders whose motives, many believed, did not serve rural interests. Lockin said Red Wing had no wish to dictate to farmers. The city's *Daily Republican* supported him editorially, commenting that "progressive farmers" want good roads and used them more than city people.[19]

The continued evolution of motorized vehicles —automobiles, trucks, tractors, buses, and motorcycles—produced more demand for good roads from vehicle owners. Local experimentation with road construction included a 1908 federally sponsored macadam highway on a section of the Featherstone road. The road, made of crushed rock bound by tar and then rolled, ran south nearly a mile from Buchanan Street in Red Wing and included five culverts and a bridge for a total cost of $45,000.[20]

Cars and trucks overtook the horse and wagon by 1920, as this Wanamingo street scene shows. The Oscar Flom garage is the first building at right. *Olson Studio, GCHS*

Henry Diercks was determined to build a functioning automobile. From his Broadway machine shop in Goodhue, the mechanic shrugged off the barbs of critics and, in 1906, pieced together his two-seater. The car was basic—no doors or fenders were necessary—and by fall he had it working.[21]

Diercks's homemade auto was not the first on Goodhue streets. In July 1905 a car came through the town, creating with its arrival a circuslike atmosphere. In June of the following year Charles A. Betcher, accompanied by William Krise and his wife, Emma, traveled from Red Wing to Goodhue. Diercks returned the favor in September by driving his car, nicknamed the "Coffee Grinder," to Red Wing and back.[22]

The county's first automobiles were attention-getting curiosities often driven by notable and wealthy citizens. Prominent businessman John Rich owned the first car in Red Wing, an electric vehicle. The 1905 car trip to Goodhue noted above included leading businessmen Charles A. Betcher and William Krise. Berton Featherstone, a Red Wing dentist, bought a car in 1906 but soon traded it for a piano. In 1906 or 1907 Cannon Falls physician Hiram Conley owned the first auto in his town, a machine made by International Harvester. Edward Hammer of Zumbrota, prominent in dairy circles, visited Goodhue by car in 1908.[23]

Red Wing issued two-dollar licenses for 20 automobiles and motorcycles in 1906. Two years later that number had more than doubled as the city licensed 30 cars and 13 motorcycles. One woman, Helen Friedrich, was among those with auto licenses.[24]

But wealth alone could not ensure the coming of age of the automobile. Nor could an industry rise merely from the skills of tinkerers like Henry Diercks. Only reliable internal-combustion engines would reach a broad audience, and they weren't available at the beginning of the auto era. One of the first major auto shows, a New York production in 1900, gave up nearly two-thirds of its space to steampowered cars, the other third to electrics. The gasoline-powered car trailed the field.[25]

The Glidden Tours, a series of well-publicized automobile trips and races, helped introduce the public to the capabilities of cars. On July 19, 1909, a cross-country Glidden group of 45 cars rumbled into Zumbrota. Confetti-tossing spectators and the music of a band welcomed them. The drivers, who had left Detroit July 12 on this sixth Glidden tour, headed toward Minneapolis.[26]

Some Red Wing drivers easily demonstrated the usefulness of their vehicles. Carl E. Betcher proved the range of the auto when he drove his father's car to Red Wing after his 1907 graduation from Yale University. Some of his friends drove their autos to Goodhue to greet him as he neared home. In 1909 Frederick W. Foote, a Red Wing attorney, drove a 60-horsepower Thomas Flyer to Chicago at an average speed of 15 miles per hour. Foote sent accounts of the journey to the *Daily Republican*.[27]

Frank Held of Kenyon converted his farm-machinery business into a car dealership. Note the horse-watering fountain. Held's original building, above, was replaced by a garage that continued service into the third millennium. *John L. Cole Collection*

Cars soon became a more common sight. Lambert Skillman began selling and servicing gasoline-powered autos in 1909 as a part of his Zumbrota machine-service business. He sold William Bevers a 22-horsepower Buick, and a Pine Island physician purchased a Ford runabout. The next year Skillman received a carload of Fords to sell. In Wanamingo, Anton Kolsum and Martin Sween dealt in Overland, Velie, and Ford cars before selling their business in 1913 to Oscar Flom. That year Henry Hellickson opened a Ford dealership in Wanamingo.[28]

Kenyon's Frank Held purchased Martin Bakko's farm-machinery business in 1894 and by 1912 considered using that enterprise as a base for selling cars. Held attended a Minneapolis auto show and signed up to handle the Everett-Metzgers-Flanders (E-M-T) line but soon switched to Chevrolets. He ran the dealership for nearly five decades.[29]

In Dennison, Austin O. Strand founded a Ford dealership and service center. Strand and his brother Fred already had experienced success with their machine shop. As an 18-year-old in 1910, A. O. had invented and patented the Faultless Litter Carrier, a device that aided farmers in cleaning barns and loading spreaders and wagons.[30]

Trucks also found a place in the local motor-vehicle picture. A 1911 shipment of grain to Red Wing by truck foreshadowed motorized farm transport.

Olaf Monson, owner of a Zumbrota dray line, used horses exclusively for hauling, but by 1919 he decided to invest in a truck. The small, underpowered vehicle proved the omen of a fleet of trucks gathered by Monson's son Gordon. Monson's Dray Line continued some use of horses into the late 1940s.[31]

William Remshardt left his father's wagon shop in Red Wing and worked assembling engines for Red Wing Motor Company before launching his "combination boat and automobile business." He became a dealer for Ford Motor Company in 1908, selling four cars that first year. His business started slowly. Farmers didn't want to change to cars, said Remshardt, as they "thought it was just humbug; they thought it would never last." After all, without proper roads, the first rainy spell in the fall immobilized most cars until spring.[32]

The transition from horse-drawn to motorized vehicle was not always smooth. During one July week in 1909, horses frightened by the new machines ran amok, injuring their owners and damaging property. In Pine Island the buggy of Mr. and Mrs. G. W. Hayward overturned when an approaching car caused their horse to bolt. A passing motorcycle spooked a team owned by Jens Smith, causing the animals to race down Red Wing's Bush Street. The sound of Pat Featherstone's auto frightened the horse drawing a carriage in which nine-year-old George Booth rode. Booth suffered head injuries when the animal panicked, pitching him out of the carriage and under the horse's hooves.[33]

Horses still ruled the road though motorized vehicles clearly threatened their dominance. By law, horses had the right of way in Red Wing. Fines to $100 cautioned automobile drivers to stop on the signal of anyone driving horses or mules. The town's auto speed limit was eight miles per hour, but that did not prevent autos from scaring the horses. Red Wing physician J. V. Anderson's new car, en route to the city from St. Paul, frightened a horse pulling a vehicle in Burnside, causing a runaway. The farmer assured Anderson he would see that the state legislature passed a law to keep cars off the roads. The farmer was not successful. By 1920 Red Wing had 600 cars. The next year 1,100 vehicles passed along Highway 3, just west of Red Wing, each day.[34]

Meanwhile on the farm, tractors powered by internal-combustion engines revolutionized agriculture. In 1900 the typical farmer relied on his own muscle and a few horses to deal with heavy work. Twenty-five years later, most farmers had cars, and many had tractors of 20 to 50 horsepower as well as smaller stationary gas engines.[35]

Local farmers got firsthand opportunities to evaluate tractors. "We demonstrated to the farmer that the tractor was as good as a horse," recalled William Remshardt, the Red Wing Ford dealer. Remshardt claimed as a sales area "practically the whole of Goodhue County." The dealer allowed farmers to take his product to their fields for a test. Later tractors, with factory-installed starters, were so easy to operate, said Remshardt, that "kids could use them and even their wives could get out and help."[36] Owners of other gasoline-powered ma-

Farmers like Andrew Heinlein, above, from the Cannon Falls area, saw productivity increase with tractors. Heinlein helped put together this plowing rig. *CFHS*

chines obtained fuel for their vehicles from suppliers of kerosene and oil. Irving Gates, Red Wing's Standard Oil agent, delivered gasoline to local residents and filled available five-gallon cans. The largest part of his business, however, still came from the sale of kerosene for home use.[37]

Electricity in Goodhue County's towns and villages became more common in the early 20th century. The new power source promised elimination of the small kerosene lamps that, despite their constant need of filling and cleaning, provided reliable light for homes and businesses. In 1887 Red Wing's first electric-light plant, which replaced the 14-year-old gaslight system, had power enough to illuminate city streets. The city paid one dollar a month for each 16-candlepower light and 40 cents a night for each of its 2,000-candlepower arc lights. Red Wing Gas Light Company soon merged with the new electricity-producing firm to form Red Wing Gas Light & Electric Company. Later, Wisconsin-Minnesota Light and Power took over the local company, bringing electricity from Menomonie, Wisconsin. The local gas plant continued to supply service during the frequent power breakdowns.[38]

Kenyon's Martin Gunderson installed an electric-power plant for his flour mill in 1896. He supplied power to the village in 1897. Gunderson and sons Raymond and Byron continued providing power to Kenyon until 1928. A flour mill owned by Loomis Irish generated Pine Island's first electricity in 1899.[39]

In 1899 E. L. Peck opened Zumbrota's first electric plant, a steampowered operation using an 80-horsepower Russell reciprocating steam engine and a 45-

kilowatt, single-phase Fort Wayne generator. The small plant required some rationing of power; consumers received daily lighting between 6:00 P.M. and midnight. During the winter months they also received power from 5:30 A.M. until daylight. In 1912 the arrival of transmission lines brought 24-hour electrical service to the city.[40]

Brothers Robert and Fred Valentine, with the backing of their father, David, built and operated the first electric-light plant in Cannon Falls. Starting in October 1896, the Valentines supplied electricity from sundown to midnight. They also sold electric irons with a sales-pitch promise to provide power on Tuesday mornings. They later sold the plant. In 1906 the facility burned down, leaving the city without power for two years.[41]

The Cannon Falls "power outage" ended when Louis F. Blinco, the manager of Zumbrota's electric operation, built a new generating plant in town. Cannon Falls Electric Service Company was a family operation, with Blinco's father-in-law, E. L. Bliss, a Nebraskan, as president, and Blinco as superintendent. Blinco's wife, Hattie, was cashier. Mary Scofield was one resident welcoming the return of electricity to Cannon Falls. She wrote, "The electric man came in the P.M. and connected us up, and we have electric light tonight." The meter was yet to be installed, hence the declaration that Scofield "would burn all the lights tonight."[42]

Smoke from the generating plant of Kenyon flour miller Martin Gunderson blew across Main Street in this ca. 1906 postcard. Gunderson began supplying electricity in 1896. The Kenyon Elevator is at left, behind the Commercial House Hotel. *John L. Cole Collection*

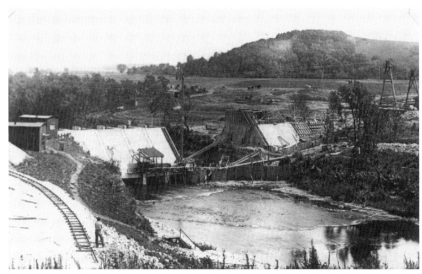

Construction of the Consumers Power Company hydroelectric facility at Cannon Falls began in 1910. The 1,125-foot-long hollow concrete dam took ten months to complete. *CFHS*

The Big Cannon River held possibilities for those interested in providing electric power, not only to Cannon Falls but also to nearby towns. In February 1910, a business consortium created Consumers Power Company through a consolidation of existing power plants in Faribault, Northfield, and Cannon Falls. This was a first step toward building a hydroelectric facility near Cannon Falls. The following month, H. M. Byllesby Company of Chicago commenced construction of a dam needed for the new power station.[43]

A crew of 500 to 600, living in quarters near the work site, completed the work in ten months despite doing most of the work by hand. The dam was of hollow concrete, 1,125 feet long and 87 feet high from its base, with 4,141 feet of spillway. A 33,000-volt line from the plant soon supplied power to Northfield and Cannon Falls. Consumers Power built lines to several towns and villages in the region, including Zumbrota in 1912, Goodhue in 1913, and Pine Island in 1916. Consumers Power became Northern States Power in April 1916.

Telephones came to the county in 1883 when Philo Jones, a Red Wing physician, connected his office and home, some five blocks apart. The telephone, considered by townspeople a modern marvel, created a sensation. Just one year later the city connected to St. Paul. Northwestern Telephone Exchange organized by 1892, and five years later a line linked Red Wing to Zumbrota. Two telephone companies served Red Wing in the first decades of the new century; they merged in 1922.[44]

August Hoff, a Zumbrota druggist, had a two-way phone system in March 1887 that linked his home and store. Physician C. H. Stearns connected his home and office by telephone in 1894. Two years later, Union Electric Company completed a long-distance line between Zumbrota and Kenyon. By May 1900, the Zumbrota area had about 60 telephone subscribers, and E. L. Peck, owner of the local exchange, published a tiny directory. After several ownership changes, Zumbrota Telephone Company was incorporated in 1908.[45]

Pine Island's telephone business began in Thomas A. Bunn's drugstore, when Bunn strung lines from his Main Street store to the offices of physicians Charles Hill and William Craddock and several other businesses. Bunn also established the Oronoco exchange, in 1901. John E. and James P. Keane acquired the Pine Island-Oronoco system in 1908 and rebuilt its rural lines. James Keane bought his brother's interest in 1912.[46]

Competition for Goodhue telephone service resulted in a 1901 lawsuit. Gustaf O. Miller, a White Rock businessman, built a telephone line from Cannon Falls through his village and Goodhue. This line provided competition for a group of Goodhue businessmen who had formed their own concern—Goodhue County Telephone Company. The Goodhue village council chose the local group over Miller and ordered his line, set up in Ahern's Hotel, severed. Miller sued Howard M. Scovell, a leader of the Goodhue consortium, and the local company for $5,000 damages. He received $250. By September, Goodhue had phone links to 23 businesses, eight residences, and 13 farmers as well as lines to Belvidere Mills, Claybank, Claypits, Wastedo, and Rice. The service cost businesses $20 and residences $10.[47]

In 1902 physician Herbert P. Sawyer connected his Goodhue office to the G. O. Miller telephone line to establish better contact west of the village. Miller still did not have council approval for a line in Goodhue, and again its members instructed the marshal to cut it. Eventually pressure from concerned citizens resolved the conflict. Goodhue authorized a link between the village and Miller's line in 1908.

In Cannon Falls, Charles and Fred Scofield, their uncle James Scofield, and Harrison Slocum began building a telephone system on March 1, 1900, in their office above Scofield Drug Store. Service commenced on June 1, with Marian Price as switchboard operator and Scofield family members providing relief. By October the outfit provided 24-hour telephone service.[48]

Goodhue County farmers added more dairy cooperatives to a list that already featured early co-ops in Sogn, Roscoe, and Minneola. Establishment of the member-owned, profit-sharing organizations followed a trend in which 560 of the state's 664 creameries became cooperatives. As World War I approached, Minnesota's creamery co-ops represented about half the nation's total.[49]

Dairy farmers around Vasa hoped to increase revenue from their herds and so formed a cooperative creamery in 1898 around the leadership of Civil War veteran and former state legislator John W. Peterson. A founder of the "The Scandinavian Transportation Company," one of the region's first farmer co-ops, he was a logical choice. They hired A. G. Swanson as first manager at $45 per month.[50]

Members voted to open Vasa Farmers Creamery in May 1898 and agreed that each stockholder should bring a load of ice to the facility. In the first year the creamery's income was nearly $6,000, a total doubled in two year's time. The combined yearly salary for the co-op buttermaker and assistant was $644.

Belle Creek's Cooperative Dairy Association organized in January 1902, under the leadership of Anton V. Anderson. The Vasa native busily drummed up the support of neighboring farmers for the venture. Members soon searched for a site for the co-op's plant. Belle Creek won out over White Rock after a fractious debate within the membership. The group decided to move when the Belle Creek building later had problems, particularly with the sewer system.[51]

Bellechester's Cooperative Creamery Association halted operations before it had a chance to begin. In the of summer 1914 construction was underway when a tornado rolled through the area, knocking down, among other things, the concrete block walls of the incomplete creamery. The owners, with no money to order replacement materials, improvised by chipping mortar from the old blocks and using them to rebuild. They had the plant open by September 1914. Fifty-two patrons brought milk in during its first year of business.[52]

Cooperative creameries in Goodhue County continued to spring up and operate successfully during the first three decades of the 20th century. From Skyberg, Kenyon, and Wanamingo in the southwest to Welch and Red Wing in the north, from Frontenac and Belvidere in the east to Dennison and Cannon Falls in the west, and in Zumbrota, Belle Creek, Goodhue, and Vasa between, co-op dairies provided farmers with production facilities in which they had a financial interest.

# 13

# *The Great War Abroad—*
# *Conflict at Home*

The threat of war in Europe held little interest for an America preoccupied with "The Good Years" of the early 20th century. Most Americans were concerned with domestic affairs and engaged with securing their place in a society boasting of opportunity for all. For those who questioned the premise of the American dream, the success of the progressive movement provided hope. Self-absorbed, inward-looking America thus took little notice when the archduke of Austria-Hungary and his wife were assassinated in Sarajevo on June 28, 1914.[1]

For more than 50 years the leaders of Europe had been spinning intricate webs of political and military intrigue. The murder of the archduke now began to entangle them in war. Austria-Hungary opened hostilities on July 28, 1914, by declaring war on Serbia and calling on Germany for support. Prewar alliances drew other nations into the conflict. On August 1 Germany declared war on Russia, and other countries marched lockstep into the conflict. On August 3, France declared war on Germany, and Germany retaliated against France. On August 4, Germany declared war on Belgium, and Great Britain on Germany. On August 6, Austria-Hungary declared war on Russia, and Serbia on Germany. On August 7, Montenegro opposed Austria-Hungary. Eleven more such declarations sounded before the end of the year, bringing Japan, Turkey, and Portugal into the melee. The suicide of empires had begun.[2]

Americans, safe on the other side of the Atlantic Ocean, were unprepared for the Great War. "To say that the outbreak of war in Europe in 1914 came as a shock to the American people would be an understatement of heroic proportions," one scholar wrote. Most Americans viewed foreign affairs as a diversion from important concerns at home.[3]

Jens Grondahl, (second from l, became the county's most prominent news-paperman during his 49 years with Red Wing's *Daily Republican*. Benjamin B. Herbert, organizer of the *Grange Advance* and founder of the National Editorial Association, stands next to Grondahl's wife, Ottonie. *GCHS*

Times of crisis inspired Jens K. Grondahl, the prolific editor and poet of the Red Wing *Daily Republican*. The outbreak of war in Europe was one such occasion. On August 5, 1914, on the paper's front page, his poem "The Madness of Monarchs" considered the commencement of fighting. His poetry was over-wrought, but his prediction of the Great War proved accurate:

Tis the Madness of Monarchs 'neath whose lash the nations groan!
And humanity, obedient, rushes on to slay its own—
Marches on, in servile millions, to appease the royal wrath—
Oh, what feast awaits the vultures in that dark and bloody path![4]

Americans were loath to be drawn into war, and they accepted their government's policy, espoused by President Woodrow Wilson, of neutrality toward belligerent nations. Although generally backing neutrality, the American public tended to favor the British, French, and Belgians. When the German military juggernaut overran tiny Belgium, widely circulated stories about the assault turned some Americans against Germany.[5]

Minnesotans mostly subscribed to neutrality. The state had large German- and Irish-American communities tending to favor Germany and its coalition of friends, the Central Powers. Such feelings balanced those of people partial to the Allied Powers—Great Britain, France, Russia, and their confederates. In Red Wing, Grondahl's August 5 comment that Germany's Kaiser Wilhelm had "taken the attitude that he can master the world" was less than neutral in tone. The *Daily Republican*, however, soon carried a German-language feature, "War Stories in German," prepared by a German-American news service.[6]

A. H. Tangen of Zumbrota and Kolben M. Larwick of Kenyon each wrote to Minnesota senator Knute Nelson in November 1914. They complained about the British naval blockade of Germany, which also affected Scandinavia. Tangen advocated "at least" asking for a change allowing American ships to travel between Iceland and the Faroe Islands to Scandinavia. Larwick claimed the blockade "an unreasonable interference, causing danger to neutral commerce between America and the Scandinavian countries." Germany, frustrated by what its leaders called the British naval "hunger" blockade of its ports, announced in February 1915 an expansion of its submarine war against Britain.[7]

Shock among Americans caused by the outbreak of war in Europe gradually lessened as the conflict continued. Secure behind a self-imposed wall of neutrality, people continued with business as usual. Minnesotans, in the first months of the war, took keen interest in two forthcoming events—the World Series of baseball and the fall elections. The "county option" that would permit the choice, through referendum, of banning or allowing licensed liquor establishments, particularly drew the attention of voters.[8]

As war continued to rage in Europe, American public opinion moved more strongly behind Great Britain and France. America, linked to Britain by language as well as cultural tradition, inevitably felt some sympathy for the island nation. Germany meanwhile had nearly crushed France. In May 1915, a German submarine torpedoed the passenger ship *Lusitania,* killing nearly 1,200, including 128 U.S. citizens. American public opinion lurched toward the Allies. That the British-owned vessel was from a nation at war did not, to most Americans, mitigate the killing of its civilian passengers.[9]

In 1916 President Wilson narrowly won reelection with the theme "He kept us out of war." But he had not kept America out of Mexico. An unstable political situation there resulted in civil war spilling over the American border. Francisco Villa, leader of one warring Mexican faction, became angry at his northern neighbor's recognition of a rival. Villa crossed into United States at Columbus, New Mexico, where he and his men killed 17 Americans. This prompted Wilson to send American troops into Mexico to capture Villa dead or

Zumbrota sent its Company D off to World War I service on August 27, 1917. *GCHS*

alive. Among the soldiers summoned to action were the men of Zumbrota's Company D, Third Minnesota Infantry, U.S. National Guard.[10]

The Zumbrota unit, under Capt. Chris Nesseth, left by train for Fort Snelling on June 18, 1916. Within 24 hours of muster, the unit was on its way to a camp in Texas, 60 miles northwest of Brownsville and six miles from the Rio Grande. The unit served six months of border duty, suffering no losses before returning to Minnesota. The American forces did not capture the elusive Villa.[11]

Shortly after Wilson's reelection, Germany announced the beginning of unrestricted submarine warfare, certain to result in shipping losses for neutral maritime nations such as the United States. Those losses came soon. Further strain between Germany and America resulted from the public exposure of a clumsy German attempt to induce Mexico to ally itself with Germany in the event of war with America. Wilson broke off diplomatic relations with Germany on February 3 and on April 2, 1917, asked for a formal declaration of war—a request approved by Congress.[12]

Citizens of Goodhue County joined other Americans in rallying to the cause. The first of about 1,500 county men enrolled in the expanding U.S. armed forces. Home-front preparations commenced, and the citizenry enlisted to support the war effort.[13] For the Mexican-expedition veterans of Zumbrota's Company D, the war meant recall to federal service. On August 26, the men assembled in front of the armory. As a hushed crowd watched, the officers commanded the men to "fall in." Captain Nesseth marched them to the train depot with an escort of three Civil War veterans carrying an American flag. The

Zumbrotans found themselves back in the American southwest at Camp Cody, New Mexico, where they began training. Red Wing's Company L became a federal unit on August 5. After three weeks of training at home, the company joined other Minnesota National Guard soldiers at Camp Cody.[14]

In New Mexico some men from the two Goodhue County companies transferred to under-strength units. Many Company L soldiers joined the 59th Field Artillery. In the meantime, volunteers with no military training swelled the ranks of America's tiny prewar army. At the war's outbreak the nation had 80,804 officers and men in the regular army. National Guard units like Company D and L boosted the army's numbers to a modest total of 127,410 men.[15]

The people of Minnesota sent their men to war, pledging to do what they could at home to aid those in the service. The momentum of their efforts produced a patriotic fervor that brought tremendous coercive pressure upon citizens apparently less committed to the war effort. President Wilson's drive to make the world "safe for democracy" did not guarantee democratic safeguards for those at home in Minnesota.

Early in the war Dick Wilkens, a neighbor of the Frederick A. Scherf family, awakened the Scherfs on a Sunday morning with the news of yellow paint splashed on their Red Wing home. The Scherfs were a prominent German-American family with roots in Hay Creek, the county's most German township. Supporters of American's growing anti-German movement targeted their house at Sixth and Bush. Rev. J. R. Bauman, pastor of St. John's German Lutheran Church, was among the first supporters to arrive at the Scherf home after the news had spread. He said the perpetrators had "put on their own color."[16]

Anti-German vandals splashed paint on Fred Scherf's Red Wing home. *MHS*

Fred Scherf was well known through the hardware and farm implement establishment he ran in Red Wing until 1907 and as Goodhue County's treasurer, elected in 1908. He was also a Nonpartisan League (NPL) candidate for the state legislature. The North Dakota-based NPL, a radical farmer-led group, was cause for worry to Minnesota's mainstream political parties. As a German-American and NPL leader, Scherf provided a prime target for those who believed either label provided grounds for suspicion in a nation now at war with Germany. The yellow-paint incident was not his last confrontation with anti-German sentiment.

Scherf had not been shy in asserting his prewar view that the American press and government was anti-German. In a 1916 letter to Senator Knute Nelson, he quoted the Swedish Minister of Foreign Affairs as disagreeing with Nelson's claim that "Germany is the chief offender" of Scandinavian neutrality. Scherf also attacked the senator for supporting arms sales to warring nations: "Can it be possible that in your declining years [Nelson was 73] you will support a policy of bloodshed and the taking of human life?"[17]

America's declaration of war with Germany had a polarizing effect in Minnesota. Some supporters of the war effort questioned the loyalty of anyone not seen as an enthusiastic backer of America's involvement. Before America's participation in the war, the leadership of the German-American community had asked for fair government and media treatment of Germany and supported the nation's neutrality policy. Did this mean they would side with Germany in a war with America? And what of NPLers who advocated state-owned terminal grain elevators and other revolutionary concepts? What of the growing power of labor unions? Strikes had closed most of northern Minnesota's iron mines in 1916. Were unions a potential problem for the nation's war effort?[18]

Loyalty leagues sprang up around the state as early as February 1917, taking a decidedly anti-German stance. The leagues countered antiwar and pro-German sentiment wherever they found it. Still, the people of Minnesota were far from united in opinion about joining the conflict. Four of the state's ten congressmen voted against President Wilson's war resolution of April 6. Three of the four were from districts with significant German-American populations.[19]

The loyalty question became a contentious issue in the state legislature, where in March 1917 a measure to establish the Minnesota Commission of Public Safety (MCPS) came forth. The proposal called for a commission of seven, headed by the governor. It also included an alien registration requirement. One political writer characterized the debate following the bill's introduction as the "most bitter in the history of the legislature." Angry lawmakers called the loyalty of other legislators into question.[20]

Some in the legislature argued against forming the MCPS while asserting their personal loyalty to the country. Others strongly backed the proposed legislation. Red Wing's Oscar Seebach, hero at the Battle of Manila during the War of 1898, proclaimed, "I am German to the backbone, but I am for this bill." Finally, Goodhue County legislator Anton V. Anderson of Vasa made a successful motion to temporarily halt the divisive debate.[21]

The house passed the state senate's bill to establish the Minnesota Commission of Public Safety on April 16, in the aftermath of America's declaration of war. It did not require alien registration but authorized the MCPS to order registration, which it did ten months later. The act also provided for a home guard, a military unit under the control of the commission. Other wartime measures included the Criminal Syndicalist Act, apparently pointed at labor unions, and HF1270, which prohibited interference with enlistment in the armed forces.[22]

In effect, the state had assigned near-dictatorial power to the Commission of Public Safety for the duration of the war. Wrote historian William Watts Folwell, "Armed with extraordinary powers, and granted an ample appropriation by a practically unanimous legislature, the commission proceeded to exercise functions the like of which the history of American law had never disclosed."[23]

The commission's report following the war gave a straightforward account of its wartime activities, describing why it was necessary to quash dissent: "Misinterpreting the constitutional guarantee of freedom of speech, these leaders thought . . . they could properly oppose the government's policies in speech and writings." The commission singled out "professional and theoretical pacifists," whom they charged with organizing antiwar activities. It called them "men of pro-German traditions and sympathies" and "professional politicians of the socialist or Nonpartisan League stamp." The report bluntly continued: "The Commission undertook to kindle the back fires of patriotism among the rank and file of this ilk . . . With the leaders it used the mailed fist."[24]

In December 1917, the Public Safety Commission demonstrated its power by intervening in a dispute between labor organizers and the owners of the Twin City Rapid Transit Company. Gov. Joseph A. A. Burnquist ordered Twin Cities Home Guard units and eight more from other Minnesota cities into Minneapolis and St. Paul. Burnquist called Red Wing's Company A, Fifth Battalion, to service on December 4, 1917, and temporarily stationed the unit in St. Paul.[25]

Minneapolis lawyer John F. McGee, a fervent supporter of the Allied war effort, led the Public Safety Commission. He voiced his belief of who was antiwar in Minnesota to the U.S. Senate Military Affairs Committee in April 1918:

> A Non-Partisan League lecturer is a traitor every time. In other words, no matter what he says or does, a League worker is a traitor. Where we made a mistake was in not establishing a firing squad in the first days of the war. We should now get busy and have that firing squad working over-time . . . The disloyal element in Minnesota is largely among the German-Swedish people. The nation blundered at the start of the war in not dealing severely with these vipers.[26]

With emotions running high, the terms *liberty sandwich* and *liberty cab-bage* replaced the familiar German words *hamburger* and *sauerkraut*. German measles became *liberty measles* and Dachshunds, *liberty pups*. In Red Wing, residents of the small Plum Street district known as "Dutchtown" (a corruption of *Deutsch,* meaning *German,* in reference to its German-American-owned businesses) wanted the old nickname removed. The *Daily Republican* reported that business people in that area declared it "100 percent loyal and patriotic."[27]

Many Americans endorsed a movement to eliminate "hyphenism"—a foreign country's name attached to the word *American* with a hyphen. The most pertinent example was *German-American,* but antihyphenists wished to do away with the concept entirely. They believed it denoted residual loyalty to one's homeland. Former President Theodore Roosevelt helped popularize the term *hyphenism* and became a spokesman for the antihyphen movement.[28]

Anti-German sentiment in Red Wing had a major effect upon the city's Lutheran Ladies' Seminary. Thirty percent of the school's student body was of German descent. The seminary was also known for the excellence of its Conservatory of Music, headed by German-born Bernard F. Laukandt. Seminary president Hans Allen resigned in June 1916 in disgust over the local anti-German movement. Laukandt left for the same reason in 1917.[29]

The limits of dissent against the war were evident in Goodhue County after speeches by Nonpartisan League secretary and manager Joseph Gilbert and NPL national organizer Louis W. Martin. A county grand jury indicted both men in Red Wing on March 14, 1918, for "discouraging enlistment" in the military. Specifically, they were charged with three counts of disloyal utterance in speeches at Goodhue village, Kenyon, and the Kenyon barbershop. The same grand jury indicted Goodhue township farmer Herman Zempke for remarks made at a Goodhue village saloon and construed as discouraging enlistment.[30]

Goodhue County grand jury members then issued a report observing that during the six months after America's entry into the war, "it seemed safe for our unpatriotic citizens and others to make statements . . . that later on would be dangerous to make. From now on an entirely different standard of patriotic citizenship is going the be DEMANDED of all in both the city and county." The grand jury also issued a thinly veiled threat stating that, "certain citizens will be expected to voluntarily assist [the war effort] to the best of their ability."[31]

Despite the unequivocal nature of the grand jury's statement in early April, a county jury found Martin innocent of sedition. Excerpts from an NPL circular printed in the Zumbrota *News* show the League blamed Martin's indictment on political persecution led by a few bankers and politicians. The circular also claimed that Kenyon physician and former state legislator Joseph Gates had boasted he would drive Martin from the county and had already assaulted him. Reported the *News*, "Sure he did, and if Martin said what he is alleged to have said, Gates ought to have broken his neck." The *News* added that the Liberty

Joseph A. Gates, M.D. *GCHS*

Loan drives in Zumbrota township and Pine Island, where Martin was active, had fallen short of their goals. Zumbrota township citizens purchased $4,200 of the $35,000 goal, and Pine Islanders, $2,500 of their $34,000 target.[32]

The threats against Nonpartisan League organizers were not idle. Townspeople chased the NPL's George Breidal out of Kenyon after a rally in which villagers proclaimed the community had "100 per cent loyalty." The crowd learned Breidal was watching a motion picture in town and went to find him. The villagers made him kneel and kiss an American flag and carry it at the head of a procession to the Chicago Great Western depot. They told him to board the next train out of town. A southbound train pulled in, and Breidal asked permission to wait for one headed north. The crowd yelled at him to get on or walk.[33]

Someone in each township in the county secretly watched for subversive activity. Fred E. Schornstein headed the county branch of the American Protective League, an arm of the War Department. He received help from the chairman of each township. Deputies searched for pro-Germans and suspected German agents. A brief history of the county organization observed, "Most people were unaware of the existence of such an organization, and it was largely through secrecy that the work of the league was so effectively performed."[34]

Gilbert's May 10, 1918, trial in Red Wing drew considerable attention. The 53-year-old NPL organizer also awaited trial in Jackson County, where he had been accused of discouraging enlistment. And he was the subject of a pending state Supreme Court decision on a similar charge in Martin County. NPL attorney James Manahan, who later represented Gilbert in a Lakeville courtroom, where he was on trial for discouraging enlistment, claimed his client was a socialist and a victim of the "spur of hate" current at the time.[35]

Six days before Gilbert's trial, a Red Wing court convicted N. S. Randall, another NPL member, of sedition, sentencing him to prison and a fine. Randall's fate dimmed Gilbert's prospects for acquittal. Judge Willard Converse said Randall's crime was a "very serious one in these times." Fred Scherf, also embroiled in the Randall case, faced charges of contempt of court. Scherf supposedly had asked Bert Rand, a member of the Randall jury, to be his campaign manager. Scherf denied any wrongdoing, and the case was later dismissed.[36]

Gilbert's Red Wing trial focused on his speech in Kenyon. At the conclusion of Gilbert's talk a bystander heckled him: "What's the matter with [President] Wilson?" Gilbert was quoted as saying "I don't know what's the matter with Wilson, do you?" The NPLer reportedly also said, "I tell you, if they conscripted wealth like they have conscripted men, the war would not last 48 hours." Among those testifying against Gilbert were Kenyon witnesses Joseph Gates, who figured in the Louis Martin trial, and banker Gilbert Flom.[37]

The defendant refuted the charges against him. Gilbert declared that the NPL stood by America against any foreign nation engaged in war with the country and that it was the duty of every American citizen to help in the war effort. O. F. Henkel, a resident of Holden, said Gilbert did not say the words written in the indictment. Under questioning, Henkel said he had opposed U.S. involvement in the war at first. Asked whether he was still against the war, Henkel answered, "As a matter of choice, yes, as a necessity, no." C. C. Lawson also testified in Gilbert's defense, saying that a prosecution witness did not take notes at the meeting as he had contended.[38]

The jury took four minutes to find Gilbert guilty. "A good piece of work quickly done," wrote the Red Wing *Daily Republican.* An editorial commented:

> Our success in winning the war depends upon cleaning out from among us the huns and shadow huns who are either paid agents of the German government, or the dupes of those who directly or indirectly represent kaiserism.[39]

In July, after his second Goodhue County trial, a jury convicted Louis W. Martin, Gilbert's NPL partner during the Kenyon incident, of sedition. Testimony against Martin referred to comments he made at the Kenyon barbershop. Martin admitted saying he was "pro-German" but said he was joking. He was accused of stating that Germany counted on the Huns in America to win the war. The court sentenced Martin to a year in jail and a $500 fine, plus costs.[40]

Just after Martin's conviction, Judge W. L. Booth sentenced John C. Seebach of Red Wing to 18 months in Leavenworth prison. Seebach stood accused of saying "This is a rich man's war" and that the Germans would win because of their men and military resources. The 60-year-old miller was convicted of violating the espionage act. Goodhue County Attorney Thomas Mohn, quoted on the day of the sentencing, said Seebach's son Carl would be tried for sedition on July 18: "Prosecution will continue until disloyalty is wiped out."[41]

The Minneapolis *Daily News* applauded the Seebach conviction with a sharp editorial reprinted in Red Wing's *Daily Republican*. The *Daily News* piece said in part: "Seebach is a German name. You or your father brought it to America for just one reason—to find BETTER CONDITIONS." It continued, "You have cashed in on American opportunity, John Seebach; you are known as a wealthy miller of Red Wing." According to the *Daily News*, Seebach was charged with speaking "contemptuously" of the United States.

The attacks on county citizens believed to be "pro-German" continued throughout the war. The Goodhue *Enterprise* reported in April 1918 that someone "displeased" with the color of Meyer's barbershop did "some painting . . . on the front of the building." The new color was yellow. Someone left a sign reading "The Hun Shop" in the window. In another incident, Ed Kolbe wrote to the *News* in November to complain that a mob of people had smeared yellow paint on his house in Zumbrota. Kolbe said he and his family had to listen to the "most vile profanity I have ever heard on the streets of any town." Five days later a group of girls and boys pounded on his door at 11:00 P.M., yelling that a "pro-German lived there." Kolbe protested the "mobism" and wrote that he and his family had been loyal throughout the war.[42]

S. S. Lewis, editor of the Cannon Falls *Beacon*, had few problems with those applying paint to the property of suspected pro-Germans. On June 14 the paper commented on a Nonpartisan League parade in Goodhue County during which yellow paint was tossed at an NPL car. The account made light of the paint attack. Two weeks later Lewis observed that "the price of yellow paint will be higher in a few months unless the sale is prohibited by law." By July 19, Lewis was backing off in his support of paint attacks, writing, "Patriots can find a better way to punish disloyalty," and "Innocent people may suffer."[43]

Concerns about subversive elements in Goodhue County were evident during the 20 months of war, but the area was comparatively free of unrest. Charles L. Parkin, mayor of Goodhue, wrote to John S. Pardee, secretary of the Minnesota Commission of Public Safety, with a request for "secret service" help. Pardee forwarded the appeal to Thomas Winter, head of the MCPS's intelligence bureau, with an explanation. Pardee wrote on August 7, 1917, that Goodhue village "is largely surrounded by German sections." Parkin wanted "two good secret service men for a month or two, especially Saturday and Saturday nights." Pardee, who had worked for a while in Red Wing as a newspaperman, was not worried about Goodhue: "I am well acquainted with that part of Goodhue County, and it is not a most pressing case before us."[44]

Goodhue County Attorney Thomas Mohn answered a request from Winter for information on a Nonpartisan League meeting in Burnside. Mohn wrote of NPL activity in the "southern end of this county," but the group was "not meeting with any success." Mohn added that a deputy sheriff had informed him about the Burnside meeting and that no one had said anything "derogatory" of the government or its officials.[45]

The Liberty Loan program, which encouraged the American public to support the war through bond purchases, began early in the war and continued past its end. Sales goals set for most counties in Minnesota were challenging. The project was a tough sell to groups such as the Nonpartisan League, which were immediately suspicious of American entanglement in a foreign war. NPL leader Arthur Townley believed that heavy taxing of business and industry profits, swollen by the conflict, could finance the war.[46]

Willingness to purchase Liberty bonds became, in the eyes of many, a test of patriotism. The bonds were, after all, securities bearing 3.5 percent interest, backed by the U.S. government. The war's supporters believed any true American would be eager to buy bonds. And for those short of cash, local bankers stood ready to provide loans to finance bond purchases—at minimal risk to the banks. The chairman of the Second Liberty Loan campaign advised bankers in the Ninth Federal Reserve District to protect themselves from the possible default of those who borrowed money to buy bonds. He suggested that the banks sell the bonds of those in default and deduct any of their losses or charges.[47]

Goodhue County's first Liberty Loan quota was set at $500,000, a sum the Goodhue County Bankers Association deemed virtually impossible to secure. They made the attempt, however, with Red Wing's William H. Putnam, president of the banker's group, assuming leadership. Putnam chaired the five county liberty loan campaigns. But the county met neither the quota of the initial bond effort nor the million-dollar goal of the second drive. A more vigorous effort during the third loan drive produced $1,550,950, carrying the county far enough over its target to make up for the shortfall of the first two attempts. At the end of the fifth and final campaign, the county had raised more than $6.3 million, surpassing the total goal by more than $250,000.[48]

Those selling liberty bonds during the first three loan drives applied considerable pressure to Goodhue County residents. Their methods could be hard to resist, even though government policy expressly prohibited coercion. Then came the Fourth Liberty Loan campaign and a change in tactics. In mid-October 1918, the Committee for Public Safety's Order 44 provided that failure of a Minnesotan to meet a Liberty Loan allotment was theoretically an indictable offense. A Red Wing newspaper account observed that "Slackers will discover that there is no avenue to escape from doing their duty."[49]

Goodhue County's loan committee, in keeping with the spirit of Order 44, got right to work. The committee, under Putnam's leadership, summoned nongivers to an October 11 meeting at the Red Wing Commercial Club. After some arm-twisting, the committee raised $20,650. When one Zumbrota farmer refused to pledge his allotted $400, the committee raised his quota to $1,000. The farmer gave in, went to his bank, and returned with $400. The committee questioned people with pro-German records who had not supported earlier loan drives. Only six "blue cards," or refusals, were necessary. A newspaper account noted that all six cards bore the names of people with German origins.[50]

Others were victims of zealous backers of the war. Charles A. Lindbergh Sr. encountered them during a 1918 campaign trip through Goodhue County. He was the NPL's choice to challenge incumbent Joseph Burnquist in the Republican gubernatorial primary. In a June cross-county motorcade, Lindbergh and 150 vehicles full of Nonpartisan Leaguers passed near Wanamingo before heading to Kenyon, Dennison, Stanton, and Cannon Falls. The caravan encountered carpet tacks strewn on the highway. Anti-NPLers hanged Lindbergh in effigy in front of the Stanton Bank, and the authorities quickly steered the caravan out of Cannon Falls when local heckling began. In Red Wing, citizens threw red paint at the cars of some NPLers, and a mob chased Lindbergh across a pasture. The engineer of a passing train facilitated his escape.[51]

To some, the primary election of June 17, 1918, was a referendum on loyalty to the nation in time of war. Burnquist pushed the patriotism issue hard throughout his gubernatorial reelection campaign. Some of his supporters believed it the only strong factor he had working for him. Whatever their reasons, Minnesota's Republicans wanted Burnquist to lead them in the general election. Record numbers took part in the June primary, giving Burnquist 199,325 votes to Lindbergh's 150,626.[52]

Goodhue County primary voters gave Burnquist 4,084 votes and a clear victory over Lindbergh's 2,177. Yet there was a pocket of Lindbergh support, centered in the heavily German-American area of Hay Creek. Members of this community were well aware of Burnquist's decision to focus his campaign on the loyalty issue, a concept many considered anti-German. Hay Creek voted 134–30 for Lindbergh, and the adjoining townships of Belvidere and Featherstone also went decisively for the NPL-backed candidate. Voters in Cannon Falls township and Roscoe picked Lindbergh by lesser margins.[53]

Governor Burnquist received overwhelming support in Goodhue County towns and villages. He claimed more than 90 percent of the vote in Cannon Falls (255–25), Kenyon (232–23), and Wanamingo (85–8). The incumbent handily won Zumbrota, Pine Island, and Red Wing. Goodhue village, with a sizable German population, voted for Lindbergh 114–80. In the general election, Burnquist defeated David H. Evans, candidate of the newly formed Farmer-Labor Party. Democratic nominee Fred E. Wheaton was a distant third. Olaf O. Stageberg, a professor at the Red Wing Seminary running as the National (Prohibition) Party candidate, polled 6,649 votes statewide.[54]

For Fred Scherf, the Nonpartisan League candidate who had been a target of anti-German sentiment, the November general election provided both redemption and revenge. The NPL standard-bearer won election to the Minnesota house, narrowly defeating David Neill, a prominent Red Wing businessman and Republican. Former president of the Red Wing Manufacturing Company and the city's Commercial Club, Neill held impeccable establishment credentials. Scherf, running a distant second to Neill in Red Wing precincts, proved dominant in the NPL strongholds of Hay Creek, Vasa, Florence, and Featherstone, where the combined vote was 472–145 in his favor.[55]

The citizens of Minnesota were clearly loyal to their country, though some opposed the war and others disagreed with the excesses of the Commission of Public Safety. Historian Theodore Blegen's assessment of their patriotism was glowing: "The Minnesota people, 70 percent of whom were immigrants and the children of immigrants, with few exceptions, gave wholehearted, generous, willing, loyal, eager, and patriotic support to the state's effort and the American success in the war."[56]

Goodhue County's Red Cross and its school-based Junior Red Cross worked throughout the conflict to assist American troops as well as civilian victims. Communities in the county raised money for Red Cross work overseas and in Minnesota. Women volunteers made surgical dressings and hospital garments and knitted sweaters and stockings at social gatherings.

A county Red Cross fund drive in mid-May 1918 had particular success. The effort began with a Red Wing parade featuring "thousands," included hundreds of children and 250 mothers with sons in the service. The parade helped the city raise $12,000 towards its $15,000 Red Cross goal. People in Kenyon, Wanamingo, Goodhue village, and Belle Creek oversubscribed their goals almost immediately. Kenyon nearly doubled its $1,400 target. An auction in Welch produced $556. Goodhue's parade helped raise $661. The Cannon Falls Red Cross scheduled a loyalty parade and displayed "Clara Barton," a Berkshire hog, for auction. The city's Red Cross sale drew hundreds of people and raised nearly $4,000.[57]

Finding ways to support the war effort was a continuing enterprise. Those with fewer resources bought saving stamps. The county's Welfare League helped in any way it could the soldiers leaving the county for military assignments. The War Advertising Board disseminated information supporting the war. Four Minute Men, a nationwide group of 75,000 volunteers who delivered patriotic speeches, had active members throughout Goodhue County. The Recruiting Board worked to enlist men, particularly those with technical skills [58]

Zumbrota and Red Wing men signed on to the Motor Corps, a division of the Home Guard, offering their cars and themselves for any duty required of the state. Officers received two dollars a day for their service, and enlisted men, one dollar. Both units traveled to northern Minnesota for relief work after forest fires there in October 1918. They spent more than a week in the Moose Lake area. Zumbrota townspeople provided nearly $1,300 for that relief work.[59]

As the war continued, citizens on the home front observed special days for conserving resources. There were wheatless Mondays and Wednesdays, meatless Tuesdays, and porkless Thursdays and Saturdays. Autos were banned on Sundays for a portion of the war. Children, including 200 from Red Wing, tended "war gardens" at school and home, under the banner "fighting with food." On October 12, the government listed 12 rules for public eating places, including no bread with the first course, one-half ounce of butter per person, and no sugar bowl.[60]

As the people at home continued to organize, the soldiers of the American Expeditionary Force (AEF) became a major factor in the fighting in France. In the spring of 1918, transport ships brought growing numbers of American troops to France—part of a force that grew to two million. Joining the men overseas were American women serving as army, navy, and Red Cross nurses. Germany, hoping to end the war before the American army fully prepared, launched a massive offensive in late May. Gen. John J. Pershing, American commander on the scene, sent his men into action.[61]

In May and June, Americans, including men from Minnesota and Goodhue County, came under fire at Cantigny, Chateau-Thierry, and Belleau Wood. American Marines advanced against the Germans holding Belleau Wood and took the position after heavy losses. Clarence Elstad of Red Wing, killed in the Marine attack, was the first Goodhue County soldier to die in combat.[62]

Back at Camp Cody, New Mexico, a feeling of impatience perplexed the men of the Minnesota National Guard. They were in their eighth month of training and beginning to feel the war would pass them by. "We have been here [Camp Cody] tossed about by sandstorms and filled with sand for months . . . we are afraid we are going to be here forever," read one complaint.[63]

The men were about to get their wish. The two Goodhue County companies, Zumbrota's D and Red Wing's L, reorganized and converted to artillery units. This shift produced "extra" soldiers who were sent to machine gun battalions or infantry regiments headed overseas. The refitted former Company L, now the 125th Field Artillery, reached France on October 10, 1918, a month before the end of the war. Old Company D reorganized, with men sent to three artillery regiments and spare soldiers fed into other combat units.[64]

American troops helped blunt the German spring offensive and readied for a major advance. On September 26, American and French troops attacked in the Argonne Forest. Combined with British efforts to the north, the offensive ended the war in six weeks. The cost was high.[65] Fourteen Goodhue County men, including soldiers from Kenyon, Dennison, Goodhue, Zumbrota, Featherstone, Welch, and Red Wing, died in two weeks of fighting in October.[66]

Total war deaths sustained by the American army were 112,432—more than half from disease. Noncombat deaths increased with the worldwide influenza outbreak, a terrible risk to soldiers and civilians alike. The "Spanish flu" pandemic killed more than 600,000 Americans, making it the most deadly in the nation's history.[67]

The flu began to hit Minnesota hard in early October 1918. A thousand cases of influenza, including 510 cases at Fort Snelling, were reported in Minneapolis on October 4. Two weeks later a flu outbreak at Kenyon afflicted 60 people, and Goodhue County officials began to prepare for the epidemic. The U.S. surgeon general reported that the death rate from the influenza strain had surged from 32.4 per 1,000 on September 27 to 81.8 per 1,000 one week later.[68]

By October 14, H. M. Bracken, executive officer of the Minnesota State Board of Health, prohibited "public funerals for all who have died of influenza." Bracken's order included the burials of soldiers victimized by the flu, whose bodies were being sent home.[69]

Among the hardest hit military bases was Camp Grant in Illinois, where 1,037 died from flu between September 21 and the third week in October. Seven army nurses also died during the epidemic. Among the dead that month were seven Goodhue County men including Christopher Shay, Charles B. Siebe, and Anton Reding, all from Goodhue. George F. Ernberg and Swan S. Brodd, a soldier who died while training in Georgia, received a joint funeral and burial in their hometown of Welch before the public funeral ban.[70]

On October 10, the U.S. military reported nearly 200,000 cases of flu in army camps, as well as 820 new deaths. During that deadly October, Goodhue County soldiers had died in Iowa, Georgia, New York, New Jersey, and Texas. Some succumbed to flu in England and France. Albert Roisum, Zumbrota, died while undergoing military training in Minneapolis, and Orrin J. Holton of Kenyon died in St. Paul, where he was learning to be a mechanic.[71]

Red Wing's City Hospital had been quiet in early October. Hospital records reported, "Nurses have busied themselves tying comforters." On October 16 Red Wing reported three cases of influenza, and within a week that number swelled to 41. Schools closed on the October 19, with instructions to parents to keep their children indoors. Health officers told city police officers to send any children on the streets back home. Incoming patients strained the staff at City Hospital, and five nurses also came down with the flu.[72]

Zumbrota officials closed all schools, lodges, churches, theaters, poor rooms, and the armory until further notice. Parents had to keep children under the age of 16 at home. The influenza outbreak had not hit the town as yet, and its leaders hoped to keep the citizens safe.[73] The Cannon Falls *Beacon,* under a headline "Gloom Prevails in Cannon Falls," reported a serious epidemic on October 30. Frank Lundberg, manager of the Pioneer Garage, had died at 9:30 that morning. Then, at 11:00 that evening Clarence Seager, who worked for

Mourners at St. John's Church in rural Goodhue watched as a military honor guard placed the casket of flu victim Pvt. Adolph Jonas in a hearse. *Phil Revoir Historical Photographic Collection*

Lundberg, succumbed to flu. Three hours later Seager's cousin and fellow worker William Ray Tanner died. Lundberg's wife, Elizabeth, and six-year-old daughter, Lorene, died shortly after that. Others in the town were sick. Meanwhile in Goodhue, eight people at Louis Meyer's home were bedridden at one time. The county health board banned all public funerals, no matter what the cause of death. In Red Wing, where the outbreak had appeared to be subsiding, the flu was back, striking 12 at the State Training School. Three deaths were reported in the city by November 1.[74]

Officials throughout Goodhue County struggled to subdue the onslaught. The Cannon Falls city council made it unlawful for "any person to be found upon the streets or in any public . . . place . . . without a face mask." The council also requested that businesses limit their hours. Cannon Falls, with 26 active flu cases, suffered through a nurse shortage. The Red Wing city council ordered "all persons" to wear influenza masks of gauze when on the streets or in public places. Kenyon, with about 40 cases of flu reported, banned all public meetings. Most of the county's rural schools closed. On November 4, Red Wing officials reported 45 new cases of flu to bring the city total to 133. Fifty-nine people were ill at the Training School, with 38 cases known and 21 suspected.[75]

The scourge weakened in Goodhue County by mid-November 1918. On November 15, Zumbrota announced the lifting of its five-week ban on public meetings, though those attending motion pictures still had to wear masks. The Red Cross of Red Wing held a meeting on November 20 as the onslaught receded. Normal routines of life resumed as fewer victims were reported. But the influenza pandemic claimed victims well into 1919 before finally subsiding.[76]

Red Wing's old high-school bell rode on a cart in the city's World War I victory parade. Dressed as George Washington was Wellington Phillips. *GCHS*

Zumbrota, long known as a temperance town, proved a center of antiliquor activism. These men rode down a Zumbrota street in a vehicle labeled "MANHOOD ABOVE MONEY" and "HOME AGAINST SALOON." *GCHS*

# 14

## *The Twenties—*
## *Years of Hope and Reform*

Word that the Great War had ended reached Red Wing in the early morning hours of November 11, 1918. The Allied armies, buoyed by the late-arriving Americans, had worn down the enemy, and Germany surrendered. Celebrations began immediately. Church bells in Red Wing rang for an hour, and workers tied down steam whistles at local manufacturing plants to add to the din. A call went out for a thousand volunteers to bring combustibles to the base of Barn Bluff by 4:00 P.M.—the city planned a mammoth bonfire. In the meantime, a victory parade, led by young women of the Lutheran Ladies' Seminary carrying a huge American flag, streamed down Main Street. The procession featured bands, impromptu floats, the home guards and other marching units as well as carloads and truckloads of what a newspaper report termed "women and girls, real war workers" from the Foot Tannery. The overworked Elks Drum Corps led spontaneous parades during the day. The crowds hanged and trampled effigies of Kaiser Wilhelm, the German leader, and, for good measure, dragged his likeness behind autos, trucks, wagons, and bikes and burned it at the stake. A steamroller repeatedly crushed a mockup of the despised autocrat.[1]

The Red Wing celebration culminated with the Barn Bluff bonfire, the Kaiser's effigy helping fuel the flames. To mark the occasion, the townspeople burned "Nov 11" into the south side of the bluff so the city could see the blazing date. In Minneola, Alton Swenson, an eighth-grader and janitor at his one-room school, heard the news of the war's end before his teacher did. When he opened the school that morning, he began ringing the school bell. His teacher approached ready to discipline him but quickly relented when he heard the war was over.[2]

Kenyon's city-hall firebell rang before daylight on November 11. Celebrations were quickly underway. When Frank Callister reached town, he found "hundreds of people milling, laughing, visiting, [and] shouting along the street." A stuffed Kaiser Wilhelm bobbed in the wind from a wire suspended above Main Street. A sword impaled the effigy. People gathered fuel for a community bonfire and placed it in the center of town. Meanwhile, municipal band members played patriotic marches and popular melodies such as "Over There" and "K-k-k-katy" throughout the day. Passing trains sounded their whistles as they steamed through town."[3]

The *Beacon* reported that the "lid flew off in Cannon Falls" in the early afternoon of November 11. Businesses closed while townspeople gathered "every conceivable thing" to produce noise. Enthusiastic crowds marched through town with their noisemakers, wildly celebrating the victory in Europe and gathering for patriotic speeches. The *Beacon's* editor S. S. Lewis, an ardent supporter of the war, was ecstatic. "Golly," he wrote, "[the celebration] was surely a terror."[4]

Zumbrotans were initially cautious about the good news. The United Press had carried an erroneous report that the war had ended on November 7, prompting premature rejoicing in many parts of the land, including Zumbrota. This time, village officials got verification from three different cities before starting to celebrate. The *News* hit the street with a special edition carrying reports from Europe, and the bells of the town began to ring.[5]

Zumbrotans hastily organized a parade, with the motor corps and a band leading the way around city streets. The entourage then headed towards Pine Island, where it encountered celebrants from that village. The Pine Island band and crowd formed a line and paraded out to meet their neighbors. Both groups then marched off to Mazeppa to stage another demonstration.

Goodhue's victory parade featured farm machinery, including Joe O'Reilly and his Titan tractor. Tom Taylor's bass drum, as well as a cannon improvised and fired by Pete Nei, George Veiths, and Carl Rosener, also provided noise. School children produced raucous music with their whistles, mouth organs, horns, and accordions. The celebrants hadn't forgotten those they believed were less than patriotic. The *Enterprise* reported, "People paraded and sang late into the night and splashed some yellow paint where it was needed."[6]

The war effort proved of assistance to those in the temperance movement working to prohibit the manufacture and sale of alcoholic beverages in the nation. The Anti-Saloon League had already secured passage of laws regulating the wartime use of alcohol. The league believed liquor to be a threat to servicemen's morals and advocated banning the use of grain in making alcoholic beverages. National and state Woman's Christian Temperance Unions (WCTUs), buoyed by prewar successes, helped pave the way to national prohibition. By

1915, as many as 18 states, including Iowa and North Dakota, had enacted prohibition. Half of Minnesota's counties at that time were also dry.[7]

Red Wing's Hobart WCTU chapter continued its activism, sponsoring regular antiliquor messages in the newspapers. During the influenza outbreak of 1918, the Hobart chapter requested closure of saloons to help stem the epidemic. The group also took out an advertisement on October 30, 1918, noting that in the six months following June 1, 1917, some 967,551 bushels of grain had been converted to "poison" alcohol. That amount of grain, the group asserted, could have produced more than 1.7 million (2.5-pound) sacks of flour.[8]

On December 17, 1917, the U. S. House of Representatives passed a resolution regarding national prohibition. That action, following the senate's concurrence, put the issue before the 48 states. On June 27, 1919, a 57-year-old Goodhue County native and congressman from Minnesota introduced a bill establishing prohibition. Andrew J. Volstead, born of Norwegian-American parents in Holden township, offered the law linking his name for all time to one of the nation's most controversial social experiments—prohibition of the manufacture and sale of alcoholic beverages—also known as the Volstead Act. [9]

Minnesota voters demonstrated their support of prohibition in the years leading to Volstead's actions in the House. Advocates of the antiliquor legislation wanted to build upon their substantial base. Nearly 75 percent of the state's counties were dry. Liquor sales remained legal in parts of Goodhue County including Red Wing, the largest city. The November 5, 1918, election gave voters throughout the state an opportunity to decide the issue, and a majority favored a dry state.[10]

The battle over prohibition in Goodhue County in the 1918 election proved close. Wanamingo, Kenyon, Holden, and Cherry Grove—the four predominantly Norwegian-American townships in the southwest corner of the county—represented the heart of dry country. They voted decisively for prohibition: Wanamingo village 70–9, Wanamingo township 130–55, Cherry Grove 89–41, Kenyon township 99–37, Kenyon village 159–87, and Holden 82–56. The county's largest antiprohibition vote came from Belvidere 112–29, Hay Creek 92–36, Pine Island township 72–32, Goodhue township 113–57, and Zumbrota township 106–51. Red Wing voted for prohibition 853–692. In the end, Goodhue County went dry by a meager 34-vote margin—2,842–2,808. [11]

The towns of Cannon Falls, Pine Island, and Zumbrota all supported prohibition, while the rural voters in the townships of the same name opposed it. The Yankee element, still strong in the towns and villages, tended to support prohibition, but the rural immigrant communities, with the exception of the Norwegian southwest, rejected it. Goodhue village provided another exception to this pattern when its voters joined Goodhue township residents in voting against prohibition. Those in town were just 46–43 against, however, while the township populace was more strongly (113–57) antiprohibition.[12]

Those backing prohibition held "Watch-night" temperance meetings on January 15, 1920. Elated dry advocates counted down the minutes to their long-awaited deadline. The National Prohibition Enforcement Act would become law at midnight. Goodhue County quietly welcomed the new law. One newspaper issued a caution about the change, commenting that authorities "expect illicit manufacturing and dealing in spirits but that will be on a small scale."[13]

More change was on the way. In 1920 the woman's suffrage movement, which had endured decades of disappointment, finally achieved success in getting the vote. Women's contributions to the war effort and the shift of women into the industrial workplace to fill gaps left by wartime labor shortages increased suffrage support.

A Zumbrota *News* article focused on women entering industry, reporting in March 1918, as "accepted fact," that before the war women industrial workers seldom stayed on the job more than five years, usually between school and marriage. Now women workers often held their jobs more than ten years without marrying. Also on the increase were "versatile women," who continued working after becoming married. The account noted, "Since the war began, women have been pouring into industries that formerly employed only men; the numbers of women in industry has increased one million during the past year."[14]

Some women achieved the vote before 1920—first in the territories of Wyoming, Utah, and Washington, then in the states of Colorado and Idaho, and finally in California, Oregon, Kansas, and Arizona. Their example bolstered the suffrage movement. In 1916, both the Democratic and Republican parties had endorsed extending the vote to women. In June 1919 the 19th Amendment, asserting that the right to vote "shall not be denied or abridged by the United States or any State on account of sex" was submitted to the states, which ratified the amendment to take effect in August 1920.[15]

The village of Goodhue wasted no time in electing Minnesota's first woman mayor. In 1921, Florence Pierce edged John Cavanaugh by a vote of 80 to 79 to become village mayor. "Let us set aside this 'I don't care' spirit that has always prevailed in Goodhue and all work together for a cleaner, prettier, and more attractive village," she wrote in the *Enterprise*. Her husband, Dwight (D. C.), had founded the newspaper in 1896, and he still edited and published it.[16]

Mayor Pierce moved the council's meeting place from the cold back room of the fire hall to the freshly painted pumping station, which boasted newly cleaned and curtained windows. Mayor Pierce also invited wives of council members to attend an early 1922 meeting followed by refreshments and a social hour. Some reproached the Pierce administration for spending tax dollars too freely. Her attempt to beautify the jail grounds with flowers drew pointed criticism. John Shelstad defeated Florence Pierce in her March 1922 reelection bid, 124–62. Katherine Hustings, Goodhue's first woman council candidate, lost to Joe O'Reilly in the same election.

Florence Cram Pierce, Mayor of Goodhue
*GCHS*

Thorstein Veblen, the prominent economist and social critic, vigorously offered support for women's equality in society. Veblen had been raised near Nerstrand in the sprawling Norwegian-American community established along the Rice County-Goodhue County line. By 1920 he was world-renowned for his unorthodox and often radical views. Called by economist John Kenneth Galbraith "the nearest thing in the United States to an academic legend," Veblen was also about the farthest thing from the hearty, pietist stock typical of the tightly knit Norwegian culture from which he sprang.[17]

Veblen's parents, Thomas and Kari, shared a mistrust of local Yankee middlemen with many of their immigrant brethren. To America's newcomers like the Veblens, those businessmen skimmed the profits created by the agribusiness system, while immigrants toiled for little reward. The Norwegian farmers saw a community in which city women were absorbed with the niceties of small-town society while farmwomen served a life sentence of hard labor beside their husbands. Yet when the Veblens sent their sons to nearby Northfield to college, they chose the Yankee stronghold of Carleton instead of St. Olaf, the college founded by their Norwegian-American neighbors. As Thorstein acquired a reputation for brilliance among his colleagues over the years, the cosmopolitan Norwegian-American did not forget his Minnesota roots. He did not forgive the storekeepers, lawyers, and bankers who made the village life of his youth "the perfect flower of self-help and cupidity."[18]

In 1899 Veblen published what became his best-known work. *The Theory of the Leisure Class* was a stinging rebuke to the upper classes and their perpetual quest for wealth and social status. He was suspicious of the existing capitalistic economic system, concluding private ownership was incompatible with the modern, technology-based industrial economy. Veblen scorned war.

His critique of Germany's socioeconomic system, *Imperial Germany and the Industrial Revolution*, first drew praise from American officials, then was banned for violating the nation's wartime Espionage Act. A careful reading of the work shows that Veblen was almost as disparaging of American and British economic structures as he was of the German.[19]

Veblen condemned the class conflict created by the capitalist system. He believed American society's treatment of women to be inequitable and foolishly wasteful of a powerful resource. He maintained that the "earliest form of ownership is an ownership of the women by the able-bodied men of the community." He contended that the time, effort, and expense necessary to acquire and maintain the refined tastes and manners so actively cultivated by the moneyed class gave evidence of their real goal—social status. The leisure-class standard of fashion, Veblen observed tartly, was that "dress . . . should not only be expensive, but it should also make plain to all observers that the wearer is not engaged in any kind of productive labor." A woman's corset, he wrote, was "substantially a mutilation, undergone for the purpose of lowering the subject's vitality and rendering her permanently and obviously unfit for work."[20]

Veblen died in 1929, before the onset of the Great Depression that lent credence to his predictions about the failure of capitalism. His influence peaked during the depression years, but the economic system he hoped to see supplanted recovered and retained many of the characteristics he criticized. The turn-of-the-century leisure class he despised expanded to include, by mid-century, a growing middle class whose members would share the "conspicuous leisure" reserved, in Veblen's time, for the wealthy.[21] Although he offered no specific remedies, Veblen's perceptive dissent led others to look more critically at existing institutions. The Norwegian-American skeptic, economist, sociologist, and satirist from the Minnesota prairie was one of the most original thinkers produced in America.

Not all who sought changes in the America of the 1920s achieved success. The World War I years affected the labor movement in a positive manner, reducing the number of immigrants and the competition they brought to the workplace, while fostering a production boom that created more jobs. Yet organized labor could not consolidate its gains, and the membership increases made between 1915 and 1920 eroded in postwar America.[22]

Two controversial Minnesota labor conflicts absorbed local attention in 1916 and 1917. In northern Minnesota, workers confronted the powerful and expanding mining and timber corporations, while in the Twin Cities, streetcar workers tried to unionize. Government and business leaders, concerned about wartime production, developed strategies to deal with labor unrest. In this antilabor atmosphere, both union conflicts were settled largely on management terms.[23]

Red Wing, the industrial center of Goodhue County, experienced minor labor unrest during the war years. Sixty employees of the Red Wing Shoe Company's bottoming and sole-leather rooms walked out in May 1914 to protest reduction in their work week from 55 to 49.5 hours. A workers' committee made up of Fred Chrisler, Richard Perrott, and Gilbert Bushwau met with manager M. T. Shaw and assistant superintendent Jesse R. Sweasy to present their position. The company asserted it would run on the nine-hours-a-day schedule until July 1 when regular hours (7:00 A.M. to 6:00 P.M.) would resume. The workers, who had reported at 7:30 A.M., walked away from the plant three hours later.[24]

Striking workers met and authorized a member to contact a Twin Cities labor organizer to come to Red Wing and establish a union at Red Wing Shoe. The employees returned to work the following day, accepting the company's offer of a 7:30 to 5:30 workday with a half-day off on Saturday, but their steps to unionize continued.[25]

The state's Department of Labor and Industry recorded five wartime work stoppages in Red Wing between December 1917 and June 1918. On December 20, 1917, five workers quit the city's Wisconsin Channel Bridge Company, when their wages were cut from $3.50 to $3.00 per day. Red Wing Linseed Company had a two-day strike in March 1918, and ten workers struck Red Wing Button Works on June 28. The actions were brief and peaceful. Early in April 1918, about 20 workers struck S. B. Foot Tannery. The *Daily Eagle* reported that the strikers "were mostly foreigners who have been doing common labor at the plant." The walkout lasted two days, less in some individual cases.[26]

Fifteen shoe cutters at Red Wing Shoe Company and Stickles Shoe Factory walked off the job in July 1918. Unlike other shoe-factory workers, cutters were paid by the hour (later, by a piece rate) plus a bonus for leather saved. They demanded a four-dollar raise to $30.00 per 55-hour week. J. R. Sweasy, now president of Red Wing Shoe, acknowledged that pay in St. Paul was higher due to war contracts there. L. D. Stickles reminded his cutters that he had raised their pay from $22.50 to $26.00 since April 1 and reduced hours from 57 to 55 per week. Red Wing Shoe lost nine employees to firms outside the city.[27]

A wartime survey of unionized workers in Red Wing showed that the largest union, the 35-member potters' group, made $3.50 per 8.5-hour day. All workers surveyed put in six-day weeks. Sheet-metal workers received $4.00 per nine-hour day. Members of the 12-worker cigar-makers' union averaged $3.00 a day for eight hours. Nineteen unionized bricklayers received $6.95 for nine hours, and their mason colleagues, $5.40. The 16 carpenters and joiners made $4.05 for a nine-hour day.[28]

A survey regarding women in the workplace showed nonunion women making considerably less. Two Red Wing companies reported on their female workforces. The 48 women at Stickles Shoe Company received wages ranging from $1.33 to $2.50 per day. The five women at Red Wing Printing Company earned $1.38 to $2.17 each day.[29]

Disputes over the length of the workday and workweek were a common problem. Workers chafed under their typical six-day schedule and its accompanying nine- to ten-hour day. But they also worried about slack times, when their employers reduced hours or shut down. Harry Nordholm, who served in several capacities as a Red Wing public official, took credit for convincing the Board of Public Works, in 1917, to allow city crew laborers "a nine-hour day working schedule with ten hours pay." Nordholm told the board, "Nine hours' toil is enough. It is time we give labor some consideration."[30]

In the 1880s the Knights of Labor had led the fight to reduce the number of hours worked and enact laws dealing with child labor, minimum wage, workmen's compensation, and other issues concerning Minnesota's organized labor. The Knights, with support from the Farmers' Alliance, had, in 1887, convinced the legislature to establish the State Board of Labor Statistics, later renamed the Bureau of Labor.[31]

The Minnesota Federation of Labor, the state's dominant labor organization by the mid-1890s, had had significant success in advancing its agenda. In 1895 the Bureau of Labor promoted a child-labor law, studied industrial accidents, and prompted improved working conditions. The state adopted a worker's compensation plan in 1913. Meanwhile Congress passed the 1916 Adamson Act, establishing an eight-hour day for the railroad industry. More than 20 years would pass before the eight-hour day was common for most workers.

The legislature designated Minnesota's Labor and Industry Department to monitor implementation of the new minimum-wage law. Myron Ohnstad, a 17-year-old Cannon Falls telephone night operator, received $40 per month for 11-hour shifts seven nights a week. He was allowed to sleep, but he still believed he was underpaid. After his complaint to state officials, Ohnstad received back pay. Clem Smart, an 18-year worker at Red Wing's Pearl Restaurant, worked for a dollar a day plus board. His June 6, 1921, complaint asserted that his day of work ran nine to 15 hours with no time off. He questioned his employer's idea of what constituted a workday.[32]

Anne Reagan believed the Red Wing Telephone Company underpaid her. She made $48 each calendar month for 9.5 hours of daily work and two nights off each month without deduction. A state official replied to her letter, saying that minimum wage was $12 per week. With four-and-one-third weeks to a month, she should get $52 a month. Reagan wrote again in March, claiming that her boss, David Neill, refused to produce the back pay.[33]

The first years of the new century were good ones for American farmers. During the war period of 1914–18, they thrived in expanding their operations to meet the increased demand created by the conflict. Progressive farmers, looking to make their work even more efficient, wished to take advantage of the steady advances made in agricultural science by colleges and universities. In 1914 Congress passed the Smith-Lever Act to create farm extension programs and underwrite the county agricultural agent movement.[34] Young Zumbrota-township farmer H. August Lohmann looked into the county-agent issue and other related questions as early as October 1913. Lohmann corresponded with A. D. Wilson, the new supervisor of the University of Minnesota's Agricultural Extension Division. Wilson detailed some of the state's preliminary work in developing a county agent system. Lohmann also requested information on cow testing, alfalfa, and liming.[35]

Lohmann wasn't the only county farmer interested in educating himself about new agricultural methods. Local farmers organized the Goodhue County Farm Bureau in April 1918. They chose as officers William J. Bryan, Burnside township, president; John P. Mark, Belle Creek, first vice president; W. Edwin Peterson, Wanamingo, second vice president; and George W. Pagel, Zumbrota, secretary-treasurer. Roy L. Olson became county agricultural agent. The bureau was to work with the Minnesota Department of Agriculture and the University of Minnesota to provide educational programs for county farmers.[36]

The county's farm bureau exhibited a long reach. Its executive committee had 15 members, including its own officers, as well as a member on the county board of commissioners. Other organized county interests—the dairy council, women's groups, the county and Cannon Valley fairs, crop improvement, livestock, commercial, shipping association, and schools—also participated. Early bureau programs focused on livestock improvement through use of purebred sires, cow testing, poultry culling, rodent control, control of diseases in rye and of smut in oats, introduction of alfalfa and sweet clover, orchard pruning and spraying, the testing of soils for lime, and ditch and stump blasting. The programs broadened to meet specific needs in the following years. By the fall of 1927, the testing of cattle for tuberculosis, begun in 1926, was complete.

The Home Extension program, a component of the Farm Bureau, provided extensive training to farm women, including instruction in the raising of productive chickens, cold-pack canning, cooking, nutrition, furniture refinishing, gardening, knitting, crocheting, and painting. Margaret Lohmann became involved in extension work in the early 1920s at the urging of county agent V. H. Kingsbury. Lohmann was a member of Zumbrota Township Group #1, one of the county's first extensions. She later recalled a lesson in making dress forms during which members put on T-shirt fabric, then pasted paper tape to the material to create the form. Lohmann noted the lessons were "extensive" and detailed how Cora Cook, University of Minnesota poultry specialist, trained women in raising chickens and making hens more productive.[37]

The Farm Bureau's Women's Camp, begun in the late 1920s by extension agent Preston O. Hale, became a popular feature of Goodhue County's Home

Extension. The camp sessions, about three days each, were seen as both vacation and educational experience.

The Home Extension program spread throughout the county in 1923. Among the leaders in other communities were Mrs. L. J. Grosse of Hay Creek, Mrs. C. J. Bang of Belvidere, Josephine Keye of Florence, Etta Featherstone and Lucy Perkins of Featherstone, Anna Hultgren of Holden, Margaret Lohmann of Zumbrota, and Caroline Uhlin of Stanton. The women elected Lucy Perkins the first home and community chairperson. She also became a member of the county Farm Bureau board.[38]

Two agricultural-based programs rapidly became popular with young people. The Farm Bureau developed 4-H clubs (Head, Heart, Hands, and Health) for rural youth, and the state public high schools created the Future Farmers of America.

Farmers looked for more ways to improve their financial picture when crop prices slumped in the postwar years. They increased the number of farmer-owned cooperatives in the county, hoping to reduce middleman costs by providing their own services. In Goodhue, a "conservative bunch of farmers" bought Edward G. Hammer's creamery in 1922 and formed Goodhue Cooperative Creamery. Fred Vollmers was its first president. By 1928 their success allowed replacement of the old plant with a new creamery. In Wanamingo township, Hader Cooperative Cheese Factory began operations in 1920. Sivert O. Haugen was president.[39]

Wanamingo-area farmers formed the Cooperative Oil Company, a petroleum consortium, in 1926. At their first meeting, the members decided to buy out the privately owned Wanamingo Oil Company and set up a cooperative. To increase revenue, the group opened membership to village residents. It later incorporated Cannon Falls and Bellechester into its operations.[40]

Farmers and the communities that supported them battled through the times of low prices. Both Kenyon and Zumbrota organized and promoted agricultural community celebrations in the 1920s. Meanwhile, the Goodhue County Fair, among the state's oldest, and the Cannon Falls Fair, inaugurated in 1916 by the Cannon Valley Agricultural Association, continued their successful operations.

Kenyon's popular Corn Show, a farm-city celebration, began in 1925 and ran annually for nearly two decades. The Commercial Club organized the festival, which invited farmers to display corn samples and compete for prizes. The Corn Show soon expanded to two days and included prizes for exhibitors of fruit, vegetables, and grains. Exhibits at the city hall and in front of stores dominated Main Street. The show eventually became too costly and unwieldy for local merchants.[41]

Zumbrota adopted the Farm Bureau's efforts to eliminate "scrub bulls" and encourage the use of purebred sires as a way to improve dairy herds. In February 1928, the town Commercial Club put together the Kow Karnival, a community celebration designed to entertain rural families. Preston Hale's "Kow Girls," a boxing match, the Red Wing Training School band, and local talent provided the entertainment. The Kow Karnival's popularity resulted in an encore the following year. This time the festival attracted 1,500 people and outgrew its armory headquarters. Zumbrota staged its final carnival in 1930.[42]

Goodhue's business community promoted its annual "Friendship Tours," in a bid to stir interest in the village. For the first tour on June 16, 1926, businesses closed at 9:30 A.M., and a parade of 60 cars and floats headed toward Zumbrota, Pine Island, Kenyon, Cannon Falls, White Rock, Stanton, and Dennison. The Goodhue Concert Band played at each stop. A second, larger tour, in June 1927, roamed north and east, with residents piloting three floats and 125 cars.[43] Merchants in Goodhue staged "Slow Auto Races" on Second Street. Spectators looked on as the racecars crept from the starting line at one end of the block and inched down the street. The winner was the last driver to get to the other end without killing his engine.[44]

The tradition of agricultural fairs had already been a long one in Goodhue County. In December 1863, organizers met in Red Wing to set up the Goodhue County Agricultural Society and Mechanics Institute—the first county fair. The annual fair did not make money, however, and it moved to Hader in 1871. Then the fair's executive committee offered to shift the operation to Zumbrota provided the town secure the deal with $500. While it sometimes struggled, the fair survived in its new Zumbrota home as proprietors adapted to the times. In 1917

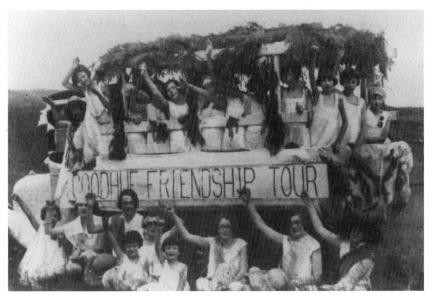

These young women joined the Goodhue "Friendship Tour" on June 6, 1926. *GCHS*

the county fair featured its first auto race, and two years later, its first airplane flight.[45]

The fair in Cannon Falls also became a fixture, giving Goodhue County what could be considered an extra county fair. The association's president, Edward A. Dibble, a Stanton farmer and later mayor of Cannon Falls, assumed its leadership. The Cannon Falls celebration soon became popular for its horse races and fireworks programs as well as its competitions in agriculture, dairy, 4-H, and culinary arts.[46]

For farmers, electricity was the most envied advantage of city folk. Rural families went without the comforts provided by electricity. Rural schools and doctors missed its advantages as well. In 1923 this began to change in Goodhue County with the establishment of what its originators believed was the "first experimental rural electric line in the world." This 6.2 mile stretch of power line served ten farms in the county's Burnside township.[47]

 Known as the Red Wing Project because of its proximity to the city, the new electrical line evolved after a state study on the increasing demand for electric service on Minnesota farms. The test project determined "whether electric service at reasonable rates could be used with profit on Minnesota farms." Its sponsors, the University of Minnesota, the Minnesota Committee on the Relation of Electricity to Agriculture (CREA), Northern States Power Company (NSP), and the farmers themselves, approved the project in November 1923. NSP started construction in December. The line began at the county poor farm, already electrified, and headed west, then south, to link ten farms to the original test high line. Nine potential customers refused the service and its expense. The university, CREA, and NSP assumed most of the $75,158.49 project cost, and the connected farmers absorbed 18 percent.

Seventy-nine manufacturers lent $2,700 worth of appliances and equipment to the participants, while the University of Minnesota monitored their use. The manufacturers' inventory of loans included ranges, motors, power saws, brooders, feed grinders, water pumps, vacuum cleaners, milking machines, and cream separators. Each of the machines had a separate meter so as to measure accurately the cost of their use.[48]

On December 24, 1923, NSP turned on the power. Electricity became an instant hit with the farm families. Later publicity photos featuring the Burnside residents showed Bernice Bryan, who kept house for her father and three brothers, demonstrating her washing machine. W. A Cady, with hands behind his back, looked on as his electric cream separator did its work. Farmwomen used electric-powered equipment to do their traditional chores of ironing, sewing, washing clothes, vacuuming, and cooking.[49]

Perhaps the most visible sign of the new electrical service stood outside the spartan, wood-frame home of W. A. Cady. In the front yard a small evergreen held a strand of Christmas tree bulbs—a colorful symbol of a change that eventually reached rural families around the nation.[50]

The five-year experiment proved useful as a source of technical information but failed to impress observers who believed the cost of such power prohibitive. The group of Burnside farmers still had electrical power, but the time for most of the state's rural farms to be "electrified" seemed far in the future.[51]

The Ku Klux Klan, the nativist hate-group born in the American South in the aftermath of the Civil War, began a comeback in 1915. The new Klan, after a fitful start, became a prominent organization by the early 1920s, and its influence spread across the nation, particularly in the Midwest. Members of the reborn KKK brandished a hatred for America's new immigrants, radicals, and communists, as well as Catholics, Jews, and African Americans. By 1923 the Klan was marching in Goodhue County.[52]

The Klan's roots were in the small towns and rural sections of America. Its membership was "mostly composed of poor people," according to Hiram Evans, who became Imperial Wizard of the organization in 1922. Evans detailed the objectives of the Klan in an Ohio speech, "The Klan's Mission—Americanism." The Klan leader proclaimed, "It is only through the maintenance in America of native, white supremacy, it is only through patriotism which will maintain the America of our fathers, that Protestantism itself can be saved."[53]

The "Invisible Empire's" presence began to grow in large cities, including Detroit, Milwaukee, Indianapolis, Pittsburgh, Denver, and Chicago. Minneapolis reportedly had ten chapters in 1923, and the Minnesota Klan published its own magazine and newspaper. The KKK also established a presence in Goodhue County and attempted to recruit new members.[54]

In 1923, Klan threats rang out even in Red Wing schoolyards. In April Julia Wiech heard the pronouncement "The Catholic Church is going to be burned" from several solemn-faced classmates during recess at Red Wing's Washington School. St. Joseph's Catholic Church was directly across Sixth Street from school, and she was frightened when she learned the arsonists would set a fire that very evening. Wiech was relieved to see the solid, limestone church still standing the next day.[55] The threat had occurred at the height of Ku Klux Klan activity in Red Wing. On April 5 young Wiech had been among those to witness a 16-by-20-foot cross burning at the highest point of Barn Bluff. Members of the Klan erected the wooden structure, drilled holes in it, and stuffed it with gasoline-soaked combustibles before setting it ablaze. The cross began burning at 8:30 P.M., its silhouette commanding the skyline. Cross burnings also occurred on Sorin's Bluff in September and November.[56]

The major county Klan event of the year took place in late September 1923. A Saturday evening parade and membership induction drew, according to *Daily*

*Republican* estimates, between 7,500 and 10,000 people to Red Wing. "Solid walls of humanity" jammed the streets as spectators observed the gathering. Klan members from the Twin Cities and southeastern Minnesota towns marched with the county group.[57]

The parade, led by three robed Klansmen on horseback, began in the downtown business district. Long, silent lines of gowned and hooded Klansmen followed the leaders. The procession moved south on Bush Street to the city circus grounds for the final ceremonies. Klansmen erected three large crosses on a knoll overlooking the site. Contrary to the usual rule of secrecy, Klan leaders conducted a public swearing in of the "large class of new members."

Fireworks erupted at the conclusion of the speeches and member induction, three crosses burned, and the audience watched "Klansmen in robes flitting like ghosts and spirits through the trees." To the *Daily Republican* observer, the ceremonies were "impressively beautiful." A *Daily Eagle* reporter agreed, writing, "the initiatory work proved very impressive."

Red Wing was the site of a Ku Klux Klan Minnesota-Wisconsin day program in September 1925. The function drew delegations from both states, and about 400 Klansmen and women marched in a parade featuring two floats. One representing the St. Paul KKK carried Klanswomen and children in regalia as well as a large, illuminated cross. One arrest occurred during the gathering. Police charged John F. Kearney with a misdemeanor for tearing down a KKK banner. Kearney was released on $100 bail and later paid a $10 fine.[58]

Klan activity elsewhere in the county was less noticeable since leaders preferred to gather members before the larger audiences that cities could guarantee. At least two speakers addressed Zumbrota audiences at a city park in the summer of 1923. In July an unidentified speaker, wearing a white robe and hat, outlined Klan "policy" and claimed the group was peaceful. He denounced some of the depredations of the southern Klan.[59]

In July 1925, a Klan rally following a band concert in Pine Island generated controversy when robed members marched through the village streets by twos, with arms folded. Cars carrying the American flag preceded and followed them. A speaker, using a car for a rostrum, gave a brief talk from north Main Street. Klansmen complained that Mayor Arthur Parkin forbade them to deliver the address. Parkin denied the charge, noting that "I did request him not to use the bandstand as a rostrum."[60]

In July 1925, Zumbrotans saw a quiet parade of about 70 Klan members on a Wednesday evening following a band concert. Those in the march, including several women and children, wore robes and hoods but no masks. The *News* reported the rumor that the marchers were citizens of Red Wing and Cannon Falls and that they had previously marched in Pine Island.[61]

Klan membership nationwide peaked at more than three million in 1925 but shrank to a fraction of that just three years later. The majority of its members in the 1920s took no part in violence. As in the case of Goodhue County, its membership mostly bought regalia, paid dues, and marched in parades. Yet the Ku Klux Klan etched a legacy of hatred into the memory of those who witnessed the intimidating parades of robed and anonymous Klansmen—and the specter of a menacing cross on Barn Bluff burning in the night.[62]

While the targets of Ku Klux Klan malice were manifold, the Klan in Minnesota focused on anti-Catholic, antiradical, and antiforeigner themes. The Invisible Empire's traditional repugnance towards African Americans was less noticeable in the state and particularly in counties such as Goodhue, with its minute black population. Their lower social and economic standing also tended to keep blacks below the Minnesota Klan's hatred horizon.[63]

Steve Bell was one of Goodhue County's first African-American residents. He came north after the Civil War with veterans of the Fifth Minnesota Infantry. He eventually settled in Pine Island with the assistance of Charles Hill, the city's first physician. Bell, born into slavery in Charleston, South Carolina, on December 25, 1850, escaped to freedom during the Civil War by making his way into Union-controlled territory.[64]

Bell worked on local farms and as a laborer in the Pine Island area until his marriage in 1880 to Sarah Elma Ford, a resident of Conway, Iowa. The Bells lived in Pine Island, where they began a family. Sarah gave birth to two daughters, Clara Mae and Edna, as well as a son who died in infancy. Steve labored in the village, digging sewers, shoveling coal, and cutting wood. The locals called him the busiest man in Pine Island. Sarah Bell became an active member of the Methodist Church. Both lived in the village until their deaths.

Sam Chambers, another black refugee from the Civil War, arrived in Zumbrota as a boy, brought by two former privates in the Eighth Minnesota Infantry, David Scofield and Jasper Dickey. Chambers lived in Zumbrota with the Scofields and went to school in the village. He died in Minneapolis in 1936.[65]

George Patterson, an African-American farmer, came to Belvidere in 1881 to work for Julia B. Nelson, the teacher and women's rights activist from Goodhue County. In 1883 he rented the Nelson farm when she returned to Tennessee for another stint of teaching in freedmen schools. Nelson established Red Wing's Equal Rights Meat Market in 1897 with Patterson's son, Jerry, but the business soon failed.[66]

A teenage black runaway known as "Lil Rastus" reached Red Wing in the mid-1890s and worked at odd jobs in the city for several years before moving on. Company G soldiers adopted Rastus as an "unofficial mascot" while he lived in Red Wing. The teenager wished to join the unit after hearing that the soldiers had gone to the Philippines in 1898. The young man earned both respect and notoriety when he stowed away on a ship to reach Manila and the welcome of Company G. He received a room, food, clothing, and "occasional tips" to take care of Capt. Oscar Seebach's room.[67]

In 1918 Dewey and Howard Patterson, whose father, Jerry, managed Red Wing's Equal Rights Meat Market, became "the only colored soldiers selected in the county" for service in World War I. The brothers had volunteered for military service several months earlier, with no vacancies found. Dewey Patterson became a private in a school for bakers and cooks. Howard was a private in the 163rd Depot Battalion at Camp Dodge, Illinois. [68]

African Americans who lived in Goodhue County, or who worked on trains or riverboats passing through, generally were laborers or held low-paying menial jobs. The treatment blacks received was at best condescending. Racial epithets such as *nigger, coon,* and *darkie* were in common usage in newspapers in the nation and Goodhue County throughout the post-Civil War years and well into the 20th century. In Minnesota, with its small population of African Americans, these terms were typically applied in the idiom of white citizens, with insensitivity and ignorance more than hatred.

Roy Wilkins, the future head of the National Association for the Advancement of Colored People (NAACP) gave an account of his growing up in a white Minnesota neighborhood—St. Paul's Rice Street. He wrote of the companions whose use of "the word 'nigger' was part of their equipment along with other brickbats." Wilkins built many friendships in his neighborhood and developed a "faith in integration." But he went on to give a chilling account of the racist 1920 lynching of three black men in Duluth and the effect it had on his view of racism's potential for violence in Minnesota.[69]

The more respectful terms applied to African Americans of the day—*Negro* and *Colored*—also became racial designations. In some cases, such as the 1907 Red Wing *Daily Republican*'s story of Nicholas Taylor's death, both words appeared. The story noted that Taylor was a "colored man" familiarly known as "Nigger Nick" and that the 69-year-old Taylor was a "well known character" who fought in the Civil War as a member the U.S. Cavalry.[70]

The Zumbrota *News,* in August 1923, gave a favorable account of a traveling group of black musicians and singers. They treated a crowd quickly gathered to "a few selections of the New Way Jazz." The entertainers passed a hat several times during the performance, and the crowd applauded the music. The *News* dubbed the performers a "traveling Coon Band."[71]

Blacks provided entertainment with road shows that covered Minnesota. Under the headline "Darkies Give Entertainment," the *Daily Republican* reported in January 1907 that a crowd nearly filled Red Wing's Sheldon Auditorium to watch as "six colored people" provided song. Not all such groups were successful. A "colored show troupe" was stranded in Red Wing in 1909 when its tent show failed to attract paying crowds. The group couldn't afford to get the act of out town and entertained in saloons for "a few stray coins."[72]

Dewey, Arthur, and Howard Patterson (front, l to r) posed with their dog. Dewey and Howard served in World War I as did Clarence Elstad (second from left on branch). Elstad's was the county's first combat death. *GCHS*

Railroad and river steamboat traffic brought some black crewmen into the Red Wing area. Nellie Allen recalled that students from the Lutheran Ladies' Seminary enjoyed the entertainment provided by excursion steamers, showboats, and workboats: "Sometimes we watched the Negro roustabouts unload freight, stopping long enough to entertain us by dancing [and] bring us a brief glimpse of the South." Herb Nordholm remembered the black stevedores who worked on river steamers, including some excellent banjo players: "Oh goll, we were entertained by them."[73] Red Wing, long proud of its baseball teams, hosted the Colored Keystones of Minneapolis in 1909. The Keystones were billed as the best "colored" team playing in the western states. The Minneapolis club defeated Red Wing 5–3 in a well-played ballgame.[74]

The number of permanent African-American residents in Goodhue County remained small. The 1930 U.S. census listed 31 "Negro" residents. That number, reported the *Daily Republican,* included 17 young men incarcerated at the State Training School as well as ten temporarily living in Florence as members a railroad section crew. That left four permanent black residents in the county—two in Hay Creek, one in Belvidere, and one in Cannon Falls township.[75]

Sinclair Lewis's Pulitzer Prize-winning 1920 novel *Main Street* provided an assault on the deeply held values of those who believed the nation's small towns and villages represented the best in America. In *Main Street*, the Sauk Centre native introduced readers to a group of typical small-town characters—the storekeeper, the doctor, and other townspeople—living a dull, futile existence. The book proved a devastating indictment of their shallow, parochial prejudices. Two years later Lewis skewered small-town businessmen with *Babbitt*, the tale of a prideful, self-absorbed realtor who built a towering self-image upon his material possessions and social contacts.

Lewis's judgment of the values of the people walking the Main Streets of middle America's small cities was too much for Red Wing's Charles P. Hall to ignore. While admitting his admiration for Lewis's descriptive powers, Hall felt the award-winning author overlooked much of value to be found on the main streets of cities like Cannon Falls and Red Wing, where he lived. He took aim at Lewis's contention that the Main Street of his fictional Gopher Prairie was a "continuation of Main Streets everywhere."[76] Hall countered Lewis by publishing *Sane Street*, a tribute to the values of small-town America.[77]

Hall's sentimental, even maudlin story tells of a couple who built a home on Sane Street in a small Minnesota town. The buildings along Sane Street did not scrape the sky, and there was some immorality and crime "proportional perhaps to the population." Yet the protagonists believed it wonderful "to feel everywhere at home: to feel that people are really friendly and helpful."[78]

For Hall, there was "no Saner Street than that which runs through the little Minnesota town." His tribute to small-town virtue took a religious turn and promised salvation to those who have traversed the street that, to him, intersected with all Minnesota's small communities. It's a "Street Eternal, which we all shall tread, the golden pavement of Life Eternal, the end of all Sane Streets."

Hall's defense of small-town Minnesota virtues has merit, especially when considered from his perspective. His father was the attorney, and later congressman, Osee Matson Hall. Hall, admitted to the bar in Minnesota in 1902, followed his father into law. He practiced in Cannon Falls and was the city attorney before returning to Red Wing, where he was elected city attorney in 1910. Hall knew well the main streets of Cannon Falls and Red Wing, along with other villages and hamlets. In 1928 voters elected Hall judge of district court in the First Judicial District.[79]

The postwar era of the 1920s continued America's transition to a more technologically advanced society, one in retreat from 19th-century Victorianism and more open to social change. By the end of the 1920s, more than 43 percent of the world's manufactured products were American-made, and the country served as the world's greatest creditor nation. Millions of improved autos and trucks using newly surfaced highways were conquering the "tyranny of distance." Airlines conducted scheduled service. Two-thirds of American homes had electricity by 1927, and every third home had a radio. Motion pictures entertained and informed wider audiences. Farm mechanization increased productivity. Workers' buying power had advanced more than a third since 1914, and purchase by the installment plan allowed some to possess coveted consumer goods such as cars, refrigerators, and washing machines.[80]

Yet there were ominous signs. The average American still worked ten to 12 hours a day, with little job security or health care protection. Prohibition was enriching liquor bootleggers who in turn brought corruption to American city halls. The end of the war and the onset of the 1920s saw crop prices plummeting and the beginnings of an agricultural depression. The value of Minnesota farm crops, which totaled $506 million in 1919, slumped to $310 million by 1929, despite acreage increases. Prohibition did not seem to be working, and a majority of Americans questioned the effectiveness of the antiliquor laws. Banks in Minnesota and elsewhere in the Midwest suffered reverses. From 1921 to 1929 more than 300 state and 58 national banks in Minnesota went under, with many depositors losing their savings.[81]

The collapse of Loomis Irish's State Bank in May 1924 rocked Pine Island. The New York-born "Lum" Irish was a leading citizen of the village. He established a brick factory and roller mill in Pine Island and in 1895 built the first business block in the community. He used its first floor as new headquarters for the private bank he opened in 1882. The Italianate commercial-style building also housed an opera house on its upper floors. Irish, in 1907, incorporated his firm as the State Bank of Pine Island.[82]

"The people of Pine Island were dazed and dumbfounded . . . when the news flashed from lip to lip that the State Bank had suspended," reported the *Record*. The newspaper described pathetic stories of people whose entire cash capital was held in the Irish bank. The shock was all the greater considering that Irish had retained control of the bank as president and principal owner since its founding 42 years earlier.[83]

Lum Irish promised to pay the depositors in full, pledging "his entire private fortune to that end." The bank had been a rock-solid institution in Pine Island, and its closing, observed the *Record*, was "a staggering blow."[84]

Trenton Island and its prohibition-era "dens and dives" lay on the Wisconsin side of the Mississippi—for Red Wing residents, a short drive or walk over the 1895 wagon bridge. This view, taken from Barn Bluff, also shows the limestone outcropping that, from certain angles, gave the appearance to some of an Indian's face in profile. *Steaffens Studio photo, MHS*

# 15

## Descent into the Great Depression

America's "noble experiment"—its attempt to ban the manufacture and sale of intoxicating liquor—was in trouble soon after the January 1920 enactment of prohibition. From the outset, authorities tried to enforce the Volstead Amendment by cracking down on the suppliers of illegal alcohol. They found themselves overmatched.

Many of those with a taste for strong drink were willing to break the law to slake their thirst. Whether they conspired to manufacture liquor or simply to consume it, some citizens found themselves involved with the alcohol "underground." The operators of hidden stills produced liquor readily available through a growing black market that also imported strong drink. Trenton Island, between the Mississippi's main channel and the Wisconsin channel, provided a popular venue for illegal sales of alcohol to residents of Red Wing and nearby townships. "The Island" was a site of liquor manufacture and sale. A trip over the Red Wing high bridge brought thirsty Goodhue County residents to the liquor source.[1]

To make matters worse for law enforcement agencies, the Volstead Act allowed breweries to produce "near beer," a product from which brewers removed all but an allowable percentage of alcohol. By spiking near beer with alcohol, consumers could create their own potent brew. The normal practice for operators of Red Wing's West End bars was to charge 25 cents to fill with alcohol the unused space in a bottle of near beer. The customer then tipped the bottle and mixed the contents.[2]

Some citizens elected to concoct "home brew," typically a dark, bitter beer, usually for their own consumption. Basement brewers mixed water with hops, malt, and yeast, all available in local stores. The combination, which could reach considerable potency, fermented for a period of days. The attendant periodically skimmed off the scum formed during fermentation. When ready, the brew was ladled into bottles, capped, and allowed to age.

"You did not make home brew in secret," recalled one Red Wing West Ender who remembered the strong smell of the concoction wafting through his neighborhood. The brewing process required delicate timing, since the drink continued to ferment in the bottle. Sometimes the caps blew off, producing beer-sprayed basements and leaving some homes smelling like breweries. Herbert Nordholm, who became Red Wing's deputy city clerk in 1923, recalled the occasional popping noise of beer-bottle explosions as he walked home at night. Nordholm claimed home brew was a staple in many Red Wing homes.[3]

A doctor's prescription provided a legal source of alcohol, including imported liquor from Canada. Large numbers of such prescriptions supplied "patients" around the nation and state, including Goodhue County. By March 1920 federal officers in Chicago complained that druggists throughout the country were buying moonshine whiskey at 18 cents a quart and selling it for four dollars. That complaint was not made in Goodhue County, but pharmacies did handle a host of liquor prescriptions. Longtime town druggist E. O. Bakko filled 314 liquor prescriptions in 1923 in Kenyon, one of the driest areas of the county. Nord's City Drug in Red Wing filled 361 prescriptions for liquor in 1921; the number mushroomed to almost 1,950 by 1923. City Drug in Red Wing served people from the entire county as well as western Wisconsin.[4]

A review of those receiving liquor by prescription revealed the names of some of the county's most influential business, civic, and political leaders. Prominent among them was Jens K. Grondahl, the editor and publisher of the *Daily Republican* and, editorially, an ardent supporter of prohibition. The Norwegian-born Grondahl, who emigrated to America at age 11, was at the height of his powers in the 1920s. He had been connected with the newspaper since 1892, the same year in which he began the first of three terms in the state legislature. Despite his public dry stance, Grondahl was "known to imbibe quite liberally on occasion."[5]

The public remembered a 1908 interstate raid against illegal liquor operations on the island. The newsman combined forces with Pierce County sheriff Oluff Halls and a score of deputies for the assault. Grondahl, Halls, and the deputies gathered at the *Daily Republican* office at 1:00 A.M., severed telephone wires to the island to ensure secrecy and marched over the bridge. The posse surprised and apprehended several lawbreakers. The owners of the island's "dens and dives" soon reestablished their operations.[6]

Violators of prohibition laws soon became the most frequent prisoners in the Goodhue County jail. Sheriff John Anderson reported incarcerating 76 people in 1921, one in three held for violating the dry laws. Twenty-six sustained liquor violations, with larceny the next most common offense, accounting for 11 jailed.[7]

Law-enforcement officials arrested and convicted county citizens for making and selling illegal alcohol but made little headway in stopping the bootleggers. Zumbrota had two convictions for moonshining in 1922 and added another two years later. All culprits paid $50 fines levied by Judge Orrin Hall. A Stanton man paid $100 for possessing a "quantity of intoxicating liquors" in 1922. In Pine Island a man served 30 days in the county jail for allowing people to drink intoxicating liquors until late hours while singing boisterously. A search warrant in Pine Island produced a keg of liquor and a gallon jug of "mash." Among those escaping authorities were some moonshine makers living in and around the old Barr Clay facility in Minneola township. Their home brew and wine had an excellent reputation.[8]

Operators of Goodhue's three pool halls frustrated village marshal Tom Taylor. The marshal knew that boys between the ages of 14 and 18 were hanging out in the establishments and that liquor was present. In April 1922, Taylor asked for help from state officials, reporting that the boys' "mothers and sisters are complaining all the time about it, but I am helpless." Two inspectors from the Industrial Commission went to Goodhue and issued stern warnings. All the boys but one heeded the call.[9]

One tough teenager still defied Taylor. He refused to stay out of one pool hall and continued to bootleg and furnish cigarettes to "small boys." Taylor couldn't handle the teenager for whom "no law of God or man has any terror." Taylor reported the recovery of one half-gallon of moonshine hidden by the delinquent.[10]

A month later, in July 1922, Taylor sought the Industrial Commission's help in shutting down "another Damnable hole running full blast now." The marshal referred to a local dance hall that allowed children inside. "[There are] little girls under fifteen years of age Dancing there," Taylor wrote. "A lot of drunken rowdies congregate here from all over the county."[11]

Marshal Frank Rew and constable Ray Stoddard made a Sunday evening raid on a Pine Island home in July 1925 to find several men and women drinking illegally—two bottles of moonshine. The female hostess had recently moved from nearby Oronoco after her husband received 90 days in jail for selling liquor in Rochester. She claimed those in her home were just friends. During that same week federal agents raided two Frontenac pool halls and soft-drink parlors. They jailed the proprietors after discovering liquor.[12]

Soft-drink parlors often sold liquor to customers. In January 1921, sheriff John Anderson, under orders of county attorney Arthur Arntson, raided a Red Wing Main Street soft-drink establishment. A federal grand jury charged the proprietor with possession of liquor in a place of business. He pled guilty and paid a $100 fine. A 1925 search of a Plum Street soft-drink business produced 150 gallons of liquor and a sentence of 90 days along with a $300 fine for its owner.[13]

Officers of the law faced an enforcement nightmare. Growing numbers of citizens violated the dry laws, and society became more accepting of such behavior. The Minnesota legislature passed a prohibition enforcement code in 1921 to little practical effect. Arrests for drunkenness nearly tripled in Minneapolis, rising from 2,546 in 1920 to 7,294 five years later. Federal agents and local police concentrated on large liquor and beer suppliers and moved against small operators on the basis of tips. Prominent leaders, including President Warren G. Harding, were regular liquor users who usually kept their taste concealed from the public.[14] To others, drinking became fashionable. Breaking Prohibition laws, they believed, involved only a small element of danger and did little harm.

An incident in Goodhue village in January of 1929 produced a quick response from authorities. A White Willow man, after a night of drinking in Goodhue, died from exposure while attempting to return home. His death prompted the sheriff and three deputies to conduct a thorough search of the village, where they discovered 20 gallons of liquor in the basement of one pool hall and two pints in a barbershop. The sheriff arrested the proprietors, who were sentenced to 30 days in jail and fined $250 each.[15]

Goodhue County law officers confronted the same challenges faced by their colleagues around the nation. They conducted liquor raids, shut down illegal operations, and arrested some, but made little headway in prevention. Historians later asserted that, compared to pre-Volstead years, Prohibition cut overall alcohol consumption by at least a third. The fact remained that Americans in massive numbers resisted the dry laws.[16]

Farmers, in their growing frustration with the stagnant prices for crops and produce in the 1920s, looked for political solutions to their woes. Some believed the answer lay in revitalizing the Nonpartisan League, champion of farmer causes. But the NPL's opponents, who labeled it as antiwar and hence anti-American, had damaged the league in 1917 and 1918. Others looked for more dramatic change. NPL veterans joined with the State Federation of Labor to support "farmer-labor" candidates for Minnesota governor in 1918 and 1920, but their candidates lost. The farmers and laborers still met as separate political organizations, but they forged the links later combined in a third-party Minnesota political powerhouse—the Farmer-Labor Party.[17]

NPL leaders conceived the new alliance during a 1922 gathering in the Minneapolis offices of the *Daily Star*, the party's newspaper. Susie Stageberg of Red Wing advocated, in a speech at the meeting, the creation of a new, independent party that would advance farmer-labor issues. Magnus Johnson, who became the first Farmer-Labor senator from Minnesota the following year, strongly backed her suggestion. Charles Lindbergh Sr. joined in support. Stageberg's address to the Minneapolis gathering earned her the title "Mother of the Farmer-Labor Party."[18]

Susie Williamson Stageberg's first political experience was as a woman's suffrage and temperance advocate. She supported the gubernatorial run of her husband, Olaf, a professor at Red Wing Seminary, in his 1918 bid as the National (Prohibition) Party candidate. She and Olaf had come to Red Wing from Waldorf College in Iowa, where he taught and she was the dean of women. Stageberg, now in her mid-forties, waded into Farmer-Labor politics.[19]

Stageberg had demonstrated her progressive instincts as a teenager, when she wrote a "sturdy defense" of bloomers, the controversial pantaloons that allowed women mobility with modesty. Traditional skirts, she argued, seemed "more suited to inanimate statues than living, moving, active women of the nineteenth century."[20]

The new Farmer-Labor Party ran Stageberg as its candidate for Minnesota secretary of state in 1922, 1924, and 1928. She lost in each of those campaigns. In 1927 she became editor of the struggling Red Wing-based farm weekly *Organized Farmer*. Fred Scherf, the Nonpartisan Leaguer who won election to the state legislature in 1918, ran the newspaper. Scherf wanted the publication to provide a voice for farmers and their issues. Stageberg decreased the paper's debt and increased its circulation but moved aside in 1929 when Scherf decided to put Francis H. Shoemaker in charge.[21]

Shoemaker, a 40-year-old Wisconsin native, was a self-proclaimed radical. As a newspaperman he recklessly attacked those he perceived as enemies. His editorial stance centered on providing relief to farmers so that they would not become "peons" and creating city-owned light and power utilities. While he received some farmer support for his views, the general public in the Goodhue County and Minnesota of the late 1920s showed little interest in his ideas.[22]

Shoemaker's hostility towards other businesses reduced the *Organized Farmer's* advertising revenue. He lashed out against the Red Wing Manufacturers Association, calling it a "gang of looting, thieving, liars." The easily ruffled editor was also unhappy with August H. Andresen, Red Wing resident and Third District congressman. Shoemaker considered a run for Congress against the Republican Andresen, known in the *Organized Farmer* as a "jellyfish," "rodent," and "Wall Street tool." In an opening volley against Andresen in December 1929, Shoemaker wrote, "Running true to form, and according to the dictates of those who live by robbing the farmers, Aug. H. Andresen . . . again stabbed the farmers, whom he misrepresents, in the back."[23]

But even Shoemaker could go too far. In spring 1930, he nearly withdrew from the race for Congress after being charged in St. Paul with sending scurrilous material through the mails. He had sent a letter to prominent Red Wing banker Robert W. Putnam addressed to "Robber of Widows and Orphans, Red

Wing, Minn. in care of Temple of Greed and Chicanery." Despite the pending charges, Shoemaker easily won the Farmer-Labor primary. He next took on Andresen, to whom he lost every county in the Third District.[24]

Following the election, the Red Wing editor reported to U.S. District Court Judge John B. Sanborn for his hearing. Shoemaker had already explained himself in print, labeling banker Putnam a hypocrite, tyrant, Jekyll and Hyde, financial dictator, and trainer of his own congressmen. Judge Sanborn, saying there was "no question" of Shoemaker's guilt, fined him $500 and sentenced him to a year in prison, suspended.[25]

Shoemaker printed his own newspaper account of the St. Paul trial, insinuating that Sanborn had treated him unfairly The aggrieved judge called the subsequently remorseful newspaperman back to St. Paul and revoked the suspension, sending him to the Leavenworth penitentiary in Kansas. This was not, however, the end of Francis Shoemaker's adventures in Goodhue County.[26]

In January 1930, the nation's farm economy continued to lag, and an economic slowdown threatened the nation's powerful industrial engine. During the prosperous 1920s manufacturers had expanded capacity to produce durable goods available to consumers, millions of whom were buying on credit for the first time. Between 1921 and 1929 average personal debt more than doubled. The Federal Reserve brought on an initial recession in 1928 and 1929 through its efforts to increase interest rates and cool rising stock-market speculation. Manufacturers then scaled back production of durable goods. Job layoffs followed, reducing consumer demand, and workers holding positions became increasingly reluctant to buy.[27]

Still, postwar optimism and the rapid pace of technological improvement seemed to guarantee a growing economy. Maintaining optimism, business leaders, economists, and politicians echoed the sentiments of Secretary of the Treasury Andrew Mellon, who expected the downturn to be short-lived: "I see nothing in the situation which warrants pessimism."[28]

But signs of catastrophe loomed. In late October 1929, panic selling on the New York City Stock Exchange staggered the nation's investment markets and caused a breathtaking drop in stock prices. The wave of selling and price dips began on Monday, October 21. With no one buying, some speculators saw only ruin. By Thursday's end, 11 men well known on Wall Street had committed suicide. The decline continued. The slump affected the nation's industries as prices for manufactured goods also fell, but this development, instead of encouraging idle entrepreneurs to begin production, had little effect. Consumers and manufacturers alike sat on their wallets, hoping to ride out the storm. As they waited, banking panics and a collapsing world monetary system shook confidence in the value of nearly everyone's credit. Increased unemployment, reduced production, and slumping prices were the result.[29]

The mood of the nation's citizens became more pessimistic as the depression deepened throughout the 1929–1933 term of President Herbert Hoover. Factory layoffs and shutdowns eroded the mass purchasing power of workers. Production was a third less than normal. The number of bank failures mushroomed. The money supply contracted. By 1933 one-fourth of America's farmers had lost their land.[30]

The humiliating financial failures of prominent industrialists created public scandal. Meanwhile, Secretary of the Treasury Mellon requested and received from the Internal Revenue Service a memo detailing 12 ways he could evade taxes. A treasury department tax expert then used five of the suggestions in filling out Mellon's return. An irate congressman threatened the secretary with impeachment upon discovery of the scheme.[31]

The economic collapse came with shocking speed. In Red Wing, where the police had registered transients and provided them shelter for years, the monthly totals of visiting tramps shot up. In January 1925, they counted 34, a typical total for a winter month in the 1920s. In January 1930, police housed 66 vagrants, and two months later, 153. The monthly total for March 1931 soared to 443. The following April, the police registered 449 transients. They came from nearly all the 48 states. Authorities estimated roughly two million Americans were "on the road" in 1932.[32]

There were few jobs for the transients. By September 1931 the Red Wing City Council unanimously approved a recommendation that employers fill out a questionnaire prepared by the Citizens Unemployment Committee. The council hoped that unemployed residents who were heads of families could substitute for "such employees who are foreign to Red Wing and not citizens." Also to be reviewed were "double-employments"—cases where a husband and wife each had work. The idea was to reduce double employment and "distribute work to those needing it."[33]

A month later the council resolved that "no man, permitting his wife to work in any factory, store, city or state institution, be allowed to hold a position under the following city departments: Board of Public Works, Board of Water Commissioners, Board of Cemeteries, Hospital Board, Board of Fire Commissioners." This resolution also passed without dissent.[34]

The Red Wing City Clerk's office registered unemployed local people in need of jobs. One method of employment involved hiring 30 people for each of two crews assigned to projects such as improving city parks. The crews worked half-days for five hours at a rate of 30 cents per hour. They received scrip that they could cash with selected city merchants.[35]

The city's cash receipts for licenses, assessments, and fees also dropped. In 1931, Red Wing took in $92,244.43, an amount that fell steadily over the next four years to a low of $70,770.04. The fees did not surpass the 1931 level until the end of the decade.[36]

J. R. Sweasy struggled to keep Red Wing Shoe Company afloat. With 275 workers, it was one of the county's largest employers. Sales were slow, and some buyers were returning goods. Retailers, unable to pay for ordered shoes, discovered they could send them back and reorder at a lower rate. Meanwhile, the company tried to cut costs. Employees straightened and saved the nails from shipping boxes. Foremen fired the plant's furnace with scrap leather. In winter, workers tacked down window shades to reduce the breeze in the barely heated building. The company kept just one telephone.[37]

Growing numbers of people were unable to buy quality footwear, so Red Wing Shoes began producing a cheap work shoe of poorer split leather to sell for 99 cents. The shoe, known as "No. 99," kept the production line going and people employed, but it tarnished the Red Wing label. Buyers expected the high quality typical of the company's other products. One worker recalled that the "99" had hard-rubber soles and leather so brittle he could nearly tear it. The company shipped 99s in barrels and did not include shoelaces. Red Wing Shoe never abandoned its high-quality boot-and-shoe line, however, and maintained customer loyalty through the depression.

Shoemaking was not a 12-month operation. Layoffs and lost hours in the off-season, usually late fall and winter, were common. To make matters worse, wages were cut 10 percent in 1929 and another 5 percent in 1938, as the depression lingered. Grocers and other retailers allowed workers to charge, but they, too, were under economic pressure. "I can still see Sundberg [a Red Wing grocer] standing outside the factory door on the first payday, and rubbing his fingers to indicate money," a shoe worker remembered. Yet Red Wing shoe employees were lucky and they knew it. They had jobs.[38]

Red Wing's Foot Tannery, another major county employer, was also in trouble. E. H. Foot saw his business "in a downhill movement from the middle of 1928 to the latter part of 1932." He had cut wages and salaries, but banks holding Foot Tannery loans required 50 cents of each sales dollar. Veteran employee Lloyd N. Nelson remembered the day Foot gathered the workers and told them a wage cut was necessary: "He had tears in his eyes, and he said he just didn't have any other way." If the men could not accept a reduction, Foot said, the factory would close. The men took the cut. Corporate officers saw their salaries decrease twice in 1931, with Foot absorbing a 17 percent reduction and the others 10 percent.[39]

The unemployed heads of families faced the challenge of finding some way to continue providing the basics. The experiences of Albin Johnson, who lost his job with the closure of Claybank's pits at Christmas in 1925, provides an example. Johnson moved his family to Red Wing but by the early 1930s could find little work. Between jobs he went into the woods and cut trees for fuel. He unloaded coal cars with a scoop shovel and hauled ash piles for neighbors. He walked three miles each way to work a full day on a dairy farm for a one-dollar book of milk tickets. He refused, however, to go the county court-house for the small handouts available for the most needy. But the need for assistance became more common. In Minnesota, relief costs in 1933 surpassed $9 million. The next year they stood at more than $33 million.[40]

Since the 1870s, the federal policy toward Native Americans had been meant to speed their assimilation into the larger culture. The government hoped to es-tablish peaceful relations using a three-part program that provided Indians res-ervation land, educated Indian children in day or boarding schools, and ex-tended law to the reservations. Officials expected this policy to pacify the Indians and help absorb them into the dominant Euroamerican society. The program was unsuccessful. Some progressive-era politicians and government officials questioned the assimilation concept. They promoted cultural pluralism, which among other things, treated with respect the rituals and ceremonies of the indigenous population. Government policy changes regarding Native Ameri-cans were in the offing by the early 1930s.[41]

Meanwhile, the Prairie Island Indian colony, which had received no signifi-cant federal aid since June 1907, suffered. The Goodhue County board of com-missioners recognized the problem and adopted a resolution on June 7, 1935. It asserted the Indian community was "at present on government relief, desti-tute and unable to support themselves, having nothing except certain lands granted to them for their support."[42]

The Prairie Island community addressed this dangerous situation by at-tempting to establish its own government under provisions of the Indian Reor-ganization Act of 1934. The Indians approved a constitution, its preamble para-phrasing that of the U.S. Constitution, by a 35–4 vote on May 23, 1936. The document began, "We, the Minnesota Mdewakanton Sioux residing on the Prairie Island Reservation." It also noted the band's determination to "enjoy cer-tain rights of home rule, to provide education in schools of higher learning in-cluding vocational, trade, high schools, and colleges for our people, and to secure the opportunities offered us under the Indian Reorganization Act."[43]

The Mdewakanton thus had more control of their lives, but their constitu-tion and corporate charter approved June 23, 1937, did little to change their lot. Individual Indians lived on small tracts deeded directly to them or their fami-lies in 1887, while the federal government held 120 acres in trust. Before a 1937–38 government-financed land purchase for the community, a survey showed that a single individual farmed 19 acres, but the remaining trust acre-age was idle or leased to whites. The community had one cow, a horse, a plow, a cultivator, and a buggy. In 1935 and 1936, average annual family income was $166.45. Of that, $97.12 came from relief and government-sponsored labor.[44]

Geography and a lingering cultural mistrust separated the Prairie Island Indian community, in its river location at the county's northern tip, from the rest of the people of Goodhue County. Poor roads and bridges only increased the isolation.

One Red Wing woman made regular trips to the reservation to continue her lifelong study of Indian culture. Frances Densmore, nearing age 70 in the mid-1930s, specialized in recording and transcribing Indian music. She had earned an international reputation for her efforts. Descended from a prominent Red Wing pioneer family, she had studied music at Oberlin Conservatory of Music and later in Boston. She became interested in Native American music after observing Indian singers and dancers at the Chicago World's Fair of 1893. Densmore began conducting her own research in 1903. Some of her earliest work was at Prairie Island, but as she later recalled, her trips ranged "across the continent from "British Columbia to the Everglades of Florida, over the plains and the mountains, across the desert."[45]

Densmore's parents taught her from an early age to respect Indians. As a child, she sometimes heard, echoing through the night, the Indian drums of the Trenton Island camps across the Mississippi from her Red Wing home. She remembered her mother, Sarah, explaining that Indians had customs "different from ours" but that there was no reason to fear them.

Frances Densmore began her journeys of music discovery lugging recording equipment to catch original performances and a notebook for transcribing what she heard. She shared her efforts with the American Bureau of Ethnology, which in 1907 provided her financial support for continued research. She paid particular attention to the Mdewakanton community at Prairie Island and the Ojibway people of northern Minnesota. As she turned 70 in the depression year of 1937, Densmore continued her work on Prairie Island. She kept at her research and writing for 20 years more until her death in Red Wing at 90.

Red Wing, the county's industrial center, withstood the depression better than many cities. Its industries, largely locally owned, were founded with the capital of its citizens. Management, thus, had considerable motivation to stay in operation and maintain its employee base. The city did not lose a business during the depression years.[46]

In the 1920s, Goodhue County farmers and their colleagues throughout the nation found themselves mired in an economic slump that showed few signs of waning. Prices for their products still did not approach wartime highs. Farm debt increased while land values declined. Meanwhile, the cost of items they needed remained steady.

Farm families had some advantages over city folk, but they still were captives of the economic downturn. They could depend on their homegrown food and meat supply for subsistence and usually had some left to barter for goods and services in town. Prices for their products, however, were low and dropping. Oats might bring 12 cents a bushel, but at that price, when one included the cost of shipping and insurance, the effort to sell was hardly worth it. Pigs and cattle fed by corn brought a price barely worth their keep. Farmers often killed pigs at birth so they wouldn't have to feed them. Some farmers claimed that using corn for fuel was cheaper than selling it to buy coal.[47]

Men hired out as temporary farm workers for $50 a month, only to find there wasn't enough money to pay them at the end of their service. On some Goodhue County farms wages dipped to 10 cents an hour, then 50 cents a day, then even lower to 10 cents—for a day of hard labor. Some worked for room and board. Richard Bohmbach, a Hay Creek native who did farm work during the depression, remembered earning $20 per month but only $5 in winter.[48]

The physical workload of farmwomen continued to be heavy. The lower the family income, the more likely the women worked in the fields. Researchers found that in 1925 more than 53 percent of Minnesota farmwomen hauled water from outside wells for use in their kitchens. The women were known for their thrift and adaptability. They preserved food through canning and kept a variety of palatable items on the table throughout the year. One Goodhue township farm wife remembered, "You couldn't buy canned goods; you couldn't buy bread. You had to bake." They could make clothes for their family and themselves and turn feed sacks into tablecloths, shirts, and dresses.[49]

The county's rural general stores, conducting business by barter and credit, became crucial to sustaining farm families. In a typical barter arrangement, the store delivered goods to the farmer and received produce in payment. Proceeds from the sale of the farmer's goods were credited to the family's store account.

Clerks Anton Carlson and Ernst Swenson tended G. O. Miller's White Rock general store during the Great Depression. *Phil Revoir Historical Photographic Collection*

Most of the county's general stores, such as Belle Creek's, above ca. 1910, survived the depression, but growing urbanization meant their days were numbered. *CFHS*

This arrangement saved the farmer the cost of transportation and enabled the store to profit enough to stay in operation. The farm family, in turn, could buy necessities on credit at the general store. Cash-flow problems also constrained the county's storeowners since they had to pay grocery wholesalers, such as Red Wing's Friedrich and Kempe, for their goods.[50]

Local farmers absorbed another blow in 1934, when one of the worst droughts in the region's history crippled production. "It was 100 in the shade the first day of May," said one county farmer. The crops "just got started and dried up," recalled another veteran of those parched days. Milk production slumped as dairy farmers hunted to find nourishment for their animals. "People saved everything they could—hay, straw, grass from road ditches. Straw went for feed instead of bedding." The desperate farmers "dug out straw piles four and five years old and used it for feed." Fall plowing of the parched ground wasn't possible. Furrows were crooked, and soil broke out in chunks.[51]

On July 2, 1931, a crowd began to gather at the Farmers State Bank of Kenyon. A notice on the door announced that the bank had closed until further notice. No other information was available. Soon the facts were out. State examiners found a shortage of $6,099.05, and the bank's board of directors ordered an investigation. Cashier Arthur B. Borlaug gave himself up at city hall and admitted to embezzling. He pled guilty in the Red Wing courtroom of Judge Charles P. Hall and received a sentence of one to three years in state prison.[52]

The nation's small rural banks, typically with assets of just $25,000 to $100,000, were susceptible to failure. They carried no deposit insurance for their customers and often held insufficient reserves. Loss of investor confidence could produce a disastrous run on a bank when too many depositors withdrew their money. American banks had failed at a rate of more than 500 a year in the more affluent 1920s. In the first four years of the depression, thousands more shut their doors.[53]

The opening of the State Bank of Kenyon, which evolved from a merger of the community's surviving banking firms, relieved some of the town's financial concerns. Leading citizens backed State Bank. In October 1932, however, the management of the new bank decided to cease operations after nervous depositors began to withdraw their funds. Nearly two years passed before organizers put together another firm, Security State Bank. This institution survived the depression.[54]

Other county banks went under. The 12-year-old Frontenac State Bank closed on October 22, 1931. Bellechester's Farmers State Bank could not re-open after the federally mandated bank holiday, a four-day closure of the nation's banks in March 1933. Goodhue's First National Bank also went into receivership at that time. Skyberg's bank, reorganized after a 1919 closure by state examiners and closed again in 1930, shut down and sold its assets. Skyberg entered a period of decline from which it never escaped.[55]

Co-op creameries such as Zumbrota's helped farmers survive the depression years by providing a market for their dairying operations. *GCHS*

First National Bank in Cannon Falls barely survived. The roots of the bank were intertwined with those of the Scriver family who, beginning with Hiram A. Scriver in 1886, operated the institution. Arthur T. Scriver, Hiram's son, was in charge at the time of the bank holiday in 1933. First National was unable to reopen after the holiday, and it appeared doomed. Yet by June the reorganized bank was back in business, opening at about 60 percent of value. Eventually it was able to fulfill its pledge to repay depositors to the penny.[56]

The citizens of Goodhue County still fared better than many of their countrymen. By 1932 the nation's cities eliminated services as tax revenues dried up. Chicago, with 600,000 unemployed, suffered through a two-year taxpayer strike and owed its teachers more than $20 million. Farm foreclosures in Mississippi resulted in the auction of an estimated one-fourth of the state's total acreage. More than a hundred Connecticut shops paid employees as little as 60 cents for a 55-hour week. In Philadelphia so many families lost their housing that children invented a doll game called "Eviction." A congressional committee discovered that in the mining counties of Appalachia, malnutrition among school children was "sometimes over 90 percent." In the hardest hit areas, starvation stalked the populace.[57]

Three years after the stock-market crash, children sang :

> Mellon pulled the whistle
> Hoover rang the bell,
> Wall Street gave the signal
> And the country went to hell.[58]

Franklin Delano Roosevelt, governor of New York and the Democratic Party's nominee for president, embarked on his 1932 campaign with a promise: "I pledge you, I pledge myself, to a new deal for the American people." This opening shot began his war on the depression. His charismatic, confident style won the support of an American public hungering for an end to the crippling economic slump. Voters swept Roosevelt and a Congress full of "New Dealers" into office. Minnesota also went for Roosevelt, the first Democratic presidential candidate to capture the state vote.

Roosevelt's New Deal, supported by a Congress dominated by his Democrat and like-minded Republican allies, produced 13 major bills in his "Hundred Days hurricane." Included were laws insuring bank deposits and the refinancing of home mortgages, legalizing liquor, and establishing the first alphabet agencies—the Civilian Conservation Corps (CCC), the Tennessee Valley Authority (TVA), and the Agricultural Adjustment Administration (AAA). New Dealers created the National Recovery Act (NRA) under provisions of the Industrial Recovery Act to stabilize and revive the nation's economy. The U.S. Supreme Court later declared some of the new programs unconstitutional, but in the heady days of 1933, the nation seemed to be moving again. NRA parades held throughout the country celebrated the promise of the new agency. A Red Wing procession on September 8, 1933, stretched ten blocks.[59]

In Goodhue County the CCC established camps in Zumbrota and Hay Creek township. A third camp, in Lake City, served Florence and Belvidere townships. The Civilian Conservation Corps accepted unemployed and unmarried young men between the ages of 18 and 25. They enrolled for six-month periods and saw a required $25 of their $30 monthly wage paid to their families. The men, organized in paramilitary fashion, worked on projects in cooperation with the Soil Conservation Service. Typically, companies included 200 men assigned to CCC camps under the supervision of U.S. Army Reserve officers. Their task was to help stem the loss of topsoil, one of Goodhue County's more pressing conservation needs.[60]

Zumbrota's CCC company formed on June 3, 1935, and temporarily encamped at the county fairgrounds. Among the first local farmers to team with the erosion control projects were Edward Goplen, Henry Hoven, Anton Holthe, Otto Olson, and Edward J. Nelson. The camp remained in operation until the fall of 1939, when it was moved to Winona.[61]

By 1938 the conservation record of the CCC helped arouse interest around the county in controlling erosion on a watershed basis. The state also attempted to enlist farmers in the organization of Soil Conservation Districts. The U.S. Army Corps of Engineers held flood control hearings in Cannon Falls and Red Wing in 1938 and 1939. By 1940 farmer efforts created the East Goodhue and Dakhue (Dakota-Goodhue) Soil Conservation Districts. The East Goodhue district included the townships of Hay Creek, Wacouta, Florence, Central Point, Featherstone, Burnside, Goodhue and Belvidere. Five townships in southeast Dakota County and Welch, Vasa, Belle Creek, Stanton, Leon, Warsaw and Cannon Falls in Goodhue County comprised the Dakhue district. South Goodhue County District, added in 1942, provided service for Roscoe, Zumbrota, Holden, Wanamingo, and Kenyon.[62]

The Works Progress Administration (WPA), established to create public-sector work for the jobless, employed nearly four million people by March 1936. The WPA focused on infrastructure improvement such as highways, bridges, public buildings, and airfields and underwrote theater, arts, music, and writers' projects. WPA officials claimed "primary" credit for the nationwide drop of families and single persons on relief from a high of 4,397,000 in July, 1935 to 1,450,000 a year later. In September 1935, Minnesotans employed on WPA projects numbered 3,569. By the end of the year 58,839 had such jobs.[63]

WPA funds in Goodhue County helped produce projects ranging from wayside parks and overlooks at Frontenac and Lake Pepin as well as Colvill and Hancock schools and the baseball-football Athletic Field in Red Wing, dams to conserve land and water at Cannon Falls and Wanamingo, sewing projects employing women around the county, a bandshell in Cannon Falls, the high school and sewage disposal plant in Goodhue, and a published inventory of Goodhue County records.

The government organized other depression-fighting governmental assistance programs. In July 1937, the state welfare department helped develop the Goodhue County Welfare Board. Henry Sathrum chaired the five-member board. The selection of Matilda Ostrem as secretary fulfilled the requirement that one board member be a woman. The Welfare Board supervised all public welfare and assistance, including direct relief, work relief, old-age assistance, care of the indigent, and child welfare.[64]

By 1932 the nation had had enough of Prohibition. The election of Franklin Roosevelt and his promise of a new deal encouraged advocates for the repeal of the dry laws. The position of Prohibition's supporters, while still formidable, was weaker than before. Congress called for upon states to ratify immediately the proposed 21st Amendment to the Constitution, an attempt to repeal the 18th (Prohibition) Amendment. By December 1933, the federal dry laws were dead, the power to control liquor returned to the states.

During the nearly 14 years of Prohibition, crime and corruption had become an increasing problem, particularly in larger cities. There criminal syndicates fought each other for greater shares of the liquor loot. They used profits from the illegal trade to bribe public officials, creating rampant corruption of the authorities in some cities. A U.S. senator eventually called the Twin Cities, within easy reach of Goodhue County, "the poison spots of American crime." Frustrated U.S. Attorney General Homer Cummings fumed, "If there are two cities in America which need cleaning up, they are St. Paul and Minneapolis."[65]

Big-city crime made two noteworthy visits to Goodhue County. In August 1931, three men discovered the body of Harry "Slim Jones" Morris in a ditch near the Wacouta store, just south of Red Wing. The corpse had bullet holes through the chest and forehead. Police found $556 in cash on the body, eliminating robbery as a motive for his murder. Morris, a lanky bank robber with a string of aliases, was involved with the gang of master bank-robber Harvey Bailey, an Oklahoman based in St. Paul.[66]

The kidnapping of St. Paul banker Edward Bremer on January 17, 1934, made national headlines. The crime was the work of the notorious Barker-Karpis gang, who chose a place five miles from Zumbrota to receive Bremer's ransom. Their activity soon brought the FBI investigators to the area.[67]

Goodhue County's most prominent federal lawbreaker, Francis Shoemaker, obtained release from the Leavenworth penitentiary in November 1931 and returned to Red Wing. There he again took the helm of the *Organized Farmer*. (See page 254.) Shoemaker returned to attacking his favorite targets—Red

Workers at Remmler's Brewery, Red Wing, showed a "Vote Wet Monday" sign to support the repeal of prohibition. *Phil Revoir Historical Photographic Collection*

Wing business leaders and Congressman August Andresen—but the newspaper, weakened by the economic depression and lack of advertisers, had to close in 1932. Francis Shoemaker, however, was far from finished.[68]

With the 1932 election looming, Shoemaker decided to make another run for Congress. The Farmer-Laborite held two advantages. The Minnesota Supreme Court had upheld Gov. Floyd B. Olson's veto of a legislative redistricting plan and forced all congressional candidates in the state to run "at large" for the nine available seats. This meant Shoemaker did not have to depend upon his home district, the old Third, for support. He could reach out to the statewide electorate. Shoemaker's image as a victim of the system that many depression-weary Minnesotans now distrusted provided another edge. To them, a man sent to prison for calling a banker a "robber of widows an orphans" wasn't a criminal but a hero.[69]

Shoemaker ran well in the 32-candidate field. Thanks to his strength in the counties of the state's north and west, he placed eighth, achieving a seat in Congress. Bragged Shoemaker, "I go from the penitentiary to Congress, not like a great majority of congressmen who go from Congress to the penitentiary." He headed to Washington, D.C., never to live again in Goodhue County.[70]

Francis Shoemaker's two-year term was an embarrassment to Minnesota. He was twice arrested while in Washington—first after a fistfight with a neighbor and second after a traffic incident in which he punched a taxi driver. Min-

Former Red Wing newspaper editor Francis H. Shoemaker seemed relaxed at the Minneapolis jail after his
arrest during the 1934 trucker's strike in that city. *MHS*

neapolis police apprehended the congressman on two occasions, once after a
high-speed chase down Hennepin Avenue and later during the 1934 trucker's
strike. He used Congress as a forum in which to vilify his enemies back home
as "ravenous fiends" and "alley cats."[71]

Shoemaker overreached in 1934 when he attempted to wrest the Farmer-
Labor Senate nomination from incumbent Henrik Shipstead. He lost after
a bitter contest and soon announced that a European news agency wanted
him as correspondent. The *Pioneer Press* responded editorially, "Never have
the citizens of the state more anxiously and passionately desired to believe the
Congressman's word." The writer added that the only thing more gratifying
than employment in Europe for Shoemaker would be the agency's "offer to
send him someplace farther away."[72]

# 16

## *Lingering Depression and New Threats of War*

America's Great Depression severely punished Goodhue County and its people, but did not inflict the level of suffering common in the hardest-hit regions. The county's comparatively strong economic base—farming and industry—provided more of the necessities for its citizens. They struggled through the calamity and persevered. They also found ways to make life more tolerable. They organized simple family activities such as picnics, games, and outings. They went to dances and watched and played on sports teams. They enjoyed the popular and inexpensive diversion of motion pictures and radio.

Fans flocked to theaters to view the first motion pictures featuring sound, later color. National Motion Picture Day, held to raise money for the unemployed, reached across America on November 24, 1931. Admission charges for movies generally declined. In Goodhue County, Kenyon's Lyric Theater admitted adults on a two-for-a-quarter basis and children for a dime. Beginning in 1936, Goodhue's Civic Club issued dime adult and nickel children's tickets for Saturday night movies. Red Wing's Sheldon Auditorium charged a quarter for adults and a dime for children. The city's Metro Theater offered matinees at a dime for everyone. Also popular were newsreels, short subjects, serials, and cartoons. Theaters lured customers with giveaway promotions including bank nights, dish nights, and bingo. The motion-picture houses offered patrons a chance to escape their everyday worries and enjoy the work of Hollywood's moviemakers, the world's most prolific and popular.[1]

Radio broadcasts also developed a large and growing audience. The nation's four large networks, NBC-Red, NBC-Blue, CBS, and Mutual, controlled 700 of the country's 900 radio stations. They provided music, drama, comedy, and news for devoted listeners. People in 28 million homes tuned in to *One Man's Family*, a Wednesday night NBC-Red staple. *Gang Busters, Amos 'n' Andy, The Shadow, Your Hit Parade,* and other hits drew huge audiences for their sponsors. Radio also carried swing music, the lively yet relaxed "sound of the Thirties." The bands of Glenn Miller, Benny Goodman, Artie Shaw, Tommy Dorsey, and others toured the nation's dance halls.[2]

High-school sports, particularly basketball, provided another entertainment staple in Goodhue County during the depression. Red Wing, not known for the modesty of its city boosters, claimed itself the "cradle and original home of western basketball."[3] As with the contention that the city was the "birthplace of skiing on the North American continent," the claims held some validity.[4]

Basketball came to Red Wing in the winter of 1895 with L. J. Cook, who had just learned the new game in Chicago. Cook, who later became basketball coach at the University of Minnesota, demonstrated the game to the men of the National Guard's Company G. In January 1896, they formed a three-team league in Red Wing. When Company G left for the Philippines in 1898, the basketballs went along.[5]

In 1905 the Red Men, a five-man team of Red Wing players, made a grueling 42-day tour through 16 western states, playing 36 games and defeating the state champions in each. The iron-man team never used a substitute during its journey. Charles Ahlers, star of Company G, teamed with Goodwin Esterly, John Fisher, Heman Bird, and Mike Kappel to finish with a 30–6 record.[6]

In 1913, Red Wing basketball players inaugurated a tradition of statewide success, playing in the first Minnesota high school basketball tournament. Two years later the Central High team won the championship at the tourney's original site, Carleton College in Northfield. Raymond "Rucca" Hanson, a rough and rebellious high-school senior doubling as the coach, led the team. In basketball's early years, the school did not hire a faculty member to run the team. The Anderson-led squad became the title favorite after upsetting Faribault's team 16–11. Faribault fans had greeted the Red Wing players with the Norwegian-laced taunt, "Red Wing! Red Wing! *Hvad Skal Du Ha? Lutefisk! Lutefisk! Ja, Ja, Ja.* "[7]

A joyful crowd greeted the Red Wing team at the city's CGW railroad station the morning after that first-round win over Faribault. The crowd carried team members down Main Street to Bush, down Bush to Third, and back to Broadway. But the mood of the team's backers changed drastically the next day. According to rumor, some underage team members were drinking beer at the city YMCA as well as selling it to other minors. School officials confirmed the rumor when they dismissed two players from the team. One was the club's player-coach, Rucca Hanson.

The weakened Red Wing team, nicknamed "speed boys" by the press, managed to overcome Fosston 27–21 in the semifinals. Then it stopped Moun-

Red Wing's 1915 basketball team won the Minnesota high-school basketball championship despite the dismissal of player-coach Raymond "Rucca" Hanson (holding ball) and another member of the team. *GCHS*

tain Lake 30–18 in the championship game. The benched Hanson had to be satisfied with the praise of his former teammates and the reporters who said he developed the team "without any assistance whatever."[8]

In 1918 Rucca Hanson had another chance to be a hero. As a U.S. Marine corporal, he took part in the assault at Belleau Wood in France. Despite being disabled by German mustard gas, he performed valiantly. Hanson received the Navy Cross on the first day of the Aisne-Marne offensive. Later he earned the Silver Star and French Croix-de-Guerre for performance under fire.[9]

Another strong Red Wing team saw influenza shrink its chance for three consecutive basketball championships. The 1920 squad crushed each of three tournament opponents, finishing with a 21–10 victory over Mankato to earn the championship. Most of that squad returned the next season, but flu knocked several from the lineup at playoff time. The Central High team could not hold its state title. Four members of the 1920 state champion team remained in 1922. Backed by a thousand followers, the club defeated Madison 34–27 for the title. Russell "Butsie" Maetzold and Oliver Nordly captained the team.[10]

Across America high-school basketball became wildly popular, with more school-sponsored teams than any other sport. Even the smallest villages could field squads and, with only a few standouts, compete with teams from larger cities. The high-school clubs carried their communities' names, which engendered loyalty. Radio coverage also helped spread basketball fever.[11]

Given the importance of basketball to so many communities, it's no surprise that the sport elicited emotional responses from fans. In February 1930, the Goodhue *Tribune* blasted the official of the Pine Island-Goodhue game under the headline, "Referee Wins Blindfolded Test." The Goodhue writer allowed, "In justice to him [the referee] we are told that he suffered snow-blindness a few years ago while escaping from a squirrel."[12]

Young women enjoyed basketball, and high schools formed teams for them. Zumbrota's tradition of girls' basketball stretches back to 1900. Its 1904 team with Pearl Anderson, Helena Biersdorf, Elsie Woodbury, Sadie Lothrop, and Eva Maley won the county championship with victories over Red Wing, Pine Island, and others. Yet by the 1930s, high-school girls' teams were dying out. Lou Henry Hoover, wife of the president, led a campaign against girls' basketball in the late 1920s. She believed it inappropriate for young women.[13]

The exploits of Red Wing's Central High School boys' team again seized headlines in March 1933. The club expected to mount another challenge for the Minnesota high-school basketball championship. No other school had won more than two state titles. The Red Wing team, known as "the midgets" for its lack of player size, was after a fourth title for its school. With all-state players Artie Lillyblad and Dick Seebach in the lead, the Wingers outlasted Minneapolis North 16–13 to win in front of 10,000 fans at the Minneapolis Auditorium. A trainload of Red Wing backers joined the audience.[14]

Red Wing's reputation as a basketball power often overshadowed outstanding teams from Goodhue County schools but not in 1942. That year Kenyon put together a dominant team. The club had developed in 1941 when the young Vikings won the subdistrict title. Virtually the whole team returned the next season. Led by Graydon "Soup" Stromme and Ray Strandemo, it won 19 straight games and the district championship. It came within one game of the state tournament, beating Rochester 33–27 before losing to Austin 48–40.[15]

In February 1944 a strong Goodhue team surprised basketball experts by overcoming an undefeated Red Wing club 49–42. A crowd of more than 700 overflowed the Goodhue gymnasium. More than 150 fans had to be turned away. To avoid overheating the players and the crowd, the custodian shut off the furnace entirely. With the gym temperature at 55 degrees, the game began. Red Wing carried a 12–0 record into the game and a share of the Big Nine championship. But it couldn't stop Goodhue's talented trio—forward Burt Eppen and guards Gerald O'Reilly and Pat Ryan.[16]

Other sporting events drew the attention of local fans. In February 1936, Red Wing's Aurora Ski Club hosted the 32nd annual National Ski Tournament.

Organizers hoped to duplicate the success of the 1928 national tourney, also held at Red Wing's Charlson Hill. The local favorite was Halvor Bjorngaard of Wanamingo. In 1924 he had helped design the jump on the Walter Charlson farm. The organizers of this ski program had to feed and house the competitors, including former Olympians, and provide a cash guarantee of $4,000. The competition drew 2,000-plus fans.[17]

But the 1936 competition was not so successful as earlier efforts. LeRoy Olson, Aurora Club president, had said, "Red Wing will be ready to take care of 100,000 visitors if need be." Yet the crowds did not appear. Tournament organizers, from their base in the St. James Hotel, conducted the competition. Red Wing fans cheered on hometown veteran Carl Ek, who in his late fifties was the nation's oldest active ski-jumper.[18]

During the 1930s the nation's campaign to end the depression continued, achieving only mixed results. The flagging confidence of Americans began to revive, spurred by President Roosevelt's New Deal programs. But for a lasting recovery, the private sector had to rebound as well. Roosevelt-backed laws, such as the Loans to Industry Act (1934), Securities Exchange Act (1934), and Banking Act (1935) were designed to reform American business methods. The National Labor Relations Act (1935) revived collective bargaining guarantees. It also created a National Labor Relations Board and helped strengthen labor unions. The Social Security Act (1935) funded, through taxes on workers and employers, a pension system and a federal-state unemployment program.[19]

The people of Goodhue County labored to rebuild an economy still haunted by the depression. One major initiative began in Kenyon City Hall on July 27, 1935. Farmers from the southwestern part of the county met to discuss how to become involved with the New Deal's Rural Electrification Administration (REA). The REA had the potential to bring electricity to nearly 90 percent of the rural American homes still lacking power. Those at the Kenyon meeting discovered that several farmers around Welch, Vasa, and Featherstone also were organizing. George F. Schwartau of Featherstone had written to the American Farm Bureau Federation on March 20 for information. By July 3 the federation mailed an application requesting that lines be built in the county.[20]

People throughout Goodhue County had to become involved if the electrification plan was to succeed. Leaders from around the county met at the courthouse in Red Wing and created, in September 1935, the Goodhue County Electric Association (GCCEA). Leading the new group was a nine-man board headed by Elmer Jacobsen, president; George Schwartau, secretary; and Bernie M. Johnson, treasurer.

Late in 1936 REA officials approved the Goodhue County project and allotted $325,000. That number was later boosted to $337,000 to cover 399 miles of line. With federal approval in hand, the county co-op board announced plans to sell shares for $10 each. Before construction could begin, farmers enough to make the project feasible had to sign on. Some proved hard to recruit.

Power came to rural Goodhue County on August 20, 1938, at the electrical cooperative's substation in Hader. A transformer there hooked into Northern States Power Company's 66,000-volt line to produce the electricity. Cooperative manager George Bleecker of Cherry Grove gave the order to "throw her in." The co-op's leadership followed him across the road to Sivert and Nettie Haugen's farmstead to watch the power turn on there.[21]

The Haugens had lived on the farm for 41 years. The prospect of electricity excited them. As a girl, Nettie Haugen helped to light her home by preparing wax and wicks for candles. When first married, she remembered, "We had just one kerosene lamp and used kerosene exclusively until about 20 years ago, when we bought a gasoline lamp." Now, she said, "We're going to have a refrigerator and not put up ice any more. We'll also have an electric iron and a motor on the washing machine. We got a toaster and floor lamp for Christmas." Electricity for the Haugens made their retired life easier. Said Nettie, "It sure is nice to have all these electric things just like they have in town."[22]

George Burch, a member of the first board of directors and secretary-treasurer of the Goodhue County Farm Bureau, offered loans to farmers still undecided about electrification. During the ceremonies at the Haugen farm, Burch promised to advance $250 to the GCCEA to help with the process. Credit would make it possible, claimed Burch, "for every farmer in Goodhue County to have electricity if he wants it." The co-op directors anticipated broad participation from farmers. They based their plans on hopes that the average consumer would use 200 kilowatt hours (KWH) per month. In the first full month of operation in 1938, 134 members received service and averaged 35 KWH. By January 1, 1945, 1,523 customers were consuming a monthly average of 150 KWH.[23]

More good news reached farmers in the state in 1933. The New Deal's WPA provided the Corps of Engineers $51 million to construct 24 locks and dams between St. Louis and Red Wing. This would enable the new generation of towboats and barges with drafts of 8.5 feet to reach Minnesota. Such barges already worked the lower river, and they carried two to four times as much cargo as freight trains. Building locks and dams would guarantee shippers a nine-foot navigation channel. This extended heavy barge traffic to the upper Mississippi and reduced freight rates.[24]

The construction of Lock and Dam No. 3 at Prairie Island, in the northernmost reaches of the county, provided a job boom. A controversy developed around the project. The Red Wing Trades and Labor Council sought changes in the ruling requiring that 90 percent of common labor employed at the dam must come from relief rolls. The WPA responded, giving preference to "union employees classed as regular employees of the contractor and who are on relief rolls."[25]

Shipping prices for agricultural commodities dropped upon completion of the lock-and-dam program. The bulk shipment of energy products helped reduce the price of manufactured goods and consumer products. In 1910, farm products made up just over 1 percent of commodities carried on the Mississippi. Sand accounted for slightly more than 50 percent of the loads, forest products for another 22 percent. At the approach of the 50th anniversary of the nine-foot channel in 1988, farm products represented 49 percent of material shipped. Coal, crude petroleum, and related products totaled just over 24 percent.[26]

As the 1930s wore on, organized labor tried to regain ground lost during the depression. By 1933, membership in construction unions had shriveled 37 percent nationwide. Rail union membership declined 32 percent. Union membership sank to a new low, just three million. But workers saw Franklin Roosevelt and his New Deal administration as friendly to organized labor. Their confidence was justified. By 1938, recovering labor unions could boast six million members.[27]

Two of Goodhue County's largest employers suffered labor unrest. On May 19, 1938, the Boot and Shoe Workers, Local 527, met at Red Wing's Labor Temple. It wanted to discuss a 5 percent wage cut about to occur at Red Wing Shoe Company. The membership was cautious. Times were still difficult. The union was not yet five years old, and its members were few. They agreed to company president J. R. Sweasy's request to form a "language" committee to discuss details of the contract offer. Yet the union also adopted a motion that the committee not accept the cut in wages. Three weeks later the local met to talk over the contract offer. In a secret ballot, the members voted 23–18 to accept the 5 percent cut for 60 days.[28]

The company agreed to restore the 5 percent when the price of shoes went back up. The prices rose, but wages remained flat. This resulted in worker unrest and growing union membership. Several years later one employee recalled, "We asked—well now, about that cut? They couldn't do it [rescind it] yet. And that went up to 1941."[29]

A prolonged and at times bitter strike began on September 6, 1940, idling 270 workers at S. B. Foot Tannery. Leather workers Union Local 32 asked for an 8 percent increase and a week's paid vacation. The union dropped an earlier request for a closed union shop at the plant. Tannery managers responded with a full-page letter in the Red Wing *Daily Eagle*. They asserted the company was still paying a voluntary wage increase in effect from August 1, 1939. They noted the plant had been in operation, with minor exceptions, for seven consecutive years, providing steady employment. The letter concluded, "The tannery is open for any of our men who wish to work."[30]

The battle line was drawn. Union picketers, at times 150, marched along the road in front of the tannery, attempting to pressure the company. Red Wing police patrolled the factory perimeter in case of trouble. Five weeks into the strike, state conciliator Lloyd Haney declared the two sides in a deadlock. Local 32 also brought a lawsuit accusing the tannery of unfair labor practices. Meanwhile, from strike headquarters across the road, the union leaders saw defections from their ranks.[31]

At the onset of the strike the tannery employed 290 workers, not counting foremen, maintenance, and office staff. After seven weeks, 203 workers remained out. Those who returned to their jobs suffered the jeers of the strikers as they entered and left the factory each day. The two sides finally hammered out an agreement on October 25. The company did not assent to the wage increase or the vacation request. It did promise a full week's bonus pay in 1941, provided profits were available to do so. The firm began recalling workers, and the plant was back to full operation in three weeks.[32]

Minnesota labor had an ally in Farmer-Labor Gov. Floyd B. Olson. In 1930 the voters handed the persuasive and popular Olson a 183,626 plurality over Republican Ray P. Chase. Reelected in 1932 and 1934, Olson became more aggressive in supporting the causes of his labor and farm constituents as well as the New Deal concepts of President Roosevelt. In August 1935, Olson addressed a crowd of 4,000 visitors and Goodhue County residents at the 53rd Convention of the Minnesota Federation of Labor in Red Wing.[33]

Olson had friends in the county, but he also had some powerful enemies. He carried the county in 1930 and 1932, forcing its Republican faithful to redouble the effort to defeat him. The election of 1934 proved Olson had worn out his welcome with conservatives in southeastern Minnesota. This included Goodhue County, home of his most potent political foe, Anton J. Rockne. Usually called "Rock" or "A. J.," the Zumbrota attorney and Republican leader also was known as "Watchdog of the State Treasury" for his tenure as chairman of the Senate finance committee.[34] Rockne's philosophy of keeping government costs low was at odds with the growing popularity of New Deal thinking. Said an Olson biographer, "More than any member of the upper house, [Rockne] symbolized unyielding opposition of rugged individualism to the encroachments of government." He added, "His horizon was limited to his native Goodhue County, which had been relatively free of starving workmen and wild-eyed farmers." Despite incurring the wrath of liberal antidepression warriors, A. J. Rockne remained one of the most powerful men in the state.[35]

Rockne was born in Fillmore County in December 1868. After studying law at the University of Minnesota, he moved to Zumbrota. There he practiced law and later acquired an interest in the Zumbrota *News*. Three years after his 1899 marriage to Susie Albertson of Wanamingo, Rockne earned election to the state House of Representatives. He was speaker of the house from 1909 through 1911, and he was elected to the state senate in 1912.[36]

A. J. Rockne of Zumbrota.*GCHS*

By early 1932 Governor Olson's ideas were on course for collision with those of the conservative Rockne. After a cautious start in his first term, Olson more vocally advocated government aid to needy citizens. While in Red Wing on June 9, 1932, the governor shared his ideas with members of the League of Minnesota Municipalities. "It is no longer a question of individualism against collectivism. In one form or another, collectivism is here to stay," he said. "The old pioneer idea of government as confined to police power has passed off the stage. We have now reached the socialized state. Only government can cope with the situation."[37]

The conservatives were worried. They lost the battle for the post of house speaker to the maneuvering of Olson allies to install radical Republican Charlie Munn. This was at the expense of the conservatives' Andrew Finstuen of Kenyon. Finstuen charged in his column in the Kenyon *Leader* that the Munn supporters were largely urban representatives trying to overpower farmers. He reported on conservative attempts in "unhorsing" Munn. Finstuen lost the speaker's post to Munn 74–56.[38]

Olson's power over the legislature was nearly irresistible in the frightening early days of 1933. Bank collapses, revolt against mortgage foreclosures, and continued miseries of the depression helped the governor overcome the legislature's conservatives. A. J. Rockne waited for an opportune time to attack Olson's programs, while trying to slow him with delaying tactics. In February 1933, Olson appeared before the senate finance committee to request support for the unemployed. Rockne wanted to know on whose authority the state had already borrowed federal funds for relief. Olson retorted, "Starving people are not interested in legal quibbles." Rockne delayed the requests in committee.[39]

Rockne finally flinched under a partisan editorial attack in the March 15 edition of the *Farmer Labor Leader*. In a story headlined "Commander-in-Chief of the Hunger Brigade," the paper charged the Zumbrota senator with preventing the distribution of federal funds. With caustic rhetoric it claimed the finance committee dealt "with the frozen blood in the veins of tiny babies." It accused Rockne with "personal and official responsibility" for blocking the "most needful legislation ever before the Minnesota legislature." Rockne's allies, according to the *Leader*, demanded that the newspaper "kill the [March 15] edition," threatening "dire consequences" if it didn't. Meanwhile Rockne sought a promise from state senator Henry Teigan, chairman of the *Leader*'s board, to denounce the charges. In exchange, Rockne offered to allow out of the finance committee the bills broadening Governor Olson's power.[40]

Defeated but still defiant, Rockne tried to delay the release of bills calling for $2 million in relief funds and the removal of municipal debt limits. Olson would have none of it. "I shall declare martial law," he asserted. "A lot of people who are now fighting the measures because they happen to possess considerable wealth will be brought in by the provost guard . . . As long as I sit in the governor's chair there is not going to be any misery in the state if I can humanly prevent it." The senator from Goodhue County again backed down.[41]

Rockne dealt Olson some setbacks. "Southerners" led by Rockne saw to the demise of the Rural Credit Bureau that made most of its loans to farmers in northern Minnesota. Olson, despite a concerted effort, could not save the bureau. The governor also failed to overcome conservative opposition to his unemployment insurance plan.

In December 1933, the governor escalated the battle by taking to the radio. He called Rockne a "leader and symbol of a dying social, economic order which brought about this catastrophe in American life, which we call a depression." The senator from Zumbrota fought back, asserting he would "not vote $5 million for a half-baked flood control program in a waterless county." His words were not well received in the state's drought-ridden areas. Olson counterpunched with another radio talk, labeling the senator a "defender of 'property rights' against 'human rights.'" The senate passed Olson's relief bill.[42]

Conservatives in Goodhue County provided Rockne a solid political home base while he wrestled with the governor in St. Paul. Newspapers around the county, especially the Zumbrota *News*, Kenyon *Leader,* and Red Wing *Daily Republican*, agreed with the senator. Jens Grondahl of the *Daily Republican* wrote of the relief issue in 1935, observing, "The dole undermines the virility of a large share of the population." He continued, "In Southern countries where people can sit by their huts and reach up for a banana whenever they are hungry, folks are lazy and slovenly . . . The dole in the North may be compared to the banana in the South—a person can eat without working."[43]

Europe struggled through the depression years with an additional challenge. It also had to recover from the human and material destruction of the Great War. Charismatic and fascist dictators emerged in Germany, Italy, and Spain by the mid-1930s, commanding the support of right-wing nationalists. The Soviet Union, a Communist state formed in 1918 from the ruins of a defeated Russia, provided the ideological enemy for the Fascists. And Russia featured an equally repressive leadership. The major democracies, Great Britain and France, vacillated, unready to accept the challenge of the dictators. Said Benito Mussolini, Italy's dictator, "Democracy is sand driven by the wind."[44]

Most Americans, preoccupied with their own problems, again had little interest in complicated European politics. Yet some activists believed the expansionist policies warranted forceful reply. They warned that the United States must modernize its armed forces in case combat in Europe again enmeshed America. Others preached isolationism—"let's mind our own business"— a philosophy strong in the Midwest.

War returned to Europe on September 1, 1939, when Adolph Hitler ordered the German military to invade Poland. Great Britain and France, which had earlier issued guarantees of protection to Poland, declared war on Germany. The Germans and their surprising but temporary ally, the Soviet Union, soon swallowed Poland. After a respite, Hitler looked west. In the spring of 1940 Germany occupied Norway, then swept through the Netherlands and Belgium and into France. The collapse of the French in June left Great Britain standing alone in the path of conquest.[45]

American opposition to involvement in Europe coalesced around the America First Committee, organized after the fall of France. Its most prominent spokesman was Charles Lindbergh Jr., the first pilot to fly nonstop solo across the Atlantic. He remembered the personal attacks suffered by his father 22 years earlier, in places like Goodhue County. "Won't it be strange," his wife, Anne, wrote to her mother-in-law, "if Charles will be fighting the same fight as his father, years ago!"[46] Other anti-interventionists included auto-maker Henry Ford and General Robert A. Wood of Sears, Roebuck. Those wishing to intervene gained the advantage, despite support for the isolationists from those skeptical about European entanglement. Congress passed the nation's first peacetime draft in 1940, with a limit for compulsory service of one year. More than 16 million men registered for possible service on October 16.[47]

In Goodhue County 5,000 men were expected to register for the 1940 draft. On October 16, 622 men enrolled in Red Wing. By the next day, 3,551 men had signed up countywide. Among them were 12 Indians from Prairie Island, including three from each of the Wells and Owen families. The *Daily Republican* quoted one unnamed enrollee: "We Indians fought for 300 years to defend our country, and we are ready to fight again if need be." The paper also reported that "the few Chinese and Negroes in the county are beyond the draft age."[48]

America reluctantly prepared for war by bolstering its small professional armed forces with National Guard units. In January 1941, Battery F, a predominantly Goodhue County unit, was deployed in California for antiaircraft duty. The following month Zumbrota's Company F and related units went in two deployments to Camp Claiborne, Louisiana. Congress meanwhile passed Roosevelt's Lend-Lease program to provide aid to cash-strapped Great Britain. That country now faced the victorious German and Italian militaries and their new ally, Japan. The Japanese government pursued its war of aggression in China and soon occupied the former southeast Asian colonies of the defeated French. Millions saw World War II muscle its way into their lives.[49]

War came suddenly to America on December 7, 1941. Japan, frustrated by American attempts to limit its expansion, struck the Pearl Harbor navy base in Honolulu. The Japanese goal, in the preemptive Sunday morning attack, was to destroy the American battle fleet and cripple its ability to respond to Japan's thrusts in the Far East.

Two Red Wing men stationed at Pearl Harbor on December 7 watched helplessly as the Japanese attack progressed. Kenneth Bolland, of the 34th U.S. Engineers, was relaxing on his bunk when he heard the first wave of Japanese planes. Army Pvt. Maurice Scripture saw Japanese planes flying so low he "could see the pilots just as plain as a car driving down the road." The first attacking planes bombed and strafed ships, airfields, and barracks. Scripture, who had not been issued a gun, could not fight back. Bolland's engineers had guns but no ammunition. Eight battleships were destroyed or crippled in the raid, and 2,403 American servicemen were killed. Bolland helped bury some of the victims two days later. Among the dead was Evan B. Brekken, a 30-year-old seaman from Dennison. He was the county's first fatality in the war.[50]

Clarence "Butch" Larson, a Kenyon native, also got a look at the war's onset. Larson had enlisted in the army air corps after graduating from Kenyon High. By December 1941, he was stationed in the Philippines at Nichols field. Japanese planes bombed the base on December 8. Two days later their assault troops were on the beach at Lingayen Gulf, 135 miles to the north. Larson became a combat soldier in a four-month struggle ending with the surrender of American forces on April 9, 1942. Their captors marched Larson and more than 50,000 Filipino and American troops a hundred miles to prison camps in what became known as the Bataan Death March. Thousands of prisoners died during and after the march from ill treatment and little food or water. Larson, assigned to the burial detail upon reaching Cabanatuan Camp No. 1, helped to inter as many as 40 U.S. military men in a single day.[51]

Another Goodhue County soldier was busy on December 7. Lauris Norstad, 1925 graduate of Red Wing High School and member of the West Point class of 1930, had just returned to Washington, D.C., from a fact-finding trip to England. He rejoined the staff of Gen. Henry H. "Hap" Arnold, commander

Zumbrota National Guard Company F leaving for combat, in early 1941. *GCHS*

of the army air corps, staying until June 1942. Then orders returned him to England to help plan for the Allied invasion of North Africa. Norstad, just 35, thus advanced in the air-corps hierarchy.[52]

After the attack on Pearl Harbor, Americans united to prepare for what looked to be a difficult challenge. The nation's enemies advanced on all fronts. Little could be done to stop them. Germany's powerful armed forces had weakened Great Britain and the Soviet Union, America's principal allies. The country was still recovering from the attack in Hawaii and the loss of the Philippines.

Two more registrations for the draft followed the first enrollment in October 1940. Those in the pool for service were called at a quickening pace. Original registrants were ages 21 to 34. The third draft reached men 34 to 45. Goodhue County would supply 2,689 soldiers to the military by war's end.[53]

The efficiency of English and Canadian women serving in noncombatant roles in the armed forces encouraged the United States to enlist women. After some congressional opposition to women in the military, Roosevelt signed legislation establishing the Women's Army Auxiliary Corps (WAAC), the navy's Women Accepted for Voluntary Emergency Service (WAVES), as well as the SPARS (Coast Guard), WAFS (Air Corps) and the Women Marines. At least 67 Goodhue County women enrolled in these units or served as nurses. Women in the military did all their male counterparts did except take part in combat.[54]

Citizens again became used to their country's involvement in world war. A Civilian Ground Observer Corps formed to watch for enemy aircraft. Government officials set a goal to place an observation post in each of the nation's townships. The townships, villages, and cities of the nation practiced "blackouts"—a way to prevent light from being seen outside a building in case of air attack. Air raids in the Midwest were "possible but not probable," according to the Minnesota's *Blackout Procedures*. But the state conducted drills anyway. Goodhue County took part in a statewide blackout on May 7, 1943, after warning residents that "no alibis" would be accepted if they did not participate.[55]

The drill of May 7 was a "semi-surprise." Local officials expected it between 9:00 and 11:00 P.M. Shortly before 10:00 the alarms sounded. Zumbrota's chief air-raid warden, Clarence Stearns, observed the town was "black as a black cat." He reported that his teams found just one light left on in Zumbrota—a bulb in the cellar of a family who was not home. Zumbrota-based National Guardsmen helped with the practice by monitoring highways to stop vehicles.[56]

Americans supported the military effort by purchasing war bonds. Goal-setting for the eight national bond efforts followed the pattern of World War I. Citizens of the county once again took an active part. Saving stamps were available in denominations as small as a dime. Savers pasted their stamps into books to purchase savings bonds when the books were filled. The county eventually sold $19,083,461 in war bonds. State sales totaled nearly $3 billion.[57]

The most visible affect of the war on the American public was the strict rationing of consumer goods. Rationing allowed the government to control materials needed for the war effort. These included food, clothing, fuel, and consumer goods. Each family member received a ration book for food. Red stamps were for meat and butter, blue stamps for other foods. When buying meat, customers often showed more interest in the points needed than in the cash cost. Men, women and children over age 12 could buy up to 2.5 pounds of meat per week. As the nation's industries concentrated on materials for the war effort, other goods including tires, refrigerators, leather shoes and boots, blankets, fabric, cigarettes, and elastic could not be bought or were rationed.[58]

The government tried to help civilians make their food last. Bulletins such as *Share the Meat for Victory* explained the system. They also provided tips on how to get the most from rationed beef, pork, veal, lamb, mutton, and products made from them. Cheese, eggs, dry beans, soybeans, and peanuts were suggested as stick-to-the-ribs substitutes. People extended their food supply through home canning. Homegrown strawberries, rhubarb, and apples proved among the most popular of preserved foods. Americans bought seasonal fruits —pears, plums, peaches and cherries—and preserved them. In summer, the government made available extra supplies of sugar, a rationed product, to encourage canning of fruit.[59]

Rationing also applied to gasoline. Those getting the smallest allotments received "A" stickers for their windshields. This qualified them for four-to-five gallons per week. Speed-limit reductions designed to conserve fuel became an everyday concern for drivers. Farmers could receive extra gasoline for their tractors. War workers, doctors, and clergymen also could receive more. Military need eventually forced a halt to wartime automobile production.

Some county women not in the military found other ways to contribute. Edna Sigrist of Pine Island moved to California to work at a Boeing aircraft

Grace Hawk and Bill Avery selling war bonds
in Red Wing. *R. J. Kosec photo, GCHS*

plant. She first assembled cockpits of B-17 bombers and later became a riveter
on C-47 cargo aircraft. Frances Haglund took a job as a teacher in the Minidoka
Japanese Relocation Center in Idaho. She taught Japanese-Americans held
(wrongfully, the nation's leaders later admitted) in the internment camp there.
Locally, women Red Cross leaders raised funds, helped equip Red Cross field
units with supplies, aided with blood donations, made hospital shirts and robes,
and obtained supplies for civilian victims of the war.[60]

The county's casualty lists were short in the first months of the war. Thus, the
death of Lt. Eric P. Nordeen, on June 5, 1942, came as a shock. The 24-year-
old flight instructor died, along with three others, in a collision of two planes
in Mississippi. His father, Phil, was a longtime game warden, well known in the
county. Hundreds of mourners filled Red Wing's St. Joseph's Catholic Church
for Nordeen's burial service.[61]

The death toll of county soldiers rose in 1943. The bad news came from all
over the world. The American invasion of North Africa produced the combat
deaths of Pvt. Mentor Johnson, the first Zumbrota soldier to die. Pvt. Paul

The death of 24-year-old flight instructor Lt. Eric P. Nordeen of Red Wing, shown here with an A-6 trainer, brought the war home to Goodhue County. Nordeen died in a collision of two planes during a Mississippi training mission. *GCHS*

Nelson of Cannon Falls and Lt. Charles F. O'Gorman of Goodhue also died there. The explosion of a Japanese mine in the Aleutian Islands of Alaska killed Pfc. Joel Stary of Zumbrota. Lt. Lloyd Manogue of Red Wing was killed in the South Pacific. Another Red Wing man, Lt. Alton G. Martenson, died on duty in Panama. Lt. Carl Carpenter, Cannon Falls, was killed in Burma. Two Red Wing men, Pfc. Eugene Baldwin and Pvt. Maynard Mehrkens, died in Italy.[62]

Thirteen Goodhue County soldiers died in 1943 and another 57 the following year. Fighting in Italy continued to claim lives in early 1944, and the Allied invasion of France in June brought more deaths to county soldiers.

For those who did not know these soldiers and their potential, the very length of the list of dead obscured the terrible cost of the war. Lt. Roger Hilstad graduated from Kenyon High School in 1940 and enlisted in the army air corps. There he trained as a P-51 fighter pilot. Stationed in England, Hilstad experienced two months of combat before being killed over Wurzburg, Germany, on March 12, 1944. Lt. James Larson, an outstanding athlete playing on Zumbrota football and basketball teams of the late 1930s, died in March 1945 when Germans shot down his B-24 bomber. In September 1944, one of Larson's Zumbrota teammates, Cpl. Richard Eberhart, had been killed in Italy.[63]

Red Wing's high-school class of 1940 sustained the combat deaths of Bob Hillesland, Dick Peterson, Ernie Betterly, and Jim Van Guilder. Hillesland was lost at sea near the Gilbert Islands, in the South Pacific. Betterly, a B-24 top turret gunner with 15 completed combat missions, was killed in England in April 1944. In November 1944, Peterson, the class vice-president, died in combat in China. Pfc. Jim Van Guilder joined the Marines after leaving Red Wing. A Bronze Star winner and member of the first Marines, he fought on the islands of Cape Gloucester, Pelelieu, and New Guinea before being killed in action on Okinawa in June 1945.[64]

Lt. Arthur Bestul of Dennison graduated from Kenyon High School and St. Olaf College and became a teacher in Zumbrota. He was wounded at Lingayen Gulf in the Philippines and recommended for a Silver Star for gallantry. Bestul was killed on Luzon on March 2, 1945. Lt. Harland T. Teigen, Wanamingo township native and 1936 Kenyon High graduate, learned to fly in nearby Randolph. He decided to join the air corps in 1939. Enemy fire brought down Tiegen's bomber over Bologna, Italy, on October 16, 1944, and he died in the crash. A training accident took the life of Sgt. Brooks Patterson, an outstanding golfer and former manager the Red Wing Country Club. Wilbur F. Scofield, from Cannon Falls, planned to become the fourth generation of his family to run the city's Scofield Drug Store. He died in May 1945 while fighting in Okinawa.[65]

Goodhue County men fell in Allied advances as the war in Europe reached its climax. Enemy forces killed Pfc. Henry Jensen of Sogn on October 17, 1944, near Aachen, Germany. A month later Sgt. Ralph Crist, Red Wing, who had battled through Normandy, Belgium, and into Germany, died in action after months of continuous combat. Less than a month before the war's end, German defenders killed Tech-4 Rolf Haugen, Kenyon, a tank-destroyer driver in Gen. George Patton's Third Army.

Cherry Grove native Clarence Morken, a gunner on a navy plane, survived 27 days on a rubber raft and 14 more on a Pacific island after being shot down on Christmas Day 1943. Two days after his rescue, a Japanese attack on the naval transport taking Morken to safety killed the Goodhue County sailor. On April, 16, 1945, Russell Haugen of Dennison and 64 others died when a wave of Japanese suicide bombers hit the destroyer *Pringle* as it was screening Task Force 58.[66]

Of the nearly 2,700 Goodhue County men who served in the military, 113 died and 135 were wounded. Allied armies freed 24 county soldiers from German prison camps at the war's end. These included Kenneth Axelson, Welch, a medic with the 101st Airborne captured in Belgium. Axelson's liberation came on his 21st birthday, April 2, 1945. When word reached Henry and Esther Axelson that their son was safe, Welch-area party-line phones buzzed with the joyous news.[67]

The unit with perhaps the most members from Goodhue County was the 91st Division of the Fifth Army. Twenty-two county men in the 91st struggled through the slow, costly advance up the Italian peninsula. Some of them recalled, in an interview 50 years later, their frightening and significant role in the war. Without bragging, they told of their fight to preserve their country and talked of their ultimate goal. "All we wanted to do was get home," said one veteran. They did get home. Yet five decades later these veterans, all in their seventies, vividly remembered the friends who did not return. And they still felt the pain of the loss.[68]

# *17*

## *Triumphant America Faces New Challenges*

At 6:00 P.M. on Tuesday, August 14, 1945, President Harry S. Truman announced Japan's surrender to the Allied forces, ending World War II. The conflict formally ceased with the signing of documents on September 2, but jubilant Americans understood the meaning of the president's announcement. The fighting was over. The nation and its allies had emerged triumphant. The president declared a two-day holiday in celebration of the news.

Town fire sirens in Pine Island, Zumbrota, Cannon Falls, Kenyon, and Red Wing screamed in unison within minutes of Truman's report. Whistles and church bells sounded through the county as citizens took to the streets for impromptu parades. Townspeople and vehicles mixed as the "procession wound round and round" the Red Wing business district. A parade of flag-waving Pine Island children hauled wagons around the village. In Zumbrota the high-school band played marches.[1] But an element of sadness and reflection gradually crept into the revels. Some wept with relief at the news. Others sought the refuge of churches to "give expression of their gratitude in prayer for the end of the greatest conflict in all history." A somber mood also had pervaded on May 8, with the announcement from Europe of German surrender. The VE Day (Victory in Europe) observances had been quiet.[2]

Reaction in Cannon Falls to the war's end typified the county's restraint. A crowd gathered at St. Angsar's Lutheran Church for a unified service of thanksgiving. Kenyon's celebration ended in an hour, reported the *Leader*, and "solemnity reigned over the village in respect to those who will not come home." All Pine Island churches held services. One observer in Zumbrota noted "joy-restrained and humble thankfulness" in the town.[3]

The costs of the war to America were terrible, the losses around the world catastrophic. The United States mobilized more than 16.3 million for its armed forces, with 292,131 killed in action. The Soviet Union sustained more than 22 million military and civilian deaths. China suffered about 12 million dead, Germany more than five million, and Japan more than two million. The cost in money and material was staggering.[4]

The United States emerged from the war in a preeminent position from a military and economic standpoint. Its armed forces, backed by the enormous output of high-quality combat equipment by industry at home, dominated the battlefield. America's use of devastating atomic weapons against Japan solidified its military superiority. The nation's manufacturing base emerged unscathed from the fighting. Meanwhile, many European and Asian countries saw much of their industrial strength damaged or destroyed.

Almost immediately the American people, aching to put war and depression behind them, began building for the future. Soldiers returned home. Some came back to wives and children. Others brought back "war brides" from other nations. The war and its demand for servicemen and women had slowed the marriage rate. Some would make up for lost time. Veterans married and began families, resulting in a postwar "baby boom." In 1946, more than half-a-million more infants were born than in 1945. In 1947, births topped the previous year's by more than 400,000. By the mid-1960s the boom resulted in "between twenty and thirty million more Americans" than planners expected.[5]

Goodhue County also experienced a boom in its younger population. The number of children under 15 years increased 40 percent from 1940 to 1960. University of Minnesota rural sociologists wrote in 1958 that Goodhue County had experienced a boom between 1950 and 1957, bringing its total population to 35,505—"a greater increase in seven years than in the preceding seventy!"[6]

Housing for veterans and their families proved an immediate problem. Red Wing brought nearly 50 small buildings to land adjacent to the State Training School for veteran housing. The first units for the "Belmont Addition" arrived on December 20, 1945. In Goodhue, the village council applied to the National Housing Agency for five trailer homes to place in the park on Fourth Street. It gave approval in March 1946. The council chose Nick Matthees to build a laundry, shower, and toilet room for couples, who paid $20 rent.[7]

Former Kenyon military men sought housing assistance for themselves and their returning comrades. On November 23, Kenyon mayor A. T. Watson learned that three army housing units from a base in Baraboo, Wisconsin, would arrive the following summer. Ex-soldiers formed part of the construction crew hired to erect three two-story units. Rent for the one and two-bedroom units in the "Vets Housing" complex ranged from $18 to $28 per month. Marcy Kvittem and her husband, Myron, were among the original residents. She recalled the

Pidgie Lee Danielson and Cheryl Eastlund (front) and Marlene and Shirley Ruhrin (rear) walk along a street in Red Wing's Belmont Addition. *MHS*

icebox, wood/coal cooking range, and heater: "I cooked mostly on a one-burner hotplate until our number came up for an electric stove." Twelve housing units from the Baraboo base went up in Zumbrota in the winter of 1945–46. [8]

Mayor Raymond F. Hedin of Red Wing called a meeting in May 1946 to address the issue of permanent housing for veterans. Hedin reported that a Rochester firm was building two-bedroom, one-story houses for $6,915 and four-bedroom, two-story homes for $8,745. Both had full basements and garage space. The mayor believed Red Wing could build similar homes if local contractors held down costs by accepting an overall profit of 10 percent.[9]

Mayor Hedin thought the homes could sell for about $5,500. He already had local builder Ben Nelson constructing two model homes on south West Avenue. The mayor reported a contractor was available to build 50 homes on secured land in the Sunnyside division. The two model homes sold before they were complete. Construction of the others quickly followed.[10]

Unfinished business with defeated Germany awaited the victors. The Allied nations put surviving members of the German leadership on trial in Nuremberg, Germany, charging them with violation of the rules of war. Twenty-four Nazi officials faced trial in 1945–1946, with 21 convicted. Twelve more trials of military men, industrialists, and government officials followed. William C. Christianson, a Red Wing judge, officiated at two of them.[11]

William Christianson practiced law in Red Wing with Clinton Bentley from 1923 to 1946. Gov. Ed Thye appointed Christianson to the State Supreme Court in 1946 to complete the term of the retiring Luther Youngdahl. After Christianson lost a reelection bid, President Truman appointed him a judge on the War Crimes Court. He left for Germany with his wife, Myrtle, and son, Bill, in February 1947.

Christianson served on the three-judge tribunal that sentenced the industrialist and owner of Mercedes-Benz, Frederick Flick, for using slave labor in his steel business. The Red Wing jurist then headed the tribunal for the "Ministries or Wilhelmstrasse Case." Twenty-one defendants represented by 68 attorneys faced 35 prosecutors conducting the 17-month case.[12]

The long "Ministries" trial drew praise for Christianson, including that of the Kansas City *Star*: "It is easy to imagine the hauteur of these men in their days of power . . . How scornful they would have been of a judge from Red Wing, Minnesota, a town they had never heard of . . . a small town in Minnesota rather than the glittering capital of Berlin . . . proved to embody the conscience of mankind."[13]

In 1949 Judge Christianson and his family returned to Red Wing after 27 months in Germany. Appointed to Minnesota's first judicial district, he served on that bench until retiring in 1963. He died at age 92 in 1985.[14]

In November 1945, three colleagues from Massachusetts Institute of Technology (MIT) arrived in Goodhue County fresh from wartime efforts in American radar research. The three men—chemist Frank Chesley, electrical engineer Gordon Lee, and physicist Demetrius Jelatis, wanted to start their own research laboratory. Chesley believed he had the perfect site—the Tower View laboratory of Alexander P. Anderson in Burnside. Chesley's wife, Jean, was a daughter of Professor Anderson and his wife, Lydia. The laboratory, idle since the death of Anderson in 1943, became the first home of the MIT trio's new Central Research Laboratories.[15]

Alexander P. Anderson was one of the county's most prominent native sons. Born in Spring Creek valley in Featherstone township, he was the son of Swedish immigrants John and Britta Anderson. At age 19 Anderson taught in rural schools while doing coursework at the University of Minnesota and helping on the family farm. He received a bachelor's degree in 1894, a master's a year later. He then traveled to Europe to earn a doctorate in botany from the University of Munich.[16]

The young professor taught botany at Clemson College in South Carolina and became state botanist there in the late 1890s. He later worked at Columbia University in New York. In 1901 he began experiments in exploding starch granules through use of their own moisture. During the winter of 1901–02, Anderson subjected nearly every known seed to a heating-exploding process.

He soon realized the commercial possibilities of puffed grain. Thus he began a process that revolutionized the American breakfast. As one observer noted, Anderson "opened the door to the cold cereal industry."[17]

Anderson reached agreement with Quaker Oats Company of Chicago to continue experimentation. In 1904 he introduced puffed rice at the St. Louis World's Fair. A year later the company marketed the product as a breakfast cereal. Between 1915 and 1921 A. P. and Lydia built a new home, Tower View farm, five miles from Anderson's boyhood residence. Tower View included a laboratory in which the professor continued his research. It also featured a house, farm buildings, water tower, and greenhouse. Anderson continued research projects there for the remainder of his life.[18]

Anderson's laboratories provided an ideal atmosphere for the researchers from MIT. The scientists first designed and produced specialized laboratory equipment but eventually began production of Master-Slave Manipulators. The long steel arms and delicate controls of the devices allowed scientists and technicians, including the Atomic Energy Commission, to handle dangerous materials in safety. The researchers added Merlin Haugen, another engineer, to the team in 1946. By the mid-1950s, 23 workers were on the payroll. Central Research outgrew the Tower View facility and in 1961 moved to a plant directly across Highway 61.

Eugenie Anderson was another prominent county resident with connections to Tower View and the Anderson family. In 1930 she married John Pierce Anderson, the artist son of Alexander and Lydia. They also lived at Tower View. She became active in Democratic Party politics and in the postwar years joined the fight to cleanse the Democratic-Farmer-Labor Party of "left wingers" and Communists. Anderson and other "Cold War Liberals," including Hubert Humphrey, Orville Freeman, and Eugene McCarthy, became prominent in Minnesota politics before moving to national leadership roles.[19]

Among those disenchanted with the DFL's move to the center was Susie Stageberg of Red Wing, the still-feisty "Mother of the Farmer-Labor Party." Stageberg, whose liberal agrarian background had shaped her belief system, continued the fight against leaders who, she thought, wanted to return the party to "the conservative policies of previous history." Stageberg was among Minnesotans at the 1944 Democratic national convention in Chicago angered to see Harry Truman replace Vice President Henry Wallace on the ticket.[20]

The bloodletting between wings of the DFL continued until the liberal Democrats, led by Minneapolis mayor Hubert Humphrey and others including Eugenie Anderson, gained control of county and state conventions in 1947 and 1948. By 1950 Susie Stageberg, lifelong advocate for temperance, women's rights, and social progress, had seen enough. She resigned from the DFL and as Goodhue County party secretary, saying the organization was "dominated by Wall Street monopolists and professional militarists." Refusing to give an inch,

Susie Stageberg (third from left), "Mother of the Farmer-Labor party," fought for liberal social programs throughout her adult life. *Fred "Scoop" Jonson photo, GCHS*

she wrote, "We . . . were called 'Red Bolsheviks' and 'Free Lovers' in the twenties. We must dare to be called 'Communists' now."[21]

Elmer A. Benson, Minnesota Farmer-Labor governor (1937–1939) who acquiesced to the merger of the Democratic and Farmer-Labor parties, later praised Stageberg for her constant socialist vision and resistance to the union. "The only Farmer-Laborites who actively opposed the merger were Victor Larson and Susie Stageberg," he wrote. "In retrospect, I am now sorry we failed to pay attention."[22]

Eugenie Anderson's star was on the rise through the DFL turmoil of the late 1940s. The 1948 election of four DFL congressmen and a U.S senator, Hubert Humphrey, helped bring Anderson to prominence in national Democratic circles. On October 12, 1949, President Truman appointed her U.S. minister to Denmark, the nation's first woman holding that rank. She continued as an American diplomat under John Kennedy and Lyndon Johnson, serving as ambassador to Bulgaria, special assistant to the Secretary of State, and U.S. representative to the United Nations Trusteeship Council.[23]

Artist Charles Biederman added his considerable talents to those of a list of creative residents in postwar Goodhue County. In 1942 Biederman, a young modernist, already known nationally, moved to Red Wing, the hometown of his wife, Mary Katherine Moore. Before his move to Minnesota, Biederman exhibited his work at galleries in New York. In 1936 artist and collector Albert E. Gallatin  selected his work for inclusion in an exhibit in London and Paris.[24]

Having studied and worked in Chicago and New York, Biederman moved to Paris in 1936. There he was disappointed in the art community's heavy reliance on tradition and history. His move to an isolated farmhouse in Red Wing allowed Biederman to internalize the "structural process level" of nature and gave him the freedom to develop his own ideas. From the early 1950s to the late 1990s, he created his signature work—three-dimensional painted aluminum constructions featuring rectangles of primary color.[25]

Biederman also started a writing career, sharing his theories with an international audience. In 1948 he published his first book, *Art as the Evolution of Visual Knowledge*, following it with ten other titles. Biederman professed that art, not science, is the most important guide to an understanding of nature. His continuing artwork frequently appeared in exhibitions during the last four decades of the century.[26]

The U.S. wartime alliance with the Soviet Union, never the most comfortable of arrangements, frayed as the fighting ended. In the aftermath of World War II, the relationship between the two nations degenerated. The Communist leaders of the USSR sought to extend its influence in eastern Europe and beyond, offering support to all their ideological allies. American foreign policy, designed to counter Communist influence in the democracies of Europe and

Harry Truman appointed Eugenie Anderson U.S. minister to Denmark. *GCHS*

anti-Communist regimes around the world, clashed with the Soviets. The resulting "Cold War" produced ever-growing threats to world peace along with brushfire wars, usually fought by proxies of the two superpowers. Complicating the ideological battle, both American and Soviet forces built stockpiles of nuclear weapons with the potential to obliterate much of the world.

Among America's "cold warriors" was Gen. Lauris Norstad, the Red Wing High graduate and World War II chief of staff for Hap Arnold, commanding general of the army air forces. After the war, Norstad became chief of plans and operations in the War Department. He helped establish the air force as an entity separate from the army. In 1950 Norstad became commander of American air forces in Europe when the United States joined European allies in forming the North Atlantic Treaty Organization (NATO). The new alliance intended to protect Europe from Communist encroachment.[27]

The Cold War heated up in June 1950 when Communist North Korea invaded South Korea. American troops stationed in Japan, including Goodhue County men, mustered to Korea to help. Draft boards around the nation prepared to induct civilians into the military. President Truman activated military reserve units, including the Zumbrota and Red Wing National Guards. The two guard units entrained for Alabama and combat preparations. This was the Zumbrota company's fourth call for wartime duty in 35 years. Fighting in Korea continued until June 1953, when an armistice ended the combat. More than 54,000 Americans died in the conflict, including ten from Goodhue County.[28]

Gen. Norstad took an increased leadership role in NATO while the war in Korea dragged on. In 1953 he became deputy commander of NATO, and in the fall of 1956, supreme commander. He maintained his role as the nation's top military officer in Europe until his retirement in 1963.[29]

The Soviet threat caused concern in the United States and action across the nation. Instructions to local authorities from the Minnesota Office of Civil Defense show how seriously government officials regarded the threat: "In the event of hostilities, which would be World War III, nothing short of TOTAL WAR would result. Every means at our disposal must be mobilized, coordinated, and used effectively and economically to gain the desired objective." The 1950 bulletin noted air-force designation of Duluth, Brainerd, Minneapolis, and Rochester as air-raid-warning centers. Plans were made to involve Minnesota counties in a coordinated evacuation plan in case of nuclear attack. Goodhue County prepared as an evacuation area in case of attack on the Twin Cities.[30]

Minnesota county air-raid plans for rural areas observed that the responsibility of "air raid warnings from each county seat to municipalities of under 5,000 population rests with the county commissioners." By spring 1954 the CONELRAD warning system was in place. In an emergency, all radio and television stations were to go off the air so that air-raid information could be broadcast on AM radio.

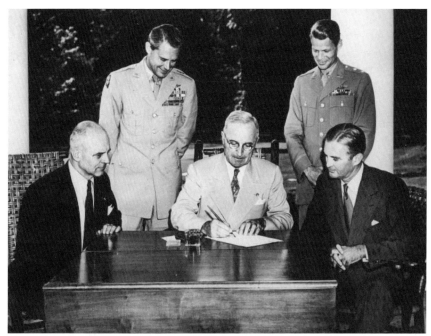

Gen. Lauris Norstad, a 1925 graduate of Red Wing High School and West Point in 1930, commanded the U.S. Air Force in Europe in 1950 and six years later was supreme commander of the North Atlantic Treaty Organization (NATO). Above are (l to r) Jimmy Doolittle, Gen. Hoyt T. Vandenburg, President Truman, Norstad, and Secretary of the Air Force Stuart Symington. *Press Association Inc., GCHS*

Federal authorities informed Civil Defense directors in cities of more than 40,000 residents of the availability of permanent identification bracelets for wear around the neck, wrist, or ankle. The steel tags could be ordered in quantity for as little as 30 cents each. Ominously, tag specifications required "an extremely high melting point"—a minimum of 2,600 degrees.[31]

*Operation You—Your Role in Civil Defense*, a kit from the Office of Civil Defense Mobilization, contained a booklet, *Personal Preparedness in the Nuclear Age*. It described how to build and equip a family bomb shelter. By the late 1960s, Minnesotans built 6,841 fallout shelters in backyards or basements. Such precautions seemed logical for adults watching newsreels of air-raid drills in the nation's largest cities. Children became familiar with "take cover" practice—under their school desks.[32]

America strengthened its military and secured alliances around the world to combat the Soviet threat. The United States created the Strategic Air Command (SAC) designed to project American power worldwide, a fact brought home to Goodhue residents in February 1956, when hometown flier Capt.

Herman Matthees's six-engine B-36 bomber went down in a storm between Iceland and Labrador. Matthees died in the crash. American military interests became stronger when Eugenie Anderson negotiated with Denmark to allow the construction of American bases in Danish-owned Greenland.[33]

Fierce competition between the Soviet Union and United States continued for three decades—during peaceful Olympic competition, in the race to outer space, in duels to secure alliances with Third World nations, in near-war showdowns in Berlin and Cuba, and in the effort to dominate militarily. The conflict persisted until the Soviet Union collapsed in 1989.

Despite the threats of the Cold War, the American public generally repressed worry about the Soviets and concentrated on everyday problems. The citizens of Goodhue County needed to provide for themselves and their families. To do so required something they were used to—hard work.

Goodhue County in 1950 had 32,118 people, a modest increase from 29,651 in 1880. The census showed that the county gained 554 residents in the previous decade and grew 2.5 percent in 20 years. The boom that would boost population by 10 percent in seven years had just begun. Meanwhile, the number of people living on farms had dropped 2,307, or 16 percent, in the 1940s. By 1950, just 37 percent of the county's citizens lived on farms, down from nearly 50 percent in 1940.[34]

The towns of Pine Island, Zumbrota, and Cannon Falls recorded the largest population increase in the 1940s. The average gain was more than 20 percent. Wanamingo jumped 10.5 percent and Kenyon was up 7.9. Cannon Falls continued as the county's second largest community with 1,831 citizens. Zumbrota (1,686), Kenyon (1,651), and Pine Island (1,298) followed. Red Wing now had 10,645 residents, just over 33 percent of Goodhue County's total population. It was the only community in the county large enough to be classified "urban" by the U.S. census.

Red Wing held its place as the county's manufacturing center. "Industry is not a new phenomenon in Red Wing," wrote economist Robert J. Holloway in a 1954 study of Minnesota towns. He asserted that the town "had probably forgotten more industry than some cities ever knew." A study by University of Minnesota researchers, led by Prof. Roland S. Vaile, showed little in the way of a wartime jobs boom, but stable employment patterns persisted.[35]

In 1954 city business leaders and community members formed the Red Wing Industrial Development Corporation (RWIDC). Its purpose was to "bring the advantages of Red Wing to the attention of industry" and to help businesses interested in locating in the city.[36] The RWIDC listed the city's industries and the total number of employees. Red Wing Shoe with 370 workers and Foot Tanning with 360 were the largest employers. Red Wing Potteries had 257 workers, Northern States Power 102, and Red Wing Sewer Pipe 100. The city was one of just three in the state with at least 40 percent of its employment in industry.

Bricklayers and plasterers held the highest-paid hourly jobs in Red Wing, each receiving $2.90. Plumbers earned $2.88 per hour followed by electricians at $2.30, carpenters at $2.15, and sheet-metal workers at $2.00. In the category "unskilled factory workers (male)," the pay range was $.93 to $1.37 per hour. For females it was $.87 to $1.14. The number of women factory workers in Red Wing had increased between 1938 and 1948 from 197 to 355. Female sales clerks were the lowest paid, at 50 to 60 cents per hour for inexperienced workers and 65 to 88 cents for experienced.

More women entered the postwar Goodhue County labor force despite the lower pay. In 1940, females made up 17.3 percent of the workers. Ten years later there were 3,160 employed women—24.7 percent of the total workforce. During that period, the number of workers in the county increased from 11,190 to 12,800.[37]

Red Wing's newer industries included Meyer Machine, a family-owned business that was expanding production, under Roy E. Meyer, of its patented tubular light towers. In 1945 Paul Riedell, a machinist and foreman at Red Wing Shoes for 19 years, started his own business. Riedell and his wife, Sophia, were avid ice-skaters who believed they could produce superior skating boots. Riedell Shoes, like Meyer Machine, flourished.[38]

As noted, the rural population of Goodhue County declined to just 43 percent of the county's total by 1950. In 1880, 72 percent of the 29,651 county's citizens lived in rural districts. The most populous townships were Wanamingo, followed by Holden, Vasa, Warsaw, Leon, Roscoe, Cherry Grove, Belle Creek, Cannon Falls, and Kenyon, all with more than a thousand. By 1950 Holden, Belle Creek, and Kenyon townships each had fewer than 600 residents. Losing ground were four other townships. Goodhue township, Warsaw, Cherry Grove, and Featherstone each had just over 600 but were dropping steadily.[39]

World War II accelerated the flight from the farm. J. S. Jones of the Minnesota Farm Bureau reported in September 1942 that hundreds of farmers around the state, as many as 200 in a single county, were going out of business. Goodhue County, with 40 to 50 farms lost in the previous year, was not hit so hard. Still, dairy farmers sent milk cows to slaughter for want of help to manage them. Finding hired hands became more difficult as workers accepted higher-paying jobs at defense plants. Jones estimated that 10,000 farmers would be out of business by 1943: "We face a situation bordering on catastrophe."[40]

Some young farmers received military deferments as essential workers. The deferment plan helped, though it was not a perfect remedy to the manpower shortage. One Goodhue County mother complained that her son, who had always done the "hard work" on the family farm, was not deferred. She contended that other families had two boys still at home. In a letter to the county draft board, she wrote, "Don't spose it does any good to tell you how the draft board done to a ex-serviceman and his wife." Draft officials faced prickly questions about classification and deferment. County agriculture agent Dick Kunau assisted the board in decisions regarding deferments for young farmers.[41]

The marked decline in county farmers and farm laborers continued through World War II and its aftermath. Farmers decreased from 3,037 to 2,765, or 9 percent, between 1940 and 1950. The total of 1,292 paid farm workers was nearly halved. Mechanization helped replace human labor and encouraged investment in larger farms. From 1940 to 1960 the average farm in the county increased from 152 to 176 acres. Meanwhile the number of farms decreased from 3,037 in 1940 to 2,849 in 1950 and 2,475 in 1960—a total loss of 562.[42]

As they had done many times before, Goodhue County farmers organized to better their condition. In 1946 the Farm Bureau, with units in 21 of 23 townships, claimed a membership of 1,396, or 44 percent of county farmers. Originally connected to the Agricultural Extension Service, the Farm Bureau later moved out on its own. By 1964 its membership had fallen to 735. The United Farmers of America in the mid-1940s had just a hundred members in the county and did not prosper. The Farmer's Union had seven local chapters and 346 members at that time. Some county farmers took an interest in the National Farmers Organization (NFO), a group advocating greater farmer power through collective bargaining. On February 28, 1961, the NFO's populist leader, Oren Lee Staley, spoke to a crowd of 500 farmers at the Wastedo school.[43]

Goodhue County farmers implemented improved conservation measures designed to protect their croplands through the war years. Federal money helped state and county agriculture officials continue work on the Hay Creek watershed project. Originally a 1935 CCC effort, the Hay Creek plan served to halt bank erosion and sediment damage to cropland and pastures, and to build fences, roads, and bridges leading to Lake Pepin. The federal government subsidized new work on the watershed at 75 percent and later facilitated work on Bullard, Wells, Belle, and Spring Creeks. Belle Creek was surprisingly powerful when flooded, washing away topsoil, fences, roads, and bridges, and even taking lives.[44]

Cash incentives provided to farmers by the Federal Cost Sharing program increased soil-conservation practices in the postwar years. Seminars featuring demonstrations, farm visits, and classes improved area farming practices. Seven soil-conservation districts held Conservation Days in southeastern Minnesota. One program drew 8,000 to the Hartwick and Orland Olson farm in Roscoe township.[45]

Fertilizer use greatly increased in the 1950s. Arnold Wiebusch, a former county farmer, joined the Goodhue County Extension staff in 1951 as a soils and conservation officer. He helped farmers capitalize on crop-fertility programs. County agent Dick Kunau later asserted that through "proper fertilizing, balancing fertilizer to soil-test indications, soil-test needs, and weed and insect control," farmers boosted corn production from 50 to 80 and later to 100 bushels per acre. They also increased alfalfa, grain, barley, and soybean yields.[46]

Herbicides and pesticides came into wider use. The chemical 2-4-D was widely used for broadleaf weed control. Atrazine came later. Dissolved in water, it was applied at corn-planting time to control broadleaf and grassy weeds. These were useless with soybeans, so scientists developed other herbicides. Insecticides that would not contaminate feeds, grains, or livestock proved valuable. Farmers also began using the first generation of weed-sprayers.[47]

Despite the loss of some dairy farms, the number of cows in the county reached 30,000 to 35,000 in the two decades after the war. Many county dairy farmers enrolled in the Dairy Herd Improvement Association (DHIA) to test their cows for butterfat. This helped farmers cull their herds and improve feeding and herd management. The separate DHIAs later combined into a single countywide operation with a central laboratory in Zumbrota. Operators of local co-op creameries and cheese plants consolidated their efforts, creating larger operations in Pine Island, Wanamingo, and Zumbrota. Mid-America Dairymen, Inc., the nation's second-largest dairy cooperative, opened a plant in Zumbrota. Milk producers also patronized the Rochester Dairy and the Twin City Milk Producers organization. Goodhue County's seven villages and towns rotated the annual Dairy Days program recognizing the top-producing cows and leading dairy farmers.[48]

American dairy farmers and hog producers achieved a major financial victory in 1949 after a successful challenge of tax laws by Roger Albright, a Kenyon farmer. In *Albright* v. *the United States*, Albright maintained the Internal Revenue Service should allow farmers a capital gains deduction on profits from the sale of dairy cows and breeding sows.[49]

After the war, modern conveniences eased life on the farm. In 1940 only 38 percent of Goodhue County farms had electricity. By 1950 it was more than 90 percent. In 1940 just 18 percent of local farms had running water, 14 percent indoor flush toilets, and 13 percent baths or showers. Twenty years later the percentages had jumped to 83, 73, and 71. Increasing numbers of rural and urban homes had appliances such as refrigerators, washers, and dryers.[50]

The role of farmwomen also changed. A 1946–47 study of Goodhue County farm families concluded that mechanization allowed "wives and daughters of a large majority of the farmers . . . to restrict their work almost exclusively to the household and care of poultry and garden." A decline in the number of women working in agriculture was another change. The number of unpaid women farm workers dropped from 435 in 1950 to 188 just ten years later.[51]

By midcentury, agriculture was becoming "a vast exporter of human labor," as surplus farm workers moved into industrial labor. In 1960, just 25.2

percent of the Goodhue County workforce engaged in agriculture. Still, the value of farm products increased, largely because of the efficient use of new technology. The decline of farm population resulted in a decreased demand for the services provided in small trade centers. Some of the county's rural hamlets and crossroads commercial centers disappeared. Others left scattered traces of their pasts.[52]

Roy W. Meyer's 1967 study of Goodhue County's ghost towns and discontinued post offices provides an overview of these communities and their decline.[53] A brief reminder of some of those hamlets, including the events signifying their fall, follows:

- Forest Mills (Zumbrota township), a once-powerful post-Civil War milling center—abandoned cheese factory razed 1943, school closed 1945. (See chapter 6 for more.)
- Eggleston (Welch township), a trading center on the Milwaukee rail line serving Prairie Island—tracks taken up in 1946.
- Fair Point (Cherry Grove township), crossroads village and trading center near the Dodge County line, known in the 1920s for award-winning cheese produced by its cooperative creamery—cheese factory closed in 1946.
- Lena (Pine Island township), begun as a trading point on the Rochester and Northern Minnesota railroad line called New Jerusalem (1878)—depot removed about 1938, cheese factory closed in 1941 and torn down in 1946.
- Belvidere Mills (Belvidere township), home of Nelson Gaylord's 1861 gristmill and general store on Wells Creek—store/tavern closed in 1942 ending 80 years of business activity, community hall torn down in 1948.
- White Willow (Zumbrota township), established as a post office in 1876 but overshadowed by Rice, a nearby trade center that grew up on the new Duluth, Red Wing & Southern line in 1889—the cheese factory organized in 1916 was shut down in 1938, train depot closing followed, houses were torn down, a 1948 Zumbrota *News* headline read: "White Willow Is No More."
- Skyberg (Kenyon township), a modest building boom fed by the construction of a train depot and grain warehouse in 1891 and a creamery in 1897—bank closed in 1930, rail agency service stopped in 1931, Evald Erickson's store and post office closed in 1951.
- Cascade (Stanton township), a prosperous Cannon River site of the 1880s resulting from the Whitson and Byrnes operation of a 45-horsepower mill with three run of stone producing 13,000 barrels of flour annually in 1870—fire of 1894 destroyed the mill, and Cascade didn't recover.[54]
- Claybank (Goodhue township), built in response to clay-digging operations supplying the county clay industry, grew in 1890s when clay pits employed 75 men—Claybank store closed August 1958, ending the community's 69-year history.

- Sogn (Warsaw township), noted first in the Cannon Falls *Beacon* in 1892: "The Sognese are bent on building a city there," by 1900 boasted a store, several small business, and the Sogn Cooperative Dairy Association, which built a modern plant in 1941—post office closed in 1903, village store and plant both closed in 1959.
- Aspelund (Wanamingo), Aurland and Wangs (Warsaw township), and Eidsvold, Holden, Nansen, and Norway (Holden township), all trading centers and post offices in the county's Norwegian-American agricultural community—significance reduced by advent of RFD, improved rail, and road links; Wangs store, the last sales point among these communities, closed in 1959.
- Wastedo (Leon township), a "paper city" built on speculation but surviving the Panic of 1857, had two stores and a blacksmith shop by 1878, two sorghum mills in business in the 1890s, and Wastedo Creamery organized in 1903—widening of U.S. Highway 52 in the 1960s resulted in the tear-down of Wastedo's remaining store and the old creamery in spring 1965.
- Hader (Wanamingo township), once a stop on the stagecoach line to Rochester, hoped to become the county seat—the failure to get rail access, the 1945 explosion of the Hader store killing manager Ed Holt and his daughter Helen, and the conversion of U.S. 52 to four lanes changed the face of the community.
- Roscoe Centre (Roscoe township), begun in August 1863 as a post office— the county's last surviving rural cheese factory, the Roscoe Center Butter & Cheese Association (1912), closed in 1966.

The metamorphosis of Goodhue County schools was another post-World War II change touching every township, village, and city. In 1946, children attended school in the county's 155 school districts. Of these districts, 146 were of the one-room, one-teacher variety. One district had four teachers, another just two. The remaining seven, in the county's largest villages and towns, were high-school districts. The average enrollment in one-room districts was 11.4 pupils. One had just three students. By 1960, there were ten districts and only a single one-room rural school (Welch).[55]

Pressure grew throughout the state to consolidate rural districts. The need for financial efficiency, as well as increased state intervention in curricular matters, produced momentum for change. In 1947 the legislature required county school boards to evaluate consolidation. Goodhue County's meeting on November 18 resulted in, as the law required, a nine-member survey committee of five rural and four urban members. Karl Tomfohr of Goodhue was chairman. County superintendent of schools Harold Diepenbrock was ex-officio secretary.[56]

Also of concern was an increasing shortage of rural teachers. High schools in Cannon Falls, Kenyon, Zumbrota, Pine Island, and Red Wing trained rural teachers through special senior-year courses and a fifth-year normal program. By 1938, Zumbrota, Pine Island, and Kenyon had closed their training programs. Red Wing followed in 1946. When Cannon Falls ended its rural teacher program in 1947, county rural schools no longer had a reliable supply of new teachers.[57]

In 1948 the school-survey committee proposed dividing Goodhue County into seven complete grade and high-school districts, with six partial districts on the county borders. Every rural student would have the legal right to attend high school under the plan. Speakers from the Minnesota Department of Education attended public meetings across the county to tell residents of the proposals.

The committee chose the Goodhue School District as the first to vote on consolidation. Pro-merger forces expected a positive vote for reorganization since some rural districts had already closed and begun transporting students

School Districts
of
Goodhue County
1948

Goodhue County's school system, before the state and local consolidation efforts began in the late 1940s, provided a patchwork of 155 separate districts. Of these, 146 districts were one-room, one-teacher operations. *GCHS*

to town. But Friends of the Rural Schools, an anti-merger, mostly Wabasha-based group, protested the end of rural schooling. They said so at a public meeting in the Goodhue school auditorium on November 15, 1949, three days before the vote. The protesters won adherents among rural citizens, who voted 441–148 against consolidation. Goodhue villagers' strong yes-vote (148–25) was not enough to secure passage.[58]

Learning from the defeat in Goodhue, the survey committee worked to address the issues raised by protesters. Advertisements in the Zumbrota *News* before the May 1951 vote there claimed "very little change in Real Estate taxes" would result from consolidation, and those that did occur would be "well justified by a much improved school system." On May 17, Alton T. Grimsrud, editor of the *News,* supported consolidation: "What we want is a school system emphasizing preparation for rural life. What we have now is some tantalizing commercial training that weans girls from the farm." He backed the merger of Zumbrota- and Wanamingo-area schools. Grimsrud noted later, "Schools are too important to be tailored to the specifications of an outmoded era."[59]

Zumbrota-area voters chose consolidation, though 41 percent of the rural voters opposed it. Goodhue-area voters reconsidered their anticonsolidation vote in April 1952, after rural district board members Joyce Ericson, Fred Benitt, and Ray Hutcheson met with their colleagues from rural districts to take the issue "into our own hands." Cannon Falls-area residents voted yes for consolidation in November 1952, followed by Wanamingo in March 1953. Wanamingo village supported the change by a 132–1 margin, while 16 of the 19 rural districts voted yes, 290–118.[60]

On May 28, 1953, Kenyon-area voters reversed their initial 1951 vote, overcoming a last-minute effort by Friends of the Rural Schools, who held an anticonsolidation meeting. The vote was 309–216 in favor of merger. Superintendent Diepenbrock announced that the Kenyon vote meant 111 of the county's 155 school districts had been "consolidated, reorganized or dissolved" during the past year.[61]

The school districts of the Pine Island area merged on May 11, 1954, following a 178–144 vote. In 1955 Red Wing annexed districts in Hay Creek and Wacouta and parts of Featherstone and Florence with little opposition. Voters in the rural districts were in favor of the change, 185–34. State senator Grover C. George of Belvidere sponsored the legislation allowing the merger.[62]

Burnside residents saw little need to reorganize. Four districts had joined in 1917 to form Burnside School District 3, which then provided eight grades plus two years of high school. A new building for eight grades opened in 1934 and still met community needs 16 years later. In 1951 six small districts joined with Burnside, necessitating an addition. The Prairie Island district also joined District 3 at the time. Burnside students in grades 9–12 attended Central High in nearby Red Wing.[63]

In 1959 Burnside voters rejected a proposed merger with Red Wing. The Red Wing school board, under the pressure of a new building program, wondered whether Burnside would continue sending students to Central High. With the matter pending, the Red Wing board announced it would not accept further high-school students from Burnside. The Burnside school board evaluated the possibility of building its own high school but found the costs "clearly beyond our means." Burnside voters approved the plan 424–138 in February 1960, and the turbulent era of school reorganization closed.[64]

Television, another form of education and entertainment, established a dominant place in American culture in the 1950s. The Age of Television swept into the nation's living rooms even faster than radio had several decades earlier. Radio enthusiasts bought 165,000 receivers a month at the high point of its expansion. Americans snapped up 200,000 televisions a month in 1949. By January 1, 1950, about three million owned TVs. Another seven million sets were installed during that year.[65]

Radio continued to rule the airwaves as the television industry struggled to find its footing. The poor reception, frequent breakdowns of TV sets, and a lack of quality programming caused some to consider television a novelty with an uncertain future.

But as improvement followed improvement, television's popularity grew. By the mid-1950s, nearly 90 percent of American families had TV sets. Thirteen percent owned two or more. The people of Goodhue County followed suit, carefully rigging antennas to pull in stations from the Twin Cities.

The effects of television on home life were monumental. Interaction between the members of many families decreased as they sat wordlessly in front of their receivers. In 1954 the invention of the oven-heatable frozen TV dinner saved viewers from leaving their sets to eat. American families, on average, watched television from four to five hours a day.[66]

Television became part of the natural rhythm of American life. The evening hours began when "prime time" network television commenced at 7:00 P.M. Time spent watching TV grew steadily, passing six hours per day and headed toward seven. Surveys found measurable reductions in the hours Americans visited friends or went to parties. Some worried that children, who formerly had learned American culture from their parents, teachers, and religious leaders, now looked to TV for information and instruction. But in the nation's rural areas, including Goodhue County, television provided an instantaneous link to the rest of the nation and the world.[67]

# 18

## Decades of Change

In October 1963, Red Wing's school board became the first in the state to establish a detailed policy on religion in public schools. This touched off a debate
in Minnesota that continued, off and on, for decades. The board decided to re-
define its procedures in light of two U.S. Supreme Court decisions that had
struck down prayer in public schools. Said Gordon Lee, school board chairman,
"Recent decisions of the U.S. Supreme Court have made it clear that it is not
the province of a public school to support or discourage religious beliefs or
practices." The board voted 5–1 to ban religious elements from holiday con-
certs, graduation exercises, and other school activities.[1]

The Supreme Court was clear in limiting religious practice in public
schools, yet no other school district in the state had revised its policies. The
rulings in 1962 and 1963 started a nationwide debate, and school leaders reacted cautiously. The Red Wing school board believed "it was time to define our
policy" though it had received no complaints.[2]

The decision in Red Wing caused a sensation in Minnesota, but local reaction was generally mild. Letters of complaint to the school board ran 2–1
against the new policy, but nearly 70 percent of the writers lived outside the city.
The Associated Press reported that the board's action "startled" local residents,
but "folks had calmed down." The Minneapolis *Tribune* included photos of Red
Wing board members in its coverage.[3]

The Rochester *Post-Bulletin* carried a vehement attack against the school
board action. Editor Charles Withers called the policy a "STUPID [and] shocking display of misguided thoughtlessness in what is after all . . . a Christian
country." Philip S. Duff, publisher of the Red Wing *Republican Eagle,* re-

sponded that the board included the president of Red Wing Shoes, a physician, the wife of a city manufacturer, and two well-regarded businessmen: "Thanks for letting me present the Red Wing school board in an other than 'stupid' light. It is never stupid to stand up for cherished American Liberties."[4]

The controversy at Red Wing prompted other districts to avoid the "religion in the schools" issue. A new debate opened in 1967 with a challenge to baccalaureate ceremonies, a traditional religious service for high-school graduates still held in some districts. The Minnesota Civil Liberties Union (MCLU) challenged school sponsorship of the ceremony, with Rochester public schools its test case, and won. Through the 1970s and 1980s the legislature assisted the education department's effort to assure secular schooling. Still, some school districts ran afoul of state policy in permitting Bible distribution and conducting Christian holiday programs.[5] By the 1990s about 70 percent of the state's public school districts followed the lead of Red Wing. But the debate about allowing prayer in schools continued.

America's urban-industrial economy, and Goodhue County's with it, began to develop in the mid-19th century with transport by railroad of huge loads of freight over great distances at comparatively low cost. Railroad giants wrestled for market share, competing for high-volume business with lower prices in large markets. But small towns and farmers on branch lines saw little competition and thus faced higher prices. Small-business owners and farmers protested what seemed to them excessive transport costs but could do little to curb the power of the railroads.[6]

In the 1930s, the continuing development of the American trucking industry began to break the rail industry's grip on freight hauling. Improved highways and roads linked Goodhue County to the growing national road network. Meanwhile, Minnesota's railroad trackage had peaked in 1929 at 9,400 miles. It shortly began a steady decline.[7]

Railroads began to abandon lines in Goodhue County in the 1930s. The Northwestern dropped the Zumbrota to Rochester link in May 1931 and pulled up tracks between Pine Island and Rochester in 1936, ending 51 years of service. The Milwaukee Road cut its link between Zumbrota and Wabasha in 1933 and abandoned its Mineral Springs to Cannon Junction line in 1937. The Chicago Great Western closed its Claybank spur in 1936.[8]

The last passenger service to Zumbrota ended in August 1950, when the Chicago Great Western halted service between Rochester and Randolph. Freight service continued, but the CGW abandoned the track in 1965. The state railroad and warehouse commission approved the elimination of the passenger service: "The commission cannot close its eyes to conditions which are well known to everyone. The day when the traveling public relied on the railroad as the chief means of transportation between towns has long since passed."[9]

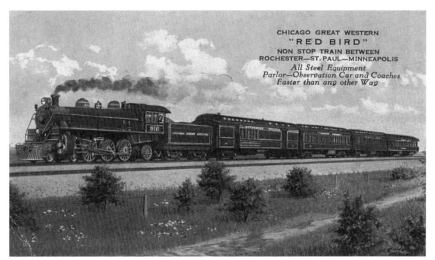

CHICAGO GREAT WESTERN
"RED BIRD"
NON STOP TRAIN BETWEEN
ROCHESTER—ST. PAUL—MINNEAPOLIS
*All Steel Equipment*
*Parlor—Observation Car and Coaches*
*Faster than any other Way*

The Chicago Great Western's Red Bird traveled from the Twin Cities to Rochester through Goodhue County beginning in 1925. *John L. Cole collection*

The Chicago Great Western's once-impressive first-class Red Bird and Blue Bird passenger trains began service from the Twin Cities to Rochester via Red Wing in 1925. By 1950 passenger traffic had dwindled and supported only daily runs by the "Doodlebug," a slow-moving engine and passenger car. The Doodlebug made its final trip in August 1950.[10]

In late September 1965 Edward M. Langemo returned to Kenyon on a mission. The Chicago Great Western was discontinuing passenger service through Kenyon, and the 89-year-old wanted to ride the route one last time. Langemo, a nine-year-old in September 1885, had earned a seat on the first passenger train on the CGW track. The boy's father Peter Langemo, a busy state legislator, sent young Edward out with ex-governor William Marshall on his search for farmers to invest in the new railroad. Eighty years after that initial trip, Langemo took a seat for a sentimental journey on the Great Western's final run through Kenyon.[11]

The Milwaukee Road's main rail passenger route through Red Wing persisted. The city had benefited from the Milwaukee's mid-1930s decision to upgrade its Chicago-to-Minneapolis connection. The new Hiawatha served the route with powerful oil-burning steam locomotives. They carried the air-conditioned, wood-paneled passenger cars at speeds of over 100 miles per hour. By the end of 1935 the afternoon and evening Hiawathas carried an average of 225 passengers per trip. Decline came in the 1950s, and the Milwaukee began losing money as early as 1957. In years following, the railroad looked for a way out. The Milwaukee shut down the afternoon Hiawatha in April 1970 with little attention from the public.[12]

The "Doodlebug," which replaced the first-class Chicago Great Western trains in the 1940s, made its final trip (above) in August 1950. *GCHS*

Trainmen attempted to get this V plow back on track after it derailed near Bombay in southern Wanamingo township in April 1951. *John L. Cole collection*

The federal government assumed control of rail-passenger service in May 1971, solving the passenger problems of the Milwaukee Road and other principal carriers by developing the Amtrak system. Red Wing's Lyle Olson, who worked for the Milwaukee for more than 30 years, remembered that by the 1960s the passenger-train lines "couldn't even give away tickets."[13]

The merged Chicago and North Western sent its freight business to the Milwaukee Road and pulled out of Red Wing in 1982. Hardees, part of a national restaurant chain, took over the CGW's 1908-era depot and converted it to a fast-food place. Cannon Falls lost its CNW depot in October 1975 as the railroad consolidated stations from Cannon Falls and Faribault with the service in Randolph.[14]

In 1983 a Goodhue County citizens' group, with help from the Minnesota Parks Foundation, bought the abandoned Chicago and North Western railroad line between Cannon Falls and Red Wing. With Charles O. Richardson of Red Wing in the lead, the group developed the former rail right-of-way into the Cannon Valley Trail—a biking, skiing, and walking path.[15]

The threat to the existence of Red Wing Potteries increased in the mid-1950s. Its future depended on its ability to compete with foreign imports and rivals' increased use of plastics. In 1956, 20 American pottery manufacturers closed while the Red Wing production line continued. Wage concessions and the firm's reputation for high-quality, hand-painted dinnerware helped keep it alive.[16]

By summer 1967, the 90-year-old firm faced a crisis. The pottery's production workers, members of Local 6-430 of the Oil, Chemical and Atomic Workers, called a strike in June. They wanted better benefits, a pension plan, and higher pay. The company countered with three proposals, estimating its offer as an increase of between $25,000 to $30,000 per year. It claimed that union demands would cost "a minimum of $100,000, not including the pension plan."[17]

As the strike dragged into its second month, union pickets parading near the pottery's salesroom became more aggressive. They shouted insults and once scattered tacks in the parking lot. Richard A. Gilmer, potteries president, warned that a continued strike could force the plant to shut. Tilfer Chastain, president of the union, countered, "If he must close the place, we'll pick a committee and help him nail the doors."[18]

The strike became more and more bitter as the summer wore on. Union leaders claimed as "blackmail" the statement that the pottery would be forced to close. Weekends brought crowds of picketers to the salesroom. Some were accused of threatening customers. On August 5, Judge John B. Friedrich granted the potteries a restraining order that limited the protests. No more than three peaceful picketers could be "at any time at each entrance."[19]

By late August the protesting workers had little room to maneuver. Gilmer still claimed that union demands could close the company. The average yearly wage before deductions was $3,500 per worker. Said one picketer, "Man, we'd rather the company died a sudden death than drag on like it has been." A last-minute mediation effort led by six Red Wing citizens raised hope of a settlement but ended in failure. [20]

On August 24, 18 shareholders, representing most of the firm's 31,444 outstanding shares of stock, met in the pottery offices. They took less than 40 minutes to vote in favor of shutting down. Gilmer met waiting newspaper and television reporters with the news. He began: "It's a very sad day."[21]

The loss of Red Wing Potteries proved a severe blow to the city and county economy. More than 100 workers lost their jobs. The city's image suffered during the 85-day strike. The county lost revenue from a top taxpaying company. The passing of this mainstay of the clay industry was indeed "a very sad day."[22]

The 1960s, one of the most turbulent decades in American history, began with four years of economic expansion. The surging economy meant greater affluence and confidence among the nation's growing middle class. It now included 60 to 70 percent of all Americans, according to studies by Cornell University's Andrew Hacker. Some observers believed a move toward "a universal middle class" was underway—a concept foreign to the rural and urban poor. Still, in June 1963 the average weekly pay for a production worker putting in slightly more than 40 hours passed $100. That was four times the amount paid during the depression. One amazed European diplomat observed, "The American economy has become so big that it is beyond imagination to comprehend."[23]

Yet there were signs of trouble. In November 1961 President John F. Kennedy sent 7,000 American troops into Vietnam to help the anti-Communist government of the south fend off the Communist government of the north. In October 1962 Kennedy received proof that the Soviet Union had installed offensive missiles on the soil of its Caribbean ally Cuba. This set off a confrontation heavy with the threat of nuclear war.[24]

Goodhue County had experienced some controversy regarding Communist Cuba. University of Minnesota student William Befort of Red Wing visited the island and wrote a *Republican Eagle* series on its new government. "Castro's Cuba—How it Looks from the Inside" ran February 9–18, 1961. An editorial on February 20 countered Befort's positive review, saying readers must have been "startled" that Befort had no criticisms of revolutionary Cuba. One writer on February 22 questioned the series as an attempt to create a "pro-Red cultural climate" and hoped Communism would "not take [Befort's] life and yours and mine in the bargain." Six years later Befort was in a combat unit fighting Communist nationalists in Vietnam.

Also in 1962, Michael Harrington's book *The Other America: Poverty in the United States* detailed the lives of the poor people overlooked by mainstream observers. Betty Friedan's *The Feminine Mystique* laid a foundation for the modern feminist movement. The growing civil-rights movement in America produced in August 1963 the March on Washington, D.C., led by the Rev. Dr. Martin Luther King Jr. And there was the assassination of the young, charismatic President Kennedy in November 1963. National television networks provided three days and nights of coverage of the murder to a stunned citizenry.

For the people of Goodhue County, the major controversy of the decade centered on the nation's growing military involvement in Vietnam. County residents, secure in the American heartland, initially experienced the war in Vietnam through the news media. Yet many of the county's young adults would encounter firsthand the effects of increased participation in the fighting in Southeast Asia.

The air war over Vietnam cost Goodhue County its first casualty. Maj. Thomas E. Reitmann of Red Wing was shot down in his F-105 jet on December 1, 1965. The air force listed Reitmann as missing and in August 1973 declared him dead.[25]

U.S. ground forces continued to arrive in South Vietnam in 1965, nearly 200,000 by year's end. The government called on local draft boards to produce the needed soldiers. Lillian Christenson, secretary for the Selective Service Office in Goodhue County, organized local conscription. The draft board included members from around the county in its attempt to distribute representation fairly.[26]

Complicating the job of the draft board was an increasing disenchantment with the war. Neither did the perception of unfair deferments help. Meanwhile, an antiwar movement gained strength on American college campuses. A 1969 *Fortune* poll indicated about 13 percent of America's 6.7 million college students were "revolutionary" or "radically dissident." This active, dedicated minority disrupted and at times paralyzed campuses across the country.[27]

In Goodhue County, citizens saw a reduction in deferments to farmers and students as the conflict wore on. Men had to register for military service on their 18th birthdays and undergo a predraft physical exam to determine physical and mental qualification. During the first years of the war, those in college or qualified educational institutions routinely received deferments. This left 18- and 19-year-olds not in school much more likely to be drafted. The inequities of the draft became a sore point. A draft lottery begun in December 1969 helped make the conscription process more fair.[28]

A heated letter to *Republican Eagle* during the potteries strike in the summer of 1967 criticized the hardship of the draft on working men and their families. Wrote H. J. Burbach of rural Red Wing, "The so-called better class, to whom we look for leadership, could well ask themselves what kind of a world they are building when the sons of working people are expected to fight and die to perpetuate the exalted living standards of the pampered so-called better class, while their fathers are paid a pauper's wage . . . Why should not the leadership (whose sons generally are provided with sufficient funds to claim exemption from military service on scholastic merit), do their part in making that dream of all servicemen a reality?"[29]

Local draft boards, including Goodhue County's, also received petitions from potential draftees for conscientious objector (C.O.) status. These came from draft-aged men usually citing religious or moral opposition to military service. C.O. exemptions grew in relation to induction from 8 percent in 1967 to 131 percent in 1972. Between 1965 and 1970, 170,000 registrants received C.O. status. Others simply refused to cooperate with the system. Of two million conscripted nationwide during the war, nearly 137,000 refused induction. More than 30,000 went into exile, mostly in Canada, Britain, and Sweden.[30]

Two brothers from Red Wing, James and David Lee, disenchanted with American involvement in Vietnam, eventually filed for C.O. status. James had already received his draft notice when he appeared before the Goodhue County Draft Board in Red Wing in June 1969. He presented a letter beginning, "On religious grounds I am opposed to warfare in any form." The board ordered James to report. David Lee sought advice from a draft counseling service as he struggled with his "revulsion against war." He notified the board that "the selective service was illegitimate and that I was going to refuse induction."[31]

Federal agents arrested both brothers that fall. On June 11, 1970, David was found guilty of draft evasion. He appealed and lost. Lee's sentence included three years of probation with two years' required service as an orderly at the University of Minnesota hospital. He later received a full pardon under a grant of executive clemency.

James Lee based his draft objection on his "strict religious" opposition to warfare, a claim the court ruled could be invoked only by men already in the service. He went into the army in November 1971 and was ordered to Fort Leonard Wood, Missouri. The army notified Lee a few weeks later that his request for C.O. status was granted. After 100 days in the army, he could leave.

More typically, the men called by the draft board reported at the appointed time. Among those inducted in the mid-1960s were Red Wing Shoe Company worker Ron Gernentz and Fred Fanslow, who farmed and worked for his father at Red Wing Implement. The draft came as no surprise to them. They had followed the growing conflict in school and in the media. Both felt a duty to their country and went to war willingly. Gernentz and Fanslow agreed that, "If the government says, 'You go'—you just go!"[32]

In the spring of 1968, four months after Gernentz arrived in Vietnam, *Republican Eagle* managing editor Arlin Albrecht interviewed him at Pleiku, 240 miles north of Saigon. Gernentz, 20, was an advocate for American aerial bombing in the north. The radio and teletype operator by this time believed his nation fought in a "foolish war." Albrecht spent a month in Southeast Asia interviewing Goodhue County soldiers and others from the paper's service area.[33]

In the spring and summer of 1970 the antiwar movement, now effectively mobilized, continued its effort to force withdrawal from Vietnam. On May 1, 1970, President Richard Nixon sanctioned an American thrust into Cambodia to clean out North Vietnamese bases and break the stalemate in Southeast Asia. It dealt the Communists a severe blow but inspired a new round of student unrest. Some Goodhue County students joined in the antiwar protests at the University of Minnesota. Patricia Chelberg, a Red Wing Central High graduate, wrote the *Republican Eagle* on May 25, discussing the student strike at the university and describing "Peace College" activity there. War protesters talked of a door-to-door campaign in Red Wing. Evan Stark, an instructor at the university, spoke to an audience of 82 in Red Wing on May 27, challenging listeners to become active in spreading the protest.[34]

The *Republican Eagle* provided a forum in spring 1970 for letter-to-the-editor skirmishes between antiwar activists and those supporting American policy. Exchanges in May and June were typical. On May 29 a letter countered the ideas professed by Evan Stark: "If we're being defeated, the underlying cause is that instead of backing the government, there are too many hacking away at it while enjoying the freedom that others have fought and died for." Four days later another writer criticized the student protests and said her generation did not run off to "escape [the] country's call to duty."[35]

On June 4 two writers wrote in support of the protest movement. They asked that community members take time to listen to those conducting a pro-peace canvass of the town. The *Republican Eagle* echoed one of the letters with an editorial encouraging people to be patient and not to throw peace activists off their property.[36]

The loss of soldiers in the increasingly unpopular war produced rancor across the nation and in Goodhue County. The death of Pfc. Gordon M. Gunhus, a 19-year-old from Kenyon, produced a bitter editorial in the *Leader*. Gunhus, who had just recovered from previous wounds, died March 29, 1970, from a mine explosion. His death, claimed the *Leader*, "brings the miserable mess in Vietnam close to home and casts a shadow of shame over those who blundered us into this undeclared war, a war which never can be won."[37]

The county's list of dead in Vietnam lengthened through the late 1960s. Russell E. Krause, a 20-year-old Marine from Pine Island, died in a truck accident on June 3, 1966. An exploding antitank mine killed Red Wing Pfc. Charles L. Hauschildt, 20, on December 8, 1967. Five weeks later, another mine killed Pfc. Frederick H. Hemphill, a 20-year-old army medic from Red Wing.[38]

In February 1968 enemy gunfire killed Cpl. Lee Kinney. Three weeks later, Spec. 4 Gerald F. Tracy of rural Dennison was killed in action northwest of Saigon. Marine Cpl. Bruce W. Staehli, a 19-year-old from Frontenac, was thought to be captured during fighting on April 30, 1968. Fellow soldiers recovered some of his personal effects but could not find Staehli. He was declared killed in action in August 1975. In April 1969 the army presented Raymond and Julia Rubin, Pine Island, the parents of Pfc. Herman Rubin, with their son's Bronze Star for bravery. The 19-year-old had died in combat.[39]

The air force declared Maj. Benjamin Danielson missing in action on December 5, 1969, when the Kenyon pilot's plane went down in Laos. His wife, Mary, a kindergarten teacher in Nerstrand, and sister, Marilyn Merseth of Zumbrota, held hope for his survival. Like many other Americans, they joined an association of families working to gain information about men missing in action or captured. In February 1976 the air force listed Danielson as presumed killed in action after examining testimony from his navigator.[40]

The painful war continued until January 1973, when the warring nations agreed to a cease-fire and the withdrawal of remaining U.S. forces from Vietnam. President Nixon said this meant "peace with honor." Without American support, the South Vietnam government collapsed, and in April 1975 the North Vietnamese occupied the south. The United States suffered more than 58,000 dead, including 1,061 Minnesotans, and more than 300,000 wounded. Eleven Goodhue County men died or were missing in action.[41]

The State Training School for Boys (STS), a fixture in the county since 1889, also faced new challenges in the 1960s. During a heat wave in August 1968 the school had its own bout with campus unrest that unsettled the state correctional system and the neighborhoods surrounding the school [42]

The problem began on the evening of August 21, when 17 boys left Stanford cottage without permission. They later returned to the building. Meanwhile in the Duke security cottage, 25 inmates, sweltering in heat that one staff member said felt like "200 degrees," began a protest that soon turned violent. The boys broke furniture and windows and armed themselves with table legs. To avoid a full-scale riot, supervisors allowed the boys out of the building. Twelve used the opportunity to escape.[43]

Authorities regained control and conducted investigations into the uprising. Controversy over the role of "The Way," a Minneapolis-based, largely African-American community organization, erupted immediately. Arnie Murray of The Way had worked at the reformatory throughout the summer and spoken to the media about problems there. He reported that The Way representatives temporarily took control of Duke and helped calm the protest. Murray also claimed a relationship with inmates superior to that of regular STS staff. "We're not Mister So and So; we're Kim and Arnie. We have established a better rapport . . . The kids are tired of being ruled. Tired of the same faces cracking the whip."[44]

Paul Keve, state corrections commissioner, countered, "Members of The Way are not running the cottage. No employee or member of The Way is a spokesman for the institution." STS superintendent Milton Olson later praised workers from the Minneapolis organization for their help in restoring order, but in less than a week officials ended The Way program at the facility.[45]

Following the disturbance, the *Republican Eagle* published a "box score." Seventy-six had left the institution. Seventeen were still missing two days after the unrest. Two were in the county jail. The newspaper also reported the number of "drifts"—those who left without permission. A total of 207 had run away since January 1, stealing 34 Red Wing cars in the process. In the previous year there had been 404 drifts and 58 cars stolen.[46]

Repercussions from the disturbances at the training school followed. On August 27, authorities led 13 handcuffed inmates from the reformatory, transferring them to the medium-security facility at Lino Lakes. One staff member was suspended, and another resigned. Gov. Harold Le Vander made an inspection of the facility as the normal routine resumed.[47]

Changes were in the works. Educational opportunities increased. The volunteer program continued to grow. The canteen, established in 1966 to supply personal needs as well as snacks, expanded its inventory. Girls were again confined at the training school in 1973, after an absence of 62 years. Starting in 1978, adult inmates, typically within a year of release, took part in a "re-entry" program at Red Wing.[48]

The dramatic but mostly nonviolent uprising at the State Training School in Red Wing had clear racial overtones. Several of those escaping from the security cottage were black teenagers from the Twin Cities. The *Republican Eagle* reported that some members of the white STS staff believed members of the Minneapolis-based group The Way agitated the boys. The controversy produced mutual finger pointing and distrust. By the summer of 1968, race relations were rocky. Across the nation, they were dangerously unstable.[49]

Throughout the 1960s African Americans became more impatient with the slow pace of reform in a society in which they received unequal and even overtly racist treatment. Martin Luther King Jr. moved to the forefront of the civil rights movement in the late 1950s and gained international acclaim for his policy of nonviolent protest. King focused on the American South, where a strictly enforced policy of racial segregation had relegated blacks to second-class citizenship. In 1964 the Nobel Prize committee awarded King its peace prize for his work. But some in the black community believed King's methods were not working. They looked to more militant forms of protest. "The day of nonviolent resistance is over," said Malcolm X, a leader of the black Muslim movement. "If they have the Ku Klux Klan nonviolent, I'll be nonviolent."[50]

Racial strife was not restricted to the South. In the nation's large urban centers, some black citizens frustrated by the slow pace of change erupted in violence. In the mid-1960s, riots became commonplace in the predominantly black ghettos and downtowns of many major cities. In April 1966 racial turmoil commenced in Washington, D.C., followed by uprisings in 27 cities. More than a hundred large cities, including Minneapolis, eventually were affected by the mid-1960s summers of rage.[51]

The assassination of Martin Luther King Jr. in Memphis on April 4, 1968, stunned the nation and touched off the worst rioting the country had ever witnessed. Black-white relations took a step backward. The racial upheaval could not be ignored. The entire nation would have to confront and overcome racism, clearly becoming more than a black-white issue. Native Americans protested the high levels of poverty, unemployment, and disease that plagued their people. By organizing a boycott of grapes in 1968, the United Farm Workers, a union and a social movement that worked mostly for the well-being of Mexican migrant workers, brought their plight to the nation's attention.

During the 1960s, Burnside proved Goodhue County's fastest-growing township, increasing its population by 50 percent. With 2,348 in 1970, Burnside's residents more than tripled those living in all but two of the county's other townships. Burnside doubled the exceptions—Cannon Falls township and Florence. Demographers attributed the expansion to the state's increasing suburban sprawl from cities of any size to nearby townships. This growth pattern changed the character of affected rural townships and soon produced a need for city services. Burnside, with its rapid growth fueled by its proximity to Red Wing, fit this picture, but, as with all stereotypes, important exceptions existed.

Burnside's growth imposed a strain on its resources. Some residents questioned the ability of the township to provide for more police and fire protection, more schools, and to develop a sewage system. Some believed consolidation with Red Wing might provide the solution. But when Red Wing officials broached the subject of a possible unification of their city and Burnside, strong opposition developed.[52]

New Red Wing mayor Demetrius Jelatis accidentally fired the opening shot in the battle for Burnside on a cold winter night in 1962. He believed the city should start talking about the growing township and its future needs and invited a member of the Minnesota Municipal Commission (MMC) to speak at a public meeting in Burnside. The topic was annexation and consolidation of lands near central cities. The speech and question period was characterized, recalled Jelatis, by the "deathly silence" of the audience of about 100.[53]

There were strong arguments for consolidation. The township form of government was not designed to serve urban areas, as much of Burnside had become. Red Wing rejected the idea of handling sewage disposal from adjoining townships unless that township agreed to unite with the city.[54]

Some Burnside residents suspected that Red Wing officials wanted to grab tax revenue from the new Northern States Power nuclear electric generating plant. The NSP plant, constructed on Prairie Island in Burnside township, would be on line by 1972. Some also remembered with bitterness the 1960 unification of the Burnside and Red Wing school districts.

At a February 12, 1970, meeting Red Wing officials, following merger talks with township leaders, took a major step to move consolidation forward. City department leaders presented cost estimates for extending services to Burnside. The township board agreed to study the figures. Eight days later, the MMC seemed to rule out one possible escape route for Burnside's anticonsolidation movement—incorporation as a village.[55]

On April 13, 1970, the Red Wing city council received a recommendation from the city's planning commission to petition MMC for consolidation. It suggested approaching Burnside township officers to sign a joint resolution. A majority of board members said they would not agree. The pro-merger Burnside Community Development Association began to explore consolidation with Red Wing. Soon the Volunteer Action Committee, a Burnside group, organized to oppose a merger. The MMC scheduled arguments for December 7.[56]

Meanwhile, Burnside residents, after a divisive debate, voted 225–142 to establish a $25,000 fund to fight the merger in the courts. On April 9, 1971, the MMC ordered consolidation. The township appealed the decision in district court but lost.[57] The first item on the MMC's order made the point—"Red Wing and Burnside are hereby consolidated into a single new municipality to be known as Red Wing."[58]

The women's rights movement in America quieted in the decades after the passage of the 19th Amendment guaranteed women the vote. Years of depression and war had preoccupied the nation. Civil rights issues slipped into the background. Still, equal rights advocates celebrated the movement of women into the workplace during World War II, their record of military service, and a growing list of firsts for women in political office.[59]

Women who joined the workforce remained there more often than in the past. The percentage of Minnesota women working by 1950 was 28.8 and rising. In Red Wing the number of women factory workers increased by 50 percent to 355 between 1938 and 1948. Cannon Falls, boosted by the Industrial Development Corporation, began an industrial expansion in the 1950s. It started modestly with Lees Manufacturing, a garment factory with a mostly female workforce.[60]

Dissatisfaction grew among equal rights advocates, who said that the existing system deprived women of equal pay, of the chance to seek jobs they wanted, and of promotions they earned. More and more women chafed under a work environment they believed was sexist. Protesters also fought against what they called male chauvinism—the belief that men were superior and women should be subservient to them. Meanwhile, the postwar baby boom subsided; the decline accelerated in 1960 with federal approval of birth-control pills. More women with college degrees were entering the workforce. In 1961 President Kennedy's Commission on the Status of Women validated the complaints of equal-rights backers showing widespread discrimination against women in the economy, legal system, and family. By the end of the 1960s the average woman worker earned just over half the salary of a man.[61]

Change came through Congress and the courts in the 1960s and 1970s. Title VII of the Civil Rights Act of 1964 prohibited employment discrimination based on race, gender, religion, and national origin and provided momentum for societal change. A series of rulings on the legal rights of American women followed. One provision allowed women meeting physical requirements to be hired for jobs formerly restricted to men (1969). Another barred excluding a person from participation, on the basis of gender, in educational programs receiving federal funds (1972). Another banned height and weight requirements for police, park service, and fire-fighting jobs. The U.S. military abolished women-only service branches (1973). Another ruling prohibited sex discrimination in consumer-credit practices (1974).

At the end of the 1960s, women engineers made up 1 percent of the national total, 2 percent of dentists, 4 percent of lawyers, and 7 percent of doctors. Yet change was in the air. By the late 1980s, one-quarter of new law and medical graduates were women. By 1992, women owned 124,143 Minnesota businesses, more than a third of the state's total. A national survey of women showed that 71 percent believed the women's rights movement had improved their lives.[62]

More than 50 percent of women were working outside their homes by 1980. Still, many women struggled in low-paying "pink collar" jobs, particularly in retail sales, clerical, and service work. In the 1980s and 1990s, more single parents, largely female heads of households, found daunting the combination of family life with work. More than a third of Minnesota's poor in 1985 lived in families headed by single women.[63] Clearly, the women's rights movement, revitalized in the 1960s, still faced formidable challenges at the century's end. Yet remarkable changes in the status of women had occurred. Said one observer, "Feminism in the last half of the twentieth century produced at least a half a revolution." She envisioned much work ahead.[64]

The women's rights movement achieved victories on both the legislative and judicial fronts through the last three decades of the 20th century. Also significant was a change in societal attitudes toward women. No longer was it a novelty to see women in many jobs and professions once considered reserved for males.

Among the important and visible changes were provisions of law forbidding the exclusion of people, on the basis of sex, from educational programs receiving federal funds. Public-school systems and state-supported post-high-school programs, colleges, and universities received federal dollars and moved to comply with the law.

In Goodhue County schools, as well as those nationwide, female students found new opportunities, especially in sports. Before 1972, girls interested in competitive sport relied on interschool athletic associations. Boys played in more visible, well-publicized leagues against teams from other communities. The premier high-school sporting event in Minnesota, almost from its inception in 1913, was the boys' high school basketball tournament. That tourney, and others held only for boys, faced the challenge of similar programs for girls.

One last hurrah remained for Goodhue County boys' basketball in March 1970. The state tournament that year was to be the last featuring a one-class system where all schools, regardless of size, competed for the championship. The State High School League ruled that future tournaments would be divided into small-and large-school classes. This new system produced two champions and, in the eyes of critics, diluted the importance of the playoffs.

Goodhue County produced two strong basketball teams in the winter of 1969–70. Sports polls rated undefeated Red Wing (22–0) the top high-school team in the state. Kenyon carried a 21–3 win/loss record into the playoffs. Red Wing, with four state championships and four runner-up trophies, found Kenyon blocking its way to the tournament. Winner of its first district playoff title since 1948, Kenyon engineered an upset in the Region One championship game at Rochester. The team came from behind to defeat Red Wing 59–57.[65]

Following the game, about a thousand people jammed into Kenyon High School for a victory party that continued past midnight. The postgame gathering had been planned before the regional final by women who "divided up the phone book and started calling everybody in town." Those in the first half of the alphabet brought cookies. The rest were asked to bring sandwiches. The happy fans listened to Joe Gates, a member of the 1926 Kenyon team that played in the regional playoffs before losing. He rejoiced in seeing the community send its first team to the state tournament.[66]

Girls' high-school sports expanded quickly after 1972, and county schools produced competitive teams. Volleyball, cross-country running, swimming, basketball, gymnastics, skiing, track, golf, and tennis attracted participants. Young women athletes now share the attention produced by the well-publicized and televised state competitions once reserved for their male counterparts.

The 1999–2000 season provided, for instance, an example of basketball excellence among the young women of Goodhue County. The merged Kenyon-Wanamingo High School team, sporting a 24–3 won/lost record, captured the Section One championship and headed into the Class-A girls' state tournament. Kenyon-Wanamingo, which also sent its 1988 basketball team to the state meet, lost in overtime in the first round.

The people of Goodhue County joined in the 20th-century movement to urban centers and away from the farms and hamlets that sustained so many of the first Euroamerican generations. Yet a journey around the county still provides the kind of landscapes familiar to earlier settlers. Those at the organizational meeting of Goodhue County Commissioners in June 1854 likely could comfortably find their way around the area nearly 150 years later. *Paul Chesley photo, GCHS*

# *19*

## *Toward the Millennium*

As a new millennium approached, the State Demographic Center viewed prospects for growth in Goodhue County as positive. Analysis showed citizens of the county would continue to take advantage of the resources that lured their predecessors—from the Mississippians to the Mdewakanton and the Euroamerican settlers—to the area. The county's natural resources provided an agricultural and transportation base that encouraged manufacturing. A strong and diverse economic system was "expected to provide jobs and attract or retain residents."[1]

The face of Goodhue County underwent change in the last decades of the 20th century. The population, while still heavily Euroamerican, included more groups with roots in other parts of the world. Between 1980 and 1990, Minnesota posted the fourth-highest minority growth rate in the nation. And the number of people of color in the state continued to grow in the 1990s. Still, Minnesota was overwhelmingly white in 1990. Caucasians accounted for 4.1 million, or 94.4 percent of the total. Minorities in Goodhue County included 276 Native Americans, 187 Asians, 173 Hispanics, and 82 African Americans.[2]

The influence of 19th-century Euroamerican settlers and their descendants deeply impressed the cultural fabric of the state and county. Most numerous statewide were citizens of German descent—2,021,854. Norwegians numbered 757,212. The Irish counted in at 574,183. There were 536,207 Swedes. At the end of the century, those ethnic groups still sustained Goodhue County.[3]

The median age of Minnesotans, prodded by the post-World War II baby-boomers, rose in the 1980s from 29.2 to 32.5 years. Of the county's 40,690 citizens in 1990, 6,284 were 65 or older. Demographers expected the county to have one of the state's highest growth rates in those 65 and older between 1995 and 2025. They predicted an increase as high as 100 percent. They also forecast a population gain of 13 percent for the county—48,170 residents by 2025.[4]

Growth patterns showed continuing movement from rural townships to villages and cities. In the 1880 U.S. census, the typical Goodhue County township had about 1,000 residents. Wanamingo (1,377) and Holden (1,183) took the lead. In 1995 most rural townships had fewer than 500. Wanamingo township was down to 472 and Holden to 460. Belle Creek at 411, Belvidere at 487, Cherry Grove at 410, and Kenyon with 423, also declined.[5]

Townships nearer cities were more likely to maintain population. Urban residents moved in, comfortable with nearby city services. The city of Cannon Falls had 1,829 residents in 1980 but 3,481 people 15 years later. Expanding industry and Twin Cities spillover triggered that 47.4 percent increase. Meanwhile, Cannon Falls township was the county's most populous with 1,435. Stanton, bordering Cannon Falls, held steady at 915. The cities of Zumbrota and Pine Island had nearly identical growth between 1980 and 1995. Pine Island moved to 2,225, a 20.6 percent increase. Zumbrota rose to 2,447, a 19.4 percent jump. Pine Island township had 702 residents, and Zumbrota township, 630. Wanamingo village grew to 881, a 44.6 percent increase between 1980 and 1995. The township of Wanamingo held 472.[6]

The hard numbers of change only hinted at the continued pressures on farmers in Goodhue County and elsewhere. More and more people abandoned farming. Those who stayed on often struggled. Statewide, the number of farms decreased from 145,662 in 1959 to 75,079 in 1992, nearly a 50 percent drop. Only 63 percent of farmers under age 55 said farming was their principal occupation. In 1959, 11.8 percent of farmers worked 200 or more days a year at outside jobs. By 1993, 37 percent worked off the farm more than 200 days.[7]

The number of farms in Goodhue County decreased, though those remaining grew in size. In 1935 the county had 3,162 farms averaging 147 acres. By 1992, there were 1,540 operations, averaging 246 acres. Goodhue County, with 45 percent of its population living on farms in 1940 had, by 1990, only 12 percent there. The nature of the county's farms also changed. A growing number of dairy operators gave up their labor-intensive livestock. They relied more on cash crops such as corn and soybeans. They also worked other jobs.[8]

Part of the reduction in county dairy farms stemmed from a 1986 U.S. Department of Agriculture program meant to slash overproduction. Nearly 10 percent of the county's dairy farmers agreed to leave the business. This process eliminated 61 county dairy farms, plus about 2,500 of its 30,000 cows.[9]

County farmers showed the same ability to adapt as their predecessors. In 1992, for example, the county ranked second in state vegetable sales ($5.2 million), including sweet corn, melons, and other produce.[10]

Kenyon farmers Linda and Mike Noble battled to keep their hog and dairy farm in the 1980s. The cost of operation, plus diseases affecting their livestock, thwarted their work. They switched to sustainable farming, allowing their 25-cow herd to graze, thus reducing expenses. By 1999 they had a contract with a cooperative to sell organically produced milk for $17.10 per hundredweight. The couple also raised 60 acres of organic soybeans for sale to Japanese buyers. And they direct-marketed Berkshire hogs to 53 families.[11]

JoEllen and Matt Voxland typified Goodhue County farmers relying on other vocations to back up farm income. In the late 1990s Matt finished 3,000 hogs and raised 300 chickens on a 500-acre farm in Holden township. He worked in partnership with his father and brother. Voxland worked at Foldcraft Company in Kenyon for nine years while tending the farm, but he began full-time farming in 1995. That left JoEllen to bolster the family income through her full-time job at Gemini, Inc., in Cannon Falls. She said, "You can't count on any kind of income with farming . . . Like my husband says, at least one person in the family has to be making some money."[12]

Jeff and Sharon Steffenhagen also faced economic uncertainty in maintaining their Frontenac-area dairy farm. By 1990 they confronted a dilemma facing many small dairy farmers—to grow by adding to their debt or sell out? When they couldn't borrow what they needed, they sold their cows and equipment. Jeff Steffenhagen went to work at the Zumbrota cheese plant run by Mid-America Dairymen, a farmer-owned cooperative. He still found time, on a small scale, to pursue farming. He tended a small herd of breeder cows at home and did mechanical work for other farmers. At age 33, Jeff died in an October 1995 accident at the cheese plant.[13]

Some observers labeled the farm crisis of the 1980s "the worst agricultural panic since the Great Depression." Others spoke of the late 1990s as the worst. Farmers were too busy trying to hang on to worry about forecasts. But by 1998, a sense of growing desperation seized farmers in every northern-tier state as prices for corn, soybeans, wheat, and barley slumped toward 1950 levels.[14]

In February 1999, U.S. Secretary of Agriculture Dan Glickman warned of a "social catastrophe" in farm country. Citing large surpluses and weak demand, the secretary predicted continued declines in U.S. farm exports. In 1996 America exported $60 billion in farm products. The projection for 1999 was just $49 billion. Hog prices were so low that one Minnesotan joked that farmers must lock their barns at night so that no one would smuggle more hogs inside. Glickman urged Congress to come to the aid of farmers. While awaiting a move by Congress, Minnesota farmers received news in April 1999 that the state legislature provided $70 million to help them.[15]

Farming in the county and state underwent much change during the 20th century. Historian Rhoda Gilman addressed the issue in recalling a time when farming was the work of the common man. In settlement days, the job required "little skill, only moderate capital, and enormous labor—labor that was normally shared by the whole family." In a state where farming once provided a living for the majority, only a few could rely on it as the year 2000 approached. A 1993 survey of income by industry showed that earnings from farming had slumped to just 1 percent of the state total.[16]

The 19th-century view of the farmer as a noble tiller of the soil seems dated in the era of competitive, high-tech agribusiness. Yet the essential tasks of the agriculturalist remains unchanged. Perhaps the farmers still deserve the praise found in the verses of an old songbook:

> Let sailors sing of ocean deep,
> Let soldiers praise their armor,
> But in my heart this toast I'll keep:
> The independent farmer.
>
> He loves his country and his friends,
> His honesty's his armor.
> He's nature's nobleman in life,
> The independent farmer.[17]

Western Goodhue County, positioned in the St. Cloud-Twin Cities-Rochester corridor, found itself in the fastest-growing region in Minnesota at the century's end. This "Golden Corridor" was expected to continue leading the state's population growth, at least until 2025. Cannon Falls showed the greatest increase in the Goodhue County portion of the corridor, with Pine Island and Zumbrota also moving up. This new path of growth traces the old St. Paul-to-Dubuque stagecoach route through the county.[18]

A group of civic leaders spurred the diversification of industry in Cannon Falls beginning in the late 1950s. Merle S. Olson, D. Fay Case, Donald Mensing, Oliver J. Althoff, and Al Johnson formed the Cannon Falls Industrial Development Corporation. It purchased 70 acres of farmland on the north edge of the city for industrial use.[19]

That first step moved Cannon Falls from its rural-agrarian roots into an era of industrial expansion. The city also relied on Minnesota Malting, in 1939 reconstituted by A. R. "Tony" Mensing and his son, Donald. The Mensing firm, crippled by Prohibition, later became a mainstay of the city and county tax base. Other entrepreneurs started successful industries. Point of Sales, and later Cannon Equipment (1960) and Midwest Importers (1964), were followed by Gemini, Inc., Fil-Mor Express, Cannon Valley Woodwork, Bergquist Company, Cannon Falls Hospital, and Manor Nursing Home. In December 1998, the city lost Kids Duds, a sleepwear supplier employing 150, to a New York company.[20]

Zumbrota, the county's third largest city, expanded its economic base in the 1990s. In 1998 alone, Coolstor Warehouse Services built a 21,000-square-foot, $1.75 million addition. The Dairy Farmers of America plant, which began in 1971 as Mid-America Dairymen, added 20,000 square feet of production space costing $200,000. The community issued 69 building permits, including three for new projects and seven for commercial/industrial rehabilitation. Four housing developments also gained approval. A $1.7 million federal grant from the Department of Housing and Urban Development had prompted a growth spurt in May 1980 [21]

The city's landmark covered bridge also came in for attention. The sturdy structure, built in 1869 over the Zumbro River, carried traffic into the 13-year-old village. Local carpenter Evander Kingsbury constructed the bridge for $5,800. By 1999 the span was the last remaining early covered bridge in the state.[22] The bridge was removed from service in 1932 after improvements to Highway 58. Eventually it was relocated in Covered Bridge Park, close to its former location. Shortly after its removal, the Committee of the American Building Survey reported that the bridge was of "exceptional historical and architectural interest." A 1989 movement by Zumbrota citizens to place the aging structure astride the river achieved success eight years later. In February 1997 the structure was back where Zumbrotans felt it belonged—spanning the Zumbro River.[23]

Pine Island, like its northern neighbor Zumbrota, saw some of the population expansion predicted for the town. In 1983 a Rochester newspaper noted, "Pine Island, once a farm town, is now part bedroom community." It referred to the influx of workers from Rochester's Mayo Clinic and IBM plant who were building in Pine Island.[24]

A 1970 Pine Island building boom caught the attention of neighboring townships. Pine Island, which contracted with nearby Olmsted County for building permits, easily led the area in permits issued and the value of projects. Construction of new Lutheran and Catholic churches was complete, and a $400,000 addition to the school underway. The Land O' Lakes plant expanded, while work started on a new municipal liquor store. About a dozen new homes were nearly finished.[25]

The city, once the heart of the Minnesota cheese industry, maintained a connection to that product. Land O' Lakes continued to make cheese with milk from local dairy farms. Another longtime city business, Pine Island Farmers Elevator, celebrated its centennial in 1996. The farmer-owned cooperative survived the crop failure of 1934 and serious fires in 1961 and 1978. It had become a multimillion-dollar operation.[26]

Kenyon and Wanamingo, to the south and west of the corridor, also grew toward century's end. Kenyon reached 1,572 residents, and Wanamingo 881, by 1995. The area, which an 1874 visitor said was inhabited by "a compact mass of Norwegians," still included descendants of those first settlers. The region maintained a high number of Norwegian Americans but not at the 1870s level. Then, for example, all but two persons in Wanamingo township were Norwegian.[27]

Agriculture remained at the economic core of Wanamingo. City leaders tried to create a more diversified business base in the 1970s by forming a development corporation. The attempt failed. Maple Island, Inc., which dried and packaged milk-based powders, took over the former town creamery in 1965. It became the city's largest employer. Kenyon depended on farming but also had the strength of Foldcraft Company, which came to the city in 1967. Harold Nielsen, who founded the corporation in Mendota in 1948, transferred ownership of Foldcraft to the factory's workers through an Employee Stock Ownership Plan (ESOP). By 1992 the business was 100 percent employee-owned.[28]

Kenyon sustained some blows in the last decades of the century. In 1982 operators of the Kern Grain Elevator filed for bankruptcy, listing unsecured debt of $742,465. Among the elevator's creditors were farmers with claims ranging to nearly $60,000. In 1998 the Kenyon Canning Company's new owners, a multinational firm, closed this local operation.[29]

Although population growth through the county's portion of the corridor was strong, Red Wing more than kept pace. The county seat had just over 33 percent of the county's population at midcentury. It held that level until the 1990s, when its share increased to 37 percent. In 1995 Red Wing, boosted by its steady economy and annexation of Burnside, had 15,701 citizens of the county's total of 42,477.[30]

Red Wing Shoe Company emerged as an innovative footwear manufacturer, growing to employ than 1,000. In 1949 William D. Sweasy assumed control of the firm upon the death of his father, J. R. Sweasy. He streamlined management while modernizing and refining production.[31]

Bill Sweasy assumed the role of chairman of the board in 1972. This allowed him to continue a leadership role while pursuing other interests. Sweasy had a deep affection for the city of Red Wing. He decided to use the financial resources of Red Wing Shoe Foundation to reinvigorate the town. In the ensuing two decades he started a breathtaking series of projects that made him, in a town known for its benefactors, Red Wing's greatest philanthropist.

Sweasy's effort to restore the St. James Hotel to Victorian grandeur started the Main Street renaissance. In 1979 the hotel reopened to acclaim from architectural critics throughout the region. The St. James and the shops and restaurants attached to it helped the city assume a new role—tourist destination. The hotel complex anchored the retail business and drew visitors from the Twin Cities and other parts. Later, architects reconfigured the block neighboring the St. James. A new city park provided views of the river from Main Street. Riverfront Centre, next to the park, became a shopping stop for visitors. Among Sweasy's other efforts were the restoration of the Sheldon Memorial Auditorium and the Milwaukee Road depot.

While revitalization of Red Wing's Main Street area continued, others pressed for a new shopping mall in Burnside. Problems arose when business owners in the city's center, represented by the Downtown Development Association, worried that a 147,000-square-foot mall would have a negative effect. In January 1982 the mall's promoter and the downtown business owners reached agreement. Revenue bonds needed to finance the Red Wing Mall were issued. The mall's anchor tenant, Kmart, opened in spring 1983.[32]

In finance, Red Wing's Goodhue County National Bank dealt with a growing threat—the challenge of "megabanks" created from mergers of the nation's largest banks. Goodhue County National, dating to 1874, began its own expansion. It acquired banks in Rushford and Lanesboro in the 1980s and operated them as branch offices. In 1994 the Red Wing-based bank merged with Signal Bank of West St. Paul to create United Community Bancshares, Inc. That alliance continued to grow.[33]

In December 1999 corporate officials announced the reorganization of United. Goodhue County National would become Signal Bank Red Wing. Scott Jones, who also served as president of the American Bankers Association in 1998, continued as chief executive of the corporation—Signal Financial.[34]

Another major project, NSP's Prairie Island nuclear power plant, produced energy, tax dollars, and controversy after opening in 1973. It announced in February 1967 that the five-year construction of a proposed 550,000-kilowatt nuclear electric-generating plant including lines would cost $100 million. The project moved forward. In less than three decades after completion, the plant supplied about 20 percent of NSP's power needs.[35]

Goodhue County and Red Wing quickly benefited from tax revenues provided by the mammoth facility. By 1974 the new Prairie Island plant produced $6.062 million, or 39 percent of county tax revenue. It accounted for $1.079 million, or 62 percent of Red Wing's city taxes. The plant generated 67 percent of the city's property tax and 69 percent of school district taxes. In the mid-1970s NSP's share of those taxes stretched to more than 70 percent.[36]

In 1996 NSP challenged its local tax liability in Minnesota Tax Court and received a large reduction for its effort. Goodhue County lost 7.2 percent of its tax base. Red Wing's base dropped 11 percent. The Red Wing school system lost 10.3 percent. County and city governments reached a settlement with NSP, which paid more than $400,000 to each in 1997 and again in 1998. Those payments saved the county and city residents from major tax increases.[37]

The national debate over disposing radioactive wastes from nuclear plants came to Minnesota and Goodhue County in 1991. The federal government, charged with developing a national repository for nuclear wastes, had failed to complete its mission. Nuclear plants like the Prairie Island facility needed, in the meantime, a safe disposal or storage method. NSP proposed an onsite, dry-cask storage system as a temporary measure.

The idea drew fire from Prairie Island Mdewakanton leaders, who cited the danger of such storage to their community and others. Environmentalists also expressed concern. A Red Wing coalition of business and labor, the Citizens Alliance for Reliable Energy, supported the NSP concept. Legislators, under pressure from both sides, eventually approved the plan. The lawmakers at once allowed NSP five onsite storage casks for Prairie Island. They agreed to allow four more casks after the company applied to the Nuclear Regulatory Commission for an alternative storage facility in Goodhue County.[38]

The search for a new location for nuclear waste caused more concern. NSP established a citizen advisory group that identified, by April 1995, three potential storage sites in Florence township. Reaction from local residents at first was restrained, but opposition soon formed. In May the town board of Florence heard a motion that the township "secede" from Goodhue County. The proposal called for Florence to unite with Wabasha County and escape NSP's reach.[39]

By September 1996 the state's Environmental Quality Board recommended scrapping the search. The EQB reported that transportation problems would make any new Goodhue County site inferior to Prairie Island. In July 1997 NSP announced it would not pursue a site in Florence township.[40]

Meanwhile the Prairie Island Mdewakanton community expressed concern with the unsolved problem of nuclear waste in their backyard. Tribal leaders worried about safety and health risks related to the power plant's operations. The Mdewakanton Tribal Council, NSP, and the Red Wing City Council addressed the issue. By 1998 they were working together to defuse the controversy. The city and tribal councils sent representatives to the proposed Yucca Mountain, Nevada, national repository for contaminated nuclear-power waste, to survey that site.[41]

The Prairie Island Mdewakanton made significant gains in the last half of the 20th century though they had begun those years mired in economic depression. A 1952 report to Gov. C. Elmer Anderson described the community as hard to access because of roads and bridges "over which one travels at his own risk." It told of citizens subsisting on the manufacture of Indian handicrafts, day labor, and trapping. In 1956 a study placed average family income there at $150–$200 per month. A 1959 estimate listed annual family income at about $1,000 per year. One expert wrote in 1961, "The Prairie Island community today, if not quite a rural slum, at least qualifies as a depressed area."[42]

Ushering in the economic resurgence of the community was a cultural reawakening and revival of Dakota traditions. Among those kindling the fires of this movement was Amos Owen. The example of this quiet, unassuming spiritual leader led others to him. In 1933 Owen moved to Prairie Island from the Sisseton Reservation in South Dakota with his mother, a member of Wabasha's band, and his brothers. He served in the U.S. Army in the Philippines during World War II, suffering critical wounds. After several surgeries and months of rehabilitation, he returned home with a 100 percent disability.[43]

Owen spent his first year back at Prairie Island trying to regain his health and restart his life. He recalled listening to his mother as she related the stories of their people. "These," said Owen, "I put in the back of my head. I knew someday I would have to use them."[44]

He began a return "to the old religion." While living at Prairie Island as a young man, Owen assisted the deacon of the Episcopal Church in reading scripture in the Dakota language. He believed he might have become an Episcopal minister had not a world war intervened. And he saw similarities to his ancestors' religion and others. "We say 'The Great Spirit,' and in the Christian world, it's 'God.' People sometime misunderstand it, and they say we worship a different God. It's all the same," he said.[45]

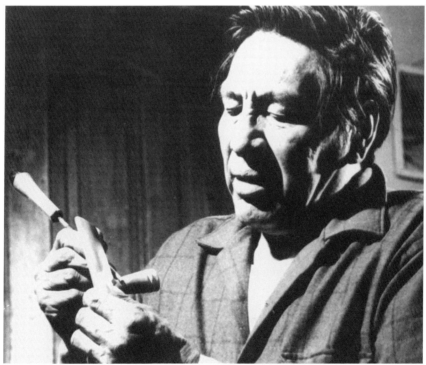

Amos Owen, whose mother was a member of the Wabasha band of Mdewakanton, returned to Prairie Island after World War II. His return to the "old religion" led him to prominence as a spiritual leader of his people. *GCHS*

While attending the Indian boarding school in Pipestone, Owen spent time with Indian stone carvers at work in the nearby catlinite (pipestone) quarries. Pipestone, sacred to his people for generations, lent itself to carving. Owen enjoyed learning from the craftsmen. He returned home with stone but began carving only after the war. His skill with pipestone soon became well known.[46]

Owen served the Prairie Island community as tribal chairman and secretary, but his renown as a spiritual leader reached other Native Americans and racial and ethnic groups. He patiently discussed Dakota religious traditions with anyone seeking to learn. Gov. Rudy Perpich declared April 23, 1990, Amos Owen Day in the state. The declaration noted that Owen "opened his home to thousands of people of all walks of life to share the belief that we are all brothers and sisters, and we can live in balance and respect for each other." Six weeks later Owen, Wiyohpeyata-Hoksina, died at age 73.[47]

Prairie Island's economic future brightened in 1984 with the opening of a bingo parlor. This marked the start of a gaming operation that grew into Treasure Island Resort and Casino, which became Goodhue County's largest employer.

Indian gaming mushroomed in Minnesota and other states during the last two decades of the century. States began to negotiate with Indian groups, using ground rules set by the U.S. Indian Gaming Act of 1988. In Minnesota those discussions resulted in 22 gaming agreements with 11 Indian bands, including the Prairie Island Mdewakanton. Prairie Island leaders soon contracted for the construction of a casino to contain the original bingo operation as well as slot machines and blackjack tables.[48]

Treasure Island played a major part in the growth of the state's Indian gaming industry. Studies show statewide tribal revenues reaching $173 million in 1991 and $300 million a year later. The prediction was $500 million by 1993. Treasure Island became the second largest employer in the state's gaming industry, with about 1,500 workers in 1993. The Mdewakanton leaders constructed a community center on the Prairie Island property. They added a hotel and marina to the complex. Individual tribal members received shares of casino profits.[49]

The success of the Prairie Island casino, especially after its expansion, prompted grumbling by some in surrounding areas. A few complaints reached the Red Wing newspaper. Those unhappy with the casino claimed people spent too much money gambling. They also said the Indian community made excessive profits and did not pay its fair share of taxes. One tribal member wrote on November 26, 1991, "With all the years of poverty that we have gone through, I would think you'd be glad that we finally have found our pot of gold." He pointed out that Indians spent considerable sums of money locally.[50]

Three citizens, identifying themselves as white, wrote the newspaper that same day, suggesting the protests about the casino were grounded in racism.

They observed, "The Indians are finally in a class of living they can be proud of. Don't take that away from them, too."[51]

In 1996 the state's advisory council on gambling reported some concerns about tribal gaming. It noted that gaming had become a source of frequent debate in the legislature, and "the state seeks to address the conditions that arise with any successful gambling enterprise." The council recommended "new discussion between the state and tribes" without a "specific outcome in mind." Some legislators hoped to renegotiate the original compacts to secure for the state a share of the profit from the casinos. The tribes, including the Prairie Island community, showed little interest in major change.[52]

The changing status of women would have impressed the Goodhue County activists who labored 100 years earlier to achieve equal rights. The NSP nuclear-storage and tax-reduction battles of the 1990s provide an example of the new environment. Among the women in leadership were the NSP project manager for spent fuel, the Florence township supervisor, the Mdewakanton tribal council president, and an assistant county attorney who served as chief negotiator in the tax case. A female judge heard the case. Several local news reporters covering the case were also female.

Women's place in the state workforce increased substantially. By 1990, workers over 16 years included 1,165,677 males and 1,026,740 females. Minnesota began the 1990s with the nation's highest rate of female employment. Married women increasingly worked out of the home. More than half the state's families had multiple workers. Just 23 percent had only one member working. The growing number with both mother and father employed resulted in debate about the effects of double employment on children.[53]

Another concern was the increasing number of children living with only one parent. In 1980, 84.1 percent of Minnesota children lived in married-couple families. This decreased to 79.3 percent by 1990. Goodhue County had 11,450 children under age 18 in 1990. Of these, 83.2 percent lived with married-couple families and 12.6 percent in single-parent homes. The proportion of births to unwed mothers also rose. In 1990, 20.9 percent of births in the state and 19.1 percent in Goodhue County were to unmarried women. Four years later it was 24.1 percent statewide and 22.6 percent in the county. Minnesota was under the national average of 32.6 percent births to unmarried mothers.[54]

In 1985 Red Wing voters elected Joanell M. Dyrstad mayor—the first woman in that office in the county's largest city. Republican gubernatorial candidate Arne Carlson chose her as a running mate in 1990, and she took part in one of the most contentious campaigns in state history. The Carlson-Dyrstad ticket won, and Dyrstad served one four-year term as lieutenant governor.[55]

Goodhue County support of Republican candidates continued at century's end but not with the constancy of the past. An important victory for county and state Republicans occurred in November 1998, when voters gave the Republicans their first majority in the state House of Representatives in a decade. Steve Sviggum of Kenyon, who had served as minority leader for the Republicans since 1993, became speaker of the house.

Sviggum embodied both the old and new political realities for Goodhue County. He came from the heavily Norwegian southwestern section of the county. This area had supported Republicans from the onset of statehood. Goodhue County sent many farmers to the House over the years and Sviggum, who operated a farm with his two brothers, continued that tradition. The new speaker lived in Kenyon with his wife, Debra, and their three children.[56]

The people of Goodhue County kept their equilibrium on the roller-coaster ride of the American adventure. They navigated through the lows of economic depression and civil and world war. They handled the highs of the King Wheat era, the exuberant 1920s, and America's emergence as a superpower.

Their geographic place in middle America echoed the citizenry's state of mind. Its people, generally conservative and usually cautious, found Goodhue County a good fit in the latter half of the 19th century. They took comfort from its peaceful rural setting and lived in relative isolation from the power, influence, and problems of the nation's urban centers. But that distance and the comparative success of county agricultural and industrial endeavors also fostered complacency and narrow-mindedness among some.

The people's pride in the achievements of the past must be tempered with the knowledge that the county's citizens displayed human frailty as well. The reluctance of many to accept Native Americans and their culture—perhaps understandable when most Euroamerican settlers viewed them as removable impediments to growth—continued during the 20th century. The emergence of a new generation of leaders and their establishment of gaming on Prairie Island brought increased respect and economic gain to the Mdewakanton.

The intolerance displayed at the mildest suggestion of dissent during the World War I years was a disgrace to the county. That such behavior was common statewide and throughout the nation mitigates it only slightly. The appearance of the Ku Klux Klan in most of the county's towns and villages in the 1920s does not mean most or even a significant number of Goodhue County residents supported it. Still, there were few signs of community protest against the activities of the Klan.

The people of Goodhue County can be justly proud of the dozens of individuals who contributed to the growth of the area while rendering service to the state and nation. Historians continue to celebrate the most famous. In some instances, including that of Col. William Colvill, theirs was but a fleeting moment of triumph. Others such as Charles Hewitt, Alexander P. Anderson, Julia Nelson, and Frances Densmore gave lifetimes of devoted service. Their efforts

Red Wing, the county seat, at the turn of the millennium. *Paul Chesley photo, GCHS*

still benefit us today. The contributions of these and other leaders, however, must rank behind those of ordinary folk. With faith in their ability and the willingness to work, they proved the true architects and construction crews—the real builders of Goodhue County. They settled, cleared and farmed the land, established businesses and industries, and labored to succeed.

The journey through the millennium past most often proved fruitful for those in Goodhue County. Their trip was not without cost, yet the people prevailed against all manner of hardship. They endured stinging setbacks and shocking tragedy, persevering in the face of disappointment and defeat. The Panic of 1857 caused terrible suffering, even starvation, while stunting the county's growth and ruining budding villages. The Civil War cost the county 122 of its finest young men. The ravaged wheat crops of the mid-1870s forced farmers of Goodhue County, the nation's "banner wheat county," to embrace new practices or fail. The Great Depression of the 1930s tested the mettle of another generation—the same who provided the leadership and personnel to triumph during World War II.

To these predecessors goes the credit for securing a place for Goodhue County in an America whose wealth and power is the envy of the world. Unresolved problems linger and unknown trials lay ahead. But the people of Goodhue County look to the future with confidence, fortified by a legacy of faith, determination, and courage.

# References

**Abbreviations**
GCHS=Goodhue County Historical Society
MHS=Minnesota Historical Society
N.c.=No city given
N.d.=No date given
N.p.=No publisher given

For convenience, all newspaper city names are printed in roman type, all newspaper names in italics.
In most cases, articles from *Goodhue County Historical News* (GCHS) and *Minnesota Collections* (MHS) are not listed separately in the bibliography.
References include full information on the first listing, author and title the first time listed in following chapters, then just the author unless the author is cited for more than one work.
For the sake of space, these references are not fully annotated. A fully annotated 37,000-word reference for this work resides at GCHS.

**Introduction**
1. Clark A. Dobbs, *The Archaeology of 21GD158: A 13th-Century Native American Village at the Red Wing Locality*, Reports of Investigations No. 250 (Minneapolis: Institute for Minnesota Archaeology, 1993), 1, 5–6.
2. Claudia G. Mink, *Cahokia: City of the Sun* (Collinsville, Ill.: Cahokia Mounds Museum Society, 1992), 16–17.
3. Mink, 13–26.
4. Clark A. Dobbs, "The Application of Remote Sensing Techniques to Settlement Pattern Analysis at the Red Wing Locality, *Minnesota Archaeologist* 50 (No. 2, 1991): 3.
5. Here and below, Clark Dobbs, *An Archaeological Survey of the City of Red Wing, Minnesota* (Minneapolis: Institute for Minnesota Archaeology, 1985), 14–19; Elden Johnson, *The Prehistoric Peoples of Minnesota*, 3rd ed. (St. Paul: MHS, 1988), 1–5.
6. Institute for Minnesota Archaeology, *Summer Field School Manual, 1995*, 5–7 (copy at GCHS).
7. Here and below, Clark A. Dobbs to Chuck Richardson, May 1, 1998, copy in GCHS Archaeological file.
8. Here and below, Charles Tooker and John Koepke, *Red Wing Archaeological Preserve: An Ancient Native American Village and Cemetery* (Minneapolis: Institute for Minnesota Archaeology, 1990), 7–9; Dobbs, *The Archaeology of 21GD158*, 164; Institute for Minnesota Archaeology, 5–6.
9. Here and below, Institute for Minnesota Archaeology, 3–4; Dobbs, "So What's So Special About the Prehistory of the Red Wing Area?" GCHS Archaeology file.
10. Tooker and Koepke, 1–2.
11. Here and below, Dobbs, "The Archaeology of 21GD158," 1–6, 162–65, and "An Archaeological Survey . . . of Red Wing, Minnesota," 4–5, 9–20; Guy E. Gibbon, "The Middle Mississippian Presence in Minnesota," in Thomas E. Emerson and R. Barry Lewis, eds., *Cahokia and the Hinterlands: Middle Mississippian Cultures of the Midwest* (Urbana: University of Illinois Press, 1991), 206–20, and "Cultural Dynamics and the Development of the Oneota Life-way in Wisconsin," *American Antiquity* 38 (April 1972): 166–85.
12. Institute for Minnesota Archaeology, 3; Guy E. Gibbon, *The Mississippian Occupation of the Red Wing Area*, Minnesota Prehistoric Archaeology Series, No. 13, MHS, 1979, 162–63.

13. Conclusions are from Guy Gibbon and Clark Dobbs as quoted in Institute for Minnesota Archaeology, *Summer Field School Manual,* 6–7.
14. Here and below, Dobbs, "An Archaeological Survey . . . of Red Wing Minnesota," 49, 53–54.
15. Mink, 66–67.
16. Gibbon, *The Mississippian Occupation of the Red Wing Area,* 161–62.

**Chapter 1**
1. R. Ernest DuPuy and Trevor N. DuPuy, *The Encyclopedia of Military History* (New York: Harper & Row, 1970), 533–53.
2. John A. Garraty and Peter Gay, eds., *The Columbia History of the World* (New York: Harper & Row, 1972), 575–80.
3. Warren Upham, *Minnesota in Three Centuries, 1655–1908,* vol. 1 (Mankato: Publishing Society of Minnesota, 1908), 127–46. Red Wing historian William M. Sweney Jr. in Franklyn Curtiss-Wedge, ed., *History of Goodhue County* (Chicago: H. C. Cooper Jr., 1909), 41–48, noted it unlikely the two Frenchmen came within 200 miles of Goodhue County.
4. Roy W. Meyer, *History of the Santee Sioux* (Lincoln: University of Nebraska Press, 1967), 6–9; Theodore C. Blegen, *Minnesota: A History of the State.* (St. Paul: University of Minnesota Press, 1975), 45–62; William W. Folwell, *A History of Minnesota,* vol. 1 (St. Paul: MHS, 1956 edition), 27–30.
5. Here and below, Meyer, 4, 10–11; Gary Clayton Anderson, *Little Crow, Spokesman for the Sioux* (St. Paul: MHS Press, 1986), 6, and *Kinsmen of Another Kind: Dakota-White Relations in the Upper Mississippi Valley, 1650–1862* (St. Paul: MHS Press, 1997 edition), 284 n; Upham, 104–05; Virginia Driving Hawk Sneve, *They Led a Nation* (Sioux Falls, S.Dak.: Brevet Press, 1975), 1.
6. This study uses *eastern Sioux* and *Dakota* interchangeably, as well as specific eastern Dakota tribal names—*Mdewakanton, Wahpekute, Wahpeton,* and *Sisseton.* The Mdewakanton dominated what would become Goodhue County. Over the centuries the word *Sioux* has lost some of its negative connotation, but as Virginia Driving Hawk Sneve wrote in *They Led a Nation* (p. 1), "Naturally the Sioux prefer their own traditional name of Dakota."
7. Douglas A. Birk and Judy Poseley, *The French at Lake Pepin: An Archaeological Survey for Fort Beauharnois,* MHS Project No. 4094 (St. Paul: MHS, 1977), 11–32; see also Louise Phelps Kellogg, "Fort Beauharnois," *Minnesota History* 8 (Sept. 1927): 243–44; Folwell, vol. 1, 1–38.
8. Here and below, Birk and Poseley, 11–32; Folwell, vol. 1, 43–52. See GCHS Oral History Collection for Mar. 10, 1987, interview with Birk.
9. DuPuy and DuPuy, 705–08; Folwell, vol. 1, 51–52.
10. Roy W. Meyer, "Who Was Red Wing?" unpublished 1964 manuscript in GCHS collections; Mark Diedrich, *Famous Chiefs of the Eastern Sioux* (Minneapolis: Coyote Books, 1987), 14–27, and "Red Wing, War Chief of the Mdewakanton Dakota," *Minnesota Archaeologist* 40 (March 1981): 19–32.
11. Joseph Woods Hancock, *Goodhue County, Minnesota, Past and Present* (Red Wing: Red Wing Printing, 1893), 78–79; C. A. Rasmussen, *A History of the City of Red Wing, Minnesota* (Red Wing: Self-published, 1934), 14; Diedrich, *Famous Chiefs of the Eastern Sioux,* 15.
12. Diedrich, *Famous Chiefs of the Eastern Sioux,* 16.
13. Thomas Anderson, "Captain T. G. Anderson's Journal," *Wisconsin Historical Collections* 9: 178, 197.
14. Mark Diedrich, "Red Wing, War Chief of the Mdewakanton Dakota," *The Minnesota Archaeologist* 40 (March 1981): 22–23; Gary Clayton Anderson, *Kinsmen of Another Kind: Dakota-White Relations in the Upper Mississippi Valley, 1650–1862* (St. Paul: MHS Press, 1997 edition), 72.
15. Gary Clayton Anderson, *Kinsmen of Another Kind,* 79–80; Diedrich, "Red Wing, War Chief of the Mdewakanton Dakota," 23–24.
16. Diedrich, *Famous Chiefs of the Eastern Sioux,* 18.
17. Donald Jackson, ed., *The Journals of Zebulon Pike* (Norman: University of Oklahoma Press, 1966), 34, 120–22, 263.
18. Here and below, Gary Clayton Anderson, *Kinsmen of Another Kind,* 66–68.
19. Diedrich, *Famous Chiefs of the Eastern Sioux,* 18–19. Diedrich believed Red Wing fought against the United States in 1812 because of his later comments to Indian Agent Lawrence Taliaferro — "I have been a fierce enemy to your nation, because I had bad advisers."
20. Ibid., 19.
21. DuPuy and DuPuy, 795.

22. Worthington *Daily Globe,* March 23, 1978, pp. 1, 4. Diedrich, *Famous Chiefs of the Eastern Sioux,* 14. See also Diedrich, "Red Wing, War Chief of the Mdewakanton Dakota," 27–28.
23. Robert Dickson to a British Officer at Fort George, June 10, 1812, Robert Dickson papers, MHS; Meyer, *History of the Santee Sioux,* 29 n. See also Louis A. Tohill, "Robert Dickson, British Trader on the Upper Mississippi: A Story of Trade, War, and Diplomacy" (Ph.D. diss., University of Minnesota, 1926), 101–02, copy at MHS.
24. Diedrich, *Famous Chiefs of the Eastern Sioux,* 20–21.
25. Thomas Anderson, "Captain T. G. Anderson's Journal," 197–98.
26. Here and below, Diedrich, "Red Wing, War Chief of the Mdewakanton Dakota," 27–30, and *Famous Chiefs of the Eastern Sioux,* 20–21; Gary Clayton Anderson, *Kinsmen of Another Kind,* 92; Edward P. Burch, "Geology of Red Wing," unpublished paper in GCHS Barn Bluff file; Meyer, *The Red Wing Indian Village,* GCHS, 6–7.
27. Gary Clayton Anderson, *Kinsmen of Another Kind,* 93–94.
28. Diedrich, "Red Wing, War Chief of the Mdewakanton Dakota," 30; Edward D. Neill, "Dakota Land and Dakota Life," *Minnesota Collections* 1: 263.
29. Diedrich, *Famous Chiefs of the Eastern Sioux,* 22.
30. Ibid.
31. Diedrich, "Red Wing: War Chief of the Mdewakanton Dakota," 30.
32. Diedrich, *Famous Chiefs of the Eastern Sioux,* 22–23.
33. Giacomo C. Beltrami, *A Pilgrimage in America,* vol. 2 of 2 (London: Hunt, 1828), 187.
34. Diedrich, *Famous Chiefs of the Eastern Sioux,* 23–24.
35. Rasmussen, 17. In May 1829, Taliaferro, who wrote that Red Wing was 84 at death, noted that 40 members of Red Wing's band traveled to Fort Snelling to inform him that their chief had died in early March. See Taliaferro Journal, March 5 and 20, April 15, and July 31, 1829, MHS. Hancock, *Goodhue County Past and Present,* 78–79.
36. Stephen Watts Kearny, "Journal of Stephen Watts Kearny," *Missouri Historical Collections* 3 (1908): 100–01, 112.
37. Meyer, *The Red Wing Indian Village,* 20–31.
38. Neill, 263–64.
39. Samuel W. Pond, *The Dakota or Sioux in Minnesota as They Were in 1834* (St. Paul: MHS Press, reprint 1986), 31–34; Meyer, *The Red Wing Village,* 25–26.
40. Pond, 34–36, 71.
41. David Humphrey to Dear Friends, July 9, 1855, David W. Humphrey Papers, MHS.
42. Ruth Landes, *The Mystic Lake Sioux: Sociology of the Mdewakantonwan Santee* (Madison: University of Wisconsin, 1968), 96–104; Gary Clayton Anderson, *Little Crow: Spokesman for the Sioux,* 15–17.
43. Meyer, *The Red Wing Indian Village,* 29–30; Landes, 40–42, 128–31.
44. Pond, 37–39: Hancock, *Goodhue County Past and Present,* 79–88.
45. Meyer, *The Red Wing Indian Village,* 26; Pond, *Dakotas . . . as They Were in 1834,* 62–63, 134–35.
46. Here and below, Pond, 26–29, 39–49, 45–47, 140–42; Meyer, *History of the Santee Sioux,* 20–21, 58–65.
47. Pond, 141.

**Chapter 2**
1. Rasmussen, *A History of the City of Red Wing,* 17–19; Diedrich, *Famous Chiefs of the Eastern Sioux,* 25; Lawrence Taliaferro Journals, July 31, 1829, MHS. Taliaferro noted the date of Red Wing's death in a letter he provided Wakute on May 17, 1829, recognizing him as the new leader of the Red Wing band. See GCHS photo collections, Historic Sites and Indians, for a copy of the document.
2. Sweney in Curtiss-Wedge, ed., *History of Goodhue County,* 132–33; Diedrich, 25. Taliaferro wrote in Taliaferro Journals, August 8, 1830, MHS: "He [Iron Cloud] wishes to be recognized as chief in place of Wahcoota. I told him in plain terms that I would have nothing to do or say in the matter in dispute between them." Riggs in "Dakota Portraits," *Minnesota Collections* 2: 517–20, provided a fairly complete look at Iron Cloud in his review of Dakota leaders. Wakute's name bears several spellings in the historic record. *Wacouta,* a more Anglicized spelling and pronunciation of his name, later came into common usage in Goodhue County.
3. Diedrich, 25; Meyer, *The Red Wing Village,* 13–15; Meyer, *The Red Wing Village,* 15.
4. Gary Clayton Anderson, *Kinsmen of Another Kind,* 155.

5. Here and below, Madeline Angell and Mary C. Miller, *Joseph Woods Hancock: The Life and Times of a Minnesota Pioneer* (Minneapolis: Dillon Press, 1980), 3; Meyer, *The Red Wing Village,* 15–17, and *History of the Santee Sioux,* 60–65; Rasmussen, 27–31; Charles M. Gates, "The Lac Qui Parle Mission," *Minnesota History* 16 (June 1935): 142–43.

6. Here and below, Meyer, *The Red Wing Village,* 16–17.

7. Angell and Miller, 1–4, 8.

8. John F. Aiton to Mary Hunter (later his wife), Feb. 20 and May 18 and 28, 1848, Aiton and Family Papers, MHS. See Patricia C. Harpole and Mary D. Nagel, eds., *Minnesota Territorial Census, 1850* (St. Paul: MHS, 1972), 73, for listing of her name.

9. Quotation from Maria Hancock's diary entry for June 13, 1849, Hancock file, GCHS; Angell and Miller, *Joseph Woods Hancock,* 3.

10. Angell and Miller, 2, 28–29; T. S. Williamson to S. L. Pomroy, Sept. 30, 1850, American Board of Commissioners for Foreign Missions Papers (hereafter ABCFM Papers), MHS. Williamson carefully explained his version of the Aiton problem to Reverend Pomroy, noting his surprise that "Brother Aiton states he was highly displeased with the decision [regarding salary policies] of the mission." Williamson indicated that Aiton was not fully candid in telling the other American Board missionaries of his reasons for wanting to leave Red Wing.

11. Quote from Aiton's account dated Sept. 3,1849, in *Annual Report of the Commissioner of Indian Affairs, 1849–1850* (Washington, D.C.: Office of Commissioner of Indian Affairs, 1850), 126; Aiton to Rev. gentlemen and Lay Members of the Sioux Mission, Oct. 5, 1849, John F. Aiton and Family Papers, MHS. Angell and Miller, *Joseph Woods Hancock,* 29–31, 73, 76.

12. Joseph W. Hancock, "Missionary Work at Red Wing, 1849–1852," *Minnesota Collections* 10: 168–69, and in *Annual Report of the Commissioner of Indian Affairs, 1850,* 82; Angell and Miller, 29–31; Meyer, *The Red Wing Village,* 19.

13. Hancock to Reverend S. B. Treat, June 23, 1852, and March (n.d.) 1853, ABCFM Papers, MHS; Hancock, *Goodhue County Past and Present,* 79, 87–88.

14. The original "Temperance Pledge" still exists; see the Aiton Papers, dated April 30, 1849.

15. Here and below, Rasmussen, *A History of the City of Red Wing,* 34: Hancock, *Minnesota Collections* 10: 174–76; *History of Goodhue County* (Red Wing, Minn.: Wood, Alley, 1878), 220–21 (hereafter Wood, Alley).

16. Angell and Miller, 70–73, 82–83.

17. Hancock to Rev. S. B. Treat, Sept. 13, 1852, ABCFM Papers; Meyer, *History of the Santee Sioux,* 68; "Mahpeya Maza, or Iron Cloud," GCHS, 4–5; Angell and Miller, 45–46. See John Aiton to wife, Mary, May 4, 1849, John F. Aiton and Family Papers, MHS, for an account of his long talk with Iron Cloud. See also Meyer, *History of the Santee Sioux,* 58, for a discussion of another terrible killer—smallpox.

18. Francis Sampson biography, GCHS biography files.

19. Meyer, *Santee Sioux,* 72–73.

20. Folwell, vol. 1, 241–48, 352; Harpole and Nagle, eds., vii–viii. June Drenning Holmquist, ed., *They Chose Minnesota: A Survey of the State's Ethnic Groups* (St. Paul: MHS Press, 1981), 8; Return I. Holcombe, *Minnesota as a Territory,* vol. 2 of *Minnesota in Three Centuries, 1655–1908* (Mankato: Publishing Society of Minnesota, 1908), 431.

21. Here and below, Folwell, vol. 1, 266–304; Meyer, *Santee Sioux,* 72–87; Hancock, *Minnesota Collections* 10: 177.

22. Lucile M. Kane, "The Sioux Treaties and the Traders," *Minnesota History* 32 (June 1951): 75–77; Meyer, *Santee Sioux,* 81.

23. Anderson, 61–62.

24. Rasmussen, 18–19.

25. Anderson, 62–63; Meyer, *Santee Sioux,* 83; Curtiss-Wedge, ed., 80.

26. Wood, Alley, 205–06; Meyer, *The Red Wing Village,* 33. Wakute referred to a strip of land near present-day Pine Island. It contained tall white pines and heavy growth of hardwod timber and was bordered by the Zumbro River and surrounding hills. The Mdewakanton wintered there, using the hills and timber as shelter from storms while hunting game in the forest. Curtiss-Wedge, ed., 202.

27. Holcombe, vol. 2, 308–16; Anderson, 63–64; Folwell, vol. 1, 285–86. In regard to the Indian refusal to sign traders' papers, the traders were aware that the Indians had been "meddled with" but didn't know what they could do about it. See Kane, "The Sioux Treaties and the Traders," *Minnesota History* 32 (June 1951): 77.

28. Anderson, 65–66; Meyer *Santee Sioux,* 84–86.

29. Meyer, *Santee Sioux,* 84–85; Wood, Alley, 218–19.
30. Anderson, 66–69; Folwell, vol. 1, 297–99, 462–70. Roger Kennedy, *Men on the Moving Frontier* (Palo Alto: American West Publishing, 1969), 39, 57, provided a more critical review of Ramsey's motivations.
31. Kennedy, 51–52.
32. Meyer, *Santee Sioux,* 87.

**Chapter 3**
1. Wood, Alley, *History of Goodhue County,* 206–08, 216–17.
2. Ibid., 216–17; Angell and Miller, *Joseph Woods Hancock,* 105.
3. Wood, Alley, 208; Angell and Miller, 85–86.
4. Joseph W. Hancock to Rev. S. B. Treat, March 1853, ABCFM Papers, MHS.
5. Here and below, Meyer, *The Red Wing Village,* 34; Angell and Miller, 100.
6. Hancock, *Goodhue County Past and Present,* 95. See also Gary Clayton Anderson, *Kinsmen of Another Kind,* 204, for more on the growing pressure on the Mdewakanton to move.
7. Meyer, History of the Santee Sioux, 88–90.
8. Joseph W. Hancock to Rev. S. B. Treat, June 14, 1853, ABCFM Papers, MHS.
9. Joseph W. Hancock to Rev. S. B. Treat, March (n.d.) 1853 and June 23, 1852, ABCFM Papers.
10. Curtiss-Wedge, ed., *History of Goodhue County,* 87–88.
11. Rev. S. B. Treat to Joseph Hancock, May 7, 1853, ABCFM Papers.
12. Folwell, *A History of Minnesota,* vol. 1, 354–57; Wood, Alley, 237–39.
13. In the words of historian Daniel J. Boorstin, "The Western "squatter" was usually the actual first settler, the preemptor, the man who had got there first." See Daniel J. Boorstin, *The Americans: The National Experience* (New York: Random House, 1965), 74. The Ramsey quotation is from Folwell, vol. 1, 355.
14. Holmquist, ed., *They Chose Minnesota,* 254.
15. Curtiss-Wedge, ed., 97–98; Wood, Alley, 237–39.
16. George S. Hage, *Newspapers on the Minnesota Frontier, 1849–1860* (St. Paul: MHS, 1967), 34–39.
17. *Minnesota Pioneer,* Jan. 16, 1851; Mary Wheelhouse Berthel, *Horns of Thunder: The Life and Times of James M. Goodhue Including Selections from His Writings* (St. Paul: MHS, 1948), 65.
18. Berthel, 63–72; Hage, 26–38.
19. Hage, 39.
20. See Roy W. Meyer, "The Discontinued Post Offices and Ghost Towns of Goodhue County," GCHS unpublished manuscript, Dec. 1967, 90–92; Hancock, *Goodhue County Past and Present,* 101–03.
21. Grace Lee Nute, "The Lore of Old Frontenac," speech given to 1939 State Historical Convention, quoted in *Minnesota History* 20 (Sept. 1939): 307; Christian A. Rasmussen, "James Wells," undated paper, *GCHS,* Frontenac file.
22. Holcombe, *Minnesota in Three Centuries,* 436–38, 441–42; Nute, "The Lore of Old Frontenac," 307; Rasmussen, "James Wells," GCHS biography file; Joseph Hancock, *History of Goodhue County,* 103.
23. Here and below, St. Paul *Pioneer Press,* Aug. 3, 1997; Folwell, vol. 1, 358–59. Theodore C. Blegen, "The Fashionable Tour," *Minnesota History* 20 (Dec. 1939): 384; Russell Blakeley, *Minnesota Collections* 8: 395–401, included a comprehensive tour passenger list, 397–99.
24. Curtiss-Wedge, ed., 98–99.
25. John G. Rice in Holmquist, ed., *They Chose Minnesota,* 55–58; Folwell, vol. 1, 359–60.
26. Holmquist, ed., 57 and table 3.1, 58.
27. See Holmquist, ed., 55; Carleton C. Qualey, "Some National Groups in Minnesota," *Minnesota History* 31 (March 1950): 18–21.
28. Folwell, vol. 1, 358–59.
29. Here and below, David Humphrey to Dear Friends, June 23 and July 9, 1855, David W. Humphrey Papers, MHS.
30. David Humphrey to Dear Friends, June 23, 1855.
31. Boorstin, *The Americans: The National Experience,* 77.
32. Carmen Johnson, "Village of Dennison," 1993 manuscript, Dennison file, GCHS.
33. Levi Hillman to Mary Hillman, May 17 and May 25, 1856, Levi Colburn Hillman and Family Papers, MHS.

34. Here and below, Helen Rudd Bunch to Mother in Michigan, May 12, 1856, in *Goodhue County Historical News* 18 (March 1984).
35. Here and below, Thomas P. Kellett, "A Brief Account of the Early Experiences of the Strafford Western Emigration Co. in Founding Zumbrota, Minn. Written by the Organizer," MHS; Wood, Alley, 474–76.
36. *Zumbrota: The First 100 Years* (Zumbrota: Centennial Book Committee, 1953), 23.
37. Holmquist, ed., *They Chose Minnesota,* 58–59.
38. S. O. Swenson, "Pioneers of Minneola Town," Zumbrota *News,* April 14, 1939.
39. Theodore L. Nydahl, "The Early Norwegian Settlement of Goodhue County, Minnesota" (master's thesis, University of Minnesota, 1929), 2. Nydahl quotes Hjalmer Holand in *De Norske Settlementers Historie* (Ephriam, Wis.: Self-published, 1908) in reference to the major Norwegian settlements: "Wisconsin Has Its Koshkonong, Minnesota Its Goodhue County, and Iowa Its Winneshiek." Holmquist, ed., 220–21.
40. Carlton C. Qualey, "Pioneer Norwegian Settlement," *Minnesota History* 12 (Sept. 1931): 266; Holmquist, ed., 221.
41. Lewis Lars Larson Reminiscences, MHS.
42. Harold B. Kildahl Sr. and Erling E. Kildahl, eds., *Westward We Came* (Orlando: Self-published, 1991), 2–8, MHS.
43. Nydahl, 27–28; Harold Severson, *We Give You Kenyon* (Kenyon: Self-published, 1976), 8–10; Wood, Alley, 461–73.
44. Nydahl, "The Early Norwegian Settlement of Goodhue County, Minnesota," 23–24, has original research but also cites Holand. Olive Ringdahl, the daughter of Mathias and Ingeborg Ringdahl, related stories of the first Norwegian settlers in Zumbrota *News,* July 5, 1940. See also Hancock, *Goodhue County Past and Present,* 308–13, and Curtiss-Wedge, ed., 220–22.
45. Ringdahl, Zumbrota *News,* July 5, 1940.
46. Qualey, "Pioneer Norwegian Settlement," 270–71. He also noted that in Wanamingo Township there were only two persons who were not Norwegian.
47. Carl Roos, "Vasa, Goodhue County, Minnesota: The First Settlers," Ernest B. Gustafson, trans., Feb. 1, 1877, Carl Roos Papers, 1–3, GCHS; Erik Norelius, *Vasa Illustrata,* Ethel Collins, trans. (Rock Island, Ill.: Augustana Book Concern, 1905), 190–92.
48. Roos, "Vasa," 8.
49. Hans Mattson, *The Story of an Emigrant* (St. Paul: D. D. Merrill, 1891), 2–3; Roos, "Vasa," 3–5.
50. Here and below, Roos, "Vasa," 6–20; Curtiss-Wedge, ed., 358.
51. Mattson, 35–40; Curtiss-Wedge, ed., 355–56.
52. Norelius, 190; Alf Aberg, *A Concise History of Sweden,* Gordon Elliott, trans. (Kristianstad: Kristianstads Boktryckeri, 1985), 31–32; Curtiss-Wedge, ed., 356.
53. Norelius, 192; Melvin Voxland, "Voxland Viking Saga: Tordal and Hafslo, Norway, to Holden-Kenyon, Minnesota," 1980 manuscript, 16, copy at GCHS.
54. Lilly Setterdahl, *Minnesota Swedes: The Emigration from Trolle Ljungby to Goodhue County 1855–1912* (East Moline: American Friends of the Emigrant Institute of Sweden, 1996), 78–81.
55. Ibid., 173–75.
56. Ibid., 180–81.
57. Holmquist, ed., 13 n.
58. Ibid., 108. See also Rice in Holmquist, ed., 261.
59. Here and below, Roos, "Vasa," 24–25. For more on mosquito onslaughts, see Curtiss-Wedge, ed., 462–63. David Humphrey in Humphrey to Dear Friends, July 20, 1855, David W. Humphrey Papers, MHS.
60. Holmquist, ed., see chapters 6 through 13 for overviews of immigration from northern and western Europe.
61. DuPuy and DuPuy, *The Encyclopedia of Military History,* 829–37; Holmquist, ed., 153. For a detailed discussion of this issue, see Hildegard Binder Johnson, "The Distribution of German Pioneer Population in Minnesota," *Rural Sociology* 6 (March 1941), reprint at MHS.
62. F. W. Kalfahs in Curtiss-Wedge, ed., 368–70.
63. Here and below, John W. Tubbesing Papers, translated copies in MHS.
64. Hildegard B. Johnson, "Factors Influencing the Distribution of the German Pioneer Population in Minnesota," *Agricultural History* 19 (Jan. 1945): 39–57; F. W. Kalfahs in Curtiss-Wedge, ed., 370.
65. Here and below, Arnold Schrier, *Ireland and the American Emigration, 1850–1900* (Minneapolis 1958): 18–42, 105–09; Holmquist, ed., 130–31.

66. James P. Shannon, *Catholic Colonization on the Western Frontier* (New Haven: Yale University Press, 1957), 3–53. See Chapter 3, "The Catholic Plan for Minnesota." Eric Foner and John A. Garraty, eds., *The Reader's Companion to American History* (Boston: Houghton Mifflin, 1991), 622, 779–81; Peter Quinn, "The Tragedy of Bridget Such-A-One," *American Heritage* 48 (Dec. 1997): 39. Livia Appel and Theodore C. Blegen, "Official Encouragement of Immigration to Minnesota during the Territorial Period," *Minnesota History* 5 (Aug. 1923): 188.

67. Margaret Hutcheson, "Irish Catholics in Goodhue County," *Goodhue County Historical News* 17 (Nov. 1983): 3–5.

68. Here and below, Hancock, *Goodhue County Past and Present*, 250–53; Richard Heaney, "Belle Creek Irish Settlement," unpublished, undated paper, GCHS biography files; W. H. Mitchell, *Geographical and Statistical Sketch of the Past and Present of Goodhue County: Together with a General View of the State of Minnesota* (Minneapolis: O. S. King, 1869), 89–92; Curtiss-Wedge, ed., 1053–54.

69. Hutcheson, "Irish Catholics in Goodhue County," 4. See also Kathryn Ericson, ed., *Map of Goodhue County Minnesota, 1877* [reprint of Warner & Foote's 1877 county map] (Red Wing: GCHS, 1991), 11, 35.

70. Heaney, "Belle Creek Irish Settlement," 3–4; Margaret Hutcheson, "Luxembourg Catholics in Belvidere," *Goodhue County Historical News* 17 (Nov. 1983): 5.

71. Here and below, William W. Sweney, in Wood, Alley, 230–31; Curtiss-Wedge, ed., 93–96; Folwell, vol. 2, 400–15.

72. Sweney, in Wood, Alley, 231.

73. Here and below, Holmquist, ed., 1, 12 n. 1, 232–33, 245 n. 30. See also Setterdahl, 145–47. Lars Goran Tedebrand, "Those Who Returned: Remigration from America to Sweden," in Nils Hasselmo, ed., *Perspectives on Swedish Immigration* (Chicago: Swedish Pioneer Historical Society, 1978), 88–98.

74. Qualey, "Pioneer Norwegian Settlement," 271; Nydahl, "Early Norwegian Settlement of Goodhue County," 36–37.

75. David Humphrey to Dear Friends, July 20, 1855, David W. Humphrey Papers, MHS; Ruby G. Karstad, *"The New York Tribune* and the Minnesota Frontier," *Minnesota History* 17 (Dec. 1936): 415–16; James M. Page Diary, 1858, March 30, 1859, entry, MHS. The Page diary is cataloged at MHS with the year 1858, but Page crossed out the last figure (8) in 1858 and replaced it with a 9. The diary, which includes many indecipherable passages and long stretches without any comment, has entries listing the year as 1859.

76. Mary Hillman to Levi Hillman, June 27, 1856, and Levi Hillman to Mary Hillman, July 4, 1856, Levi Colburn Hillman and Family Letters, 1822–1861, MHS.

77. John Tubbesing to relatives, letter marked "Red Wing, 1866," John W. Tubbesing Papers, MHS; Swen Olson to family in Sweden, Nov. or Dec. 14, 1855, in Setterdahl, *Minnesota Swedes,* 175. The original Olson letters are in the Svenska Emigrantinstitutet in Vaxjo, Sweden.

78. For overviews of early immigration and its continuing influence, see "Yankees in Goodhue County," *Goodhue County Historical News* 22 (July 1988), and "Century Farms," *Goodhue County Historical News* 29 (Winter 1995). See also Jacob Hodnefield, "A Danish Visitor of the Seventies," *Minnesota History* 10 (Dec. 1929): 416–17.

**Chapter 4**

1. Wood, Alley, *History of Goodhue County*, 413; Holmquist, ed., *They Chose Minnesota,* 254.

2. Nydahl, "The Early Norwegian Settlement of Goodhue County," 26–27; Rasmussen, *A History of Goodhue County*, 201; Hancock, *Goodhue County Past and Present,* 314.

3. Lucius F. Hubbard, "Early Days in Goodhue County," *Minnesota Collections* 12: 154. Hubbard founded the Red Wing *Republican*. He later gained fame as a Civil War hero and became the ninth governor of Minnesota.

4. Wood, Alley, 413–14. David Hancock was the older brother of the early missionary Joseph Hancock. Philander Sanford, a Red Wing lawyer, served as secretary of the group, and a county commissioner, the Rev. Resin Spates, served as assistant secretary.

5. Here and below, *Annual Report of the Commissioner of Indian Affairs, 1849–1850* (Washington: 1850), 81–82; Minnesota Historical Records Survey, *Inventory of the County Archives of Minnesota, No. 25, Goodhue County, Red Wing* (St. Paul: The Survey, 1941), 11–12. Hancock, *Goodhue County Past and Present,* 119–24. See also Gary Clayton Anderson, *Kinsmen of Another Kind,* 150–56.

6. Curtiss-Wedge, ed., *History of Goodhue County*, 90–91. For more on vigilance clubs, see Boorstin, *The Americans: The National Experience,* 72–78.

7. William C. Christianson, "The Land Office and the Banks," *Goodhue County Historical News* 12 (Feb. 1978): 1–2. Phelps and Graham were later mayors of Red Wing. On May 13, 1857, Phelps became a member of the House of Representatives from Minnesota following a contentious House debate. Minnesota had sent Phelps and two other men to Congress, only to find the territory's bid for statehood bogged down by political maneuvering. See Folwell, *History of Minnesota,* vol. 2, 9–19, for an overview of the controversy involving Minnesota statehood and Phelps.

8. Here and below, Hancock, 122–24. See also Minnesota Historical Records Survey, *Inventory of the County Archives . . . Goodhue County,* 12.

9. Hancock, *Goodhue County Past and Present,* 331–32.

10. Swenson, *Pioneers of Minneola Town,* 3–6.

11. Severson, *We Give You Kenyon,* 7. Curtiss-Wedge, ed., 155–56; Meyer, "The Discontinued Post Offices and Ghost Towns of Goodhue County," 37–38.

12. Edward J. Letterman, *Farming in Early Minnesota* (St. Paul: Ramsey County Historical Society, 1966), 3.

13. Nydahl, 39–40.

14. Lettermann, 11–13; Nydahl, 40–41; Rasmussen, 51; Hancock, *Goodhue County Past and Present,* 58.

15. Levi Hillman to Mary Hillman, June 1, 1856, Levi Colburn Hillman and Family Papers, MHS.

16. Nodland, "Farm Life among the Early Norwegian Settlers in Minnesota with Particular Reference to Goodhue County," 4–6; Rasmussen, 53; Nydahl, 36–37.

17. Lettermann, 52–53; Nodland, 10; Rasmussen, 51–53; Lettermann, 22–23, 39.

18. Hancock, 67–68.

19. Boorstin, *The Americans: The Democratic Experience,* 19–20.

20. Karstad, "The New York Tribune and the Minnesota Frontier," *Minnesota History* 17 (Dec. 1936): 415–16.

21. Ole E. Rolvaag became chair of the Department of Norwegian Language and Literature at St. Olaf College in 1906. See Merrill E. Jarchow, *Private Liberal Arts Colleges in Minnesota* (St. Paul: MHS, 1973), 84–86.

22. Nydahl, 37–38; Rasmussen, 55. Nydahl cited Ingrebrikt F. Grose, "A Pioneer Boy's Experience in a Corner of Goodhue County," *Jul I Vesterheimen* (1919): 31.

23. David W. Humphrey to Dear Friends," July 9, 1855, David W. Humphrey Papers, MHS.

24. Bicentennial Heritage Committee, *Chronicles of Cannon Falls* (Cannon Falls, Minn.: Cannon Falls *Beacon,* 1976), 15; Wood, Alley, 595; Rasmussen, 191–92. Charles Parks, a 26-year-old lawyer and later the first president of Cannon Falls village, described the burial of Mrs. Season and her child. The child lay on her mother's chest as the two were buried together. A group of mourners, largely male, looked on, making no effort "to hide their tears."

25. Bicentennial Heritage Committee, 15; Wood, Alley, 631.

26. *Holden through One Hundred Years, 1856–1956* (Holden: Holden Lutheran Church, 1956), 69.

27. Glenda Riley, *The Female Frontier: A Comparative View of Women on the Prairie and the Plains* (Lawrence: University Press, 1988), 14–22; Anne B. Webb, "Forgotten Persephones: Women Farmers on the Frontier," *Minnesota History* 50 (Winter 1986): 135.

28. Here and below, Kenneth M. Stampp, *America in 1857: A Nation on the Brink* (New York: Oxford University Press, 1990), 213–18.

29. Folwell, vol. 1, 362–63; Stampp, 218; Karstad, 412.

30. Stampp, 218; Holcombe, *Minnesota in Three Centuries,* vol. 2, 508.

31. Mattson, 52–53.

32. Folwell, vol. 1, 363–64.

33. Mattson, 53–54.

34. Albert C. Johnson, "Panic of 1857," *Chronicles of Cannon Falls,* 24.

35. Kellett, "A Brief Account . . . Founding Zumbrota," 3; Rasmussen, 218.

36. Hubbard, "Early Days in Goodhue County," *Minnesota Collections,* 12: 15–59.

37. Carmen M. Johnson, *The Days of Dennison: A History of a Small Village in Southern Minnesota* (Dennison, Minn.: Self-published, 1992), 5–6, quoting B. Lampson to Dear Aunt, March 21, 1858.

38. Karstad, 417.

39. Ibid., 461.

40. Holcombe, vol. 2, 513.

**Chapter 5**

1. Allan Nevins, *The Emergence of Lincoln: Douglas, Buchanan, and Party Chaos 1857–1859* (New York: Charles Scribner's Sons, 1950), 90–95; Stampp, *America in 1857,* 100.
2. H. M. Rice to W. H. Welch, Jan. 15, 1858, Abraham E. Welch and Family Papers, MHS.
3. Folwell, *A History of Minnesota*, vol. 2, 10–11.
4. Ibid., 16–17.
5. Bruce White, et al., *Minnesota Votes: Election Returns by County for Presidents, Senators, Congressmen, and Governors, 1857–1977* (St. Paul: MHS, 1977), 65; Folwell, vol. 2, 18.
6. Goodhue County *Republican*, April 26, 1861; Hancock 140–42; Curtiss-Wedge, ed., *History of Goodhue County*, 507–08; Grace Lee Nute, *In Hamline Halls, 1854–1954* (St. Paul: Hamline University, 1954), 56.
7. James A Wright, "The Story of Company F, First Regiment," unpublished manuscript, MHS, 210; Nute, 63–64.
8. Richard Moe, *The Last Full Measure: The Life and Death of the First Minnesota Volunteers* (New York: Henry Holt, 1993), 11–12; Curtiss-Wedge, ed., 520–21; Nute, 56; Hancock, 161; Wright, 74.
9. Goodhue County *Republican*, May 10, 1861. Leading the new Red Wing unit were A. D. Whitney, captain, and Edward L. Baker, first lieutenant.
10. Wright, 11.
11. Ibid., 19, 22–24.
12. Goodhue County *Republican,* May 10, 1861.
13. Moe, 28–31; Wright, 34.
14. John Quinn Imholte, *The First Volunteers* (Minneapolis: Ross & Haines, 1963), 47–49; Wright, 36.
15. Moe, 47–64; William Colvill, "Bull Run: Address to Survivors at the Reunion of the First Minnesota," June 21, 1877, MHS. Another Colvill account of the battle at Bull Run is in William Lochren, "Narrative of the First Regiment," *Minnesota in the Civil and Indian Wars, 1861–1865,* vol. 1, 9–11.
16. Nute, 55–58; Amos Scofield diary, July 21,1861, quoted in undated newspaper article, GCHS "Scofield Brothers" biography file; Goodhue County *Republican*, July 26, 1861.
17. Nute, 57.
18. Lochren, "Narrative of the First Regiment," vol. 1, 11.
19. Rasmussen, *A History of Red Wing*, 70–71; Goodhue County *Republican*, Sept. 20, 1861; Wood, Alley, *History of Goodhue County*, 291.
20. Gen. Christopher C. Andrews, "Narrative of the Third Regiment," in *Minnesota in the Civil and Indian Wars*, vol. 1, 151–58.
21. Ibid.
22. Andrews, "Narrative of the Third Regiment," 157–58. See also *Minnesota in the Civil and Indian Wars,* vol. 2, 116–24, 178, and Folwell, vol. 2, 92–94.
23. Hans Mattson to Dear Wife (Cherstin), July 25, 1862, Hans Mattson and Family Papers, MHS.
24. David Humphrey to Dear Friends," July 20, 1855, David W. Humphrey papers, MHS.
25. Gary Clayton Anderson, *Little Crow: Spokesman for the Sioux*, 89–134. This author believes the Wakute mentioned was the son of the first Wakute, the man who led the Red Wing band to the Minnesota River territory. The first Wakute died in 1858, according to the Wood, Alley *History of Goodhue County*, an account Meyer, "The Red Wing Village," 35, believes "plausible." In June 15, 1868, the second Wakute told the Indian Peace Commission he had been chief for ten years. See *Papers Relating to Talks and Councils Held with the Indians in Dakota and Montana Territories in the Years 1866–1869* (Washington, D.C.: Government Printing Office, 1910), 94. A contemporary account by Mrs. J. E. Decamp Sweet notes that Wakute and his *mother* helped whites during the Dakota wars in 1862, *Minnesota Collections*, 6: 358–63. DeCamp lived near Wakute's village. The St. Paul *Daily Globe* (Aug. 27, 1880, p. 1) reported that "Wa-ku-ta" died "recently" at the Santee Agency in Nebraska.
26. Return I. Holcombe, "Big Eagle's Story of the Sioux Outbreak of 1862," *Minnesota Collections* 6: 384.
27. Kenneth Carley, *The Sioux Uprising of 1862* (St. Paul: MHS, 1976), 10–16; Anderson, 71–73, 116–18, 130–34; Folwell, vol. 2, 109–11.
28. Anderson, 132.
29. Folwell, vol. 2, 109–24.

30. Here and below, "Mrs. J. E. DeCamp Sweet's Narrative," 358–63; Gary Clayton Anderson and Alan R. Woolworth, eds., *Through Dakota Eyes: Narrative Accounts of the Minnesota Indian War of 1862* (St. Paul: MHS, 1988), 87–91. Wabasha noted in 1868 that he immediately "sent word" to Wakute, who had not yet heard an uprising had begun. See *Papers Relating to Talks and Councils Held with the Indians . . . "* June 15, 1868, 90–91.

31. "Mrs. J. E. DeCamp Sweet's Narrative," 363.

32. Anderson and Woolworth, eds., 154.

33. Folwell, vol. 2, 109–46; Carley, 21–52.

34. "Reminiscences of Mrs. A. F. Andersen [1927]," A. F. Andersen family papers, GCHS biography files. The Andersen interview is from Frances Densmore, "Interviews with Early Red Wing Pioneers," Frances Densmore Papers, MHS. Cleng J. Dale's account from Curtiss-Wedge, ed., 335–36, in error, gives the year of the attack as 1852 instead of 1862. No "pioneer" settlements existed in that part of the county in 1852.

35. *Minnesota in the Civil and Indian Wars,* vol. 1, 304–11; Folwell, vol. 2, 147–56.

36. Maj. Gen. John Pope to Col. H. H. Sibley, Sept. 17, 1862, in *Minnesota in the Civil and Indian Wars,* vol. 2, 234–35.

37. Here and below, Folwell, vol. 2, 174–78; Henry Sibley, "Battle of Wood Lake," in *Minnesota in the Civil and Indian Wars,* vol. 2, 240–43, and E. T. Chaplin's account, 244–47. See also Hubbard and Holcombe, *Minnesota in Three Centuries,* vol. 3, 401–07.

38. Undated newspaper clipping, in Harry W. Wilson family history, GCHS; Hubbard and Holcombe, *Minnesota in Three Centuries,* vol. 3:403–06.

39. Folwell, vol. 2, 183–85.

40. Ibid., vol. 2, 182–85, 191.

41. Carley, 67–75; Folwell, "The Punishment of the Sioux," in vol. 2. 190–211.

42. Wright, "The Story of Company F, " 255, 269, 357.

43. Anne A. Hage, "The Battle of Gettysburg as Seen by Minnesota Soldiers," *Minnesota History* 38 (June 1963): 245–57.

44. Moe, 260.

45. Ibid., 266.

46. William Colvill, "The Old First at Gettysburg," Minneapolis *Tribune,* July 28, 1884. Hancock's words to Colvill are in a letter written by Colvill to John R. Bachelder, June 9, 1886. See Harry W. Pfanz, *Gettysburg: The Second Day* (Chapel Hill: University of North Carolina Press, 1987), 410–11.

47. Moe, 266–69, 296–97; Pfanz, 410–14.

48. Colvill, "The Old First at Gettysburg"; Pfanz, 411.

49. Colvill, "The Old First at Gettysburg."

50. Pfanz, 411–12. There have been questions about the casualty figures of the First Minnesota at Gettysburg. Both Moe (p.275) and Pfanz (p. 414) reported 215 wounded and killed, or 82 percent of those in the action. Folwell discussed the issue in vol. 2: 450–52 (Appendix 17). He believed that the casualty figures for the unit's two days of battle were consolidated. Thus, the report of 215 casualties during the July 2 charge seemed high. A Minnesota researcher concluded that, at most, 179 were killed and wounded during the battle, a casualty rate of 68 percent (see Moe, 275 n).

51. Wright, 599–600.

52. Ibid., 603.

53. Edwin B. Coddington, *The Gettysburg Campaign: A Study in Command* (New York: Charles Scribner's Sons, 1968), 493, 502–12; Moe, 286–88.

54. Lochren, "Narrative of the First Regiment," vol. 1, 37–38; Wright, "The Story of Company F," 610–12; Moe, 287–89.

55. Wright, 610, 615.

56. Ibid., 614, 616.

57. Ibid., 616.

58. Folwell, vol. 2, 311.

59. Wright, "The Story of Company F," 873–74. Wright soon moved away from Goodhue County but became the historian of Company F. He wrote in the preface to his 875-page manuscript: "May I also express the hope that the boys and girls of Red Wing, and Goodhue County, will try to get interested in what I write."

60. Moe, 309–10.

61. Lucius F. Hubbard, *Minnesota in the Civil and Indian Wars,* vol. 1, 260–82.

62. Abraham E. Welch and Family Papers, MHS. Rasmussen, *A History of Red Wing*, 77; Andrews, *Minnesota in the Civil and Indian Wars*, vol. 2, 343.
63. Dr. A. C. Wedge, *Minnesota in the Civil and Indian Wars*, vol. 1, 174–75 n.
64. Albert Marshall, "Roster of Men From Goodhue County Who Enlisted in the Civil War," unpublished manuscript, GCHS. Chauncey Hobart, chaplain of the Third Regiment, noted a measles outbreak during the winter of 1861–62 that affected 190 men, killing six, in *Recollections of My Life: Fifty Years of Itinerancy in the Northwest* (Red Wing: Red Wing Printing, 1885), 315.
65. C. T. Taylor, "Goodhue County in the Civil War," copy of Taylor's speech given at GCHS meeting, Nov. 4, 1929, GCHS, p. 10.
66. Rasmussen, *A History of Goodhue County*, 85–87; Hubbard and Holcombe, *Minnesota in Three Centuries*, vol. 3, 215; Rasmussen, *A History of Red Wing*, 238–39.
67. Moe, 313. On June 12, 1905, Colvill died in his sleep at age 78. He was attending a regimental reunion in St. Paul at the time.

## Chapter 6
1. Hancock, *Goodhue County Past and Present*, 159–61; *Zumbrota: The First 100 Years,* 31–32.
2. Nodland, "Farm Life among the Early Norwegian Settlers in Minnesota with Particular Reference to Goodhue County," 10–11; Nydahl, *The Early Norwegian Settlement of Goodhue County*, 41; Folwell, *A History of Minnesota*, vol. 3, 1.
3. John Jordan in Hancock, 132–35.
4. Alan Nevins, *The War for the Union: War Becomes Revolution, 1862–1863* (New York: Charles Scribner's Sons, 1960), 462–66.
5. Rasmussen, *A History of Goodhue County*, 86–87; Hancock, *Goodhue County Past and Present*, 279, 318 (Walter and Johanna Doyle of Belle Creek sent four sons into the military service during the Civil War. A fifth paid for a substitute, p. 252).
6. C. T. Taylor, "Goodhue County in the Civil War," unpublished paper, Nov. 4, 1929, GCHS.
7. Here and below, Wood, Alley, *History of Goodhue County,* 500–02, 596, 624; Curtiss–Wedge, ed., *History of Goodhue County*, 798–99, 925; Joseph C. Dickey and Family Papers, MHS.
8. Julia Wiech Lief, "A Woman of Purpose: Julia B. Nelson," *Minnesota History* 47 (Winter 1981): 304.
9. Here and below, Lief, "A Woman of Purpose," 303–04; Hancock, 304–08.
10. Henry L. Swint, *The Northern Teacher in the South, 1862–1870* (Nashville: Vanderbilt University, 1941), 3–6.
11. Lief, "A Woman of Purpose," 306. Nelson's request for more teachers is in the Goodhue County *Republican,* Mar. 14, 1872.
12. Ericson, "Jane Elizabeth Colvill: A Woman of Means," Cannon Falls *Beacon*, July 28, 1994.
13. Curtiss-Wedge, ed., 520; White, *et al., Minnesota Votes*, 68.
14. Here and below, Ericson, "Jane Elizabeth Colvill: A Woman of Means."
15. Mattson, *Story of an Emigrant,* 97–100; Holmquist, ed., *They Chose Minnesota*, 258.
16. Eric Foner, *Reconstruction: America's Unfinished Revolution* (New York: Harper & Row, 1988), 463.
17. Folwell, vol. 3, 66; Hancock, 252. The Goodhue County *Republican* of Nov. 11, 1859, noted that wheat-buying continued despite the winter close of navigation.
18. Jean Chesley, "The Story of Milling in Goodhue County," GCHS; Nydahl, "Early Norwegian Settlement of Goodhue County," 43–44; Henrietta M. Larson, "The Wheat Market and the Farmers in Minnesota, 1858–1900" (Ph.D. diss., New York: Columbia University, 1926), 23–24, copy at MHS. See also Ingebrikt F. Grose in Albert M. Marshall, *Goodhue County's First Hundred Years* (Red Wing: *Daily Republican Eagle,* 1954), 31.
19. Larson, 33–40, 68.
20. Folwell, vol. 3, 68–69; Merrill E. Jarchow, "King Wheat," *Minnesota History* 24 (Mar. 1948): 16–17; Larson, 128.
21. James J. Hill, "History of Agriculture in Minnesota," *Minnesota Collections* 8: 252; A. T. Andreas, *An Illustrated Historical Atlas of the State of Minnesota* (Chicago: A. T. Andreas, 1874), 217.
22. Here and below, Jarchow, "King Wheat," *Minnesota History* 24 (Mar. 1948): 6.
23. Austin A. Sanderson, "Red Wing of the '60s," 1929 paper in GCHS biography files; Larson, 35.
24. Mrs. Harold R. Ullrich, "James Marshall: Father of Grain Futures," *Goodhue County Historical News* 4 (Feb. 1970): 2. Marshall later moved to Minneapolis, where he was a founding member of the Minneapolis Grain Exchange, then known as the Chamber of Commerce, and served two terms as president of the organization. Marshall, 48.

25. Larson, 68; Andreas, 235–36; Rasmussen, *A History of Red Wing*, 107.

26. Larson, 35, 97.

27. Rasmussen, *A History of Red Wing,* 97; Sanderson, 2.

28. Jarchow, "King Wheat," 13, 24–25.

29. Folwell, vol. 3, 36–37; Foner and Garraty, eds., *The Reader's Companion to American History*, 464–65.

30. Larson, 104; Mitchell, *Past and Present in Goodhue County,* 130; Hazel Anderson and Archie Swenson, *How it All Began* (White Rock: White Rock State Bank, 1985), 1.

31. Mitchell, 130; Wood, Alley, 582–83.

32. John C. Luecke, *Dreams, Disaster and Demise: The Milwaukee Road in Minnesota* (Cannon Falls: Cannon Falls *Beacon,* 1988), 19–20; Larson, 61.

33. Here and below, Larson, 74–75, 139.

34. D. Jerome Tweton, "The Business of Agriculture," in Clifford Clark Jr., ed., *Minnesota in a Century of Change: The State and Its People since 1900* (St. Paul: MHS Press, 1989), 265–69; Larson, 74–75.

35. Curtiss-Wedge, ed., 31–32; Margaret E. Hutcheson, *Goodhue: The Story of a Railroad Town* (Red Wing: Self-published, 1989), 6–8; Meyer, "Some Historical Facts about White Willow" ( sketch of the village included with Roy W. Meyer's 1955 self-published *History of Forest Mills,* 96–104). See ledger books, Theodore B. Sheldon Papers, MHS.

36. Wood, Alley, 378–81. The authors claim (p. 378) Diamond Mill was the first American mill to use the Hungarian process. It was certainly among the first. This source gives a detailed description of the inner workings of both mills. See also Donald Gregg Flour Milling Collection, Red Wing file, MHS; Andreas, 236; Marshall, 47.

37. Here and below, "Hurrah for Rollers! Genuine Roller Mill to be Built in Minnesota," *Northwestern Miller* 5 (July 20, 1877); Wood, Alley, 378–81.

38. Rasmussen, *A History of Red Wing*, 233.

39. Here and below, Carlene Stewart, "Cannon Falls Was Once a Prominent Thriving Flour Milling Center," *Goodhue County Historical News* 9 (Feb. 1975): 3. See also Donald Gregg Flour Milling Collection, Cannon Falls file, MHS, and Hancock, 258–59.

40. Donald Gregg Flour Milling Collection, Oxford Mill file, MHS; Frances Heglund, "The Old Oxford Mill, *Goodhue County Historical News* 9 (Feb. 1975).

41. Here and below, Charles E. and Hattie Raymond, *Kenyon, Minnesota, Located on the Chicago Great Western Ry, 1885–1887* (Kenyon: Self-published, 1897), 8; Henrietta M. Gunderson, "Martin T. Gunderson," *Goodhue County Historical News* 3 (June 1969): 2; Frank Callister, "Martin T. Gunderson House, Kenyon," *Goodhue County Historical News* 9 (Nov. 1975): 1.

42. Folwell, vol. 3, 2.

43. Agnes Flom Doebler, "Early Stage Routes in Goodhue County," *Goodhue County Historical News* 7 (Mar. 1973): 1–3; C.A. Rasmussen in Curtiss-Wedge, ed., *History of Goodhue County,* 298–304.

44. Doebler, "Early Stage Routes in Goodhue County," 1–3; Hancock, 252, 289.

45. Here and below, Red Wing *Daily Republican,* July 1, 1936; Sanderson, "Red Wing of the '60s," 1. See also Rasmussen, *A History of Red Wing*, 87–88.

46. "The Concord Coach," *Goodhue County Historical News* 7 (March 1973): 4.

47. Doebler, "Early Stage Routes in Goodhue County," 2–3. See *Zumbrota: The First 100 Years*, 191.

48. Folwell, vol. 3, 32.

49. John C. Luecke, *Dreams, Disaster and Demise: The Milwaukee Road in Minnesota* (Cannon Falls: Cannon Falls *Beacon,* 1988), 19–20; Folwell, vol. 3, 2.

50. Here and below, Red Wing *Republican,* June 22, 1871; Luecke, *Dreams, Disaster and Demise,* 20; Rasmussen, *A History of Red Wing*, 100.

51. Luecke, *Dreams, Disaster and Demise,* 23; Hastings *Gazette,* Dec. 9, 1871.

52. Chris Graham to Dear Daughters, Jan. 7, 1871, GCHS collections.

53. Luecke, *Dreams, Disaster and Demise,* 87–88.

54. "State Builders of the West, Lucius Frederick Hubbard," *Western Magazine* 14 (July 1919): 6–38; Meyer, "The Discontinued Post Offices and Ghost Towns of Goodhue County," 46–47.

55. Meyer, "The Discontinued Post Offices and Ghost Towns of Goodhue County," 46–47; Rasmussen, *A History of Goodhue County,* 215–16.

56. Roy W. Meyer, *History of Forest Mills* (N.c.: Self-published,1955), 23–25, copy in GCHS Chesley Library; Wood, Alley, 628–29.

57. Meyer, *History of Forest Mills,* 23–25.

58. Ibid., 25–26.

59. Luecke, *Dreams, Disaster and Demise*, 88–89.

60. Here and below, John C. Luecke, *The Chicago and Northwestern in Minnesota* (Cannon Falls: Cannon Falls *Beacon,* 1990) 114–117; Meyer, *History of Forest Mills*, 25–26. Reports from the Wabasha County *Sentinel* of May 28, 1878, and the Red Wing *Argus* of May 30, 1878, vary in their timelines. The account used here relies on the analysis of Meyer and Luecke.

61. Goodhue County *Republican,* May 23, 1878. The report, dated May 21, came from the *Republican's* Zumbrota correspondent "O.H.P.," likely O. H. Parker.

62. Luecke, *Dreams, Disaster and Demise*, 94; Meyer, *History of Forest Mills*, 26–27.

63. Goodhue County *Republican,* Feb. 3, 1876.

64. Curtiss-Wedge, ed., *History of Goodhue County,* 225–26; Wanamingo Town Records, 1869–1894, GCHS collections.

65. Cannon Falls *Beacon,* Oct., 27, 1882; Mrs. R. N. Nelson, "The Development of the Railroads," *Goodhue County Historical News* 11 (June 1977): 2, 5.

66. H. Roger Grant, *The Corn Belt Route: A History of the Chicago Great Western Railroad Company* (DeKalb: Northern University Press, 1984), 50–51.

67. Rasmussen, *A History of Goodhue County,* 141–42, 164–66.

68. Red Wing *Daily Republican,* July 1, 1936; Meyer, "The Discontinued Post Offices and Ghost Towns of Goodhue County," 51–56; Wood, Alley, 611.

69. Meyer, "The Discontinued Post Offices and Ghost Towns of Goodhue County," 69–75, 96–100.

70. Marshall, ed., 41–42.

71. *Duluth, Red Wing and Southern Railroad from the Rich Mines of Lake Superior and the Great Lake Port of Duluth through the Belts of Timber, to the Grain, Stock and Dairy Regions of Minnesota and Iowa* (Red Wing: Red Wing Printing Company, 1887), 5–6, MHS.

72. Hutcheson, *Goodhue*, 1–6.

73. Grant, *The Corn Belt Route,* 52.

74. Ibid., 53.

75. Annette Atkins, *Harvest of Grief: Grasshopper Plagues and Public Assistance in Minnesota, 1873–1878* (St. Paul: MHS Press, 1984), 2, 13. The "hoppers" quote on the title page of Atkins's book comes from Minnesota author Meridel Le Sueur's *North Star Country.*

## Chapter 7

1. Marshall, ed., *Goodhue County's First 100 Years,* 37–41. In 1870 Goodhue County's 54 manufacturing establishments employed 310 and produced an annual payroll of $100,780, an average of $325 per worker.

2. Foner, *Reconstruction: America's Unfinished Revolution,* 512; Ralph K. Andrist, ed., *The American Heritage History of the Confident Years* (New York: American Heritage, 1987), 84.

3. Andrist, ed., *The Confident Years,* 84–85.

4. "From Rails to Trails," *Goodhue County Historical News* 29 (April 1995): 7; Foner, 512–13.

5. Folwell, *A History of Minnesota*, vol. 3, 72–73; Larson, *The Wheat Market and the Farmer in Minnesota,* 61.

6. St. Paul *Pioneer Press,* July 21, 1878.

7. Laura M. Hamilton, "Stem Rust in the Spring Wheat Area," *Minnesota History* 20 (1939): 156–59.

8. Here and below, Hamilton "Stem Rust in the Spring Wheat Area, 158–59. Stem rust was later linked to a popular imported ornamental shrub, the barberry bush. By the time the barberry was outlawed in 1918, more than 600,000 bushes had been planted in the state. The development of wheat strains resistant to stem rust helped farmers.

9. Larson, 119.

10. Meyer, *History of Forest Mills,* 31.

11. Folwell, vol. 3, 97–112, 140–41.

12. James J. Hill, *MHS Collections,* 8: 275–90.

13. Caroline A. Danielson Morgan, "The Beginning of the Clay Industry," GCHS undated, unpublished manuscript. The author of this account was born in Goodhue County in 1857 and had first-hand knowledge of Paul, a neighbor of her family, and his work. Morgan died on February 20, 1939, at age 81. See also Goodhue County, *Book R of Deeds* (p. 42), for Paul's warranty deed for the school dated July 23, 1862.

14. John Schwartau, "The Red Wing Clay Industry: How it All Began, John Paul 1819–1900," 1993 manuscript, pp. 1–5, copy at GCHS; Hancock, *Goodhue County Past and Present*, 221. There has been confusion over the name of the county's first potter. Curtiss-Wedge's *History of Goodhue*

*County*, 619, listed this man as Joseph Pohl, another early resident in Goodhue township, as did G. Hubert Smith in "Minnesota Potteries: From Pioneer Craft to Modern Factory," *Minnesota History* 33 (Summer 1953): 231–32. The work of John Schwartau, who lived within a few miles of the original Paul and Pohl homesteads for more than 50 years, produced proof that John Paul was the first potter. Schwartau found county records and census information detailing Paul's life in the township. In interviews with Schwartau, grandchildren of Pohl stated "emphatically" that Joseph Pohl was not a potter. Schwartau provided this author with the information gathered in that research. See also John Schwartau, "Our Pioneer Potter," GCHS, 1993, 1–4.

15. G. Hubert Smith, "Minnesota Potteries: From Pioneer Craft to Modern Factory," *Minnesota History* 33 (Summer 1953): 232; Hancock, 221; Marshall, ed., 51. See Mabel Densmore letter Sept. 2, 1952, regarding Philleo in Densmore (Benjamin Densmore and Family) Papers, 1797–1955, Box 5, MHS. For Philleo's attempt to secure a new base in St. Paul, see Philleo to Willius, Dec. 14, 1877, and Jan. 9, 1878, in Ferdinand Willius and Family Papers, MHS.

16. Marshall, ed., 51.

17. Curtiss-Wedge, ed., 620, 669; Wood, Alley *History of Goodhue County,* 505, 515.

18. Marshall, ed., 51.

19. Here and below, Smith, "Minnesota Potteries," 234–35; Marshall, ed., 51.

20. C. J. Sansome, "Goodhue County's Geologic Story," *Goodhue County Historical News* 10 (Feb. 1976); Frank R. Holmes, *Minnesota in Three Centuries*, vol. 4, 387.

21. Clinton R. Stauffer and George A. Thiel, *The Limestone Marls of Minnesota,* University of Minnesota Geological Survey Bulletin No. 23 (Minneapolis: University of Minnesota, 1933), 39–40; Andreas, *An Illustrated Historical Atlas of the State of Minnesota*, 235–36. See also Rasmussen, *A History of Goodhue County*, 150.

22. Oliver Bowles, *The Structural and Ornamental Stones of Minnesota,* Bulletin 663 (Washington: Government Printing Office, 1918), 168–69. See also Stauffer and Thiel, *The Limestone Marls of Minnesota,* 40, and Centennial Book Committee, *Zumbrota: The First 100 Years*, 364.

23. Stauffer and Thiel, *The Limestone Marls of Minnesota,* 39; Curtiss-Wedge, ed., 634–35; Andreas, *An Illustrated Historical Atlas of the State of Minnesota,* 236.

24. Here and below, Berndt M. Eide, "History of the Lime and Stone Industry in Red Wing, Minnesota, 1850–1916," GCHS, 10–18. Eide, as a young man, worked as a quarryman in Red Wing. His history of later quarries lists the "Siberia," based on the old "Little Carlson" site at Sorin's Bluff; the short-lived North Barn Bluff, a quarry opened in 1888 by Twin Cities Lime and Cement Company; the Malmberg, later Dahl, quarry on Sorin's; the Hickman or Lawther quarry along Highway 58; the "New Bellman" adjoining the Hickman operation; the John Peterson quarry near Oakwood Cemetery; and the Budensiek quarry owned by Ben Budensiek, located atop a hill near his residence at the end of Greenwood Street. In 1940 C. A. Rasmussen, GCHS president, asked Eide to write a history of the city's lime industry. For assistance with his 45-page study, he conferred with experienced city quarrymen August Bellman and Aaron Bjork.

25. Ibid., 13–17, 20.

26. Andreas, 236; Curtiss-Wedge, ed., 635; Eide, 11, 29–30, 45; Wood, Alley, 393, 500, 506.

27. Eide, 18–20.

28. Sam Blondell, "Foundation of the Lime Industry in Red Wing," unpublished, undated paper in GCHS Industry and Organizations file.

29. Eide, 8–9.

30. Red Wing *Daily Republican*, Nov. 27, 30, 1906. See also Red Wing *Daily Republican*, Aug. 21, 1929, for a summary of the battle to save the bluff.

31. Red Wing *Daily Republican,* March 9 and 11, 1907; April 20, 1907; and Aug. 21, 1929.

32. Red Wing *Daily Republican,* March 17, 1907.

33. Red Wing *Daily Republican,* March 16, 1907.

34. Red Wing *Daily Republican,* Aug. 21, 1929; Rasmussen, *A History of Goodhue County*, 271.

35. W. C. Werner, "Survey and Test on Limestone Quarries in Minnesota," Minnesota Highway Department Bulletin No. 2, 1921, 73.

36. E. G. Cheyney, "The Development of the Lumber Industry in Minnesota," *Journal of Geography* 14 (Feb. 1916): 189.

37. Curtiss-Wedge, ed., 670–72; Wood, Alley, 448.

38. Curtiss-Wedge, ed., 672–73.

39. Wood, Alley, 384–85.

40. Orrin Densmore to son Benjamin, Dec. 27, 1856, and Jan. 14, 1857, Densmore (Benjamin and Family) Papers, MHS; Wood, Alley, 385–86.

41. Folwell, vol. 3, 63–64.
42. George B. Engberg, "The Rise of Organized Labor in Minnesota," *Minnesota History* 21 (Dec. 1940): 372–73; Carl N. Degler, *Out of Our Past: The Forces That Shaped Modern America*, rev. ed. (New York: Harper Colophon, 1970), 238.
43. Engberg, "The Rise of Organized Labor in Minnesota," 375–81.
44. *Ninth Census of the United States, 1870*, 40; Franklin Coyne, *The Development of the Cooperage Industry in the United States* (Chicago: Lumber Buyer Publishing, 1940), 33.
45. Stillwater *Gazette*, Feb. 19, 1879; Engberg, "The Rise of Organized Labor in Minnesota," 392. See George B. Engberg, "The Knights of Labor," *Minnesota History* 22 (Dec. 1941): 371–73.
46. *Northwestern Miller* 7 (March 14, 1879): 163; Eames's modern cooperage grew rapidly, expanding three times from its 1872 start to 1877. It featured a 12-horsepower engine and boiler made by Densmore Brothers of Red Wing and averaged nearly 150,000 barrels per year. Eames's plant included a heating room for barrels and employed 50 men. George Reichert's three Red Wing cooper shops employed 25 to 30 men, including a four-man operation that produced "tight work" barrels (beer barrels and casks); see Wood, Alley, *History of Goodhue County*, 391, and GCHS Oral History Collection interview with Fritz Reichert, June 2, 1979.
47. *Northwestern Miller* 14 (Nov. 11, 1882): 401; Stillwater *Gazette*, Feb. 19, 1879.
48. Coyne, 33–34.
49. Engberg, "The Rise of Organized Labor in Minnesota," 394.
50. Goodhue County *Republican*, June 8, 1876; Engberg, "The Rise of Organized Labor in Minnesota," 393.
51. Engberg, "The Knights of Labor," 367–71.
52. Marshall, ed., 40; Engberg, "The Knights of Labor," 389–90.
53. *Grange Advance* (Red Wing), Jan. 10, 1877; Albrecht, "Early Newspapers and Editors," *Goodhue County Historical News* 13 (Nov. 1979): 1–3.
54. W. H. Bruce, History of the Farmer's Guild, Grange No. 84, Goodhue, Minnesota, 1871–1877, minute book, GCHS; Record Book of Burnside Grange, No. 148, of Patrons of Husbandry, GCHS.
55. Folwell, vol. 3, 54–55.
56. Andrist, ed., 244.
57. Ibid.
58. Folwell, vol. 3, 168–69.

**Chapter 8**
1. O. M. Hall speech given in Zumbrota, July 3, 1880, O. M. Hall Papers, GCHS Manuscript Collection.
2. *Zumbrota: The First 100 Years*, 101–37.
3. Theodore C. Blegen, *Norwegian Migration to America: The American Transition* (Northfield: Norwegian-American Historical Association, 1940), 266; *Holden through One Hundred Years*, 14–16.
4. Curtiss-Wedge, ed., *History of Goodhue County*, 408.
5. Here and below, Blegen 263–66.
6. Goodhue County *Republican*, May 5, 1870.
7. Goodhue County *Republican*, June 2, 1870.
8. Here and below, Blegen, 266; *Holden through One Hundred Years*, 14–16. See Halvor Ronning, *The Gospel at Work* (Minneapolis: Self-published, 1943), 25–28, for more on B. J. Muus.
9. Here and below, Kathryn Ericson, "Triple Jeopardy: The Muus vs. Muus Case in Three Forums," *Minnesota History* 50 (Winter 1987): 299–308. Oline Muus's pronouncements about her husband came from a long statement she issued in 1880 during the public breakup of their marriage.
10. Here and below, Charles O. Richardson, "Landmark Cases in Goodhue County," *Goodhue County Historical News* 15 (Feb. 1981), 4; Ericson, "Triple Jeopardy," 304–06.
11. Here and below, *Holden through One Hundred Years*, 18; Rasmussen, *A History of Goodhue County*, 226; Blegen, 263–66.
12. Kildahl, *Westward We Came*, 17–20, MHS; GCHS Oral History Collection, #117 Lyle Teigen, 2–3.
13. Ericson, "Triple Jeopardy," 306; Kenyon *Leader*, April 26, 1894; *Holden through One Hundred Years, 1856–1956*, 19. See also GCHS Oral History Collections, #117, 3, and Kildahl, *Westward We Came*, 31–32.
14. Ericson, "Triple Jeopardy," 307–08.
15. Rev. Muus would have been pleased with a story of a teacher in 1936 who was assigned to a

Holden school. For the first school program of the year, the new teacher decided to allow the students to sing in Norwegian a song taught them by a nearby resident. When the children began singing, the audience "just went wild" and insisted upon three encores. See GCHS Oral History Collection, #21, interview with Orville Olson, 6–7.

16. A rare incident involving conflict with Indians occurred in 1855 when a Wanamingo woman reported that an Indian woman had taken her infant child. The settler said her child was dropped to the ground without injury during a subsequent pursuit. See Wood, Alley, *History of Goodhue County,* 186.

17. GCHS Oral History Collection, #216, "Swedish Men and Women," 5.

18. GCHS Oral History Collection, #217, "Irish Men and Women," 9.

19. Curtiss-Wedge, ed., *History of Goodhue County,* 154.

20. GCHS Oral History Collection, #193, "Norwegian Men," 6.

21. Bruce M. White, "Indian Visits: Stereotypes of Minnesota's Native People," *Minnesota History* 53 (Fall 1992): 99–111.

22. Here and below, GCHS Oral History Collections #216, "Swedish Men and Women," 13–15; #217, "Irish Men and Women," 6, 11; and #193, "Norwegian Men," 11.

23. Here and below, GCHS Oral History Collection, #218 "German Men and Women," 11.

24. Ibid., 12.

25. Phil Revoir, *The Early History of St. John's Evangelical Lutheran Church,* excerpted in *Goodhue County Historical News,* 17 (June 1983): 3–4.

26. Andrea Brekke, untitled memoir on Wanamingo school days, ca. 1900, Nov. 8, 1961, GCHS; GCHS Oral History Collection, #216, "Swedish Men and Women," 12–13.

27. Goodhue County *Republican,* Oct. 22, 1874; O. N. Nelson, *History of the Scandinavians and Successful Scandinavians in the United State* (Minneapolis: O. N. Nelson, 1900), 434.

28. GCHS Oral History Collection, #216 "Swedish Men and Women," 12–15; GCHS Oral History Collection, #217 "Irish Men and Women," 10.

29. Here and below, GCHS Oral History Collection, #216 Swedish Men and Women," 14; GCHS Oral History Collection, #217 "Irish Men and Women," 10; GCHS Oral History Collection, #218 "German Men and Women," 5. Henry C. Hinrichs related the story of his family's fighting Swedish hired hand. See GCHS Oral History Collection, #74, 9.

30. Alf Peterson Papers, MHS, "Story of the Peterson Family," p. 13.

31. GCHS Oral History Collection, #217 "Irish Men and Women," 10–11.

32. Nydahl, "The Early Norwegian Settlement of Goodhue County," 29–30; GCHS Oral History Collection, #193, "Norwegian Men," 2.

33. Harold Severson, *Goodhue County Heritage* (N.c.: Self-published, 1963), 139.

34. "The Norwegian Element," undated (ca. 1875) paper in the GCHS Dr. Justus Christian Gronvold biography file.

35. Revoir, "The Early History of St. John's Evangelical Lutheran Church," 4.

36. Here and below, "Pioneer Churches in Goodhue County, 1850–1900," *Goodhue County Historical News* 17 (Feb., June, and Nov. 1983). The author relied on the comprehensive overview of pioneer churches found in the successive issues listed above. Specific citations are also used. See also Curtiss-Wedge, ed., 380–83, 404–67.

37. Holmquist, ed., *They Chose Minnesota,* 57–59; Curtiss-Wedge, ed., *History of Goodhue County,* 437–48; Jeanne Ode, "Pioneer Yankee Churches," *Goodhue County Historical News* 17 (Feb. 1983): 2–3, 8. See also Chapter 3 of this book for more detailed information on settlement patterns in Goodhue County.

38. Ode, "Pioneer Yankee Churches," 2–3, 8; Roy W. Meyer, "The Prairie Island Community: A Remnant of Minnesota Sioux," *Minnesota History* 37 (Sept. 1961): 277.

39. Margaret Hutcheson, "Irish Catholics in Goodhue County" and "Luxembourg Catholics in Belvidere," *Goodhue County Historical News* 17 (Nov. 1983): 3–5; Curtiss-Wedge, ed., 431–36.

40. Here and below, Meyer, "The Prairie Island Community," 274–75. Meyer observes that Prairie Island in the 1890s was not an island at all but part of the Mississippi's right bank "cut off from the upland by an arm of the Vermillion River." After the 1938 construction of Lock and Dam No. 3 in the Mississippi and the subsequent diversion of the Vermillion, the island became a peninsula.

41. The Henton quote is from Meyer, "The Red Wing Indian Village," 38.

42. "History of Prairie Island Sioux," *Goodhue County Historical News* 2 (June 1968): 2. This article is based on the papers of Rev. Thomas Rouillard, which were kept by his daughter Eliza Rouillard Wells and translated by her grandson Norman R. Campbell. The Campbell and Wells families became prominent in the Prairie Island community.

43. Meyer, "The Red Wing Indian Village," 38–39.
44. Here and below, Meyer, "The Prairie Island Community," 276–78.
45. Red Wing *Daily Republican*, Feb. 15, 1895, reprinted from the Hastings *Democrat*; Meyer, "The Prairie Island Community," 276–77.
46. Curtiss-Wedge, ed., 321.
47. "History of Medicine in Goodhue County," *Minnesota Medicine* 28 (no. 2–6, 1945): 134–36.
48. Ibid., 136–37; Goodhue County *Volunteer*, Feb. 25, 1863.
49. Goodhue County *Volunteer*, Aug. 17, 1864.
50. "History of Medicine in Goodhue County," 137; Mrs. John Stone, "Charles Nathaniel Hewitt, 1836–1910," *Goodhue County Historical News* 6 (Feb. 1972): 2–4.
51. Here and below, William Watts Folwell, "Biographic Memorial of Dr. Charles N. Hewitt," *Minnesota Collections* 15: 669–86. Stone, "Charles Nathaniel Hewitt," 2–3; Folwell, 154–55. Thomas E. Keys, "The Medical Books of Dr. Hewitt," *Minnesota History* 21 (Dec. 1940): 357.
52. George M. B. Hawley, "Charles Nathaniel Hewitt: The Man and His Profession," *Goodhue County Historical News* 6 (Feb. 1972): 6; Folwell, *Minnesota Collections* 15: 677.
53. Stone, "Charles Nathaniel Hewitt," 3.
54. Folwell, *Minnesota Collections* 15: 677. Gov. David M. Clough dropped Hewitt from the State Board of Health in a move denounced by historian Folwell as political and "simply brutal." Folwell concluded, "It will be long before Minnesota shall look upon his like again." Hawley, "Charles Nathaniel Hewitt: The Man and His Profession," 6. After his death in 1910, Hewitt's professional library was put under the care of his long-time friend William J. Mayo, M.D. The libraries of Hewitt and Mayo "form the nucleus of the present library of the Mayo Clinic." See Keys, "The Medical Books of Dr. Hewitt," 353–71, for the specific titles from Hewitt's collection.
55. Walter Washburn, "Leprosy Among Scandinavian Settlers in the Upper Mississippi Valley, 1864–1932, *Bulletin of the History of Medicine* 24 (Baltimore: John Hopkins Press, 1950): 123–28: Frank Callister, "Dr. Just Christian Gronvold Estate," *Goodhue County History Society News* 7 (Nov. 1973): 4; *Minnesota Medicine* 27 (March 1945): 211–13, and (May 1945): 381; Goodhue County Oral History Collection, #37, Hilda Gronvold.
56. *Minnesota Medicine* 27 (March 1945): 214.
57. Here and below, ibid., 215; Folwell, *Minnesota Collections* 15: 676; Goodhue County *Republican,* June 4, 1881.
58. Curtiss-Wedge, ed., 910–11.
59. Here and below, Red Wing *Daily Republican,* Aug. 23, 26, and 28, and Sept. 5, 9, 12, 13, 15, 16, and 18, 1893.
60. Here and below, *Minnesota Medicine* 27 (April 1945): 304–05.
61. *Red Wing Hospital Association Minutes,* 1891–93; MHS Goodhue County: City of Red Wing records; Helen Bell, "Beginnings of Hospitals and Nursing," *Goodhue County Historical News* 12 ( Nov. 1978): 3, 5.
62. *Minnesota Medicine* 27 (April 1945): 305–06. See Curtiss-Wedge, ed., 627, 674, 731, for information on Foot, Sterling and Smith. *Zumbrota: the First 100 Years,* 253–54.
63. J. Arthur Myers, *Invited and Conquered: Historical Sketch of Tuberculosis in Minnesota* (St. Paul: Minnesota Public Health Association, 1949), 356–57; Helen Clapesattle, "When Minnesota was Florida's Rival," *Minnesota History* 35 (March 1957): 214–15.
64. Lucille Lohmann, "Mineral Springs: National Leader in TB Care," *Goodhue County Historical News* 21 (Winter 1997): 7.
65. Jesse E. Douglass, "History of the Mineral Springs Sanatorium," May 29, 1970, unpublished paper in GCHS Mineral Springs files. See also Edythe Beckman, "Activities at Mineral Springs Sanitarium [*sic*] as recalled by Harriet Wickey who worked there for 22 years," undated, unpublished paper, GCHS in Mineral Springs files.
66. "Deaths from Tuberculosis in Goodhue County, Minnesota," Minnesota Department of Health data compiled in the GCHS Mineral Springs files.
67. Ethel McClure, *More Than a Roof: The Development of Minnesota Poor Farms and Homes for the Aged* (St. Paul: MHS, 1968), 20–22, 81.
68. Red Wing *Daily Republican,* Feb. 5, 1864 (quoting Goodhue *Volunteer*), and April 1, 1864; McClure, 23.
69. William D. Erickson, "Establishing Minnesota's First Hospital for the Insane," *Minnesota History* 53 (Summer 1992): 47–48.
70. McClure, 88; Harold Harrison, "Rest Homes and Care Facilities," *Goodhue County Historical News* 13 (Feb. 1979): 1.

## Chapter 9

1. Here and below, Andrist, ed., *Confident Years, 1865–1916,* 246. See also Lawrence Goodwyn, *The Populist Moment: A Short History of the Agrarian Revolt in America* (New York: Oxford University Press, 1978), 105–06.
2. James Marshall, "An Unheard Voice: The Autobiography of a Dispossessed Homesteader and a Nineteenth-Century Cultural Theme of Dispossession," *The Old Northwest* 6 (Winter 1980–81): 303–29.
3. White, et al., *Minnesota Votes,* 79–80; Andrist, ed., 246.
4. Folwell, *A History of Minnesota,* vol. 3, 187–90. For details on how a divided and weakened Alliance Party came together for its strong showing in the 1890s, see Donald F. Warner, "Prelude to Populism," *Minnesota History* 32 (Sept. 1951): 129–46.
5. Here and below, White, *et al.,* 65–80.
6. O. M. Hall, speech of acceptance, 1890 Democratic Third District Convention, O. M. Hall Papers, GCHS Manuscript Collection.
7. Steven J. Diner, *A Very Different Age: Americans of the Progressive Era* (New York: Hill and Wang, 1998), 12–13, 200–201; John D. Hicks, "The Birth of the Populist Party," *Minnesota History* 9 (Sept. 1928): 238.
8. Here and below, Marjorie Bingham, "Keeping at It: Minnesota Women," in Clifford E. Clark Jr. (ed.), *Minnesota in a Century of Change* (St. Paul: MHS, 1989), 437–38.
9. Bingham, 438.
10. Bessie Lathe Scovell, ed., *Yesteryears: A Brief History of the Minnesota Woman's Christian Temperance Union from Its Organization, September 6, 1887 to 1939* (St. Paul: WCTU, 1939), 70–71.
11. Red Wing *Republican,* Dec. 9, 1882, and Feb. 3, 1883; Lief, "A Woman of Purpose," *Minnesota History* 47 (Winter 1981): 309.
12. Red Wing *Republican,* Aug.11, 1893; Lief, 309.
13. Curtiss-Wedge, ed., *History of Goodhue County,* 1024–25.
14. Scovell, ed., 230–63.
15. GCHS Oral History Collections, #41, 13.
16. Here and below, see the series of annual reports *Proceedings of the Annual Catholic Total Abstinence Union of the Archdiocese of St. Paul,* 1879, 1882–1886, 1888 –1889, and 1891 for more information related to Goodhue County. For specific notes on formation of both the men's and women's chapters, see the 1888 report, p. 18, and appendix, p. 1. For details on women's membership surpassing men, see 1891 report, pp. 13–14. For the quote from Nellie Igoe, see 1891 report, pp. 33–34. See also Curtiss-Wedge, ed., 434, and Heaney, "Belle Creek Irish Settlement," GCHS collections, 5.
17. Here and below, Hancock, *Goodhue County Past and Present,* 264–66; Meyer, "Discontinued Post Offices and Ghost Towns of Goodhue County," 66–69.
18. Meyer, "Discontinued Post Offices and Ghost Towns of Goodhue County," 68–69; Curtiss-Wedge, ed., 158.
19. Betty Kane, "The 1876 Legislature: A Case Study in Lively Futility," *Minnesota History* 45 (Summer 1977): 232.
20. Rasmussen, *A History of Goodhue County,* 202.
21. Marshall, ed., *Goodhue County's First 100 Years,* 11; *Zumbrota: The First 100 Years,* 33; *The United States Biographical Dictionary and Portrait Gallery of Eminent and Self-Made Men,* Minnesota vol. (New York: American Biographical Publishing, 1879), 48–49; Meyer, *History of Forest Mills,* 101.
22. Here and below, Hutcheson, *Goodhue,* 11.
23. Ibid., 12.
24. Red Wing *Daily Republican,* April 7, 8, 1891.
25. S. J. Nelson, letter to the editor, Red Wing *Daily Republican,* April 11, 1891.
26. Here and below, Hutcheson, 14–15; Red Wing *Advance Sun,* Aug. 31, 1892.
27. Barbara Stuhler, "Organizing for the Vote: Leaders of Minnesota's Woman Suffrage Movement," *Minnesota History* 54 (Fall 1995): 293.
28. Red Wing *Daily Republican,* April 11, 1891.
29. Mark Sullivan, *Our Times: America at the Birth of the Twentieth Century* (New York: Charles Scribner's Sons, 1926, abridged 1996), 37.
30. Chris Graham to Miss Helen Graham and Miss Jennie Graham, Jan. 10, 1871, GCHS collections.
31. Goodhue County *Republican,* May 25 and 18, 1876.

32. Here and below, Red Wing *Daily Republican,* Oct. 29, 1887.
33. Stuhler, 293–95.
34. Lief, 309.
35. Ibid., 310.
36. Here and below, Hurd, *Woman Suffrage in Minnesota,* 29, 26–27.
37. Hurd, 8; Lief, 314.
38. Here and below, Sullivan (abridged), 69, 72.
39. Sullivan (abridged), 72.
40. *Zumbrota: The First 100 Years,* 40.
41. Jeannette Scriver Burch, "The Dressmakers," in Connie Bickman, ed., *Roots & Wings: A Scrapbook of Time* (Cannon Falls: Yatra Publications, 1996), 161.
42. Red Wing *Daily Republican,* Jan. 11, 1907.
43. Chris Graham to Mattie Graham, March 10, 1869, GCHS collections.
44. Todd Walsh, "The Lutheran Ladies' Seminary of Red Wing, Minnesota (1894–1920)," 19–20; GCHS collections, 30–31, 40.
45. Frederick L. Johnson, "Unlocking the Mysteries of the Sea Wing," *Minnesota History* 52 (Summer 1990): 75–77.
46. Red Wing *Daily Republican,* Aug. 9, 1894.
47. Ibid.
48. Charlotte O'Kelly, *Women and Men in Society* (New York, Van Nostrand, 1980), 238; Mechele Peterson, "The Development of a Medical Specialty: Obstetrics," unpublished paper, 1984, GCHS "medicine" collection.
49. Ruth Hodgson, "Midwifery," *Goodhue County Historical News* 13 (Feb. 1979): 1, 7.
50. Helen E. Bell, "Beginnings of Hospitals and Nursing," *Goodhue County Historical News* 12 (Nov. 1978): 4; Hodgson, "Midwifery," 1.
51. Here and below, Amanda Johnson reminiscences, 9–12, GCHS collections.
52. Here and below, Mary Scofield to "My Dear Children," Feb. 23, 1908, Mary Scofield Papers, MHS; Cannon Falls *Beacon,* Feb. 28, 1908.
53. Scofield to "My Dear Children," Feb. 23, 1908, Mary Scofield Papers, MHS; Cannon Falls *Beacon,* Feb. 28, 1908.
54. Goodwyn, 230.
55. Ivan Musicant, *Empire by Default: The Spanish-American War and the Dawn of the American Century* (New York: Henry Holt, 1998), 16–20; Marshall, ed., 41–42.
56. Foner and Garraty, eds., *Readers Companion to American History,* 341; Musicant, 28.
57. White, *et al.,* 15.
58. Paul Johnson, *A History of the American People* (New York: HarperCollins, 1998), 609–10; Sullivan, *Our Times* (abridged), 46–47.
59. *Eleventh Census of the United States, 1890,* Part I, Table 15, p. 197. See also Table 94, p. 296.
60. Holmquist, ed., *They Chose Minnesota,* 2–3; Diner, 77.
61. *Eleventh Census of the United States, 1890,* Part I, Table 15, p. 197. See also *Twelfth Census of the United States, 1900,* 762, Table 15.
62. Here and below, Andrist, ed., 361–62; Foner and Garraty, eds., 868–71.

**Chapter 10**
1. Here and below, G. J. "Dick" Kunau, "The Agriculture of Goodhue County," *Goodhue County Historical News* 4 (Feb., 1970): 4.
2. Here and below, Martin J. Anderson, "The Development of the Dairy Products Industry in Minnesota," *Minnesota Dairy and Food Department Bulletin No. 52, Minneapolis,* 1914, 1, 1 n, 16.
3. Ibid., 30–37.
4. Here and below, Anderson, 2–3; Severson, *Goodhue County Heritage,* 86.
5. Pine Island *Record*, Sept. 24, 1936, see "History Cheese Industry."
6. Ibid. See also Curtiss-Wedge, ed., *History of Goodhue County,* 808.
7. Curtiss-Wedge, ed., 994–995; Pine Island *Record,* July 24, 1936; Ruth Mondale, "Pine Island Cheese Industry," *Goodhue County Historical News* 2 (Nov. 1968): 1–3.
8. Marshall, ed., *Goodhue County's First Hundred Years,* 33.
9. S. Charlson, "History of the Sogn Cooperative Dairy Association," 1940 manuscript in GCHS Sogn Files; Peter Brandvold, Sr., "Sogn," *Goodhue County Historical News* 9 (Feb. 1975): 6.
10. Charlson, 1–2.

11. "National Register of Historic Places Recognizes Goodhue County Buildings," *Goodhue County Historical News* 15 (Nov. 1981): 3.
12. *Zumbrota: The First 100 Years,* 363.
13. Anderson, 4–5. Mrs. J. M. Monrad's account of women in dairying is found in the Red Wing *Daily Republican,* Oct. 16, 1889.
14. Anderson, 4–5.
15. Ibid. 4, 30–37.
16. Anderson, 16, 38.
17. Severson, 39–40.
18. Here and below, Mondale, 1, 3; Pine Island *Record*, Aug. 3, 1911, and Sept. 24, 1936.
19. Pine Island *Record*, Aug. 3, 1911, and Sept. 24, 1936.
20. Here and below, Curtiss-Wedge, ed., 621–22.
21. Red Wing Sewer Pipe Company, *Raw Clay Tells the Story* (Red Wing: Minn.: Red Wing Sewer Pipe Company, 1927), 5 (pamphlet). A 1919 *U.S. Geological Survey Bulletin* noted, "Goodhue County is remarkable for having more workable high-grade clays than any other county in Minnesota." See Frank F. Grout, *Clays and Shales of Minnesota, Bulletin 678* (Washington, D.C.: Government Printing Office, 1919), 165.
22. *Zumbrota: The First 100 Years,* 364.
23. Harriet Erickson, "Barrclay," 16, 28, unpublished manuscript, June 5, 1971, in GCHS clay industry collection; *Zumbrota: The First 100 Years,* 363–65.
24. Erickson, "Barrclay," 16; Zumbrota *News*, March 22, 1912.
25. *Zumbrota: The First 100 Years,* 365; Erickson, "Barrclay," 29, from an interview with Lewis Hellickson; Curtiss-Wedge, ed., 934, 975.
26. Marshall, ed., 39.
27. GCHS Oral History Collection, #40, Harold and Hazel Swarthout interview.
28. Here and below, Vernold L. Johnson, *History of the Clay Pits near Clay Bank and Bellechester* (Red Wing, Minn.: Self-published, 1986), 3–14.
29. Johnson, 11; Mrs. Vincent Deden, "The Clay Pits," *Goodhue County Historical Society News* 5 (June 1971): 3; GCHS Oral History Collection, Township Days Interview series.
30. Here and below, Red Wing *Republican Eagle*, Oct. 27, 1973. See "Bellechester Clay Pits Obsolete." Johnson, 5.
31. Johnson, 12–14.
32. James Burt, "The Red Wing Clay Line, Part I DRW&S Beginnings," *North Western Lines* (Fall 1991): 21–22.
33. Red Wing *Republican Eagle*, Oct. 27, 1973; Johnson, 12.
34. Madeline Angell, "Leader in Leather: The S. B. Foot Tanning Company of Red Wing," *Minnesota History* 47 (Fall 1981): 263–65; Curtiss-Wedge, ed., 674–75.
35. Here and below, Marshall, ed., 41; Angell, *Minnesota History* 47 (Fall 1981): 268–70.
36. Angell, "Leader in Leather," 270.
37. Here and below, Patrice A. Martin and Nicholas C. Vrooman, *Heart and Sole: A Story of the Red Wing Shoe Company* (Red Wing, Minn.: Red Wing Shoe Co., 1986) 4; Red Wing *Daily Republican*, Jan. 26, 1905.
38. Marshall, ed., 37.
39. Here and below, Marshall, ed., 49–50; Curtiss-Wedge, ed., 625–26.
40. Donald Mensing, "History of the Minnesota Malting Company of Cannon Falls, Minnesota," in Burch, ed., *Chronicles of Cannon Falls,* 78–79; Hutcheson, *Goodhue*, 38.
41. Marshall, ed., 38–39.
42. Charles and Hattie Raymond, *Kenyon, Minnesota: A Review of its Growth, Resources, Manufactures, Financial Interests, Public Buildings and Prospects* (Kenyon, Minn.: Raymond Series, 1897), 10.
43. Marshall, ed., 49.
44. Paul Johnson, *A History of the American People*, 594–95.
45. GCHS Oral History Collections, Lloyd Spriggle, #121, 25–26.
46. Frank Callister, *Recollections* (Kenyon, Minn.: Self-published, 1978). 61.
47. Here and below, "Contaminants in the Upper Mississippi River," *Goodhue County Historical News* 19 (Nov. 1985): 3; Mrs. R. H. Nelson, "Clamming in County Area Water," *Goodhue County Historical News* 4 (Nov. 1970): 1–2.
48. Cecil O. Monroe, "Baseball in Minnesota," *Minnesota History,* 19 (June 1938): 165–81; Goodhue County *Republican*, April 12, 1867.

49. *Historical Sketches of Cannon Falls, 1854–1954* (Cannon Falls: Cannon Falls *Beacon,* June 1954) 87; Goodhue County *Republican*, July 26 and Aug. 2, 1867.
50. Hutcheson, *Goodhue,* 51; *Goodhue County Historical News* 24 (April 1990): 2–3. Frank Held became a well-known automobile dealer in Kenyon. *Zumbrota: The First 100 Years,* 255, 388.
51. *Zumbrota: The First 100 Years,* 296.
52. Andrist, ed., *Confident Years, 1865–1916,* 210; *Zumbrota: The First 100 Years,* 299.
53. Here and below, Elaine Robinson, "Bicycling at the Turn of the Century," *Goodhue County Historical News* 24 (April 1990): 1–2; "They brought bikes to Red Wing," undated newspaper article, GCHS, Red Wing transportation file.
54. Barbara Tittle, "Horses and Boats," *Goodhue County Historical News* 24 (April 1990): 5, 8.
55. Frederick L. Smith, "The Philosopher of Frontenac," *The History of Frontenac* (Frontenac, Minn.: Self-published, 1951), 7–9.
56. Ibid.
57. Marshall, ed., 45.
58. Red Wing *Daily Republican*, Jan. 31, 1928. Bertha L. Heilbron credited Norwegian settlers at Red Wing with organizing the "nation's pioneer ski group" in 1883. See Heilbron, "Minnesotans at Play," *Minnesota History* 36 (Sept. 1958): 91.
59. "U. S. Central Championship Meet Program, Red Wing, Feb. 21, 1932," 3, GCHS collections; Red Wing *Daily Eagle*, Feb. 2, 1928.
60. Harry Borgen, "Ski Tournament Sites Used by the Aurora Ski Club, Red Wing, Minnesota," 2–3, GCHS Collections; "24th National Ski Tournament Program," Feb. 3–5, 1928, Red Wing, Minnesota," 8, GCHS Collections.
61. *Zumbrota: The First 100 Years,* 264.
62. Ibid., 266.
63. Here and below, Ross Hankins, "Show-Boats on the Upper Mississippi, 1905–1920," 1976, unpublished manuscript, GCHS collections.
64. Ross Hankins, "Excursion Boats on the Upper Mississippi, 1910–1927," 1976, unpublished manuscript, GCHS collections.

**Chapter 11**
1. Here and below, Frederick L. Johnson, *The Sea Wing Disaster,* 2nd ed. (Red Wing: Goodhue County Historical Society, 1990), 1–12.
2. Red Wing *Daily Republican,* July 14, 1890, 3; Johnson, 11–12.
3. St. Paul *Pioneer Press,* June 13, 1926.
4. St. Paul *Pioneer Press*, July 14, 1890.
5. St. Paul *Dispatch*, July 14, 16, 1890; St. Paul *Pioneer Press,* July 15, 17, 1890; *In Memory of Those Who Perished in the Disaster of the Steamer Sea Wing on Lake Pepin, July 13, 1890* (Red Wing: Red Wing Printing, 1890), 3.
6. Red Wing *Argus,* Aug. 27, 1890; St. Paul *Pioneer Press,* Aug. 23, 1890.
7. Johnson, 87–91.
8. Frederick L. Johnson, "Unlocking the Mysteries of the *Sea Wing*," *Minnesota History* 52 (Summer 1990): 75–77.
9. Cannon Falls *Beacon*, May 23, 1884. Norwegian-born Sather and his wife, Carrie, had come to Cannon Falls in 1877. See Wood, Alley, *History of Goodhue County*, 596.
10. Here and below, Cannon Falls *Beacon,* May 27, 1884.
11. Jeanette Burch, "The Cannon Falls Fires of 1884 and 1887," *Goodhue County Historical News* 16 (Nov. 1982): 4; Cannon Falls *Beacon,* May 27, 1884.
12. Burch, "The Cannon Falls Fires of 1884 and 1887," 4.
13. Here and below, Hutcheson, *Goodhue,* 21–22.
14. Kenyon *Leader*, April 1, 1908.
15. *Northwestern Miller* 15 (March 1883); Hancock, *Goodhue County Past and Present,* 211–12; Curtiss-Wedge, ed., *History of Goodhue County,* 506.
16. Curtiss-Wedge, ed., 144, 211; Hancock, 335.
17. Aileen Sethre, "The Fury of Winter," *Goodhue County Historical News* 16 ( June 1982): 1–2; Goodhue County *Republican*, Jan. 16, 1873; Cannon Falls *Beacon*, March 13, 1888.
18. Alexander P. Anderson, *The Seventh Reader* (Caldwell, Idaho: Self-published, 1941), 361–62.
19. Here and below, *Grange Advance* (Red Wing), July 9, 1879.
20. *Grange Advance,* July 9, 1879; Curtiss-Wedge, ed., 490–91.
21. Red Wing *Republican*, July 3, 1879; Curtiss-Wedge, ed., 490–91; Anderson, 362–64.

22. Marshall, ed., *Goodhue County's First Hundred Years,* 14–15.
23. Wood, Alley, 275–77.
24. Zumbrota *News*, Sept. 8, 29, 1905.
25. Here and below, Red Wing *Daily Republican,* extra and evening eds., Jan. 15, 1907; Curtiss-Wedge, ed., 502–03.
26. Here and below, Musicant, *Empire by Default,* 78–86; Franklin F. Holbrook, *Minnesota in the Spanish-American War and the Philippine Insurrection* (St. Paul: Minnesota War Records Commission, 1923), 1–8; Dupuy and Dupuy, *The Encyclopedia of Military History,* 907.
27. Holbrook, 2–8; Dupuy and Dupuy, 907.
28. Here and below, *Zumbrota: The First 100 Years,* 204–06; Curtiss-Wedge, ed., 249–51; Holbrook, 198, 245, 309–14.
29. Holbrook, 19; Folwell, *History of Minnesota,* vol. 3, 231–232.
30. Dupuy and Dupuy, 907.
31. Here and below, Holbrook, 47–48.
32. Ibid., 73–78.
33. Ibid., 79–86.
34. Holbrook, 50–52; Vincent J. Esposito, ed., *The West Point Atlas of American Wars*, vol. 1 (New York: Praeger, 1972), 158.
35. Esposito, ed., vol. 1, 158; Holbrook, 52–53. Details on the wounded during the Battle of Manila came from the regiment's acting surgeon (1st Lt.) Harry Richie's account in Goodhue *Enterprise*, Sept. 30, 1898.
36. Sgt. Charles Burnsen to Uncle Ole, July 5, 1898, and Burnsen to Uncle Ole, undated, both in GCHS Small Collections, Box 4.
37. Elwood Karwand, "Company G fights for Soldier's Proper Burial," Red Wing *Republican Eagle,* Aug. 31, 1998.
38. Here and below, Holbrook, 55–56. A copy of the May 22, 1898, Seebach letter to "Jens" is in the GCHS Seebach biography file.
39. Goodhue *Enterprise*, Aug. 13, 1898.
40. Musicant, 626–30.
41. Here and below, Folwell, vol. 3, 237–240; Holbrook, 60–72.
42. Karwand, "Soldiers Question Censorship," Red Wing *Republican Eagle,* Oct. 19, 1998.
43. Bruce Dickey to Father and Mother, Dec. 12 and 20, 1899, Joseph C. Dickey and Family Papers, MHS.
44. Bruce Dickey to Father and Mother, June 18, 1900, Dickey Papers, MHS.
45. Bruce Dickey to Father and Mother, Sept. 7, 1900, and Dec. 16, 1900, Dickey Papers, MHS.
46. Bruce Dickey to Father and Mother, Jan. 13, 1901, Dickey Papers, MHS; Trevor N. Dupuy, Curt Johnson, and David L. Bongard, *The Harper Encyclopedia of Military Biography* (New York: Castle Books, 1995), 16.
47. Holbrook, *Minnesota in the Spanish-American War,* 72.
48. Carl H. Chrislock, *The Progressive Era in Minnesota, 1899–1908* (St. Paul: MHS, 1971), 12; Curtiss-Wedge, ed., 731; Nelson, *History of the Scandinavians and Successful Scandinavians in the United States,* 430–34. See also Folwell, vol. 3, 219–22, for details of Lind's fusion candidacy of 1896.
49. Folwell, vol. 3, 241–242; George M. Stephenson, "The John Lind Papers," *Minnesota History* 17 (June 1936): 159–61.
50. Andrist, ed., *The Confident Years,* 290–94.
51. White, *et al.,* 170–71.
52. The Curtiss-Wedge history of Goodhue County contains nearly 700 biographies of county men and a handful of women. Many list political affiliations.
53. Hancock, 113–14; White, *et al.,* 64.
54. Goodhue County *Republican*, Oct. 14, 1859; White, *et al.,* 65–66, 153–54.
55. *Legislative Manual,* 1885, 196–236; J. A. Thatcher obituary, unidentified newspaper clipping, John H. Webster scrapbook, GCHS collections; Curtiss-Wedge, ed., 1057; Wood, Alley, 661–62.
56. Ferdinand Willius to Charles Betcher, Aug. 22, 1879, Willius (Ferdinand and family) Papers, MHS.
57. Here and below, Charles Betcher to Ferdinand Willius, Aug. 23 and 27, 1879, Willius Papers, MHS.
58. Ibid., Sept. 3, 1879.
59. Folwell, vol. 3, 246; *Legislative Manual,* 1897, 432–33.
60. Curtiss-Wedge, ed., 363–64, 1002.

61. Leonard A. Rosing and Family papers, biography, MHS; *Historical Sketches of Cannon Falls,* 82–83; H. E. Graham, *Cannon Falls, Minnesota* (Red Wing, Minn.: Wall & Haines, 1900), 8, 10.
62. Minneapolis *Tribune,* June 26, 1902; White, *et al.,* 173–74.
63. Char Henn, "The Training School: A Centennial Activity of the Minnesota Correctional Facility, Red Wing," (Red Wing: Self-published, 1989), 2.
64. Red Wing *Daily Republican,* Oct. 11, 1889; "The Training School," 3.
65. "The Training School," 4.
66. Ibid., 3–8.
67. Marshall, ed., 84.
68. Here and below, Smith, *History of Frontenac,* 4–9; Rasmussen, *A History of Goodhue County,* 146–47. For a summary of Israel Garrard's wartime service, see Stewart Sifakis, *Who Was Who in the Civil War* (New York: Facts on File, 1988), 238. Mrs. W. F. Fritze, "Old Frontenac," *Goodhue County Historical News* 7 (Nov. 1973): 3.
69. Marshall, ed., 84.
70. Walsh, "The Lutheran Ladies' Seminary of Red Wing, Minnesota" 19–20, GCHS collections.
71. Ibid., 12–15, 22–23, 26.
72. Ibid., 45–46.

**Chapter 12**
1. Sullivan, *Our Times (* abridged), 60–61.
2. Theodore C. Blegen, *Minnesota: A History of the State* (St. Paul: University of Minnesota, 1975), 446; Lowry Nelson, Charles E. Ramsey, and Jacob Toews, *A Century of Population Growth in Minnesota,* Bulletin 423 (St. Paul: University of Minnesota Agricultural Experimental Station, Feb. 1954), 4–7.
3. Sullivan (abridged), 56; Blegen, 464–65.
4. Here and below, Johnson, *A History of the American People,* 593–95.
5. Here and below, Foner and Garraty, eds., *The Reader's Companion to American History,* 694; Johnson, 594–95.
6. Nass, "The Rural Experience," in Clark, ed., *Minnesota in a Century of Change,* 133–34.
7. Ibid., 136.
8. Meyer, "The Discontinued Post Offices and Ghost Towns of Goodhue County," 5.
9. Pamphlet from Third Annual Meeting of the Postmaster's Association of Minnesota, June 9, 1908, 24–26, GCHS collections. See Rasmussen, *History of Goodhue County,* p.120, for routes and patron numbers in 1935.
10. Rasmussen, *A History of the City of Red Wing,* 153; *Zumbrota: The First 100 Years,* 178–80.
11. Here and below, Hutcheson, *Goodhue,* 40–41.
12. *Minnesota Department of Highways, 1921–1971, 50th Anniversary* (St. Paul: Minnesota Department of Highways, 1971), 20 (pamphlet); Marshall, ed., *Goodhue County's First Hundred Years,* 69.
13. Here and below, C. A. Rasmussen, "Beginning of Good Roads Movement," GCHS "Roads" file. See also Goodhue *Enterprise,* May 29 and June 26, 1897.
14. Ibid.
15. Here and below, Red Wing and Trenton Transit Company, "Corporate Minute Book, 1875–1890," MHS (see April 20, 1878, entry). See also Red Wing *Daily Republican,* May 1, 1895; Marshall, ed., 62–63.
16. GCHS Oral History, #40, p. 6.
17. "Minnesota Department of Highways, 1921–1971," 6, 20.
18. Red Wing *Daily Republican,* April 2, 1914 (see M. K. Kindseth's letter to the editor); Red Wing *Daily Republican,* April 14, 1914. See also Folwell, *History of Minnesota,* vol. 3, 309–12.
19. Red Wing *Daily Republican,* May 20, 1914.
20. Marshall, ed., 69–70.
21. "Goodhue," *Goodhue County Historical News* 28 (June 1994): 6.
22. Ibid.
23. "The Horseless Carriage Comes to Goodhue County," *Goodhue County Historical News* 28 (June 1994): 1–7.
24. *License Book, 1906–1908,* Goodhue County, City of Red Wing, MHS State Archives Notebooks.
25. Sullivan (abridged), 56.
26. Red Wing *Daily Republican,* July 12, 1909.
27. Red Wing *Daily Republican,* July 7, 1909; Marshall, ed., 73.

28. Curtiss-Wedge, ed., *History of Goodhue County,* 268–70, 1015–16; *Zumbrota: The First 100 Years,* 312–13.
29. Severson, *Goodhue County Heritage,* 132–33.
30. Johnson, *Days of Dennison,* 54.
31. Severson, 175–76.
32. "The Reminiscences of Mr. William Remshardt," Ford Motor Company Archives, Oral History Section, Oct. 1956, 1–3 (copy at GCHS).
33. Red Wing *Daily Republican,* July 3 and 7, 1909.
34. Marshall, ed., 70.
35. Sullivan (abridged), 56; GCHS Oral History Collection, #69, June 29, 1970, interview with Willard Dibble, Sr.; Severson, 126.
36. "The Reminiscences of Mr. William Remshardt," 6–7.
37. Marshall, ed., 70.
38. Rasmussen, *History of Red Wing,* 133; Marshall, ed., 57.
39. Severson, 150; Rasmussen, *History of Goodhue County,* 179.
40. *Zumbrota: The First 100 Years,* 187, 301; *Goodhue County Historical News* 5 (June 1971): 2.
41. *Historical Sketches of Cannon Falls,* 90.
42. Curtiss-Wedge, ed., 914; Mary Scofield to My Dear Children, March 4, 1908, Mary P. Scofield Papers, MHS.
43. Here and below, Cannon Falls *Beacon,* Feb. 4, 1910; Herbert W. Meyer, *Builders of Northern States Power Company,* 1972 ed. (Minneapolis: Northern States Power, 1957), 17–18.
44. Marshall, ed., 72.
45. Wood, Alley, *History of Goodhue County,* 624; Curtiss-Wedge, ed., 785.
46. Severson, 158–59.
47. Here and below, Goodhue *Enterprise,* Jan., 1, 1901, Feb. 5, 1901; Hazel Anderson and Archie Swenson, *How It All Began* (White Rock, Minn.: White Rock State Bank, 1985), 1–2; Hutcheson, *Goodhue,* 39–40; Curtiss-Wedge, ed., 862, 870.
48. *Historical Sketches of Cannon Falls,* 73–74; Curtiss-Wedge, ed., 925–26.
49. Tweeton, "The Business of Agriculture," in Clark, ed., 272.
50. Severson, 80.
51. Ibid., 87.
52. "Bellechester Clay Pits Obsolete," Red Wing *Republican Eagle*, Oct. 27, 1973; Severson, 77–78.

**Chapter 13**
1. Walter Lord's popular history provides an overview of prewar America, using "the good years" in his title. See Walter Lord, *The Good Years: From 1900 to the First World War* (New York: Harper, 1960); Blegen, *Minnesota: A History of the State,* 469, also uses the expression in his assessment of prewar Minnesota.
2. George B. Manhart, *Alliance and Entente, 1871–1914* (New York: F. S. Crofts, 1932); Sullivan, *Our Times* (abridged), 431–33.
3. The quotation is from Arthur S. Link, *Woodrow Wilson and the Progressive Era, 1910–1917* (New York: Harper, 1954), 145; Carl H. Chrislock, *The Progressive Era in Minnesota, 1899–1918* (St. Paul: MHS, 1971), 66.
4. Red Wing *Daily Republican,* Aug. 5, 1914.
5. Here and below, Blegen, 469–70; Chrislock, *The Progressive Era in Minnesota,* 70.
6. Chrislock, *The Progressive Era in Minnesota,* 68–70; Red Wing *Daily Republican,* Aug. 5, 1914.
7. A. H. Tangen to Knute Nelson, Nov. 11, 1914, and Kolben M. Larwick to Knute Nelson, Nov. 12, 1914, Knute Nelson Papers, MHS; Martin Gilbert, *The First World War: A Complete History* (New York: Henry Holt, 1994), 102–03, 127–28.
8. Here and below, Red Wing *Daily Republican,* Sept. 29, 1914; Chrislock, *The Progressive Era in Minnesota,* 76–83.
9. Andrist, ed., *Confident Years,* 381–82.
10. Oscar T. Barck Jr., and Nelson M. Blake, *Since 1900: A History of the United States in Our Times* (New York: MacMillan, 1959), 172–76.
11. *Zumbrota: The First 100 Years,* 209–10.
12. Barck and Blake, eds., 212–15.
13. *Goodhue County in the World War* (Red Wing: Red Wing Printing, 1919), 6–7.
14. Zumbrota *News*, Aug. 31, 1917. The newspaper also lists each of the men who left with the company. *Zumbrota: The First 100 Years,* 209–10; *Goodhue County in the World War,* 183–86.

15. Sullivan (abridged), 491.
16. Here and below, Mildred Scherf, "Reminiscing—Hectic Days During World War I," GCHS Scherf biography file. Mildred Scherf was the daughter of Fred Scherf. On June 24, 1987, this author interviewed Ms. Scherf regarding Farmer-Labor politics. She told of the yellow-paint incident (notes in author's possession). See also Curtiss-Wedge, ed., *History of Goodhue County,* 1033–34.
17. Fred Scherf to Knute Nelson, Jan. 6 and Feb. 1, 1916, Knute Nelson papers, MHS.
18. For an overview of the prewar political climate in Minnesota, see Carl H. Chrislock, *Watchdog of Loyalty: The Minnesota Commission of Public Safety during World War I* (St. Paul: MHS Press, 1991), 1–60. Historian Carl Chrislock was born in Goodhue County and became emeritus professor of history at Augsburg College in Minneapolis. For more on the NPL's philosophy and goals, see "Rural Americans and Industrial Capitalism" in Diner, *A Very Different Age,* 102–24.
19. Chrislock, *Watchdog of Loyalty,* 40–48.
20. Ibid., 52–54.
21. Seebach quotation from Carl H. Chrislock, *Ethnicity Challenged: The Upper Midwest Norwegian-American Experience in World War I* (Northfield, Minn.: Norwegian-American Historical Association, 1981), 57–58.
22. Chrislock, *Watchdog of Loyalty,* 54–60.
23. Folwell, *History of Minnesota,* vol. 3, 557.
24. Ibid., 557–58. Folwell's Appendix 19 to his history provides more detail of the Public Safety Commission's activities.
25. Chrislock, *The Progressive Era in Minnesota,* 157–60; Chrislock, *Watchdog of Loyalty,* 187–98. See also Cannon Falls *Beacon,* June 7, 1918, for a strong anti-NPL editorial, and Robert L. Morlan, "The Nonpartisan League and the Minnesota Campaign of 1918," *Minnesota History* 34 (Summer 1955): 229. *Goodhue County in the World War,* 160–61.
26. Chrislock, *The Progressive Era in Minnesota,* 169–70.
27. Sullivan (abridged), 564; Red Wing *Daily Republican,* July 8, 1918.
28. Here and below, Chrislock, *Ethnicity Challenged,* 38–41.
29. Walsh, "The Lutheran Ladies Seminary," 49–53; Jeanne Ode, "The Professor," *Goodhue County Historical News* 19 (July 1985): 5.
30. Red Wing *Daily Eagle,* March 14, 1918; Zumbrota *News,* March 22, 1918.
31. Ibid.
32. Zumbrota *News,* April 12, 1918.
33. Zumbrota *News,* March 15, 1918.
34. *Goodhue County in the World War,* 177.
35. Folwell, vol. 3, 571–75. Gilbert shared the Jackson County docket with Arthur C. Townley, founder of the NPL. For information on Gilbert's Lakeville trial, see James Manahan, *Trials of a Lawyer* (Minneapolis: Self-published, 1933), 232–38. The Manahan book is in the MHS collection.
36. Red Wing *Daily Republican,* May 4, 1918.
37. Ibid., May 9, 1918. Dr. Gates, who had been accused during Martin's trial of assaulting the Nonpartisan Leaguer, later joined the war effort when he was appointed to the medical reserve as a captain. Gates also had two sons in military service. The well-known physician built the Kenyon telephone exchange in 1901 and served as president of the village council. Gates was killed in a car-train accident in June 1922. A crowd reportedly numbering 4,000 attended his funeral. See Kenyon *News,* June 22, 1922; Cannon Falls *Beacon,* July 26, 1918; *Goodhue County in the World War,* 92.
38. Red Wing *Daily Republican,* May 10, 1918.
39. Red Wing *Daily Republican,* May 15, 1918. After long and unsuccessful appeals, Gilbert reported to the Goodhue County jail in February 1921 to serve his one-year sentence. See Red Wing *Sunday Republican,* Feb. 6, 1921. Gilbert stayed loyal to his socialist beliefs. In 1950, at age 86, he was still a columnist for *Co-op* magazine. See Meridel Le Sueur, *Crusaders: The Radical Legacy of Marian and Arthur Le Sueur* (St. Paul: MHS Press, 1984 ed.), 61.
40. Red Wing *Daily Republican,* July 1, 2, 1918. Some men in Goodhue County did refuse induction into the armed services. In October 1918, for example, Carl Danielson, 33, withdrew his declaration to become a citizen. Danielson said he wanted to return to Sweden to die there rather in France. Sjur Larson-Husby of Zumbrota also renounced his citizenship when faced with the draft. See Red Wing *Daily Republican,* Oct. 18, 1918.

41. Minneapolis *Journal,* June 27, 1918; Red Wing *Daily Republican,* July 2, 1918. The *Daily Republican* reprinted the Minneapolis *Daily News* editorial "The Sentence of John C. Seebach" on July 3, 1918. Johannes (John) Christian Seebach was an uncle of Spanish-American war hero Oscar Seebach, who, during World War I, helped organize the Red Wing Home Guard. According to a family history, John refused to allow sons Carl, 24, and Walter, 27, to fight against "the mother country" and placed both sons on a farm in Goodhue. See Seebach family records, GCHS biography file.

42. Zumbrota *News,* April 19 and Nov. 15, 1918. The "Hun Shop" report is carried in April 19 Zumbrota *News.*

43. Cannon Falls *Beacon*, June 14 and 28 and July 19, 1918. See also CGHS Oral History Collection #74 (interview with Henry C. Hinrichs), 36, 44. Hinrichs reported that in Featherstone several houses and buildings were splashed with yellow paint.

44. John S. Pardee to T. G. Winter, Aug. 7, 1917, Minnesota Commission of Public Safety, Agents' Reports to T. G. Winter, 1917–1919, MHS.

45. Thomas Mohn to T. G. Winter, Aug. 28, 1917. Minnesota Commission of Public Safety, Agents' Reports to T. G. Winter, 1917–1919, MHS.

46. Chrislock, *The Progressive Era in Minnesota,* 148–49.

47. Chrislock, *Watchdog of Loyalty*, 222.

48. *Goodhue County in the World War,* 153–54.

49. Chrislock, *Watchdog of Loyalty*, 287–89. See also Red Wing *Daily Republican,* Oct. 14, 1918.

50. Red Wing *Daily Republican,* Oct. 11, 1918.

51. Cannon Falls *Beacon,* June 14, 1918; Le Sueur, xvii. See also Scherf, "Reminiscing—Hectic Days during World War I," GCHS Scherf biography file. Goodhue County did have active Nonpartisan League strongholds, particularly in Hay Creek, Belvidere, and Featherstone. Henry Hinrichs, who farmed on the Featherstone prairie with his wife, Esther, recalled that farmers there were "100% Non-partisan Leaguers" with the exception of a small nucleus living around the town hall. See GCHS Oral History Collection #74, 32–33, 35–37, 54.

52. Chrislock, *Watchdog of Loyalty,* 307–08, and *The Progressive Era in Minnesota,* 169–70.

53. Here and below, *Legislative Manual,* 1919, 124. For an overview of the 1918 campaign, see Robert L. Morlan, "The Nonpartisan League and the Minnesota Campaign of 1918," *Minnesota History* 34 (Summer 1955): 221–32.

54. White, *et al.,* 183–84.

55. Red Wing *Daily Republican,* Nov. 6, 1918.

56. Blegen, 473.

57. Red Wing *Daily Republican*, May 10, 13, 18, 20, and 21, 1918; Hutcheson, *Goodhue,* 68; *Goodhue County in the World War,* 154–55.

58. *Goodhue County in the World War,* 159–78.

59. Zumbrota *News,* Oct. 25, Nov. 1, 1918; Red Wing *Daily Eagle,* Oct. 18, 1918; *Goodhue County in the World War,* 161–64: *Zumbrota: The First 100 Years,* 214.

60. Blegen, 471–73; Red Wing *Daily Republican,* May 24, 1918; Esposito, ed., *The West Point Atlas of American Wars,* vol. 2, 64–65; Sullivan (abridged), 547–50; Gen. John J. Pershing, "Report of General Pershing," in *Goodhue County in the World War,* 44–46.

61. Among the Goodhue County women to serve overseas were Esther and Ellen Jorstad, two Kenyon sisters stationed at Hospital No. 65 in France, and Ellen Teele and Ada Anderberg of Red Wing, a part of the AEF in France.

62. *Goodhue County in the World War,* 145, 150. Captain William F. Rowles, Goodhue, was listed as killed in action on August 30, 1918, at Juvigny in France.

63. Red Wing *Daily Republican,* May 9, 1918.

64. Lt. Harvey Johnson, "Company L," in *Goodhue County in the World War,* 183–84. Company D's history is given on page 186–87. No author is listed. Individual photos are also included; see 52–62 (Company L) and 62–65 (Company D).

65. Esposito, ed., vol. 2, 69–70.

66. War Records Commission, Box 6, "Killed and Wounded by County," MHS; *Goodhue County in the World War,* 143–51; GCHS World War I file.

67. The influenza virus killed 642,000 Americans during the two-year period at the end of war, according to Dr. Keiji Fukuda, chief of the influenza branch of the epidemiology section of the Centers for Disease Control and Prevention. See St. Paul *Pioneer Press,* Nov. 9, 1997. Foner and Garraty, eds., *The Reader's Companion to American History,* 356, 1172.

68. Red Wing *Daily Republican,* Oct. 4, 7, and 12, 1918; Zumbrota *News,* Oct. 11 and 18, 1918.

69. Zumbrota *News,* Oct. 18, 1918.
70. Red Wing *Daily Republican,* Oct. 12, 1918; *Goodhue County in the World War,* 143–51; Cannon Falls *Beacon,* Oct. 11, 1918.
71. Red Wing *Daily Republican,* Oct. 10, 1918; *Goodhue County in the World War,* 144, 149–50.
72. Red Wing Hospital Minute Book, 1914–1922, GCHS. See entries for Oct. 8 and Dec. 10. Red Wing *Daily Eagle,* Oct. 19, 1918; Red Wing *Daily Republican,* Oct. 24, 1918.
73. Zumbrota *News,* Oct. 18, 1918.
74. Cannon Falls *Beacon,* Nov. 1, 1918; Red Wing *Daily Republican,* Oct. 30 and 31 and Nov. 1, 1918.
75. Cannon Falls *Beacon,* Nov. 1, 1918; Red Wing *Daily Republican,* Nov. 1, 4, and 6.
76. Zumbrota *News,* Nov. 15, 1918; *Red Cross* (Red Wing) *Minute Book, 1917–1950,* Nov. 20, 1918 entry, GCHS.

**Chapter 14**
1. Here and below, Red Wing *Daily Eagle,* Nov. 12, 1918; Red Wing *Daily Republican,* Nov. 12, 1918; *Goodhue County in the World War,* 171; Walsh, *The Lutheran Ladies Seminary,* 53.
2. Clara L. Hellickson and others, "Memories of Wanamingo," (Wanamingo, Minn.: Wanamingo Historical Society, 1978), 74.
3. Callister, *Recollections,* 14–15.
4. Cannon Falls *Beacon,* Nov. 15, 1918.
5. Here and below, *Zumbrota: The First 100 Years,* 213–14; Zumbrota *News,* Nov. 18, 1918. See Sullivan, *Our Times* (abridged), 567–68, for details on the erroneous report of the war's end on November 7.
6. Hutcheson, *Goodhue,* 68.
7. Scovell, ed., *Yesteryears,* 96–97; Red Wing *Morning Republican*, April 21, 1915.
8. Red Wing *Daily Republican,* Oct. 24 and 30, 1918.
9. Folwell, *A History of Minnesota,* vol. 3, 302–03; *Goodhue County Historical Society News* 1 (June 1967): 4; White, et al., *Minnesota Votes,* 88–102.
10. Scovell, ed., *Yesteryears,* 97.
11. Ibid., 96; *Legislative Manual* 1919, 556. Blocker notes "the pietist Norwegian farmers who colonized the Upper Midwest and Plains states employed total abstinence to set themselves apart from their native–born neighbors." See Jack S. Blocker Jr., *American Temperance Movements: Cycles of Reform* (Boston: Twayne Publishers, 1989), 67.
12. *Legislative Manual* 1919, 556.
13. Scovell. ed., *Yesteryears,* 98; Red Wing *Daily Republican,* Jan. 16, 1920.
14. Zumbrota *News,* March 29, 1918. The account, written by Fredric J. Harkin, was reprinted from the Rochester (New York) *Union and Advocate.*
15. Barbara Stuhler, "Organizing for the Vote, Leaders of Minnesota's Woman Suffrage Movement," *Minnesota History* 54 (Fall 1995): 291–92; Johnson, *A History of the American People,* 658–60.
16. Here and below, Goodhue County *Tribune,* July 11, 1984; Goodhue *Enterprise*, May 3, 1921; Hutcheson, *Goodhue,* 69.
17. "The Last Man Who Knew Everything: Thorstein Veblen," *The Carleton Voice* 45 (Fall 1980): 5–14; Callister, 7.
18. Sondra Herman, *Eleven against War: Studies in American International Thought, 1898–1921* (Stanford, Calif.: Hoover Institute, 1969), 152.
19. Ibid., 162–64.
20. "The Last Man Who Knew Everything: Thorstein Veblen," 14.
21. Here and below, "The Last Man Who Knew Everything, Thorstein Veblen," 14; Blegen, *Minnesota: A History of the State,* 510–11.
22. Daniel Nelson, *Shifting Fortunes: The Rise and Decline of American Labor, from the 1820s to the Present* (Chicago: Ivan R. Dee, 1997), 91–92.
23. Peter Rachleff, "Turning Points in the Labor Movement: Three Key Conflicts," in Clifford E. Clark Jr., ed., *Minnesota in a Century of Change,* 196–205.
24. Red Wing *Daily Republican,* May 18, 1914.
25. Ibid., May 19, 1914.
26. Here and below, Minnesota Department of Labor and Industry, *Trade Union Reports-Strikes and Lockouts, December, 1917 through June, 1918,* MHS; Red Wing *Daily Eagle,* April 2, 1918.
27. Here and below, Red Wing *Daily Eagle,* July 8, 9, 10, and 11, 1918; Martin and Vrooman, *Heart and Sole,* 44–45, 68–69; Red Wing *Daily Republican,* July 8, 1918.
28. Labor and Industries, "Trade Union Reports as of May 1, 1918, Goodhue County," MHS.

29. Public Safety Commission, "Survey of Women in Industry, 1918–1919," Goodhue County.
30. Goodhue County *Daily Republican,* Nov. 1, 1918. See Nordholm's political advertisement, a part of his campaign for Clerk of District Court.
31. Here and below, Nelson, *Shifting Fortunes,* 92–94; Blegen, 454–55.
32. Myron Ohnstad to Industrial Commission of Minnesota, Sept. 10, 1914; Lorrine E. Schultz to Myron Ohnstad, Sept. 14, 1921; Clem Smart to Commissioner of Labor, June 6, 1921; Labor and Industry, Minimum Wage Correspondence, 1921, MHS.
33. Anne Reagan to Minimum Wage Commission, Feb. 12, 1921; Secretary of the Minimum Wage Commission to Reagan, Feb. 23, 1921; Reagan to Secretary of the Minimum Wage Commission, March 24, 1921, MHS.
34. Nass, "The Rural Experience" in Clark, ed., *Minnesota in a Century of Change,* 136; Blegen, 400.
35. *Zumbrota: The First 100 Years,* 119–20.
36. Here and below, GCHS Oral History Collection #44, G. J. "Dick" Kunau, 1–6; Marshall, ed., *Goodhue County's First Hundred Years,* 29.
37. Here and below, Lois Scharpen, "Memories of Extension, Margaret Lohmann," *Goodhue County Historical News* 20 (Nov. 1986): 3–4.
38. Here and below, Marshall, ed., 27; Zumbrota *News,* Oct. 4, 1918.
39. Severson, *Goodhue County Heritage,* 81, 88.
40. Ibid., 82.
41. Callister, 28–29.
42. *Zumbrota, The First 100 Years,* 121, 125, 328–29.
43. Hutcheson, *Goodhue,* 80–81.
44. Frederick K. Johnson, "Our Old Model 'T' Ford," *Goodhue County Historical News* 28 (June 1994): 1–2.
45. *Zumbrota, The First 100 Years,* 110–13.
46. Marshall, ed., 106; Rasmussen, *History of Goodhue County,* 299.
47. Here and below, E. A. Stewart, J. M. Larson, and J. Romness, *The Red Wing Project on Utilization of Electricity in Agriculture* (St. Paul: University of Minnesota Agricultural Experiment Station, 1923), 1–2; Nass, 137. Nass is more equivocal about the project's claim to be the first rural electric line in the world, calling it "one of the first."
48. "Rural Red Wing Experimental Lines Brought Electricity to the Farmer," Red Wing *Daily Republican Eagle,* Oct. 30, 1973.
49. Jeanne Pearson, "A Revolution—Electricity Reaches the Farm," *Goodhue County Historical News* 20 (Nov. 1986): 5.
50. "Rural Red Wing Experimental Lines Brought Electricity to the Farmer," Red Wing *Daily Republican Eagle,* Oct. 30, 1973.
51. Harold Severson, *The Night They Turned on the Lights* (Kenyon, Minn.: Midwest Historical Features, 1964), 229–30.
52. Arnold S. Rice, *The Ku Klux Klan in American Politics* (Washington, D.C.: Public Affairs Press, 1962), 11–18; Foner and Garraty, eds., *The Reader's Companion to American History,* 625–26.
53. H. W. Evans, "The Klan's Mission—Americanism," *The Kourier Magazine* 1 (Nov. 1925): 5; Geoffrey Perrett, *America in the Twenties—A History* (New York: Simon & Schuster, 1982), 72–76. Perrett (page 74) quotes Evans, who said the Klan was "mostly composed of poor people."
54. Blegen, 482; Perrett, 75.
55. Julia Wiech Lief, "Gone Are the Sinister Years," Red Wing *Daily Republican Eagle,* May 22, 1981.
56. Lief, Red Wing *Daily Republican Eagle,* May 22, 1981; Red Wing *Daily Republican* and Red Wing *Daily Eagle,* April 6, 1923.
57. Here and below, Red Wing *Daily Republican,* Sept. 24, 1923; Red Wing *Eagle,* Sept. 24, 1923.
58. Here and below, Red Wing *Daily Republican,* Sept. 24, 26, and 28, 1925.
59. Zumbrota *News,* July 13, 1923.
60. Pine Island *Record,* July 23, 1925.
61. Zumbrota *News,* July 24, 1925; Red Wing *Daily Republican,* Aug. 3, 1925.
62. Foner and Garraty, eds., 626.
63. Blegen, 482.
64. Here and below, Ruth C. Mondale, "The Pine Island Rifles," *Goodhue County Historical News* 11 (Feb. 1977): 6; Mrs. C. T. [Ruth] Mondale, "Pine Island, 1854–1971," *Goodhue County Historical News* 5 (June 1971):1.
65. Zumbrota *News,* Feb. 21, 1936.
66. Red Wing *Republican,* May 12, 1897; Red Wing *Republican Eagle,* May 21, 1957.

67. Red Wing *Daily Republican Eagle*, Dec. 15, 1998. See Karwand's Spanish American War feature. GCHS has a photograph of Rastus in its files.
68. Red Wing *Daily Republican,* July 22, 1918.
69. Roy Wilkins, *Standing Fast: The Autobiography of Roy Wilkins* (New York: Viking Press, 1994), 31.
70. Red Wing *Daily Republican,* Jan. 8, 1907.
71. Zumbrota *News*, Aug. 10, 1923.
72. Red Wing *Daily Republican,* Jan. 14, 1907, and July 8, 1909.
73. Walsh, "The Lutheran Ladies' Seminary of Red Wing, Minnesota," 21; Goodhue County Oral History Collections, #41, 24.
74. Red Wing *Daily Republican,* July 7 and July 12, 1909.
75. *Fifteenth Census of the United States, 1930,* Table 21, 1237.
76. Sinclair Lewis, *Main Street* (New York: Harcourt, Brace and Howe, 1920), preface.
77. Charles P. Hall, *Sane Street: A Short Story of Minnesota* (Red Wing: Red Wing Advertising, 1922), 1–14.
78. Ibid., 5, 7, 9, 11.
79. Rasmussen, *History of Red Wing*, 269–70.
80. Harold Evans, *The American Century* (New York: Alfred A. Knopf, 1998), 182–83.
81. Blegen, 480–82; Thomas Harvey, "Small Town Minnesota," in Clark, ed., *Minnesota in a Century of Change,* 109; Evans, 183.
82. *Goodhue County Historical News,* 15 (Nov. 1981): 4; Curtiss-Wedge, ed., *History of Goodhue County,* 806–07.
83. Pine Island *Record,* May 29, 1924. See "Banking in Pine Island," *Goodhue County Historical News* 12 (Feb. 1978): 2–3. See also *The Security State Bank of Pine Island Newsletter*, Sept. 27, 1982: 2–3.
84. Pine Island *Record,* May 29, 1924.

**Chapter 15**
1. GCHS Oral History Collections, #41, 14–16. See also Red Wing *Daily Republican Eagle*, April 22, 1983.
2. Frederick K. Johnson, *This I Remember* (1992 memoir), GCHS collections, 30–31.
3. Ibid., 32. See also GCHS Oral History Collections, #41, 14 and GCHS Oral History Collections, #36, 29.
4. *Index to Sellers and Purchasers of Liquor,* vol. 1 (1921–1933), 43–59, 79–106; *Liquor Prescription Record, Aug. 1, 1924 – Oct.1, 1930,* state archives notebooks (Goodhue County District Court records), MHS collections. These volumes list the liquor-prescription-filling agency and those for whom they were filled. For example, City Drug is under Tab C in the first section of the volume, and Grondahl is under Tab G.
5. Rasmussen, *History of Goodhue County*, 247. The source of the quote on Grondahl is newspaperman Albert Marshall (Red Wing *Daily Republican Eagle*, July 7, 1954), who took over the city's *Daily Eagle* and merged it with Grondahl's *Daily Republican* in November 1940.
6. "Purifying the Island Opposite Red Wing," *Tidsskrift, for Kirke og Samfund* (newspaper for church and society, Oct. 1914): 229–30; Red Wing *Daily Republican Eagle,* Sept. 28, 1908.
7. Zumbrota *News,* Jan. 5, 1922.
8. Goodhue County District Court Records, Certificates of Convictions, Book B, 133–34, 136, 149, 166, MHS; Goodhue County District Court Records, Pine Island Justice Court, 1906–1938, MHS; Callister, *Recollections*, 127–28.
9. T. W. Taylor to Industrial Commission of Minnesota, April 5, 1922, MHS.
10. T. W. Taylor to Henry McColl, Industrial Commission of Minnesota, June 4, 1922, MHS. Taylor later reported that the pool-hall situation had been corrected.
11. T. W. Taylor to Henry McColl, Industrial Commission of Minnesota, July 26, 1922, MHS.
12. Pine Island *Record,* July 23, 1925; Red Wing *Daily Republican*, July 25, 1925; Goodhue County District Court Records, Certificates of Convictions, Book B, pages 166–67, 171, 173, MHS.
13. Red Wing *Daily Republican*, Jan. 3, 1921; Red Wing *Daily Republican*, July 24, 1925.
14. Blegen, *Minnesota: A History of the State*, 481; Evans, *The American Century*, 200–02.
15. Hutcheson, *Goodhue*, 70–71.
16. Richard Chin, "Prohibition Worked, Say Some Historians. Could It Come Back?" St. Paul *Pioneer Press*, April 13, 1997.

17. Blegen, 477–79. See also Arthur Naftalin, "The Tradition of Protest and the Roots of the Farmer-Labor Party," *Minnesota History* 35 (June 1956): 53–63.
18. Virginia Dustin, "As a Woman Sees It," *The Friend* 21 (Sept. 1944): 5. For an overview of the role of farmwomen in the NPL, see Karen Starr, "Fighting for the Future, Farm Women of the Non-partisan League," *Minnesota History* 48 (Summer 1983): 255–62.
19. Rolf Stageberg, "Olaf Stageberg and Family," 1–2, 31–32, unpublished manuscript, GCHS Stageberg biography file; White, *et al.*, *Minnesota Votes*, 183–84.
20. Susie Stageberg's article, "A Sturdy Defense," was printed in the Fort Dodge (Iowa) *Messenger*.
21. Rolf Stageberg, "Susie W. Stageberg," 32, in GCHS Stageberg file; notes about Scherf and the *Organized Farmer* from June 24, 1987, interview with Scherf's daughter Mildred, in author's possession.
22. Frederick L. Johnson, "From Leavenworth to Congress: The Improbable Journey of Francis H. Shoemaker," *Minnesota History* 51 (Spring 1989): 167–68.
23. *Organized Farmer*, Oct. 4 and Dec. 27, 1929.
24. *Minnesota Union Advocate* (St. Paul), April 3, 1930.
25. Frederick L. Johnson, 169; St. Paul *Dispatch*, Dec. 22 and 29, 1930.
26. St. Paul *Pioneer Press*, Dec. 30, 1930.
27. Foner and Garraty, eds., *The Reader's Companion to American History*, 279–81; Evans, 220–23.
28. Barck and Blake, *Since 1900*, 409; Foner and Garraty, eds., 279–81.
29. Paul Johnson, *A History of the American People*, 735; Foner and Garraty, eds., 279–80.
30. Evans, 218–23.
31. William Manchester, *The Glory and the Dream: A Narrative History of America, 1932–1972* (Boston: Little, Brown, 1973), 43–45; Paul Johnson, 735.
32. Goodhue County, City of Red Wing, Jail Register (see "Tramps Lodged" books for 1925–30, 1930–31, and 1931–32; later records are incomplete), MHS. In 1925 the total number of tramps registered was 341. The number was 1,062 in 1930; 2,570 in 1931; 3,062 in 1932; and 3,252 in 1933. Manchester, 19; Evans, 220–21.
33. "Dream into Nightmare," *Goodhue County Historical News* 26 (April 1992): 2.
34. Ibid.
35. "Registering for Work," *Goodhue County Historical News* 26 (April 1992): 5.
36. *Annual Report of the City Clerk of the City of Red Wing, Minnesota for the Year Ending December 31, 1932* (see also subsequent volumes for 1933 through 1940), MHS; Red Wing *Daily Republican*, July 25, 1931.
37. Here and below, Marvin, Vrooman, *Heart and Sole*, 106–12.
38. Ibid., 119–20.
39. Angell, "Leader in Leather, S. B. Foot Tanning Co.," *Minnesota History* 47 (Fall 1981): 271–72.
40. Frederick K. Johnson, *This I Remember*, 28–29; Blegen, 526.
41. Henry E. Fritz, "Assimilation vs. Cultural Pluralism: Making Federal Policy toward Native Americans, 1869–1933," 1–3, 11–14. A copy of this 1997 paper by Professor Fritz is in GCHS Chesley Library. In his book, *The Movement for Indian Assimilation* (Philadelphia: University of Pennsylvania, 1963), Fritz wrote that the "government approach to the Native Americans in the 1870s was "with a Sharps' carbine in one hand and a Bible in the other." For more on the issue of assimilation, see W. Roger Buffalohead, "The Indian New Deal: A Review Essay," *Minnesota History* 48 (Winter 1983): 339–41.
42. Roy E. Meyer, "The Prairie Island Community, A Remnant of Minnesota Sioux," *Minnesota History* 37 (Sept. 1961): 278.
43. Ibid.
44. Meyer, 279–80.
45. Here and below, Mary Biederman, "Dr. Frances Densmore, 1867–1957," *Goodhue County Historical News* 5 (Nov. 1971): 1–2; Angell, *Saga of a River Town*, 218–19.
46. "Registering for Work," *Goodhue County Historical News* 26 (April 1992): 5.
47. Eva Million, "The Rural Areas," *Goodhue County Historical News* 26 (April 1992): 4.
48. Jeannette Scriver Burch, "The Depression Years," *Goodhue County Historical Society News* 27 (April 1993): 3–5; GCHS Oral History Collections, #129, 13.
49. Red Wing *Daily Republican Eagle*, Nov. 1, 1984; Burch, "The Depression Years," *Goodhue County Historical Society News* 27 (April 1993): 4. See also Marjorie Bingham, "Keeping at It: Minnesota Women," in Clark, ed., *Minnesota in a Century of Change*, 448–49.

50. "The Great Depression," *Goodhue County Historical Society News* 26 (April 1992): 2. See the comments of Bruce Akerson, whose father Rudolph B. Akerson ran Vasa General Store, in "The Rural General Store," *Goodhue County Historical Society News* 27 (April 1993): 6–8.
51. Red Wing *Daily Republican Eagle*, Nov. 1, 1984. See also "1934—Year of the Drought," *Goodhue County Historical Society News* 26 (April 1992): 5, and Evans, 227.
52. Kenyon *Leader*, July 3, 1931; Red Wing *Daily Republican* (rural edition), July 3, 1931; Harold Severson, "Banking in Kenyon," *Goodhue County Historical Society News* 12 (June 1978): 5.
53. Evans, 223–24.
54. Severson, "Banking in Kenyon," 5.
55. "The Banks in Goodhue and Bellechester," "Frontenac State Bank," *Goodhue County Historical Society News* 12 (June 1978): 6. See also Hutcheson, *Goodhue*, 85; Meyer, "The Discontinued Post Offices and Ghost Towns of Goodhue County," 81.
56. Jeannette Scriver Burch, "Banks of the Cannon Falls Area," *Goodhue County Historical Society News* 12 (June 1978): 3–4.
57. Manchester, 36–43.
58. Ibid., 43.
59. Manchester, 80–87; Evans, 246, 272–73; Angell, 313. *Minnesota Department of Highways, 1921–1971, 50th Anniversary* (St. Paul: [Minnesota Department of Highways.]. 1971), 20 (pamphlet); *Minnesota Department of Highways, 1921–1971, 50th Anniversary* (St. Paul: [Minnesota Department of Highways.]. 1971), 20 (pamphlet);
60. GCHS Oral History Collections, #44, 7–10; Frederick K. Johnson, "The Civilian Conservation Corps: A New Deal for Youth," *Minnesota History* 48 (Fall 1983): 296–97.
61. *Zumbrota: The First 100 Years*, 103–04. Minnesota's CCC camps were constituted as follows: U. S. National Forest Service (24), state forests (24), state parks (three), private lands or forests (one), erosion and flood control (nine). See Rolf T. Anderson, *Federal Relief Construction in Minnesota, 1933–1941*, MHS.
62. "Conservation at Work in Goodhue County," *Goodhue County Historical News* 22 (Nov. 1988): 1, 6.
63. *Works Progress Administration, Minnesota: Progress of WPA in Minnesota, August 1935–December, 1936*, 5–8, MHS. WPA employment in Minnesota averaged more than 55,000 a month from January through November 1936. See the graph "Minnesota Emergency Relief and Emergency Employment Case Load, 11/32–11/36," page 8.
64. Minnesota Historical Records Survey, *Inventory of the County Archives of Minnesota, No. 25, Goodhue County, Red Wing* (St. Paul: The Survey, 1941), 147–48; Angell, 316.
65. Paul Maccabee, *John Dillinger Slept Here: A Crooks' Tour of Crime and Corruption in St. Paul, 1920–1936* (St. Paul: MHS, 1995), 250.
66. Red Wing *Daily Republican*, Aug. 17, 1931.
67. Maccabee, 200.
68. Frederick L. Johnson, 170–71.
69. Ibid., 171.
70. White *et al.*, 113–20; New York *Times*, April 20, 1933.
71. Frederick L. Johnson, 173–76.
72. Here and below, St. Paul *Pioneer Press*, April 4, 1934; St. Paul *Pioneer Press*, May 6, 24, 1934; Minneapolis *Journal*, May 21, 1934; St. Paul *Dispatch*, July 3 and 5, 1934; St. Paul *Pioneer Press*, July 30, 1934.

**Chapter 16**
1. "Escape from Bleakness," *Goodhue County Historical Society News* 26 (April 1992): 3; Kenyon *Leader*, Dec. 15, 1932; Hutcheson, *Goodhue*, 92; Manchester, *The Glory and the Dream*, 119–20.
2. Manchester, 119–22.
3. Andrew M. Lyons, "Red Wing Basketball" in Rasmussen, *History of Red Wing*, 231.
4. Red Wing *Daily Republican*, Jan. 31, 1928.
5. Edmund P. Neill, "Red Men Basketball," GCHS.
6. Dick and Nancy Deden, "The Red Men Basketball Team," 2–7, GCHS.
7. Here and below, Red Wing *Daily Republican*, March 16 and 17, 1915.
8. Red Wing *Daily Republican*, March 23, 1915.
9. Alfred J. Lindsay, *Rock Hanson: The Life of a Hero* (Macomb, Ill.: Cedar Street Press, 1993), 6–9, 16–21.
10. Red Wing *Daily Republican*, March 18, 1920, and March 18, 1922.

11. Steve R. Hoffbeck, "Hayloft Hoopster: Legendary Lynd and the State High School Basketball Tournament," *Minnesota History* 55 (Winter 1997–98): 336.
12. Goodhue *Tribune*, Feb. 27, 1930.
13. "Early in the Game," St. Paul *Pioneer Press*, July 7, 1998; *Zumbrota: The First 100 Years*, 261, 330; Red Wing *Daily Republican*, March 18, 19, and 20, 1920, and March 18, 1922; Callister, *Recollections*, 120.
14. Here and below, Red Wing *Republican Eagle* (weekly), March 8, 1933; Red Wing *Republican Eagle* (Progress Edition, Section A) "Looking Back," Feb. 26, 1993.
15. Kenyon *Leader*, March 14, 1941, and Jan. 9 and March 27, 1942.
16. Goodhue *Tribune*, Feb. 3 and March 16, 1944; Red Wing *Republican Eagle*, Feb. 1, 5, and 6, 1944.
17. Solberg, "Aurora Ski Club of Red Wing," 9–12; Red Wing *Daily Republican*, Jan. 31, 1928. See also Harry Borgen, "Ski Tournament Sites used by the Aurora Ski Club, Red Wing, Minnesota" (unpublished manuscript, 1972), 2–3, GCHS files.
18. Red Wing *Daily Republican*, Jan. 30, 1936; Solberg, "Aurora Ski Club of Red Wing," 10–11.
19. Johnson, *A History of the American People*, 754–59; Nelson, *Shifting Fortunes*, 112–17; Foner and Garraty, eds., *The Reader's Companion to American History*, 1006–08, 1095–96.
20. Here and below, Harold Severson, "Bright Lights for a Dark Countryside," *Goodhue County Co-operative Electric Association 45th Anniversary Report, 1936–1981* (Zumbrota: The Association, 1981): 4–5. See also "Rural Electrification in Goodhue County," 1–3, Goodhue County Electric Power Distribution file, GCHS, and Zumbrota *News*, Aug. 26, 1938.
21. Zumbrota *News*, Aug. 26, 1938; Severson, *Goodhue County Heritage*, 83–85.
22. Zumbrota *News*, Aug. 26, 1938.
23. Severson, "Bright Lights for a Dark Countryside," 6; "Rural Electrification in Goodhue County," 3.
24. Here and below, U. S. Engineer District, St. Paul, Minnesota, *Old Man River, 50th Anniversary, Nine-Foot Navigation Channel, Upper Mississippi River* (St. Paul: U. S. Corps of Engineers, 1988), 4–7.
25. Red Wing *Daily Republican*, Aug. 21, 22, and 26, 1938.
26. U. S. Engineer District, St. Paul, Minnesota, 14.
27. Nelson, 104, 111–12.
28. Minutes, Boot and Shoe Workers Union, Local 527, May 19, June 7, 1938 (copies in author's possession). The local also advocated adopting a 40-hour work week (Aug. 24, 1938) and continued its efforts to get the 5 percent pay cut restored.
29. Marvin and Vrooman, *Heart and Sole*, 121–22.
30. Madeline Angell Johnson, *History of the S. B. Foot Tanning Company* (Red Wing: Foot Tanning Company, 1979), 108–11; Red Wing *Daily Eagle*, Sept. 6, 1940.
31. Madeline A. Johnson, 112; Red Wing *Daily Republican*, Oct. 16, 18, 1940.
32. Madeline A. Johnson, 112–14.
33. Red Wing *Daily Republican*, Aug. 19, 20, 1935; White *et. al.,* 191–95.
34. Joseph H. Ball, "Powerful Ally, Fearsome Foe, Is Rockne, Dean of State Senate," undated newspaper profile labeled "1943," Zumbrota file, GCHS; White *et. al.,* 192–95.
35. George H. Mayer, *The Political Career of Floyd B. Olson* (St. Paul: MHS, 1987, reprint of original 1951 edition), 130–31.
36. "Bedridden 'Treasury Watch-dog' Is Subject of Article in Austin Daily," Zumbrota *News*, May 4, 1950; Rasmussen, *History of Goodhue County*, 322.
37. Speech to the League of Minnesota Municipalities at Red Wing, June 9, 1932, Floyd B. Olson papers, MHS; *Farm Labor Leader*, June 15, 1932.
38. Kenyon *Leader*, Dec. 16, 1932. See Finstuen's column "Legislative News," and Mayer, 117–19, for an account of the conservatives' attempt to derail the Munn candidacy.
39. Here and below, Mayer, 130–34. Mayer claims of Rockne, "The possibility that depression could strike down energetic and lazy alike never occurred to him." In 1935, the Zumbrota senator saw his first bread line when he visited a depressed Minneapolis neighborhood. Rockne was surprised by the suffering among the unemployed, but, says Mayer, "he never really comprehended the magnitude of the economic crisis."
40. *Farmer Labor Leader*, March 15, 30, 1933. See the March 30 issue for Teigan's letter to Rockne regarding the newspaper attack. The *Farmer Labor Leader* continued its assault on Rockne with a page one editorial entitled "Rockne's Plot." See also Mayer, 130–33.
41. Here and below, St. Paul *Pioneer Press*, April 13, 1933; Mayer, 162–64.
42. Minneapolis *Journal*, Dec. 27, 28, 1933; Mayer, 163–64, 266–68.

43. Red Wing *Daily Republican,* July 30, 1935. See also Zumbrota *News*, Oct. 6, 1945. Anton Rockne died in 1950.
44. Evans, *The American Century*, 297.
45. Within four days of the outbreak of war in Europe, a German submarine torpedoed the British passenger liner *Athenia*, making world headlines and bringing the war home to Goodhue County. Bernice Jansen, a former Red Wing resident, was among the ship's survivors. Rescuers took Jansen, suffering from head injuries, to an Irish hospital. See Red Wing *Daily Republican*, Sept. 5 and 6, 1939.
46. A. Scott Berg, *Lindbergh* (New York: Putnam, 1998), 396–432. Following his dramatic solo journey across the Atlantic, Lindbergh returned in triumph to Minnesota. He made a scheduled flyover of Red Wing on August 23, 1927, circling for ten minutes before dropping a message to excited onlookers below. See Bruce L. Larson, "Lindbergh's Return to Minnesota, 1927," *Minnesota History* 42 (Winter 1970): 143. Red Wing *Daily Republican*, Aug. 22 and 23, 1927.
47. Red Wing *Daily Republican*, Oct. 16 and 17, 1940; Manchester, 224.
48. Manchester, 222–25; Red Wing *Daily Republican*, Oct. 16 and 17, 1940.
49. "Goodhue County Goes to War, 1941," *Goodhue County Historical News* 24 (Nov. 1990): 3. The 159-man Battery F included Goodhue County men from Welch, Goodhue, Pine Island, Frontenac, Red Wing, Cannon Falls, and Zumbrota. *Zumbrota, The First 100 Years*, 224–26; Evans, 304–05.
50. Red Wing *Republican Eagle*, Dec. 7, 1991, Esposito, ed., *The West Point Atlas of American Wars*, vol. 2, 114–15.
51. Clarence K. Larson, *A Long March Home* (N.c.: Self -published, 1998), 1–13, 32–33. Larson was kept prisoner in the Philippines until August 1944, when he was shipped to Japan. He survived and returned home. Wayne Spriesterbach, an army private from Pine Island also captured in the Philippines, died while in captivity, on July 16, 1943; see Kenyon *Leader*, Sept. 10, 1943.
52. GCHS Oral History Collections, #84, interview with Lauris Norstad, Oct. 11, 1975, 1–10.
53. Red Wing *Daily Republican Eagle*, Aug. 21, 1945.
54. Bernie Melter, "Women in the Service in World War II," GCHS World War II file; "Women in the Armed Forces, World War II," GCHS World War II file; Stephen E. Ambrose, *D-Day, June 6, 1944: The Climactic Battle of World War II* (New York: Simon & Schuster), 488.
55. Kenyon *Leader*, March 27, 1942, May 7, 1943; Adjutant General, *State of Minnesota Manual for Organization and Instruction of Blackout Procedure* (St. Paul, 1942), ii; "Airplane Spotting," GCHS Welch file.
56. Zumbrota *News*, May 7, 14, 1943.
57. Minnesota War Finance Committee, "Victory Is Ours," 5, 31.
58. Memoir of Marion Nelson Glew, 1990, GCHS World War II files. Glew's 15-page reminiscence thoroughly reviews the war years on her family's Burnside farm. See also "Remembering Rationing," *Goodhue County Historical News* 24 (Nov. 1990): 2.
59. Here and below, "Share the Meat for Victory," copy in GCHS small collections, Box 4. The Kenyon *Leader* reported on Feb. 26, 1943, that 858 local people had registered for ration book No. 1. GCHS Oral History Collections, #20, 16–17. Memoir of Marion Nelson Glew, 7–14; "General Motors Reports to the Women of America," copy in GCHS small collections, Box 4.
60. Paul E. Stanton, "Reminiscences of the Past," April 1993, copy at GCHS; Frances Haglund memoir, 1988, copy at GCHS. Information on Red Cross activities in the county is from GCHS World War II files and *Goodhue County Historical News* 24 ( Nov. 1980): 5.
61. Red Wing *Republican Eagle*, June 6, 7, and 10, 1942.
62. Here and below, "The Honored Dead," 1–3. See Bernie Melter, "The Military and Cannon Falls," in Bickman, ed., *Roots & Wings,* 314.
63. Albert Hilstad to Goodhue County Historical Society, Oct. 10, 1944, GCHS World War II file; *Zumbrota, The First 100 Years*, 258; "The Honored Dead," 1–3.
64. M. Dale Larsen, Red Wing *Republican Eagle*, May 7, 1990.
65. Here and below, see GCHS World War II Service files for accounts of county soldiers killed in action. Background information on the assault against Aachen, Germany, is from Esposito, ed., vol. 2, 59.
66. The story of the sinking of the *Pringle* is in Samuel Eliot Morison, *The Two-Ocean War: A Short History of the United States Navy in the Second World War* (Boston: Little, Brown, 1963), 552.
67. Red Wing *Republican Eagle*, Aug. 21, 1945; Gwen Haugen, "Prisoner of War," *Generations of Today* (April 1998): 24–29.
68. Red Wing *Republican Eagle*, Aug. 22, 1945.

**Chapter 17**

1. Pine Island *Record*, Aug. 16, 1945; Zumbrota *News*, Aug. 17, 1945; Cannon Falls *Beacon*, Aug. 17, 1945; Kenyon *Leader*, Aug. 17, 1945; Red Wing *Republican Eagle*, Aug. 15, 1945.
2. *Zumbrota, The First 100 Years,* 342–43; Red Wing *Republican Eagle,* May 8, 1945.
3. Pine Island *Record*, Aug. 16, 1945; Zumbrota *News*, Aug. 17, 1945; Cannon Falls *Beacon*, Aug. 17, 1945; Kenyon *Leader*, Aug. 17, 1945.
4. Evans, *The American Century*, 384–85.
5. Manchester, *The Glory and the Dream,* 429.
6. Lowry Nelson and George Donohue, "Social Change in Goodhue County, 1940–65," University of Minnesota Agriculture Experiment Station Bulletin (St. Paul: U of M, 1966), 14–16; Lee Taylor, Marvin J. Taves, and Gordon Bultena, "Changing Goodhue County, 1946–1958," in *Sociology of Rural Life* (University of Minnesota Agriculture Experiment Station, Jan. 1959), 2.
7. Hutcheson, *Goodhue*, 96; Angell, *Saga of a River Town*, 336.
8. Kenyon *Leader,* Feb. 7, 1996; *Zumbrota, The First 100 Years,* 343.
9. Red Wing *Republican Eagle*, May 1, 2, 1946.
10. Ibid. In 1932 Raymond Hedin, M.D., a native of Red Wing, and Dr. Edward H. Juers, M.D., of Lake City, began a medical partnership that grew rapidly. Hedin and Juers, later joined by other physicians, opened Red Wing's Interstate Clinic in September 1940. See "Recollections of Dr. Edward H. Juers," *Goodhue County Historical News* 13 (Feb. 1979): 3–4.
11. Here and below, William L. Christianson, "Goodhue County Judge Serves on Nürnberg Tribunal," *Goodhue County Historical News* 3 (Nov. 1991): 1–2; Foner and Garraty, eds., *The Reader's Companion to American History*, 802.
12. For details on the work schedule of Judge Christianson and information about the family's first several months in Germany, see Myrtle Christianson to Sara and A. P., April 21, 1947, in GCHS Judge William C. Christianson file.
13. Christianson, "Goodhue County Judge Serves on Nürnberg Tribunal," 2.
14. Rochester *Post Bulletin*, May 27, 1985.
15. GCHS Oral History Collections, #62, 1–2, interview of Dr. Demetrius Jelatis; Angell, 342–43.
16. Jayne Smythurst, *Alexander P. Anderson and the History of Tower View* (pamphlet). GCHS.
17. Marshall, ed., *Goodhue County's First Hundred Years,* 18; Deborah L. Gelbach, *From This Land: A History of Minnesota's Empires, Enterprises, and Entrepreneurs* (Northridge, Calif.: Windsor Publications, 1988), 108–09.
18. Angell, 342–43.
19. See John Earl Haynes, *Dubious Alliance: The Making of Minnesota DFL Party* (Minneapolis: University of Minnesota Press, 1984). Haynes uses the phrase "Cold War liberals" to define the more moderate progressives such as Eugenie Anderson and Hubert Humphrey as they struggled to purge the DFL of Communists and their allies. See also Blegen, *Minnesota: A History of the State*, 577–58. Angell, 338–39, provides biographical data on Anderson.
20. See Stageberg's letter to Goodhue County DFL chairman Frank O'Gorman in a newspaper article, "Mrs. Stageberg Resigns as D-F-L County Secretary," dated only "1950," in GCHS Stageberg biographical file. For Stageberg's view on Wallace and his politics, see Susie W. Stageberg, "Henry Wallace," *The Friend* 24 ( Feb. 1947): 8–9.
21. Stageberg to Goodhue County DFL Chairman Frank O'Gorman, 1950.
22. Elmer A. Benson, "Politics in My Lifetime," *Minnesota History* 4(Winter 1980), 154–57.
23. Angell, 338–39, 365–66, 395–97.
24. Susan C. Larsen, "Charles Biederman and American Abstract Modernism," 2–7; Patricia McDonnell, "Charles Biederman: A Tribute to the Life of the Mind," in *Charles Biederman*, a guide to the exhibit of the artist's work held at the Frederick R. Wiesman Art Museum, University of Minnesota, March 27–May 23, 1999.
25. McDonnell, 8.
26. "Art and science reflect nature," Red Wing *Republican Eagle*, March 27, 1998; Lyndel King, "Director's Foreword," in *Charles Biederman*, 1.
27. GCHS Oral History Collections, #42, interview with Lauris Norstad, Oct. 11, 1975, #42, 12–13.
28. Red Wing *Republican Eagle*, July 8, 1950, and Jan. 22, 1951. See also Manchester, 663.
29. GCHS Oral History Collections, #42, 15–16.
30. "Minnesota Civil Defense and Disaster Relief Plan" (State of Minnesota, Office of Civil Defense, 1950), 3, 6, 22, MHS. Here and below, "Civil Defense Planning Advisory Bulletins, 1950–1954" (Minnesota Office of Civil Defense), Bulletins No. 3 (Jan. 12, 1951), 8 (July 23, 1951), and 2 (1953). The same office's "Minnesota State Civil Defense Plan," revised April 30, 1954, contains

information on CONELRAD. "Relics of Cold War gather dust," St. Paul *Pioneer Press*, June 14, 1999, reports on Twin City residents and their bomb shelters.

31. Minnesota Office of Civil Defense, "Civil Defense Memorandum, No. 1–19, June 6, 1951–Aug. 28, 1952. Memo 8 contains information on the identification tags.
32. Manchester, 575–76. The preparation kit from Office of Civil Defense Mobilization, "Operation You—Your Role in Civil Defense" and "Personal Preparedness in the Nuclear Age," are in MHS collections. St. Paul *Pioneer Press*, June 14, 1999.
33. Details on Matthees's death are in GCHS "WWII Service People file." See also Red Wing *Republican Eagle*, Feb. 10, 1956; Angell, 365; Johnson, 930.
34. Here and below, *Seventeenth Census of the United States,* vol. 2 *(Characteristics of the Population),* part 23: "Minnesota," 23–16. See also Nelson and Donohue, 14–16, and Taylor, Taves, and Bultena, 2–3.
35. Thomas Harvey, "Small-Town Minnesota," in Clark, ed., *Minnesota in a Century of Change*, 115; "Sample Small City Has a Good Record in Postwar Years," Minneapolis *Star*, Sept. 10, 1952.
36. Here and below, Red Wing Industrial Development Corporation, "Assistance for New Red Wing Industry" (1954), 7–8, 19; Red Wing League of Women Voters, *Women in the Work Force* (Red Wing: The League, 1991).
37. Taylor, Taves, and Bultena, 6.
38. "Meyer Industries, Inc." in GCHS Meyer Machine file; "Riedell Shoes, Inc. of Red Wing," in GCHS Riedell Shoes file.
39. *Eleventh Census of the United States (1890),* Part 1,197; *Seventeenth Census of the United States (1950),* vol. 2, part 23, pp. 23–16.
40. Red Wing *Republican Eagle*, Sept. 23, 1942.
41. Mrs. Oscar Kappeldahl to the Goodhue County Draft Board, "WWII Service People" file, GCHS Oral History Collections, #44, 33.
42. Taylor, Taves, and Bultena, Table I; Nelson and Donohue, 9–10.
43. Nelson and Donohue, 9, 22; Nass, "The Rural Experience," in Clark, ed., 146–47; Red Wing *Republican Eagle*, Feb. 24, 28, 1961.
44. Vince Deden, "The Hay Creek Watershed," *Goodhue County Historical Society News* 22 (Nov. 1988): 4; GCHS Oral History Collections, #44, interview with Goodhue County Agent G. J. "Dick" Kunau, 8–10, 13.
45. Ibid., 6.
46. GCHS Oral History Collections, #44, 30.
47. Ibid., 31–32.
48. Kunau, "Recollections of a County Agent," *Goodhue County Historical News* 20 (Nov. 1986): 2–3; Tweton, "The Business of Agriculture," in Clark, ed., 274.
49. "Albright v. The United States," *Goodhue County Historical News* 15 (Feb., 1981): 5. Kenyon lawyer Allan E. Finseth represented Albright as well as Isaac Emerson, who was bringing a similar tax issue to court. Emerson also won. See Kenyon *Leader*, June 3, 1949.
50. Nelson and Donohue, 11–12.
51. Frank D. Alexander and Lowry Nelson, "The Social Organization of Goodhue County," University of Minnesota, Agriculture Experiment Station Bulletin (St. Paul: 1949), 33; Nelson and Donohue, 26.
52. Nelson and Donohue, 23, 61.
53. See Roy W. Meyer, "The Discontinued Post Offices and Ghost Towns of Goodhue County," 8–107, for more detail on the stories behind the hamlets and post offices listed here. See also "Ghost Towns of Goodhue County," *Goodhue County Historical News* 21 (March 1987): 1–5, which includes a map based on Roy W. Meyer's listings.
54. Meyer, "The Discontinued Post Offices and Ghost Towns of Goodhue County," 23–28.
55. Goodhue County School Survey Committee, "School Survey Report: A Study of School Reorganization in Goodhue County, Minnesota," 1948 (copy at MHS), 5; Nelson and Donohue, 64; Thomas Harvey, "Small-Town Minnesota," in Clark, ed., 120.
56. Goodhue County School Survey Committee, "School Survey Report," 2–4; Harold Diepenbrock, "Old Goodhue County School Districts," *Goodhue County Historical News* 4 (June 1970): 3.
57. Here and below, Margaret Hutcheson, "A Century of Organization and Reorganization," *Goodhue County Historical News* 25 (Aug. 1991): 2–3, 8.
58. Ibid., 3.
59. Zumbrota *News*, May 10, 17, and 24, 1951.
60. Zumbrota *News,* May 31, 1951; Hutcheson, *Goodhue*, 108; Kenyon *Leader*, April 3 and May 22, 1953; Hutcheson, "A Century of Organization and Reorganization," 3.

61. Kenyon *Leader*, May 29, 1953; Severson, *Goodhue County Heritage*, 164.
62. Pine Island *Record*, May 13, 1954; Hutcheson, "A Century of Organization and Reorganization," 3.
63. Burnside township Consolidation files, GCHS; Hutcheson, "A Century of Organization and Reorganization," 8. See also Arthur Harlans, I. Karon Sherarts, and Richard G. Woods, "Public Education of the Prairie Island Sioux: An Interim Report," University of Minnesota, 1969.
64. "A Letter from the Burnside School Board," undated letter ca. 1959 to the "Voters of the Burnside School District" found in Burnside Township Consolidation files, GCHS; Red Wing *Republican Eagle*, Aug. 14, 1959; Hutcheson, "A Century of Organization and Reorganization," 8.
65. Manchester, 583–84.
66. Ibid., 586–87.
67. Stephen Seplow and Jonathan Storm, "TV at 50: Dominating Americans' Free Time," St. Paul *Pioneer Press*, Dec. 28, 1997.

**Chapter 18**
1. Bruce J. Dierenfield, "Rooting Out Religion: Church-State Controversies in Minnesota Public Schools since 1950," *Minnesota History* 53 (Winter 1993): 301; Red Wing *Republican Eagle*, Oct. 30, 1963.
2. Ibid.
3. Minneapolis *Sunday Tribune*, Nov. 3, 1963; Red Wing *Republican Eagle,* Nov. 4, 1963.
4. Rochester *Post-Bulletin*, Nov. 4, 1963; Red Wing *Republican Eagle*, Nov. 7, 8, 1963.
5. Here and below, Dierenfield, "Rooting Out Religion," 302–11.
6. John Steele Gordon, "R. I. P., ICC," *American Heritage* 47 (May/June 1996): 22–24.
7. Harvey, "Small Town Minnesota," in Clark, ed., *Minnesota in a Century of Change*, 109.
8. James Burt, "The Red Wing Clay Line: Part II—Enter the Great Western," *North Western Lines* (Winter 1992): 58. See also Roy W. Meyer, "The Railroads of Goodhue County" (map), *Goodhue County Historical News* 29 (April 1995): 7. "'Those Were the Days,' says Ed Davis in Reminiscences on Early Railroading," Zumbrota *News*, March 13, 1952.
9. Zumbrota *News*, Aug. 17, 1950.
10. Frederick K. Johnson, "From Rails to Trails," *Goodhue County Historical News* 29 (April 1995): 3–4.
11. Kenyon *Leader*, Sept. 30, 1965.
12. "Transportation," 1976, 13–16; manuscript in GCHS transportation file, prepared by Thomas L. Olson of the University of Minnesota for the Red Wing Bicentennial Project.
13. Red Wing *Republican Eagle*, Sept. 21, 1979.
14. Ibid., Sept. 15, 1982; Cannon Falls *Beacon*, Oct. 16, 1975, and April 19, 1984.
15. Charles T. Tooker and John A. Koepke, *Cannon Valley Trail* (Red Wing, Minn.: N.p., 1985), 1, 4 (pamphlet).
16. "Forecast of Doom Came in 1957," Red Wing *Republican Eagle*, Aug. 25, 1967; Angell, *Saga of a River Town*, 403.
17. Red Wing *Republican Eagle*, July 3 and Aug. 25, 1967.
18. "Pottery Strike Slows Tourism in Red Wing," Minneapolis *Tribune*, July 24, 1967.
19. Red Wing *Republican Eagle*, Aug. 4, 5, and 25, 1967.
20. Minneapolis *Tribune*, July 24, 1967; Red Wing *Republican Eagle*, Aug. 11, 1967; Red Wing *Republican Eagle*, Aug. 22, 1967.
21. Red Wing *Republican Eagle*, Aug. 25, 1967.
22. Richard A. Gilmer's son reported on the pottery's demise from the company's viewpoint. See Richard S. Gilmer, *Death of a Business: The Red Wing Potteries* (Minneapolis: Ross & Haines, 1968).
23. John Brooks, *The Great Leap: The Past Twenty-five Years* (New York: Harper & Row, 1966), 138; Manchester, *The Glory and the Dream*, 1001; Irwin Unger and Debi Unger, eds., *The Times Were a Changin': The Sixties Reader* (New York: Three Rivers Press, 1998), 13–19.
24. Red Wing *Republican Eagle*, Feb. 9–18, 20, 22. Interview with William Befort, March 28, 1999, notes in author's possession.
25. Summary of Service, Maj. Thomas E. Reitmann, U.S. Air Force. GCHS Vietnam War file.
26. GCHS Oral History Collections, #160, 11–12 (interview with Lillian Christenson); Red Wing *Republican Eagle*, Dec. 20, 1971 (Phil Duff column).
27. Manchester, 1167, 1174–75.
28. GCHS Oral History Collections, #160; Foner and Garraty, eds., *The Reader's Companion to American History*, 218.

29. H. J. Burbach to the editor, Red Wing *Republican Eagle*, Aug. 23, 1967.
30. Foner and Garraty, eds., 218; Paul Johnson, *A History of the American People*, 884.
31. Here and below, Red Wing *Republican Eagle*, June, 12, 16, 1970. GCHS Oral History Collections, #84, interview with James and David Lee, Aug. 15, 1981.
32. GCHS Oral History Collections, #85, interview with Ron Gernentz and Fred Fanslow, July 8, 1981.
33. Arlin Albrecht, "Gernentz Foresaw Red 'Peace Talk Offensive,'" Red Wing *Republican Eagle*, May 14, 1968. See also Albrecht's series of articles, written when he was in Vietnam, in the Red Wing *Republican Eagle*, April 23–May 24, 1968.
34. Red Wing *Republican Eagle*, May 25, 27, 1970.
35. Red Wing *Republican Eagle*, May 29 and June 2, 1970.
36. Red Wing *Republican Eagle,* June 4, 1970.
37. Kenyon *Leader*, April 9, 1970.
38. Pine Island *Record*, June 9, 1966; Red Wing *Republican Eagle*, Dec. 17, 1967; Jan. 19, 1968; Feb. 11, 1968; and May 3, 1985.
39. Red Wing *Republican Eagle,* Feb. 11, 1968, March 2, 1968, and Aug. 13, 1975. Information on Staehli is from a March 29, 1999, interview with his cousin Char Henn, notes in author's possession. Pine Island *Record*, April 17, 1969.
40. Red Wing *Republican Eagle*, Oct. 16, 1970; Rochester *Post-Bulletin*, May 28, 1984.
41. Robert S. McNamara, *In Retrospect, the Tragedy and Lessons of Vietnam* (New York: Random House, 1995), 321; Red Wing *Republican Eagle*, May 3, 1985.
42. Red Wing *Republican Eagle*, Aug. 23, 1968.
43. Ibid., Aug. 23 and 24, 1968.
44. Ibid. See also Char Henn, *The Training School: A Centennial Activity of the Minnesota Correctional Facility, Red Wing* (Red Wing, Minn.: Self-published, 1989), 16–17.
45. Red Wing *Republican Eagle*, Aug. 24, 28, 1968.
46. Ibid., Aug. 24, 26, 1968.
47. Ibid., Aug. 28, 1968.
48. Henn, 28–29.
49. Red Wing *Republican Eagle*, Aug. 28; Interview with Edna Martenson, Dec. 22, 1998.
50. Manchester, 983.
51. Evans, *The American Century*, 547; Manchester, 1064–65.
52. Edward L. Henry, "Urban-Suburban Clash in Minnesota," 1–2 (copy in GCHS "Burnside Township Consolidation" collection); Red Wing *Republican Eagle*, May 8, 1970.
53. GCHS Oral History Collections, #84 (interview with Dr. Demetrius Jelatis), 8–9.
54. Here and below, Charles O. Richardson, "Landmark Cases in Goodhue County," *Goodhue County Historical News* 15 (Feb. 1981): 3.
55. Red Wing *Republican Eagle*, Oct. 18, 1971; GCHS Oral History Collections, #84, 12–13; Red Wing *Republican Eagle*, March 11, 1970.
56. Red Wing *Republican Eagle*, June 2, 3, 1970.
57. Richardson, "Landmark Cases in Goodhue County," 3; Red Wing *Republican Eagle*, Oct. 18, 1971.
58. Red Wing *Republican Eagle*, April 12, 1971.
59. Foner and Garraty, eds., 394–97; Here and below, St. Paul *Pioneer Press*, July 20, 1998. See the special feature "Conventional Wisdom."
60. Marjorie Bingham, "Keeping at It: Minnesota Women," in Clark, ed., *Minnesota in a Century of Change*, 452; Red Wing League of Women Voters, *Women in the Work Force* (Red Wing, Minn.: The League, 1991).
61. Manchester, 1109–10; Bingham, "Keeping at It," 453–57; "Conventional Wisdom," St. Paul *Pioneer Press*, July 20, 1998; Evans, 597.
62. Foner and Garraty, eds., 396. See also Bingham, 455. Flora Davis, *Moving the Mountain: The Women's Movement in America since 1960* (New York: Simon & Schuster, 1991), 493; Diana Telschow, "Economic Census Sampler," *Population Notes* (St. Paul: Minnesota Planning, Nov., 1996), 5.
63. Davis, 335; Bingham, 457–62.
64. Davis, 491.
65. Here and below, Kenyon *Leader*, March 12, 19, and 26, 1970. Red Wing *Republican Eagle*, March 14, 1970. Another of Goodhue County's standout basketball teams was the 1952 Wanamingo club led by Roger Hostager, the team's center. Hostager scored 24 points in the Bulldogs 48–47 vic-

tory over Owatonna in the District Four title game. "Wanamingo Seized by Cage Hysteria," read a newspaper headline as townspeople snapped up tickets for the regional tournament in Rochester. Joining Hostager in the lineup were Gunder Froyum, David Fossam, Roger Naeseth, and Bill Lund. See Zumbrota *News*, March 6 and 13, 1952; Red Wing *Republican Eagle*, March 6, 10, and 12–15, 1952.
66. Red Wing *Republican Eagle*, March 14, 1970.

**Chapter 19**
1. Here and below, Martha McMurry, *Faces of the Future: Minnesota County Population Projections, 1995–2025* (State Demographic Center, Sept. 1998), 1–2, 10–11; Martha McMurry, *Population Notes* (St. Paul: Minnesota Planning Office, Sept. 1997), 6; and Minnesota Extension Service, *Goodhue County, Profile of Demographic, Social and Vital Statistics, 1997*, 2.
2. McMurry, *Population Notes* (Sept. 1991): 1–4.
3. Diana Telschow, *Population Notes* (St. Paul: Minnesota Planning Office, Feb. 1993), 1. In 1998 the Minnesota Historic Preservation Office nominated 75–square miles of Sogn Valley in Warsaw township as a Rural Historic Landscape District. The picturesque valley, heavily settled by Norwegians in the 19th century, was largely unspoiled by new development. If approved, the Sogn site would become the first recognized rural historical district in Minnesota. See Red Wing *Republican Eagle*, Oct. 28, 1998.
4. McMurry, *Population Notes* (Jan. 1992): 1–4; McMurry, *Faces of the Future*, 4.
5. *Tenth Census of the United States, 1880*, 226; Minnesota Extension Service, *Goodhue County, Profile of Demographic, Social and Vital Statistics, 1997*, 2.
6. Ibid.
7. Barbara Ronningen, "Highlights of 1992 Census of Agriculture," *Population Notes* (St. Paul: Minnesota Planning Office, Nov. 1995), 4.
8. *Minnesota Agricultural Profile, 1995*, vol. 1, *Goodhue County* (St. Paul: University of Minnesota Department of Applied Economics, 1996), 1–5, 10.
9. Red Wing *Republican Eagle*, April 3, 1986.
10. Ronningen, 6.
11. "Nobles Find Sustainable Farming Fits," Red Wing *Republican Eagle*, March 19, 1999; *1992 Census of Agriculture, Geographic Area Series*, part 23, *Minnesota State and County Data*; Bureau of Census, Aug. 1994, Table 1, 165.
12. "Farm economics add up to city job," Red Wing *Republican Eagle*, March 19, 1999.
13. St. Paul *Pioneer Press*, March 7, 1999.
14. "Root Causes," Sept. 21, 1997, and "Free Markets or Political Fixes?" St. Paul *Pioneer Press*, July 15, 1998.
15. "Agriculture secretary: Farm Crisis Worsening," St. Paul *Pioneer Press*, Feb. 23, 1999; Minnesota House of Representatives, *Session Weekly* 16 (May 21, 1999): 6.
16. Rhoda R. Gilman, "Interpreting Minnesota's Farm Story," *Minnesota History* 46 (Spring 1978): 31–32; *Minnesota Agricultural Profile, 1995*, vol. 1, 6.
17. The verses are in Gilman, "Interpreting Minnesota's Farm Story," 32.
18. McMurry, "Faces of the Future, Minnesota County Population Projections, 1995–2025," 3–4; Red Wing *Republican Eagle*, Feb. 4, 1991; *Goodhue County, Profile of Demographic, Social and Vital Statistics, 1997*, 2.
19. "Three Groups Formed to Help Industry," Cannon Falls *Beacon*, Aug. 15, 1991.
20. Marshall, ed., *Goodhue County's First Hundred Years*, 49–50. The August 15, 1991, issue of the Cannon Falls *Beacon* contains more information on the firms listed. Red Wing *Republican Eagle*, March 19, 1999.
21. "Zumbrota experiences residential and commercial development," Red Wing *Republican Eagle*, March 19, 1999. Zumbrota *News*, Nov. 12, 1980. Red Wing *Republican Eagle*, July 22, 1980.
22. "Zumbrota Covered Bridge last of its kind," Red Wing *Republican Eagle*, Feb. 1, 1997.
23. *Zumbrota, The First 100 Years*, 249–50. Charlie Buck recalled another covered bridge, about half-a-mile upstream from the surviving covered bridge, built by the Duluth, Red Wing and Southern Railroad in the 1880s. See Red Wing *Republican Eagle*, Feb. 1, 1997.
24. Rochester *Post-Bulletin*, Dec. 24, 1983.
25. Ibid., Sept. 5, 1970.
26. Ibid., Dec. 24, 1983; *News-Record*, Aug. 14, 1996.
27. Goodhue County, Profile of Demographic, Social and Vital Statistics, 1997, 2; Carlton C. Qualey, "Pioneer Norwegian Settlement," *Minnesota History* 12 (Sept. 1931): 270–71.

28. Rochester *Post-Bulletin*, Feb. 15, 1983; Kenyon *Leader*, Sept. 9, 1998.
29. Kenyon *Leader*, Jan. 21, March 4, 1998.
30. Taylor, Taves, and Bultena, "Changing Goodhue County, 1946–1958," 3; *Goodhue County, Profile of Demographic, Social and Vital Statistics, 1997*, 2.
31. Marvin and Vrooman, *Heart and Sole*, 139–41, 173–80, 246.
32. Red Wing *Republican Eagle*, Jan. 15, Nov. 18 and 21, 1981, Jan. 20 and Feb. 3, 1982, and Jan. 25, 1983.
33. "Survival of the Small," St. Paul *Pioneer Press*, Aug. 23, 1998; Red Wing *Republican Eagle*, May 24, 1993.
34. Red Wing *Republican Eagle*, Sept. 28, 1998, and Dec. 24, 1999. See also Red Wing *Republican Eagle*, Sept. 11 and Nov. 2, 1992.
35. "NSP-Prairie Island 25 Years," Red Wing *Republican Eagle* (supplement), Dec., 1998, 2.
36. Red Wing League of Women Voters, *Nuclear Power Plant Next Door: The Prairie Island Nuclear Plant and Its Influence upon Our Community* (Red Wing: The League, May 1981), 4–5.
37. Red Wing *Republican Eagle*, Dec. 21, 1996. NSP expected to see a tax increase between 1998 and 2000 after installing more nuclear spent fuel casks and new turbines. See also Kenyon *Leader*, Dec. 25, 1996.
38. Red Wing *Republican Eagle*, May 7, 1994.
39. Ibid., April 10 and May 23, 1995. The goal of the secession backers was to put the issue before Goodhue and Wabasha County voters in the next general election. See Cannon Falls *Beacon*, June 15, 1995.
40. Red Wing *Republican Eagle*, Sept. 12, 1996, and July 23, 1997.
41. "NSP-Prairie Island 25 Years," Red Wing *Republican Eagle* (supplement), Dec. 1998, 3. See also Red Wing *Republican Eagle*, Sept. 28, 1998.
42. Governor's Interracial Commission of Minnesota, *The Indians in Minnesota: A Report to Gov. C. Elmer Anderson*, rev. ed. (St. Paul: The Commission, 1952), 23, 31–32. The report also noted that the state's Dakota population was just 656 in 1950, while the Ojibway total was 10,255 (p. 39). Meyer, "The Prairie Island Community," *Minnesota History* 37 (Sept. 1961): 280, reported that the president and vice-president of the community council believed the 1959 estimate of yearly family income at $1,000 to be low. See 280, n31.
43. Jane B. Katz, ed., *This Song Remembers: Self Portraits of Native Americans* (Boston: Houghton Mifflin, 1980), 64–66; GCHS Oral History Collections #93 (Sept. 17, 1984, interview with Amos Owen), 2; Jim Parsons, "Spiritual Man of 2 Cultures Dies at 73," Minneapolis *Tribune*, June 6, 1990.
44. GCHS Oral History Collections #93, 17–18.
45. Ibid., 2, 7, 41. See also Robert A. Murray, *A History of Pipestone National Monument Minnesota* (National Park Service, 1965), 11.
46. GCHS Oral History Collections #112 (Amos Owen, Sept. 10, 1988), 5–6; Rochester *Post-Bulletin*, Sept. 13, 1978.
47. GCHS Oral History Collections #93, 2, 12. Owen comments extensively on Dakota spirituality and religious customs in this 43-page transcription.
48. Tribal State Negotiating Committee, Tom Gilbertson, chair, "Report to the Legislature on the Status of Indian Gambling in Minnesota," Sept. 5, 1991, 3–6; Red Wing *Republican Eagle*, March 18, 1999; "Getting Dealt Back In," St. Paul *Pioneer Press*, Aug. 6, 1998.
49. Minnesota Planning, *Minnesota Gambling, 1993* (May 1993): 3, 6.
50. Red Wing *Republican Eagle*, Nov. 26, 1991.
51. Ibid.
52. State of Minnesota Advisory Council on Gambling, "Final Report to the Legislature and Governor" (Feb. 1, 1996): 32; "Getting Dealt Back In," St. Paul *Pioneer Press*, Aug. 6, 1998.
53. Telschow, 2, 5; "A Division Problem," St. Paul *Pioneer Press*, April 11, 1999.
54. McMurry, *Population Notes* (March 1997): 1, 3–4; Minnesota Extension Service, *Goodhue County, Profile of Demographic, Social and Vital Statistics, 1997*, 3.
55. *Legislative Manual*, 1991–1992, 165. By 1998 the legislature had 57 female members, 28.4 percent of the combined bodies. Four of the six executive offices were led by women. See Commission on the Economic Status of Women, *Women in Office* (St. Paul:The Commission, 1998), 1.
56. Sandy Donovan, "Sviggum Promises Balance, Openness in House," *Session Weekly* 16 (Jan. 8, 1999): 7; Grant Martin and Sarah Tellijohn, "Historic Session Ends with Action on Tax Cuts, Major Bills," *Session Weekly* 16 (May 21, 1999): 3–4.

# Bibliography

GCHS=Goodhue County Historical Society
MHS=Minnesota Historical Society
N.c.=No city given
N.d.=No date given
N.p.=No publisher given

For convenience, all newspaper city names are printed in roman type, all newspaper names in italics. In most cases, articles from *Goodhue County Historical News* (GCHS) and *Minnesota Collections* (MHS) are not listed separately in the bibliography.


## Manuscripts
**Goodhue County Historical Society (GCHS), Red Wing, Minnesota**

A. F. Andersen Family Papers
Alexander P. Anderson, biographical file
Eugenie Anderson, biographical file
August Andresen, biographical file
Charles Betcher, biographical file
Lena Whipple Campbell, biographical file
Chris Graham correspondence
Just C. Gronvold, biographical file
Martin Gunderson, biographical file
O. M. Hall Papers
Charles N. Hewitt, biographical file
Joseph Woods Hancock, journal
Amanda Johnson Reminiscences
Mildred Lair, biographical file
Julia Bullard Nelson, biographical file
Lauris Norstad, biographical file
Amos Owen and Family, biographical file
Anton Rockne, biographical file
Carl Roos Papers
Susie Stageberg, biographical file
Harold and Ruth Severson, biographical file
John H. Webster scrapbook, ca. 1885
Harry W. Wilson family history

**Minnesota Historical Society (MHS), St. Paul, Minnesota**

John F. Aiton Papers
American Board of Commissioners for Foreign Missions Papers (transcripts)
Benjamin Densmore and Family Papers
Frances Densmore Papers
Joseph C. Dickey and Family Papers

Robert Dickson Papers
William Watts Folwell Papers
Donald Gregg Flour Milling Collection
Charles Hewitt and Family Papers
Levi Colburn Hillman and Family Papers
David W. Humphrey Papers
Thomas P. Kellett (account books)
Lewis Lars Larson Reminiscences
James A. Manahan and Family Papers
Hans Mattson and Family Papers
Knute Nelson Papers
Floyd B. Olson Papers
James M. Page Diary
Alf Peterson Papers
Red Wing and Trenton Transit Company "Corporate Minute Book," 1875–1890
Leonard A. Rosing and Family Papers
Mary Scofield Papers
Theodore B. Sheldon Papers (Ledger Books)
Strafford Immigration Company (minute book, 1856–1865)
Lawrence Taliaferro Journals and Papers
John W. Tubbesing Papers
Abraham E. Welch and Family Papers
Thomas S. Williamson Papers (microfilm)
Ferdinand Willius and Family Papers
James A. Wright Papers

## Oral Histories

The author used transcriptions of these numbered, tape–recorded interviews from the Goodhue County Historical Society Collections:

20. Frank Callister, Jan. 1, 1974
21. Orville Olson, Feb. 1, 1975
36. Herb Nordholm, Aug. 21, 1975
40. Harold and Hazel Swartout, Sept. 22, 1975
41. Walt Lindell, Herb Nordholm, July 31, 1975
42. Gen. Lauris Norstad, Oct. 11, 1975
44. G. J. "Dick" Kunau, Mar. 9, 1976
45. Herbert Kolberg, Mar. 10, 1976
48. Lloyd Wilford, July 2, 1976
62. Demetrius Jelatis, Jan. 27, 1979
68. Fritz Reichert, June 2, 1979
69. Willard Dibble, Sr., June 29, 1970
74. Henry C. Hinrichs, July 26, 1978
84. James and David Lee, Aug, 15, 1981
85. Ron Gernentz and Fred Fanslow, July 8, 1981
90. Richard Gilmer, Sept. 23, 1982
93. Amos Owen, Sept. 17, 1984
97. William D. Sweasy, Feb. 22, 1985
112. Amos Owen, Sept. 10, 1988
121. Lloyd Spriggle, Nov. 1, 1990
129. Township Days interviews, June 17, 1987
160. Lillian Christenson, Sept. 25, 1985
193. Norwegian Men, June 10, 1980
216. Swedish Men and Women, Aug. 21, 1980, Aug. 28, 1980
217. Irish Men and Women, Oct. 14, 1980
218. German Men and Women, Aug. 14, 1980, Sept. 18, 1980
422. Mabel and Margaret Lohmann, Aug. 21, 1984

Newspapers

Cannon Falls *Beacon*, 1882, 1884, 1888, 1908, 1910, 1918–1921, 1942–1945, 1951–1952, 1962–1964, 1978, 1984, 1991, 1994–1995
*Farmer Labor Leader*, 1932
Goodhue *Enterprise*, 1897–1898, 1901, 1918–1921
Goodhue County *Republican* (Red Wing), 1857–1861, 1867, 1870, 1873–1874, 1876–1878, 1881
Goodhue County *Tribune* (Goodhue), 1930, 1944, 1984
Goodhue County *Volunteer* (Red Wing), 1863–1864
*Grange Advance* (Red Wing), 1876–1877, 1879
Hastings *Democrat*, 1895
Kenyon *Leader*, 1894, 1908, 1931–1932, 1941–1943, 1945, 1949, 1953, 1963–1965, 1970, 1996, 1998
Kenyon *News*, 1922
Minneapolis *Journal*, 1918, 1934, 1939
Minneapolis *Star*, 1952
Minneapolis *Tribune*, 1884, 1902, 1963, 1967, 1990
Minnesota *Union Advocate*, 1930
New York *Times*, 1933
Northfield *News*, 1925
*Organized Farmer* (Red Wing), 1929
Pine Island *Record*, 1911, 1918–1920, 1924–1925, 1936
Red Wing *Argus*, 1878–1880, 1890
Red Wing *Advance Sun*, 1892
Red Wing *Daily Eagle*, 1914–1918, 1920, 1922–1923, 1927, 1930–1931
Red Wing *Daily Republican*, 1871, 1879, 1887, 1889–1891, 1893–1895, 1906–1909, 1914–1918, 1921, 1925, 1927–1929, 1931, 1933, 1936–1940
Red Wing *Republican Eagle*, 1944–1946, 1948, 1950–1952, 1956, 1959, 1961, 1963, 1967–1970, 1973, 1979, 1981–1982, 1983–1985, 1990–1999
Rochester *Post–Bulletin*, 1963, 1970, 1978, 1983–1985
St. Paul *Daily Globe*, 1880, 1890
St. Paul *Dispatch*, 1890, 1930, 1934
St. Paul *Pioneer Press*, 1878, 1890, 1930, 1933–1934, 1997–1999
Stillwater *Gazette*, 1879
Wabasha County *Sentinel*, 1878
Worthington *Daily Globe,* 1978
Zumbrota *News*, 1905, 1918, 1919–1923, 1925, 1938–1939, 1940, 1942–1943, 1950, 1952

Government Records and Documents

*Annual Report of the City Clerk of the City of Red Wing, Minnesota for the Year Ending December 31, 1932*. Also volumes for 1933–1940. MHS.
*Annual Report of the Commissioner of Indian Affairs, 1849–1850*. MHS.
Bureau of Census. *1992 Census of Agriculture, Geographic Area Series, Part 23 Minnesota State and County Data*. Washington, D.C.: Aug. 1994, Table 1.
Goodhue County, City of Red Wing, Jail Register—"Tramps Lodged," 1925–30, 1930–31, and 1931–32. MHS.
Goodhue County Court Records, 1846–1983, MHS.
Goodhue County District Court Records. *Index to Sellers and Purchasers of Liquor,* vol. 1 (1921–1933), and a second volume, *Liquor Prescription Record, Aug. 1, 1924–Oct.1, 1930*. State Archives notebooks. MHS.
Goodhue County District Court Records, Certificates of Convictions, Book B. MHS.
Goodhue County District Court Records, Pine Island Justice Court, 1906–1938. MHS.
Goodhue County School Survey Committee. "School Survey Report: A Study of School Reorganization in Goodhue County, Minnesota." 1948.
Governor's Interracial Commission of Minnesota. *The Indians in Minnesota* (revised)*: A Report to Gov. C. Elmer Anderson*. St. Paul: 1952.
Industrial Commission of Minnesota, correspondence, 1914, 1922. MHS.
*License Book, 1906–1908,* Goodhue County, City of Red Wing. State Archives notebooks. MHS.
Minnesota Board of Commissioners on Publication of History of Minnesota in the Civil and Indian

Wars. *Minnesota in the Civil and Indian Wars, 1861–1865.* 2 vols. St. Paul, 1890–93.
Minnesota Commission of Public Safety Papers (Main Files). Minnesota State Archives, MHS.
Minnesota Commission of Public Safety. Agents' Reports to T. G. Winter, 1917–1919. MHS.
Minnesota Commission of Public Safety. "Survey of Women in Industry, 1918–1919," Goodhue County. MHS.
Minnesota Department of Civil Defense. "Minnesota State Civil Defense Plan," revised April 30, 1954.
Minnesota Department of Labor and Industry. Minimum Wage Correspondence, 1921. MHS.
Minnesota Department of Labor and Industry. Trade Union Reports–Strikes and Lockouts, December 1917–June 1918. MHS.
Minnesota Department of Labor and Industry. "Trade Union Reports as of May 1, 1918, Goodhue County." MHS.
Minnesota Extension Service. *Goodhue County, Profile of Demographic, Social and Vital Statistics, 1997.* St. Paul: University of Minnesota, 1997.
Minnesota Historical Records Survey. *Inventory of the County Archives of Minnesota, No. 25, Goodhue County, Red Wing.* St. Paul: The Survey, 1941.
*Minnesota Legislative Manual,* 1885, 1897, 1919, 1991–1992.
Minnesota Office of Civil Defense. Civil Defense Memorandum, No. 1–19, June 6, 1951–Aug. 28, 1952.
Minnesota Office of Civil Defense. Civil Defense Planning Advisory Bulletins, 1950–1954.
Office of Civil Defense Mobilization. *Operation You—Your Role in Civil Defense.* Washington, D.C.: Office of Civil Defense Mobilization, 1960. Pamphlet.
Office of Civil Defense Mobilization. *Personal Preparedness in the Nuclear Age.* Washington, D.C.: Office of Civil Defense Mobilization, 1960. Pamphlet.
*Papers Relating to Talks and Councils Held with the Indians in Dakota and Montana Territories in the Years 1866–1869.* Washington, D.C.: Government Printing Office, 1910.
Red Wing Hospital Association Minutes, 1891–93. Goodhue County: City of Red Wing records. State Archives notebooks.
State of Minnesota Advisory Council on Gambling. "Final Report to the Legislature and Governor," Feb. 1, 1996.
State of Minnesota, Office of Civil Defense. "Minnesota Civil Defense and Disaster Relief Plan," 1950.
Tribal State Negotiating Committee, Tom Gilbertson, chair. "Report to the Legislature on the Status of Indian Gambling in Minnesota." Sept. 5, 1991.
*Wanamingo Town Records,* 1869–1894. GCHS.
*Works Progress Administration, Minnesota: Progress of WPA in Minnesota, August 1935–December, 1936.* State Archives, MHS.
War Records Commission, Box 6, "Killed and Wounded by County." MHS.

*Ninth Census of the United States, 1870.*
*Tenth Census of the United States, 1880.*
*Eleventh Census of the United States, 1890,* part 1.
*Twelfth Census of the United States, 1900.*
*Fifteenth Census of the United States, 1930*
*Seventeenth Census of the United States, 1950,* vol.2, *Characteristics of the Population,* part 23, *Minnesota,* 23–16.

## Books, Articles, and Pamphlets

Aberg, Alf. *A Concise History of Sweden.* Translated by Gordon Elliott. Kristianstad: Kristianstads Boktryckeri, 1985.
Adjutant General. *State of Minnesota Manual for Organization and Instruction of Blackout Procedure.* St. Paul: 1942.
Alexander, Frank D., and Lowry Nelson. *The Social Organization of Goodhue County.* St. Paul: University of Minnesota, Agriculture Experiment Station Bulletin, 1949.
Ambrose, Stephen E. *D–Day, June 6, 1944: The Climactic Battle of World War II.* New York: Simon & Schuster, 1994.
Anderson, Alexander P. *The Seventh Reader.* Caldwell, Idaho: Privately published, 1941.
Anderson, Gary Clayton, and Alan R. Woolworth, eds. *Through Dakota Eyes: Narrative Accounts of the Minnesota Indian War of 1862.* St. Paul: MHS, 1988.

Anderson, Gary Clayton. *Kinsmen of Another Kind: Dakota–White Relations in the Upper Mississippi Valley, 1650–1862*. St. Paul: MHS, 1997 ed.

——. *Little Crow: Spokesman for the Sioux*. St. Paul: MHS, 1986.

Anderson, Hazel, and Archie Swenson. *How it All Began*. White Rock: White Rock State Bank, 1985.

Anderson, Martin J. *The Development of the Dairy Products Industry in Minnesota*. Minnesota Dairy and Food Department Bulletin No. 52, Minneapolis, 1914.

Anderson, Thomas. "Captain T. G. Anderson's Journal." *Wisconsin Historical Collections* 9: 178–97.

Andreas, A. T. *An Illustrated Historical Atlas of the State of Minnesota*. Chicago: A. T. Andreas, 1874.

Andrist, Ralph K., ed. *The American Heritage History of the Confident Years*. New York: American Heritage, 1987.

Angell, Madeline, and Mary C. Miller. *Joseph Woods Hancock: The Life and Times of a Minnesota Pioneer*. Minneapolis: Dillon, 1980.

Angell, Madeline. "Leader in Leather: The S. B. Foot Tanning Company of Red Wing." *Minnesota History* 47 (Fall 1981).

Appel, Livia, and Theodore C. Blegen, "Official Encouragement of Immigration to Minnesota during the Territorial Period." *Minnesota History* 5 (Aug. 1923).

Atkins, Annette. *Harvest of Grief: Grasshopper Plagues and Public Assistance in Minnesota, 1873–1878*. St. Paul: MHS, 1984.

Barck, Oscar T., Jr., and Nelson M. Blake. *Since 1900: A History of the United States in Our Times*. New York: MacMillan, 1959.

Beckman, Edythe. "Activities at Mineral Springs Sanitarium [*sic*] as Recalled by Harriet Wickey Who Worked There for 22 Years." N.d. GCHS Mineral Springs files.

Beltrami, Giacomo, C. *A Pilgrimage in America*, vol. 2 of 2. London: Hunt, 1828.

Benson, Elmer A. "Politics in My Lifetime." *Minnesota History* 47 (Winter 1980).

Berg, A. Scott. *Lindbergh*. New York: Putnam, 1998.

Berthel, Mary Wheelhouse. *Horns of Thunder: The Life and Times of James M. Goodhue Including Selections from His Writings*. St. Paul: MHS, 1948.

Bicentennial Heritage Committee. *Chronicles of Cannon Falls*. Cannon Falls: Cannon Falls *Beacon*, 1976.

Bickman, Connie, ed. *Roots & Wings, A Scrapbook of Time*. Cannon Falls: Yatra Publications, 1996.

Birk, Douglas A., and Judy Poseley. *"The French at Lake Pepin: An Archaeological Survey for Fort Beauharnois,"* MHS Project No. 4094. St. Paul: MHS, 1977.

Blegen, Theodore C. "The Fashionable Tour." *Minnesota History* 20 (Dec. 1939).

——. *Minnesota: A History of the State*. St. Paul: University of Minnesota, 1975.

——. *Norwegian Migration to America: The American Transition*. Northfield: Norwegian–American Historical Association, 1940.

Blocker, Jack S., Jr. *American Temperance Movements: Cycles of Reform*. Boston: Twayne, 1989.

Blondell, Sam. "Foundation of the Lime Industry in Red Wing." N.d. GCHS.

Boorstin, Daniel J. *The Americans: The National Experience*. New York: Random House, 1965.

——. *The Americans: The Democratic Experience*. New York: Random House, 1973.

Borgen, Harry. "Ski Tournament Sites Used by the Aurora Ski Club, Red Wing, Minnesota." N.d. GCHS Collections.

Bowles, Oliver. *The Structural and Ornamental Stones of Minnesota,* Bulletin 663. Washington: Government Printing Office, 1918.

Bray, Edmund C. *A Million Years in Minnesota: The Glacial History of the State*. St. Paul: Science Museum of Minnesota, 1962.

Brooks, John. *The Great Leap: The Past Twenty–five Years*. New York: Harper & Row, 1966.

Bruce, W. H. *History of the Farmer's Guild, Grange No. 84, Goodhue, Minnesota, 1871–1877*. Minute book. GCHS.

Buffalohead, W. Roger. "The Indian New Deal, a Review Essay." *Minnesota History* 48 (Winter 1983).

Burnsen, Sgt. Charles, to Uncle Ole, July 5, 1898, and Burnsen to Uncle Ole, undated. GCHS Small Collections, Box 4.

Burnside Township Consolidation files. *A Letter from the Burnside School Board*. Ca. 1959. GCHS.

Burt, James. "The Red Wing Clay Line, Part I DRW&S Beginnings." *North Western Lines* (Fall 1991).

——. "The Red Wing Clay Line: Part II—Enter the Great Western." *North Western Lines* (Winter 1992).

Carley, Kenneth. *The Sioux Uprising of 1862*. St. Paul: MHS, 1976.

Centennial Book Committee. *Zumbrota: The First 100 Years*. Zumbrota: The Committee, 1956.

Charlson, S. "History of the Sogn Cooperative Dairy Association." 1940. GCHS.

Cheyney, E. G. "The Development of the Lumber Industry in Minnesota." *Journal of Geography* 14 (Feb. 1916).

Chrislock, Carl H. *Ethnicity Challenged: The Upper Midwest Norwegian–American Experience in World War I.* Northfield: Norwegian–American Historical Association, 1981.

——. *The Progressive Era in Minnesota, 1899–1908.* St. Paul: MHS, 1971.

——. *Watchdog of Loyalty: The Minnesota Commission of Public Safety during World War I.* St. Paul: MHS, 1991.

Christianson, Myrtle, to Sara and A. P., April 21, 1947. Judge William C. Christianson file, GCHS.

Clapesattle, Helen. "When Minnesota Was Florida's Rival." *Minnesota History* 35 (March 1957).

Clark, Clifford, Jr., ed. *Minnesota in a Century of Change: The State and Its People since 1900.* St. Paul: MHS, 1989.

Coddington, Edwin B. *The Gettysburg Campaign: A Study in Command.*

Colvill, William. "Bull Run: Address to Survivors at the Reunion of the First Minnesota." June 21, 1877. MHS.

Coyne, Franklin. *The Development of the Cooperage Industry in the United States.* Chicago: Lumber Buyer, 1940.

Curtiss–Wedge, Franklyn, ed. *History of Goodhue County.* Chicago: H. C. Cooper Jr., 1909.

Davis, Flora. *Moving the Mountain: The Women's Movement in American since 1960.* New York: Simon & Schuster, 1991.

"Deaths from Tuberculosis in Goodhue County, Minnesota." Minnesota Department of Health data. GCHS Mineral Springs files.

Deden, Richard, and Nancy. "The Red Men Basketball Team." N.d. GCHS.

Degler, Carl N. *Out of Our Past: The Forces That Shaped Modern America.* Rev. ed. New York: Harper Colophon, 1970.

Diedrich, Mark. *Famous Chiefs of the Eastern Sioux.* Minneapolis: Coyote Books, 1987.

——. "Red Wing, War Chief of the Mdewakanton Dakota." *The Minnesota Archaeologist* 40 (March 1981).

Dierenfield, Bruce J. "Rooting Out Religion: Church-State Controversies in Minnesota Public Schools since 1950." *Minnesota History* 53 (Winter 1993).

Diner, Steven J. *A Very Different Age: Americans of the Progressive Era.* New York: Hill and Wang, 1998.

Dobbs, Clark A. *An Archaeological Survey of the City of Red Wing, Minnesota.* Minneapolis: The Institute for Minnesota Archaeology, 1985.

——. "The Application of Remote Sensing Techniques to Settlement Pattern Analysis at the Red Wing Locality." *Minnesota Archaeologist* 50 (No. 2, 1991).

——. *The Archaeology of 21GD158: A 13th Century Native American Village at the Red Wing Locality,* Reports of Investigations Number 250. Minneapolis: Institute for Minnesota Archaeology, 1993.

Donovan, Sandy. "Sviggum Promises Balance, Openness in House." Minnesota House of Representatives *Session Weekly* 16 (Jan. 8, 1999).

Douglass, Jesse E. "History of the Mineral Springs Sanatorium," May 29, 1970. GCHS Mineral Springs files.

Driving Hawk Sneve, Virginia. *They Led a Nation.* Sioux Falls: Brevet, 1975.

*Duluth, Red Wing and Southern Railroad from the Rich Mines of Lake Superior and the Great Lake Port of Duluth through the Belts of Timber, to the Grain, Stock and Dairy Regions of Minnesota and Iowa.* Red Wing: Red Wing Printing, 1887.

DuPuy, R. Ernest, and Trevor N. DuPuy. *The Encyclopedia of Military History.* New York: Harper & Row, 1970.

Dupuy, Trevor N., Curt Johnson, and David L. Bongard, *The Harper Encyclopedia of Military Biography.* New York: Castle Books, 1995.

Dustin, Virginia. "As a Woman Sees It." *The Friend: A Family Magazine* (Minneapolis: Lutheran Periodicals) 21 (Sept. 1944).

Eide, Berndt M. "History of the Lime and Stone Industry in Red Wing, Minnesota, 1850–1916." N.d. GCHS.

Engberg, George B. "The Knights of Labor." *Minnesota History* 22 (Dec. 1941).

——. "The Rise of Organized Labor in Minnesota." *Minnesota History* 21 (Dec. 1940).

Erickson, Harriet. "Barrclay." June 5, 1971. GCHS.

Ericson, Kathryn, ed., *Map of Goodhue County Minnesota, 1877.* Red Wing: GCHS, 1991. Reprint of Warner & Foote's 1877 county map.

——. "Triple Jeopardy: The Muus vs. Muus Case in Three Forums." *Minnesota History* 50 (Winter 1987).

Esposito, Vincent J., ed. *The West Point Atlas of American Wars*, vol. 1. New York: Praeger, 1972.

Evans, H. W. "The Klan's Mission—Americanism." *The Kourier Magazine* 1 (Nov. 1925).

Evans, Harold. *The American Century*. New York: Alfred A. Knopf, 1998.

Folwell, William Watts. *A History of Minnesota*. 4 vols. St. Paul: MHS, 1956 ed.

Foner, Eric and John A. Garraty, eds. *The Reader's Companion to American History*. Boston: Houghton Mifflin, 1991.

Foner, Eric. *Reconstruction: America's Unfinished Revolution*. New York: Harper & Row, 1988.

Fritz, Henry E. "Assimilation vs. Cultural Pluralism: Making Federal Policy toward Native Americans, 1869–1933." GCHS.

——. *The Movement for Indian Assimilation*. Philadelphia: University of Pennsylvania, 1963.

Garraty, John A., and Peter Gays, eds. *The Columbia History of the World*. New York: Harper & Row, 1972.

Gates, Charles M. "The Lac Qui Parle Mission." *Minnesota History* 16 (June 1935).

Gelbach, Deborah L. *From This Land: A History of Minnesota's Empires, Enterprises, and Entrepreneurs*. Northridge, Calif.: Windsor, 1988.

Gibbon, Guy E. "Cultural Dynamics and the Development of the Oneota Life–way in Wisconsin." *American Antiquity* 38 (April 1972).

——. "The Middle Mississippian Presence in Minnesota," in Thomas E. Emerson and R. Barry Lewis, eds., *Cahokia and the Hinterlands: Middle Mississippian Cultures of the Midwest*. Urbana: University of Illinois, 1991.

——. *The Mississippian Occupation of the Red Wing Area*. Minnesota Prehistoric Archaeology Series, No. 13. St. Paul: MHS, 1979.

Gilbert, Martin. *The First World War: A Complete History*. New York: Henry Holt, 1994.

Gilman, Rhoda R. "Interpreting Minnesota's Farm Story." *Minnesota History* 46 (Spring 1978).

Gilmer, Richard S. *Death of a Business: The Red Wing Potteries*. Minneapolis: Ross & Haines, 1968.

Glew, Marion Nelson. 1990 memoir. GCHS World War II files.

*Goodhue County Historical News*. 33 vols. Red Wing: GCHS, 1967–1999.

*Goodhue County in the World War*. Red Wing: Red Wing Printing, 1919.

Goodwyn, Lawrence. *The Populist Moment: A Short History of the Agrarian Revolt in America*. New York: Oxford University, 1978.

Gordon, John Steele. "R. I. P., ICC." *American Heritage* 47 (May/June 1996).

Graham, H. E. *Cannon Falls, Minnesota*. Red Wing: Wall & Haines, 1900.

Grant, Roger H. *The Corn Belt Route: A History of the Chicago Great Western Railroad Company*. DeKalb: Northern University, 1984.

Gronvold, Just Christian. "The Norwegian Element." Ca. 1875 paper. GCHS Gronvold biography file.

Grout, Frank F. *Clays and Shales of Minnesota,* Bulletin 678. Washington, D.C.: Government Printing Office, 1919.

Hage, Anne A. "The Battle of Gettysburg as Seen by Minnesota Soldiers." *Minnesota History*, 38 (June 1963).

Hage, George S. *Newspapers on the Minnesota Frontier, 1849–1860*. St. Paul: MHS, 1967.

Haglund, Frances. 1988 memoir. GCHS.

Hall, Charles P. *Sane Street: A Short Story of Minnesota*. Red Wing: Red Wing Advertising, 1922.

Hamilton, Laura M. "Stem Rust in the Spring Wheat Area." *Minnesota History* 20 (June 1939).

Hancock, Joseph Woods. *Goodhue County, Minnesota, Past and Present*. Red Wing: Red Wing Printing, 1893.

Hancock, Maria, to Capt. William Houghton, June 19, 1849. GCHS.

Hankins, Ross. "Excursion Boats on the Upper Mississippi, 1910–1927." 1976. GCHS.

——. "Show-Boats on the Upper Mississippi, 1905–1920." 1976. GCHS.

Harlans, Arthur, I. Karon Sherarts, and Richard G. Woods. *Public Education of the Prairie Island Sioux: An Interim Report*. University of Minnesota, 1969. GCHS.

Harpole, Patricia C., and Mary D. Nagel, eds., *Minnesota Territorial Census, 1850*. St. Paul: MHS, 1972.

Hasselmo, Nils, ed. *Perspectives on Swedish Immigration*. Chicago: Swedish Pioneer Historical Society, 1978.

Haugen, Gwen. "Prisoner of War." *Generations of Today* (Red Wing, April 1998).

Haynes, John Earl. *Dubious Alliance: The Making of Minnesota DFL Party*. Minneapolis: University of Minnesota, 1984.

Heaney, Richard. "Belle Creek Irish Settlement." N.d. GCHS.

Heilbron, Bertha. "Minnesotans at Play." *Minnesota History* 36 (Sept. 1958).

Hellickson, Clara L. and others. *Memories of Wanamingo*. Wanamingo: Wanamingo Historical Society, 1978.

Henn, Char. "The Training School: A Centennial Activity of the Minnesota Correctional Facility, Red Wing." Red Wing: Privately published, 1989.

Henry, Edward L. "Urban–Suburban Clash in Minnesota." Burnside township consolidation collection, GCHS.

Herman, Sondra. *Eleven Against War: Studies in American International Thought, 1898–1921*. Stanford: Hoover Institute, 1969.

Hicks, John D. "The Birth of the Populist Party." *Minnesota History* 9 (Sept. 1928).

Hilstad, Albert to GCHS, Oct. 10, 1944. World War II file.

*Historical Sketches of Cannon Falls, 1854–1954*. Cannon Falls: Cannon Falls *Beacon,* June 1954.

*History of Goodhue County*. Red Wing, Minn: Wood, Alley, 1878.

"History of Medicine in Goodhue County." *Minnesota Medicine* 28 (No. 2–6, 1945).

Hobart, Chauncey. *Recollections of My Life: Fifty Years of Itinerancy in the Northwest*. Red Wing: Red Wing Printing, 1885.

Hodnefield, Jacob. "A Danish Visitor of the Seventies." *Minnesota History* 10 (Dec. 1929).

Hoffbeck, Steve R. "Hayloft Hoopster: Legendary Lynd and the State High School Basketball Tournament." *Minnesota History* 55 (Winter 1997–98).

Holand, Hjalmer. *De Norske Settlementers Historie*. Ephriam, Wis.: Self-published, 1908.

Holbrook, Franklin F. *Minnesota in the Spanish–American War and the Philippine Insurrection*. St. Paul: Minnesota War Records Commission, 1923.

Holcombe, Return I. *Early History–Minnesota as a Territory*, vol. 2 of *Minnesota in Three Centuries, 1655–1908*, edited by Lucius F. Hubbard, William P. Murray, James H. Baker, and Warren Upham. Mankato: Publishing Society of Minnesota, 1908.

*Holden through One Hundred Years, 1856–1956*. Holden: Holden Lutheran Church, 1956.

Holmquist, June Drenning, ed. *They Chose Minnesota: A Survey of the State's Ethnic Groups*. St. Paul: MHS, 1981.

Hubbard, Lucius F. "Early Days in Goodhue County." *Minnesota Collections*, vol. 12 (1908).

Hubbard, Lucius F., and Return I. Holcombe. *Minnesota as a State, 1858–1870*, vol. 3 of *Minnesota in Three Centuries, 1655–1908*, edited by Lucius F. Hubbard, William P. Murray, James H. Baker, and Warren Upham. Mankato: Publishing Society of Minnesota, 1908.

"Hurrah for Rollers! Genuine Roller Mill to be Built in Minnesota." *Northwestern Miller* 5 (July 20, 1877).

Hutcheson, Margaret E. *Goodhue: The Story of a Railroad Town*. Red Wing: Privately published, 1989.

Imholte, John Quinn. *The First Volunteers*. Minneapolis: Ross & Haines, 1963.

*In Memory of Those Who Perished in the Disaster of the Steamer Sea Wing on Lake Pepin, July 13, 1890*. Red Wing: Red Wing Printing, 1890.

Jackson, Donald, ed. *The Journals of Zebulon Pike*. Norman: University of Oklahoma, 1966.

Jarchow, Merrill E. "King Wheat." *Minnesota History* 24 (March 1948).

——. *Private Liberal Arts Colleges in Minnesota*. St. Paul: MHS, 1973.

Johnson, Carmen M. *The Days of Dennison: A History of a Small Village in Southern Minnesota*. Dennison: Privately published, 1992.

——. "Village of Dennison." 1993 manuscript, GCHS.

Johnson, Elden. *The Prehistoric Peoples of Minnesota*. St. Paul: MHS, 1988 (3rd ed.).

Johnson, Frederick K. "The Civilian Conservation Corps: A New Deal for Youth." *Minnesota History* 48 (Fall 1983).

——. "This I Remember," 1992 memoir. GCHS.

Johnson, Frederick L. "From Leavenworth to Congress: The Improbable Journey of Francis H. Shoemaker." *Minnesota History* 51 (Spring 1989).

——. "Unlocking the Mysteries of the Sea Wing." *Minnesota History* 52 (Summer 1990).

——. *The Sea Wing Disaster*. Red Wing: GCHS, 1990 (2nd ed.).

Johnson, Hildegard Binder. "Factors Influencing the Distribution of the German Pioneer Population in Minnesota." *Agricultural History* 19 (Jan. 1945).

——. "The Distribution of German Pioneer Population in Minnesota." *Rural Sociology* 6 (March 1941).

Johnson, Paul. *A History of the American People*. New York: HarperCollins, 1998.

Johnson, Vernold L. *History of the Clay Pits near Clay Bank and Bellechester*. Red Wing: Privately published, 1986.

Kane, Betty. "The 1876 Legislature: A Case Study in Lively Futility." *Minnesota History* 45 (Summer 1977).

Kane, Lucile M. "The Sioux Treaties and the Traders." *Minnesota History* 32 (June 1951).

Kappeldahl, Mrs. Oscar, to the Goodhue County Draft Board, n.d. WWII Service People file. GCHS.

Karstad, Ruby G. "The New York Tribune and the Minnesota Frontier." *Minnesota History* 17 (Dec. 1936).

Katz, Jane B., ed. *This Song Remembers: Self Portraits of Native Americans*. Boston: Houghton Mifflin, 1980.

Kearny, Stephen Watts. "Journal of Stephen Watts Kearny." *Missouri Historical Collections* 3 (1908).

Kellogg, Louise Phelps. "Fort Beauharnois." *Minnesota History* 8 (Sept. 1927).

Kennedy, Roger. *Men on the Moving Frontier*. Palo Alto: American West, 1969.

Keys, Thomas E. "The Medical Books of Dr. Hewitt." *Minnesota History* 21 (Dec. 1940).

Kildahl, Harold B., Sr., and Erling E. Kildahl, eds. *Westward We Came*. Orlando: Privately published, 1908 (rev. ed. 1991).

Landes, Ruth. *The Mystic Lake Sioux: Sociology of the Mdewakantonwan Santee*. Madison: University of Wisconsin, 1968.

Larsen, Susan C. "Charles Biederman and American Abstract Modernism." In *Charles Biederman*, a guide to the exhibit of the artist's work held at the Frederick R. Wiesman Art Museum, University of Minnesota, 1998.

Larson, Bruce L. "Lindbergh's Return to Minnesota, 1927." *Minnesota History* 42 (Winter 1970).

Larson, Clarence K. *A Long March Home*. N.c.: Privately published, 1998.

Larson, Henrietta M. "The Wheat Market and the Farmers in Minnesota, 1858–1900." Ph.D. diss., Columbia University, 1926.

"The Last Man Who Knew Everything: Thorstein Veblen." *The Carleton Voice* 45 (Fall 1980).

Le Sueur, Meridel. *Crusaders, the Radical Legacy of Marian and Arthur Le Sueur*. St. Paul: MHS, 1984 ed.

Letterman, Edward J. *Farming in Early Minnesota*. St. Paul: Ramsey County Historical Society, 1966.

Lewis, Sinclair. *Main Street*. New York: Harcourt, Brace and Howe, 1920.

Lief, Julia Wiech. "A Woman of Purpose: Julia B. Nelson." *Minnesota History* 47 (Winter 1981).

Lindsay, Alfred J. *Rock Hanson: The Life of a Hero*. Macomb, Ill.: Cedar Street, 1993.

Link, Arthur S. *Woodrow Wilson and the Progressive Era, 1910–1917*. New York: Harper, 1954.

Lord, Walter. *The Good Years: From 1900 to the First World War*. New York: Harper, 1960.

Luecke, John C. *Dreams, Disaster and Demise: The Milwaukee Road in Minnesota*. Cannon Falls: Cannon Falls *Beacon*, 1988.

—. *The Chicago and Northwestern in Minnesota*. Cannon Falls: Cannon Falls *Beacon*, 1990.

Maccabee, Paul. *John Dillinger Slept Here: A Crooks' Tour of Crime and Corruption in St. Paul, 1920–1936*. St. Paul: MHS, 1995.

Manahan, James. *Trials of a Lawyer*. Minneapolis: Farnham, 1933.

Manchester, William. *The Glory and the Dream: A Narrative History of America, 1932–1972*. Boston: Little, Brown, 1973.

Manhart, George B. *Alliance and Entente, 1871–1914*. New York: F. S. Crofts, 1932.

Marshall, Albert M. *Goodhue County's First Hundred Years*. Red Wing: *Daily Republican Eagle,* 1954.

Marshall, James. "An Unheard Voice: The Autobiography of a Dispossessed Homesteader and a Nineteenth–Century Cultural Theme of Dispossession." *The Old Northwest* 6 (Winter 1980–81).

Martin, Grant, and Sarah Tellijohn. "Historic Session Ends with Action on Tax Cuts, Major Bills." Minnesota House of Representatives *Session Weekly* 16 (May 21, 1999).

Martin, Patrice A., and Nicholas C. Vrooman. *Heart and Sole: A Story of the Red Wing Shoe Company*. Red Wing: Red Wing Shoe Company, 1986.

Mattson, Hans. *The Story of an Emigrant*. St. Paul: D. D. Merrill, 1891.

Mayer, George H. *The Political Career of Floyd B. Olson*. St. Paul: MHS, 1987 (reprint of 1951 ed.).

McClure, Ethel. *More Than a Roof: The Development of Minnesota Poor Farms and Homes for the Aged*. St. Paul: MHS, 1968.

Patricia McDonnell. "Charles Biederman: A Tribute to the Life of the Mind." In *Charles Biederman*, a guide to the exhibit of the artist's work held at the Frederick R. Wiesman Art Museum, University of Minnesota, 1998.

McMurry, Martha. *Faces of the Future: Minnesota County Population Projections, 1995–2025*. St. Paul: State Demographic Center, 1998.

——.*Population Notes*. St. Paul: St. Paul: Minnesota Planning Office, Sept. 1991, Jan. 1992, and Sept. 1997.

McNamara, Robert S. *In Retrospect: The Tragedy and Lessons of Vietnam.* New York: Random House, 1995.

Melter, Bernie. "Women in the Service in World War II." N.d. GCHS World War II file.

Meyer, Herbert W. *Builders of Northern States Power Company.* Minneapolis: NSP, 1972.

"Meyer Industries, Inc." N.d. GCHS Meyer Machine file.

Meyer, Roy W. "The Discontinued Post Offices and Ghost Towns of Goodhue County," Dec. 1967 manuscript. GCHS.

——. "The Prairie Island Community: A Remnant of Minnesota Sioux." *Minnesota History* 37 (Sept. 1961).

——. "Who Was Red Wing?" 1964 manuscript. GCHS Collections.

——. *History of the Santee Sioux.* Lincoln: University of Nebraska, 1967.

——. *History of Forest Mills.* N.c.: Privately published, 1955. Copy in GCHS Chesley Library.

Mink, Claudia G. *Cahokia: City of the Sun.* Collinsville, Ill.: Cahokia Mounds Museum Society, 1992.

*Minnesota Agricultural Profile, 1995,* vol. I, *Goodhue County.* St. Paul: University of Minnesota Department of Applied Economics, 1996.

*Minnesota Department of Highways, 1921–1971, 50th Anniversary.* St. Paul: Minnesota Department of Highways, 1971.

Minnesota Historical Society. *Minnesota Collections.* 17 vols. St. Paul: The Society, 1860–1920.

Minnesota House of Representatives. *Session Weekly* 16 (May 21, 1999). St. Paul: Minnesota House of Representatives.

Mitchell, W. H. *Geographical and Statistical Sketch of the Past and Present of Goodhue County.* Minneapolis: O. S. King, 1869.

Moe, Richard. *The Last Full Measure: The Life and Death of the First Minnesota Volunteers.* New York: Henry Holt, 1993.

Monroe, Cecil O. "Baseball in Minnesota." *Minnesota History* 19 (June 1938).

Morgan, Caroline A. Danielson. "The Beginning of the Clay Industry." N.d. GCHS.

Morison, Samuel Eliot. *The Two-Ocean War: A Short History of the United States Navy in the Second World War.* Boston: Little, Brown, 1963.

Morlan, Robert L. "The Nonpartisan League and the Minnesota Campaign of 1918." *Minnesota History* 34 (Summer 1955).

Murray, Robert A. *A History of Pipestone National Monument Minnesota.* N.c: Pipestone Indian Shrine Association, 1965.

Musicant, Ivan. *Empire by Default: The Spanish–American War and the Dawn of the American Century.* New York: Henry Holt, 1998.

Myers, J. Arthur. *Invited and Conquered: Historical Sketch of Tuberculosis in Minnesota.* St. Paul: Minnesota Public Health Association, 1949.

Naftalin, Arthur. "The Tradition of Protest and the Roots of the Farmer–Labor Party." *Minnesota History* 35 (June 1956).

Neill, Edmund P. "Red Men Basketball." N.d. GCHS.

Neill, Edward D. "Dakota Land and Dakota Life," *Minnesota Collections* 1: 263.

Nelson, Daniel. *Shifting Fortunes: The Rise and Decline of American Labor, from the 1820s to the Present.* Chicago: Ivan R. Dee, 1997.

Nelson, Lowry, and George Donohue. *Social Change in Goodhue County, 1940–65.* St. Paul: University of Minnesota, Agriculture Experiment Station Bulletin, 1966.

Nelson, Lowry, Charles E. Ramsey, and Jacob Toews. *A Century of Population Growth in Minnesota.* St. Paul: University of Minnesota Agricultural Experimental Station Bulletin 423, Feb. 1954.

Nelson, O. N. *History of the Scandinavians and Successful Scandinavians in the United States.* Minneapolis: O. N. Nelson, 1900.

Nevins, Allan. *The Emergence of Lincoln: Douglas, Buchanan, and Party Chaos 1857–1859.* New York: Charles Scribner's Sons, 1950.

——. *The War for the Union: War Becomes Revolution, 1862–1863.* New York: Charles Scribner's Sons, 1960.

Norelius, Erik. *Vasa Illustrata.* Rock Island: Augustana Book Concern, 1905.

Nute, Grace Lee. *In Hamline Halls, 1854–1954.* St. Paul: Hamline University, 1954.

Nydahl, Theodore C. "The Early Norwegian Settlement of Goodhue County, Minnesota." Master's thesis, University of Minnesota, 1929.

O'Kelly, Charlotte. *Women and Men in Society.* New York: Van Nostrand, 1980.

Olson, Thomas L. "Transportation." 1976. GCHS Transportation file.

Perrett, Geoffrey. *America in the Twenties: A History.* New York: Simon & Schuster, 1982.

Peterson, Mechele. "The Development of a Medical Specialty: Obstetrics." 1984. GCHS.

Pfanz, Harry W. *Gettysburg: The Second Day*. Chapel Hill: University of North Carolina, 1987.

Pond, Samuel W. *The Dakota or Sioux in Minnesota as They Were in 1834*. St. Paul: MHS reprint 1986.

Postmaster's Association of Minnesota, Third Annual Meeting, June 9, 1908. GCHS.

*Proceedings of the Annual Catholic Total Abstinence Union of the Archdiocese of St. Paul,* 1879, 1882–1886,1888–1889, 1891. MHS.

"Purifying the Island Opposite Red Wing." *Tidsskrift, for Kirke og Samfund*. Red Wing: Newspaper for Church and Society, Oct. 1914.

Qualey, Carlton C. "Pioneer Norwegian Settlement." *Minnesota History* 12 (Sept. 1931).

——. "Some National Groups in Minnesota." *Minnesota History* 31 (March 1950).

Quinn, Peter. "The Tragedy of Bridget Such–A–One." *American Heritage* 48 (Dec. 1997).

Rasmussen, Christian A. *A History of the City of Red Wing, Minnesota*. Red Wing: Privately published, 1934.

——. "Beginning of Good Roads Movement." N.d. GCHS Roads file.

——. *History of Goodhue County*. Red Wing: Privately published, 1935.

Raymond, Charles E., and Hattie Raymond. *Kenyon, Minnesota, Located on the Chicago Great Western Ry, 1885–1887*. Kenyon: Privately published, 1897.

——. *Kenyon, Minnesota: A Review of its Growth, Resources, Manufactures, Financial Interests, Public Buildings and Prospects*. Kenyon: Raymond Series, 1897.

Record Book of Burnside Grange, No. 148, of Patrons of Husbandry. Ca. 1874. GCHS.

Red Wing Hospital Minute Book, 1914–1922. GCHS.

Red Wing Industrial Development Corporation. "Assistance for New Red Wing Industry." Red Wing: RWIDC, 1954. GCHS.

Red Wing League of Women Voters. *Nuclear Power Plant Next Door: The Prairie Island Nuclear Plant and Its Influence upon Our Community*. Red Wing: The League, May 1981. GCHS.

——. *Women in the Work Force*. Red Wing: The League, 1991. GCHS

Red Wing Sewer Pipe Company. "Raw Clay Tells the Story." Red Wing: Red Wing Sewer Pipe Co. 1927. GCHS.

Reitmann, Maj. Thomas E. Summary of Service, United States Air Force, Vietnam War file. GCHS.

"Reminiscences of Mr. William Remshardt." October 1956. GCHS.

Revoir, Phil. The Early Hisotry of St. John's Evangelical Lutheran Church. Red Wing: Self-published, 1983.

Rice, Arnold S. *The Ku Klux Klan in American Politics*. Washington, D.C.: Public Affairs, 1962.

"Riedell Shoes, Inc. of Red Wing." N.d. GCHS Riedell Shoes file.

Riley, Glenda. *The Female Frontier: A Comparative View of Women on the Prairie and the Plains*. Lawrence, Kans.: University Press of Kansas, 1988.

Ronning, Halvor. *The Gospel at Work*. Minneapolis: Privately published, 1943.

Ronningen, Barbara. "Highlights of 1992 Census of Agriculture." *Population Notes*. St. Paul: Minnesota Planning Office, Nov. 1995.

Roos, Carl. "Vasa, Goodhue County, Minnesota: The First Settlers." Translated by Ernest B. Gustafson. Feb. 1, 1877. Carl Roos Papers GCHS.

"Rural Electrification in Goodhue County." GCHS Electric Power Distribution file.

Ryan, Ron. "Airplane Spotting." GCHS Welch file.

Scherf, Mildred. "Reminiscing—Hectic Days during World War I." N.d. GCHS Scherf biography file.

Schmeckebier, Laurence E. *Art in Red Wing*. Minneapolis: University of Minnesota, 1946.

Schmidt, Edward W. "Visiting among the Mounds in the Red Wing Area." Unpublished manuscript, ca. 1908. GCHS.

Schrier, Arnold. *Ireland and the American Emigration, 1850–1900*. Minneapolis: University of Minnesota, 1958.

Schwartau, John. "The Red Wing Clay Industry: How It All Began, John Paul 1819–1900." Unpublished manuscript, 1993. GCHS.

Scovell, Bessie Lathe, ed. *Yesteryears: A Brief History of the Minnesota Woman's Christian Temperance Union from Its Organization, September 6, 1887 to 1939*. St. Paul: WCTU, 1939.

Setterdahl, Lilly. *Minnesota Swedes: The Emigration from Trolle Ljungby to Goodhue County 1855–1912*. East Moline, Ill.: American Friends of the Emigrant Institute of Sweden, 1996.

Severson, Harold. "Bright Lights for a Dark Countryside," *Goodhue County Cooperative Electric Association 45th Anniversary Report, 1936–1981*. Zumbrota: The Association, 1981.

——. *Goodhue County Heritage*. N.c.: Privately published, 1963.

——. *The Night They Turned on the Lights*. Kenyon: Midwest Historical Features, 1962.

——. *We Give You Kenyon*. Kenyon: Privately published, 1976.

Shannon, James P. *Catholic Colonization on the Western Frontier*. New Haven: Yale University, 1957.

Sifakis, Stewart. *Who Was Who in the Civil War*. New York: Facts on File, 1988.

Smith, Frederick L. *The History of Frontenac*. Frontenac: Privately published, 1951.

Smith, G. Hubert. "Minnesota Potteries: From Pioneer Craft to Modern Factory." *Minnesota History* 33 (Summer 1953).

Smythurst, Jayne. "Alexander P. Anderson and the History of Tower View." N.d. GCHS.

Solberg, Nancy. "Aurora Ski Club of Red Wing," 1969. GCHS Aurora Ski Club file.

Stageberg, Rolf. "Olaf Stageberg and Family." GCHS.

——. "Susie Stageberg."GCHS Stageberg file.

Stageberg, Susie W. "Henry Wallace." *The Friend: A Family Magazine* 24 (Feb. 1947).

——. "A Sturdy Defense." Fort Dodge (Iowa) *Messenger*, n.d. GCHS Stageberg file..

Stampp, Kenneth M. *America in 1857: A Nation on the Brink*. New York: Oxford University, 1990.

Stanton, Paul E. "Reminiscences of the Past." April 1993. GCHS.

Starr, Karen. "Fighting for the Future: Farm Women of the Nonpartisan League." *Minnesota History* 48 (Summer 1983).

"State Builders of the West: Lucius Frederick Hubbard." *Western Magazine* 14 (July 1919).

Stauffer, Clinton R., and George A. Thiel. *The Limestone Marls of Minnesota*. Minneapolis: University of Minnesota Geological Survey Bulletin No. 23, 1933.

Stephenson, George M. "The John Lind Papers." *Minnesota History* 17 (June 1936).

Stewart, E. A., J. M. Larson, and J. Romness. *The Red Wing Project on Utilization of Electricity in Agriculture*. St. Paul: University of Minnesota Agricultural Experiment Station, 1923.

Stuhler, Barbara. "Organizing for the Vote: Leaders of Minnesota's Woman Suffrage Movement." *Minnesota History* 54 (Fall 1995).

Sullivan, Mark. *Our Times: America at the Birth of the Twentieth Century*. New York: Charles Scribner's Sons, 1926, abridged 1996.

Swint, Henry L. *The Northern Teacher in the South, 1862–1870*. Nashville: Vanderbilt University, 1941.

Taylor, C. T. "Goodhue County in the Civil War." Unpublished paper. GCHS.

Taylor, Lee, Marvin J. Taves, and Gordon Bultena. "Changing Goodhue County, 1946–1958." *Sociology of Rural Life*. St. Paul: University of Minnesota, Agriculture Experiment Station, Jan. 1959.

Telschow, Diana. "Economic Census Sampler. " *Population Notes*. St. Paul: Minnesota Planning Office, Nov. 1996.

——. *Population Notes*. St. Paul: Minnesota Planning Office, Feb. 1993.

*The Security State Bank of Pine Island Newsletter*. Sept. 27, 1982. GCHS.

*The United States Biographical Dictionary and Portrait Gallery of Eminent and Self–Made Men,* Minnesota vol. New York: American Biographical, 1879.

Tohill, Louis A. "Robert Dickson, British Trader on the Upper Mississippi: A Story of Trade, War, and Diplomacy." Ph.D. diss., University of Minnesota, 1926.

Tooker, Charles, and John Koepke. *Red Wing Archaeological Preserve: An Ancient Native American Village and Cemetery*. Minneapolis: Institute for Minnesota Archaeology, 1990.

Tooker, Charles T., and John A. Koepke. *Cannon Valley Trail*. Red Wing, Minn.: N.p., 1985.

U. S. Army Engineer District, St. Paul, Minnesota. *Old Man River, 50th Anniversary, Nine–Foot Navigation Channel, Upper Mississippi River*. St. Paul: U. S. Army Corps of Engineers, 1988.

Unger, Irwin, and Debi Unger, eds. *The Times Were a Changin': The Sixties Reader*. New York: Three Rivers, 1998.

Upham, Warren. *Descriptions and Explorations,* vol. 1 of *Minnesota in Three Centuries, 1655–1908*, edited by Lucius F. Hubbard, William P. Murray, James H. Baker, and Warren Upham. Mankato: Publishing Society of Minnesota, 1908.

Voxland, Melvin. "Voxland Viking Saga: Tordal and Hafslo, Norway to Holden–Kenyon, Minnesota," 1980. GCHS.

Walsh, Todd. "The Lutheran Ladies' Seminary of Red Wing, Minnesota (1894–1920)." 1982 manuscript, GCHS.

Warner, Donald F. "Prelude to Populism." *Minnesota History* 32 (Sept. 1951).

Washburn, Walter. "Leprosy among Scandinavian Settlers in the Upper Mississippi Valley, 1864–1932." *Bulletin of the History of Medicine* 24 (Baltimore: John Hopkins, 1950).

Webb, Anne B. "Forgotten Persephones: Women Farmers on the Frontier." *Minnesota History* 50 (Winter 1986).

Werner, W. C. "Survey and Test on Limestone Quarries in Minnesota." Minnesota Highway Department Bulletin No. 2, 1921.

White, Bruce M. "Indian Visits: Stereotypes of Minnesota's Native People." *Minnesota History* 53 (Fall 1992).

White, Bruce M., et al. *Minnesota Votes: Election Returns by County for Presidents, Senators, Congressmen, and Governors, 1857–1977.* St. Paul: MHS, 1977.

Wilkins, Roy. *Standing Fast: The Autobiography of Roy Wilkins.* New York: Viking, 1994.

Winchell, Newton H. *The Aborigines of Minnesota.* St. Paul: MHS, 1911.

"Women in the Armed Forces, World War II." N.d. GCHS World War II file.

Wright, James A. "The Story of Company F, First Regiment." Unpublished manuscript, 1911. MHS.

# Index

Welch as 1054 1 in school
(28?

121, 198, 213,
251, 259, 271,
286-7